W. J. (William John) Robertson

History of England

W. J. (William John) Robertson

History of England

ISBN/EAN: 9783742832955

Manufactured in Europe, USA, Canada, Australia, Japa

Cover: Foto ©ninafisch / pixelio.de

Manufactured and distributed by brebook publishing software (www.brebook.com)

W. J. (William John) Robertson

History of England

This is a reproduction of a book from the McGill University Library collection.

Title: History of England
Author: Buckley, Arabella B. (Arabella Burton), 1840-1929
Publisher, year: Toronto : Copp, Clark, c1891

The pages were digitized as they were. The original book may have contained pages with poor print. Marks, notations, and other marginalia present in the original volume may also appear. For wider or heavier books, a slight curvature to the text on the inside of pages may be noticeable.

ISBN of reproduction: 978-1-926846-75-0

This reproduction is intended for personal use only, and may not be reproduced, re-published, or re-distributed commercially. For further information on permission regarding the use of this reproduction contact McGill University Library.

McGill University Library
www.mcgill.ca/library

Irene R. Joseph
1899

Map of Great Lakes showing various
provinces of Canada. "" t map.
Watercolor...
maps of Europe with... That.

HISTORY OF ENGLAND.

HISTORY OF ENGLAND,

BY

ARABELLA B. BUCKLEY,

AND

W. J. ROBERTSON, B.A., LL.B.

AND

HISTORY OF CANADA,

BY

W. J. ROBERTSON, B.A., LL.B.

Authorized by the Protestant Committee of the Council of Public Instruction for the Province of Quebec.

TORONTO:
THE COPP, CLARK COMPANY, Limited.

Entered according to Act of the Parliament of Canada, in the year one thousand eight hundred and ninety-one, by THE COPP, CLARK COMPANY (LIMITED), in the Office of the Minister of Agriculture.

PREFACE

In the small space allowed me in this little book, I have tried to set before young readers a connected history of the rise and development of England. While giving as far as possible the chief facts required by students, I have been especially anxious to present a vivid picture of the life, the difficulties, and the achievements of our ancestors; showing how our laws, our constitution, our trade, and our colonies have arisen. If this short sketch opens the way to the study of more comprehensive histories, leading those now growing up into citizens of a widespread empire to take a lively interest in the past, present, and future of our nation, it will have done its work.

At the same time, as it is necessary in school teaching that dates and facts should be firmly rooted in the memory, I have endeavoured, with the help of Messrs. Acland and Ransome's admirable *Outlines*, so to arrange the Table of Contents at the beginning of the volume that it may offer a clear abstract of the facts of each chapter, and also serve as a Chronological Table, giving the dates in their due succession. Among so many figures, both in the table and the text, there must inevitably be some errors in spite of every care. When any such are discovered, I shall be grateful to those who will point them out that they may be corrected.

Upcott Avenel, Highampton.

CANADIAN AUTHOR'S PREFACE.

A brief explanation of the Canadian author's share in this History is, perhaps, desirable.

The revision and classification of the matter of Miss Buckley's History of England has been carried out with a scrupulous regard to maintaining intact the essential features of the work. Particular attention has been given to retaining the "woven whole" of the style and diction of the author, a style and diction at once simple, graphic, and interesting. Therefore, the changes made have been principally in the direction of the classification of the contents of the paragraphs, the excision of minor dates and names, and in the giving of fuller details of some important events and measures somewhat briefly treated by Miss Buckley.

As to the part of this work dealing with Canada, it is but fair to state that no attempt has been made to give a full and complete account of all the events that occur in our history. The "leading events" alone have been sketched; the task of giving important details being left to the intelligent teacher. No one feels more keenly than the author, the impossibility of giving in the space of eighty pages, an account of the growth and life of the Canadian people. An effort, however, has been made to give a fair and impartial outline, in language so simple as to be easily understood by the junior pupils of our High Schools.

W. J. ROBERTSON.

St. Catharines, June 1st, 1891.

SOVEREIGNS OF ENGLAND SINCE THE NORMAN CONQUEST.

(For fuller details see Tables at beginning of each Part.)

```
                                    WILLIAM I., 1068.
           ┌────────────────────────────────┼────────────────────────────┐
      Robert,                         WILLIAM II., 1087.          HENRY I., 1100.         Adela.
   Duke of Normandy.                                                  │                      │
   William, d. 1128.                                               Matilda.              STEPHEN, 1135.
                                                                 HENRY II., 1154.
                         ┌──────────────┬──────────────┬──────────────┐
                    Henry, d. 1183.  RICHARD I., 1189.  Geoffrey.    JOHN, 1199.
                                                          │        HENRY III., 1216.
                                                       Arthur,          │
                                                     (murdered).        │
                                           ┌────────────────────────────┼──────────────┐
                                       EDWARD I., 1272.                        Edmund Lancaster.
                                       EDWARD II., 1307.                            │
                                       EDWARD III., 1327.                     Thomas Lancaster.
                                              │                                     │
                                                                              Henry Lancaster.
                                                                                    │
                                                                              Henry Lancaster.
                                                                                    │
                                                                                Blanche,
                                                                           Duchess of Lancaster.
                                                                                    │
                                                                              HENRY IV., 1399.
                                                                              HENRY V., 1413.
                                                                              HENRY VI., 1422.
                                                                                 (deposed)
```

Edward, d. 1376, | Lionel, | John of Gaunt, | Edmund, Duke of York.
Black Prince. | Duke of Clarence. | 1st wife— |
 | │ | 3rd wife— |
RICHARD II., 1377. | Philippa, | Katharine Swynford. | Richard,
 | m. Earl of March. | │ | Earl of Cambridge.
│	John, Earl of Somerset.
Roger,	│
Earl of March.	John, Duke of Somerset.
│
Anne Mortimer, m. ································
│
Edmund,
Earl of March.

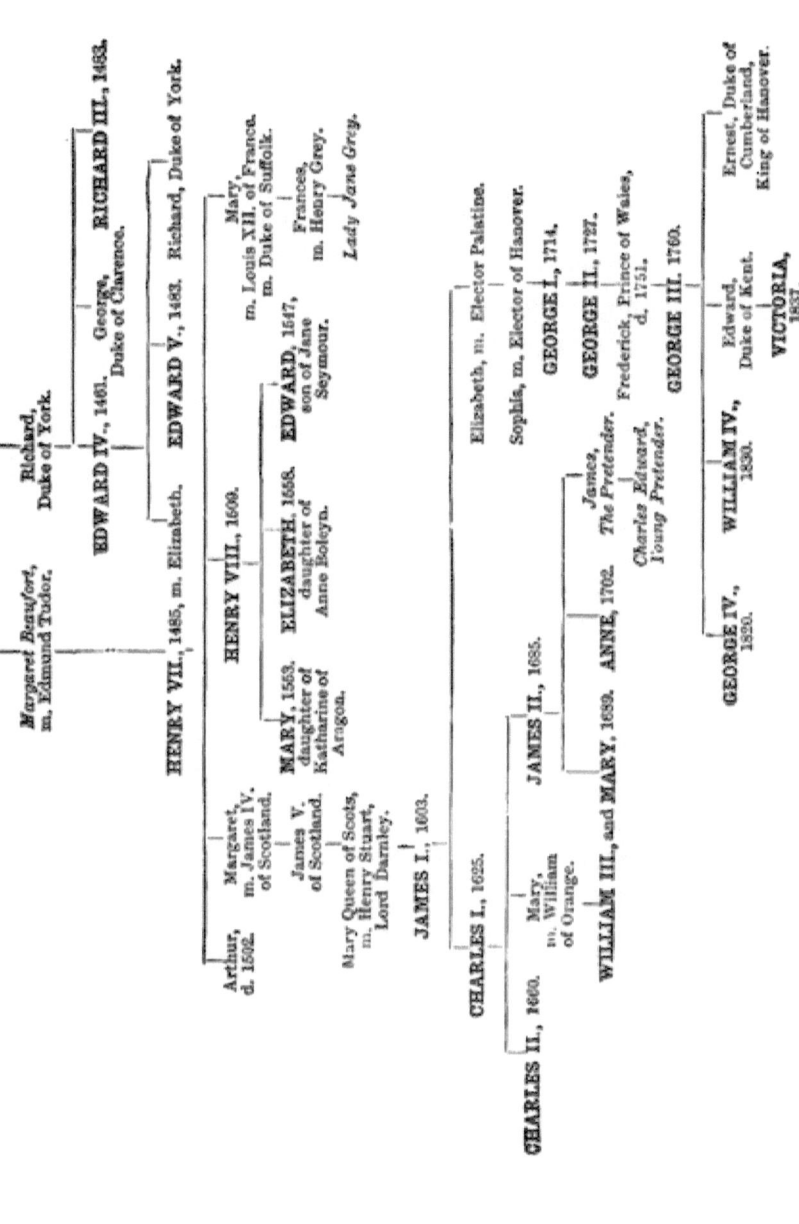

GENEALOGIES[1]

	PAGE
SOVEREIGNS OF ENGLAND—*General Outline*	vi
RACES OF EARLY BRITAIN	xxxiv
SOVEREIGNS FROM THE CONQUEST TO GREAT CHARTER	32
SOVEREIGNS FROM GREAT CHARTER TO HOUSE OF LANCASTER	60
SOVEREIGNS OF LANCASTER AND YORK	91
SOVEREIGNS OF THE HOUSE OF TUDOR	112
SOVEREIGNS OF THE HOUSE OF STUART	150
SOVEREIGNS OF THE HOUSE OF HANOVER	232

MAPS

MAP I. ENGLISH KINGDOMS IN 600	*Facing page*	8
II. ENGLAND AND THE DANELAGH	"	18
III. DOMINION OF THE ANGEVINS	"	48
IV. MAP OF HUNDRED YEARS' WAR	"	78
V. BATTLES AND SIEGES OF THE CIVIL WAR	"	172
VI. INDIA IN THE TIME OF CLIVE	"	244
VII. NORTH AMERICAN COLONIES AT DECLARATION OF INDEPENDENCE	"	258
VIII. AUSTRALASIA	"	288

[1] In these genealogies no attempt is made to give all the children of each king. Only those are named who are concerned in the succession to the throne.

CONTENTS

ARRANGED IN CHRONOLOGICAL ORDER WITH DATES.

(In referring from this table to the text, make use of the *dates* in the side notes.)

PART I.

EARLY BRITAIN AND OLD ENGLAND.

CHAPTER I.

EARLY BRITAIN.

	B. C.
ENGLAND defined—Britain before England—Palæolithic men—Neolithic men—Cromlechs—Celts—Visits of Phœnicians, sixth century B. C.—Invasions of **Julius Cæsar**, B. C. 55-54—Homes of Britons—Druid religion—**Roman Conquest**, A. D. 43—Caractacus, A. D. 50—Boadicea, A. D. 61—Three hundred years of Roman rule—**Romans leave**, A. D. 401-410—Picts and Scots grow troublesome . . . Pages 1-7	55 to A. D. 410

CHAPTER II.

HOW THE ENGLISH CAME.

Saxon pirates in fourth century—**Landing of Jutes in Britain, 449**—Kingdom of Kent founded, 449—**Arrival of Saxons, 477**—King Arthur defeats the Saxons, 520—Saxon Settlements, Essex, Wessex, etc.—**Settlements of Angles**—Northumbria, 603—East Anglia and Mercia—Terms Welsh and English—**Early English villages**—Eorls and ceorls—Laets	449 to

CONTENTS.

	and slaves—Compurgation and ordeal—Folkmoot and Witan-
	gemot—Kings elected, with thegns for bodyguard—Heathen
	gods—**Conversion to Christianity** of Ethelbert of Kent, 597
627	—Of Edwin of Northumbria, 627—Irish Missions, 634-664—
673	**English Church organised,** 673—Origin of towns—Rise of monasteries and towns—**Bede the historian,** 673-735—
839	**Egbert of Wessex Lord of all the English.** 802-839.

Pages 7-14

CHAPTER III.

STRUGGLE BETWEEN ENGLISH AND DANES.

789 — **Invasion of Danes or Northmen,** 789-879—Ethelwulf of Wessex fails to check them, 839-858—Ethebald, Ethelbert, Ethelred I. struggle against them, 858-871.

871 — **ALFRED THE GREAT,** 871-901—After seven years' fighting is forced to hide in the marshes—Returns, defeats
879 — the Danes, and forces them to sign **Treaty of Wedmore,** 878—Alfred's government—He translates works—Encourages education—Forms a navy—Collects and improves the laws—Promotes foreign trade and travel—Peter's Pence—**Alfred**
901 — **dies, 901.**

Making of England under Alfred's family—Edward the Elder, 901-925, and his sister Ethelfled conquer the Danelagh—Athelstan, 925; Edmund, 940; Edred, 946; Edwy, 955; gradually conquer the northern counties—Edgar the Peace-
959 — able, 959-975, has **Dunstan, Archbishop of Canterbury,** as minister—Increased power of king—Shire-reeves his officers—His thegns numerous—Ceorls sink into villeins—Frith-guilds—Yeomen—Great nobles and bishops—Danes and English settle down together—**Firm government of Dunstan**—Laws of Edgar—Lothian put under Kenneth, King of the Scots=Increase of trade—**The land first called Engla-land**—Edward
975 — **the Martyr,** 975-979—Fall of Dunstan, 978—He dies, 988.

979 — **ETHELRED THE UNREADY,** 979-1016—Quarrels with his thegns—**Second Danish invasion,** 991—**Danegeld first**
1002 — **levied,** 991—Massacre of Danes, 1002—Sweyn's revenge—Ethelred flies to Normandy—Government divided between Cnut, Sweyn's son, and Edmund Ironside, son of Ethelred—**Edmund dies, 1016.**

CNUT THE DANE elected king, 1017—Divides England into four earldoms—Eighteen years of peace, **1016-1035**—Cnut's sons, Harold, **1035**, and Harthacnut, **1040**, rule badly—On death of Harthacnut the English recall Ethelred's son Edward, **1042** . . . . Pages 15-24

1017

1042

CHAPTER IV.

NORMAN INFLUENCE IN ENGLAND.

EDWARD THE CONFESSOR, son of Ethelred the Unready, and Emma of Normandy—Origin and character of Normans—Edward favours Norman nobles—**Earl Godwin of Wessex outlawed, 1051**—William of Normandy visits Edward, **1051**—Godwin returns and Norman favourites flee to France, **1052**—Harold, Godwin's son, rules in Edward's name, **1053**—Welsh king subdued—Northumbrian rebellion—Tostig, Harold's brother, outlawed, **1065**—Harold's oath in Normandy—**Death of Edward, 1066.**

HAROLD is king for nine months—William of Normandy claims the crown—Harold defeats King Hardrada of Norway and Tostig at Stamford Bridge, **Sept. 25**—**Battle of Hastings, Oct. 14**—Noblest of English nation killed—Harold slain—**William crowned at Westminster Dec. 25.**

Pages 25-31

1042

1051

1053

1066
Jan. 5

Dec. 25

PART II.

FROM THE CONQUEST TO THE GREAT CHARTER.

CHAPTER V.

ENGLAND UNDER NORMAN RULE.

WILLIAM THE CONQUEROR, hard and stern, but a wise statesman—Confiscation of land—Folk-land becomes king's land—Feudal system—Building of castles—Norman nobles oppress the people—English revolt—**Struggle with English patriots, 1067**—William subdues Exeter, **1068**—Retakes York, and wastes the north country, **1069**—**End of Patriot leaders, 1071**—Laws of the English declared by twelve men from each shire—William lays waste land in Hampshire for New Forest—Lanfranc, Archbishop of Canterbury, rules well, but appoints

1066

1067

1087	foreign bishops, 1070—William's eldest son Robert rebels, 1078—General survey of England—**Domesday Book**, 1086—Troubles and death of William at Rouen, **Sept. 9, 1087**—Robert has Normandy and Maine—William, the third son, is elected king in England.
1087	**WILLIAM II.**, surnamed **Rufus**, crowned at Westminster by Lanfranc, **Sept. 26**—He was brave but lawless and vicious—Barons rebel in Robert's favour, 1088—English support the king—**Defeat of Normans at Pevensey**, 1088—Death
1089	of Lanfranc, 1089—Ralph Flambard, justiciar, oppresses the people—War against Robert in Normandy, 1090—Conquests in Wales—Annexation of Cumberland, 1092—Malcolm of
1093	Scotland does homage—**Anselm made archbishop**, 1093, tries to check William's oppressions—Robert goes to the crusades, and pledges Normandy to William, 1096—Anselm retires
1097	to Rome, 1097—**William killed when hunting, Aug. 2, 1100**—Henry, fourth son of the Conqueror, seizes the throne.
1100	**HENRY I.** is chosen King and crowned at Westminster, **Aug. 11, 1100**—A learned and cautious man—First Norman king born in England—**Grants a charter of liberties**—Marries a princess of English blood—Imprisons Flambard—Quiets Robert with a pension—Colony of Flemings planted in Pembroke, 1105—Norman barons rise for Robert—**Battle of
1106	Tenchebrai**, 1106—Robert imprisoned in England—Bishop Roger, justiciar, 1107—Restores just laws—Court of the Exchequer—Blending of Normans and English—**Henry's son
1120	William drowned**, 1120—Henry makes barons swear allegi-
1125	ance to Matilda—**Pope's legate received in England**, 1125—Cistercian monks settle in England, 1128—Death of Robert's only son, 1128—Death of Robert, 1134—**Death of Henry**,
1135	1135 . . . . Pages 33-45

CHAPTER VI.

ANARCHY UNDER STEPHEN.

1135	**STEPHEN**, grandson of William the Conqueror, seizes the throne—Popular but unstable—Well received by the people of London—Some of the barons support Matilda, whose uncle, David of Scotland, is defeated in the **Battle of the Standard**,

CONTENTS.   xiii

1138—Stephen arrests Roger the justiciar and others, 1139. | 1138
Matilda lands in England, 1139—Civil war—Stephen a prisoner, | 1139
1141—Siege of Oxford, 1142—Matilda leaves England, 1147—
Barons ravage the land—Religious revival—**Theobald, Archbishop of Canterbury**, mediates between Stephen and Prince | 1147
Henry—Treaty of Wallingford, 1153—Death of Stephen, **Oct.** | 1153
25, leaving the crown to Henry . . . Pages 45-48 | 1154

CHAPTER VII.

HENRY PLANTAGENET AND HIS SONS.

HENRY II., grandson of Henry I., crowned at Westminster, | 1154
Dec. 19—A strong, wise king—**Issues a charter**—Destroys barons' castles—Restores courts of justice—Establishes **circuits and juries**, and scutage in lieu of military service—**Thomas Becket chancellor, 1154**—Made Archbishop of Canterbury, 1162—Opposes trial of clergy in law-courts—**Quarrel of Henry** | 1162
and Becket, 1163—Becket flies to France, 1164—Constitutions | 1163
of Clarendon, 1164—Assizes of Clarendon, 1166, and Northampton, 1169—Students at Oxford—Return and **murder of Becket,** | 1166
1170—**General league against Henry, 1173**—His penance, | 1170
1174—Subdues the King of Scotland, the rebel barons, and his own sons—Militia established, **1181**—**Death of Henry, 1189**— | 1181
Henry and Geoffrey having died, Richard, the third and eldest | 1189
surviving son, succeeds.

RICHARD I., Cœur de Lion, crowned **Sept. 3**—Brave and | 1189
popular, but a foreigner in heart and speech—Sold all offices he could, and left in December for the **Crusades**—His brother John tries to supplant him in England—Longchamp, justiciar, deposed, 1191—**First Mayor of London, 1191**—**Richard** | 1191
taken prisoner by Austria, 1192—Five kinds of taxes imposed for his ransom—He visits England for four months, **1194**, and | 1194
then never again—**Hubert Walter and Geoffrey Fitz-Peter**, justiciars—Bishops oppose unjust taxes—**Death of Richard from an arrow-wound at Chaluz, April 6.** | 1199

JOHN, fourth son of Henry II., succeeds in England— | 1199
Handsome, cruel, and treacherous—Makes war on Arthur of Brittany, Geoffrey's son, who has succeeded to Anjou—**Arthur, aged fifteen, is taken prisoner, and disappears, 1203**—John | 1203

1206	refuses to account to Philip of France for his death—**Philip takes Normandy and Anjou,** 1204—Archbishop Hubert dies, 1205—Stephen Langton elected archbishop, 1206—John refuses to admit him to England—**Pope lays England under an interdict,** 1208—Excommunicates John, 1209—Deposes
1212	him, 1212—John submits and becomes the **Pope's vassal,** 1213—Growing strength of the nation—Barons demand a charter
1215	—**John forced to sign Magna Charta,** 1215—War between king and barons—**Louis of France comes with an army,** 1216—Loss of crown jewels in the Wash—**Death of John,**
1216	Oct. 19, 1216 . . . . . . Pages 48-59

PART III.

RISE OF PARLIAMENT.

CHAPTER VIII.

THE BARONS' WAR.

1216	**HENRY III.**, son of John, aged nine, crowned at Gloucester with gold circlet—Well-meaning, but weak and suspicious—William Marshall, Earl of Pembroke, Regent—The French
1217	defeated at Lincoln and in the Channel, return home, 1217—Good government of Hubert de Burgh, justiciar—**Privy Council**—Prosperity of country—Fairs—Highwaymen—Death
1228	of Archbishop Langton, 1228—Pope levies money in England
1232	—Henry dismisses Hubert, last great justiciar, 1232, and favours foreigners—To obtain money summons earls, barons, and bishops in a **Parliament**—**Extravagance of Henry drives**
1258	barons to resist—Mad Parliament, 1258—**Provisions of Oxford**—Simon de Montfort, king's brother-in-law, leader
1264	of the barons—**Mise of Amiens,** 1264—**Battle of Lewes,** 1264—King made prisoner—Prince Edward surrenders at **Mise of Lewes** after the battle—**Montfort's Parliament, origin of**
1265	**Commons,** 1265—Escape of Prince Edward, May 28—**Battle of Evesham, Montfort killed,** Aug. 4, 1265—Dictum of Kenilworth, king restored, 1266—Prince Edward goes to
1272	crusades—**Death of Henry,** 1272 . . . Pages 61-66

CHAPTER IX.

STRUGGLE WITH WALES AND SCOTLAND.

EDWARD I., a brave and wise king—two years' regency —Edward returns and is crowned, **Aug 12, 1274**—Office of justiciar is dropped—Burnell Chancellor—Halfpennies and farthings first coined—**Llewellyn of Wales refuses homage** —**Conquest of Wales, 1277-1282**—**First English Prince of Wales, 1301** — Organisation of law-courts — Statute of Mortmain, 1279—**Keepers of the Peace established, 1285** —**Expulsion of Jews, 1290**—**Struggle with Scotland**— Scots have no king, 1290—Edward, as umpire, chooses **John Baliol, 1292**—**First complete English Parliament, 1295**— Edward raises heavy taxes, and Parliament in return exacts new charters, 1297—Edward requires Scotch law-appeals to be heard in England—**War with Scotland, 1296**—Insurrection under Wallace, 1297—**Battle of Falkirk, 1298**—Wallace hanged, **1305**—Rebellion under Robert Bruce, who is crowned king 1306—**Edward**, marching to Scotland, **dies at Burgh-on-Sands, July 7, 1307.** | 1272 1274 1277 1290 1295 1296 1297 1306

EDWARD II., son of Edward I., a weak, headstrong king, governed by favourites—Neglected the Scotch war—**Rule of Piers Gaveston, 1308**—Driven out by **Lords Ordainers, 1310** —Returns and is beheaded, 1312—Knights Templars abolished, 1309—**Battle of Bannockburn**, English defeated, **1314**— Famine and trouble, 1315—**Rule of Hugh le Despenser, 1320** —Barons rebel—**Lancaster beheaded, 1322**—**Commons gain a share in making laws, 1322**—Edward's queen Isabella brings troops from France, 1326—**King deposed Jan. 7, and murdered Sept. 21, 1327.** . . . . Pages 66-77 | 1307 1310 1314 1322 1327

CHAPTER X.

THE HUNDRED YEARS' WAR.

EDWARD III., son of Edward II., aged fifteen, crowned Jan. 29, 1327—Rule of Queen Isabella and Mortimer, 1327-1330—Independnce of Scotland recognised, 1328—Fall and death of Mortimer, 1330—King of France, coveting Guienne, | 1327 1330

	interferes in Scotland—**Edward claims French crown, 1337**
1338	—Hundred Years' War begins, 1338— Naval victory off Sluys, 1340—Battle of Crecy, 1346—**Bravery of Black Prince—Surrender of Calais,** 1346—Order of Garter instituted, **1348**—Home affairs—Freedom of serfs and leases granted—Growth
1344	of industries—Gold coins first used, 1344—**Parliament gains power by the king's need of money for the war**—Defeat of
1348	Scots at Neville Cross, 1346—**Black Death, 1348**—Struggle between capital and labour—**Statute of Labourers, 1349**—State of people seen in writings of Chaucer and Langland—Wiclif preaches equality—First statute of *præmunire*, 1353—**Renewal**
1355	**of French war, 1355**—**Battle of Poitiers, 1356**—**Peace of**
1360	**Bretigny, 1360**—**Statutes of Kilkenny oppress the Irish,**
1367	1367—**Disastrous third campaign with France, loss of**
1376	**French territory, 1376**—Decline of the king—**Good Parliament impeaches the ministers**—Death of Black Prince,
1377	1376—First poll-tax, 1377—**Death of Edward III., June 21, 1377.**
1377	**RICHARD II.**, son of Black Prince, aged eleven, crowned July 16—Brave and strong-willed, a good king till spoilt by absolute power—His uncle, John of Gaunt, Duke of Lancaster,
1381	has great influence—**Peasants revolt against poll-tax, 1381**—Wat Tyler and John Ball—Richard appeases the people—Villeinage dies out gradually—**Struggle between Richard and**
1386	his uncles—Council of Eleven appointed, **Dec. 1, 1386**—**Lords Appellant** attack the king's friends in the Merciless Parliament,
1388	1388—**Richard takes the Government, 1389**—Second law of *præmunire*, 1393—A truce with France, 1396—**Richard's re-**
1397	**venge, 1397**—An absolute—He banishes Norfolk and Henry of Hereford and Lancaster, surnamed Bolingbroke—Henry returns
1399	to claim his lands—**Fall and imprisonment of Richard, 1399**—**Bolingbroke declared king, Sept. 30, 1396.** . Pages 77-90

CONTENTS. xvii

PART IV.

WARS OF THE ROSES.

CHAPTER XI.

THE HOUSE OF LANCASTER.

HENRY IV., of Lancaster, grandson of Edward III. and son of John of Gaunt—An able king under many difficulties—Unsettled succession for eighty years—English nobles rebel, 1400—Death of Richard—Owen Glendower rebels in Wales, 1400—Persecution of Lollards, 1401—Battle of Homildon Hill against the Scots, 1402—Revolt of Percies and Glendower, 1403—Battle of Shrewsbury, 1403—Rebellion of Mowbray and Scrope, 1405—**Commons gain power by troubles of the king,** 1407—Beauforts, sons of John of Gaunt, were chancellors—Death of Henry, March 20, 1413.   1399 / 1400 / 1402 / 1407

HENRY V., of Lancaster, son of Henry IV., a brilliant soldier and wise statesman—**Granted to the Commons that their Bills should not be altered,** 1414—Alien Priories granted to king, 1414—People prosperous—Revolt of Lollards, 1414—Henry revives the war with France, 1415—Siege of Harfleur, 1415—Battle of Agincourt, 1415—Siege of Rouen, 1418—Henry Regent of France, 1420—Death of Henry 1422.   1413 / 1414 / 1415 / 1420

HENRY VI. of Lancaster, son of Henry V., aged ten months—**Duke of Bedford, Protector of the Realm,** goes to the French war—Duke of Gloucester and Cardinal Beaufort quarrel at home, 1425—Decline of Parliament—Parliament of the "Bats," 1425—Siege of **Orleans,** 1428—Siege raised by Jeanne Darc—Charles crowned at Rheims—**Jeanne Darc burnt,** 1431—**The king good but weak**—Ruled by his queen, Margaret—**Gloucester and Suffolk murdered,** 1447, 1450—People rebel under Jack Cade against foreign favourites, 1450—**End of Hundred Years' War,** 1453—Calais alone remains to the English—Madness of the king—**Duke of York protector,** 1454—He is displaced for Somerset—York takes up arms—**Wars of the Roses begin,** 1455—Battle of St. Albans, 1455—**Bills of attainder introduced**—Battle of Northampton, **July,**   1422 / 1425 / 1431 / 1450 / 1453 / 1455

B

CONTENTS.

1460 1460—Battle of Wakefield, Dec. 1460—Richard, Duke of York, killed—His son Edward takes up the contest—Battle of Mortimer's Cross, 1461—Edward of York declared
1461 king, March 4, 1461—Battle of Towton, March 29, 1461—Henry and Margaret fly to Scotland. . . Pages 92–103.

CHAPTER XII.

THE HOUSE OF YORK.

1461 **EDWARD IV.** of York, great-great-grandson of Edward III.—Brave and popular but dissolute—Battle of Hedgeley Moor and Hexham, 1464—**Quarrel with Earl of Warwick,**
1469 **the king-maker**—Battle of Edgecote, 1469—Edward flies to Flanders—**Henry VI. restored for six months, 1470**—Ed-
1471 ward returns, 1471—**Warwick killed at Barnet, April 14, 1471—Battle of Tewkesbury, May 4, 1471**—Margaret defeated and her son killed—**Death of Henry VI.**—Margaret imprisoned—Rise of a middle class—Edward rules despotically—Collects benevolences—**Introduction of printing by**
1476 **Caxton, 1476**—Duke of Clarence put to death, 1478—**Death of Edward, April 9, 1483.**

1483 **EDWARD V.**, son of Edward IV., aged thirteen—Enters London, **May 4, 1483**—Reigns three months, but is never
May 4   crowned—**Richard, Duke of Gloucester, protector**—Lodges
to king and his brother in the Tower—**Puts Lord Hastings to**
June 25 **death, June 13**—Pronounces the princes illegitimate—**Accepts the crown, June 25.**

1483 **RICHARD III.**, brother of Edward IV., crowned **July 6**—Brave but cruel and treacherous—**Murder** of the young princes—Richard rules well—**Introduces Consuls** and a **running post**—Duke of Buckingham plots to bring in Henry Tudor of the house of Lancaster—**Buckingham beheaded, Nov. 1,**
1485 1483—**Henry Tudor arrives, 1485**—Nobles rally round him—**Battle of Bosworth Field, Aug. 22, 1485—Richard killed—End of Wars of Roses, 1485.**

Close of Middle ages—Destruction of old nobility in the wars—Use of gunpowder and rise of middle class mark modern era.
Pages 103–111

PART V.

THE TUDORS.

CHAPTER XIII.

HOUSE OF TUDOR.

HENRY VII., descended from Edward III. through John of Gaunt, Duke of Lancaster, Crowned **Oct. 30**—Married Elizabeth of York, daughter of Edward IV—**Union of Houses of York and Lancaster**—A wise, unpopular, and avaricious, but strong king—**Crown settled on his heirs**—Futile rebellion of Lambert Simnel, 1487—**Court of the Star Chamber established**, 1487—Rebellion of Perkin Warbeck, 1492-1497—**Poyning's Act applies English laws to Ireland**, 1494—King heaps up wealth by **benevolences, statute of liveries, and appropriating disputed estates**—Empson and Dudley his tools—Rules without Parliament — Voyages of Christopher Columbus, Vasco de Gama, and Cabot, 1492-1498—Warbeck and Earl of Warwick executed, 1499 — Royal marriages — Katharine of Aragon is married to Arthur, Prince of Wales, 1501—He dies and Henry, now Prince of Wales, is betrothed to his brother's widow—Princess Margaret marries James IV. of Scotland, 1502; from her descends Mary Queen of Scots—**Introduction of new learning in England**—**Death of Henry VII, April 21, 1509.** | 1485
1487
1494
1498
1501
1502

HENRY VIII., son of Henry VII., united in himself houses of York and Lancaster—Affable, popular, and with plenty of sense, but selfish and coarse—Puts Empson and Dudley to death—Builds ships and dockyards—Trinity House established, 1513—War of the Holy League—**Battle of the Spurs,** 1513—Scots attack England—**Battle of Flodden Field, 1513,** James IV. killed—Margaret, Henry's sister, becomes Regent of Scotland for James V —**Administration of Wolsey, 1515-** 1529—Intrgiues with Francis I. of France and Charles V, of | 1509
1510
1513
1515

1520	Spain—**Field of the Cloth of Gold, 1520**—War with France, 1522—Alliance with France, 1525—Henry seeks divorce from
1529	Katharine, 1527—**Fall of Wolsey, 1529**—Seven Years' Parliament, 1529—**Administration of Thomas Cromwell, 1530-**
1533	**1540**—**Henry breaks with the Pope**—Divorce Katharine and marries Anne Boleyn, 1533—**Is declared Supreme Head of**
1535	**the Church, 1535**—Cromwell's law of high treason—Execution of Sir Thomas More and Fisher, 1535—Wales put under English law, 1536—English people suffer from corn-lands being turned into pasture—**Luther and Zwingli**—Religious changes in
1536	England—**Destruction of monasteries, 1536-1549**—Execution of Anne Boleyn and marriage of king with Jane Seymour, 1536—Rebellion in north and west of England—
1537	**Birth of Prince Edward, 1537**—Death of Jane Seymour—Six Articles passed against the Protestants, 1539—**King marries**
1540	**and puts away Anne of Cleves, 1540**—**Fall and execution of Cromwell, 1540**—King marries Katharine Howard, 1540— She is executed, 1542—King assumes the title of King of Ireland, 1541—**James V. of Scotland attacks England**—Dies
1542	after defeat at Solway Moss, 1542, leaving an infant, **Mary Queen of Scots**—Henry marries Katharine Parr, 1543—English liturgy introduced—Debasement of coinage—**Act of Succession** sets aside Mary Queen of Scots—**Death of Henry, Jan.**
1547	**28, 1547** Pages 113-127

CHAPTER XIV.

STRUGGLE BETWEEN THE TWO RELIGIONS.

1547	**EDWARD VI.**, son of Jane Seymour, aged ten—Thoughtful and deeply religious—A strict Protestant—**Duke of Somerset protector**—Battle of Pinkiecleugh, 1547—Protestant
1548	reforms—English Prayer-book and Act of Uniformity, 1548— Rebellion in Devon for the old religion, 1549—Agricultural
1549	insurrection in Norfolk, 1549—**Earl Warwick protector**— Made Duke of Northumberland, 1551—**Somerset executed,**
1552	**1552**—Second Act of Uniformity, 1552—**Edward VI.'s** grammar schools founded—Young king names Lady Jane Grey his successor—**Death of king, July 6, 1553.**

MARY, daughter of Katharine of Aragon—Conscientious but narrow-minded and bitter—**Lady Jane Grey proclaimed, July 10**—**Mary proclaimed, July 19**—Northumberland executed—Roman Catholic religion restored—Wyat's rebellion—**Lady Jane Grey beheaded, 1554**—Mary marries Philip of Spain, July 1554—Cardinal Pole, papal legate, made Archbishop of Canterbury—Nobles refuse to give up Church lands—**Persecution of Protestants**—Latimer, Ridley, and Cranmer burnt at the stake, 1555-1556—Philip draws England into a war with France—Lords of the Congregation in Scotland, 1557 (*see* p. 136)—**Loss of Calais, 1558**—**Death of Mary, Nov. 7, 1558.** | 1553
1554
1556
1558

Pages 127-134

CHAPTER XV.

PEACE AND PROGRESS UNDER ELIZABETH.

ELIZABETH, daughter of Anne Boleyn—Vain and obstinate, but a wise and great queen, devoted to her people—Weak state of England, and danger from struggle between Roman Catholics and Protestants on the continent—**Cecil, Lord Burleigh, Secretary of State**—Act of Supremacy—Queen leans towards liberty of conscience—Calvinists of Scotland quarrel with the regent Mary of Guise, 559—Treaty of Edinburgh, July 1560—**Mary Queen of Scots arrives in Scotland, 1561**—**First English poor-law established, 1562-1601**—Advance in agriculture, trade, and manufactures—Increase of comfort—Oath of allegiance established, 1563—Elizabeth will not marry—Shan O'Neill's Revolt in Ireland, 1565—**Mary Queen of Scots marries Darnley, 1565**—Murder of Rizzio, 1566—Murder of Darnley, 1567—**Mary escapes to England and is imprisoned by Elizabeth, 1568**—Growing strength of Parliament—Revolt of the Netherlands, 1568—Plot for Mary in north of England, 1569—Elizabeth excommunicated—Ridolfi plot, 1571—Massacre of St. Bartholomew, 1572—English help the Netherlands by land and sea—**Voyages of discovery, 1576-1583**—Frobisher, Raleigh, Hawkins, Drake—Roman Catholic mission and plots against Elizabeth, 1576-1583—Association to protect her, 1584—**Execution of Mary Queen** | 1558
1559

1560
1562

1563

1566

1568

1571

1576
1584

xxii   CONTENTS.

1587 | of Scots, 1587—The Spanish Armada attacks England and
       is dispersed, 1588—England united and at peace—Fresh
1598 | rebellion in Ireland, 1595—Edict of Nantes in France, 1598—
       Growth of knowledge: Copernicus, Galileo—Age of literature:
       —Spenser, Sir Philip Sidney, Sir Walter Raleigh, Shakespeare
       —Death of Lord Burleigh, 1598—East India Company
1601 | founded, 1599—Insurrection and death of Earl of Essex, 1601
       —Ireland brought under English rule, 1602—Abolition of
1603 | monopolies—Death of the great queen, March 23, 1603.
                                                 Pages 134-149

PART VI.

STRUGGLES AGAINST ABSOLUTE MONARCHY.

CHAPTER XVI.

PREROGATIVE AND PARLIAMENT.

1603 | JAMES I., son of Mary Queen of Scots, came to England
       and was crowned on the sacred stone of Scone, July 25, 1603
       —Shrewd and amiable, but undignified and wise in his own
       conceit—Believed in his **divine right** to reign, and did not
       understand the English people—Three parties—Puritan—English
       Church — Roman Catholics — **Hampden Court conference,**
1604 | 1604—Proposed union with Scotland, 1604—Difficulties with
       the first Parliament, 1604-1610—**Gunpowder Plot,** 1605—
       James issues proclamations and levies impositions—
       Great Contract and dissolution of Parliament, 1610—**Addled**
1614 | **Parliament,** 1614—Rule of favourites, 1612-1621—Somerset
       —George Villiers—Disaster and execution of Sir Walter
       Raleigh, 1616-1618—Outbreak of Thirty Years' War, 1619—
1620 | **Emigration of Puritans to America,** 1620—Proposed Spanish
       marriage of Prince Charles broken off, 1623—**King levies**
1621 | **money illegally**—Third Parliament, 1621-1622—Pym, Hampden, Eliot, and Coke—Impeachment of Bacon, 1621—Parlia-

CONTENTS. xxiii

ment dissolved, 1622—First weekly newspaper, 1622— | 1622
Fourth Parliament, 1624—Disastrous expedition to Holland,
1625—Death of James I., **March 27, 1625** . Pages 151-159 | 1625

CHAPTER XVII.

KING AND PEOPLE.

CHARLES I., son of James I.—Grave and dignified, but | 1625
obstinate and insincere—Marries Henrietta of France—First
Parliament, **June 18**—"Tonnage and Poundage"—**Parliament
dissolved, Aug. 12**—Disastrous expedition to Cadiz, Oct.—
Second Parliament, 1626—Buckingham impeached—**Parlia-** | 1626
ment dissolved—War with France, 1627—King levies forced
loans—Buckingham fails to relieve La Rochelle, 1627—Oppo- | 1627
sition to forced loans—**Petition of right**, 1628—Assassina- | 1628
tion of Buckingham, 1628—Laud made Bishop of London,
1628—Parliament defiant—Tumult and dissolution, 1629 | 1629
—**Rule of Wentworth and Laud**—Great emigration of
Puritans, 1630-1634—Eliot dies in the Tower, 1632—**Went-** | 1630
worth in Ireland, 1633-1639—Inland Post, 1635—Laud
made archbishop, 1635; quarrels with Puritans—King
levies ship-money, 1634-1638—Hampden appeals against it | 1634
—Sentences on Prynne and Bastwick, 1637—Charles tries to | 1637
force the Prayer-book on the Scots—**Renewal of Covenanters**,
1638—Wentworth, now Lord Strafford, recalled to Eng- | 1638
land, proposes to bring Irish troops over—Short Parlia-
ment, 1640—Victory of Scots at Newburn—**Long Parliament** | 1640
begins, 1640—Execution of Strafford, 1641—Triennial | 1641
Act, 1641 — Star Chamber abolished — Massacre in Ireland,
Oct. 1641—**Grand Remonstrance, Nov. 1641**—King at-
tempts to seize five members, Jan. 4, 1642—London train- | 1642
bands defy the king—**Outbreak of civil war, Aug. 22**
—Cavaliers and Roundheads—Prince Rupert's Horse—Powick
Bridge and Edgehill battles, **Sept. Oct. 1642**—Train-bands
turn the king back from London—Royalist successes—Death
of Hampden, **June 1643**—Parliamentary successes—Falkland | 1643
killed, Sept. 1643—**League with the Scots and death of Pym**,
Sept. 1643—Oliver Cromwell and his Ironsides—Battle
of Marston Moor, July 1644—Self-denying Ordinance, 1645 | 1644

1645	—Parliamentary victory at Naseby, June 1645, ends the war—Charles takes refuge with the Scots—**They give him up**
1647	**to Parliament, 1647**—He is seized by the army—Plots with the Irish and Scots—Second civil war, 1648—Battle of Preston—Pride's Purge, Dec. 1649—**Trial and execution of the**
1649	**king, Jan. 30, 1649** Pages 160-176

CHAPTER XVIII.

THE COMMONWEALTH.

1649	Commonwealth or Free State proclaimed, May 19, 1649—Leading men, Cromwell, Bradshaw, Fairfax, Vane—Europe stands aloof—*Eikón Basiliké* published—Scotland and Ireland proclaim Charles II. their king, 1649—Prince Rupert in the Channel—**Cromwell in Ireland, 1649**—He sacks Drog-
1650	heda and Wexford—**Charles II. in Scotland, June, 1650**—Cromwell's Campaign in Scotland, 1650—Battle of Dunbar, Sept. 3, 1650—Charles II. marches to England—Battle
1651	of Worcester, Sept. 3, 1651—Flight of Charles II. to France, Oct. 16, 1651—Commonwealth Recognized by
1651	Europe—Navigation Act, Oct. 1651—Dutch War, 1651—Blake defeated by Van Tromp, 1652—Dutch completely
1653	defeated, Feb. 1653—Abuses of the republican Government—Members refuse to have a general election—Cromwell clears the House, **April 20, 1653**—Military rule—Barebone's Parliament, **July 4 to Dec 16**—**Cromwell protector, Dec. 16, 1653**—His ordinances—Peace with Holland, 1654—First Par-
1655	liament dissolved in five months—Taking of Jamaica, **1655**—Government by major-generals, 1655—Second Parliament, 1656—Cromwell refuses title of king—Parliament dissolved,
1658	Feb. 1658—Battle of the Dunes, Dunkirk taken—Country at peace, but discontented—**Death of Cromwell, Sept. 3, 1658**—**Richard Cromwell protector for ten months**—The
1659	Rump recalled—Anarchy—**General Monk enters London, Jan. 1, 1660**—Long Parliament expires, **March 16,**
1660	**1660**—**Charles lands at Dover, May 25,** and is restored as king, May 29, 1660 . . . . . Pages 176-184

CHAPTER XIX.

THE RESTORATION.

CHARLES II., son of Charles I., witty, sagacious, easy-tempered, and wary, but selfish and indolent—Resolved never to be driven out—**Clarendon**, leading minister, 1660-1667—Act of Indemnity, 1660—Abolition of feudal tenures, 1660—Charles keeps first nucleus of standing army—Cavalier Parliament, 1661—A dissolute court—The people rejoice at release from Puritan rule—Sufferings in Scotland and Ireland—**Corporation Act and Act of Uniformity**, 1661-1662—Acts against Dissenters 1662-1665—Bunyan and Milton—Nonconformists emigrate—Foundation of Royal Society, 1662—Charles's marriage with a Roman Catholic unpopular—Execution of Vane—Sale of Dunkirk, 1662—War with Holland, 1665—**Plague of London**, 1665 Battle of the Downs, 1666—**Fire of London, Sept. 2, 1666**—New River supply adopted—While Peace of Breda was in progress the Dutch fleet burnt ships in the Medway, 1667—Anger of people and **banishment of Clarendon**, 1667—**Cabal ministry**, 1667-1673 — Triple Alliance with Holland and Sweden, 1668—**Secret treaty of Dover between Charles and Louis**, 1670—National bankruptcy, 1672—Declaration of Indulgence, 1672—Second war with Holland, 1672—Duke of York declares himself a Roman Catholic—**Test Act**, 1673—End of Cabal ministry—Beginning of "ministry" and "opposition"—**Danby's administration**, 1673—Marriage of William and Mary, 1677—Charles receives French pension—Popish plot, 1678—Treaty of Nimeguen, 1678—**Fall of Danby**, 1679—Struggle to exclude James, Duke of York, a Roman Catholic, from the throne, 1679-1681—"Habeas Corpus" Act, 1679—Lord Shaftesbury supports Duke of Monmouth for succession—Parliament dissolved, 1681—Names Whig and Tory arise—**Oxford Parliament threatened violence**, 1681—Fall of Shaftesbury—Penn founds Pennsylvania, 1682—Rye House Plot, 1683—Execution of Russell and Sydney—Doctrine of **passive obedience** preached by clergy—**Death of Charles II., Feb. 6, 1685**

1660

1661

1662
1662

1665
1666

1667

1668
1670
1672

1673

1678
1679

1681

1683

1685

Pages 184-199

CHAPTER XX.

THE REVOLUTION.

1685 — JAMES II., brother of Charles II., well-meaning but obstinate and unreasonable—Wanted to restore Roman Catholicism—Commits arbitrary acts—**Whigs invite Monmouth as a Protestant to claim the crown, 1685**—Failure of Argyll's rebellion in Scotland, May, 1685—Monmouth lands and is proclaimed king at Taunton—Defeated at Battle of Sedgemoor, June, 1685—Cruel revenge by Kirke and by Judge Jeffreys in Bloody Assizes, Sept. 1685—James appoints Catholic officers—Parliament remonstrates against violation of Test Act, 1685—Revocation of Edict of Nantes in France startles the English—Politics of the coffee-house—**Blind fanaticism of James**—Claims power of dispensation—Puts Catholics into office—

1686 — **Establishes an Ecclesiastical Court under Jeffreys, 1686**—Overawes London with troops—**Declaration of Indulgence,**

1687 — 1687—Expels Fellows of Magdalen, 1687—**Nation turns secretly to William of Orange and his wife Mary**, James's daughter—Birth of James's son destroys hope of Protestant succession, 1688—Trial of the seven bishops exasperates

1688 — the people, June 1688—Landing of William, Nov. 5, 1688—Flight of James—**Interregnum,** Dec. 1688 to Feb. 1689—

1689 — **Declaration of Rights** drawn up, 1689—**William and Mary declared king and queen, Feb. 13, 1689.**

1689 — **WILLIAM and MARY** crowned April 11, 1689—William stern and unpopular, but a good king—James II. crosses from France to Ireland—Non-jurors and Jacobites stand aloof from William—William and Mary proclaimed in Scotland, April 11—Dundee's rebellion—Battle of Killiecrankie, July 27

1689 — —Civil war in Ireland—Siege and relief of Londonderry, April to Aug. 1689—James reigns in Dublin—Toleration Act passed in England—Annual voting of supplies—Mutiny Bill—

1690 — William crosses to Ireland—**Battle of the Boyne, July 1, 1690**—Defeat of James and flight to France—Battle of Beachy Head, 1690—Ireland subdued—**Treaty of Limerick, 1691**—Mas-

1692 — sacre of Glencoe, 1692—William goes to Netherlands to fight against James's ally, Louis of France, 1692—Plots against

CONTENTS. xxvii

William—Battle of La Hogue cripples the French fleet, 1692—Greenwich Hospital founded by Mary—Origin of National Debt, 1692—Rise of Party Government, 1693—Bank of England established, 1694—New Triennial Act, 1694—Death of Queen Mary, 1694—Freedon of Press, 1695—Law of treason amended—New Coinage, 1696—Window tax, 1696—Plot to murder William, 1697—Peace of Ryswick, 1697—Reduction of the army—Judges made independent, 1701—Spanish succession—Two Partitions treaties—Anjou becomes King of Spain—Louis takes Netherland fortresses—Act of settlement, 1701, settles the crown after Anne on Electress Sophia of Hanover, granddaughter of James I.—Death of James II. in France—The claims of his son the Pretender to the English crown supported by Louis, 1701—England eager for war to keep out the Pretender—Death of William, Feb. 2, 1702. Pages 199-222

	1694
	1696
	1697
	1701
	1702

CHAPTER XXI.

THE LAST OF THE STUARTS.

ANNE proclaimed queen—Slow-minded, affectionate, and good—Ministry of Marlborough and Godolphin, 1702—Grand Alliance against France—Marlborough hampered by the allies—Occasional Conformity Bill, 1702-1711—Queen Anne's Bounty, 1704—Battle of Blenheim, 1704—Taking of Gibraltar, 1704—Battle of Ramillies, 1706—Whigs refuse peace with Louis, 1706 Pretender threatens Scotland—Fall of the funds, 1708—Growth of large towns—Decrease of yeomen—Union of Scotland and England, 1707—Penal laws afflict Ireland—Battles of Oudenarde and Lille, 1708—Malplaquet, 1709—The people weary of war—Marlborough and the Whigs dismissed, 1710—Tory Government under Harley and St. John—Peace of Utrecht ends the war, 1713—England gains Gibraltar and Nova Scotia—Tory plot for the Pretender—Death of Anne, July 30, 1714—Whig dukes proclaim George I. son of Electress Sophia—Struggle of seventeenth century ends in a powerful constitution—Literature of seventeenth century Pages 222-231

	1702
	1704
	1706
	1707
	1708
	1710
	1713
	1714

PART VII.

THE EXPANSION OF ENGLAND.

CHAPTER XXII.

ENGLAND STRENGTHENED.

1714	**GEORGE I.** of Hanover, great grandson of James I., honest and well-meaning—Impeachment of Tory ministers—A Whig Parliament—People restless—**Riot Act passed**,
1715	1715—Jacobite plots in the north, 1715—Death of Louis XIV. rendered France harmless, 1715—**Septennial Parlia-**
1716	**ment established**, 1716—Defeat of Spaniards at Cape Passaro, 1718—Spread of English trade—**South Sea Bub-**
1721	**ble bursts**, 1721—**Walpole**, who had opposed the scheme,
Walpole, March 1721	becomes **Prime Minister**, 1721-1742—Having influence with great Whig families, he gives rest to the country—Wood's halfpence cause trouble in Ireland, 1723—**Death of George I.**, 1727.
1727	**GEORGE II.**, son of George I., stubborn and passionate—His queen upheld Walpole—Walpole's good finance measures—Failure of Excise Bill, 1733—Walpole alienates
1737	his friends—**Rise of Patriot Party**, 1737—Death of Queen Caroline, 1737—Preaching of Whitefield and Wesley,
Wilmington, 1742	1739—Family Compact of France and Spain—War of Jenkin's ear, 1739—**Fall of Walpole**, 1742—War of the Aus-
Pelham, July 1743	trian succession—England drawn in to defend Hanover, 1743—Battle of Dettingen, 1743—Anson returns from voyage
1745	round the world, 1744—Battle of Fontenoy, 1745—**Jacobite Rebellion of 1745**—Battles of Falkirk and Culloden,
1746	1746—Prince Charlie escapes to France—Disarming of
1748	Highlanders, 1746—Peace of Aix-la-Chapelle, 1748—Death of Prince of Wales, 1751—Reform of Calendar—**History of East India Company**—Struggle between **English and French in India**—Dupleix and Clive, 1749-1751—

CONTENTS.

Daring campaign of Clive, 1751—Peace in India, 1759— | 1751
Skirmishes between English and French in Canada,
1754 — French build Fort Duquesne, 1754—Defeat of | 1754
English general Braddock, 1755—War in Canada inevitable | *Duke of*
—**Seven Years' War in Europe**, 1756—Panic in England | *Newcastle,*
—French seize Minorca, 1756—News of disaster of Black | *1754*
Hole of Calcutta, 1756—Admiral Byng executed, 1757— | 1756
English defeated on continent, 1757—General despair— | *Duke of*
Rise of Pitt, afterwards Earl of Chatham, 1757— | *Devonshire,*
Takes vigorous measures—Gives support to King Frederick | Nov. 1756
of Prussia—Victories of Rossbach and Luethen, 1757—Clive | *Newcastle,*
retakes Calcutta, 1757—Battle of Plassy, 1757—**English** | *June, 1757*
Power established in India—Pitt sends troops to Canada, | 1757
1757—Fort Duquesne taken, 1758—**Wolfe takes Quebec,** | 1758
1759—Montreal surrenders, 1760—**Canada becomes English** — First canals made, 1758—Constant victories in | 1760
Europe—**Death of Geo. II.**, Oct. 26, 1760.

GEORGE III., son of Geo. II., wants peace—Pitt | 1761
retires because war with **Spain is not declared,**
1761—**Earl of Bute minister**—War with Spain is forced | *Lord Bute,*
on England, 1672—Peace of Hubertsburg and Treaty | *1762*
of Paris end the Seven Years' War, 1763. | 1763
Pages 231-251

CHAPTER XXIII.

INDEPENDENCE OF AMERICAN COLONIES.

At Peace of Paris George III. had been king for three | 1763
years—Ministers were all powerful—Parliament did not
represent the people—State of England—Machines and | *Lord Bute.*
steam engines—Land enclosures—Increase of paupers—
Growing importance of the middle class—Geo. III., religious, simple-minded, and a good father, shrewd
and persevering, but obstinate and arbitrary; he
became insane—He retarded progress of England—Tory
party revived under Bute—Bribery and injustice—Bute | *Grenville,*
resigns, 1763—Contest of Parliament with Wilkes, 1763— | *April 1763*
Quarrel with American colonists begins, 1764—Stamp Act,

CONTENTS.

Rockingham, 1765
Grafton, July 1766
Lord North Jan. 1770

1765—First Regency Bill—Stamp Act repealed, 1766—Townshend's Revenue Act causes irritation in America, 1767—Wilkes elected for Middlesex, 1769—Parliament refuses to admit him, and wrongfully gives the seat to Colonel Luttrell—Wilkes fights the battle of reporters in Commons, 1771—Contest between Parliament and the city—Reporting continues—Modern newspapers.

1773

1775

1777

1780

Rockingham, March 1782
Shelburne, July 1782

Restless feeling increases in America, 1770—Duty on tea—Tea thrown in Boston Harbour, 1773—First Congress in America, 1774—Skirmish at Concord, April 19, 1775—War begins between colonists and England—Battle of Bunker's Hill, May 1775—George Washington commander-in-chief—Declaration of American Independence, July 4, 1776—Surrender of Burgoyne's army, Oct. 1777—Last efforts of Chatham for peace—His death, 1778—Siege of Gibraltar, 1779-1782—All Europe against England—Grattan obtains free export for Ireland, 1780; and repeal of Poyning's law, 1782—Gordon riots, 1780—Surrender of English Army at Yorktown, Oct. 1781—Lord North resigns, 1782—Rodney's naval victories, 1782—England acknowledges independence of America, 1782—Treaty of Versailles, Jan. 1783.

Portland, April 1783
William Pitt, Dec. 1783

Extension of English rule—Cook's voyages, 1768-1779—Convict settlements in Australia, 1788—The younger Pitt Prime Minister, Dec. 1783—Pitt and Fox—Warren Hastings Governor-General of India, 1773—First Mahratta war, 1779-1782—Defence of Madras—East India Bill passed—Government Board of Control appointed, 1784—Trial of Warren Hastings, 1787-1795.

Pages 251-265

CHAPTER XXIV.

THE FRENCH REVOLUTION—NAPOLEON AND ENGLAND.

William Pitt
1784
1785

Pitt remained minister from 1783 to 1800—Adam Smith's *Wealth of Nations*—Pitt reduces National Debt—Offers free trade to Ireland, 1785—Tries without success to pass a Reform Bill—King has attack of insanity, 1788—

CONTENTS.

Second Regency Bill—King recovers, 1788—**French Revolution breaks out, May 5, 1789**—Bastille stormed, July 14—Trouble between Orange Lodges and United Irishmen, 1790-1791—**Execution of Louis XVI.**, 1793—Burke rouses England to her danger—**War between England and French republic**, Feb. 1793—Naval victory of Lord Howe, 1794—French take Amsterdam and Dutch fleet, 1795—**England captures Cape of Good Hope, Ceylon, and Malacca**, 1795—Distress in England caused by the war—Pitt grows alarmed—"Habeas Corpus" Act suspended—Trial of Horne Tooke and others—**French invasion of Ireland fails**, 1796—French refuse terms of peace, 1796—**Naval Battle of St. Vincent**, Feb. 1797—Mutiny at the Nore, May—**Naval Victory of Camperdown**, Oct. 1797—Napoleon Bonaparte crosses to Egypt, 1798—**Nelson's victory of the Nile**, Aug. 1798—Irish rebellion of 1798—**Union of Ireland and England**, 1800—Pitt resigns because the King will not recognise Catholic rights, Jan. 1801—King insane for a short time—Victories of Alexandria and Copenhagen, 1801—**Peace of Amiens** ends war with French republic, 1802—Sir A. Wellesley in Second Mahratta war, 1803—**War between England and Napoleon**, who is now Emperor of France, 1803-1815—Napoleon's threatened invasion of England, 1805—**Victory of Trafalgar, death of Nelson**, Oct. 1805—Defeat of Austerlitz, Dec. 1805—Death of Pitt, Jan. 1806—Death of Fox, Sept. 1806—Napoleon defeats Prussians at Jena and issues **Berlin decree** against French vessels, Nov. 1806—**Abolition of slave trade**, 1807—Invades Portugal, 1808—**Peninsular War begins**, 1808—Retreat of Corunna, 1809—Death of Sir John Moore—King becomes hopelessly insane, 1810—**Prince of Wales Regent**, 1811—**Wellington's victories in Spain**, 1809-1813—Ciudad Rodrigo, Badajos, Salamanca, 1812—Vittoria, Battle of Pyrenees, St. Sebastian, 1813—Perceval shot, 1812—War with United States, 1812—Burning of Moscow and French retreat, 1812—Allies victorious—**Napoleon sent to Elba**, April 28, 1814—He escapes—**Battle of Waterloo**, 1815—Peace of Paris, 1815—Napoleon dies a prisoner in St. Helena, 1821—Distress from effects

1789	
1790	
1793	
1795	
1796	
1798	
1800	
Addington, May 1801	
1802	
Pitt, May 1804	
Lord Grenville, Feb. 1806	
Duke of Portland, March 1807	
1808	
Perceval, Dec. 1809	
Lord Liverpool, June 1812	
1815	

xxxii   CONTENTS.

	of the war—The Farmers' Corn-law, 1815—Gas introduc-
	ed, 1816—Riots, 1816—Death of Princess Charlotte
1817	and her baby, 1817—Manchester massacre, 1819—Six
1819	Acts passed, 1819—Term "Radical" arose—**Death of**
1820	**George III., Jan. 29, 1820.** Pages 266-284

CHAPTER XXV.

THE HISTORY OF OUR OWN TIMES.

1820	GEORGE IV., son of George III.—Trial of Queen Caroline—Cato Street conspiracy, Feb. 23—Suicide of
1822	Lord Londonderry (Castlereagh), 1822—Canning as Foreign Secretary keeps England at peace—Catholic Association, 1823—First Mechanics' Institute, 1823
1824	—Peel reforms criminal laws, 1824—Huskisson passes Reciprocity of Duties Bill and reforms trade laws, 1823-
1826	1824—Speculation, panic, and famine, 1824-1826—Emigra-
Canning, April 1827	tion, 1826—Foundation of Australian colonies, 1803- 1836—Canning Prime Minister, 1827—Death of Canning,
Goderich, Sept. 1827	1827—Sliding-scale duties on corn, 1828—Wellington
Wellington, Jan. 1828	Prime Minister, 1828-1830—Election of O'Connell, 1828 —Catholic Emancipation Bill passed, 1829—New police
1830	introduced, 1829—George IV. died, June 1830.
1830	WILLIAM IV., second son of George III., genial, homely sailor—Second French Revolution made England restless, 1830—Huskisson killed at opening
Lord Grey, Nov. 1830	of Manchester railway, 1830—Resignation of Wellington, Nov. 1830—Reform Bills: 1st in March; 2nd in Sept.
Melbourne, July 1834	3rd, which was carried, Dec. 18, 1831—Terms Conservative and Liberal arose—Abolition of Slavery Act
Sir R. Peel, Dec. 1834	passed Aug. 30, 1833—Factory and Education Acts, 1833 New poor-law, 1834—Municipal reform, 1835—Changes
Melbourne, April 1835	produced distress—Canada rebellion, 1837—Death of William IV., June 20, 1837. Pages 284-297

CHAPTER XXVI.

ENGLAND AND HER COLONIES.

| *Melbourne,* 1837 | VICTORIA, daughter of Duke of Kent, succeeded, June 20, 1837, crowned June 28, 1838—Married to Prince |

CONTENTS. xxxiii

Albert, **Feb. 10, 1840**—Hanover passes to Duke of Cumberland—Electric telegraph invented—Lord Durham sent as governor-general to Canada, **1838**—Rise of Chartists—Anti-corn-law League, **1838**—Penny Post, **1839**—Opium war with China, **1839** — **Constitution granted to Canada, 1840**—Massacre in Kabul Pass, Afghanistan, **1842**—**Peel establishes income-tax, 1842**—Free Church of Scotland established, **1843**—**Potato disease in Ireland, 1845**—Peel supports free trade, **1845**—**Repeal of corn-laws, 1846**—Protection Party throw Peel out of office, **1846**—**French Revolution of 1848 rouses the Chartists**—Failure of Chartist Demonstration, **April 10, 1848**—Annexation of the Punjab, **1849**—Free Libraries, **1850**.

Constitution given to Cape Colony, **1850**—Australian Colonies Bill, **1850**—Rise of New Zealand, **1839-1850**—Discovery of gold in California and Australia, **1849-1851**—Constitution granted to New Zealand, **1852**—Maori wars, **1861-1868**.

Great Exhibition in Hyde Park, 1851—*Coup d'Etat* of Louis Napoleon, **Dec. 2, 1851**—First English volunteers, **1852**—Eastern Question grows troublesome, **1853**—**Crimean War, 1854**—Battle of Alma, Sept. 20—Balaclava, Oct. 25—Inkermann, Nov. 5, 1854—Confusion and mismanagement—Help of Miss Florence Nightingale—**Sebastopol taken, Sept. 8, 1855**—**Treaty of Paris ends the war, March 30, 1856**.

Grievances of Indian Sepoys—**Indian Mutiny, 1857**—Massacre of Cawnpore, **July 15**—Justice of Canning, governor-general—Relief of Lucknow, **Sept. 23**—Campaign of Sir Hugh Rose, **1858**—East India Company ceases, 1858—Queen proclaimed sovereign of India, **Nov. 1**—**Took title of Empress of India, 1877**.

Orsini quarrels with France—**Volunteers are organized and made part of the British army, 1858**—United States Civil War breaks out, **1861**—Causes cotton famine in Lancashire, 1861—The *Alabama* claims—Death of Prince Consort, **Dec. 14, 1861**—Marriage of Prince of Wales, **1863**—Public Health Act, **1866**—Wars in Afghanistan and Africa, **1867-1886**—Reform Bills, **1867**-

	1838
	1839
	1840
	Sir R. Peel, Sept. 1841
	1845
	Lord John Russell, July 1846
	1848
	1850
	1851
	Lord Derby, Feb. 1852
	Lord Aberdeen, Dec. 1852
	Lord Palmerston, Feb. 1855
	1856
	1857
	Lord Derby, Feb. 1858
	Lord Palmerston, June 1859
	Lord Russell, Nov. 1865
	Lord Derby July 1866
	Disraeli, Feb. 1868

CONTENTS.

Gladstone, Dec. 1868
Deraeli, Feb. 1874
Gladstone, April 1880
Lord Salisbury, June 1885
Gladstone, Feb. 1886
Salisbury, Aug. 1886

1885—Fenian and Trades Union outrages, 1867—Irish Church disestablished, 1869—Franco-Prussian War, 1870—Irish Land Act, 1870—Education Act, 1870—Religious Tests abolished at universities—Army Purchase abolished, 1871—Disraeli becomes Lord Baconsfield, 1876—**Irish obstruction begins**, 1877—Murder of Cavendish and Burke by Irish, 1882—**Reform Bill brings in 2,485,667 new voters**, 1885—" Home Rule " of Gladstone and Parnell defeated, 1886—Depression of trade and agriculture, 1879-1886—Science, literature, and general advance of nineteenth century—**Colonial and Indian Exhibition of 1886 representing the English Empire.**

Pages 286-322

CANADIAN HISTORY.

CHAPTER I.

EARLY SETTLEMENT OF CANADA.

1608
1635

Dominion of Canada defined—Early inhabitants—North American Indians—Discovery of America—Jacques Cartier—**Champlain—Founding of Quebec, 1608**—Company of One Hundred Associates—Quebec taken by Sir David Kirke, 1629—Death of Champlain, 1635.

Pages 323-327

CHAPTER II.

CANADA UNDER FRENCH RULE.

1642

Indian missions—Indian wars—Destruction of Huron missions—Martyrdom of Brébœuf and Lalement—Founding of Montreal, 1642—Story of Dulac des Ormeaux—Laval in Canada—**Royal Government**—Custom of Paris—Military or feudal tenure—Carignan regiment settles in Canada—**Talon's Administration**—Paternal Government—Count de Frontenac—Marquette and Joliet—**Sieur** de la Salle—Discovery and exploration of the Mississippi—Frontenac's first Administration—**Massacre of Lachine,** 1689—Frontenac's second Administration—Sir William Phips tries to take Quebec, and fails, 1690—Border warfare—**State of the colony**—Condition of the people—Louisburg taken, 1745—Restored, 1748—**Braddock's expedition,** 1755—Baron Dieskau defeated, 1755—Seven years' war begins, 1756—Massacre of Fort William Henry, 1757—**Louisburg captured,** 1758—Ticonderoga, 1758—Fort Du Quesne taken, 1758—Niagara taken, 1759—Wolfe appears before Quebec—**Battle of Plains of Abraham, Sept. 13, 1759**—Montcalm and Wolfe killed—**Quebec surrendered, Sep. 18, 1759.** . . Pages 328-346

| 1689 |
| 1690 |
| 1748 |
| 1755 |
| 1757 |
| 1758 |
| 1759 |

CHAPTER III.

LAYING THE FOUNDATIONS OF THE CANADIAN CONSTITUTION.

The British spend the winter in Quebec—Second battle of Plains of Abraham, 1760—**Peace of Paris,** 1763—Conspiracy of Pontiac—Detroit besieged by the Indians—**Military rule**—State of the colony—Government of Canada, 1763-74—**Quebec Act, 1774**—Declaration of Independence, 1776—Invasion of Montgomery and Arnold—Montgomery killed at Quebec—Boundaries of Canada fixed, **1783**—United Empire Loyalists settle in Canada, **1784**—British settlers dissatisfied with Quebec Act—**Constitutional Act of 1791**—Boundary between Upper and Lower Canada defined—Terms of Constitutional Act—Act goes into force, 1792. . . Pages 346-355

| 1763 |
| 1774 |
| 1776 |
| 1783 |
| 1784 |
| 1791 |
| 1792 |

CHAPTER IV.

THE WAR OF 1812.

The beginning of Parliamentary Government—First Parliament of Upper Canada meets at Newark (Niagara), Sep., 1792—Legislation—Abolition of slavery in Upper Canada—First Parliament of Lower Canada meets, Dec., 1792—Legislation—Chief Justice Osgoode's decision regarding slavery—

1792

xxxvi   CONTENTS.

1812 | Founding of Upper Canada—Life of settlers—Political discontent—**Cause of War of 1812**—War declared, June—Plan of campaign of Americans—Tecumseh and Brock—Surrender of Detroit by Hull—**Battle of Queenston Heights, Oct. 13, 1812**—Death of Brock and Macdonnell—Dearborn defeated at
1813 | Lacolle—American successes at sea—**Campaign of 1813**—Army bills issued—York captured—Stony Creek—Beaver Dams—Mrs. Laura Secord—Captain Barclay defeated on Lake Erie by Commodore Perry—Battle of Moraviantown, Oct. 5, 1813—Tecumseh killed—Battle of Chrysler's Farm, Nov. 11, 1813—Battle of Chateauguay, Sept. 26, 1813—Niagara burned by Americans—Buffalo, Lewiston, and other American villages
1814 | burned by the British—**1814 and the close of the war**—Lacolle Mill—Chippewa—**Lundy's Lane, July 25, 1814**—Failure of attack on Plattsburg—Washington taken—**Treaty of Ghent, Dec. 24, 1814**—Repulse of British at New Orleans.
                                                              Pages 355-369

CHAPTER V.

THE STRUGGLE FOR RESPONSIBLE GOVERNMENT, AND THE REBELLION 1837-38.

1822 | **Growth of the colony**—Immigration—Inland navigation and canals—Banks founded—Canada Trade Act, 1822—Educational growth—**Political abuses and troubles**—Causes of discontent in Lower Canada—Discontent in Upper Canada—The Family Compact—Clergy Reserves question—William
1837 | Lyon Mackenzie—**Rebellion in Lower Canada, 1837-38**—Papineau—St. Denis—St. Eustache—Lord Durham sent to Canada—Illegal Acts of Durham—**Durham's Report**—**Rebellion in Upper Canada, 1837**—Sir Francis Bond Head—Montgomery's Tavern—Mackenzie escapes to the United States—
1838 | "**Patriot War,**" 1838—Burning of the "Caroline"—Battle of the Windmill, Nov. 16, 1838—Execution of Von Schultz and his companions.   .   .   .   Pages 369-379

CONTENTS.   xxxvii

CHAPTER VI.

THE GROWTH OF RESPONSIBLE GOVERNMENT.

Act of Union, 1840—Charles Poulett Thompson, Governor—Union takes place, 1841—**Terms of Union**—**Municipal Act of 1841**—Other measures—Sir Charles Metcalfe—Disagrees with his Ministers—Governs without a Ministry—**Ashburton Treaty, 1842**—Terms of Treaty—Educational progress in Upper Canada—Dr. Ryerson and Public School system—Colleges founded—Lord Elgin's Administration—**Rebellion Losses Bill**—Parliament Buildings burned—Commercial progress—Railway era—Municipal Loan Fund Act—Uniform Postage, 1851—**Reciprocity Treaty, 1854**—**Clergy Reserves and Seignorial Tenure Acts, 1854**—Increase of members of Parliament—Legislative Council becomes elective, 1856—**Representation by population agitation**—Political deadlock—Steps towards Confederation—**British North America Act passed, 1867**—Volunteer system, 1854—**Decimal Currency, 1858**—Reciprocity Treaty expires, 1866—Fenian raids, 1866—**Ridgeway, 1866**—Effect of raids. Pages 379-391	1840 1841 1842 1846 1849 1852 1854 1853 1856 1864-6 1867 1858 1866

CHAPTER VII.

NOVA SCOTIA AND NEW BRUNSWICK.

Change of names of Upper and Lower Canada—**Nova Scotia**—First settlement at Port Royal, 1605—Port Royal taken by English colonists—Old name of province, Acadia—Called Nova Scotia by Sir William Alexander—Given to England by Treaty of Utrecht, 1713—Halifax founded, 1749—**Acadians expelled, 1755**—Constitution given, 1758—New Brunswick, Cape Breton, and Prince Edward Island secede, **1784**—Cape Breton returns, 1819—**Responsible Government granted, 1848**—Joins Confederation, 1867.	1605 1713 1749 1758 1784 1848 1867
New Brunswick—First settlement near St. John River—U. E. Loyalists settle in province, 1783-84—Made separate	1784

1825 1867	province, 1784—Great fire at Miramichi, 1825—**Responsible Government**, 1848—Joins Confederation, 1867.

Pages 391-396

CHAPTER VIII.

CANADA SINCE CONFEDERATION.

 1869-70 1873 1871 1873 1874 1878 1882 1885 1886	British North America Act—Terms—**New provinces**—Red River Rebellion—Manitoba Act passed—British Columbia joins Confederation, 1871—Prince Edward Island joins, 1873—Political changes—**Washington Treaty**, 1871—**Halifax Commission**, 1878—Pacific Railway—"Pacific Scandal," 1873—Mackenzie Government formed—"National Policy" agitation, 1878—Mackenzie Government defeated, 1878—**Ballot Act** passed, 1874—**Redistribution Bill**, 1882—**Dominion Franchise Act**, 1885—Increase of Dominion Parliament members—Municipal Loan Fund indebtedness settled—Crooks' Act—"Jesuits' Estates" question settled—Manitoba secures right to construct railways—**North-West Rebellion, 1885**—**Batoche**—Riel executed—**Material progress**—Canadian Pacific Railway completed, 1886—Literary and social progress.

Pages 396-408

HISTORY OF ENGLAND

CHAPTER I.

EARLY BRITAIN

1. England defined.—Before beginning to study the history of England we must first inquire what we mean when we speak of England—a question not so easy to answer as many people would suppose. The sovereign of the British Isles, Queen Victoria, is styled "Queen of the United Kingdom of Great Britain and Ireland," showing that Ireland is a country distinct from Great Britain; and this is not merely because it is an island, but because a large part of it is inhabited by a people of a different race from the English, who have a language of their own called "Gaelic," which they still often speak among themselves. But how about Great Britain? is this all England? Certainly not; for the northern half is Scotland, which, until about three hundred years ago, was a separate kingdom; and although the Lowlanders of Scotland are of the same race as the English, the Highlanders, living in the north, speak Gaelic, and are a branch of the same race as the Irish. There remains, then, only the south of Great Britain—from Northumberland to the English Channel. Surely this at least is England? Yes, but only if we add, "the principality of Wales;" for here again we must take out a large slice of country, inhabited by a people who have a language of their own, called "Cymric," sufficiently like that of Ireland and the Highlands to show that the Welsh, Irish, and Highlanders sprang from the same stock, which remains to this day to a great extent separate from the English. *[margin: Ireland and Scotland]* *[margin: Wales.]*

Strictly speaking, then, England is only the southern half of the island of Great Britain, covering an area of 50,922 square miles and divided into fifty-two English counties, with the twelve counties of

Wales (covering an area of 7398 square miles) nestling into her western side. Eighteen hours in the railway will carry you from the extreme south of the country to the northern boundary at Berwick-on-Tweed, and on to Edinburgh, the chief city of the Lowland Scotch; while in eight hours you can cross the widest part of England from east to west. Yet this small country is the fatherland of the millions of Englishmen now spread over the globe; and a history of England is the history of the rise of this great people, with its struggles and its mistakes, its sufferings through ignorance and crime, and its rewards for courage, perseverance, and endurance.

Area of England.

2. Britain before England.—Now if the English had lived in this country from its very beginning, we could start at once with their doings. But the races which we now call Welsh, Irish, Highlanders, and Cornish have been in these islands at least two thousand years, as we know from scattered notices of them in Greek and other writers, and some of them probably very much longer, before we have any written account of them; while it is not fifteen hundred years since the "Angles" or "Engles" came over the sea from Angeln, on the shores of the Baltic, and, with their companions, the Jutes and the Saxons, took possession of the southern half of Britain, giving it their name. Therefore, before we can speak of England, we must sketch very briefly the history of Britain before the English came.

. . .

In ages long gone by—how long none can tell—the land we now inhabit was a wild country, in different parts of which lions and tigers, bears and hyænas, elephants, hippopotami, elks, and reindeer roamed in the forests and over the plains, disputing the ground with savage men who killed them as best they could with weapons made of rough flints rudely chipped to a point. We know this was so, because we find these weapons in ancient caves and river gravel-beds in many parts of England, together with the broken bones of the wild animals which were killed; while charcoal at the mouths of the caves tell us that fires were kindled there. We call these savages the men of the "Palæolithic" or "Ancient Stone" Period, and we know very little about them.

Palæolithic men.

They were followed, in after ages, by men who made better weapons, still of stone, but well shaped and highly polished. These are called the men of the "Neolithic" or "New Stone" Period. We find the bones and skeletons of these later *Neolithic men.* men buried in long chambers or barrows in many parts of England, Wales, and Ireland, together with polished arrow-heads, hatchets and axes of stone, and needles and pins of bone. The bones of dogs and pigs, sheep, oxen, and goats show that they kept domestic animals; and pieces of rough pottery and woven flax and straw prove that they were learning the arts of pottery-making and weaving.

The skulls of these men were long and narrow, like the skulls of a small, dark-skinned, curly-haired people called the Basques or Iberians, who still live in some wild mountainous parts of Spain, and speak a different language from every other nation except the Finns in the far north of Europe. So we have reason to suppose that the "Neolithic" men belonged to a widely-spread race, from which these Iberians also sprang; especially as the skeletons the ancestors of the Iberians are found with polished stone weapons in long barrows in Spain just like those in Britain. There is even a small dark type of men among a certain class of Irish and Welsh of to-day which is probably a remnant of this same ancient people.

We can picture these Neolithic men, then, to ourselves, keeping their cattle, fashioning their weapons and rude pots, living in caves with their wives and children, and burying their dead in long chambers made of huge uncut stones covered with earth. When this earth is dug away the stones remain, forming those *Cromlechs.* rude tables which have been called "cromlechs," and were long mistaken for altars. It is also probable that the strange circles of gigantic stones at Stonehenge on Salisbury Plain in Wiltshire, and elsewhere, were raised by these men, though how and why is a mystery.

Time passed on, and another race with rounder skulls began to mingle with the long-headed men. We find their skeletons in round barrows formed entirely of earth, and with them both *Celts.* stone and bronze weapons, showing that they were learning the use of metal. In some of the later barrows we even find tools made of iron, which is much more difficult to work than bronze. For by this time a new people had come over into Britain, bringing with them a higher civilisation. Strange as it may seem, we must go right away to the East, probably somewhere near Persia, to find these people called "Celts," some of whom, after long migrations, came and settled in our island. Scholars tell us that an Aryan people—so called from the old name *Arya* (the noble people) anciently applied to part of Persia—started in the East long before the time of history, and spread out in two directions; into Persia and India on one side, and across Europe on the other, where we can follow the traces of their language. First these people made their homes a little to the West; then, as they became too numerous, the stream of migration flowed on, and parties of them settled farther and farther West, till some crossed over the sea into Britain, conquered the inhabitants and settled down, a large-limbed, fair-haired race among the smaller and darker natives.

Here history first tells us of them, when the Phœnicians, sailing through the Straits of Gibraltar (then called the Pillars of Hercules),

Visits of Phœnicians, 6th cent. B.C. about six hundred years before Christ was born, came to trade for tin with the Scilly Isles near Cornwall, called by Greek writers the "Cassiterides" or Tin Islands. About a hundred years later the Greeks came overland from Massilia or Marseilles, and from this time we find our island called "Albion" and Ireland "Ierne," while the whole group was named BRITANNIA.

Here then, at last, we arrive at BRITAIN, which became gradually known to other nations. About three hundred and fifty years

Julius Cæsar came B.C. 55. later the great Roman general, Julius Cæsar, came in the years 55 and 54 before Christ, and, defeating the Britons under their great chief, Cassivelaunus, made them promise to pay tribute to Rome. He went away again that same year, and the Britons had their country to themselves for another hundred years, and then never again.

By this time the people of the south of Britain had become fairly civilised. They had war chariots, and fought with spears, pikes, and axes, defending themselves with a shield of skin and wickerwork. They wore mantles and tunics of cloth, and arm-rings of gold and silver, and lived in scattered huts of wood and reeds on a stone foundation. Each tribe had a *din* or stronghold, surrounded by a wall or high bank for refuge in time of war, and one of these—the "Lynn-din" or lake-fort, pronounced Lundun—seems to have been the beginning of our great city. They grew corn and stored it in cavities of the rocks, and they made basket-work boats and canoes hollowed out of tree-trunks. The inland people were more ignorant; they dressed in the skins of beasts, and lived on milk and meat; while those still further to the north were mere naked savages—fearless, cruel, and revengeful. Homes of Britons.

There was something grand and yet horrible in the religion of the Britons. They had priests called Druids, who had secret doctrines of their own, and who are said to have offered up men and women as sacrifices; but the people seem chiefly to have worshipped nature. They adored the genii of the streams, woods, and mountains. The oak, with the mistletoe growing on it, was their emblem of Divinity; and they met for worship in caves and in the depths of the forest. Druid religion.

3. Roman Rule.—Such were the Britons when the Romans came a second time, under the Emperor Claudius, and took possession of the south of the island. The Britons struggled bravely for many years, and harassed the Romans in the woods and marshes. For seven years it seemed doubtful which side would win, and then the great British chief, Caractacus, was defeated and sent a prisoner to Rome. When the Romans had once gained a footing they advanced, till in a few years more they reached the island of Anglesey, then called *Mona*, where they massacred the Druids in their stronghold. But they nearly lost the country, for Boadicea, the widow of a British chief, roused the people in the east of England; and it was only after London, then an open British town, had been burnt, and the Romans were almost exhausted, that they won the day. Queen Boadicea is said to have poisoned herself to escape the shame of being taken. Roman conquest of Britain, A.D. 43. Caractacus, A.D. 50. Boadicea, A.D. 61.

After this the Romans ruled over the Britons for about three hundred years, much as the English govern India now. They made good laws, and laid down solid roads, which remain to this day. One of these, called Watling Street (*see* Map II.), stretched from Dover to Chester, passing through London. They built houses and villas, public baths and theatres; and large towns such as York, Lincoln, and Chester sprang up in different parts of the country. To this day we can trace many of these towns—such as Doncaster, Leicester, Manchester—by the termination *caster* or *cester*, from the Latin *castra*, a camp or fortified place. They cleared the forests and encouraged the growth of corn, so that Britain was called "the granary of the North;" and they introduced many new fruits, worked the mines, and taught the Britons civilised habits. It was during this time that missionaries visited our island, and both Britons and Romans became Christians.

<small>300 years of Roman rule.</small>

But though Roman roads, the pavements of Roman villas, and Roman walls remain to this day, the influence of these people on the Britons did not last. Britain was, after all, only a conquered province of Rome. The natives lived happily under their conquerors, imitating their customs, speaking Latin as a fashionable language, and relying upon the Romans to defend them. Yet they clung at heart to their own laws and their own chiefs; and when in the year 401 the Romans, much troubled by enemies at home, gradually took away their troops from South Britain, the people would have been glad to see them go, if they could have defended themselves without their help from their wild Celtic neighbours in Northern Britain. These neighbours, the "Picts" or Caledonians, and the "Scots"—who came originally from Ireland, and afterwards gave Scotland its name—were savage and warlike. Even the Romans had only kept them out by strong fortified walls, of which the most famous is the wall of Hadrian, from the Solway Firth to the mouth of the Tyne, parts of which remain to this day. No sooner were the Romans gone than these Picts and Scots broke through the walls and harassed the South Britons, who found it difficult to defend themselves, for the Romans had always sent away the British soldiers to serve in the Roman army abroad. So they sent for Roman soldiers to defend them, who came once and drove back the Picts and

<small>Romans begin to withdraw, A.D. 401.</small>

<small>Picts and Scots.</small>

<small>Romans leave, A.D. 410.</small>

Scots; but after this, the Romans withdrew entirely, and left the Britons to their fate.

This brings us to the point where the history of England begins; for the Britons in their despair invited some still more formidable enemies, who were hovering about their shores, to come over and help them. These were our ancestors, who founded the English nation, and we must now learn where they came from and how they came.

CHAPTER II.

HOW THE ENGLISH CAME

1. Early Saxon Invasions.—For more than a hundred years before the Romans left Britain, they had been much troubled by pirates, who came in large flat-bottomed boats across the German Ocean from the country around the River Elbe. Swooping down upon the shores of the north of Gaul and of the south-east of Britain, these marauders carried off men, women, and children, together with any plunder upon which they could lay their hands. So fierce and cruel were these Saxon pirates that the Romans built strong fortresses from the River Humber all around to the Isle of Wight to keep them away; and an officer, called the "Count of the Saxon shore," was appointed specially to superintend the defence of the coast.

The invaders belonged to the Teutonic race, quite different from the Celts, although they came originally from the same stock in the East. When we first hear of them in history they had spread gradually across Europe, as the Celts had done in ages before; and as the Celts drove out an earlier race, so these Teutons now drove the Celts out of the plains of Germany, as far south as the Romans would let them, and then made their way northwards to the country between the rivers Weser and Elbe, and up into Jutland, Sweden, and Norway. Here,

Origin of the Teutons.

with the Baltic on one side and the North Sea on the other, they naturally became bold sea-rovers, and from the shores of Jutland and Germany they came in their flat-bottomed boats driven by at least fifty oars, and ravaged the fair shores of Gaul, and the scarcely less fertile coasts of Britain.

They had little chance of gaining a footing on the island while the Romans were there; and even after the Roman troops had left, the Britons kept them off for nearly forty years. At last, however, worn out by the attacks of the Picts and Scots by land, and of these Saxon pirates by sea, the Britons determined to set one enemy against the other; and a British chief named Vortigern is said, to have invited Hengest and Horsa, two chiefs of the sea-pirates from Jutland, to settle in the Isle of Thanet, in the north of Kent, and fight his battles against the Picts. This the Jutes did, but no sooner had they conquered the Picts than they turned their arms against the Britons themselves. Horsa was killed in the first battle, but Hengest led the Jutes on, and after thirty years of fighting, his son Eric founded the two small kingdoms of East and West Kent (see Map I.), of which the chief city was Cant-wara-byrig or Kentmensborough, now our city of Canterbury. So the Jutes were the first of our ancestors to settle in this country.

Landing of Jutes, A.D. 449.

But meanwhile other pirate boats cruising in the Channel carried back, year after year, tidings of a land to be conquered; and the Saxons, who also came from the opposite shores between the rivers Elbe and Weser, landed with their chiefs on the south coast of Britain. Long before this the Britons had bitterly regretted calling in foreign allies, for these new invaders killed or drove back all before them, and when Cissa, their chief, took the town of Anderida, near where Pevensey now is, he left not a single Briton alive. The Saxons moved forward very slowly, for the land was covered with dense forests, marshes, and swamps, and the Britons fought desperately. In those days battles were hand to hand fights, and the ground which was won one day was often lost the next. In the year 520 the British King Arthur (about whom the legends of the knights of the round table are told) defeated the West Saxons so completely that he stopped them for many a year.

Arrival of Saxons, A.D. 477.

Struggle with the Britons.

HOW THE ENGLISH CAME.

It was, however, only a question of time. The Britons were divided among themselves, and were helpless against the numbers which came over the sea, fresh every year, to strengthen the invaders, bringing with them their wives, children, and cattle, and settling down stubbornly to make new homes whenever they gained a fresh piece of country. It is true they took sixty long years to win Southern Britain, but at the end of that time they had founded the kingdoms of the South Saxons or Sussex, West Saxons or Wessex, East Saxons or Essex, and Middle Saxons or Middlesex, and the Britons were driven westward into the part now called Somerset, Devon, and Cornwall. *[Saxon settlements.]*

Meanwhile, on the north-east of Britain, another tribe called the "Angles," who came from the small country of Angeln in Schleswig, north of the River Eyder, were settling down in large numbers. This tribe is specially interesting to us; first, because almost the entire people came over with all they had and made our country their home, and secondly, because they gave their name of Angles or Engles to our nation. *[Settlements of the Angles.]*

We do not know exactly when they first landed, but we know that some of them sailed up the Humber and founded a kingdom called Deira; while in 547 another portion of the tribe came in fifty boats from Angeln, under a chief called Ida the flame-bearer, and going farther north founded the kingdom of Bernicia; and, after a struggle of fifty years or more, Bernicia and Deira were united into the kingdom of North-Humber-land, which stretched from the River Humber right up to the Firth of Forth. This explains why the Lowland Scotch are Teutons, while the Highlanders are Celts. The Angles drove the Celts into the Highlands and took the Lowlands for themselves, and the city of Edinburgh itself took its name Eadwinesburh from one of the later Anglian kings, Eadwine or Edwin. Meanwhile other Angles were settling to the south of the Humber. The North-folk and South-folk settled in the counties still called by their names, and formed the kingdom of East Anglia (*see* Map I.); while others pushed into the middle of England, into that part now called the Midland Counties. These middle-Angles were called Marchmen or Bordermen, as living on *[Northumbria, A.D. 603.]* *[East Anglia and Mercia.]*

the borders of the land still held by the Britons, while their land was called March-land or Mercia.

And so it came to pass that about the end of the sixth century, two hundred years after the Romans left, the Britons had been driven right over to the west of England, into Devonshire and Cornwall (or West Wales) on the south, into the mountains of North Wales on the west, and into Cumberland, Westmoreland, and Lancashire, then called "Strathclyde," farther to the north. They also began about this time to be called *Welsh*, which was the name the Angles used for *strangers*, or those whose language they did not understand. The rest of the country was in the hands of the Jutes, Angles, and Saxons, who were called *Saxons* by the Welsh, but who, as they grew into one people, were sometimes called Anglo-Saxons, but among themselves more commonly *English*.

<small>Welsh and English.</small>

They held all the east of the island, from the English Channel to the Firth of Forth, and it was roughly divided into seven chief kingdoms—Kent, belonging to the Jutes; Sussex, Wessex, and Essex, belonging to the Saxons; Northumbria, Anglia, and Mercia, belonging to the Angles—and these seven kingdoms have been called the "Heptarchy." We must not, however, suppose that these were fixed and settled divisions, as we should understand kingdoms now. The Anglo-Saxons were free men who had come over in separate bands, under favourite leaders, to take what they could, each for themselves. When they were not fighting against the Britons, they were struggling with each other, trying to get the upper hand, so that the different kingdoms were broken up and pieced together over and over again before the English became one nation.

<small>Term Heptarchy misleading.</small>

To understand the history of these times we must picture to ourselves a wild country, with dense forests, wide swamps and marshes, and waste land in the plains. The Roman roads still remained in the more civilised parts, but the only roads in the west were narrow rugged passes through the mountains, where the Britons had taken refuge. Here and there, over the plains and undulating ground in the east of the country, would be grouped the villages of one or other of the English tribes,

<small>Early English villages.</small>

HOW THE ENGLISH CAME. 11

with some cultivated land around them, while the towns which the Romans had built had very few people in them, and were falling into ruin.

2. Social and Political Condition of the English.— The people in the villages were rough, sturdy freemen, only just settling down from a sea-life. The largest house would belong to the Etheling or *Eorl*, a man of nobler family and wealthier than the rest. But even the *Ceorls* or churls, who were lowlier freemen, had each his own house, built on his own land which was portioned out to him to cultivate. Some late-comers, who had no land of their own, worked for the ceorls, and were called *Laets;* while there were a good many *slaves*, either conquered Britons or men who had sold or lost their freedom, and these men might be sold by their masters either in the country or into foreign lands. On the whole, however, the greater number were free men, having their own house and land, and a voice in the village *Moot* or meeting, which was held around the sacred tree, to settle disputed questions and to divide the land. A man who had committed a crime was judged by his fellows, and acquitted if he could get a number of honest men to swear that he was innocent. This was called "*compurgation.*" If he could not clear himself in this way, he was allowed to appeal to the "*ordeal*" or "judgment of God," by walking blindfold over red-hot ploughshares, or dipping his hand into boiling water. If he was unhurt, then he was declared not guilty.

Eorls and Ceorls.

Laets and slaves.

Village moot.

Compurgation and ordeal.

Each village or township was surrounded by a rough fence called a "*tun*," and was separated from the next by a piece of waste ground called the "*mark*" or march which no one might claim. If a stranger crossed this mark he blew a horn, otherwise any one had a right to kill him. The townships were grouped into "*hundreds,*" and when the people had to gather for war, or to settle any great question, some of the freemen from each of the villages meet together in the great "*Folkmoot*" or meeting of the tribe, and choose ealdormen or aldermen from among the eorls to lead them to battle, or to speak for them in the "*Witangemot*" or meeting of wise men,

Hundreds.

Folkmoot and Witan.

where laws were framed, and questions of peace or war decided. Before the English came to Britain each band was governed separately by its own alderman. Now, however, that they were obliged to unite against another nation, they elected one alderman to be superior to the others, as "king" over a large number of bands. But though the king had his own *"Thegns"* or chosen bands of warriors, he could do nothing without the consent of the Witan and all the people. He could not even say who should reign after him. The kings were elected, <small>Elected kings.</small> though they were generally chosen from the same family, because the people believed that certain families were descended from Woden, their great god of war.

3. Religious Condition of the English.—For these Angles were still heathen, and although the Britons whom they conquered were Christians, yet they did not learn from them. Our <small>Heathen gods.</small> days of the week still remind us of the gods of our ancestors—Wednesday is Woden's day; Thursday, the day of Thor, the god of thunder; Friday, the day of Freya, goddess of peace and fruitfulness; while Eostre, goddess of the spring, gave her name to our Easter. Besides these chief gods, they believed in water-nixies and wood-demons, in spirits of earth and air, in hero-gods and in weird women. The real religion, however, of these ancient English was not in these superstitious beliefs, but in their deep sense of right, of justice, of freedom, and of the mystery of life and death; and it was because they were so much in earnest that the Christian religion, when it came, took such a deep hold upon them.

It came very slowly and with many a struggle. Pope Gregory the Great, when he was quite a young man, had once seen some <small>Christianity.</small> young fair-haired boys who were being sold as slaves in the market-place of Rome. Touched by their beauty, he asked where they came from, and when he heard that they were Angles, "Not Angles, but angels," said he, "with faces so angel-like." When he became Pope he remembered those lovely heathen boys, and in the year 596 sent a Roman abbot named Augustine, with forty monks, to preach the gospel to the English people. Augustine landed in Kent, where a king named Ethelbert was then

HOW THE ENGLISH CAME. 13

reigning, who had married a Christian wife, Bertha, the daughter of a Frankish king. Ethelbert met Augustine on the Isle of Thanet, in the open air for fear he should cast a spell upon him, and listened to him patiently. In the end he was baptised with many of his people, outside the chief gate of Canterbury, where the little Church of St. Martin now stands. From that time the kingdom of Kent became Christian, and Augustine was the first Archbishop of Canterbury. *Conversion of Kent, A.D. 597.*

From Kent the new religion spread to Northumbria. Edwin, king of that land, married Ethelbert's daughter, and she took a monk named Paulinus with her to the north. Here Edwin called together his Witan, and they listened to this faith which told them of a life after death, and accepted Christianity. Edwin was a very powerful king, for all the other kings, except the King of Kent, acknowledged him "overlord" or, as they called it, "Bretwalda." He ruled so well that in his days "a woman with her babe might walk scatheless (unhurt) from sea to sea," which was saying a great deal in such a turbulent land. *Conversion of Northumbria.*

4. Irish Missions, 634-664.—The Irish had been converted by St. Patrick a hundred years before, and an Irish monk, Columba, built a mission-station on a small rocky island called Iona on the west coast of Scotland, from which teachers went out to all the north of England. Cuthbert, monk of Montrose, who wandered on foot among the Northumbrians, and Cædmon, the cowherd of Whitby, our first English poet, were trained under these Irish monks, who did good work among the people. In the year 664, however, some questions arose about minor Church matters between these Irish monks and the Roman missionaries, and King Oswi of Northumbria decided in favour of the Roman teachers. Most of the Irish monks then went back to their home, and monks and bishops from Rome took up the work. The Pope sent Theodore of Tarsus as Archbishop of Canterbury, and he marked out the sees of the bishops and appointed priests to each village, or cluster of villages, which were then probably first called "*parishes.*" An archbishop was afterwards appointed to York for the north of England, and archbishops, bishops, and priests sat in the "moots" and took a part in govering the people. *English Church organised, 673.*

14   HISTORY OF ENGLAND.

Monasteries now sprang up rapidly, and the monks settling among the rough freemen taught them to love quiet work and respect learning. Carpenters and other artisans and traders settled round the monasteries and abbeys; markets were held before the abbey gates; and in this way small towns began to grow up. It was in the
Origin of towns. monastery of Jarrow, on the coast of Durham, that Bede, the first writer of English history, spent his whole life, and trained six hundred scholars, beside strangers. He wrote forty-five works all in Latin, some text-books for his students,
Bede, 673-735. some treatises on the Bible, and one was his famous *Ecclesiastical History of the English Nation*, which tells what happened for a hundred and fifty years after Augustine landed in Kent. Bede's was a loving, patient nature, and it was such men as he who were gradually civilising the English people, while the various petty kings were struggling for power and conquering more and more land from the Welsh.

5. Supremacy of Wessex.—At first, as we have seen, Northumbria was the most powerful kingdom; then Mercia got the upper hand under her great king, Offa the Mighty; and lastly in 827 Egbert, King of Wessex, conquered both the Mercians and Northumbrians, and became king of all the English south of the Thames, and Bretwalda right up to the Firth of Forth. Kent, Sussex, and Essex had altogether ceased to be separate kingdoms, and thus for the first time all the English were overruled by one king. We shall see that the kings of Wessex had the chief power over the English people for the next two hundred years.

CHAPTER III.

STRUGGLE BETWEEN ENGLISH AND DANES

1. Origin of Danes.—Hardly, however, were the English beginning to settle down from their own petty wars than a new danger threatened them, and threw them back for a long time, although in the end it helped to unite all the kingdoms into one. It will be remembered that when the Teutons spread over Europe many of them went northwards into the countries now called Denmark, Sweden, and Norway. These people had remained barbarians and heathen, worshipping Woden, and having a hard struggle to live in the cold barren countries of the north. They too became sea-rovers, as their countrymen the Saxons had done before them, and they were known as the Northmen, Danes, or "Vikings," which last means *creek-dwellers*. Already they had settled in the Orkneys and the Isle of Man, and after a long struggle had taken possession of the coast of Ireland, with Dublin, Limerick, and Waterford as their chief towns.

2. Danish Invasions.—Now they began to harass the English, sometimes joining with the Welsh on the west, sometimes making raids on the east coast, sailing up the rivers, and throwing up earth works round their head-quarters. From these they sallied out over the country, burning towns and monasteries, killing men and children, and carrying off the women as slaves. At first they only came in the summer time, and went away with their spoils; but after Egbert's death they became more troublesome, and when his son Ethelwulf was king, they remained all the winter in the Isle of Sheppy, at the mouth of the Thames. In 866 a great Danish army attacked East Anglia, and, crossing the Humber, took York and overran all the south of Northumbria. Then they pushed their way south into Mercia as far as Nottingham, and, taking complete possession of the country, wintered at Thetford in Norfolk, where they murdered Edmund, King of East Anglia, tying him to a tree and shooting at him with arrows till he died, because he refused to give up the Christian faith.

Having conquered a large part of Northumbria, Mercia, and East Anglia, bringing ruin and misery wherever they went, they next turned their arms against Wessex. But here they met with their match. Four brothers, sons of Ethelwulf, had reigned one after another in Wessex during the last thirteen years. The third of these brothers, Ethelred I., fought bravely, with the help of his younger brother Alfred, against the Danes, subdued the Welsh in Cornwall and Wales, and went even as far as the island of Mona, which had been named Anglescy (*Angles' Ey or Island*) by King Edwin of Northumbria. But in spite of all Ethelred's efforts the Danes gained ground, and when he died in 871, and Alfred was chosen king, matters were growing desperate.

3. Alfred the Great.—The history of Alfred shows what a good and wise man can do under great difficulties. He was born at Wantage in Berkshire. As quite a little child he used to repeat old Saxon poems to his mother, Osburgha, who said one day, "The one among you children who can first say this book by heart shall have it ;" and the story goes that little Alfred carried the book to his teacher, and, when he had learnt it, repeated it to his mother. If this be true, it must have happened before the boy was four years old, for at that age his father sent him to Rome, and he never saw his own mother again. It was probably in Rome, where Alfred afterwards went a second time with his father, that he learnt much which was of use to him afterwards. Before he was twenty he married happily, but he had to struggle against ill health and attacks of epilepsy, and was only twenty-two when he became king over a country laid waste by the ravages of the Danes.

<small>Alfred's childhood.</small>

Within a month of his brother's death he fought a battle against them, but was defeated, and from that time he struggled in vain to overcome them, sometimes fighting, sometimes buying them off. But in spite of bribes they came in endless numbers over the sea. The monks and clergy, turned out of their homes by the invaders, wandered about the country, or carried off their treasures to the continent; the people were worn out and reduced to beggary, the land was laid waste, and the Welsh, of whom there were still a great many in Wessex, were half disposed to help the Danes. At last, in 878, after seven years' almost ceaseless fighting, Alfred was so completely defeated at Chippenham, in Wiltshire, that he was forced to fly in disguise into the woods and marshes of Somersetshire. But he would not leave the country, as the King of Mercia had done, to die a pilgrim in Rome. His people were in distress, and he must help them.

It is at this time that Alfred is said to have taken refuge in a swineherd's cottage, where he let the good woman's cakes burn on the hearth as he mused how to save his country. At any rate he mused to good purpose, and gradually collecting a band of faithful friends in Athelney, an island in the swamps of Somersetshire, he set forth in the spring to reconquer his kingdom. As he went, men flocked to his standard; and, after a desperate struggle, he completely defeated the Danes at Edington, near Chippenham, and made their leader, Guthrum, enter into a solemn treaty at Wedmore. By this treaty the Danes bound themselves not to pass south of a line drawn from the mouth of the Thames to Bedford, from there along the Ouse to the old Roman road of Watling Street, and by Watling Street to Chester. Even this gave them all Northumbria and East Anglia, together with a part of Mercia called the Five Boroughs of the Danes, and this tract of country became known as the Danelaw or "Danelagh" (see Map II.); while Alfred kept only Wessex and part of Mercia. But he had gained peace for the sorely-troubled land, and as Guthrum was baptised a Christian, together with many of his nobles, the Danes and English settled down more happily together. *Treaty of Wedmore, 878.*

Alfred now set himself to govern Wessex well and to strengthen his kingdom. He collected the old laws of the English, and adding to them the ten commandments and some of the laws of Moses, he persuaded the Witan to adopt them as the law of the land, and took great pains to see that justice was done to rich and poor alike. He restored the monasteries and schools and built new ones, inviting learned men from all parts to teach in them, among whom was the famous Welshman, Asser. *Alfred's government.*
He himself superintended the palace school for his nobles, and encouraged every freeborn youth who could afford it to "abide by his book till he can well understand English." He translated Bede's

History and other works into English, and prepared selections for the scholars, and under his direction the compilation of the Saxon Chronicle was begun in earnest. Thus he became the Father of English literature, for till then all books except the old Saxon poems and Cædmon's song had been in Latin.

Nor was his work merely among books. He divided his people into two parts, to take turns in going into battle and in guarding the homesteads, while he kept one troop always under arms to defend the fortresses. He built ships, by which he repulsed a severe attack by the Danes, and which formed the first beginning of our English navy. He rebuilt London, which had been nearly destroyed by fire and pillage. He encouraged travellers to go to Norway, Jerusalem, and even India. In his day the famous Peter's Pence, were collected annually and sent to the Pope as a tribute. Only a few years ago (1883) a hoard of silver Saxon coins was dug up in Rome bearing the stamp of Alfred's grandsons, Athelstan and Edmund. Alfred set his people an example of industry, self-denial, and patient endurance, and won their affection as no king had done before him. His day was divided into regular duties; candles, burning each two hours, marked the time devoted to prayer, to learning, or to active work. His was a deeply religious mind, and he educated his children to a high sense of duty. He had a large family, of whom two were important in history—Ethelfled, who married an ealdorman, and as a widow governed Mercia; and Edward. who succeeded his father when Alfred died in 901.

4. Alfred's Successors.—And now for eighty years the English were almost free from invasions of the Northmen. But the country could not be at peace while it was composed of so many different kingdoms, all jealous of each other; especially as they had the Welsh, the people they had conquered, as a thorn in their side on the west; and the Danes, the people who had half conquered them, on the east. Ethelfled, the "Lady of Mercia," set valiantly to work soon after her father's death, and conquered the five Danish boroughs—Derby, Lincoln, Leicester, Stamford, and Nottingham. After her death Edward conquered the rest of the Danelagh, while the Northumbrians,

Map II.

ENGLAND
AND
THE DANELAGH

STRUGGLE BETWEEN ENGLISH AND DANES.

both Danes and English, and the princes of Wales, Strathclyde, and Scotland, "chose him to father and lord."

Thus he really governed the whole country, and his son Athelstan, who succeeded him, often called himself Emperor of Britain. Still Athelstan had serious difficulties with the Scots and Welsh of Strathclyde, who leagued themselves with the Danes against him, but were defeated. Athelstan's three successors, Edmund, Edred, and Edwy, sons and grandson of Edward, all had to struggle more or less, during their short reigns, against revolts on all sides. At last, in 959, when Edgar, Edwy's brother and Alfred's great-grandson, came to the throne, there was peace for twenty years. *Athelstan, 925.*

5. Dunstan.—This was chiefly owing to a very remarkable man named Dunstan, who was born at Glastonbury in 925, and helped Edgar to rule wisely. Let us first see what kind of people he had now to govern; for by degrees, as things settled down, changes had taken place. The king had become more powerful than in earlier times. The village hundreds were now grouped in sections or "*shires*," each with their own *shire-reeve* or "*sheriff*," who was the king's own officer, collecting his taxes and sitting in the shire-moot with the alderman and the bishop, who was also always appointed by the king. The number of the king's thegns had also increased, and as he gave them lands to hold from him, he could call upon them to help him at any time. These thegns formed a new nobility, having rank, not like the old eorls because they were of ancient family, but because the king made them noble. Another change was among the ceorls, who during the troubled times had found it very difficult to defend their homes, and were glad to put themselves under the protection of some man richer and more powerful than themselves. In the towns this did not happen so much, for there the men formed themselves into frith-guilds or peace-clubs and stood by each other. But in the country the smaller freemen sought out a lord and became his "men," and had to do him service, being called "villeins," from the Latin *villanus*, husbandmen, while they called *State of the Nation. King's sheriff. Increased importance of thegns. Frith-guilds.*

their master *hláford* or lord, meaning "giver of bread." They were not badly off on the whole, having their own houses and land, and feeding on barley-bread, honey and fish, with vegetables and fruit, and buttermilk to drink. But whereas formerly they received their land as a right from the village-moot, and each man held his head as high and gave his vote as freely as any other man, now they received it from their lord, and were bound to one spot, having little or no share in the government except through him.

Ceorls sink into villeins.

Nevertheless there were still many free ceorls in their own homesteads; the master in his linen shirt and embroidered blue cloth frock, linen-swathed legs and leather shoes, ruling his labourers and slaves on his own freehold; and the mistress, in her embroidered robe and linen veil, guiding her maidens, who span in the woman's bower, or performed household duties in house and kitchen. These men were still as independent as in the olden days, and were the forefathers of the sturdy yeomen of later times. Their homes were often as well kept as those of the nobles themselves. Beef and mutton, ale and mead, were to be seen on their long hall tables, where master and servant sat together; and no man had a right to claim their services or restrain their liberty. These free ceorls lived chiefly in the north of England; and, led by the bishops, they often quarrelled with the great nobles of the south, who gradually became more masterful as they controlled a larger number of villeins.

Yeomen of the North.

The nobles lived idle and often riotous lives each on his own manor; they had villeins to work for them as tillers or carpenters, smiths or shoemakers; and slaves, which they bred for sale. They had meat and game in plenty, with good ale, mead, and wine. Hunting, hawking, wrestling, and racing were their favourite pursuits in times of peace, while the ladies span or embroidered, and the gleeman sang ballads in the ancestral hall, or travelling jugglers and tumblers amused the company. In time of war they gathered at the king's command, and they were now, together with the bishops, the chief people in the Witangemot. They had power to elect or depose the king, to deal out justice, conclude treaties, dispose of the lands, and govern the state. Thus the nobles and the bishops became of great import-

Nobles and bishops.

ance, standing between the people and the king; and it was only in the large towns of London and Winchester, where the Witans were held and the people could be present, that the voice of the freeman still made itself heard.

Another great change since the time of Alfred was caused by the mixture of Danes and English all along the east coast; for the Danes had settled down as conquerors, and were very jealous of any interference with their rights, acknowledging no one as their superior but the king, and rebelling against him whenever they were not satisfied. Thus they were like the freemen of the north, sturdy and independent. *Mixed population of Danes and English.*

This was the state of the people when Dunstan, as yet a lad, came to the court of Athelstan, and was driven away by the insolent nobles who were jealous of his knowledge and ability. After a severe illness, he became a monk, and was made Abbot of Glastonbury by Edmund, and when he became the king's minister, he ruled with a firm hand. First he secured the friendship of Malcolm, King of the Scots, by giving him Cumberland, and so kept him from helping the Danes. Then he pleased the Danes themselves by allowing them to have their own laws and customs; and by dealing fairly and justly with rich and poor alike, he kept some kind of justice in the troubled land. Edmund was murdered by an outlaw named Leof, but Dunstan remained minister during Edred's reign, and though Edwy banished him for objecting to his marriage with a kinswoman, the Witangemot of Wessex soon recalled him as minister to Edgar, who was only a boy of fourteen when he came to the throne. *Dunstan's government.*

Under Dunstan's rule as Archbishop of Canterbury the people began gradually to grow into one nation. Edgar was surnamed "the Peaceable," and the "laws of Edgar" were remembered for generations as wise and just, while in his reign the country was for the first time called ENGLALAND, the land of Englishmen. The unruly people of the north were quieted by giving the north part of Northumbria, called Lothian, to Kenneth, King of the Scots, who held it under Edgar; so that the Scotch kings now lived more in the Lowlands, and Edinburgh became the capital of *Edgar the Peaceable, 959-975.* *Lothian given to the Scots.*

Scotland. In Wales, the rebellious King Idwal was subdued and made to pay a yearly tribute of 300 wolves' heads. Commerce with
Increase of trade. other nations now began to flourish: the laws protecting trade from robbers and wreckers were very severe, and Edgar had three fleets continually guarding the coast against the Vikings, so that traders from France and Germany could safely visit London. There handicraftsmen began to form themselves into societies or *guilds*, and the parishes became united into *wards*, each with its own alderman, and the *burghers* or householders in the *burh* or borough claimed the right to govern themselves.

Dunstan revived education, and strove to make the monks in the monasteries and schools lead purer lives, and be more diligent in teaching. His zeal for the Church, however, drove him from power. He favoured the monks, or unmarried clergy, and tried to make the married clergy give up their wives, as was being done in Rome, while he took many lands to endow abbeys and monasteries. This caused great discontent, and when Edgar died, and his young son Edward, after a reign of only four years, was murdered by order of his stepmother Elfrith, the thegns, tired of the quarrels of the Church, crowned Ethelred, Elfrith's young son, and looked to her and to her favourite alderman Ethelwine to govern them. Dunstan retired to Canterbury, and died nine years after.

6. Danish Conquest and Rule.—And now the unfortunate country was thrown back into a sea of troubles. Ethelred, called
Ethelred the Unready, 979-1016. the "Unready" or "Uncounselled" because he would not listen to the *rede* or advice of others, quarrelled with his clergy as soon as he was old enough to govern, and tried to rule despotically and break the power of his thegns. But they were too strong for him, and the country fell apart again into a number of petty states, offering an easy prey to the Danes, who began once more to come over in great numbers under the two kings of Denmark and Norway, Sweyn (or Swegen) and Olaf. No
Second Danish invasion. doubt, under a good king, the English would have kept them at bay, for we read how Brithnoth the Old, alderman of the East Saxons, fought them, and died fighting in the famous Battle of Maldon in 991. But Ethelred only

STRUGGLE BETWEEN ENGLISH AND DANES.

levied a land-tax called "Danegeld," and bought them off, first with a sum equal to £16,000 and a few years later with £24,000. Then he married Emma, daughter of Richard, Duke of Normandy, in hopes the Normans would help him; and lastly, he persuaded the Witan, only too glad to fall upon the hated Danes, to give secret orders for a general massacre of large numbers of them on St. Brice's Day, 13th November, 1002. *Massacre of Danes, 1002.*

Among those murdered was Sweyn's sister Gunhild, with her husband and child, and he swore to be revenged. He came over with a large force, and Earl Thurkill followed soon after with a horde of Vikings. They ravaged the country, and Alphege, Archbishop of Canterbury, was savagely murdered by the Danes. Twice more Ethelred bought off his enemies, but the English were weary of his bad government. Northumbria and Mercia joined Sweyn, and even the thegns of Wessex submitted to him. Ethelred fled to Normandy with his wife and family, and Sweyn became king of the country. It is true that when Sweyn died a month afterwards Ethelred came back, but only to be attacked by Cnut, Sweyn's son. He struggled on for two years and died in 1016. Then the people of London chose Ethelred's son, Edmund Ironside, for their king, but the rest of England choose Cnut. Edmund fought bravely, and after six pitched battles divided the kingdom with Cnut, but he died after seven months' reign, and Cnut was acknowledged king by Danes and English alike. *Struggle for the kingdom.* *Edmund Ironside, 7 months' reign, 1016.*

Now, after a weary strife of thirty six-years, a strong hand was once more over the people, and the land had quiet for eighteen years. Cnut resolved to govern as an English king. Though he was cruel in the early part of his reign, before he was secure of the throne, he showed himself just and wise afterwards. He received his crown from the Witangemot, as all English kings had done; he governed by "Edgar's laws," and he bound himself still more to the people by marrying Emma, Ethelred's widow. On the other hand, the Danes were satisfied, because he was a king of their own race. Cnut divided England into four earldoms—*Earl* or *Jarl* being the Danish title answering to the English *alderman.* These earldoms, Mercia, Northum- *Cnut, 1016-1035.*

berland, Wessex, and East Anglia, were governed by Englishmen, of whom the most powerful were Leofric, Earl of Mercia, and Godwin, Earl of Wessex, who was Cnut's minister, and married his niece. Cnut dismissed his Danish army, and kept only a body of "hus-carls" or household troops, and he even took English soldiers with him to fight in Denmark. Meanwhile the people at home had peace, and time to reclaim marshes, clear forest-land, cultivate their homesteads, and increase their trade and manufactures. Cnut even tried, as Edgar had done before him, to stop the shameful sale of Welsh and English as slaves, but in vain. From Bristol whole shiploads of young men and women were still sold to the Danes in Ireland, in spite of the laws and of the preaching of the bishops.

<small>Eighteen years of peace.</small>

If Cnut's sons, Harold and Harthacnut, had been as wise as he, Danish kings might have continued to reign in England. But they were brutal, and caused nothing but misery during their short reigns; and when Harthacnut fell down and died at a wedding-feast in 1042, his half-brother Edward, the son of Ethelred and Emma, was welcomed by the English as belonging to the old stock. From this time the Danes who lived in England were gradually absorbed into the English nation, so that after a few generations it was difficult to say which were Danes and which were English. Yet to this day we may see traces of Danish blood in the fair-haired sturdy yeomen of Yorkshire and Lincolnshire; and the towns which they founded are marked by names ending in *by*, which has the same meaning as *tun* and *ham* in Saxon. Thus Derby, Whitby, and Rugby are towns which once belonged to the Danes, while Nottingham, Durham, and Bridlington mark old English settlements.

<small>Danish towns.</small>

CHAPTER IV.

HOW THE NORMANS BEGAN TO HAVE INFLUENCE IN ENGLAND.

1. Norman Incursions.—But though the people rejoiced at having once more one of Alfred's descendants as their king, Edward was really more a foreigner than even Cnut had been. To understand this we must go back about a hundred and fifty years, and see what had been taking place on the north coast of France. About the time when Alfred the Great was so hard pressed by the Danes or Northmen in England, large boat-loads of these same sea-pirates were swooping down upon the country round the River Seine in France, plundering and ravaging just as their comrades did in England. One band of these marauders, under the command of a famous Viking, Rolf or Rollo, sailed up the Seine, and took possession of Rouen; and there are many traditions of the havoc which Rolf wrought on all sides. But all that we know for certain is, that in 913, Charles the Simple, King of France, made a treaty with this adventurer Rolf, and gave him land on each side of the Seine, with Rouen for his capital. Rolf then married the king's daughter and became a Christian; the land over which he reigned, as count or duke, became known as Normandy, or the Northman's land, and descended to his heirs.
<small>The Normans in France, 900.</small>

The Normans, then, in France, were of the same race as the Danes in England, but the French people among whom they settled, and with whom they intermarried, were very different from the English. Though less sturdy and earnest, they were more civilised and polished, from having seen more of the world and of the cultivated people of Rome. They were clever in art and architecture, and were lively, quickwitted, bright, and gay; and in a very short time the Normans, except in one little spot round Bayeux, adopted the French language, habits, and customs, blending their own robust and resolute natures with those of the more refined Franks.
<small>Normans become French.</small>

So after a hundred years had passed, when Ethelred the Unready married Emma (who was the daughter of Richard, Duke of Normandy, and thus the great-grandchild of the Viking Rolf), the Normans were already Frenchmen; and Edward, the son of Emma and Ethelred, though born in England, was half a foreigner. Moreover, when he was only nine years old, he and his brother Alfred fled with their father and mother into Normandy. His mother Emma went back to England and married Cnut when Ethelred died; and his brother Alfred, who went over in Harold's reign, had his eyes treacherously put out by Harold's men, and died at Ely. But Edward remained at the Norman court. He was there when his cousin William, a boy only seven years old, became Duke of Normandy, and the two cousins were fast friends.

Edward half a Norman.

Naturally, then, when Edward was invited to England by his half-brother Harthacnut six years afterwards, and soon after was elected King of England, many Normans, both priests and nobles, followed him, and were given high offices in the land. Edward was gentle, timid, and very devout, and soon he made a Norman monk, Robert of Jumièges, Bishop of London; then another, named Ulf, Bishop of Rochester. A few years later he even promoted Bishop Robert to be Archbishop of Canterbury, and this man became a very hurtful influence in the country.

Edward the Confessor, 1042-1066.

2 Godwin, Earl of Wessex.—The only person who held these Norman favourites in check was Godwin, Earl of Wessex, whose daughter, Edith, Edward had married. Godwin really ruled the country, and ruled it well; but unfortunately his eldest son Sweyn was a wild and lawless man, and committed crimes which offended both the king and the people, and Godwin's enemies were only too glad to make this a pretext against him.

It happened just then that Count Eustace of Boulogne, who had married Edward's sister, had a dispute with the men of Dover, and in a fight which followed many people were killed. Godwin refused to punish the men of Dover without a fair trial; and though he was in the right, the Normans, and even the other English nobles, jealous of his power, sided with the king against him. He and his sons were declared outlaws, and

Goodwin outlawed, 1051.

sooner than provoke a civil war he withdrew to Flanders, and was away about a year. This was a memorable year in English history; for while Godwin was away the Norman knights and priests had everything their own way, and William, Duke of Normandy, now a tall handsome young man, came over to England to visit Edward. It was during this visit that Edward, who had no child, is said to have promised that William should succeed him on the English throne. Being so friendly with his cousin, it seems very natural that he should do this, though the crown was really not his to give. The Witan only could give it, and as William had not a drop of English blood in his veins, he had absolutely no right to it.

Meanwhile things went very badly in the country without Godwin, and when he came back next year with his younger sons, the people flocked to meet him. He refused to let them fight the king's men, but claimed to be heard in his own defence, and though the king was very unwilling to receive him, the Witan gladly gave him back his estates and power. As soon as the Norman favourites heard that he was taken back into favour they fled to France, though a large number of less note remained.

And now during fourteen years, from 1052 to 1066, England was once more really governed by her own people; and as a flame often leaps up brilliantly before it dies out, so these years were bright ones for the nation. Godwin died very suddenly the next year at a feast, but his second son Harold, a brave soldier and an able ambitious statesman, took his place. Edward spent all his time in hunting, and in watching the building of the grand Church of St. Peter at Westminster, on the spot where the Abbey now stands. Meanwhile Harold governed England with the help of Leofric, Earl of Mercia, and Eldred, Archbishop of York. Leofric's house was the rival of the house of Godwin, and his sons gave Harold much trouble, but the old man himself loved his country too well not to uphold such an able ruler as Harold.

Government of the Saxon Harold.

3. Harold.—So contented were the people, on the whole, that there is little to tell, except of some disturbances in Wales and Northumberland. The Welsh King, Gruffyd, had been harassing the west of England ever since Godwin's banishment, but now

Wales subdued. Harold, with the help of his brother Tostig, conquered him and made him recognise Edward as overlord. In Northumberland matters were less happy. The great Earl Siward, who had helped young King Malcolm of Scotland, to conquer the usurper Macbeth, died and Tostig was made earl in his place. But Tostig was a great favourite with King Edward, and was always at *Northumbrian* court instead of governing his earldom, and a great *rebellion.* rebellion arose. The people held an assembly of their *Tostig outlawed.* own, choose Morkere, Leofric's grandson, as their earl, and marching south in large numbers demanded the banishment of Tostig. Harold saw that he could not shield his brother, and Tostig was outlawed, and went with his family to Flanders. From that time he was his brother's enemy, and was one of the chief causes of Harold's downfall.

By this time Harold was really supreme governor of England; the people were happy under his firm rule, and as Edward had no children they began to look to him as their future king. If Edward *Claimants for* had ever really promised William the crown, he evi- *the crown.* dently saw now that he could not keep his promise, for he invited over Edward, the son of Edmund Ironside, from Hungary to be his successor This man died, however, only a few days after his arrival, before he had even seen the king, and he left only a little boy, Edgar, of whom we shall hear again by and by.

Meanwhile Duke William still counted upon Edward's promise; and when Harold was once shipwrecked on the coast of Normandy, *Harold's oath* and the Count of Ponthieu sent him a prisoner to Rouen, William is said to have made Harold swear to support his claim to the throne, and even to have tricked him, by hiding the relics of the saints under the altar on which he swore, so as to make the oath more sacred. Be this as it may, neither Edward *Edward's death.* nor Harold had power to promise the English crown. Edward died in 1066, only a week after the consecration of his beloved Minster, where his body was soon to be laid. He had been a poor, feeble king, but Harold had governed well in his name during the last fourteen years, and people reverenced him as a saint, and named him "the Confessor." Before he died he recommended Harold as his successor; and the Witan which was then assembled in London carried out the election the same day. Harold was crowned at Westminster by Archbishop Eldred.

4. Norwegian and Norman Invasions.—Harold, son of Godwin, was now by consent of the people King of England, although the only royal blood in his veins came from his mother, a Danish princess. But he had little time to enjoy his new honours. Duke William no sooner heard what had happened than he swore he would force Harold to keep his oath, and give up the throne to him. Without loss of time he began to build a fleet, and to collect a great army throughout France, and sent to Pope Alexander to crave a blessing on his expedition against the man who had broken a vow taken over the relics of the saints. Meanwhile a cruel fate brought Harold's own brother to increase his difficulties. Tostig, who had gone to Norway, chose this time to come and try to recover his earldom. After plundering the south coast, he went north and sailing up the Humber with the Norwegian king, Harold Hardrada, landed in Yorkshire.

Harold II., Jan. 5, Oct. 14. 1066.

Threatened on all sides, Harold watched the south coast for some months, but as William did not arrive, he was obliged to allow the fishing vessels which formed his fleet to disperse, while he himself hastened north against Tostig. He defeated the Norwegian army at Stamford Bridge, in Yorkshire, and Tostig and King Hardrada were both killed. But the feast of victory was not over when a messenger arrived with the news that the Normans had landed at Pevensey, in Sussex.

Battle of Stamford Bridge.

5. Battle of Hastings.—South again hastened the king to London, where he called the people together to defend the country. Only the men of the south came, and with these he marched to Hastings where the Normans were encamped. His brother Gurth begged him not to run the risk of a battle without a stronger force, and urged him to lay waste the land and starve William out. But Harold would not desolate English ground, and on Oct. 14 on a hill called Senlac, about seven miles distant from the town, was fought the memorable "Battle of Hastings." It was a stubborn contest. The English soldiers fought stoutly on foot, clad in coats of mail, and armed with javelins and two-handed axes. The country folk fought as they could with pikes and forks, while the Norman archers let fly their arrows, and the mailed and helmeted horsemen, headed by Taillefer, the Norman minstrel, who was the first to fall, pressed up the hill, trying to break through the English ranks. The sturdy Saxons stood like a wall, striking death-blows on all sides, and once the Normans began to yield, and a cry arose that the duke was slain. "I live" shouted William, tearing off his helmet, "and by God's help I will conquer yet;" and by making his men pretend to flee he drew the English down the hill in disorder. Then the Normans turned and cut them to pieces, driving back a small band of the noblest men in England to the top of the hill, where they gathered round the king and the royal standard, on the spot where Battle Abbey was afterwards built. There William brought forward his archers and bade them shoot upwards, so that the arrows fell upon the English from above. One struck Harold's right eye and he fell, and though his men defended him bravely, the last of the Saxon kings died under the blows of four Norman knights, leaving William conqueror. Gytha, the aged widow of Godwin, craved her son's body, and William allowed him to be buried in a purple robe beneath a heap of stones among the rocks of Sussex.

Death of Harold.

William marched to London, and there were few to oppose him, for the flower of the English nation lay dead on Senlac Hill. The people of London did indeed choose little Etheling Edgar for king; but their hearts failed them as William approached with his army, burning Southwark on his way, and they "bowed to him for need." At Christmas William was chosen by the Witan, and received the crown at Westminister from the same Archbishop Eldred who had crowned Harold.

William crowned.

6. English and Normans.—England had lost her freedom Six hundred years before, the English had come in hordes from their homes on the shores of the North Sea, and had conquered the Britons at Anderida, near Pevensey. Now, on nearly the same spot, they had been conquered themselves, and had to bow their heads to foreign rule. But it was a different kind of conquest. The Normans came indeed in great numbers, but not as a whole nation, nor did they drive out the English, who really belonged to the same race as themselves. Moreover, William the Conqueror was a wise and great man, and we shall see that he protected the English, both because they were useful to him and because he really wished to rule them well. Lastly, the English were by this time a strong nation of sturdy determined men, too independent and earnest to be crushed, even under the tyranny they suffered. And so in about a hundred years the Normans became Englishmen and were proud to call England their country.

PART II.

FROM THE CONQUEST TO THE GREAT CHARTER.

CHAPTER V.

ENGLAND UNDER NORMAN RULE.

1. William of Normandy.—And now came important changes in our country, bringing great suffering with them. The old English line of West Saxon kings was over, and from that day to this no king of pure Anglo-Saxon race has sat upon the throne of England. Their place was taken by William, Duke of Normandy, though he was not in any sense an Englishman, for his father was Robert, surnamed "le Diable," Duke of Normandy, and his mother was Arlotta, the daughter of a Norman tanner. As a mere boy he had succeeded his father, and as he grew up he mastered the turbulent Norman barons and conquered the territory of Maine. In 1053 he married Matilda, daughter of the Count of Flanders, and was always a kind husband and good father. When he came over to be King of England he was a tall stately man, about forty years of age. He was hard and stern, and did many cruel deeds to gain his end, but in most things he was a just ruler, a great general, and a wise statesman. He tried to rule England well, and made no changes in the laws and customs when he could avoid it. But he had come with an army of foreigners to take possession of the country, and he could not do this without crushing the free English life and causing misery.

Even during his coronation at Westminster the shouts of the people inside the Minster alarmed the Norman soldiers outside, and they set fire to the houses around, showing that the reign of fear had begun; and these same soldiers and their leaders were all waiting to be rewarded for fighting William's battles. *Burning at the Coronation.*

2. Extension of Feudal System.—They had not long to wait. Very soon after his coronation William made a royal visit to the south and east of England, which was the only part really conquered, and divided the land among his barons, knights and common soldiers. He said that he had been the rightful king ever since Edward's death, that the nation had rebelled against him by obeying Harold, and that therefore all the lands, except that which belonged to the Church was forfeited. This was of course absurd, but it gave an appearance of justice to the changes he made.

<small>Confiscation of the lands.</small>

The *folk-land*, or common land of the people, had ever since the time of Alfred come more and more under the king's control, and now it became altogether the *terra regis*, or land of the king, while the private estates of those who lay dead on the battle-field, or had fled the country, were given to the Norman nobles. In this way all Kent, and nearly all Surrey and Sussex, passed into the hands of Norman masters, as well as much land in the other shires. In some cases William gave back portions to widows, orphans, and small landowners. But those among the English who kept any land received or bought it back, and held it as *vassals*. And so, instead of the old English freedom of the time of Alfred,—when a man had his own land as his right, which he helped to defend by military service, while he chose his own alderman, who in his turn helped to choose the king,—now it began to be all the other way. The old English system worked from below upwards, from the freeman to the king. The Norman system on the contrary, worked from above downwards. All the land belonged to the king, who gave it to his earls, barons, and knights (who took the place of the English thegns) and they held it under him, while the smaller owners held it from them in the same way. The vassal knelt unarmed and bareheaded before his lord, with his hands in his, and swore to be his liegeman, and to keep faith and loyalty to him in life and death. Then, with a kiss, the lord gave him the land as a *fief* or *feudum* for himself and his heirs for ever, and in return he was bound to provide a certain number of men to fight for his lord.

<small>Folk-land becomes king's land.</small>

<small>Feudal system.</small>

Now, although many of these changes were made gradually and not with force or cruelty, yet we can imagine the distress of those, who saw all or nearly all they had given to strangers; while even the villeins and slaves were now at the mercy of foreigners, for

ENGLAND UNDER NORMAN RULE.   35

each man took with the land all the rights which belonged to it.
The Norman barons, even in their own land, had always
been wild and unruly; and being used to handsome   *Normans looked down upon the English.*
houses, delicate food, and courtly manners, they had a
great contempt for the rough homes, coarse food, and
heavy drinking of the English; and they often brought with them
their own cooks and tailors, architects and stewards.

Moreover, strong castles began now to be built all over the land.
When William went back to Normandy, three months after his
coronation, he left his brother, Bishop Odo, Earl of Kent, and his
friend Fitz-Osbern, Earl of Hereford, to govern the land in his
absence, telling them to hasten the building of castles everywhere.
In London the White Tower rose up on the banks of
the Thames; and at Hastings, Norwich, Canterbury, *Building of castles.*
Rochester, Bramber, Lewes, Carisbrooke, Windsor,
and other places, huge battlemented towers soon arose, in which
were put large forces of foot and horse soldiers, with trusty Norman
captains, to keep the conquered land. The English, who had always
hated stone walls and loved their freedom, saw with dismay these
huge fortresses rising up among them. So, when in William's
absence the barons began to oppress the English, taking their
property and insulting their wives and daughters, serious rebellions
arose in Kent and Hereford; while Harold's sons in
the west, and the great English earls in the north, *English revolt.*
began to make attempts to reconquer the kingdom.
At last, when William heard that Sweyn, King of Denmark, was
coming over to help the English, he hastened back.

3. English Revolts.—The next four years were one long
struggle between the conqueror and the English patriots. First,
the king put down the rising in the west, and ordered
a strong castle to be built at Exeter. Then Leofric's   *Struggle with English patriots, 1067-1071.*
grandsons Edwin and Morkere, and Waltheof, son of
the brave Siward, helped by Malcolm III. of Scotland,
rose in the north; and at last, in 1069, the people of Northumbria
chose Edgar Etheling as their king, and with the help of the Danes
stormed York and killed three thousand Normans.

William took a terrible revenge. He was hunting in the forest of Dean when he heard the news, but he set off at once, and bought off the Danish fleet. Then, after retaking York, he marched his troops over the whole land between York and Durham ravaging the country. Towns, villages, cattle, crops, all were destroyed, and the unfortunate people either killed or driven over the Scottish border. More than one hundred thousand innocent people are said to have died of famine alone, and the land was so desolate that no one attempted to till the ground for nine years. But William had gained his point— the north of England was conquered. Then, sparing neither himself nor his troops, he marched in the depth of winter through snowdrifts and swollen rivers, and across desolate moors, to Chester, and conquered this, the last city which held out against him. In all these places we must remember that those who rebelled forfeited their land, and so the Norman landowners increased.

William lays waste the North Country.

Still the English patriots, though only a small band of outlaws, gathered hundreds of their countrymen in the Isle of Ely, surrounded by streams and fens, and under their leaders, Morkere, and Hereward-the-Wake the famous outlaw, held out for nearly a year. At last William made a causeway, two miles long, across the Fen, and after a desperate resistance this last stronghold was taken in 1071. The patriot leaders were scattered. Edwin had been already killed. Morkere lived in captivity. The poor, weak Etheling Edgar, after remaining some time abroad, returned to England and lived on a pension, and William is said to have made friends with the brave Hereward. But Waltheof was beheaded five years later, for having known of a conspiracy of the Norman earls against the king. This was the only cold-blooded execution of William's reign, and probably he was alarmed because Waltheof was much beloved by the people.

End of patriot leaders, 1071.

4. Sixteen Years of Peace.—So the last of the patriots died a martyr, and after the surrender of Ely the land was comparatively at peace during the rest of William's reign. The king ruled with a firm hand. He assembled twelve men in each shire to declare the laws of the English, and adopted these. He kept the work of the shires in the hands of his own sheriffs, the accounts being made up by the clerks of the royal chapel or *chantry*, the chief secretary being called the *chancellor*, because he had his seat behind a screen called in Latin *cancelli*; and he kept the barons in check by allowing complaints to be referred to the King's Court, where justice was done to Norman and English alike. Moreover, in the year 1086 he made all the English land-owners swear allegiance to him at his great court at Salisbury, so that they might look upon him as their first and supreme master, and this, as we shall see by and by, prevented England falling a prey to the barons as happened in other countries. Oath of allegiance to the king.

He also took good care to keep the Church under control. He refused to do fealty to the Pope since no English king had done so before him, nor would he allow any of his vassals to be *excommunicated*, or deprived of the benefits of the Church, without his leave. In 1070 he appointed Lanfranc, a wise and learned Lombard, to be Archbishop of Canterbury, and gradually filled the bishoprics with foreigners, making them do homage to him for their lands as the barons did. He also gave the clergy courts of their own, and no longer allowed them to sit in the ordinary courts with the aldermen and sheriffs. Under Lanfranc's good government the clergy and monasteries were brought into better order, and some check was kept on the barons, although Lanfranc "often longed to leave the country, seeing so much misery and wrong in it." Many of our finest Norman cathedrals were begun at this time, and, what was better, Lanfranc and the king did their best to put down the shameful slave trade at Bristol. Archbishop Lanfranc, 1070.

Thus William, though he was a stern master, ruled fairly. Only in two things he did injustice for his own benefit. First he laid waste more than 90,000 acres of land in Hampshire to make the New Forest for his hunting, and ordered that any man who killed a deer should have his eyes put out; and secondly, he oppressed the people with taxes to add to his hoard of wealth at Winchester, levying the Danegeld again which Edward the Confessor had abolished. The New Forest.

The people were very angry with him for making a general survey of England to learn how the land was divided and cultivated, and what taxes each man ought to pay. Yet this was really a fair thing to do. The results of this survey were entered in a book called Domesday Book, and from it Domesday Book, 1086.

we learn how much land passed into Norman hands. It tells us, too, that there were at that time not more than two million people in England, that is less than half the number now living in London alone. Nor did the population increase for many generations. A great many Flemings, together with traders from Rouen and Caen, came over during the next two reigns, and the Jews began to make homes in England, living in Jewries, or separated quarters in the towns, under the protection of the king. Yet with all this the numbers did not increase, and this shows how many must have died in the wars and famines of the hard times which followed the Norman conquest.

The last part of William's reign was full of troubles to himself. His eldest son Robert rebelled against him in Normandy in 1078, and nearly killed his own father in battle before he recognised him. His step-brother, Bishop Odo, conspired with the barons against him, and had to be imprisoned; and lastly, in 1087 William had to defend his Norman frontier against Philip of France. Here, while riding over hot ashes in the burning town of Mantes, his horse stumbled, throwing him violently against his saddle. He was carried back to Rouen and died Sept. 9, 1087, and was buried at Caen. He had four sons—Robert, Richard, William and Henry. Richard died young. Robert succeeded to Normandy and Maine; to Henry he left £5,000; while William he sent at once with a letter to Lanfranc, praying him to place the crown upon his head; for he knew that Robert was too headstrong and too weak to govern England.

5. William Rufus or the Red King, 1087-1100.— William the Second, the Conqueror's third son, who came to Lanfranc with his father's ring to be made King of England, was a strong fierce man, with a red face, yellow hair, and keen gray eyes. He had been a dutiful son, and was as brave as his father, but he was no statesman; he cared little for law or religion, and his life was wild and vicious.

Appearance and character.

Lanfranc, who had been his tutor, crowned him at once at Westminster, fearing lest Robert should put in a claim. He made him promise to give the people good laws; and for the next two years, until Lanfranc died in 1089, this promise was kept. But the barons were not content. They wanted the weak, good-natured

Robert to rule over them. Before three months were over they rebelled, and with the troublesome Bishop Odo at their head, fortified their castles, wasted the land, and seized the king's taxes and fines. Now was seen the wisdom of William the Conqueror's good government of the English, for they looked upon the king as their protector against the barons. When William called upon all who were not "*nithing*" or worthless to help him, and promised to govern well and repeal the cruel forest laws, the people flocked to his standard. Not only were the barons defeated, but the English even drove back the soldiers whom Robert sent over with a fleet from Normandy; and the curious sight was seen at Pevensey—where first the Normans had landed in 1066—of an army of Englishmen defeating an army of Normans in support of a Norman king.

<small>Rebellion of barons, 1088.</small>

<small>English people uphold the king.</small>

6. Oppressive Rule of Rufus.—But William forgot his promises. When Lanfranc died he left his seat or "see" vacant for more than four years, and had no one to check him. In 1090 he went to war with Robert in Normandy, and when the two brothers at last made peace, and agreed that whichever lived the longer should have both Normandy and England, then they both went to war with Henry. Meanwhile English money and English soldiers were used freely, although soldiers in those days were men with farms and homesteads, called away from work to serve the king. William was a brave commander, kind to his followers and often generous to his enemies. Nobles from all parts flocked to serve him, and he rewarded and entertained them lavishly, never heeding that he was spending his people's money.

<small>People taxed to pay for Norman wars.</small>

The law was administered by justices, and in the reign of William the Conqueror the chief of these was first called a *Justiciar*, and had great power. He ruled in the king's stead when he was abroad, and writs were issued in his name. William II. appointed a rough, coarse man named Ralph Flambard to be his justiciar, and when money ran low in the treasury, this man oppressed the people in every way. When bishops and abbots died he sold their posts or left them vacant, and put the money in the king's treasury. He exacted heavy tributes from the

<small>Ralph Flambard justiciar.</small>

nobles, making every heir pay exorbitant fines when he came into property, or a father when he asked the king's permission to let his daughter be married; while he levied unjust taxes from the people, and the very thieves could escape punishment by paying a fine. Nor was this all, for the king's courtiers lived upon the country folks wherever they went, taking their food, using their horses, selling their crops, and laying hands on everything they could get. "*All that was hateful to God and oppressive to man,*" says the Chronicle, "*was customary in this land in William's time, and therefore he was most hateful to almost all of his people and odious to God.*" The unfortunate English had only one consolation, and this was that at least the king kept the barons quiet, and there was peace in the land.

<small>Oppression of the people.</small>

Two things, indeed, the king did for the good of England. In 1090 he granted land in Wales to all who could conquer it, and made two expeditions there himself. Many new lands were won and castles built, especially in Pembroke and Cardigan. Also in 1092 he took possession of Cumberland, which had till then been part of Strathclyde. Building a large castle at Carlisle he settled peasants from Hampshire in the county, and made it an English earldom. He also obliged Malcolm III. of Scotland to do homage for his kingdom.

<small>Conquests in Wales.</small>

<small>Cumberland joined to England.</small>

And now in the year 1093 William, being seriously ill, repented of his evil ways and his robbery of the poor, and appointed a very good and learned man, Anselm, Abbot of Bec, to the archbishopric of Canterbury. Anselm was very unwilling to accept the office, saying that for him and William to govern together would be to link a poor, weak sheep with an untamed bull. The bishops had to force the crozier or crook into his hand. Yet he proved anything but weak when the king, recovering from his illness, began again to govern badly. Anselm refused to pay an exorbitant sum for his see, and boldly rebuked the king's extortions from his people; but at last, after struggling for four years against wickedness which he could not prevent, he retired to Rome in 1097, and William was left once more to work his own evil will.

<small>Anselm archbishop.</small>

7. First Crusade.—Meanwhile William had again gone to war with Robert, and spent a large sum of money in buying off the French king, who took Robert's side; while he gave yet another sum of ten thousand marks, or £6,666, to Robert himself, who made peace and pledged Normandy to William in order that he might get money to go to Jerusalem. Just then, in the year 1096, all Europe was wild to go and conquer the Holy City, and punish the Turks who were ill-treating Christian pilgrims. Pope Urban IV. encouraged Peter the Hermit, one of the insulted pilgrims, to preach of the terrible suffering of those who went to worship at the Holy Sepulchre, and called on all men who sought forgiveness of their sins to sew a coloured cross on their left arm and go on a *crusade* (from *crux*, cross) to free the Holy Land. So Robert went, and many English and French people with him, and William became for the time governor of Normandy and of some of the best parts of France. *Robert goes on the first crusade, 1096.*

Heavily the poor English people paid for it. The Chronicle relates how the year 1096 was dismal through manifold taxes and sad famine, and the same tale is told for the next three years. But the end was near. William went hunting in the New Forest, though he had been warned not to do so. There he became separated from his companions, and was found soon afterwards by some peasants, dead with an arrow in his breast. Some thought that a French knight, Walter Tyrell, had killed him by accident; but Tyrell denied it on oath, and it is more likely that William was assassinated by one of those poor men to whom he was "*most hateful by the oppressions he wrought.*" His body was carried in a peasant's cart to Winchester and buried without any religious service, since he died "unabsolved in the midst of his sins." His brother Henry, who was one of the hunting party, galloped off to Winchester to secure the throne before any one should propose Robert, who was still in the Holy Land. *Death of William Rufus, 1100.*

8. Henry I., Surnamed Beauclerc, 1100-1135.—After this for thirty-five years the land was well governed, although times were hard and taxes heavy. Henry, the youngest son of the Conqueror—a quiet, cautious man, with thoughtful intelligent eyes, fond of learning, and with a good head though not much heart,—saw that his seat on *Character of Henry I.*

the throne depended on his governing his subjects well. He seized the royal treasure at Winchester on the very day that William was killed, and then hastening to London was elected king after some discussion, and crowned at Westminster. The people were delighted for he was the only one of the Conqueror's sons born and educated in England. Moreover, he hastened at once to arrest the infamous Ralph Flambard and send him to the Tower, and to recall good Bishop Anselm.

Then he put forth a "*charter*," or written promise, that he would restore the good laws, and relieve the people and the Church from their unjust burdens; not forcing widows and heiresses to marry against their will, and allowing people to leave their property as they liked. He also made the barons promise to do as much for their feudal tenants as he did for them. He still further won the love of the English people by marrying Edith —the daughter of Malcolm of Scotland and of his wife Margaret, grand-daughter of Edmund Ironsides—so that the queen was of English royal blood. Through her all our kings and queens to this day can trace their descent from Cerdic, the first West Saxon king. To please the Normans, however, Edith changed her name to Maud or Matilda.

His charter.

He marries an English princess.

All this was done before Robert, who was always too late, came home. Then the barons as usual rebelled in his favour. This time, however, the insurrection was soon put down. Robert landed with troops at Portsmouth, but Anselm and Robert of Meulan made peace between the brothers, and Robert went back with a pension of 4,000 silver marks from Henry. Still for five years more the barons, both in England and Normandy, kept stirring up the people. Duke Robert governed so badly that little by little Normandy was falling to pieces. Then in 1106 Henry went over with an English army, and at the famous Battle of Tenchebrai, thoroughly conquered the nobles and brought Robert to England, where he remained in prison the rest of his life. So ended poor Robert, so headstrong and reckless, yet so generous and warmhearted! The English were proud of the Battle of Tenchebrai, for they considered that by conquering the Normans in their own land they had wiped out the reproach of the Battle of Hastings.

Battle of Tenchebrai, 1106.

Robert imprisoned.

ENGLAND UNDER NORMAN RULE. 43

Normandy and England were now once more under one ruler, and this struggle with the Norman barons was very important to our country, not only because Henry taught his English soldiers how to fight the French cavalry so that they lost their fear of them, but also because he took away the English estates of the rebellious barons, and divided them among less powerful men who would be loyal to him. These new nobles often became sheriffs of the counties, and although they were Normans, yet not being of the old nobility, nor having land in Normandy, they looked upon England as their home, and married among the English. So the distinction between Norman and English began to fade away, especially as the English language became more used everywhere, except at court. To this day we may often trace how the French language was for some time the language of the nobles; as, for instance, *sheep, oxen,* and *calf,* are old English names, because the villeins reared the animals; but when they came to the Norman dinner-table, they were called *mutton (mouton), beef (bœuf),* and *veal (veau).* So also *sovereign, homage, palace,* and *castle* are Norman words, while *hearth* and *home* are old English. Thus our language became richer and more graceful by the introduction of Romance or French words, in the same way that the English people became more lively, enterprising, and refined by the introduction of Norman blood into England.

New nobility become English.

French words in our language.

9. Administration of Justice.—The two nations were also brought nearer together by the even-handed justice of Henry's reign. In 1107 he made Bishop Roger of Salisbury his justiciar, and this famous man brought the revenue and laws of the kingdom into excellent order. He gave the people back their shire-moots, and the sheriffs came up each year to pay the rents, taxes, and fines into the King's Court or "*Curia Regis,*" receiving in return *tallies,* or little strips of wood (so called from *tailler,* to cut), which were notched exactly alike on each side to mark the money paid, and split down the middle, so that the court kept one half and the sheriff the other. The table on which the money was counted had a chequered cloth like a chess-board, on which, when certain of the king's accounts were

Roger of Salisbury justiciar.

made up, the sums were scored by counters. From this the counting-house became known as the "Court of the Exchequer." If any one was wronged by the sheriffs he could complain before the justices or officers of the King's Court, who went round the country once every year to settle the taxes and inquire into disputes.

<small>Court of the Exchequer.</small>

The towns bought many new privileges from Henry I., and London secured a special charter, with a sheriff and justiciar of its own. Its citizens could not be judged outside its walls; they had not to pay any Danegeld, and their trade was free from toll; nor could they be made to undergo "*trial by battle*" or duelling, which the barons had introduced in some parts of the country instead of the trial by ordeal. Even the country people were much better off, though the forest laws were still very strict, on the other hand thieves and robbers were hanged, and evil practices severely punished. "*Good man was Henry,*" writes the Chronicle, "*and great awe there was of him, no man durst do against another in his time.*"

<small>Town and country.</small>

In consequence of the good laws, peaceable arts began to flourish in England. Two curious settlements took place in this reign. In 1105 Henry planted a colony of Flemings—driven by floods from their own country—in Pembrokeshire, where they remain to this day; and in 1128 the Cistercian monks, a strict, hard-working order, founded first at Citeaux, near Rouen, began to settle in the wildest parts of England, at Waverley in Surrey, and afterwards in the north and west. The Cistercians bred sheep and redeemed waste lands, while the Flemings brought the art of weaving wool, and so these two settlements were useful to the country.

<small>Flemings and Cistercians.</small>

10. Henry and the Church.—Two other acts of Henry's reign we must mention, because they were important in later reigns. After much discussion with Archbishop Anselm he consented to let the clergy of the cathedrals elect their own bishops, so that the king could not keep bishoprics vacant, as William Rufus had done. But the election had to take place in the King's Court, and the bishops did homage to the king for their lands. Henry also allowed the Pope to send a legate or ambassador to England.

<small>Election of bishops. Pope's legate.</small>

11. Closing Years of the Reign.—And now, when all was at peace at home, a great sorrow fell upon Henry. He had been fighting for three years in Normandy against the barons, and on his return his only son William was drowned in the *White Ship*, which struck on a rock and sank with all on board. It is said that the king never smiled again. If he had now been wise and generous he would have taken young William of Normandy, Duke Robert's son, as his successor, for William was a good, honest young man, and the nearest heir to the throne. But Henry schemed to keep the crown in his own family. He married his daughter Matilda, widow of the German Emperor, to Geoffrey, Count of Anjou, the only man whose enmity he feared ; and then he made the English barons swear that she, and her baby-boy after her, should succeed to the throne. This they did most unwillingly, even after young William of Normandy had been killed in battle, for these turbulent nobles did not want a woman over them. The prospect looked very gloomy, and it turned out even worse than it appeared. On Dec. 1, 1135, Henry died at his hunting-seat in Normandy, from a fever caused by eating lampreys. His body was brought to England and buried in Reading Minster, but even before it arrived, another king sat on the English throne.

Henry's only son drowned, 1120.

Henry forces Matilda and her son on the barons.

CHAPTER VI.

NINETEEN YEARS OF ANARCHY UNDER STEPHEN, 1135-1154.

1. Civil War.—Truly England never saw before, and may she never see again, nineteen years of such misery, bloodshed, and cruelty as now followed. Stephen of Blois, who hastened to England as soon as his uncle died, was the son of William the Conqueror's daughter Adela, who married a count of Blois. He and Matilda's little son Henry were the only male heirs to the throne, Stephen being a grandson, Henry a great-grandson of the Conqueror. Stephen was very popular, brave and generous, and had been a great favourite with Henry I.; but he was impetuous

Stephen's claims.

and unstable, and quite unfit to reign. The people of London welcomed him, because they did not want a queen, and Roger, Bishop of Salisbury, and Henry, Bishop of Winchester, who was Stephen's own brother, supported him. He was elected and crowned on midwinter day, promising to govern well and put down the quarrels among the barons.

But he had promised what he could not perform. The barons, now Henry's strong hand was removed, broke into open rebellion; they fortified their castles and took sides, some for Matilda whom they had sworn to support, some for Stephen who was their crowned king, while they really cared only to be able to ravage the country for themselves. David, King of Scotland, who was Matilda's uncle, took up arms for her, but was defeated at Cowton Moor in Yorkshire, in the famous "Battle of the Standard," so-called because the English had as their standard sacred banners hung from a ship's mast.

Battle of the Standard, 1138.

Then Stephen did a very foolish thing. As the barons became more and more riotous, the bishops were alarmed for their property, and began to fortify their castles. Stephen, seized with a panic lest they should betray him and join Matilda, arrested several of them, among others Roger the justiciar, his best friend; Roger's son, who was chancellor; and his nephew, the Bishop of Ely, who was treasurer. He put Roger in irons and threatened to hang his son unless their castles were given up. Bishop Roger retired broken-hearted, and Stephen lost his most useful allies. From that moment all law and order were at an end.

Stephen arrests the justiciar and chancellor.

Meanwhile Robert, Earl of Gloucester, Matilda's half-brother, took up arms on her side, and so did the barons in the north and west, while the east and south fought for Stephen. Matilda landed at Portsmouth, and civil war began in earnest. Battle followed battle. It is impossible to speak of them all, for during eight years there was not a week in which fighting was not going on in some part of the country. At one time Stephen was a prisoner in Lincoln Castle, and Matilda entered London and was proclaimed queen in 1141, but she was so stern and haughty that the citizens rose against her, and she was never crowned. Then Stephen's brave wife, Matilda of

Matilda lands in England, 1139.

Boulogne, stirred up the people of London to send a thousand mail-clad men to the siege of Winchester. They sacked the town, took the Earl of Gloucester prisoner, and exchanged him for Stephen. Once more free, Stephen next besieged Matilda in Oxford Castle in 1142, and she was so sorely pressed that she had to escape by night in a white cloak across the deep snow. Wearied out at last, after many skirmishes, she left England, and about the same time Earl Robert died. Matilda leaves England, 1147.

2. Misery of the People.—Still there was no peace, for the barons were fighting one against another. Every castle was a kingdom of its own, whose lord coined his own money, made his own laws, and ravaged the country round. "They cruelly oppressed the wretched men of the land with castle-building," says the Chronicle, "and when the castles were made they filled them with devils and evil men. Then they took those whom they supposed to have any goods, both by night and by day, labouring men and women, and threw them into prison for their gold and silver, and inflicted on them unutterable tortures. Many thousands they wore out with hunger. I neither can, nor may I, tell all the pains which they inflicted on the wretched men in this land. And this lasted the nineteen winters while Stephen was king, and it grew continually worse and worse. Then was corn dear, and flesh, and cheese, and butter, for none there was in the land. After a time they spared neither church nor churchyard, but took all the goods that were therein, and then burnt the church and all together. The earth bare no corn, for the land was all laid waste by such deeds, and men said openly that Christ and his saints slept."

Trouble and death pressed hard upon the people, and awoke the old spirit of earnest devotion which had slumbered so long under foreign clergy. In town and country men banded themselves together for prayer, hermits flocked to the woods, and noble and churl alike welcomed the austere Cistercians as they spread over the woods and forests. As the barons grew more wicked the people became more earnest, and relief came at last. Religious revival.

In 1150, when a new Pope was elected in Rome, he appointed

Theobald, Archbishop of Canterbury, a man of strong moral sense, to be his legate. Theobald at once used his new influence to persuade Stephen to acknowledge Matilda's son Henry, now twenty years of age, as his successor. Just at this time Stephen's own son Eustace died, and young Henry landed in England, where an army gathered round him at once, in hopes of gaining a settled peace.

Treaty of Wallingford, 1153. Stephen saw he must yield, and by the Treaty of Wallingford, he acknowledged Henry as heir to the throne. Then justice was restored, for all who longed for peace joined to put down the rebels. Moreover, Stephen was sinking into the grave. On Oct. 25, 1154, he died, leaving the crown to Henry. It was in this year that the Old English Chronicle ceased, the last records being made in Peterborough Abbey.

CHAPTER VII.

HENRY PLANTAGENET AND HIS SONS (THE ANGEVIN KINGS).

1. Henry II.—Young Henry was abroad when Stephen died, but Archbishop Theobald kept good order till he arrived, and on Dec. 19, 1154, at the age of twenty-one, he was crowned with his queen at Westminster and issued a charter. Although his possessions in France were larger than all England, and out of thirty-five years of his reign he spent eighteen years or more than half his time abroad, yet he was one of the best English kings.

He was the first of a new line of kings called by some the PLANTAGENETS, because Geoffrey of Anjou, Henry's father, wore a sprig of broom or *planta genista* as his device; and by others the ANGEVIN kings, or descendants of the counts of Anjou. The name Plantagenet seems to me the best, because it is only a symbol, whereas the other name sounds as if a new foreign race had come to rule over us. Now Henry, on the contrary, was the first king since the Conquest with West Saxon blood in his veins, for though he was the son of the Count of Anjou, yet his mother was both Norman and Saxon, being the granddaughter of William the Conqueror and great-great-granddaughter of Edmund Ironsides. Moreover, as we shall see, Henry's descendants soon ceased to be counts of Anjou.

HENRY PLANTAGENET AND HIS SONS. 49

Henry himself, however, ruled over a vast territory, and had in him a good deal of the fiery French nature. He inherited Anjou and Touraine from his father, and Maine, Normandy, and England from his mother and grandfather; while he ruled Brittany through his brother Geoffrey, husband of Constance, heiress of Brittany; and gained Poitou, Aquitaine, and Gascony with his wife Eleanor, a woman older than himself, whom he married only a few weeks after she was divorced from Louis VII. of France.

Possessions and marriage.

He was a stout, square-built man, with short red hair and prominent grey eyes, so active that he scarcely ever sat down except to meals, and his subjects never knew where he might next be found, so that he always kept a ruling hand over them. He was well educated, a good man of business, and a clever statesman when his fiery temper did not override his prudence. He was a good father to his children, who behaved ill to him; but he was neither kind nor faithful to his wife, and from this sprang many troubles.

Appearance and character.

The English people soon began to feel the benefit of a strong and just king. Under Theobald's advice Henry forced the barons to destroy all the castles built without royal permission; he took back the royal lands with which Stephen had bribed his followers, and sent away the foreign troops which he had brought into England. He restored the courts of justice and chose a good and loyal justiciar, Richard de Lucy, who served him for twenty-five years. For his chancellor he took Thomas Becket, Archdeacon of Canterbury—the son of a rich Norman merchant, Gilbert Becket, portreeve of London, and the pupil and friend of Archbishop Theobald.

Thomas Becket chancellor.

For the next ten years England was quiet, though Henry had several wars abroad and was away for five years, from 1158 to 1163. But even when away he was occupied with English matters, and during these ten years he made many good laws for the people. He wanted to check the power of the barons, and to get money to pay soldiers for his wars abroad, and this he did by allowing the smaller tenants to pay a fine called "scutage" or shield-money (*scutum*, shield), instead of being obliged to follow their lord to the wars. This was a great boon to the farmers, who

Scutage.

4

could reckon safely on staying at home to sow and reap their crops, while the barons had fewer armed men at their beck and call.

2. Administration of Justice.—The visiting justices now began to make their rounds more regularly than before, for Henry divided the country into six districts or "circuits," and arranged that four knights in each shire, and twelve men in each neighbourhood, should present all evil-doers and disputers about property before these judges, and swear to their guilt, or to the truth about the dispute. This was the Grand Jury, the men being called "*jurors*" from the Latin *juro*, I swear. In cases of property, when they acted as a "civil jury," their evidence decided the matter; but people accused of crime were afterwards sent to the trial by "ordeal" as in old Saxon times. Forty years later, in John's reign, ordeal was abolished, and then this "Grand Jury" sent the prisoner on to the "Petty Jury," or another twelve men who were most likely to know all the facts of the case, and who declared of their own knowledge as to whether the accusation of the Grand Jury was true. This was called giving their "*verdict*," which means *truly said*. Later still the Petty Jury found that they wanted to inquire more closely what others knew, and so the practice arose of hearing witnesses.

Circuits and juries.

Assizes of Clarendon, 1166.

The people had now every opportunity of complaining if they were ill-used, and the assizes or edicts of Clarendon in 1166 and of Northampton in 1176, in which all these changes were confirmed, must be remembered as important to the liberty of Englishmen even in our own day. The quiet state of the country under these good laws allowed many now to think of gaining knowledge as they could not in troubled times, and we hear for the first time of students at Oxford hearing lectures from the Friars, who were the chief teachers. It was a small beginning, but it was the first step towards a great school of learning.

First Oxford students.

3. Thomas Becket.—In his zeal to improve the courts of justice, however, Henry brought a great trouble on himself. Thomas Becket, his chancellor, had become a great man and his dearest friend; and when Theobald died, and Henry saw that he must reform the clergy as well as the nobles, he made Becket Archbishop of Canterbury, thinking he

Becket archbishop.

would assist him. But Becket was a man who put his whole heart into whatever he had to do. When he was chancellor he was the king's servant, and served him well; when he became archbishop he was the servant of the Church, and he put off his gay clothing, wore a hair-shirt, and determined to uphold the clergy.

It will be remembered that William I. gave the clergy courts of their own. This had worked badly, for nearly all educated men in those days were clerks or clergy, though they held many lay offices; and whatever crimes these men committed, even thefts and murders, they got off very easily, for these courts had no heavy punishment, and the ordinary judges had no power over them. Henry insisted that clerks should be tried for ordinary offences in the King's Court, and punished like other men as in the days of Edward the Confessor. The bishops consented, but Becket would not, and though he was persuaded to put his seal to the "Constitutions of Clarendon," drawn up in 1164 for the government of the clergy, he repented next day, and applied to the Pope to free him from his promise. *Trial of the clergy.*

Henry was furious with his friend. He put all kinds of indignities upon him, and Becket was forced to fly to France, where he remained six years, while Henry in petty spite banished all his friends and relations. Meanwhile, in 1170, the king wished to have Prince Henry crowned, that he might govern during the king's absences abroad; and Becket being in exile, Roger, Archbishop of York, performed the ceremony. This was a deep insult to the Archbishop of Canterbury, and the Pope threatened to excommunicate Henry unless he recalled Becket. *Prince Edward crowned.*

So Henry, who was then in France, was obliged to make up the quarrel, and allow Becket to return to England. But Becket, now furious in his turn, no sooner landed than he suspended the Archbishop of York for crowning the prince. It was a foolish quarrel, and still more foolish Henry's mad passion which made him exclaim, "Will no one rid me of this turbulent priest?" Four knights took him at his word, and crossing to England murdered Becket, calm and brave, on the floor of his own cathedral at Canterbury. *Murder of Becket, Dec. 29 1179.*

Such were the effects of passion and revenge. Henry was right in altering the law, and Becket did only what he thought his duty in opposing him. But it was revenge for his persecution which misled Becket at last, and passion which made Henry the murderer of his friend. He was full of remorse when he heard what had been done, and sent off messengers at once to the Pope to declare that he had not intended the murder to be committed, then, wishing to keep out of the way till he was absolved, he crossed over to England and from there to Ireland.

4. Conquest of Ireland.—In Ireland great changes were taking place. Ever since the Danes in 795 invaded that country the people, oppressed and plundered, had drifted back into barbarism. In 1014 the Irish hero, Brian Boru, had driven out the Danes, and died himself in the battle; and since then the petty kings and chieftains had been always at war with each other. Quite early in his reign Henry had gained the Pope's permission to go over and conquer Ireland; but he did nothing till, in 1166, one of the Irish kings, Dermot of Leinster, asked for help against his neighbours. Then Henry allowed Richard de Clare, Earl of Pembroke, surnamed 'Strongbow,' to take over an army of adventurers, and he conquered nearly the whole of Leinster. It was to take possession of this new land that Henry now went over with an army. He lived for a year outside Dublin, gave away lands to his followers, ordered castles to be built, and received the homage of the chiefs as Lord of Ireland. Five years later he sent his favourite son John to rule, but John made so many enemies that he had to return to England. Though this was the beginning of the conquest of Ireland, it was more than three hundred years before the English really governed the country.

Conquest of Leinster.

Henry II. Lord of Ireland, 1171.

5. Domestic Troubles.—While Henry was thus adding to his kingdom, his sons and his enemies at home took advantage of the horror caused by the murder of Becket to rebel against him. Young Prince Henry wanted to rule at once over England or Normandy, Geoffrey and Richard wanted lands of their own in France, and Queen Eleanor hated her husband who neglected her, while the King of France was only too ready to help the rebels. Added to this William the Lion, King of Scotland, was eager to reconquer the northern counties of England, and the

Rebellion of Henry's sons.

HENRY PLANTAGENET AND HIS SONS. 53

English barons hoped in the turmoil to get back some of their power.

But Henry was equal to them all. He went from Ireland to Normandy to meet the messengers bringing the Pope's pardon, then with his army he conquered his rebellious sons, and put Queen Eleanor into confinement, where she remained till after his death. He next won the hearts of his people by doing severe penance at Becket's tomb; and just as he left Canterbury he learned that William of Scotland was taken prisoner. William did not get his freedom again till he had done homage as a vassal of England. From Canterbury Henry hastened to Huntingdon, and meeting his rebellious barons, made them return to their allegiance. In less than a year he was again master of the situation. *Henry's penance and triumph.*

But he had learnt that he must have an English army on which he could rely, and in 1181 he reintroduced the old West Saxon law of *fyrd* or military service, by which all freemen had armour, and pledged themselves to protect king and country in times of danger. This was quite different from feudal service to a lord, and it was the foundation of our "*militia*," a body of national soldiers trained as a regular army, but only called out to defend the country. The remainder of Henry's life was spent chiefly abroad. *Militia established, 1181.*

Henry's sons still gave him much trouble. At last the two eldest Henry and Geoffrey, died, Richard and John only remained, and Richard, with the help of Philip of France, drove his father, now breaking in health, out of Touraine. Henry, sick at heart and ill with fever, asked to see the list of the conspirators against him, and when he saw at the head the name of his favourite son John, "Now," said he, "let all things go as they will, I care no more for myself or the world," and two days after he died. To England he had been a true king and lawgiver. He gave the English peace and justice, and made good laws, which have lasted to our own times. *Henry's death, 1189.*

6. Richard Cœur de Lion (*Lion-hearted*).—In everything except being a good soldier Richard, who succeeded to the throne, was the very opposite of his father. Though born in England, yet, as he had two elder brothers, he had been educated abroad as the future Duke of Aquitaine. It is doubtful if he could even speak an English sentence, and during his ten years' reign he was only twice in England, for a few months at a time. Brave and chivalrous, though mean and covetous, a born soldier, a warm friend but a dangerous enemy, careless of his people while full of zeal for religion, Richard behaved nobly in the Crusades, and the English were proud of him; but he played no part in English history; that went on without him.

Richard no king to England.

7. Richard's Rule.—He was crowned on Sept. 3, 1189, and began at once to sell all the offices, honours, and church and crown lands on which he could lay his hands. He even sold the homage of the Scotch king, that he might get money for his crusade. "I would sell London," he said, "if I could find a buyer." Then he joined Philip, King of France, on his way to the Holy Land, and left his mother Eleanor and his justiciar, William of Longchamp, a man of low birth who bought the chancellorship, to rule in his absence. Fortunately the good laws of his father really governed the kingdom. Longchamp ruled only two years, for the barons hated him, and when Queen Eleanor went to Sicily in 1191 Prince John, with the help and goodwill of the London citizens, turned him out of office, and he fled to Normandy. It was most likely to this that we owe our Lord Mayor of London, for John, as a reward to the London citizens, took an oath to their "communa" or governing body, and gave them for the first time a "Mayor," with power in the city almost equal to that of the king. Henry Fitz-Alwyn was the first mayor of London, and when he died twenty-three years afterwards, John, who was then king, sold to the London citizens the right to elect their own mayor.

Richard sells preferments.

Longchamp deposed, 1191.

First mayor of London, 1191.

Meanwhile Richard, who had heard that Longchamp was unpopular, sent another justiciar; Queen Eleanor returned, and John, who would have liked to seize the throne, was obliged to remain quiet. News came from time to time of the king's brave doings in the Holy Land, till one day the English people heard that on his way home he had been seized by the Duke of Austria, who had

HENRY OF PLANTAGENET AND HIS SONS.

sold him to the German Emperor, and they must provide money to ransom him. To raise the £100,000 required, every man had to give a quarter of his yearly income and goods, besides paying four other kinds of taxes. *Richard's ransom, 1194.* John treacherously tried to persuade the emperor to keep Richard a prisoner, but he did not succeed, and the ransom being paid, Richard landed at Sandwich. He spent the four months of this second visit in raising money for foreign wars, received the archbishop's blessing after his *Richard's second visit March-May, 1194.* captivity, and then went to Normandy, never again to return. He took away John's lands and castles, but otherwise forgave his base treachery.

For the next four years Hubert Walter and Geoffrey Fitz-Peter, faithful justiciars, governed the country; levying as justly as they could the enormous sums Richard required. One good came from this. The people, now they were at peace, began to consider whether it was wise to let a king tax them so heavily, and the justiciars had to call lawful meetings when they levied money. The two bishops of Lincoln and Salisbury actually once refused to pay money on church *Bishops refuse money for foreign wars.* lands to be spent in foreign wars, and the idea grew up that the nation ought to have some voice in settling what taxes should be raised.

At last, quite suddenly, came the news of Richard's death from an arrow-wound, while he was besieging the castle of Chalus, near Limoges. He died bravely, as he had lived, pardoning the man who shot him; but after his *Death of Richard, 1199.* death the order was disobeyed, and the man cruelly killed.

8. John, surnamed Sansterre or Lackland.—

We now come to the one English king about whom nothing good can be said; though his reign was very important to England, because he was so bad that the whole nation was roused to insist on justice and right. John was absolutely mean and selfish. He was handsome, gay, well educated, and had ability; but he was cruel, licentious, avaricious, and treacherous, caring for none but himself. He had betrayed his father and his brother, and as a king he was false to his nephew, his people, and his own kingly word. *Character of John.*

9. War with France.—He was with Richard when he died, and received the homage of the barons who were there; and in England he was elected to the crown without any difficulty, for Arthur of Brittany, Geoffrey's son, was only twelve years old, and no one seriously upheld him. But in France it was different. John with some difficulty secured Normandy, Poitou, and Aquitaine; but Arthur was the true Count of Anjou, and Anjou, Maine, and Brittany stood by him. Old Queen Eleanor, now eighty years of age, sided with John, while Philip, King of France, fought for Arthur. The war lasted on and off for three years, till Prince Arthur, when besieging his grandmother Eleanor in the castle of Mirabel, in Poitou, was defeated by John and taken prisoner.

Then followed a black deed at which we shudder even now. Arthur, then fifteen, was imprisoned in the new Tower at Rouen, but he stoutly refused to give up his claim to the English throne. From that time he was never seen again. Shakespeare has made us all thrill with anger and pity at the shameful murder of the brave young prince; but all that we really know is, that throughout Europe the whisper grew louder and louder that John had murdered the boy, and there seems little doubt that the accusation was true. Philip of France, from whom John held his French lands as a vassal, summoned him to clear himself of the murder before the peers of the realm; but John refused, and then Philip declared all *his lands in France forfeited.

Murder of Arthur, 1203.

Loss of Normandy and Anjou. Most of the barons turned against him, his mother died, and in the end John lost all his possessions in the north of France except the Channel Islands (see Map III.). There remained to him only his mother's lands of Gascony and a small part of Aquitaine in the far south. He made, indeed, several attempts to regain Normandy and Anjou, but in vain; and so by the base murder which he committed to secure the English crown, he lost in one great swoop all the inheritance of his ancestors. England gained by his loss. For the future her kings and her nobles belonged to her alone; they could no longer live abroad fighting on English money; they had to make their home and their friends among the English people.

10. Struggle with the Pope.—John, however, was soon involved in a new quarrel. For the last five years Archbishop

HENRY PLANTAGENET AND HIS SONS. 57

Huoert, as chancellor, had done well for the nation; but he died in 1205, and the monks of Canterbury, knowing that John would try to choose some minion of his own, secretly elected an archbishop. John, when he heard it, forced some of their number to elect another, and both archbishops appealed to Pope Innocent III. But the Pope set them both aside, and made the six monks who came to consult him elect Stephen Langton, an English cardinal then in Rome, and a good and upright man. John refused to receive Langton in England, and as he remained obstinate, the Pope, in 1208 laid the whole kingdom under an "*interdict;*" that is, he forbade the clergy to marry the people in church, or bury them in the churchyard, or to read any church services except the baptismal services and prayers for the dying. For four long years no church bell was rung, no prayers were offered up in church, and the dead were buried without a service in ditches and meadows. *Election of Stephen Langton.* *England laid under an interdict, 1208.*

But John did not care; he only revenged himself by seizing the goods of the bishops and clergy, and spending the money on wars in Ireland, Scotland, and Wales. Then Innocent, excommunicated John, forbidding any one to serve him. Still he paid no heed, but punished all who followed the Pope's orders, crushing under a cope of lead an archdeacon of Norwich who refused to obey him. When his barons withdrew from his court, he seized their castles and their children, and shamefully treated their wives and daughters. At last, the Pope declared John to be deposed from his throne, and gave Philip of France orders to conquer England. *John excommunicated, 1209.* *Pope deposes John, 1212.*

Then at last John became uneasy, because he was going to lose something himself. If his subjects had loved him he could have defied the Pope and Philip, but all men detested him for his crimes. In abject alarm at a prophecy that he would cease to reign before Ascension Day, which was the anniversary of his coronation, he not only received Langton as archbishop, but actually gave up the English crown to the Pope's legate, Pandulph, and received it back as a vassal. In doing this he gave rise to a long struggle between the popes and the English kings, which lasted more than three hundred years. *John submits and becomes the Pope's vassal, 1212.*

11. National Progress.—But in accepting Langton he had brought more immediate trouble on himself. For many years, all through the quiet reigns of Henry II. and Richard, the nation had been growing stronger. In the towns the citizens discussed freely when the town-bell called them to meeting. The merchant-guilds settled the laws of trade, the craft-guilds protected the
<small>Growing strength of the people.</small> workmen from oppression, and many new privileges were bought when the kings wanted money. At the universities, too, scholars, English and Norman, Irish and Welsh, noble and peasant, met as friends and equals. Even in the country the duties of a man to his lord were now fixed by law, so that each had his rights, while the farmer was often free and paid his master instead of working for him. The nation was now united enough for the people and the barons to make common cause against a tyrannical king.

12. Magna Charta.—They only wanted a leader, and they found one in Langton. On Aug 4, 1213, a council of bishops, barons, and reeves of the towns, was called to settle what was due to the bishops whom John had robbed, and then Geoffrey Fitz-Peter, the justiciar, told the barons it was their own fault if they
<small>Barons demand a charter.</small> submitted to John's tyranny, for they had a right to insist on his obeying the laws of Henry I. A few weeks later, at a meeting held at St. Paul's, Stephen Langton produced the charter of Henry I., in which these laws were given, and Fitz-Peter laid the claims of the two councils before the king. Unfortunately just then Fitz-Peter died, and John took as justiciar a foreign friend of his own. But Archbishop Langton continued the fight, and the barons from both north and south took a secret oath at St. Edmundsbury to make John sign a charter of rights or to take up arms against him. In January 1215 they laid their demands before the king.

Taken by surprise, John asked to have till Easter to consider, and spent the three months, not in learning what rights they had, but in secretly engaging hired troops and enrolling himself among the crusaders, so that it would be sacrilege to fight against him. But the barons were too much in earnest to mind this. They flew to arms, the whole country joined them, and John saw his case was hopeless. Almost alone, having only seven knights true to him, he met the barons at Runnymede on the Thames, near Windsor, and on June 15, 1215, sorely against his will, signed the "MAGNA CHARTA" or Great Charter, by which the liberties of Englishmen have been defended from that day down to our own. Most of the laws in this Great Charter were not new, but had been in others before it. The two main clauses were, *first*, that the king could not imprison and punish his subjects as he pleased, but that each man must be judged by his equals ; and, *secondly*, that he might not levy taxes without the consent of the bishops, earls, and greater and lesser barons. The other clauses chiefly renewed old rights. But the great point gained was, that while the other charters had been mere declarations made by kings when they were crowned of the laws by which the people should be governed, this was a treaty forced on a bad king by his people. The nation was now strong enough to insist that the king, as well as his subjects, should obey the laws and respect the rights of others. So determined were the barons to enforce their rights and those of the people, that twenty-five of their number were appointed to see that the promises were kept, and were authorised to seize the royal castles and lands if the king broke them.

John signs the Great Charter, 1215.

Benefits of the Great Charter.

Of course John did not mean to keep his word. He put off the barons with excuses while he collected his foreign troops, and appealed to the Pope to help him, and at last civil war broke out. John gained several victories, and in the north of England burned and destroyed all before him. Then at last, exasperated at his treachery, the barons invited Louis, the eldest son of the King of France, to come over and be their king and he came with a large army. But a few months later death freed England from the tyrant. Crossing the Wash, in the Fens of Lincolnshire, John lost all his baggage, his jewels, and his crown, far dearer to his heart than his people. The next day he was taken ill at Swineshead Abbey, but he pressed on, and died at Newark, leaving two young sons, Henry and Richard, and a country full of civil war and foreign troops.

War between John and the barons.

Louis comes with an army.

Death of John, 1216.

HISTORY OF ENGLAND.

PART III.

RISE OF THE ENGLISH PARLIAMENT.

KINGS FROM THE GREAT CHARTER TO THE HOUSE OF LANCASTER.

CHAPTER VIII.

THE BARONS' WAR.

1. Henry III.—King John was dead. He could no longer either make promises or break them; and the barons, who were already beginning to see that Prince Louis would give their lands to his French nobles, were willing enough to take little Prince Henry of England, only nine years old, for their king. The Bishop of Winchester crowned him at Gloucester ten days after his father's death, with a plain gold circlet (for the crown was lost), and he did homage to the Pope's legate, Gualo, for his kingdom. The Great Charter was republished, but the clause about asking the consent of the people to the taxes was left out. William Marshall, Earl of Pembroke, a wise old man, who had been the friend of Henry's father and grandfather, was elected "governor of the king and kingdom."

Little by little all the barons came back to their allegiance. Prince Louis still fought for the crown, but his army was defeated in the streets of Lincoln by the Earl of Pembroke, and his fleet in the Channel by Hubert de Burgh, so he was glad to make a treaty at Lambeth and return to France with a sum of money. *Prince Louis returns to France, 1217.*

Two years later the old Earl of Pembroke died, and Peter des Roches, Bishop of Winchester, became the young king's guardian. Hubert de Burgh as justiciar, and good Stephen Langton as archbishop, governed the kingdom. Henry was crowned a second time by the archbishop in 1220; and in 1227, when he was twenty, he began to govern in his own name. At first this made no real difference, for his advisers continued as his "private Council" and this was the beginning of the "*privy Council*" of our day.

2. State of the People.—Both in town and country the people were prosperous. It is true the civil war had left the land very disturbed. Highwaymen and robbers, such as bold Robin

Hood and his companions, Little John and Friar Tuck, infested the roads; but these free-booters attacked chiefly wealthy travellers, and left the homesteads in peace. The harvests were on the whole good; even the labourers had plenty of oaten and sometimes wheaten bread, and drank barley beer with their herrings and cheese. They wove their own clothing, tanned their own leather, and made their own wooden tools in the winter; amusing themselves with wrestling, throwing, and archery, which the law required them to learn; while several times a year the hundred and manor-courts broke the monotony of their lives. From time to time some villager bought permission of his lord to go and trade in a town, or another served the king in foreign wars, or the village priest taught another and sent him to the university. In the towns, too, trade both with home and abroad was increasing, in spite of the heavy tolls often levied by the king. Such articles as the country people could not make for themselves were bought by the steward of the

Fairs. manor at the annual fairs held in different parts of the kingdom by special permission of the king, who levied tolls on all the goods sold. These fairs were very useful to the people, although sometimes, when Henry wanted money, he ordered them to be held where they were not needed, as, for example, in London, to the hurt of the shop-keepers. It was in this reign, in 1257, that gold coins were first struck in England, though they did not come into general use till 1344. But while the people were quiet and prosperous, a storm was again brewing between the barons and the king. Archbishop Langton died in 1228, and after his death Pope Gregory IX. filled English bishoprics and livings with Italian priests, also sending over to England for money from both barons and clergy for his own wars. Two new orders of "Friars"

The Friars. or "Brothers," came to teach the people. These were the *Dominicans* or *Black Friars*, the followers of *Dominic*, a Spaniard, and the *Franciscans* or *White Friars*, the disciples of Francis of Assisi, an Italian. They were men of all nations, who made a vow of poverty, and wandered over Europe and Asia barefoot, and with a hempen girdle round their serge frock. One of these *Friars* was the famous Roger Bacon, whose great work, the *Opus Majus*, first drew men's thoughts to science

3. Henry governs alone.

—In 1232 the king became jealous of Hubert de Burgh, and depriving him of his justiciarship, took the government into his own hands, putting mere clerks in the place of the great ministers. From that time all went badly, for Henry was a capricious man, vain, extravagant, and easily led by favourites. He was amiable and fond of poetry and art. He caused Westminster Abbey to be rebuilt as it now stands, and improved English architecture. But he was no statesman. He would trust a man one day, and be suspicious of him the next; and though kindly and well-meaning, he was so miserably weak that he was never true to himself or others.

In 1236, he married Eleanor of Provence, and her relations had their share of good things, while a swarm of foreigners crowded to his court, whom he married to English heiresses. *Influx of Foreigners.*

The king himself was very extravagant at home, and was always trying to get back his father's possessions in France. To obtain money for all these purposes he was obliged to call together the earls, barons, and bishops, in assemblies now first called "Parliaments," from the French *Parlement* (parler, to talk). The nobles gave him grants very unwillingly, urging him each time to allow them to appoint a proper justiciar, chancellor, and treasurer to look after the expenditure. The king made many promises, and six times confirmed the charters—but did not keep them. Year after year as he came for money the same difficulties arose, growing worse as he asked for more and more, till the barons began to see that a stop must be put to the constant drain and to the increase of foreign favourites. *Parliament first so called.*

The chief leader of the barons was Simon de Montfort, Earl of Leicester, who was the king's brother-in-law, having married his sister Eleanor. Earl Simon, curiously enough, was the son of foreign parents, but his grandmother had been English, and he was a true friend to England. A man faithful in word and deed, and resolute to defend the right, he had learned from his friend Grosseteste and from Adam Marsh, an earnest Franciscan friar, to long for a better government of the people. During many years he ruled in Gascony for the king, *Simon de Montfort.*

though Henry treated him shamefully, leaving him without men or money. When he returned to England he tried to check the king in his weakness and folly, but in vain! For twenty-two years things went from bad to worse. In 1253 Grosseteste died, but not before he had drawn up a list of grievances, and had made Simon swear that he would stand up even to death for justice and right. And Earl Simon kept his word.

<small>Twenty-two years of bad government.</small>

The storm burst a few years later. Pope Innocent IV wanted to drive Conrad, the German Emperor, out of Sicily; so he offered the crown of Sicily to Henry for his second son Edmund, only nine years old. Henry was foolish enough to accept, and though Innocent died just then, the next Pope, Alexander IV., made war on Conrad in Henry's name and at his expense. The king had to confess to his Parliament that he owed the pope 135,000 marks, or £90,000.

<small>Pope offers Edmund the crown of Sicily.</small>

4. Provisions of Oxford.—The barons were very indignant, for they had not been consulted, and the country was drained of money. They only granted 52,000 marks; and they came to the Parliament at Oxford fully armed, and insisted that twenty-four barons—twelve chosen by the king and twelve by themselves,—should reform the Government; that there should be three Parliaments every year; that the castles should be given back to Englishmen; that the king should have a standing Privy Council to advise him; and that the justiciar, chancellor, and treasurer whom they appointed should give an account to this Privy Council at the end of each year. Though the king's party were very angry, and called this the "Mad Parliament," yet Henry was obliged to submit; and he and his eldest son Edward, now nineteen, swore to accept these "Provisions of Oxford." Earl Simon, as a foreigner, was the first to offer to give up his castles, and most of the foreign favourites fled to France, their posts being filled by Englishmen.

<small>Mad Parliament 1258.</small>

The barons now governed; but their power lasted only four years, for most of them were satisfied with having turned out the foreigners, and took no trouble about the reforms, while Earl Simon really wished for good government. Prince Edward, who was naturally just and honourable, was inclined to support Simon. The

THE BARON'S WAR.   65

king, on the contrary, had already sent to the Pope to absolve him
from his promise of keeping the "Provisions," and when the absolution came he seized the Tower, and ordered the counties not to
obey the barons' officers. Then the barons flew to arms; the queen,
alarmed, took refuge in the Tower, and civil war was imminent,
though there was no great battle. At last it was agreed to refer the
whole question to Louis IX. of France. Louis thought _{Mise of Amiens,}
that a king had the right to govern absolutely, and at _{1264.}
the *Mise* (or arbitration) *of Amiens* he decided altogether in favour
of Henry.

5. The Barons' War.—Then the famous "Barons' War"
broke out. Fifteen thousand Londoners joined Earl Simon. Some
of the barons joined the king, and Prince Edward, now that it had
come to open war, stood by his father with all the foreign troops.
But Earl Simon had also a large following. After many smaller
encounters, the armies met face to face near Lewes. At _{Battle of Lewes,}
first the royalists had the advantage; but the young _{1264.}
prince who opened the battle having routed the Londoners, pursued
them fiercely. When he came back the battle was lost, and the
king a prisoner. Edward himself could do nothing but surrender.

6. De Montfort's Parliament.—For more than a year
after this Earl Simon ruled England in the king's name, keeping
Henry with him. On Jan. 20th, 1265, he held a Parliament at
Westminister, which, although it was composed of those only who
upheld his power, was very important. For Simon summoned not
only two knights from each shire, but two citizens, of burgesses,
from every borough, to sit with the nobles in Parliament; and so
for the first time the city communities or *commons* had members of
their own. The knights were chosen in the county court, as in the
shire-moot of old, by the freeholders of the county, and they
answered to our *county members* now, who are still called *knights of
the shire*. The *borough members* were elected by the citizens.

7. Death of Earl Simon.—But Simon could not keep
his party together. The barons were jealous of his power, and
Simon's sons gave offence by their pride, while the people did not
like the king being a prisoner. At last Prince Edward, who was

kept under guard, set his keepers to run races, and when their horses were tired he escaped from them.

Once free, his old friends rallied round him, and the Earl of Gloucester having joined him with a large force, he drove Simon to take refuge with the Welsh prince Llewellyn. Then pushing on to Kenilworth, he defeated young Simon, who was coming to his father's help; and putting the banners taken from young Simon's knights in front of his army, he came close upon the old Earl at Evesham, in Worcestershire, before he knew that an enemy was approaching. Simon had but a small force of undisciplined Welshmen with him, and he saw that all hope was over. "Let us commend our souls to God," said he to the few barons around him, "for our bodies are the foe's," and he died fighting bravely, with the cry, "It is God's grace," upon his lips. With him died all hope of success. The civil war lingered on for a year, and then at the peace, or *dictum* of Kenilworth, most of the barons received back their lands from the king. In 1267, Henry renewed the *Provisions*, and the next six years were peaceful. Prince Edward went to the Crusades, and while he was gone the king died after a troubled reign of more than half a century, during which he had never meant to do any harm, but had worked endless ills by being simply a "worthless king." Battle of Evesham, Aug. 4th, 1265.

CHAPTER IX.

STRUGGLE WITH WALES AND SCOTLAND.

1. Edward I.—When Henry died the Royal Council proclaimed Prince Edward king, and ruled the land peaceably for nearly two years till he returned to England, and was crowned. He was then thirty-five, a tall, strong man, with dark hair and gentle eyes, which, however, could flash angrily when he was roused. He was one of England's best kings, and made many useful reforms in the laws. A good son, husband and father, we have proof of his loyal heart in his indignation at the insult to his mother, and in the crosses remaining to this day, which he erected wherever the body of his first wife Queen Eleanor Appearance and character of Edward I.

STRUGGLE WITH WALES AND SCOTLAND. 67

rested between Lincolnshire and Westminster. Charing Cross receives its name from one of these. Brave, truthful, and constant, his motto was "Keep Troth," and having seen his father's mistakes, he wished to win the love of his people and give them good laws. When he failed it was because the old idea still clung to him that a king might overrule the law.

The office of justiciar was not revived after the Barons' War. The chancellor was now next in authority to the king, and Robert Burnell was the first great Chancellor of England. Edward began at once to reform abuses; he forbade the barons to drive cattle into their castles without paying for them, or to levy money unjustly; and made a law that the people should be left free in electing the sheriffs and others who dealt out justice. He also improved the money of the country, and caused silver halfpennies and farthings to be coined. Up to this time, ever since the days of Alfred, the silver penny had been marked with a deep cross, and people broke it in half or in quarters when they wanted small change.

<small>First great chancellor, 1274.</small>

<small>Halfpennies and farthings coined.</small>

2. Conquest of Wales.—Edward next turned his attention to Wales, which was a constant source of trouble. Little by little the Britons had lost nearly all the land which once was theirs. Strathclyde and Cumbria had long been swallowed up in England and Scotland. West Wales, or Devon and Cornwall, had become part of South England; and even the southern counties of Wales itself had been conquered by Norman barons, who, living on the borders of Wales were called "Lords of the Welsh Marches," from *mark* or *march*, a boundary. In North Wales alone the Welsh were still governed by their native chiefs, while their bards sang of the hated Saxon and of the days of good King Arthur. The head of these chiefs,—Llewellyn, Lord of Snowdon and Prince of Wales,—had helped Earl Simon, and governed as an independent prince, during the Barons' War, and now he refused to come to England and do homage to Edward. After trying all peaceful means for more than two years, the king at last, in 1277, marched to Wales with an army, and drove Llewellyn into the mountain fastnesses. Then he was forced to

<small>Llewellyn refuses homage.</small>

submit, and Edward allowed him to keep his title and power under certain conditions, and to marry Simon de Montfort's daughter.

But four years later rebellion broke out again. Llewellyn was a brave and noble chief, but his brother David was a restless adventurer, who had once been false to Llewelyn and sided with the English. Now, being dissatisfied, he turned traitor the other way, broke into Hawarden Castle in Flintshire, took the English chief-justice of Wales prisoner, and persuaded Llewellyn and the Welsh princes to revolt and plunder the Marches. There was a Welsh prophecy that when English money became round a Welsh prince would be crowned in London, and the coining of smaller round coins instead of broken pennies made the people think this would come true. Again the king took an army into Wales, and endured severe suffering during the cold Welsh winter, but would not quit his position. Chance favoured him, for in a small skirmish on the banks of the Wye, brave prince Llewellyn was killed, and with his death Wales was conquered. A few months later David was taken and justly suffered the death of a traitor. Edward remained in Wales a whole year introducing good laws, and while he was there his son Edward was born at Caernarvon in 1284. From this time Wales was joined to England, though it had its own laws. In 1301 Edward gave the people as their prince his Welsh-born son Edward, the only one who survived of Eleanor's four sons. This boy was the first English Prince of Wales. *First English Prince of Wales, 1301.*

3. Law Reforms.—The next twelve years, during three of which Edward was away from England, were spent chiefly in law reforms, which have lasted to our day. The land laws were carefully regulated, and the famous "Statute of Mortmain" was passed, forbidding land to be held by *dead hand* without license. The law prevented men from pretending to give their land to the Church and to religious societies, so as to avoid rendering feudal service for it. About this time the law courts, which used to be united under the justiciar, were divided into three—the *King's Bench*, where public questions were tried; the *Court of Common Pleas*, where people brought their private suits; and the *Court of the Exchequer*, for all questions of the king's revenue. The *Statute of Mortmain, 1279.* *Organisation of law courts.*

Chancellor also now examined all cases of law where people appealed for "grace and favour" to the king, and so he gradually became, by the reign of Edward III,, the head of what was called the *Court of Chancery*. Lastly, such disputes as were not settled by any of these courts came to the king himself in his Privy Council, so that all injustice might be corrected.

Edward's next care was to put down robbery and assault. Large bands of lawless men at that time lived by plunder and black-mail. On one occasion a body of country gentlemen actually broke into Boston fair in Lincolnshire, robbed and murdered the merchants, and carried off the goods to ships they had brought up to the quay. To stop such outrages as these, a law was made binding every man to arm himself and join in the "hue and cry" to arrest marauders; and in 1285 a knight was elected in each shire to act as "Keeper of the Peace," and to watch the sheriff to see that crime was punished. These keepers afterwards became our "Justices of the Peace," or "County Magistrates," who now judge and punish crime, each in his own neighbourhood. *Keepers of the Peace, 1285.*

4. Expulsion of the Jews.—Among these useful reforms one sad blot was the expulsion of the Jews. Through many reigns the Jews, specially protected by the kings, had become richer and richer by usury. They were often employed by the nobles to ruin small landowners by lending them money and seizing their land in payment, and this made them hated by the people. They were also accused, perhaps justly, of clipping coin and of many dishonest practices. Already when Richard I. was crowned there had been a terrible massacre of Jews in London and York, and during the "Barons' War" Jewry after Jewry was sacked. Simon de Montfort had wished to banish the Jews, and now Edward ordered all who would not become Christians to leave England. He allowed them to keep their wealth, and he himself lost one means of getting money by sending them away. But it was a cruel deed, and as they crossed to France many of them were robbed and wrecked, the better class suffering with the rogues. From that time till the days of Cromwell there were no Jews in England.

5. First full Parliament.—If this, however, was a tyrannical step, Edward made a much more important one towards freedom

when he adopted Simon de Montfort's plan of calling knights and
citizens to Parliament. He could only get grants of money in
Parliament from the barons and bishops. The shires, citizens, and
clergy had each to be asked separately out of Parliament, and this
was often very troublesome. Now, by summoning two knights from
each shire, two burgesses from each borough, and two clergymen
from each bishop's diocese, these members could make promises for
the people who elected them, and grant money. Besides, as Edward
justly said, it was right that "what concerned all should be
approved by all." So in 1295 a full and perfect Parliament was first
summoned by order of a king—the nobles each by name, the knights
and burgesses by a sheriff's writ. This Parliament was much like
ours now, only the nobles and commoners sat together, and there
were clergy present. Afterwards the clergy refused to come; they
preferred to vote money in their own assembly or *Convocation*, and
this is why there are now no clergy in the House of Commons. In
some other ways these early Parliaments were different from ours.
There was a fresh election every time they met, and the people had
to pay for the members' expenses—two shillings a day
to a burgess and four to a knight. This was equal to   Members were paid.
about five shillings and ten shillings of our money, and
neither the members nor the people much liked the trouble or
expense. Besides they looked on each Parliament only as a fresh
demand to supply the king with money, and little thought what
power they were one day to gain by having members to speak for
them.

6. War with Scotland.—A year after the meeting of the
first full Parliament, Edward was drawn into a war with Scotland,
after there had been peace between the two countries for nearly a
hundred years. In 1286 Alexander III. of Scotland   Scots left
died, and the only direct heir to the throne was his   without a
little grandchild Margaret, daughter of Eric, King of   king, 1290.
Norway. In the summer of 1290 this little "Maid of Norway"
was coming over to be betrothed to Prince Edward of Caernarvon,
when she died, and the Scots were left without a sovereign. The
Scotch Council asked Edward to decide between the five nobles who
now claimed the crown. Edward therefore met the Scotch Parlia-

STRUGGLE WITH WALES AND SCOTLAND.

ment at Norham, near Berwick on the border, and after he had made them acknowledge him as feudal lord, he examined carefully the claims of the three chief rivals. These were John Baliol, Robert Bruce, and John Hastings—the descendants of three sisters who sprang from the line of King David I. of Scotland. Edward chose John Baliol, grandson of the eldest of the three sisters, who did homage to Edward under the name of King John of Scotland, and for a short time all went well. But Edward wanted more power as feudal lord than was fair. He insisted that the Scotch nobles and citizens might appeal to him against decisions in the Scotch law courts; and when he was drawn into a war with the King of France about Guienne, he summoned the Scotch nobles to follow him and fight. They refused indignantly, and being anxious to throw off the control of England, they made a secret treaty with the King of France, crossed the English border, and ravaged Cumberland.

John Baliol elected king, 1292.

Edward was very angry. Sending his brother in his stead to Gascony, he marched north with a large army, stormed the town of Berwick, and maddened by the taunts of the inhabitants, cruelly massacred them all. Then, as Baliol still defied him, he seized Edinburgh, Stirling, and Perth, and at Montrose took Baliol prisoner and sent him to England. He then appointed an English council to govern the kingdom, and carried off to England the crown jewels and the "Sacred Stone" of Scone, on which the Scotch kings were crowned. This stone was made into the seat of the regal chair in Westminster Abbey, and our kings are crowned on it to this day. The Scots declared that wherever it went, there, sooner or later, Scottish kings would reign; and their prophecy came true when James I. was crowned.

First war in Scotland, 1297.

Edward thought that Scotland was now conquered, as Wales had been, but he did not know the people with whom he had to deal. The high-spirited Scots chafed under their loss of freedom, and when William Wallace, a brave outlawed knight, raised the standard of rebellion, the people flocked to him. Wallace was bold and skilful. He cut to pieces the English garrison at Lanark, made a dash at Scone, and drove out the English justiciar. Then, with the help of Sir William Douglas,

William Wallace, 1297.

another outlaw, he defeated the English army at Stirling, and proclaimed himself "Guardian of the Realm" in King John's name.

At this time Edward was in Flanders, where he had gone to uphold the Flemings against Philip IV. of France, who was seizing English wool in the Flemish ports. Edward's troubles were heavy just then; Ireland was restless, there was a rebellion in Wales, and Philip was trying to cheat him out of Guienne. Hampered for money, he applied to the clergy for half their yearly income, but they refused by the Pope's order, until he made them submit by refusing them justice or protection in the law courts unless they paid. Then some of the English nobles refused to go and fight in Guienne. They did not care for these foreign possessions, and thought there were wars enough at home. Edward, anxious to hold his own against the French king burdened the people with taxes. He raised the duty on wool to six times what had been paid before, ordered the counties to send in large supplies of food, and called upon the country gentlemen to be knighted, for which they paid heavy fees; he also summoned all landowners to bring soldiers for the war. At this Parliament rebelled; and when they accused him of levying unjust taxes, Edward, with that generous feeling which made his people love him, owned he had been wrong, but pleaded he had done it for England's honour, and appealed to their loyalty to help him. Then they gave their consent to the war, but they sent a charter after him to Flanders which he signed, promising among other things that he would *never more levy money without consent of Parliament, and that the grievances of the people should always be redressed before a fresh grant was made.*

Edward levies heavy taxes, 1297.

Parliament exacts new charters, 1297.

And now, with all this on his hands, he heard how the Scots were wasting the north of England. He returned home at once, and marching to Scotland, met Wallace with his forces near Falkirk, where a famous battle took place. The Scots fought bravely, and Wallace with great skill drew them up in blocks, something like the *square* in which our soldiers still fight. But the English were three to one, and their archers, the finest in the world, cleared a gap, into which the English horsemen dashed in overwhelming numbers. The Scots were cut to pieces

Battle of Falkirk, 1298.

STRUGGLE WITH WALES AND SCOTLAND. 73

and their army destroyed. Edward forgave the rebel nobles, but Wallace escaped and refused the king's mercy. Seven years later he was betrayed by his servant, Jack Short, to Sir John Monteith, governor of Dunbarton Castle, and hanged on Tower Hill.   *Wallace hanged, Aug. 24, 1305.*

For eight years after the battle of Falkirk, Edward tried in vain to unite the Scots and English into one nation. The nobles, led by John Comyn, nephew of Baliol, rebelled constantly, but at last there seemed some chance of peace. Meanwhile, however, there had been growing up in Edward's court a brave young Scotch nobleman, Robert Bruce, Earl of Carrick and Lord of Annandale, who was the grandson of that Robert Bruce who had been a competitor for the crown in 1291. Edward, half afraid of him, kept him about his person, and was just planning a mixed Parliament of English and Scots at Carlisle, when one day rumours reached him through Comyn that Bruce was plotting with the Scots. The following morning young Bruce was missing, and the next that was heard of him was that he had quarrelled with Comyn in a church at Dumfries, that Comyn was killed, and the English judges driven out of the town.

It was a bad beginning, for the slaying of Comyn in a church was both murder and sacrilege, but a band of nobles gathered round Bruce, and he was crowned at Scone six weeks later, by the courageous Countess of Buchan, who was a Macduff; and tradition said that a Macduff must always place the crown on the head of the King of the Scots. King Edward heard the news at Winchester. He was ill, old and careworn, but he determined once more to invade Scotland. Before he went he knighted his son, the Prince of Wales, with great ceremony. At the banquet which followed, he swore to exact vengeance for Comyn's murder, and bade his people, if he died, to carry his body before the army till Scotland was subdued.   *Robert Bruce crowned King of Scotland, Mar. 25, 1306.*

Travelling slowly to Carlisle, he sent the army forward under the Earl of Pembroke, who took many of the Scottish nobles prisoner, and drove Bruce a fugitive into the Grampian Hills. Once more Edward's anger led him to bitter vengeance; the nobles were hanged, and the Countess of Buchan was placed in a wooden cage on the walls of Berwick   *Edward's last journey, 1307,*

Castle. But the hand of death was on the avenging king, and though he tried to push forward, he died at Burgh-on-the-Sands, within sight of Scotland, July 7, 1307. Besides his eldest son, Edward, Prince of Wales, he left two sons by his second wife, Margaret of France.

7. Edward II. (of Caernarvon).—The death of the old king altered the whole course of events. Edward II., the son of good and able parents, was a frivolous, indolent youth, who had been indulged in childhood, and had already given his father much trouble. Now at twenty-three, he was handsome, headstrong, and fond of low companions, revelry and folly. Even his sad end twenty years later, can scarcely make us feel an interest in so pitiful a king.

His father, on his deathbed, left him three commands. First, to carry on the war till Scotland was subdued; secondly, to send his heart to the Holy Land; thirdly, never to recall from exile a profligate Gascon—Piers Gaveston, whom Edward I. had banished. He disobeyed all three. Returning south at once, he left Bruce for three years to gather strength for a struggle. He buried his father at Westminster, and within a month of his death had recalled Gaveston, loaded him with riches and honour, and left him as regent for two months, while he went to France to marry Isabella, daughter of Philip IV.

On his return he and his young queen were crowned, and Gaveston was put at the head of the Government. Gay, insolent and ambitious, the favourite held revels and tournaments with the king, and insulted the nobles. Twice he was banished, but Edward always recalled him. One year, Parliament actually took the Government out of the king's hands, and gave it to a committee of bishops and peers, called "the Lord's Ordainers," who drew up a set of ordinances limiting the king's power. This Parliament is the first on record that was *prorogued* (*prorogo*, I prolong), that is, dismissed for a time and called together again without a fresh election. Gaveston remained in exile for a time, but at last he returned again, and was taken prisoner by the barons at Scarborough. Falling into the hands of his mortal enemy, the Earl of Warwick, he was beheaded on Blacklow Hill, in presence of the king's cousin, Thomas, Earl of Lancaster.

<small>The Ordainers, 1310-1311.</small>

<small>Murder of Gaveston, 1312.</small>

STRUGGLE WITH WALES AND SCOTLAND.

8. Battle of Bannockburn. June 24, 1314.—During this time, while the king was fooling, Scotland was slipping from his grasp. Town after town had been taken by Bruce, and an expedition by Edward and Gaveston against him in 1310 had been an utter failure. At last, Bruce was master everywhere, except at Stirling and Berwick; and the Governor of Stirling Castle was so hard pressed that he had promised to surrender on St. John's Day, June 24, if he were not relieved. Then Edward, who had lost his favourite, and who, although so indolent, was brave enough when roused, marched north, and met Bruce within sight of Stirling Castle, by the little brook or *burn* called the Bannock. The moment had come when the freedom of Scotland was to be won or lost, and the Scots were in terrible earnest. The battle was fought on St. John's Day. Burns' famous song,

"Scots, wha hae wi' Wallace bled,
Scots, wham Bruce has aften led,"

written more than 400 years later, tells us how it is remembered in Scotland to this day. King Robert had dug pits in front of his army, and covered them with sticks and turf; and, like Wallace, he drew up his spearmen in hollow squares or circles, with the front men kneeling. The arrows of the English bowmen punished them sadly, but they closed in bravely. When the English horsemen charged, their horses were met again and again by such a mass of bristling spears that at last they were thrown into hopeless disorder. At that moment the English mistook a body of Highland servants coming over the hill for a fresh enemy; a panic arose, and the brilliant array of nobles and knights turned and fled. Edward himself escaped to Berwick, but his army was scattered and his nobles prisoners, while rich spoils remained with the enemy. The Scots had thrown off the English yoke. *Scotland free.*

9. Deposition and Death of Edward II.—The humiliation to England was bitter, and six unhappy years followed. The country had been drained of men for soldiers; bad seasons, cattle plague, and the greed of the king's servants, brought scarcity of food. Parliament unwisely tried to keep down the price of food by law; the consequence was, that food being cheap, was bought up too freely, and a famine *Famine and trouble.*

followed in which many died. The Scots, too, were ravaging the north of England; Edward Bruce, Robert's brother, was invading Ireland; and Edward took a new favourite—Hugh le Despenser—who with his father supplanted the chief minister, Thomas, Earl of Lancaster, and ruled the kingdom. The Despensers were superior men to the former favourite, but the barons soon quarrelled with them, and taking up arms under Roger Mortimer, and the Earls of Hereford and Lancaster, they conspired with the King of the Scots to seize the government.

The favourite Hugh Despenser, 1320-1327.

But this time Edward was on the alert; he marched against the rebels before the Scots could join them. The Earl of Hereford was killed, Mortimer sent to the Tower, and Thomas of Lancaster, whom Edward had never forgiven for Gaveston's death, was beheaded. Then the king held a Parliament at York, revoking the Ordinances; and because he wished to curb the power of the barons, he persuaded Parliament to pass a very important law, that "all matters should be established by the king, prelates, earls, barons, and *commonality* of the realm." This was the first time that the Commons were given a share in making the laws; hitherto they had only been consulted about taxes. The Despensers now governed, but they were hated by both the queen and the people, and misrule and confusion reigned in the land. Queen Isabella went to France to settle a dispute about the duchy of Guienne with her brother Charles IV., and a few months later she sent for her son Prince Edward, thirteen years of age, to come and do homage for the duchy. But neither the queen nor the prince returned, for she was intriguing with Lord Mortimer (who had escaped to France), to overthrow Edward and put his son in his place. In 1326, she landed in Suffolk with a small body of troops, and was joined at once by the archbishop and the barons.

Lancaster beheaded, 1322.

Commons gain a share in legislation, 1322.

Deserted by all, the wretched king fled with the Despensers to Wales, and was taken prisoner at Glamorgan. Both the Despensers were hanged, and the king was declared unfit to reign by a Parliament held at Westminster. His staff of office was broken, and young Edward was proclaimed king in his stead. The king's words are sadly touching. "It

Edward II. dethroned and murdered, 1327.

grieved him much," he said, "that he had deserved so little of his people, and he begged pardon to all who were present; but since it could not be otherwise, he thanked them for electing his eldest son." Then he was imprisoned in one castle after another, and on Sept. 21, 1327, he was cruelly murdered in Berkeley Castle by order of Mortimer.

CHAPTER X.

THE HUNDRED YEARS' WAR—THE PEASANT REVOLT.

1. Edward III.—On Jan. 29, 1327, the young prince was crowned; guardians were appointed to govern for him, but during the first four years Queen Isabella and her favourite, Lord Mortimer, usurped the real power. After that Edward took his own place. In 1328 he had married Philippa, daughter of the Count of Hainault; in 1330, his first son, afterwards so well known as the Black Prince, was born; and in November, of the same year—his eyes being opened by the execution of his uncle, the Earl of Kent, through Mortimer's influence—he entered Nottingham Castle at midnight with a band of friends and seized Mortimer, who was condemned by the peers for many crimes, and hanged at Tyburn (then called "The Elms"). Queen Isabella was sent to Castle Rising, in Norfolk, for the rest of her life. *King's minority, 1327-1336. Fall of Mortimer.*

Thus Edward, before he was nineteen, was a husband, a father, and a responsible king. His reign has a double history—one of wars abroad, the other of great events at home—and we must take these separately. Although Scotland was now independent, yet skirmishes continued on both sides, and when King Robert died leaving only a little son seven years old, Edward III. invaded Scotland, and put Edward, eldest son of John Baliol, on the throne. Baliol was soon driven out again, but as the French were allies of the Scots, King Philip VI. of France, who wanted Guienne, made Edward's invasion of Scotland an excuse for invading Gascony. About the same time *Causes of quarrel with France.*

the people of Flanders, who had now a large wool-trade with England, wanted protection from the extortions of their worthless ruler, Count Louis. Their leader, James van Artevelde, named "the Brewer of Ghent," called on Edward to help them, and to take the title of "King of France," so that they might transfer their allegiance to him.

Flemings ask Edward's help.

2. War with France.—This Edward did. He put the French fleur-de-lis on his shield, with the motto "*Dieu et mon Droit*," and claimed the throne of France by right of his mother Isabella, who belonged to the elder branch of the French royal family, Philip VI. belonged to the younger. The claim was worthless, for by French law the succession could not pass through a woman. But, on the accession of Philip VI., Edward, whilst he admitted that a woman could not herself succeed tot he throne of France, contended that her male heir, if nearest of kin to the last sovereign, was entitled to the French crown. This gave rise to the famous "HUNDRED YEARS' WAR," which lasted on and off through the reigns of five English kings. It soon ceased to have anything to do with the Flemings, and was a sad war, for it was a mere struggle for power, without any thought of doing good to either nation.

Chivalry. These were the days of chivalry, when, even in tournaments, the nobles loved to risk their lives and perform feats of bravery and daring. There was a great deal that was good in this high-spirited courage and knightly honour, but the nobles only exercised it among themselves. When they went to war they cared but little for the burning villages and the ruined crops and vineyards, nor for the suffering people, who were called "rascals" in those days, and counted for nothing.

3. First Campaign.—In Edward's reign the war was divided into three campaigns. The first began when the French attacked Portsmouth in 1338, and lasted till 1347, and the English were on the whole successful. In 1340 they gained a great naval victory off Sluys, on the Flemish coast; and, on Aug. 26, 1346, another at Crecy, in Northern France, in which the English archers overpowered the knighthood of France. Gunpowder was first used in this battle, and Edward, Prince of Wales—called the Black Prince—won his knightly spurs there at sixteen years of age by his bravery. It is

FAMOUS BATTLES & SIEGES OF HUNDRED YEARS WAR

said, but on doubtful authority, that it was after this battle that the Black Prince adopted the three plumes and the motto "*Ich Dien*," which the Prince of Wales still uses. Then followed the Siege of Calais, which lasted eleven months—from Sept. 1346, to Aug. 4, 1347—on which day, when the town could hold out no longer, six brave burgesses came out barefooted and with halters on their necks to beg mercy for the inhabitants. Edward would have hanged them, but for the prayer of good Queen Philippa, who begged him on her knees to spare them. Edward peopled Calais with Englishmen, and for two hundred years it remained an English town, and was a great protection to ships in the Channel. It was about this time, and perhaps in memory of the Siege of Calais, that Edward III. established the famous Order of the Garter, comprising twenty-five knights, the king himself being the twenty-sixth.

<small>Siege of Calais.</small>

<small>Order of the Garter, 1348.</small>

4. Second Campaign.—The second outbreak of war began in 1355, when John II. was King of France. The most memorable battle in it was the Battle of Poitiers, when, on Sept. 19, 1356, the Black Prince, with only 12,000 men, defeated the French with 60,000, by drawing up his army at the end of a narrow lane among vineyards, across which the archers let fly their arrows as the French approached. From that moment of confusion, though the French fought bravely, they had no chance. King John and his little son Philip were taken prisoners to England, where John died eight years later in the Savoy Palace in London. Two years after the Battle of Poitiers, the English pushed on to Paris, across a wasted country which had been ravaged by lawless soldiers, called "Free Companies"; and at Bretigny, south of Paris, a peace was signed on May 8, 1360. By this treaty Edward gave up his claim to the French crown, but ruled Aquitaine, Poitou, Gascony and Calais, as an independent sovereign. Thus, at the end of the second campaign, the English held a large part of France.

5. Third Campaign.—But they lost it in the third. The Black Prince, who had gone to rule at Bordeaux as Duke of Aquitaine, interfered in a quarrel in Spain, and Charles V. of France began the war afresh. More wily than his father John, Charles avoided battles, while he harassed the English by long marches across the wasted country. The Black Prince was ill and irritable; he tarnished his fame by a massacre of the people of Limoges who had gone over to the enemy; while Charles got the better of him at every turn. At last ill-health drove him back to England, and from that time the English were unsuccessful. Their fleet was defeated by the Spaniards in 1371, and by 1374 the French had reconquered everything except Calais, Bordeaux, and Bayonne. So at the end of this part of the war the English held less of France than at the beginning, thirty-six years before.

6. Rise of the People.—We must now take up the history at home during the early part of Edward's reign. It may seem strange that the French war was popular in England. But the nobles liked war in itself, and the people thought if the king had more subjects they would help to pay the taxes, while they were proud of the brave Black Prince. Moreover, the lower classes really gained at first by the war. The knights and barons wanted money for their costly armour and splendour abroad, and were

<small>Leases granted and freedom to serfs.</small> willing to let their manors for *leases*, or long terms, receiving rent, called *feorm*, in return, and this was the beginning of the *farm* and independent farmer. They were also willing to sell freedom to their serfs or villeins, and even the king sent commissioners to his enormous estates to raise money by allowing his serfs to buy their discharge.

Edward had brought over a number of Flemish weavers, who settled in Norfolk, Suffolk, and Essex, and taught the people to

<small>Growth of industries and trade.</small> weave cloth. This soon became an important industry, and, as any serf who could escape to a town and dwell there for a year and a day was free, many began in this way to earn a free livelihood. Trade also began to flourish with foreign countries. The fish and timber trade with Normandy, the wool trade with Flanders, the wine and salt trade with Gascony, gave new openings for employment. The coinage was improved about this time, and in 1344 gold coins first began to be used as money. The nobles, busy with their wars, did not observe that, in consequence of all this advance, the freed serfs, and independent workmen and farmers were becoming a strong body of free men, with wants they had never felt, and rights they had never claimed before.

THE HUNDRED YEARS' WAR. 81

This went on for more than twenty years, and meanwhile the king was always appealing to Parliament for money for the war. In 1340 he came from France in a great rage, turned out the ministers and chief-justices, and accused his chancellor, Stratford, Archbishop of Canterbury, of having misused the money he had collected. He wanted Stratford to answer to *him* for the money, but Parliament replied that no minister could be judged except in full Parliament before his peers; and in 1341 they insisted that they should help to choose ministers, who should swear before them to keep the law. *Lords and Commons protect the minister.* For the last nine years the knights and burgesses had sat in the Painted Chamber, separate from the lords and bishops, who sat in the White Chamber, so that there were now two Houses, the Lords and Commons; and we find that the Lords consulted the Commons, who spoke their mind freely. Parliament was now really taking some control of government, and for the time all worked well. The people were pleased at the victory of Crecy, and at a defeat of the Scots at the Battle of Neville Cross, near Durham, where King David of Scotland was taken prisoner in 1346; and still more at the taking of Calais, which protected the Channel.

7. **Statute of Labourers.**—But great sorrow was at hand. In 1348 a terrible plague, called the "Black Death," swept over the continent to England, and in the crowded streets of the towns and the hovels of the country the people died so fast that it was difficult to bury them. *The Black Death.* In the end more than one-third of the population of England was swept away, without reckoning the numbers killed in the wars. How now were the landowners to get their work done? In the panic, fields had been left uncultivated and farms abandoned, and the labourers, now there were so few, asked higher wages for their work. Then came the first struggle between those who had money and lands, or the owners of *capital*, and those who lived by *labour*. *Struggle between capital and labour.* During the plague a number of sturdy beggars had arisen who would not work, and Parliament justly passed a law that every man under sixty must do work of some kind. But the "Statute of Labourers," which they passed, went further, and said that *the labourers should work for the same wages as before the Black Death.*

6

82   HISTORY OF ENGLAND.

This they would not do; and they managed to evade the law, and work for those who paid them best. The landowners were in a difficulty, for they had to pay more heavily for labour, tools, and everything made by labour, while they did not get any more money for the corn and meat grown on their land, because there were fewer people in the country to feed. So Parliament, in which, of course, the landowners were powerful, brought back the old laws which bound each man to work on his lord's estate. The labourer was forbidden to leave his parish, and any man who ran away was to have an *F* (*fugitive*) stamped with hot iron on his forehead. Many escaped serfs were brought back from the towns, and some even who had bought their freedom were unjustly claimed. The labourers, who now knew that they could earn more money if left free, chafed under the tyranny, while they tried to evade it.

<small>Statute of Labourers.</small>

8. John Wiclif, 1324-84.—The works of our great poet Chaucer, who about this time wrote the *Canterbury Tales*, and a strange poem, *The Vision of Piers Plowman*, written by the people's poet Langland, show how, while the knights, courtiers, wealthy abbots and monks were holding tournaments and revels, the lower classes were growing more and more restless. At this time, John Wiclif, Master of Baliol, Oxford, the first English religious reformer, began to write against the wickedness of the clergy, and especially of the friars, many of whom had grown hypocritical and greedy. A few years later he translated the Bible into English, and sent out "simple priests," barefooted and in russet gowns, who taught that each man must answer by his own conscience to God, that men are equal in His sight, and that nobles and priests must rule justly for the good of all. We can easily understand how all these stirring thoughts of freedom worked in the minds of the discontented peasants, and bore bitter fruit in the next reign.

<small>Works of Chaucer and Langland.</small>

9. Important Statutes.—Still all remained outwardly quiet, and during the next twenty years Parliament made many good reforms. In 1351 it was enacted that the Pope (who was at this time a Frenchman, living at Avignon in France, among enemies of England) should no longer give English livings to foreigners, nor

exact heavy tributes as he had done since the reign of John. In
1353, people were forbidden to carry English questions of law to
foreign courts; and this statute of *Præmunire*, a name
given from the first word used in the writ, became very
important in later times. In 1362 it was ordered that
English should be used in the law-courts, and not French, as
formerly; and that the king should no longer levy tolls on wool
without consent of Parliament.

First Statute of Præmunire.

The Government also tried to make laws for Ireland, but from
the first these were mistaken and cruel. There were three classes
of subjects at that time in Ireland—1st, the original Irish; 2nd,
the English who had gone there long ago, intermarried with the
natives, and made Ireland their home; and 3rd, the English who
went over to rule. The Irish and Irish-English were no doubt a wild,
half-barbarous people, but they were shamefully treated by their
rulers. By the statute of Kilkenny the English were
forbidden to marry with the Irish, all national
games were prohibited, and the Irish were ordered
to speak English and adopt English customs. The King's son
Lionel, Duke of Clarence, who went to govern them, would not
even allow any man born in Ireland to come near his camp. Under
such government it was impossible that the Irish should become a
contented people.

Statute of Kilkenny, 1367.

10. The Good Parliament.—Ten or more years passed away.
The war-disasters of the third campaign happened in France; the
king was growing old; good Queen Philippa was dead; and a
worthless woman, Alice Perrers, influenced Edward. The Black
Prince, who was the king's eldest son, was dying, and his little son
and heir was only ten years old. The king's third son, John of
Gaunt, Duke of Lancaster, was really governing with ministers of
his own choosing, and people suspected that he wished to seize the
throne. At last, in 1376, the "Good Parliament"
met, and the Commons made bold for the first time to
impeach the ministers, or, in other words, to prosecute
them before the House of Lords, who acted as judges. They
accused them of misappropriating the public money, levying taxes
without permission, and lending the poor old king money, for
which they made him pay them a hundredfold. The Duke of

The first Impeachment.

Lancaster did all he could to stop these attacks, but the Black Prince, though dying, upheld the Commons. The ministers were removed and Alice Perrers sent away from the king, though she soon came back again; and when the Prince died two months later, little Prince Richard was brought by the archbishop before Parliament, and acknowledged as heir-apparent. Nevertheless John of Gaunt came back to power, and the Parliament of 1377 undid all that had been done, and laid a new tax upon the people, called the poll-tax, of so much a head for every person in the kingdom. It was in this Parliament that the foreman or chairman of the Commons was first called the "Speaker." That same year, Edward III. died, and young Prince Richard, only eleven years old, succeeded to an uneasy throne.

Death of Black Prince, 1376.

First poll-tax, 1377.

11. Richard II.—Richard was crowned, July 16, 1377, and a council appointed to rule the kingdom. The king's uncles were not on this council, but John of Gaunt had still much influence. The war with France was drifting on, very badly for England, and there were heavy taxes to pay for it. The poll-tax was again levied. The Duke of Lancaster paid £6 : 13 : 4, the earls £4, and so on down to the poorest person over sixteen years of age, who paid a groat or four-pence. But this did not bring in enough, and next year a still larger poll-tax was collected. This pressed heavily upon the poor; and ever since the "Statute of Labourers," thirty years before, discontent had been increasing among the villeins, the labourers, and even the smaller tenants, who had to pay heavy dues and tolls. Secret associations were being formed all over the country, and Wiclif's priests, now called "Lollards," travelled from place to place, and were messengers between the restless people. John Ball, one of these priests, had even been put in prison by the Bishop of London for seditious preaching.

Hatred of poll-tax.

12. Peasant Revolt, 1381.—Still all was quiet till John of Dartford, a tiler by trade, killed a poll-tax collector, who insulted his daughter. At once all England was in an uproar, and it was clear there was some secret understanding, for the people rose all at once in Yorkshire, Lancashire, Devon, Suffolk, Essex, and Kent.

The men of Kent, under Wat Tyler (of the same trade as John of Dartford), rose in a mass, released John Ball from Maidstone gaol, and marched to Blackheath, where he preached to them that all men were equal, repeating the two lines,

> "When Adam delved, and Eve span,
> Who was then the gentleman?"

The men of Essex, under Jack Straw a thatcher, came armed with clubs, rusty swords, and bows, and joined the throng, and so did the men of Hertfordshire. A hundred thousand men moved on to London, and the mob within opened the gates to them. They ransacked the prisons, burnt the Savoy Palace (the home of John of Gaunt, whom they detested), and the new Inn at the Temple, and destroyed the houses of the Flemings. Yet they did not plunder or steal, but settled down quietly for the night —the Kentish men on Tower Hill, the Essex men at Mile End, the Hertfordshire men at Highbury.

Taken by surprise, the nobles and council were paralysed with fear. Only the young king kept his presence of mind. Though not yet sixteen years of age, he showed wonderful courage. Early the next morning he rode out to Mile End to meet the rioters. "I am your king and lord, good people," said he, "what will ye?" They asked for freedom, for the abolition of the oppressive tolls and market dues, and to be allowed to pay rent instead of giving labour. He promised all they asked, and set thirty clerks to write letters of freedom for each parish; with these papers in their hands the people dispersed. But while Richard was gone the Kentish men had broken into the Tower Palace and murdered the archbishop who was chancellor, and the treasurer whom they hated because of the poll-tax; while thirty thousand men still remained in London under Wat Tyler. These Richard met the next day in Smithfield, and when Wat Tyler laid his hand on the rein of the king's horse, the Mayor of London struck him and he was killed. "Kill, kill," shouted the crowd, "our captain is killed." "I am your captain," cried Richard, "follow me;" and they followed him quietly to Islington. Here he would not allow the troops, which had at last assembled, to interfere with them, but gave them written charters, and they returned home. So

Richard meets his people.

the revolt ended in London, but many lives were lost and much damage done in the distant counties during the next fortnight. Then the king marched through Kent and Essex with a large army; John Ball, Straw, and hundreds of others were arrested and put to death; and when Parliament met all the king's charters were declared to be valueless, because he could not give away what belonged to the nobles.

So the people seemed to have gained nothing; but, in truth, though at first the oppression was worse than ever, the nobles soon saw that *Villeinage dies out gradually.* it would be dangerous to force villeinage any longer on the people. Gradually during the next hundred and fifty years it died away entirely, and free labour took its place.

13. Power of Parliament.—Yet though young Richard began so bravely, the history of his reign was sad for him. To understand it we must notice that the Commons were now strong enough to force the king to listen to their advice before they granted him money but they did not yet know how to use their power; and were swayed this way and that by the great lords who were the real rulers in the land. Now Richard's uncles loved power, and wanted to keep him under their control, while Richard, as we see, had a high spirit of his own. Edward had seven sons, but only five grew to manhood.

The two first died before the king, and the Black Prince's son, as we have seen, became Richard II. His ministers and his council were never first-rate men, probably because his mother and friends were afraid of choosing friends of his uncles. But the uncles ruled nevertheless. John of Gaunt had power at first, but after the people showed in the Peasant Revolt how much they hated him, he withdrew to Spain for three years, leaving in England his son Henry Bolingbroke, Earl of Derby, who was beloved by the people. After John of Gaunt left, Thomas, Duke of Gloucester, took the lead; and while Richard was still under guardians, this duke and the Earl of Arundel stirred *Council of Eleven, 1387.* up Parliament in 1387 to impeach Richard's minister, the Duke of Suffolk, for wasting the public money; and to appoint a *Council of Eleven* to look after the king's affairs.

Richard was furious; he set the Parliament at defiance, and tried to rouse the people to join him. This was foolish and headstrong, for he had as yet no power, and the next year, in a Parliament, called the "Merciless Parliament," five lords—Gloucester, Arundel, Warwick, Nottingham, and Derby, who were called the "Lord's Appellant"— appealed against the king's friends, and accusing them of treason, hanged seven of them, among others a brave old knight, Sir Simon Burley, whom the king loved and honoured, and for whom the queen, and even Henry of Derby, begged in vain. Gloucester was merciless, and Richard saw that he must be wary. *The Merciless Parliament, 1388.*

14. Richard's Rule.—The next year, 1389, he took them all by surprise, by announcing suddenly in the council, that as he was twenty-three, he would govern in future himself. He called upon the Earl of Arundel to give up the Great Seal; and, staggered at his boldness and his just right, the lords yielded, and he took everything into his own hands.

For eight years he ruled wisely and well, making good laws. It was during this time that the second law of *Præmunire* was passed, enacting that all persons introducing bulls or sentences of excommunication from the Pope into England, should be liable to be imprisoned and lose their property. This statute, as we shall see, had important effects in Henry VIII's reign. Richard also visited Ireland, where he behaved kindly to the people. Meanwhile he did not show any ill-feeling towards those who had killed his friends. But he had not forgotten. His wife, Anne of Bohemia, died, and he married the little daughter of the King of France, only eight years old, so as to arrange a truce for twenty-five years. *Second law of Præmunire, 1393. Richard makes a truce with France, 1396.*

Now his hands were free, and when the great lords were angry at the war being broken off, and began to intrigue against him, he took his revenge. Gloucester, Warwick, and Arundel, were taken prisoners in a few hours. Gloucester was sent off to Calais, and in a fortnight news arrived that he died there. Arundel was tried before Parliament on the charge of treason and beheaded, while Warwick was imprisoned *Richard's revenge, 1397.*

for life. Then Parliament, left without its leaders, granted all the king asked, gave him a promise of an income for life, and allowed him to form a special committee of his own friends to overrule the petitions sent to Parliament. In a word, Richard had made himself an absolute king. But this was the cause of his downfall. From that moment there was no check on his extravagance or his strong will, and he began to oppress the people with taxes, and to interfere in the courts of justice. Even when he was right, as in protecting the labourers against the landowners, or in preventing the Lollards from being persecuted, the people grew to hate him, because he did it of *his own will*, and made them feel he would do as he chose.

<small>Richard an absolute king.</small>

Meanwhile two of the "Lords Appellant" still remained in England—Nottingham, now Duke of Norfolk, and Henry Bolingbroke, now Earl of Hereford, John of Gaunt's son and Richard's cousin. They were friendly to the king, but he did not feel safe, and took advantage of a quarrel between them to banish them both—Norfolk for life, and Henry for six years. This was most unjust, and as the people loved Henry, it angered them. But Richard was blind to all but his own power; and the next year, when John of Gaunt died, he seized all his estates which by right, belonged to Henry. Then, thinking that he had swept England clear of all his enemies, he went over again to Ireland, May 1399.

<small>Banishment of Henry, Earl of Hereford, 1398.</small>

15. Richard's Fall.—At the moment when he thought all was safe, his power crumbled to dust. Henry, now Duke of Lancaster, landed in Yorkshire to claim his estates. In a moment, at the news that he was in England, the Percies from Northumberland, Earl Neville from Westmoreland, and even the Duke of York, Richard's uncle, whom he had left as regent, all gathered round him. Richard had shown himself a tyrant, and England rose against him. When he landed in Wales a fortnight later he found his kingdom was lost. The nation, tired of Richard, welcomed Henry to rule over them.

Richard fell into Henry's hands at Flint Castle in Wales, through the treachery of the Earl of Northumberland. He was sent to the Tower, and signed a deed of resignation on Sept. 29, 1399. The next day Parliament declared Henry king. A year later, when a rebellion arose to restore Richard, he was said to have died, and his body was shown to the people; but how he really came to his end no one knows to this day, though it seems most probable he was secretly put to death. So the kingdom passed to the house of Lancaster; but it must always be remembered that Henry and his descendants held the crown because Parliament elected him, and that the nearest heir belonged to the house of Clarence; for this caused all the trouble which ended in the "Wars of the Roses."

<small>Disappearance of Richard.</small>

16. Summary—1216-1399.—We have now passed over nearly two hundred years since the Great Charter laid the foundation of English liberty. During that time we have seen Parliament take its rise, admit members elected by the Commons of the land, take the control of the taxes, insist that the people's grievances should be redressed before grants were made, and that the king's ministers should answer to Parliament for their actions. We have seen the two Houses of *Lords* and *Commons* begin to sit separately, but act together by consultation; and two kings set aside because they tried to act wilfully without the consent of their subjects. But in both these cases it was the great lords who led the way; for still, as in the days of John, it was the nobles who ruled the land whenever the king was weak or wilful. During this period, too, we have seen Wales become joined to England, while Scotland gained her liberty and her own line of kings. We have seen England gradually freeing herself from the heavy money grants, which the Popes levied ever since John took his kingdom from Pope Innocent III. as his vassal; while commerce was extending itself by the large wool-trade with Flanders, and profiting by the gradual rights which the towns acquired of trading, without the vexatious tolls levied by the earlier kings. We have also seen the first beginning of the rise of the masses of the people; how the villeins were gradually obtaining their freedom, and the tenants paying rent instead of giving labour; and how, by Wiclif's teaching of the freedom of conscience, and his translation of the Bible, the first seeds of the Reformation were sown. Wiclif himself, after a long contest with the Bishop of London, withdrew to his own parish at Lutterworth, and died in 1384. We shall still hear of his followers, the Lollards, in the next reign.

Lastly, we leave England in the midst of a war with France (for the truce made by Richard ended with his death), and on the eve of a struggle at home, which grew out of Henry having taken the throne, although he was not the direct heir. We shall see that in the war abroad, and in this struggle at home so many of the great families suffered, that when it was ended there was no longer the same barrier of great lords between the king and his people.

PART IV.

HOUSES OF LANCASTER AND YORK,
WARS OF THE ROSES

KINGS OF LANCASTER AND YORK.

CHAPTER XI.

THE HOUSE OF LANCASTER.

1. Henry IV.—The year 1400, which we have now reached, begins one of the most unsettled periods of our history. No king during the next eighty years held undisputed possession of the throne. There was always some one else who had a claim to be king, and this caused endless struggles and civil wars, in which the greater number of the old families were destroyed.

Unsettled succession for eighty years.

Henry IV. had already two rivals—Richard II., a prisoner in Pontefract Castle in Yorkshire, and the little Edmund Mortimer, Earl of March, the king's cousin, who, with his younger brother, was being brought up in Windsor Castle. Before three months were over, the Earls of Kent, Huntingdon, and Salisbury, together with Lord Despenser, entered into a conspiracy to restore Richard, but the plot was betrayed, and they were all executed. We shall probably never know whether this conspiracy hastened Richard's death or whether he died naturally. A few weeks later it was announced that he was dead, and his body was shown to the people, though many still doubted whether it were really he. Soon after this the Welsh prince, Owen Glendower, who was a descendant of Llewellyn, and had been a faithful squire to Richard II., rebelled in Wales, and the Welsh from all parts of the country flocked to support him. King Henry made several expeditions against him, and sent his son, the young Prince of Wales, with a large army. But Glendower always retreated to the mountains, and left the inclement weather to fight for him, coming back as soon as the English were gone, and really ruling the country.

Owen Glendower rebels, 1400.

Meanwhile the Percies—that is, the Earl of Northumberland and his warlike son, Harry Hotspur—who had helped to put Henry on the throne, had been defending the North against the Scots. At the Battle of Homildon Hill, on the Tyne, they defeated the Scotch army, and took many important prisoners, for whom they hoped to get large ransoms. But Henry seems to have claimed these prisoners, and also to have offended the Percies by leaving Edmund Mortimer, who was Hotspur's brother-in-law, a prisoner in Wales. Irritated at what they considered the king's ingratitude, the proud Percies turned against him and joined Glendower. The cry was raised that Richard was still alive in Scotland; the French sent troops to Wales to help the insurgents, and again Henry had to defend his crown. In the famous Battle of Shrewsbury he, with his two young sons, Henry, Prince of Wales, and John, Duke of Bedford, defeated the rebels. Harry Hotspur was killed and many noblemen were taken and executed. *Battle of Homildon Hill, 1402.* *Revolt of Percies and Glendower, 1403.* *Battle of Shrewsbury, July 21, 1403.*

But the old Earl Percy of Northumberland still remained, and in the year 1405, when the unfortunate Henry had only just recaptured the little Earl of March, whom Lady Despenser had carried off from Windsor, he heard that a fresh rebellion had broken out in the north. Again, however, the king's forces met the rebels and dispersed them, and this time Earl Mowbray and Richard Scrope, Archbishop of York, were beheaded for treason. *Rebellion of Mowbray and Scrope, 1405.*

After this Henry held his throne in peace. That same year, Prince James, heir to the Scotch throne, was taken prisoner by English ships on his way to France, and by bringing him up at the English Court, Henry kept a hold over the Scotch. France, too, ceased to trouble him. Young Henry, Prince of Wales, already a good general, gradually drove Glendower out of South Wales, and he became a wanderer in the mountains. Lastly, Northumberland was killed in battle, and no one again attempted to overthrow Henry's power. *Time of peace, 1405-1413.*

2. Important Measures.—But these seven years of constant uncertainty had been very hard for the king. Not daring to trust his nobles, he was obliged to keep good friends with Parliament and the Church. The long French war had made the Commons very unwilling to grant much money, and the king was often short of funds. *Commons gain the right of making money grants, 1407.*

So they could make their own terms, and they not only required the king to change his council and arrange his household as they dictated, but they succeeded at last in forcing the Lords to leave to them the sole right of making money grants after their grievances had been considered.

This was a step towards freedom, but another measure, passed chiefly to please the Church, was a cruel tyranny which lasted for more than a hundred years. By the advice of Archbishop Arundel, the first *Convocation* (or assembly of clergy), after Henry was crowned, sent him a petition, begging him to put down the Lollards; and in the next Parliament a law was passed by which a heretic, if he continued in his opinions after the first warning, was to be given over to the officers of justice and *burnt alive*. There were probably three causes for this terrible law: first, the clergy believed that the Lollards would ruin men's souls and take the property of the Church; secondly, the Parliament dreaded them, because they wished to alter the land-laws and the taxes, and to free the remainder of the serfs; thirdly, Henry was afraid of them because they had been favoured by Richard. And so in February 1401 the first fire was lighted to destroy a fellow-creature on account of his belief. William Sawtre, a rector of Norfolk, who had come to London to preach Lollard doctrines, was burnt at the stake.

<small>Law against heresy, 1401.</small>

3. Death of Henry IV.—Yet Archbishop Arundel, who persecuted the Lollards, was in other matters a wise and able chancellor, and so too were the Beauforts, Henry's half-brothers, who were chancellors during his reign. Now, when Henry's health was failing and he was afflicted with fits, they were good and faithful advisers to the young prince. It is said that they wished the king to resign the crown to his son, but this he would not do. He rallied for a time, and the prince, who had taken a prominent part in the council, retired, Arundel again becoming chancellor. So things remained, till one day, while praying in Westminster Abbey, the king was seized with a fit and died, March 20, 1413. He left four sons—Henry, who succeeded him; Thomas, Duke of Clarence; John, Duke of Bedford, a wise and noble prince; and Humfrey, Duke of Gloucester, the evil genius of his family.

<small>Thomas Beaufort chancellor, 1409.</small>

4. Henry V.—For nine years England was now once more to be dazzled by foreign victories. Henry V., a man of five and twenty when his father died, was already a brilliant soldier and an experienced statesman. It was said that he had been wild in his youth, and that Judge Gascoigne had once sent him to prison for defying the law. If this was so, he had done good work besides, conquering Glendower, boldly opposing the Commons when they wished to confiscate the property of the Church, and governing wisely in the council. *[Bills not to be altered in becoming statutes, 1414.]* Now he succeeded to a throne which his father had made strong by his firm but moderate rule, and he had the wisdom to follow in his steps. In the first year of his reign he granted to the Commons a boon they had long wished for, namely, that their petitions, now called *bills*, should become *statutes* after they had passed them, without garbling or alterations, and that the king should refuse or accept them as they came before him. This Parliament also agreed that *[Alien Priories granted to the king, 1414.]* the king should take all the property of the "alien Priories," that is, property in England which had till then been held by religious houses abroad.

Thus his reign began happily. He had an able friend and helper in his brother the Duke of Bedford, and a faithful chancellor in Henry Beaufort, Bishop of Winchester; and being himself truthful, brave, and self-denying, he became during his short reign the idol of the English people. He even felt strong enough to give back the Mortimer estates to the young Earl of March, and the earldom of Northumberland to Harry Hotspur's son, and he had King Richard's body removed with royal honours from Abbots Langley to Westminister Abbey. *[Henry V. strong and beloved.]* A feeble conspiracy was indeed formed by Richard, Earl of Cambridge, brother-in-law to Mortimer, but it was soon discovered, and he was beheaded, together with his fellow-conspirators, Lord Scrope and Sir Thomas Grey.

5. State of the People.—In spite of famines and a visitation of the Black Death in 1407, the nation had now for many years been prosperous. Labour was becoming free, the yeoman and the farmer could rent their farms, and we can see by the statutes passed to prevent extravagance in dress that money was not wanting. No labourer's wife, for example, was to wear a girdle garnished with silver nor a dress of material costing more than two shillings (about twenty shillings of our money) a yard. The many new treaties made to promote trade with Holland, the Baltic towns, Flanders, Venice, and other countries, show that shipbuilding and commerce were flourishing. The coal-trade of Newcastle was becoming important, and although the English kings were foolishly beginning to debase the coin—that is, to use less silver and more alloy, —money was circulating freely. The merchants, among whom was the famous Dick Whittington, thrice Lord Mayor of London, were rich and powerful; and the craft-guilds protected the workmen and encouraged good work.

6. Revolt of the Lollards.—The only restlessness among the people seems to have been caused by the Lollards, whose opinions had spread very widely. A sturdy knight, Sir John Oldcastle, who became Lord Cobham by marrying the heiress of Cobham, had now for many years upheld the Lollards. He was a brave soldier and a respected member of Parliament, and it was difficult to interfere with him, although his castle at Cowling in Kent had become the headquarters of the sect. At last, after Henry V. had tried in vain to convert him, he was arrested and condemned to death, but before the day arrived he escaped from the Tower. His escape was a signal for revolt. A large body of Lollards assembled at St. Giles' in the fields outside London, but Henry was too quick for them. He closed the city gates, and the royal forces dispersed the meeting. Thirty-nine of the chief Lollards were executed, and Lord Cobham fled to Wales; in 1417 he was taken, hanged in chains, and burnt.

7. Renewal of the French War.—After this Lollardism gradually disappeared. But the general restlessness of the country was one of the reasons why the French war began again. The bishops wished to divert the attention of the people from the Lollards, and of Parliament from their idea of confiscating Church property; the merchants wanted to open new channels for their goods, and the nobles were tired of peace. In these times war and conquest were considered honourable to a king and nation, and Henry was ambitious, and really believed that he was doing wisely in trying to

Causes of the renewal of the French war.

THE HOUSE OF LANCASTER. 97

put an end to the wretched civil war then raging in France. So, although he had far less right than even Edward III., he made a formal claim to the throne of France, and war began once more.

On Aug. 14, 1415, he landed near Harfleur in Normandy, and took it after a terrible siege, during which sickness broke out in his army, and he lost many thousand men. Then he marched on towards Calais, and met on the plains of Agincourt, in Picardy, an army of 60,000 Frenchmen, who had united for the time against the common enemy. Henry had, at the most, only 9,000 men, yet once more the English bowmen scattered the French cavalry, and 11,000 Frenchmen lay dead on the field, of whom more than a hundred were princes and nobles. Yet Henry was obliged to return to England, for his army was exhausted; and it was only two years after, that he returned with 32,000 men and conquered Normandy, with its strongholds, cities, and seaports. The siege of Rouen alone in 1418 lasted six months. The starving city held out, although the governor was obliged to turn 12,000 men, women, and children outside the gates, where they lay dying between the walls and the English army. At last the brave citizens threatened to fire the city, and Henry made terms with them, but he put to death their gallant captain, Alan Blanchard. The next year Henry took Pontoise and threatened Paris, and just at this time fortune favoured him. John, Duke of Burgundy, had gone to a conference with Charles, the dauphin or heir of France, and there was treacherously murdered by the friends of Orleans in the dauphin's presence. The Burgundians, furious at the treachery, joined Henry, and even Queen Isabel, wife of the mad French king, turned against her son, and gave her daughter Katharine to Henry as his wife. By the Treaty of Troyes, Henry was made Regent of France, and named as the successor to the throne.

Siege of Harfleur, Aug. 1415.

Battle of Agincourt, Oct. 1415.

Siege of Rouen, 1418.

Treaty of Troyes, 1420.

England was proud of her king when he returned, with his young French wife, as the Regent of France. Few or none of the people then thought how heavily they would pay in the next reign for all this conquest and glory. In 1421, a little prince was born and named Henry. The king was abroad fighting against the dauphin, his health was

Death of the kings of England and France, 1422.

7

failing fast, and he died at Vincennes, Aug. 31, 1422, at the early age of thirty-four. Two months later the unhappy Charles VI. of France also died, and the English baby-prince, only ten months old was King of England and France.

8. Minority of Henry VI.—England was at the height of her fame when Henry V. died. The parliament, clergy, and nation had made vigorous efforts to support the king in his glorious victories, and he had won for them a grand position in the eyes of Europe. But it was a false glory; the crown was deeply in debt, and the country exhausted and drained both of men and money. By Henry's last wishes the Duke of Bedford became Protector of the Realm and guardian of the young prince: but he was also to be Regent of France, and the Duke of Gloucester was to govern England in his absence, with the help of the council. Henry bade the two brothers never to make peace with the dauphin nor quarrel with the Duke of Burgundy, and he warned Gloucester to care for the country's interest before his own. He judged him only too truly. Before a year was over Gloucester had quarrelled with the Duke of Burgundy, about his wife's inheritance, and three years later Bedford was obliged to come back from France to make peace between him and his uncle the chancellor, Henry Beaufort.

Bedford, on the contrary, did his work well abroad. He married the Duke of Burgundy's sister, and with much difficulty steered clear of Gloucester's quarrel. By victory after victory he conquered, in five years, the whole of France north of the Loire and was on the point of succeeding in the siege of Orleans, when that wonderful rescue took place, of which the story will be told as long as the world lasts.

Siege of Orleans, 1428, 1429.

9. The Story of Jeanne Darc.—A simple village girl of eighteen, Jeanne Darc (called in English by a curious mistake Joan *of* Arc), the child of a labourer of Domremi, on the borders of Champagne and Lorraine, was filled with pity for the misery and ruin of her country. Dwelling on an old prophecy which said that a maid from Lorraine should save the land, she believed that she saw in visions the archangel Michael bidding her go to the dauphin and promise him that she would lead him to Rheims to be anointed and crowned king. In spite

History of Jeanne Darc, 1429-1431.

of the village priest and people, she persuaded the captain of Vaucouleurs to lead her to the camp, and there she told her mission; and the dauphin, catching at any hope in his despair, let her have her way. Then, without fear or shrinking, she put herself at the head of the rough soldiers, and clad in white armour, with a banner studded with fleur-de-lis waving over her head, she burst through the English army with 10,000 men-at-arms. Though she herself was wounded in the action, she raised the siege of Orleans. The English were panic-stricken; the French believed her to be a messenger from God; and, not heeding the French generals, who wished to remain fighting on the Loire, she led the victorious army to Rheims, conquering all before her. There, Charles VII. was crowned King of France. Then Jeanne begged to go home to her sheep and village. Her voices, she said, had left her, her mission was over. But Charles would not let her go, so she fought bravely on, though her confidence was gone. At the siege of Compiégne, in 1430, she was taken prisoner by the Burgundians, who sold her to the English, and Charles made no effort to save her. The end was a tale of shame—to the French whom she rescued, to the English who had seen her bravery —to all except to the simple maid herself. She was burnt as a witch at Rouen, and the noble spirit escaped, from false friends and cruel foes, to where "the wicked cease from troubling and the weary are at rest."

<small>Death of Jeanne Darc, 1431.</small>

10. End of Hundred Years' War.—The war was not yet at an end, for Charles had not reached Paris, and the very year of Jeanne Darc's death Henry VI. was crowned in that city by Beaufort. But from that time the English lost ground. Bedford died two years later, and Richard, Duke of York, with John Talbot, carried on the war; but there was little hope of success, for Burgundy after Bedford's death went over to the French king. In 1445, when Henry VI. married Margaret of Anjou, the English promised to give up Anjou and Maine to her father René, and a truce was made with France. But it was constantly broken. In 1449 Charles VII. reconquered Normandy, and in four years more he was master of Guienne and Bordeaux. When Talbot was killed, and the Hundred Years' War ended in 1453, Calais alone remained to England.

While disaster and loss were thus falling on the English abroad, the Duke of Gloucester and Chancellor Beaufort were quarrelling at home. Gloucester was popular, ambitious, and not an able statesman, while Beaufort tried in vain to keep matters straight. At one time he withdrew from England altogether, because it was impossible to work with the duke. Bedford even got out of patience with his brother, and the poor little king, when only eleven years old, had to beg his uncles to be reconciled. After Henry was crowned in 1429 Gloucester's control came to an end, and Beaufort, who was now a cardinal, had great influence in the state till he died in 1447.

Quarrels of Gloucester and Beaufort.

11. Decline of Parliament.—During this time Parliament was becoming weaker, and the king's Privy Council more powerful. One reason of this was, that in the eighth year of Henry VI.'s reign the *franchise* or power of voting for knights of the shire was no longer given to all who attended the county court at which the election was held, but was restricted to freeholders of land or houses worth forty shillings (between twenty and thirty pounds of our money), while the borough elections were gradually getting into the hands of a "select body" of burgesses, and were very much governed by the sheriffs, so that the king and leading men could easily influence them. Thus the House of Commons became little more than an instrument of the ministers, and when these quarrelled among themselves the members even came armed to Parliament. One Parliament in 1425 was called the "Parliament of bats," because the members, being forbidden to bring arms, brought cudgels or bats in their sleeves. Lastly, in 1437, the king for the first time chose his council himself, instead of allowing Parliament to do so, and this really gave the power into his hands.

Parliament of the "Bats."

12. Weak Rule of Henry.—Not, however, really into his *own* hands, for Henry, who came of age in 1442, had no will of his own. Pure-minded, patient, humble, merciful, and generous, he was nevertheless weak both in body and mind. On his mother's side, he was the grandson of poor mad Charles VI. of France, and during the last part of his life had frequent attacks of insanity. He took great interest in Eton School,

Character of Henry VI.

THE HOUSE OF LANCASTER.

and King's College, Cambridge, both of which he founded, and he tried hard to fulfil his official duties, striving to keep the peace among his advisers; but in all State matters he was driven hither and thither by people stronger than himself.

After he married Margaret of Anjou she chiefly ruled him, and her favourite ministers were first the Duke of Suffolk and afterwards the Earl of Somerset. When the war began to go badly for England, Gloucester wished to try and recover what was lost, but Margaret, being French, naturally wished for peace. Gloucester was charged with high treason, and five days after was found dead in his bed, probably murdered. Suffolk now had the chief power, and used it well, but secret enemies raised the cry that he was making a disgraceful peace with France. He too was impeached and banished, but he did not live to reach the continent; he was murdered while crossing the Channel. *Murders of Gloucester and Suffolk, 1447-1450.*

13. Jack Cade's Rebellion, 1450.—Then the people, weary of the heavy taxes, yet angry at the truce with France, and having no strong hand over them, rose in rebellion. A certain Irishman named Jack Cade, who called himself a Mortimer, led a body of 20,000 men out of Kent, Surrey, and Sussex on to Blackheath Common, and from there to London. We can see how much better off these people were than those had been who rose under Wat Tyler seventy years before, for they made no complaints of villeinage nor of their wages, but asked for the parliamentary elections to be free, the foreign favourites to be sent away, and for a change of ministry. They entered London and murdered Lord Saye, the treasurer, but were in the end defeated in a battle on London Bridge, and dispersed with pardons. Jack Cade was afterwards killed near Lewes. It was in November of this year that the first Lord Mayor's Show was held at the election of the Lord Mayor.

14. Wars of the Roses.—Jack Cade's rebellion made it clear that some strong hand must now take the Government; and a few years later Richard, Duke of York, who had been away in France and Ireland, came to England, and taking the place of Somerset, whom the queen favoured, was made protector in 1454, to rule for the unhappy king, who was out of his mind. This Richard of York had been *Richard Duke of York, Protector, 1455.*

heir to the throne since Gloucester's death, for he was Henry's nearest relation, until the king's son Edward was born. Even then, strictly speaking, Richard had in one sense the best claim, for his mother belonged to that elder branch of Mortimer, descended from the Duke of Clarence which had always been set aside. But the Lancasters had reigned for three generations, and York at present came forward only to help the king. The next year, when Henry recovered, Margaret persuaded him to send away York and recall Somerset. The loss both of the chance of succession and of influence in the Government was too bitter. York took up arms, and being joined by the Earls of Salisbury, Neville, and Warwick, he defeated the queen's party at St. Albans, where Somerset was killed.

<small>Battle of St. Albans, May 22, 1454.</small>

The Wars of the Roses had begun. The Lancastrians, or the queen's party, wore a red rose, which had always been their badge; the Yorkists chose a white rose; and in the struggle that followed, now one, now the other, had the advantage. In 1455 the king was once more insane, and the Duke of York protector. Then when Henry recovered he tried to make peace between the duke and the queen. But Margaret was anxious for her son's rights, and plotting against York, persuaded the Parliament to pass a "*bill of attainder,*" judging him and his friends to be guilty of death as traitors. An attainted person was condemned by Parliament without the usual forms of law, and their family was tainted and deprived of property for ever. Each party during these wars attainted the leaders of the other party when it held the power, and almost as many nobles were killed in this way as in battle. The bill of attainder did not injure York, for he was out of reach in Ireland; and in 1460 he came back with an army, and was victorious in the Battle of Northampton, when Henry VI. was made prisoner and Margaret fled with her son to Scotland.

<small>Bills of attainder.</small>

<small>Battle of Northampton, July 1460.</small>

Then the Duke of York laid claim to the throne, and a Parliament which met that autumn named him as Henry's successor, setting aside young Edward, Prince of Wales. A battle at Wakefield, however, five months later, reversed all this; the Lancastrians were victorious, the Duke of York was killed, and his son, the Earl of Rutland, murdered after the battle.

<small>Battle of Wakefield, Dec. 24, 1460.</small>

Then Edward, Richard's eldest son, who became Duke of York, by his father's death, took up the contest. He defeated the Earl of Pembroke at Mortimer's Cross, in Herefordshire, and marched straight to London. Though the north of England favoured the Lancastrians, the great merchant towns were steady supporters of the house of York. While the Earl of Warwick was attacking the queen, who defeated him and carried Henry VI. off safely to the north, Edward had entered London, and was greeted by the people with the cry, "Long live King Edward." The citizens were tired of Henry's feeble government, and hoped to find rest under a strong king. Two days later the Earl of Warwick arrived in the city, the Yorkist lords assembled, and Edward was declared king. *Battle of Mortimer's Cross, 1461.* *Edward declared king, 1461.*

But he could not wait to enjoy his triumph, for the queen was raising a large army in the north, and thither Edward and Warwick hastened. The two armies met at Towton Field, in Yorkshire, and the bloodiest battle of the whole war took place; 20,000 Lancastrians lay dead on the field, and the Yorkists lost nearly as many, but they gained the victory. Henry and Margaret took refuge in Scotland, many nobles were killed or executed, and Edward returned to London and was crowned at Westminster, June 28, 1461. *Battle of Towton, Mar. 29, 1461.*

CHAPTER XII.

THE HOUSE OF YORK.

1. Wars of the Roses, Continued.—The next ten years are one long history of skirmishes and battles. Margaret struggled bravely to recover the throne for her husband and son. In 1463, at the Battles of Hedgeley Moor and of Hexham, she was defeated, though she had help from the French and Scots. She fled with her son to Flanders, and King Henry, while hiding in Lancashire, was taken prisoner and sent to the Tower, then used as a palace as well as a fortress. There he was kindly but safely kept. *Henry VI. in the Tower.*

Meanwhile, however, Edward had given great offence to the Earl of Warwick by marrying Elizabeth Woodville, the widow of Sir John Grey. Warwick had hoped to marry the king to some French princess, and so to strengthen his power; or, if that failed to have given him a daughter of his own. Now Edward had not only married a lady of no great wealth or standing, but he soon began to give important posts to her father, Lord Rivers, and her other relations. Warwick, on his side, married his daughter, Isabella Neville, to the Duke of Clarence, Edward's brother, who was the next heir to the throne, and this displeased the king.

Royal marriages.

About this time a Lancastrian rising took place in the north of England, and spread very widely; in a battle at Edgecote, in Oxfordshire, Edward's party was defeated, and a large number of his nobles, among whom were several of the queen's relations, were killed. He himself, left alone without a protecting army, was for a short time a prisoner in the hands of Archbishop Neville, Warwick's brother. He was, however, allowed to return to London, and soon after he issued a proclamation against Warwick and his own brother Clarence, as traitors, which obliged them to escape to France. There Warwick met the deposed queen Margaret, and proposed to her that his daughter Anne should be betrothed to her son, Edward of Lancaster, Prince of Wales, and that he would then help Margaret to recover the throne. By this means Warwick hoped to secure the succession for one of his daughters, either Isabella, married to Clarence, a Yorkist, or to Anne betrothed to the Prince of Wales, a Lancastrian.

Battle of Edgecote, 1469.

Warwick joins Margaret.

The Queen agreed. Warwick landed at Dartmouth, and Edward IV., finding himself betrayed, fled to Flanders. His queen, Elizabeth Woodville, took refuge in the sanctuary at Westminster, and there her eldest son, afterwards the unfortunate Edward V., was born.

Flight of Edward.

Poor weak Henry was taken out of the Tower, and for six months, he reigned again, thus gaining for Warwick the nickname of the "King-maker." But we are now at last nearing the end of the wearisome seesaw of victories and defeats. Edward obtained help from the Duke of Burgundy, who had married his sister, and landing in

Henry VI. reigns again for six months.

Yorkshire with a small body of foreign troops, on the same spot where Henry IV. had landed seventy-two years before, was joined by his brother Clarence. They marched to London, where Edward was again received with acclamation. He gave battle to Warwick at Barnet, and Warwick was killed in the fight. Then Margaret gathered all the soldiers she could, and met Edward at Tewkesbury in Gloucestershire. There she too was completely defeated, and her young son, the Prince of Wales, was stabbed to death on the battle-field in the presence of King Edward. A fortnight later Henry VI. died in the Tower, probably murdered, and the long struggle was over. Margaret was imprisoned, but was ransomed by her father René in 1475, and returned to France.

<small>Battle of Tewkesbury, May 4, 1471.</small>

2. Progress of the Middle Class.—At last the country was quiet; though, indeed, all this time, while the nobles and their retainers were destroying each other, the new middle class, the farmers, yeomen, small landowners, tradespeople, and merchants had been progressing. The battles going on did not concern them, but were mere party fights, and the mass of the people took no part in them, although they found it difficult to get redress when their houses were broken into and goods taken, as we learn from some interesting letters written at this time by Margaret Paston, a lady in Norfolk, but on the whole the wealth of the middle class was increasing, and when Edward had finished struggling for his throne, and thought of invading France (which, however, in the end, he did not do, but turned back on receiving an annual pension from the French king), he found plenty of rich merchants and others from whom he could obtain money under the name of a *benevolence* or present, showing that there was no want of money. These benevolences were given willingly at first, for the citizens welcomed a peaceful government, but after a time they became a grievance. On the whole, however, the country flourished in spite of a terrible plague called Sweating Sickness, of which a large number of people died in 1479.

<small>Benevolences.</small>

As Edward had secured an income for life early in his reign, he only summoned Parliament once during eight years, and the power of the king and the council was almost without any check. The king, who led an immoral and dissolute life, began, as Richard II.

had done, to be very exacting, and to govern with an iron rule. Still he was popular, and by sacrificing all those who opposed him he managed to keep peace. But he bought it dearly, for his fear of treason led him to cause his own brother, the Duke of Clarence, to be impeached and put to death in the Tower; drowned, it is said, in a butt of Malmsey wine.

<small>Execution of Clarence, 1478.</small>

3. Caxton.—Meanwhile in a small corner of the sanctuary at Westminster, where stood a chapel and some almshouses, a man was doing a greater work than the king and his nobles with their quarrels; nay, even perhaps than the merchants and craftsmen in the city. This was William Caxton, who as a boy had gone from Kent to Flanders, where he spent thirty years, and brought back with him to England in 1476 the first printing press. The history of the rise of printing abroad, and how wood-blocks used for printing block-books were gradually replaced by moveable type, is a long one. But all this was done when Caxton began his printing in England. Before 1476 all new copies of books made in this country had to be written out by hand, and we can imagine how rare and costly they were. But now in his quiet corner Caxton, under the patronage of King Edward and Richard, Duke of Gloucester, printed many books of poetry, while he earned his daily bread by printing "service-books for the preachers, and histories of chivalry for the knights and barons." The *Dictes and Sayings of the Philosophers* was the first book he printed in England in 1477, and Chaucer's works and the romance of the Saxon hero Arthur, the *Morte d'Arthur*, followed. Besides this he translated and printed many foreign works, such as the story of *Reynard the Fox* and the *History of Troy*. But more important than the actual books he produced was the fact that when he died about 1491, the art of printing, which has worked such wonderful changes in the world, was established in England.

Before that time, however, troubles had again broken out. In 1483, Edward IV died leaving two young sons, Edward, Prince of Wales, aged thirteen, and his brother Richard, Duke of York, aged ten, and over these two poor little boys another struggle began.

4. Edward V.—When the king died there were two parties

ready at once to bid for power, the queen and her relations on the one hand, and the king's brother, Richard, Duke of Gloucester, on the other. The Prince of Wales was at Ludlow under the guardianship of his mother's brother, Lord Rivers, and his own half-brother, Sir Richard Grey. The Queen, who was at Westminster, claimed that the Council should make her guardian of her son and of the realm; but they wished Richard to be protector, and sent for him from York, where he was governing as lord-lieutenant. Richard seems to have determined at once to crush the queen's party. On his road he and the Duke of Buckingham met Rivers and Grey, who were coming to London with the young prince, arrested them, and sent them to Pontefract Castle in Yorkshire. Richard then told the young prince that his uncle and half-brother had conspired to betray him and seize the Government. The poor boy burst into tears and defended his friends, but it was of no avail; he never saw them again.

When the queen heard that her brother had been arrested she was alarmed, and fled with her younger boy and her daughters to the sanctuary of Westminster Abbey; and when the young king and the dukes entered London, Richard was appointed protector, chiefly through the influence of Lord Hastings, one of the new nobility, who was opposed to the queen. Edward V. was at first lodged in the Bishop of London's palace at St. Paul's, but was soon moved to the palace of the Tower, and unfortunately the queen was persuaded to allow the Duke of York to join him. Richard appointed protector, May 4.

So far all is clear. But now it becomes very difficult to say whether Richard intended from the first to seize the crown, or began by defending himself against the plots going on all around him, and then was led on by ambition. He was not by any means so repulsive-looking or unpleasing as his enemies have described him. Delicate and slightly deformed in one shoulder, he had a thoughtful but nervous expression, pleasing manners, and intellectual habits. No doubt he was crafty and unscrupulous, but he had always been true to his brother Edward when he was alive, and we may hope that he did not in the beginning plan the crimes he afterwards committed. Character of Richard.

A month passed. The queen's party were intriguing and watching their opportunity, and Lord Hastings appears to have changed sides, thinking that Richard was taking too much upon himself. Suddenly, Richard, entering the Council Chamber, accused Hastings of conspiring against him, and without allowing him to defend himself, called in a body of armed men and caused him to be beheaded on a log of timber on Tower Green before noon. Nine days later a preacher at St. Paul's Cross, and the Duke of Buckingham in Guildhall, pretended to the people that Elizabeth Woodville was not Edward IV's legal wife, because he had been betrothed to another lady before he married her, and that therefore the princes were illegitimate, and not true heirs to the crown. Even then, however, the young Earl of Warwick, son of Clarence, stood between Richard and the throne, but he was set aside because his father had been attainted. A body of Lords and Commons, with the mayor, aldermen, and citizens, offered Richard the crown, and he entered Westminster Hall and took his place in the marble chair as Richard III. A few days later Earl Rivers and Sir Richard Grey were executed at Pontefract. This closed the reign of Edward V.

The princes declared bastards.

5. Richard III.—But the sad end had not yet come. Richard was crowned 1483, with all the pomp which had been prepared for his nephew. Then he set out with his queen for the north of England, where he had always been a great favourite. While he was gone the Duke of Buckingham seems to have repented having helped him to seize the throne, and the people began to murmur at the imprisonment of the young princes. Soon the report spread far and wide that they had been murdered in the Tower. Yet people refused to believe that such a horrible deed could have been committed, and expected Richard to produce them and clear his fame. He never did. Nearly two hundred years afterwards, in the reign of Charles II., the bodies of two boys of the ages of the young princes were found under the staircase of the White Tower, and were moved to Henry VII.'s chapel in Westminster Abbey. Though we know nothing certainly, there can be little doubt that Sir James Tyrrel told the truth when he confessed that the boys were smothered in their beds by Richard's order, and buried under the stairs,

Report of the murder of the princes.

From this time Richard's peace of mind was gone. Not only did he suffer from remorse, so that his attendants said that he started and cried aloud in his dreams, but the horrid deed he had committed gave his enemies a hold over him. He governed well during the two years of his short reign. He passed good laws for the protection of commerce, and was the first to establish a protection for the English in foreign countries, by appointing a Florentine merchant to act as what we should call "*consul*" for the English inhabitants of Pisa. He was also the first to employ regular couriers to run with letters from the North of England, a kind of primitive post; and he passed a law against the "benevolences" which Edward IV. had imposed. Added to this, he promoted printing and the sale of books. But he knew that he was hated, and that plots were afloat to destroy him. *(Improvements in Richard's reign.)*

The Duke of Buckingham, who was now quite opposed to Richard, had at first thought of claiming the crown for himself, being of royal descent. But he soon saw it would be wiser to support the claims of Henry Tudor, Duke of Richmond, whom the Lancastrians invited over from abroad; while the Yorkists, hating Richard, proposed that Tudor should marry Elizabeth, daughter of Edward IV., and so unite the two parties. To understand who this Henry Tudor was, we must go back a century to the sons of Edward III., for *his mother, Margaret Beaufort, was the great-granddaughter of John of Gaunt, Duke of Lancaster, and Catharine Swynford.* It was a long way back to go for a title, and even then it was but a poor one, for the Beauforts had only been made legitimate by Richard II., while Henry Tudor's father was merely a Welsh gentleman, the son of Owen Tudor who married Katharine of France, the widow of Henry V. It shows how eager the English were to be rid of Richard that they were willing to accept Henry of Richmond. *(Henry Tudor invited to England.)*

The first attempt was a failure. Richard was on the watch, and Buckingham was arrested and beheaded. For two years longer Richard reigned, losing his son and heir in 1484. A year later, Henry of Richmond landed at Milford Haven, in Pembrokeshire, with barely two thousand men, and marched forward, his forces increasing rap- *(Landing of Henry of Richmond, Aug. 7th, 1485.)*

idly as he went. Richard scarcely believed in the danger, but he advanced to Leicester, and the two armies met at Market Bosworth, some distance outside the town. The battle had scarcely begun when Lord Stanley left Richard and joined the enemy with all his followers, and a second body went over with Earl Percy of Northumberland. Richard saw all hope was over. He was no coward, and dashing into the thick of the battle with a cry of "Treason, treason," he died fighting. His crown was found under a hawthorne bush, and was placed on Henry's head. The Wars of the Roses with all their deeds of bloodshed, treachery, and murder were over. Henry of Richmond soon after married Elizabeth of York, Edward IV.'s daughter, and while thus he gained a firm title to the crown, he united the two rivial houses of Lancaster and York.

Battle of Bosworth Field, Aug. 22, 1485.

End of Wars of the Roses.

6. Summary.—The conclusion of the Wars of the Roses brings us to the end of MEDIEVAL HISTORY, or the HISTORY OF THE MIDDLE AGES, in England. Throughout those ages the nobles had been very powerful, and the king had been, as it were, their chief, often controlled by the *bishops* or peers of the Church and the *barons* or peers of the realm. Moreover, England had been during this time scarcely more than part of the continent. The nobles of England and France were often near relations, and whether at war or at peace, they belonged to one great family of knighthood under one bond of chivalry. The Church, too, was one from Rome to England; our learned men and clergy were often foreigners or educated abroad; our most powerful body of merchants in London was the "Hanseatic League," of Germans from the shores of the Baltic; and it had been a constant complaint of English people that foreigners held the highest posts in the courts of the English kings.

Close relations of England and the continent in the middle ages.

But now already for some time the old ties were gradually loosening. For the last fifty years the old nobility were being destroyed, some in the Hundred Years' War, but by far the larger number in the Wars of the Roses. In these civil wars no less than eighty princes of royal blood alone were killed; and when, as so often happened, a noble

Destruction of the old nobility.

was attainted his estates passed to the king. When Henry VII. came to the throne there were only twenty-seven dukes, earls, viscounts, and barons in his first Parliament; and though, no doubt, some were absent because they would not acknowledge him, yet even among these twenty-seven several were newly-created nobles.

Some of these were, it is true, very powerful, owing to a custom called *maintenance*, by which a nobleman gave liveries and badges to the yeomen and gentlemen of the neighbourhood who fought for him while he protected them. But the day of these powerful nobles was nearly over. The use of gunpowder, which had now become common, put a new power into the king's hands, for he and his ministers had the control of the cannon, and the arsenal where ammunition was kept; and a single train of artillery would soon disperse the archers and pikemen of the nobles and destroy their castles. *Custom of maintenance.*

Meanwhile the gentry and middle class of England were increasing in wealth and importance, and those who held good positions because they were rich, or of use in the Government, were more obedient to the king than the ancient haughty nobility, and cared more for peace and commerce than for foreign wars. So we find that one of the chief differences between the middle ages and modern times is, that the old barons cared more for war and chivalry abroad, the new aristocracy for personal freedom, commerce, knowledge, art and science at home. We pass from one to the other as we enter on the reign of Henry VII., and he was in many ways the right man to pave the way for the beginning of a new state of things. *Transition from middle ages to modern times.*

PART V.

STRONG GOVERNMENT OF THE TUDORS.

SOVEREIGNS OF THE HOUSE OF TUDOR.

CHAPTER XIII.

HOUSE OF TUDOR—THE REFORMATION.

1. Henry VII.—The reign of Henry VII. begins a new epoch in our history. He was crowned at Westminster, Oct. 30, 1485, and the next year he married Elizabeth of York, thus uniting the two rival houses. He was a lean, spare man, with an intelligent countenance, grey eyes, and a bright, cheerful expression. On his mother's side he was descended from the Beauforts, a family of wise and famous statesmen, and he inherited their talent. From his French grandmother he inherited tact and diplomatic skill, and during his exile in France he had learned to understand foreign politics. Now his chief aim was to keep peace at home and abroad, that he might accumulate wealth and establish a strong monarchy. *Appearance and character.*

Parliament settled the crown upon him and his heirs, and even Wales was satisfied, since the king's father was a Welshman. But the Yorkists were still very restless, because they were only represented by the king's wife ; and with the help of Margaret of Burgundy, Edward IV.'s sister, and James IV. of Scotland, they actually set up two impostors, one after the other, to claim the throne. There was a real heir of the house of York still alive— young Edward, Earl of Warwick, son of that Duke of Clarence who was drowned in the butt of Malmsey— and Henry had taken the precaution to keep him in the Tower. But in 1487 a sham Earl of Warwick appeared in Ireland, and being supported by the Earl of Kildare, was actually crowned in Dublin Cathedral. Henry soon put down the imposture by showing the real earl to the people of London, and defeating the army of the pretended earl at Stoke, near Newark, June, 1487. He proved to be a lad named Lambert Simnel, the son of a joiner at Oxford, and became a scullion in the king's kitchen. *Yorkists rebellions.* *Lambert Simnel, 1487.*

2. Poynings' Act, 1497.—This rebellion turned Henry's attention to Ireland, where for many years the English, who lived on a strip of land along the coast called the "Pale," were constantly fighting among themselves and with the Irish chieftains in the interior of the island, and passed what laws they chose in their own Parliament. In 1494 Henry sent Sir Henry Poynings, an able soldier, to make another attempt to settle the country. Poynings established English judges and other officers, sent the rebel Kildare to England, and passed an Act that English laws should apply to Ireland, and that the Parliament of the Pale should not make any new law without the consent of the king's council. Then Kildare, who promised to be loyal, was allowed to return as lord deputy, and govern the country.

State of Ireland.

3. Court of the Star Chamber.—Another effect of Simnel's rebellion was that Henry made haste to have Elizabeth crowned Queen, hoping in this way to quiet the Yorkists. Then, with the consent of Parliament, he chose a committee out of the Privy Council, with authority to examine and punish the numerous powerful offenders whom the law-courts were afraid to touch. This committee was called the "Court of the Star Chamber," from the room in which it was held. In future reigns it became very hurtful, but at this time it was of great use in restoring order. Riotous assemblies and attempts at rebellion were put down much more quickly by a court which could punish without long trials, and by means of it Henry abolished the custom of "maintenance," which had enabled the lords to oppress the people, overawe the judges, and control the election of the sheriffs. He was determined to be master of the great lords, and now there were not so many, he was able to deal with them.

4. Perkin Warbeck.—Meanwhile another conspiracy was brewing. A young man, called Perkin Warbeck, who proved afterwards to be a native of Tournay, pretended that he was Richard, Duke of York, the younger of the two little princes in the Tower, and that he had escaped when his brother Edward V. was murdered. He persuaded the King of France and Margaret of Burgundy to acknowledge him, and was not only received at the foreign courts, but, after failing in Ireland, he went to Scotland, where James IV. married him to his own cousin Catharine Gordon, and helped him to invade England in 1496. The invasion was defeated, however, by the Earl of Surrey, and then Perkin went back to Ireland, and crossed over to Cornwall, where the people had revolted against the heavy taxes. There he raised an army and marched to Exeter, but meeting the king's troops at Taunton, he lost courage, and fled to the Abbey of Beaulieu, where he was taken prisoner and sent to the Tower in 1497.

5. Arbitrary Rule.—These conspiracies, though they gave the king some trouble, had very little effect upon the country, in which much more serious changes were going on. Henry, with the help of his able minister Archbishop Morton, was heaping up wealth in his treasury. Any lords who broke the law by keeping too many retainers were heavily fined. <small>Henry extorts money.</small> The Earl of Oxford is said to have been obliged to pay £15,000 for making too great a show of liveries when the king visited him. The "benevolences," which Richard had abolished, were again collected, and Henry took advantage of the confusion which had grown up in the civil wars to claim many money arrears due to the crown, and to take possession of estates of many landowners who had not a good title to show for them. Thus he gained two things; he weakened those who were too powerful, and filled his own treasury. He even made use of the old claim to the crown of France, and obtained a large sum of money from the French king for withdrawing his troops from Boulogne. In this and other ways he collected large sums of money, and as he spent little or nothing on foreign wars, he left nearly two millions when he died for his son to spend. Unfortunately much of his wealth was gained by unjust extortion, and two lawyers, named Empson and Dudley, who did the king's dirty work, were much hated by the people. But Henry gained another advantage. By <small>Governs without Parliament.</small> getting his money in this way, he was not dependent on Parliament, which was called only once during the last thirteen years of his reign, so that he was almost an absolute king.

6. Foreign Alliances.—His next ambition was to secure peace with foreign countries, and in this he showed much cleverness. The great rivals in Europe were Charles VIII. and his successor Louis XII., Kings of France, and Ferdinand, King of Aragon. Now that France was so powerful, it was important for England to have an ally against her, especially as the French were always ready to help the Scots. Ferdinand was equally anxious to have the support of England, so in 1501 a marriage was arranged between Henry's eldest son Arthur, Prince of Wales, and Katharine of Aragon, Ferdinand's daughter. Before this marriage took place the young Earl of Warwick and Perkin Warbeck were executed, on the ground that they had tried to escape from the Tower, but probably because Ferdinand insisted that all rivals to the throne should be removed. The next year Henry also married his daughter Margaret to James IV. of Scotland, and thus secured the friendship of that country.

Marriage of Arthur with Katharine of Aragon.

Margaret marries James IV. of Scotland.

Unfortunately Prince Arthur died three months after the Spanish marriage. What was to become of Katharine? Both Ferdinand and Henry were unwilling to break the alliance, so it was agreed that, as she had been only formally married to Arthur, she should stay in England to marry his brother, the king's second son, afterwards Henry VIII. A dispensation was obtained from the Pope, and Henry, still only a boy, was betrothed to his brother's widow, a woman six years older than himself. We shall see by and by what unforeseen consequences grew out of this unnatural marriage.

Henry, Prince of Wales, marries his brother's widow.

7. Discoveries.—While the monarchs of Europe were trying in this way to strengthen their power by royal marriages, some adventurous men were making new discoveries, which were in the end to be very important to the whole world. In the year 1492 Christopher Columbus, a native of Genoa, tried to find his way to India across the Atlantic, and discovered those islands off the American coast which he called the West Indies. A few years later, a Portuguese, named Vasco de Gama, discovered the sea route to India round the Cape of Good Hope; and that same year, Sebastian Cabot, a Venetian, sailed from Bristol with leave from Henry VII. to explore the north-western seas, where he had been with his father the year before. Sailing

Discoveries of Columbus, 1492.

Vasco de Gama and Cabot, 1497-1498.

THE HOUSE OF TUDOR. 117

up the coast of Labrador, and among the icebergs where the Polar bears were feeding, he opened up the cod-fisheries of Newfoundland.

8. The New Learning.—Side by side with these discoveries, new learning was coming to England from Italy. In 1453 Constantinople was taken by the Turks, and many learned Greeks fled into Italy, bringing Greek literature to the people of the west. This new knowledge, and the spread of printed books, led men to study the Greek philosophers and the Greek Testament, whereas before this even the priests had only read the Vulgate or Latin version of the Bible. In 1486 Colet, an English priest who had visited Italy, delivered a course of lectures in Oxford full of new thoughts. In 1497 Erasmus, the Dutchman, a famous Greek scholar and a great reformer, visited England for the first time; while Sir Thomas More, the great English lawyer and friend of these men, wrote in 1504 his life of Edward V., the first work published in modern English prose. The universities were full of new stirring life, and Luther had just began to lecture in Germany when Henry VII. died in the palace he had built at Richmond, and was buried in the beautiful chapel which bears his name in Westminster Abbey. He left three children— Margaret, wife of James IV. of Scotland; Mary, who afterwards married Louis XII. of France; and Henry, a handsome youth of eighteen, whose reign was to be an eventful one for our country.

<small>Death of Henry VII., April 21, 1509.</small>

9. Henry VIII.—All England was pleased when Henry VIII. became king. He had in his veins the blood of both York and Lancaster. He was hearty and affable, with a kind word and jest for every one, and a generous disposition which seemed to promise he would not be grasping like his father. He had been well educated for, while his elder brother lived, it had been intended that Henry should become Archbishop of Canterbury. He was an excellent musician and an admirable horseman and wrestler. Though he had a strong will, and was extremely vain, yet he had plenty of sense, and wished to be popular with his people, who never entirely ceased to love "Bluff King Hal" in spite of the many wrong things he did. His chief fault was a monstrous selfishness. To gain anything he wanted, or

<small>Character of Henry VIII.</small>

to keep up his popularity, he relentlessly sacrificed those who had served him most faithfully; and as the love of self, if indulged, increases with age, he became, in the latter part of his life, a coarse, brutal tyrant, only kept in check by his dread of unpopularity.

He married his betrothed, Katharine of Aragon, soon after his father's death, and was crowned with his queen on June 24, 1509. One of his first acts was to order the prosecution of Empson and Dudley, who were put to death. Then he turned his attention to the ships of England. As yet he possessed only one ship of war, *The Great Harry*, built in his father's reign; but in 1511 a large ship, *The Lion*, was captured from the Scots, and the next year another, *The Regent*, was built, carrying 1000 tons. This was destroyed by the French, but a larger one, *Henry Grace de Dieu*, was built in its place, and many others followed. Besides this the king founded the first Navy Office, and the corporation of the Trinity House, which has done so much good work in erecting beacons and lighthouses, licensing pilots, framing laws for shipping, and placing buoys in dangerous spots. When it is added that he established dockyards at Deptford, Woolwich, and Portsmouth, we see that Henry has a claim to be called the founder of our modern navy.

Henry VIII. the creator of our modern navy.

10. Foreign Wars.—With less wisdom he plunged into foreign wars, joining in the Holy League formed by Spain and Germany, to protect the Pope's domains against France. The war was very costly, and the English only gained the town of Tournay, in Flanders, which was won in the "Battle of the Spurs," so called because the French soldiers were seized with a panic. In 1514 peace was made with France, and Henry's youngest sister Mary was married to Louis XII. Three month's later Louis died, and his son, Francis I., became King of France.

Battle of the Spurs, Aug. 16, 1513.

Meanwhile the Scots, who were always friendly with France, had attacked England in 1513, and Henry being away, the Earl of Surrey met and defeated them at the famous Battle of Flodden, where James IV. was killed. Margaret, Henry's sister, was now left Regent of Scotland, her little son, James V., being only two years old. For many years the

Battle of Flodden Sept. 9, 1513.

Scotch nobles were too busy quarrelling among themselves to annoy England, but twenty-nine years later, towards the end of Henry's reign, this young James V again attacked England, and was defeated at the Battle of Solway Moss, and died of grief. He left a baby daughter, the unfortunate Mary, the Queen of the Scots. <small>Battle of Solway Moss 1542.</small>

11. Wolsey.—And now we must keep our attention alive to follow the changes which took place, for Henry VIII.'s reign is like a play acted in a theatre, as one man or woman after another influenced the king for a time, and then gave place to a rival. The first and most powerful of these was a young man named Wolsey, a son of a wealthy citizen of Ipswich. He had been chaplain to Henry VII., and was very useful to Henry VIII. in France. As soon as they returned to England the king made him Archbishop of York and chancellor, and the Pope afterwards created him cardinal and papal legate. This gave him great power. As chancellor he was chief officer of the state; as legate, he had the highest authority in the Church, even over the Archbishop of Canterbury. Wolsey was an able, enlightened man. He encouraged learning, and founded Christ Church College, Oxford, and he was very skilful in foreign politics. Unfortunately, though he devoted all his energy to the government of the country, he was not single-minded. He was too anxious to strengthen the power of the king and to gain honor and wealth for himself. He raised money by benevolences and forced loans, and used the law-courts to wring fines from the people; and while he filled the king's treasury, he grew rich himself on presents from Henry, so that he was able to build the magnificent palaces of Hampton Court and York House (afterwards Whitehall) for his own residences. <small>Administration of Wolsey, 1515-1529.</small>

He did not, however, get all this wealth from England. The greatest ruler in Europe was now the Emperor Charles V., who had succeeded his maternal grandfather Ferdinand as King of Spain, and had been elected Emperor of Germany after the death of his paternal grandfather Maximilian, while he inherited the Netherlands from his father's mother, Mary of Burgundy. This powerful emperor was the nephew of Henry's queen, Katharine, and both he and Francis I. of <small>Politics of Europe.</small>

France were very anxious to get the support of England. Wolsey took presents from both, and played them off one against the other. In 1520 Charles V. visited the king at Canterbury. A few months later Francis invited Henry to meet him in France, and the two kings entertained each other with tournaments and feasts at

<small>Field of the Cloth of Gold, 1520.</small> Guisnes, not far from Boulogne, on the "Field of the Cloth of Gold," so called from the splendour displayed there. Nevertheless, on his way home, Henry met Charles V. again at Gravelines, and two years later helped him to fight against Francis.

The secret of all this was that Henry wanted to balance the power of one monarch against the other, while Wolsey, who wished to be Pope, wanted to side with the one who would help him the best. Charles V. had promised to use his influence, but when two chances had slipped by, Wolsey began to doubt him, and changed sides. In 1525 the emperor took Francis prisoner at the Battle of Pavia in Italy, and was becoming so powerful that Henry and Wolsey were alarmed, and after treating first with one side and then with the other, ended by making an alliance with France. This displeased the English people, for as Charles V was <small>Alliance with France.</small> ruler of the Netherlands, it checked their trade with Flanders. Henry let Wolsey bear all the blame, and as the taxes were heavy, the cardinal began to be unpopular.

12. Henry Seeks a Divorce from Katharine.—It was now proposed to marry Henry's only child, the Princess Mary, to one of the sons of the French king. But the Bishop of Tarbes objected, saying that Mary was illegitimate because Henry had married his brother's widow. This set Henry thinking. He was tired of Katharine; they had been married eighteen years, and her only living child was Mary, while he wanted a son. Moreover he had fallen in love with Anne Boleyn, one of Katharine's maids of honour. So in 1527 he told the Pope, Clement VII., that he felt Katharine was not really his wife, and he ought to be divorced from her. He thought the Pope would support him, for only five years before Henry had written a treatise against the reformer Luther, and Leo X. had given him the title of "Defender of the Faith." The Pope sent a special legate, Cardinal Campeggio, to England,

THE HOUSE OF TUDOR. 121

who tried to persuade Katharine to go into a nunnery, but she stood up for her rights and those of her child, so the Pope summoned Henry to Rome to try the question.

13. Fall of Wolsey.—Now Wolsey, though he wished to serve the king, did not think it wise for him to marry Anne Boleyn. She knew this, and, as her influence was by this time the strongest, she set Henry against his faithful minister. Wolsey saw that he was in danger. He hastened to give his handsome palaces to the king, and retired to his archbishopric of York. But there he was so popular that Henry grew still more jealous of him, and a year later he was arrested for high treason. Ill and worn out with work, though only fifty-nine, the cardinal was obliged to pause on his way to London at the Abbey of Leicester. "I come to lay my bones among you," said he to the monks; " had I but served God as diligently as I have served the king, He would not have given me over in my gray hairs," and there he died, Nov. 28, 1530.

His place as chancellor was already filled by Sir Thomas More, a just and good man, who, however, could do little against Henry's will. For six years there had been no Parliament, because the last one had refused to grant as much money as the king wanted. Now in 1529 a Parliament was summoned, which lasted for seven years, because it was composed of men willing to do the king's bidding. During this Parliament some very important changes were made in England. <small>Seven years' Parliament, 1529-1536.</small>

14. Act of Supremacy.—Henry's great wish was now to get free from the Pope, so that he might carry out his divorce, and he found a new and able minister who helped him out of his difficulty. Thomas Cromwell, a man who had formerly been in Wolsey's service, became the king's secretary in 1530, and he reminded Henry of that law of "Præmunire" of Edward III. and Richard II. which condemned all people to forfeiture and imprisonment who allowed the authority of the court of Rome to interfere with the king or his realm. Wolsey had broken this almost-forgotten law by acting as the Pope's legate, and though the king had allowed it, yet now it was made an accusation against the cardinal and, after his death, <small>Administration of Thomas Cromwell, 1530-1540.</small>

against all the clergy for having followed him. The clergy, alarmed lest they should lose their incomes and be imprisoned, fell into the trap. They sent a petition to beg mercy of the king, and in this petition Cromwell made them call Henry "PROTECTOR AND ONLY SUPREME HEAD OF THE CHURCH." Then Parliament, passed two separate Acts in 1533-1534, in which they entirely abolished the Pope's authority in England. They forbade the clergy to pay him any longer the "annates" or first fruits of their livings, and the clergy, on their side, gave up the right of making laws in Convocation. An Act was passed in 1534, called the "Act of Supremacy," creating Henry Supreme Head of the Church; and the sovereign, with Parliament, has ever since ruled all questions of the English Church.

<small>Henry declared Supreme Head of the Church, 1534.</small>

Meanwhile Henry was able to go on with his divorce. Cranmer, a Cambridge scholar who had already sided with the king, had been made Archbishop of Canterbury, and with the help of a council of bishops, he now declared the marriage with Katharine void. In 1533 Henry married Anne Boleyn, and in September of that year Princess Elizabeth was born.

<small>Divorce of Katharine and marriage with Anne Boleyn, 1533.</small>

From this time Henry, freed from Wolsey's control, and complete master of Church and state, followed his own will and the guidance of Cromwell, who was a hard, stern man, anxious to increase the king's power. Cromwell had spies all over the kingdom, and spared no one who stood in his way. Yet it is but just to say that he devoted himself to governing the country, and did not even enrich himself as Wolsey had done. It was under his rule that Wales was at last made entirely one with England, having English laws and liberty.

<small>Wales under English law, 1536.</small>

But on the other hand, it was he who caused the infamous law to be passed forbidding people accused of high treason to be heard in their own defence. Strange to say, when he fell he was the first to suffer under this law.

<small>Law of high treason.</small>

15. Sir Thomas More.—As soon as Henry's marriage was declared, two Acts were passed, one setting aside Princess Mary and settling the succession on Anne's children; the other making it treason to deny the Act of Supremacy. As a man might be called upon at any time to swear to these Acts, many suffered for conscience sake. One of the first was Henry's best friend and councillor, Sir Thomas More, who was much respected for his uprightness and learning, and his simple, honest character. Yet the king pressed him so hard, he was obliged to acknowledge that he did not approve of the divorce, nor of the way it had been brought about; both he and Fisher, Bishop of Rochester, were sent to the Tower and executed. More died cheerfully, as he had lived. "See me safe up," he said to the governor of the Tower, as the ladder trembled; "coming down I can take care of myself." And he moved his beard aside on the block. "Pity that should be cut," said he, "that has not committed treason."

16. State of the People.—This was a sad time for England, as everything was unsettled. For some time past the poor had been suffering. The new men who had taken the land of the old nobles were able to make more money by grazing sheep than by growing corn, so that less land was under cultivation and less labour was employed. Many tenants and labourers were turned out of their homes; even much of the common land, over which their animals used to graze, was now enclosed for the benefit of the rich. Besides these, the retainers of the old nobility were thrown out of service, causing a great increase of paupers and vagabonds, so that many men gained their livelihood by robbery and murder.

17. Religious Changes.—Added to this, men's minds were much unsettled about religion. The old ties were broken, and new ones were not yet formed. People in England were much moved by the great events happening in Germany and Switzerland, where Luther and his fellow-reformer, Zwingli, *were protesting* against many things done by the Pope and priests, and taking the Bible for their guide instead of the teaching of the Church. Those who followed this new teaching were first called *Protestants* in 1529, and among them were many German princes. Now Henry had no wish to bring the reformed religion into England, for he himself had answered Luther; but having thrown off the power of the Pope, he had set a great movement going which he could not stop. Under Cromwell and Cranmer a series of articles of religion were drawn up, the worship of images and relics was forbidden, and Tyndale's translation of the Bible,

Luther and Zwingli.

corrected by Miles Coverdale, was published and put in all the churches. The friends of the new learning, and those who remembered the teaching of Wiclif and the Lollards, were pleased with these changes, and this made it more easy for Cromwell to carry out a plan he had in his mind to abolish the monasteries.

<small>Destruction of the monasteries 1536-1539.</small> We have seen how much good the monks did in olden times among the uncivilized English: but as the monasteries grew wealthy, and there was less real work to be done, indolence and self-indulgence had crept in among them. Many of the monks and nuns were very ignorant and immoral, and Wolsey had already with the Pope's sanction, suppressed some monasteries and built colleges instead. Cromwell, who wanted money for the king, went farther, and, with the help of Cranmer, put down these retreats altogether, the smaller monasteries in 1536, the larger ones in 1539. The monks and nuns were dispersed, sometimes with small pensions, sometimes without. Part of the remaining money went to build ships and endow cathedral chapters and bishoprics, and to found Trinity College, Cambridge; but most of it went to the king, while the land was either given to the nobles or bought by them for very little. All this was not done without tumults, although Cromwell ruled with an iron hand, and the monks made no resistance.

<small>Execution of Anne Boleyn, and marriage with Jane Seymour, 1536.</small> Meanwhile Henry had taken a new wife. In 1536 (a few months after Queen Katharine had died in her solitary palace) he accused Anne Boleyn of being unfaithful to him, and of having several lovers. She was tried and beheaded on May 19, 1536. The next day Henry married Jane Seymour, one of the ladies in waiting, and Princess Elizabeth was declared illegitimate, as her half-sister Mary had been before her.

18. Rebellions in the North and West.—Such injustice and gross want of feeling could not fail to shock the nation. In the north of England the people were already restless from want of work and from the sudden destruction of the monasteries, besides hating the new religion; and now a serious rebellion broke out, in which both nobles and peasants joined. They demanded that Mary should be heir to the throne, that the old religion should be restored, and that Cromwell should be dismissed. But the minister was too strong for them. Through his spies he knew all their plans, and after making many promises, he dispersed the rioters. A few months later he arrested the ringleaders of this "Pilgrimage of Grace," as it was called, and many of the northern nobles were executed. About the same time Cromwell repressed another rebellion in the west of England, where he arrested the Marquis of Exeter, a grandson of Edward IV., and the old Countess of Salisbury, Margaret Plantagenet, who were both afterwards beheaded.

19. Death of Cromwell.—Meanwhile, at last, a young prince was born. On October 12, 1537, Jane Seymour gave birth to a son, who was named Edward, and two hours after she died. There were now two parties in the state. One was the party of the *Protestant* or new religion, headed by the Earl of Hertford, Jane Seymour's brother and Edward's uncle, and to this party Cromwell inclined. The other party held to the *Roman Catholic* or the old religion, and was headed by the Duke of Norfolk and his son the Earl of Surrey, who belonged to the old nobility. Cromwell, anxious to make a league with the Protestant princes of Germany, chose a Protestant princess, Anne of Cleves, for Henry's next wife. Unfortunately she was plain and awkward, and Henry liked her so little that he put her away after six months. This ruined Cromwell. Henry was so angry with him for having placed him in a false position that he caused him to be arrested in the Council Chamber, where all the lords hated him. Cromwell flung his cap to the ground. "This then," he exclaimed, "is the guerdon for the services I have done. On your consciences I ask you, am I a traitor?" Then when he received no answer, "Make quick work," said he, "and do not leave me to languish in prison." He was attainted in parliament a few days later, without being allowed to speak in his own defence, and executed on Tower Hill. Marriage and separation of Anne of Cleves, 1540.
Execution of Cromwell. July 28, 1540.

On the very day that his faithful minister suffered, Henry married his fifth wife, Katharine Howard, niece of the Duke of Norfolk. He had already begun to be afraid that he had gone too far towards the

Reformation, and now leant towards the supporters of the old religion. He caused Parliament to pass a bill against the Protestants; and two days after Cromwell's death, the curious sight was seen of six men carried in a cart to execution—three Catholics for denying the Supremacy, and three Protestants as heretics. In the year 1541 Henry first took the title of King of Ireland instead of "Lord," which had been the title ever since the time of Henry II. His marriage with Katharine Howard did not last long, for it was discovered that she had had a sad early life, which, though she was much to be pitied, made her unfit to be the king's wife. She was beheaded, and the next year Henry married Katharine Parr, who outlived him.

Marriage with Katharine Howard, 1540.

Execution of Katharine Howard, 1542.

20. Death of Henry.—The king was now getting anxious about the future of his little son Edward. He had tried to betroth him to the baby Mary Queen of Scots, after the death of her father in 1542. But he did not succeed, and wars both with Scotland and France dragged on, by the last of which Henry gained the town of Boulogne. He now selected a council, composed of men of both opinions, to govern after his death till his son should be of age. Among those was the Earl of Hertford, Edward's uncle, who about this time began to have great influence over the king, and with help of Cranmer the Protestant party succeeded in introducing an English liturgy (or service), composed of the Litany, Creed, Commandments, and Lord's Prayer, to be read every morning and evening instead of the Latin service.

English liturgy introduced.

Hertford was much afraid of the influence of the Duke of Norfolk, and he persuaded the king that the duke meant to seize the regency, and this caused Henry to perform his last cruel act. He put the duke in the Tower, and executed his son, the Earl of Surrey. It is said that he had even fixed the day for Norfolk's execution, when his own death stayed the power of his hand. He had long been growing unwieldy and infirm, and he died on Jan. 28, **1547**.

By his will Edward was to succeed him, and if he had no children, then Mary, and after her Elizabeth. If they all three died without issue, then the crown was to pass to the children of his younger sister Mary, the widow of Louis XII., who had married the Duke of Suffolk. Thus we see

Act of Succession.

Henry set aside Mary Queen of Scots the grandchild of his eldest sister Margaret. This "Act of Succession," in which the king left his crown by will, shows what a change had now grown up since the early days when the people elected their own king.

CHAPTER XIV.

STRUGGLE BETWEEN THE TWO RELIGIONS.

1. Edward VI.—The next two reigns, which lasted only eleven years, were one continued struggle between the two religions. Edward VI. was only ten years old when he became king. He had been educated by men of strong Protestant opinions, and as he was thoughtful and intelligent, he took an interest in these matters beyond his age. His uncle, the Earl of Hertford, who was created Duke of Somerset by Henry's will, managed to become President of the Council of Regency, and soon persuaded the boy king to make him protector, so that he had almost supreme power. He was an earnest man who meant well, but he was a bigoted reformer, greedy of wealth and not a wise statesman. _{Edward VI, a strict Protestant.} _{Duke of Somerset protector.}

He began by making a treaty with the Protestants in Scotland, and gathered an army to try and force the Scots to give their queen in marriage to Prince Edward. He did indeed defeat them at the famous Battle of Pinkiecleugh near Edinburgh, Sept. 1547, but he was obliged to return to England, and his campaign did no good. The Scots, enraged at the defeat, made haste to send little Queen Mary to France, where she married the Dauphin ten years afterwards. _{Useless attack on Scotland, 1547.}

2. Protestant Reforms.—In England Somerset and Archbishop Cranmer began at once to push on the Protestant reforms vigorously. An Act was passed repealing all the laws against the Lollards, and the six articles of Henry VIII. against the Protestants. Permission was given to the priests to marry; the use of the Roman Catholic mass was forbidden in the churches, and all images were destroyed. In 1549 the first English book of Common Prayer was brought into use, and by an "Act of Uniformity" the clergy were forbidden to use any other service-book in the churches, and people were required to follow the new religion. Moreover, Cranmer welcomed to England the foreign Protestants who were now escaping from Spain and the Netherlands, where all heretics were being tortured under Charles V. before the secret tribunal called the Inquisition.

3. Popular Discontent.—In the towns, where the people understood how much freedom the new religion gave them, these changes were welcome. But in the lonely country districts people cried out for the "mass" to which they were accustomed; and on Whitmonday 1549, an insurrection broke out which spread all over Devonshire and Cornwall. The insurgents besieged Exeter, and were with difficulty defeated by Lord Grey, with the help of German and Italian troops.

Insurrection in the west.

At the same time another rising took place in Norfolk, among the agriculturists. There was everywhere great discontent The enclosure of the commons and the want of work filled the country with vagrants, paupers, and thieves; and the misery was increased by the small supply of corn and the debasing of the coinage. In the last part of Henry VIII.'s reign he had raised £50,000 by mixing a great deal of alloy with the silver of which coins were made, so that each coin was really worth less than it pretended to be; and now the mass of gold and silver coming in from America lowered the value still more. By degrees a shilling became only worth sixpence, while wages, or the number of coins each man received for work, remained the same. Yet Parliament passed a severe law against vagrancy in 1548, as if men could work and pay when neither work nor money was to be had. At last, in 1549, twenty thousand men collected near Norwich under Robert Ket, a tanner, and defeating the royal troops, demanded that the grievances of the poor should be redressed, enclosures forbidden, and the ministers dismissed.

Rebellion in Norfolk 1549.

Debasement of the coinage.

Lord Warwick put down the rebellion with German troops; but so many disturbances made Somerset very unpopular. He had become rich and overbearing, and had built himself in the Strand a grand palace called Somerset House. Moreover, just at

STRUGGLES BETWEEN THE TWO RELIGIONS. 129

this time, he arrested and executed his own brother, Admiral Seymour, who had married Katharine Parr, and after her death had tried to marry Princess Elizabeth, and to supplant his brother with the young king. This murder of a brother, even if necessary, shocked the nation, and the council forced Somerset to resign the protectorship. He remained on the council three years longer, and then Earl Warwick, fearing his influence, caused him to be attainted and executed. *Somerset executed, 1552.*

This Earl of Warwick, John Dudley, who now became protector, was the son of the Dudley who extorted money for Henry VII. He was a selfish man; but even if he had been a ruler, he could scarcely have prevented the troubles caused by the low value of money and want of work. He too favoured the Protestants. Gardiner, Bishop of Winchester, and Bonner, Bishop of London, were imprisoned in the Tower for upholding the old beliefs, while Latimer and Ridley, two Protestant Bishops, took their places. A second Prayer-book and Act of Uniformity were issued in 1552, and the young prince in his zeal nearly caused a war with Spain by insisting that his sister Mary, who was a Roman Catholic, should give up hearing "mass" in her chapel. *Earl of Warwick becomes protector.* *Second Act of Uniformity, 1552.*

4. Edward VI.'s Grammar Schools.—Turning from these religious disputes, it is pleasant to see how learned men were trying to give education to poor children. Already, in Henry VIII.'s reign, Dean Colet had founded St. Paul's School, and now many private people began to establish foundation schools. Edward VI. endowed no less than eighteen grammar schools, with grants obtained from the suppression of various monasteries. The Blue Coat School, or Christ Church Hospital, was founded in 1553 for foundlings and orphans, in consequence of a sermon preached by Bishop Ridley before the king, pointing out the sad condition of the London poor.

Already, however, the young king's reign was drawing to a close. Consumption had seized upon him, and his councillors saw that he could not live long. Warwick, who had been made Duke of Northumberland (the Percies had lost the earldom by being attainted), now saw that if Mary came to the throne she would bring back the Roman Catholic religion, and he would be ruined. So he persuaded Edward to sign a paper, putting aside his sisters Mary and Elizabeth, and naming as his successor Lady Jane Grey, the granddaughter of Henry VIII.'s sister Mary (*see* table p. 112).

Lady Jane Grey named to succeed.

Lady Jane Grey had married Lord Guildford Dudley, the Duke of Northumberland's son, a few weeks before, and thus the duke hoped to keep his power. All the great men round Edward signed this paper, though it was really valueless without the consent of Parliament. On July 6, 1553, the young king died at the early age of sixteen, having reigned only six years.

5. **Mary.**—As soon as the king was dead Northumberland sent off a body of soldiers to Hundson, in Hertfordshire, to take Mary prisoner, and prevent her coming to claim the throne. Then he hastened off with four other lords to Sion House, and kneeling before Lady Jane Grey hailed her as queen. The beautiful, accomplished girl of sixteen had never a thought or wish for the crown, and she was terrified at the greeting. It was only by working upon her feelings as a Protestant that she could be persuaded to oppose Mary. Northumberland proclaimed her queen in London, but the people listened sullenly, for they hated Northumberland, and looked upon Mary as their lawful sovereign.

Lady Jane Grey proclaimed in London, July 10, 1553.

Meanwhile Mary had not been idle. Warned by secret friends, she had escaped before Northumberland's soldiers arrived, and taken refuge with the Duke of Norfolk's family, the Howards. There she soon gathered thousands around her, and marching into London, was received with shouts of joy. Even Northumberland, who had retreated to Cambridge, was obliged, when she was proclaimed there, to throw up his cap and shout with the rest. He was arrested and sent to the Tower, together with his son and Lady Jane Grey, and was executed a month later, regretted by none.

Mary proclaimed in London, July 18, 1553.

6. **The Roman Catholic Religion Restored.**—The Duke of Norfolk, and the Bishops Bonner and Gardiner, were now set free from the Tower, and the Protestant Bishops, Latimer and

STRUGGLES BETWEEN THE TWO RELIGIONS.   131

Cranmer were sent there in their place. When Parliament met Mary was declared legitimate, and all the laws passed in Edward's reign repealed. The married priests were driven from their churches, the Prayer-book was forbidden and the mass restored, though Parliament discussed this last change for many days. Bonner was made Bishop of London, and Gardiner was made chancellor, while the queen was much guided in all she did by Simon Renard, the Spanish ambassador.

So far, except in London and some of the large towns, the country was well satisfied to have back the old religion. But Mary wished to go much further. To understand and pity her for the cruelties which took place in her reign we must put ourselves in her place. She was a conscientious but narrow-minded woman, thirty-seven years of age, who had suffered from her childhood upwards. Half a Spaniard, and devoted to her mother and her mother's people, she had seen that mother divorced and disgraced from no fault of her own, and Anne Boleyn, Elizabeth's mother, made queen in her stead. Mary had been taught to connect this great sorrow of her life with the decrees against the Pope and the introduction of the new religion. Her father had always been harsh with her: and her half-sister Elizabeth, whom she always refused to speak of as princess, was named as the future queen. Then came her little brother Edward, who took precedence of both his sisters, and during his reign tried to force Mary to give up her religion. Can we wonder that she felt bitter against those who oppressed her? *Character of Queen Mary.*

7. The Queen's Marriage.—By her brother's death everything was now altered. The people, disgusted at Northumberland's conduct, hailed Mary gladly as their queen, and for the first time she was free and had power. Her great wish was to restore the Pope's rule in England, and as a step towards this, she listened to Renard when he proposed she should marry her cousin Philip of Spain, son of the Emperor Charles V. and the chief supporter of the Roman Catholics. This engagement displeased the people and the Parliament very much, for they wished her to marry Edward Courtenay, Earl of Devon, great-grandson of Edward IV. They were afraid of a Spanish king, who might claim too much power in England, and also introduce the cruel Inquisition.

The people in all parts of England became very uneasy, and a conspiracy was formed in Devonshire, Wales, the Midland Counties, and Kent to marry Princess Elizabeth to the Earl of Devon, and place them on the throne instead of Mary. But through mismanagement only the people of Kent rose, under a brave Kentish gentleman, Sir Thomas Wyat. They seized the cannon and the ships in the Thames; and even the militia, whom the Duke of Norfolk led against them, deserted and joined the insurgents, crying, "A Wyat, a Wyat." It was Mary herself who saved the day. She rode boldly to Guildhall and appealed to the loyalty of the citizens, promising not to marry without the consent of Parliament. When Wyat arrived in London his way was barred by 25,000 men. He was taken prisoner at Temple Bar and sent to the Tower.

Wyat's rebellion, Feb. 1554.

A terrible revenge followed. Mary, who had till now spared Lady Jane Grey, consented that she and her husband should be put to death. They were both executed on Feb. 12, 1554. Lords Grey, Suffolk, Wyat, and other leaders were beheaded soon after, and more than a hundred commoners were hanged. Princess Elizabeth was sent to the Tower, and Renard wished her also to be put to death, but Chancellor Gardiner prevented it. She was placed under care at Woodstock in Oxfordshire, and afterwards at Hatfield in Hertfordshire.

Execution of Lady Jane Grey and others.

A few months later, July 1554, Mary was married to Philip. It was not a happy union. Parliament would not allow Philip to be crowned king, and he did not love his middle-aged wife, though he was always courteous to her. He remained in England a year, hoping she might have a son, but grew weary at last and went back to his kingdom. Meanwhile Mary pushed on her designs. She managed to get a tolerably obedient Parliament elected, which consented to receive a legate from the Pope, and Cardinal Pole, son of that Marchioness of Salisbury who was beheaded in Henry VIII.'s reign, sailed up the Thames with a silver cross on the bow of his barge, and granted absolution in the Pope's name to the Lords and Commons who knelt to receive it. Thus far there was no opposition. In 1554 Cardinal Pole became Archbishop of Canterbury, and took a chief

Arrival of a legate from the Pope.

STRUGGLES BETWEEN THE TWO RELIGIONS.

place in the Council. But when the Pope Paul IV. demanded that every acre of Church property in England should be given back, this was too much. Mary gave what she could, but the great nobles swore that they would keep their land as long as they had a sword by their side. So, by dividing the estates of the monasteries among the nobles, Henry VIII. had put an effectual stop to the Pope regaining any real hold on England.

<small>Nobles refuse to give up Church lands.</small>

8. Persecution of the Protestants.—A sad story of cruelty and suffering remains to be told. Mary thought it her duty to try and root out those heretics who stood in the way of the holy faith. The old statutes of Henry IV. and V. against the Lollards were put in force again, and the first victims, Rogers, a canon of St. Paul's, and Hooper, Bishop of Gloucester, were burnt at the stake, Feb, 1555. Others followed rapidly, four in April and May, six in June, eleven in July, eighteen in August,—the roll of martyrs went on increasing. In October Latimer and Ridley were chained back to back at the same stake.

"Play the man, Master Ridley," said Latimer, "we shall this day light such a candle in England as by the grace of God shall never be put out." And so they did. It was not the question which religion was right, or which wrong, that mattered so much to England. It was whether a man has a right to believe according to his conscience, and has the strength to stand by that right. The burning of these men, and of Archbishop Cranmer in 1556, when he thrust his right hand first into the flame because he had once weakly signed a recantation, did light the candle of truth and courage amid the deep gloom of persecution. At least two hundred and eighty honest and God-fearing people perished for their religion in three years. But they did not die in vain, for the terror which overshadowed the land, while it sent away good men as exiles to Frankfurt and Geneva, made Roman Catholics as well as Protestants in England reflect how dangerous it is to allow either Pope or Sovereign to sacrifice men's lives for honest religious opinions.

<small>Burning of Latimer, Ridley and Cranmer.</small>

9. Loss of Calais.—People now began to speak in whispers of the queen's feeble health, and to long for a time when horrors would cease. Nor did Philip's second visit to England in 1557 tend to improve matters. He came to persuade Mary to join him in a war against France. It was undertaken sorely against the will of the Council, and Mary in the end regretted it bitterly; for in 1558 Calais, which was not properly defended, was retaken by the French, after having been English for more than two hundred years. When the fortress of Guisnes within the pale of Calais was surrendered soon after, the English no longer possessed a foot of land on the continent. Mary is said to have exclaimed that when she died the name of Calais would be found engraven on her heart. Her death took place in the same year, on Nov. 17, 1558, and Cardinal Pole died twenty-two hours after.

CHAPTER XV.

PEACE AND PROGRESS UNDER ELIZABETH.

1. Elizabeth.—Princess Elizabeth was sitting under a tree in Hatfield Park, Nov. 17, 1558, when she received the news that she was Queen of England. She fell on her knees and exclaimed, "It is the Lord's doing, and it is marvellous in our eyes," and these words were stamped on the gold coinage all through her reign.

As a woman Elizabeth had many and great faults; as a queen we can scarcely admire her too much. She could truly say at the end of her reign, "I have ever used to set the last judgment-day before mine eyes, and so to rule as I shall have to answer before a higher Judge, to whose judgment-seat I do appeal that never thought was cherished in my heart that tended not to my people's good."

Character of Elizabeth. From her father she inherited a strong will, courage, self-confidence, and a love of popularity, together with great want of sincerity and of gratitude towards those who served her. Her fondness for gaiety, fine dress, and coquetry, she had from her mother; and vanity from both parents. But Elizabeth was not a mere vain coquette. She had a deep sense of her duty as a queen, and the wisdom to choose good councillors; while she often saw even more clearly what was for her people's good than they did themselves. The work she had before her was to keep her place on the throne, to free the country from foreign enemies and heavy taxes, and to restore civil and religious order, so that England might be a strong and united nation. If in doing this she was often untruthful and capricious, it is some excuse that she was, as she herself said, "a weak woman," who had to play her game against powerful enemies.

2. Weak State of England.—Nothing could be worse than the state of England when Elizabeth came to the throne. By giving up the Church lands, and by the ruinous war with France, Mary had drained the treasury. The terrible persecutions had driven the best men into exile and the country to the verge of rebellion, while the general discontent made life and property insecure. Added to these troubles within, there were serious dangers from without. Civil war was raging in Ireland, and Scotland's queen, Mary Stuart, who was now married to the French dauphin, declared Elizabeth to be illegitimate, and claimed the English throne for herself. On the continent a great struggle was going on between Roman Catholics and Protestants, which lasted all through Elizabeth's reign. Henry II. of France was struggling to put down his Protestant subjects, the Huguenots; and Philip was burning heretics in Spain. Though Philip was at first friendly to Elizabeth, because he was afraid of France, he never really wished her well. Moreover, Philip's father Charles V. had inherited the Low Countries or Netherlands from his grandmother, Mary of Burgundy, who married Maximilian of Austria. Now the Netherlanders had become staunch Protestants, and were already beginning to grow restless under the rule of Philip II. and the Inquisition. Thus Europe was divided into two hostile camps, Roman Catholic and Protestant, and the Pope, Paul IV., who had regained much power in England during Mary's reign, was waiting to see which side Elizabeth would take.

Religious struggle on the continent.

She wisely took neither at first. She kept many of the ministers who had been on Mary's Council, adding to them an able statesman, Sir William Cecil, afterwards Lord Burleigh, who became Secretary of State, and served her faithfully all his life. She refused to alter the Church service until Parliament had met, and meanwhile she declared she would not

Sir William Cecil Secretary of State.

meddle with the consciences of her subjects, but would leave each one free to hold his own opinions so long as he attended the public worship prescribed by the law. When Parliament met on Jan. 25, 1559, its first act was to declare Elizabeth legitimate and true Queen of England, and to pass "Acts of Supremacy and Uniformity." The first required all the clergy to take the oath of the queen's supremacy. The second restored the Prayer-book of Edward VI., with some changes agreeable to the Roman Catholics, and obliged all the people to attend service or pay a heavy fine.

Freedom of opinion with outward conformity.

The Bishops were staunch Roman Catholics, and all but one refused to take the oath of supremacy. As this was denying the queen as their Head, they were deprived of their sees, and Protestant bishops were put in their places. But Elizabeth was careful not to press the lower clergy too hard. No notice was taken of those who neglected to come and take the oath, and in many places the parish priest went on holding mass in his house for the Roman Catholics, while he used the English service in the Church. Matthew Parker, a learned and prudent man, was made Archbishop of Canterbury, and so for a time Elizabeth avoided religious disputes such as were going on abroad.

Oath of supremacy.

3. State of Scotland.—The next difficulty was Scotland, where Mary of Guise was reigning as regent, because her daughter, Mary Stuart, was now Queen of France. For many years Scotland had been gradually adopting Protestantism. Many of the monasteries had become corrupt, and the nobles were jealous of the wealth and power of the Church. Many of them therefore encouraged the new religion, and those English Protestants who had escaped over the border during the persecutions of the last reign were welcomed. Stern and earnest by nature, the Scotch went farther than the English, and became followers of the great teacher, John Calvin, of Geneva. In 1557 a large body of nobles met at Edinburgh, and pledged themselves to support each other and spread the new doctrine. The pledge they signed is called the "First Covenant," and they took the name of the "Lords of the Congregation." Now Mary of Guise was a staunch Roman Catholic, and when she tried to put down the

Lords of the Congregation in Scotland, 1557.

PEACE AND PROGRESS. 137

new doctrines, the people, led by the famous Calvinist preacher, John Knox, destroyed the images in the churches and broke out into open rebellion. The regent tried to enforce her rule by the help of a French army, but the Lords of the Congregation occupied Edinburgh and held a Parliament. They were anxious to be free from their old allies, the French, and asked Elizabeth to help them.

Elizabeth hesitated, for she did not like to support rebels against their sovereign. But a French army in Scotland was a serious danger to England, so at last she sent the English fleet to the Firth of Forth, and 8000 men under Lord Grey to help in the siege of Leith. Just then the queen regent died, and the Council of Lords who took the Government, signed a treaty at Edinburgh by which the French promised to leave Scotland, and the Lords promised that Mary Stuart should not claim the English crown. *Treaty of Edinburgh, July, 1560.* But Mary herself would never consent to sign this promise. The Scotch Parliament then formally adopted the Geneva Confession of Faith and Protestantism has been the religion of Scotland ever since. A few months later, Mary's French husband, King Francis II., died, and the next year she returned, to take her place as Queen of Scotland. *Return of Mary Queen of Scots, Aug. 1561.* But for the moment Elizabeth had nothing to fear from Mary, having the Protestant lords on her side.

4. Prosperity of England.—Meanwhile peace at home was giving England time to grow prosperous. The treasury was refilled by claiming back the Church lands and by great economy; while by calling in the base coin, and giving money once more its true value, Cecil removed a heavy burden from the people. In 1561 a commission was sent to inquire into the causes of the great distress, and in 1562 the mayor of each town and the church-wardens of each village were ordered to raise a fund among the inhabitants to provide for their own poor. This was the beginning of the first "Poor-law" which was confirmed *Poor-law established, 1562-1601.* by Act of Parliament in 1601, and lasted down to our century in 1834. Though it became at last a serious burden, it was then a wise measure, and helped to restore order.

But it was by making property secure that Elizabeth did most for her people. The landowners and gentry now began to work their farms better, to study the use of manures, and how to plant different crops in succession; and though it was no doubt a misfortune that the labourers no longer had land of their own, yet better farming gave better crops and employed more hands.

Improvements in agriculture.

Industries, manufactures, and trade began also to revive, giving work to many. The religious troubles in the Netherlands drove many Flemings over to England, and the English learnt from them how to weave cloth and silk better, to make soap and oil for dressing it, and to dye their cloth at home. The northern towns began to flourish, and Manchester friezes, Halifax cloth, and Sheffield cutlery became famous. Moreover, goods and money which used to go to Antwerp now came direct to England. Raw gold and silver from America, gold dust and ivory from Africa, silks and cottons from the East, found their market in London, where Sir Thomas Gresham built the Royal Exchange in 1566, as a hall in which the merchants might meet. The encouragement, too, given by the queen to shipping adventure caused a regular merchant navy to spring up, led by daring commanders.

Trade and manufactures.

England was in fact now beginning that conquest of the sea which has made her so great. In 1576 Frobisher, a west country seaman, sailed northwards to try and find a north-west passage to India, and discovered the straits in Hudson's Bay, which still bear his name. In the same year the brave Sir Humphrey Gilbert made a voyage of discovery to America, and another in 1583, when he took possession of Newfoundland, and was afterwards lost with his ship and all on board. Davis, Raleigh, Hawkins, and Drake—who was the first Englishman to sail round the world—are all names famous for discoveries on the sea, though Hawkins is unfortunately chiefly remembered as having been the first to carry slaves from Africa to America in 1562. All these men led the way to new countries, and opened out new roads for commerce.

Voyages of discovery.

The result of this increase of prosperity was that people lived more comfortably. Instead of fortified and battlemented castles, fine Elizabethan villas were built for the gentry, with carved staircases and rich carpets on the floors; the yeoman and farmers had houses of stone and brick, with glass windows and chimneys, instead of mere holes in the roof. The dress of all classes, and especially of the gentry, was richer and more costly. The queen herself, thrifty as she was, loved splendour and show, and as she travelled from one courtier's house to another, gay revels and pageants gave new brightness to the lives of her subjects.

Increase of comfort.

5. Religious Discord.—But while the people were in peace and prosperity, Elizabeth herself had endless anxieties. The Pope, Pius IV., finding she would neither have a legate in England nor send ambassadors to his Council at Trent in 1561, began to treat her as a rebellious sovereign, and told the Roman Catholics that they must not go to the English churches. Parliament was jealous of this interference, and passed an Act requiring every member of the House of Commons, every public officer and every parish priest, to take an oath of allegiance to the queen, and deny the Pope's authority in England. This, of course, kept all strict Roman Catholics out of the House of Commons. The Thirty-nine Articles of Faith, drawn up in Edward VI's reign, were now adopted, and all the clergy were required to sign them. Thus, sorely against Elizabeth's will the seed of religious discord was sown among her people.

Oath of allegiance established, 1563.

6. Mary Queen of Scots.—Mary Queen of Scots, too, now again began to give trouble. She was still the next heir to the throne, for though Elizabeth was often pressed by Parliament to marry, and she coquetted with an offer from the Archduke of Austria, and with her favourite courtier, Robert Dudley, Earl of Leicester, yet it all came to nothing. In truth, she could not marry, for whether she choose a Protestant or a Roman Catholic, she must have offended half her subjects.

Elizabeth would not marry.

So Mary Stuart was still a thorn in Elizabeth's side. When she first returned to Scotland all the people adored their lovely young queen, and allowed her to follow her own Roman Catholic religion, especially as her half-brother, Earl Murray, who was a Protestant, helped her to govern. She soon began to think of marrying a second time, and chose her young cousin, Henry Stuart, Lord

Darnley, who was descended like herself from Margaret Tudor, Henry VIII.'s sister. Darnley had been brought up in England and his family, the Lennoxes, were old Roman Catholics. The Roman Catholic lords now had the upper hand in Scotland, Murray was obliged to quit the country, and Elizabeth saw that at any time Mary and Darnley might try to seize the English throne.

Mary Queen of Scots marries Lord Darnley, 1565.

But Mary ruined her own chances. Darnley was a weak, vicious man, and she soon tired of him. She was eager to bring back Roman Catholicism and to be Queen of England, and her clever Italian secretary, David Rizzio, helped her to carry on a secret correspondence with the Pope and Spain. Darnley was so angry because Mary would not allow him to be crowned king, and so jealous of Rizzio, that he plotted with some of the Protestant lords, who entered the queen's chamber at Holyrood, dragged Rizzio from her presence, and murdered him upon the staircase. Then they seized the palace gates, and Mary was in their power. She was wise enough to yield, and to make friends again with Darnley, but she did not forget. Three months later, her son was born, and she had now an advantage over Elizabeth in having an heir to succeed her.

Murder of Rizzio, Mar. 9, 1566.

All went on quietly for the next nine months, and then a terrible thing happened. Darnley had an illness, and Mary, who appeared anxious about him, brought him for change of air to an old priory called Kirk-o'-Field, close to Holyrood Palace, outside Edinburgh. There one evening she left him with a young page, while she went to a servant's wedding-dance at Holyrood. Soon after midnight an awful explosion shook the city. The Kirk-o'-Field had been blown up, and Darnley and the page lay dead in a field hard by. How much the queen knew no one could tell. But there is no doubt that a bold and worthless young noble, James Hepburn, Earl of Bothwell, did the deed, and Mary married him three months after.

Murder of Darnley, Feb. 9, 1567.

All Scotland shrank from her in horror, even though many believed her innocent of the murder. She spent a month gathering an army to meet the lords, but when the time came none would fight for her. Bothwell fled to the Orkneys, and afterwards to Denmark where he died; and Mary was made prisoner, and put in a strong castle in the middle of Loch Leven, a lake in Kinross-shire. The lords forced her to abdicate, and her baby son was crowned as James VI., Earl Murray being made regent. A year later she escaped and gathered an army. But she was defeated at Langside, near Glasgow, and galloping ninety miles, only stopping to change horses, she crossed the Solway Firth, and took refuge at Carlisle. Mary escapes to England, May 1568.

To have her rival in England was the last thing Elizabeth wished. Only the year before this she had had another discussion with Parliament about her marriage and her successor. As the nation prospered the House of Commons grew bolder. Country gentlemen now coveted seats, and members, instead of being paid, offered themselves freely to represent their neighbours. These men were independent and looked to their rights. Soon after Mary's son was born they began again to urge the queen to settle the succession; and when Elizabeth sent them a sharp message to leave the matter to her, Wentworth, a member of the House of Commons, rose and asked if this was not "against their liberties." At last the queen quieted them with promises, and they voted the supplies she wanted for sending an army to Ireland. That country had been in open revolt ever since 1565, under a bold and able leader, Shan O'Neill. But with men and money in 1567 Sir Henry Sidney put down the rebellion, and there seemed some hope of peace. The English Parliament grows stronger.
Shan O'Neill's revolt, 1565-1567.

Just then Mary Stuart's escape to England put Elizabeth into fresh difficulties. What was to be done with her? Mary asked for an army to take her back to Scotland, or for a free passage to France. This last Elizabeth could not grant, for it would have given the French a fresh hold upon Scotland. She did try to get Murray to receive his queen back, but he refused, and produced letters between Mary and Bothwell which, if genuine, proved that she had plotted her husband's murder. So Elizabeth kept her in England, putting her under care, first in one country-house, then in another. Mary a prisoner in England, 1568-1587.

Many have blamed Elizabeth for keeping Mary a prisoner, while others condemn Mary for the plots in which she took part against Elizabeth during the next eighteen years. To me it seems that neither queen could be expected to act otherwise than she did.

Mary, as a Roman Catholic and the friend of the Roman Catholics, believed she would do right to seize the throne if she could, while Elizabeth was bound to use every effort to keep her place over the subjects who loved her. The difference between the two queens which gave Elizabeth the advantage was that, though hard, she always looked to the good of her people, while Mary, attractive and lovable as she was, ruined her chance by her own uncontrolled passions. From the moment when Mary married her husband's murderer her cause was lost.

Mary and Elizabeth.

7. Plots against Elizabeth.—All this time Elizabeth, by great diplomacy, had kept clear of foreign wars, but it was becoming more difficult every day. Just at the time when Mary Stuart escaped to England, the brave Netherlanders, the people of Holland, Zealand, and Flanders began a long and bitter struggle under William of Orange against their Spanish tyrants. They fought, suffered and starved; and at last breaking down their dykes, flooded their country and turned out the enemy. During this struggle it would have been useful to Philip II. to have a Roman Catholic queen on the English throne; while it was very difficult for Elizabeth not to take one side or the other in the contest. Her own Council were divided. Cecil and the Protestant lords wished to help the Netherlanders; the Duke of Norfolk and the Roman Catholic lords wanted peace with Spain, and wanted Mary to be named as Elizabeth's successor. The queen tried to keep the balance between them, but the Roman Catholic lords grew impatient. A plot was formed to marry Mary to Norfolk, and when this was discovered and Norfolk was sent to the Tower, a rebellion broke out in the north of England, under the Earls of Northumberland and Westmoreland, with the design of setting Mary free. The earls were defeated and fled to Scotland, and more than six hundred people were put to death as rebels.

Revolt of the Netherlands, 1568.

Revolt in north of England, Nov. 1569.

But still the Roman Catholics were restless, and the next year, 1570, Pope Pius V excommunicated Elizabeth and absolved her subjects from their allegiance. Parliament in return made more stringent laws against the Roman Catholics, and the Pope, angry, that his "Bull of excommunication" had so little effect, made use of a banker named Ridolfi to revive the plan of Mary's marriage with Norfolk, and to plot

Excommunication of Elizabeth and the Ridolfi plot, 1570-1571.

with Spain to dethrone Elizabeth. A man was found in Madrid who agreed to assassinate the queen: and the Spanish general, Alva, was to cross over from the Netherlands and seize the kingdom. But before they could do anything Lord Burleigh learnt their secret. Norfolk was executed, and the Spanish ambassador was ordered out of England. Still, though Parliament urged Elizabeth to try Queen Mary for treason, she would not.

Though undermined in this way by Spain, Elizabeth still kept a hold on France by proposing to marry, first the Duke of Anjou and afterwards his younger brother. But meanwhile an awful thing happened. The French king's mother, Catharine de Medici, and the Roman Catholic dukes, the Guises, fearing that the Huguenots were growing too strong, excited the mob in Paris against them. On Aug. 24, 1572, the massacre of St. Bartholomew took place, when all the Huguenot leaders were murdered in Paris, and the fury spread from town to town till more than a hundred thousand Huguenots perished. *Massacre of St. Bartholomew, Aug. 24, 1572.*

This terrible triumph of the Roman Catholic party alarmed both Elizabeth and her people. Yet she would not even now openly side with the Protestants, but refused the Netherlanders when they invited her to be their queen in 1575, although she sent some money to help them.

8. Privateering.—But she did not forbid her subjects from giving them assistance. The London merchants sent half a million of money to William of Orange, and more than five thousand young Englishmen crossed over to the Netherlands to stand by the brave patriots. Others put out to sea in their own ships, and the channel swarmed with "sea-dogs," as they were called, who attacked the trading vessels of France and Spain. *The English help the Netherlanders.* These privateers cared probably as much for the plunder as for the cause. The Spanish and Portuguese had possession of those parts of the New World where gold and treasure were to be found, and Francis Drake, the son of a Devonshire clergyman, sailed in 1572, and again in 1577, to Spanish South America, and sacked the gold ships. *English privateers rob Spanish vessels.* Philip vowed revenge, especially as England welcomed Drake as a hero, and Elizabeth made him a knight. But Philip had too much on his hands already, and eight years passed by, till Elizabeth at last sent the Earl of Leicester to help the Netherlanders, and allowed Drake to sail again in 1585 with twenty-five vessels to Spanish America, from which he returned laden with plunder. From this time Philip began really to prepare for war with England, but it was three years more before his famous "Spanish Armada" or *armed fleet* was ready, and in those years much happened.

9. Seminary Priests.—For some time past a number of young English Roman Catholics had been in training at Douai in France, on purpose to be sent as missionaries to England. These men firmly believed that the salvation of the country depended on bringing the people back under the Pope's authority. In 1576 they began to travel secretly over the land, holding services and distributing tracts against the queen, inciting men to rebellion. The Government became seriously alarmed; the priests were taken prisoners wherever they were found, and during the next twenty years a large number were put to death. But their work bore its fruit. In 1583 a plot was discovered, headed by a Roman Catholic, Francis Throgmorton, to murder Elizabeth and put Mary on the throne, and it was clear that the Spanish ambassador knew of it. Throgmorton was executed, and the leading men of England now thoroughly afraid of harm to their queen, formed an association in which they pledged themselves, with the consent of Parliament, "to pursue to the death any one plotting against the queen, *as well as any person in whose behalf they plotted.*"

<small>Catholic mission to England, 1584.</small>

<small>Association to protect the queen, 1584.</small>

10. Execution of Mary Queen of Scots.—We see at once that this was a warning for Queen Mary, and she herself was made to sign the document. Three years later, however, Sir Francis Walsingham, the Secretary of State, discovered that, sick and weary with long imprisonment, Mary had given her consent to another plot, headed by a young man named Anthony Babington, and, as before, encouraged by Spain. This plot caused Mary's death. The proofs were laid before a commission of peers at Fotheringay Castle, Northamptonshire, where Mary was imprisoned, and she was condemned to death by Parliament, Nov. 1586. The people rejoiced

PEACE AND PROGRESS. 145

that now the continual conspiracies would be stopped, and the streets of London blazed with bon-fires. But it was a long time before Elizabeth would sign the warrant; she was afraid all Europe would condemn her. At last she signed it, and on Feb. 8, 1587, the lovely and unfortunate Queen of Scots was beheaded. "Do not weep," she said to her ladies, "I have given my word for you. Tell all my friends that I died a good Catholic."

11. Spanish Armada.—Elizabeth had now only one enemy left to deal with, and this was Philip of Spain, who was making serious preparations to attack England. The queen, afraid, as usual, of spending money, would scarcely give enough to make the English fleet effective. But Lord Howard of Effingham and his admirals spared no exertions. Sir Francis Drake in 1587 made a bold dash at Cadiz harbour, and burnt part of the Armada, and many private English gentlemen fitted out vessels at their own expense. At length the time came. Philip's great general, the Duke of Parma, gathered 30,000 Spanish troops in the Netherlands, ready to cross as soon as the Armada arrived, and Philip, confident that all the English Roman Catholics would join him, started his monster fleet of one hundred and twenty-nine ships, under command of the Duke of Medina Sidonia, on July 12, 1588. *The Spanish Armada starts, July 12, 1588.*

He had reckoned wrongly. No sooner, on July 19, did the beacon fires along the coast spread the news that the Armada was coming, than all England, Roman Catholics as well as Protestants, rose to defend their country and their queen. Though Lord Howard had only eighty vessels and 9000 seamen, these were commanded by such daring spirits as Lord Henry Seymour, Frobisher, Drake, and Hawkins. The light English ships harassed the Spanish heavy galleons, and eight fire-ships, sent adrift at night into Calais harbour, made the Spaniards slip their cables and stand out to sea. Then the English fleet, dashing among them, cut off their return, raking them with a terrible fire as long as ammunition lasted. The spirit of the Spaniards was broken, and a great wind obliged the duke to try and find his way round the north of Scotland back to Spain. Near the Orkneys the fury of the storm burst upon them; the ships were driven on the rocks, the *Defeat of the Armada, 1588.*

10

shores of the Scottish isles were strewn with bodies. 11,000 Spaniards perished off the coast of Ireland, and only a shattered fleet of fifty-three vessels found its way back to Corunna. The dreaded Armada was defeated, and the joy and gratitude of the English was expressed on the coin struck by Elizabeth, in the words "Afflavit Deus, et dissipati sunt," "God breathed and they were scattered."

Now at last Elizabeth was comparatively at rest. All nations recognised her power; her fleet was "mistress of the seas"; her people had withstood all temptations to treason: and even the Roman Catholics, convinced at last that peace and toleration under their own sovereign was better than plotting with foreign powers, settled down quietly, contented to be Englishmen. The people most difficult to deal with were the extreme Protestants or "Puritans," who had brought back from Geneva a dislike to even the simplest ceremonies, but they were kept fairly quiet during Elizabeth's reign. In France Henry IV., by the famous "Edict of Nantes," gave his Protestant subjects freedom to worship as they wished, and thus helped to quiet Europe.

England united and at peace.

Edict of Nantes, April 13, 1598.

12. National Growth.—And now the growth of the nation, which had been going on unnoticed for the last thirty years, began to bear fruit. On the sea English ships sailed far and wide. Sir Walter Raleigh sent seven expeditions to North and South America, which brought back new fruits, as well as tobacco and the potato; and though the colony of Virginia, which he founded, did not flourish, it paved the way for others. Sir Francis Drake opened up the way to the East Indies, and ship after ship, both from Holland and England, began to trade with the East. Elizabeth granted a charter to a company of London East India merchants, who formed the beginning of our famous East India Company.

East India Company, Dec. 31, 1599.

And side by side with this outward growth, an inward growth of mind and thought was going on. During the hundred years which had passed since Henry Tudor came to the throne, great events had happened, and wonderful discoveries had been made which could not fail to excite men's minds. Copernicus and Galileo had shown that our little world is not the centre of the universe, while at the same time voyages of discovery

Copernicus and Galileo.

had proved how much grander and larger even this little world is than the ancients had believed. America, with all its riches of gold and silver, and its strange races of people, had been discovered; while at home the new religion, the spread of printing, and the study of Greek and Latin, had stirred the minds of the English people to high thoughts, which expressed themselves in stirring works of prose and poetry. And so towards the end of Elizabeth's reign we find the study of history reviving. Archbishop Parker tried to collect together the old English chronicles, and Sir Walter Raleigh began his great *History of the World*, written during the next reign. Then again, besides pamphlets, novels, and short-lived works of all kinds, we have such great writers as Sir Francis Bacon, who gave new life to philosophy and science; the poet Spenser, who wrote the "Faerie Queen"; and Sir Philip Sidney, who died from a fatal wound received at the Battle of Zutphen in the Netherlands, wrote the "Arcadia." To crown all,—among a host of play-writers and poets of the Elizabethan period of literature, whose plays were acted and poems recited in barns, booths, and courtyards, or in the theatres which now sprang up in London,—came our great Shakespeare, born in 1564, who gave us those plays, so true to nature, so full of deep wisdom, so powerful in language, and so noble in thought, that not only England, but all the world has been the richer for them ever since.

Writers of Elizabeth's reign.

Shakespeare, 1564.

13. Irish Revolts.—We are now nearing the end of Elizabeth's reign. In 1598 Cecil, Lord Burleigh, died, and younger men gathered round the queen. There was Sir Walter Raleigh, brave and able; Robert Cecil, Burleigh's son, a wise statesman; and Robert Devereux, Earl of Essex, a wild, headstrong young man, whom Elizabeth petted and scolded like a child. The old troubles were still going on in Ireland, and matters had been made worse by the unwise attempt to carry out the penal laws against Roman Catholics and to force the English Prayerbook and service on the people. Moreover, when the Pope excommunicated Elizabeth, the Irish scarcely knew which way to lean. The Spaniards were always exciting them against England, and in 1595 Hugh O'Neill, Earl of Tyrone, a brave Irish chief, rose in rebellion, as-

Death of Burleigh, 1598.

Rebellion of Hugh O'Neil, Earl of Tyrone, 1595-1602.

sisted by Philip II. He defeated the English near Armagh, and the queen sent Essex against him with an army of 30,000 men. But Essex, finding many difficulties, and won over by flattery, made a foolish peace with Tyrone, and then hastened back to England, hoping to persuade the queen he had done wisely.

Insurrection and death of Essex, 1601.
She, however, was very angry, and he was kept a prisoner in his own house. Sore at this treatment, the foolhardy young man gathered his friends together and marched to the city, hoping to raise a revolt. He failed utterly, and being found guilty of treason, was beheaded.

Meanwhile Lord Mountjoy was sent to Ireland, where Tyrone at last surrendered. From this date the whole of Ireland has been governed by England, and during the next reign large

Ireland governed by England from 1602.
numbers of English and Scotch settlers had lands given them in Leinster and Ulster on condition that they preserved order. These are known as the Ulster and Leinster "plantations," and by them two-thirds of the North of Ireland passed to strangers. But though this change brought outward prosperity, it was unjustly carried out, and raised a bitter spirit, which caused serious trouble some years after.

14. Death of the Queen.—And now the queen lay dying. Vain and fickle, vacillating and often untruthful, she had no doubt been, but she found England weak and divided—she left it strong and united. Even Parliament had regained much of the independence it had lost under Henry VIII. In her last Parliament

Abolition of monopolies, Oct. 1601.
Elizabeth had to yield to the House of Commons when they insisted on abolishing the "monopolies" or right which were held by many nobles to be the only persons to sell certain articles, wine for example, and so wringing money from the people.

But on one point Elizabeth was stubborn to the end. She would not name her successor. As her life was fading away in the evening

Death of Elizabeth, Mar. 24, 1603.
of March 23, 1603, it was only by a slight motion of the head that her ministers could conclude she was willing to allow James VI. of Scotland to fill her place. In the early morning of March 24, the great queen died.

15. Summary of The House of Tudor.—The reign of the family of Tudors was now over, and the family of Stuarts was coming in their place. For more than a hundred years England had been rising to a leading position among nations. Henry VII. laid the foundation by keeping clear of foreign wars and holding a firm hand over the nobles at home. Henry VIII. followed in his footsteps by shutting out foreign influence. The troubled reigns of Edward and Mary did their work in leading men to long for freedom of thought and to abhor persecution, while Elizabeth, carefully shielding her people from the wars of religion raging all around, gave them time to grow strong and develop. Trade flourished, agriculture improved, comfort and well-being increased. Daring seamen explored distant oceans and scoured the seas, till England's name stood high for courage and adventure, while the new thoughts and widening knowledge, filling the minds of men, broke out in a grand literature, which has never been surpassed even in our day. The Goverment, however, under which all this advance was made, had one weak side. It depended almost entirely on the character of the king or queen who happened to reign. So long as a wise and able sovereign was on the throne, things went well; but the reigns of Edward and Mary had shown that the monarchy was so strong, that when its power was unwisely used, the nation was thrown into confusion. After Elizabeth's death came monarchs who did not reign wisely, and so, as we shall see, a struggle arose with Parliament and the people, causing England to be once more torn by civil war and suffering.

PART VI.

THE STRUGGLE AGAINST ABSOLUTE MONARCHY

SOVEREIGNS OF THE HOUSE OF STUART

CHAPTER XVI.

PREROGATIVE AND PARLIAMENT.

1. James I.—As soon as Elizabeth died the Council sent off post-haste for James VI. of Scotland, son of Mary Stuart and Darnley, and great-grandson of Margaret, eldest daughter of Henry VII. Though Henry VIII. had passed over Margaret in his will yet James was not only the next heir, but the choice of the nation. So the Scotch prophecy was fulfilled at last, and a Scotch king once more sat on the sacred stone of Scone, on July 25, 1603, when James VI. of Scotland was crowned as James I. of England in Westminster Abbey.

Though no very remarkable events happened in James's reign, yet it is important, because his constant disputes with Parliament prepared the way for the unhappy reign of his son Charles I. James was not a bad man, and he was a misguided rather than a bad king. In every-day matters he was shrewd enough. We owe to him the draining of the fen country, making useless land profitable, the first establishment of the post-office (for foreign countries only), and the encouragement of many useful manufactures, such as silk-weaving and the cultivation of silk-worms. But he never understood the English people, and he had such an overwhelming idea of his own superior wisdom that, being already thirty-six when he came to England, he was not likely to learn to know them. He was amiable and kindly by nature, and we shall see that the persecutions in his reign were never brutal as they had been formerly. But he was ungainly and undignified, fond of coarse jokes and of showing his learning, which was great. He was very obstinate and impatient of advice, yet, as he loved flattery and hated exertion, he was easily governed by favourites. *[Character of James I.]*

He looked upon the English crown as his by inheritance, and believed that he ruled by "*divine right*"; or, in other words, that he was not responsible to any earthly power, but had absolute authority over the nation and the laws. The Tudors had been despotic, and the "Star Chamber" *[Question of divine right.]*

of Henry VII., and the "Court of High Commission" which
Elizabeth founded to govern the Church, gave the sovereign great
power. But Henry VIII. and Elizabeth had understood their
people, and were popular; James, on the contrary, vexed his
subjects unnecessarily. He tried to overrule Parliament, and
told the Commons that, as it is "atheism to dispute what God
can do so it is presumption and high contempt in a subject
to dispute what a king can do, or say that a king cannot do this
or that."

We see at once that this would irritate the free English people who,
although they revered and loved their kings, had been accustomed
from Saxon times upwards to cry, *Aye, aye,* or *Nay, nay,* to any
new measure, at first in the Witangemot, and afterwards through
their representatives in Parliament. Moreover, at the time when
James became king, the people, prosperous after the long peace,
and accustomed to be governed by strong and popular princes, were
not likely to yield to a weak and pompous sovereign.

State of the nation. In the country, gentlemen, farmers, and labourers were
well off. In the towns trade was increasing. London
had spread so fast that Elizabeth had tried to stop fresh building,
and twice in his reign James ordered the country gentlemen and
their families "to go home and bide there, minding their duties."
This gathering of the people in large towns, and the spread of
printed books, especially of the English Bible, led people to think
and talk freely of many things, which before had been left chiefly
to statesmen and priests.

2. Religious Parties.—Roughly speaking, there were at this
time three parties in England. *First,* the Puritans, earnest self-
denying men, who led serious lives, and condemned the
The Puritans. swearing, gambling, drinking, and other vices which,
unfortunately, were common at court. These men disliked all
church ceremonies, and thought it wrong to make the sign of the
cross in baptism or to wear a surplice; and, as the Act of
Uniformity forbade any services to be used except those in the
Prayer-book, the Puritans wanted some parts of the
English Church party. services to be altered. With regard to the state, these
men upheld very strongly the liberty of Parliament.
The second, and by far the largest party as yet, was the High Church

party, as we should call it now. It consisted of those who wished matters in the Church to remain as Elizabeth had left them and as the bishops advised, and who upheld the power of the king. Lastly, there was a *third* party—the Roman Catholics—who wanted to restore the Roman Catholic religion and the power of the Pope in England. *[The Roman Catholics.]*

Elizabeth had cleverly managed to keep these three parties quiet, but James was unable either to understand or deal with them. He did not like the Puritans, because they held much the same opinions as the Scotch Protestants or Presbyterians (so called because they had no bishops, but were governed by "presbyters" or elders). These Presbyterians had given James much trouble in Scotland, and when he invited four of the English Puritans to meet the bishops at a conference at Hampton Court, he found they were equally obstinate in their views. He grew angry that they would not yield to his arguments, and declared he would "make them conform, or harry them out of the land." The only good result of the conference was that James ordered a revised translation of the Bible to be made. This "authorised version," published in 1611, has been used down to our time, and the beautiful language contained in it together with the writings of Shakespeare, has done more to form our modern English speech, and keep it pure, than all other writings. The evil result of the conference was that James carried out his threat. Ten of the men who had petitioned for changes were imprisoned by order of the Star Chamber, and three hundred Puritan clergymen were turned out of their livings. *[Hampton Court conference, Jan. 1604.]* *[Persecution of the Puritans.]*

3. Puritan Emigration.—The people, seeing that there was little chance of their being allowed to worship in their own way, began to think of leaving the country. A small congregation of Puritans escaped over the sea to Amsterdam and Leyden, under the guidance of their minister, John Robinson, and William Brewster, one of their chief men or *elders*. Twelve years later this little colony of one hundred and twenty souls, afterwards known as the "Pilgrim Fathers," sailed across the Atlantic in a ship called the *Mayflower*, *[Emigration of Puritans to America, 1620.]*

and settled some way to the north of Virginia, which was already a flourishing colony. They took with them the Bible as their law, and brotherhood as their charter, and though they suffered terrible hardships on the barren coast of Massachusetts, they prepared the way for those who came after, and founded the free states of New England.

4. Gunpowder Plot.—Almost directly after the conference, James summoned his first Parliament, and unfortunately he began by trying to dictate to the people what members to elect. Then, during the next session, the Commons petitioned that the Puritan clergymen might be allowed to preach again, but James refused to let them discuss the subject.

<small>Difficulties with the first Parliament, 1604-1620.</small>

They retorted by making stronger laws against the Roman Catholics, and James was obliged to banish some of the priests, and to begin again to levy £20 a month from all "*recusants,*" that is, Roman Catholics who refused to attend the English service.

This so troubled the Roman Catholics that a small knot of men, not more than fifteen in all, led by an enthusiast, Robert Catesby, proposed to blow up Parliament while it was being opened in state by the king and his eldest son Henry, and to set one of the younger children on the throne and restore the Roman Catholic religion. The plot went on for several months, arms were brought from Flanders, and Roman Catholic gentlemen invited to come over and join in a rebellion.

<small>Gunpowder Plot, Nov., 1605.</small>

But just at the last moment one of the conspirators, Francis Tresham, wrote to warn his brother-in-law, Lord Monteagle, to stay away from Parliament. James saw this mysterious letter, and guessed that something was wrong. A search was made, and Guy (or Guido) Fawkes, a Yorkshireman, who had served in Flanders, was discovered in a vault under the Houses of Parliament, with barrels of gunpowder stacked ready to be exploded. The result of this foolish plot was that the conspirators were killed, or taken prisoners and executed, and the Roman Catholics were in a much worse position for many generations.

5. Crown and Parliament.—But it was not only about Church questions that James and the Commons could not agree. The

PREROGATIVE AND PARLIAMENT.

English were jealous of the Scots, who came flocking to court; and when the king proposed to unite the two kingdoms, under the title of "Great Britain," there was a violent opposition. All that Sir Francis Bacon, then a rising barrister in Parliament, could obtain from them was that Scotchmen born after James came to throne should be naturalised Englishmen.

<small>Proposed union with Scotland, 1604.</small>

On this point James was more in the right than his people, but they opposed him partly because he was always trying to be independent of them. He insisted on making proclamations and imposing customs on merchandise without the consent of Parliament. Thinking to improve the dyeing of cloth, he issued a proclamation in 1608 forbidding undyed cloth to be sent abroad, and at the same time he granted to Alderman Cockayne the sole right of dyeing and dressing cloth. The result was he nearly ruined the trade, and had to take back the patent. Then, as he wanted money, he obtained an opinion from the judges that he had a right to levy "impositions" on goods, and in one year he raised in this way £70,000. The expenses of his court were very heavy, and he had to keep a large army in Ireland, where people were very restless at the "plantation" of Ulster. So he had at last to apply to the Commons, who refused to give him any money till he had promised to give up the proclamations and impositions. This James would not do, so Cecil, who was now Lord Salisbury and chief minister, tried to make a bargain with the Commons, called the "Great Contract." The king was to give up certain rights, and they were to give him £200,000 a year for life. But they would not consent, and at last James dissolved Parliament in Feb. 1611 without getting any money. Two years later he called a second Parliament, and dissolved it again in a few weeks, because the Commons again refused any grant till the "impositions" were given up. This was called the "Addled Parliament," because it did not pass a single bill.

<small>Proclamations and impositions.</small>

<small>Great Contract and dissolution, 1610.</small>

<small>Second or Addled Parliament, 1614.</small>

For seven years after the "Addled Parliament" James tried to rule without one. In 1612, when Lord Salisbury died, he raised a young Scotchman, Robert Carr, to high offices in the state, and

made him Earl of Somerset. But this did not last long. Somerset married the divorced wife of the Earl of Essex,
and was accused of helping her to poison Sir Thomas
Overbury, a man she hated. So he was disgraced, and
was succeeded in the king's favour by George Villiers, afterwards
Duke of Buckingham. Buckingham was young, handsome, and
brave, but very rash and headstrong. He had so much influence
over James and his second son Prince Charles, that all who wanted
promotion at court bribed and flattered him, and in a few years he
became the richest and most powerful peer in England. Things
might have been different if the king's eldest son, Henry, Prince
of Wales, had lived, for he was a bright, adventurous, and able
young prince, much beloved by the people. But he died in 1612,
and Charles, a weakly and reserved lad, became the heir to the throne.

<small>Rule of favourites, 1612-1621.</small>

6. Proposed Spanish Marriage.—James, who sincerely
loved peace, had long ago ended the war with Spain, and now wished
to marry Prince Charles to the Infanta Maria, daughter of Philip III.
This was very unwise, for the English hated the Spaniards,
and did not want a Roman Catholic princess. Queen Elizabeth
would have felt this at once and given way, but James went on for
twelve years trying to arrange the match, and constantly irritating
his people. After all it came to nothing, for though "Baby Charlie
and Steenie," as James called Charles and Buckingham, made a
romantic journey to Spain, the Infanta did not like the prince,
and the Spanish king wanted to make him a Roman Catholic, so
the match was broken off in 1623. But for a great part of James's
reign it made his people uneasy, and this same foolish project led
the king to commit the one really cruel act of his life.

The brave Sir Walter Raleigh had been condemned to death in
1603 for being concerned in a conspiracy to put Arabella Stuart (a
great-great-grandchild of Henry VII.) upon the throne, and he had
remained in prison for thirteen years writing his *History of the
World*. In 1616 he told the king that he believed
he could find his way to a gold mine in Guiana; and
James, always in want of money, set him free to make
the voyage. But he told him he must not fight the
Spaniards, or he would lose his head. The expedition was most

<small>Disaster and execution of Raleigh, 1616-1618.</small>

PREROGATIVE AND PARLIAMENT.   157

unfortunate. Raleigh stayed to guard the mouth of the River
Orinoco, and sent the other ships up to search for the mine. They
could not find it, but destroyed a Spanish village, and Raleigh's son
was killed. Sooner than come back empty-handed, Raleigh wished
to seize some Spanish treasure-ships, but his crew mutinied, and he
returned to England broken-hearted, and was beheaded under his
sentence of thirteen years before. The people, who knew that this
was done merely to please the King of Spain, were very indignant
at the death of the great explorer and historian, who, whatever
might have been his faults, was a brave and noble man.

7. Thirty Years' War.—Three years after Raleigh's death
James found he should be obliged to call another Parliament. He
had married his eldest daughter Elizabeth in 1613 to the Elector
Palatine Frederick V., one of the chief Protestant princes of
Germany, who ruled over the Rhine country near
Heidelberg. A few years later the Bohemians revolted   Outbreak of Thirty Years' War in Germany, 1618.
against Ferdinand, Emperor of Germany, and chose
Frederick as their king. But the King of Spain, with
other Roman Catholic princes, joined with the Emperor
against the Protestants, and the terrible Thirty Years' War began.
Very early in this war Frederick lost not only Bohemia, but the
Palatinate as well, and he and his wife were fugitives. They came
to James for assistance, and he could not give it without Parliament.

But now came a serious reckoning. During the last seven years
the king had been levying money by heavy fines,   Illegal levying of money.
benevolences, forced loans, and other illegal means.
He sold peerages for enormous sums, allowed the Dutch
towns to pay back their debts at half their value, and created the
new order of "baronet," which any man might buy for £100.
Moreover, he had granted "monopolies" of all kinds to Buckingham
and his friends, by which the people were greatly oppressed and the
law-courts were shamelessly corrupt. The judges, appointed by the
king, were underpaid, and took gifts from the suitors before cases
were decided.

8. Third Parliament, 1621-1622.—Now among the men
elected to the new Parliament were many who saw that it was time
to stop this despotic government of the king. The chief of these

were John Pym, member for Calne and afterwards for Tavistock, and John Hampden, a Buckinghamshire squire. Both were upright, resolute, and brave men, who from this time were to struggle till death for the liberty of England. With them were also Sir John Eliot, vice-admiral of the fleet, fiery and outspoken by nature; Coke and Selden, the famous lawyers; and Wentworth, who only sided with the patriot party for a time because he hated Buckingham. All these men were to play a great part in the struggle of the next forty years.

They granted a small sum to prepare for war, and then remonstrated against the illegal fines and monopolies, and the corruption of the judges. The monopolies James was forced to abolish, and the Commons impeached Sir Francis Bacon, then Lord Verulam, for bribery and corruption.

Impeachment of Bacon, 1621.

Bacon, who had been Lord Chancellor for three years, had just published his famous work, the *Novum Organum*, and ranked first among the writers of the day. Unfortunately he was not as upright as he was able. When tried before the House of Lords he did not deny having taken bribes, but said he had only followed the custom. He was condemned, deprived of his offices, and heavily fined; but the king pardoned him, and he retired on a pension of £1200, and devoted himself to science.

Meanwhile the king was preparing, in a half-hearted manner, for war. He still clung to the idea that he might fight the Emperor Ferdinand, and yet remain friends with Spain, Ferdinand's ally. This was folly, for the King of Spain would never fight against the Emperor. Pym and Coke drew up a petition which the Commons sent to the king, telling him boldly that he ought to break with Spain, and marry Charles to a Protestant. Deeply offended, the king treated their advice as an impertinence. They in their turn protested that they had a right to freedom of speech, and James in a rage tore their protestation out of the Journal Book of the House, and dissolved Parliament, sending Pym, Coke, Selden, and other leading members to prison. So ended the third Parliament, in which the Commons had certainly gained some advantages. They had abolished

Dissolution of third Parliament, 1622.

monopolies, reformed the law-courts, and revived their power of impeachment and their right to give an opinion on matters of state. But the breach between the crown and Parliament was growing wider. It was about this time that sheets of news first began to be printed, and on May 23, 1622, the first weekly newspaper appeared.

First weekly newspaper, 1622.

9. Last Years of James.—The next year the Spanish marriage was broken off, and Charles and Buckingham came back eager for war with Spain. The king was very unwilling to fight, knowing how difficult it was to get money; but Buckingham urged him on, and he called his fourth and last Parliament to vote supplies. Now that all danger of the Spanish marriage was over, the Commons did not want war, especially as James proposed to make an alliance with France to recover the Palatinate, and to marry Prince Charles to Henrietta of France, who was a Roman Catholic. They voted just enough money to help the Dutch against Spain and to defend the English ports, and then adjourned, promising to meet in the winter and vote more if it was wanted. Meanwhile the treaty of marriage between Charles and the Princess Henrietta was signed, and James was afraid to face Parliament now that his son was pledged to marry a Roman Catholic. With the little money he had, he sent in the spring 12,000 men to the Palatinate under Count Mansfeld, a German officer. The expedition was badly managed, supplies ran short, and disease broke out among the troops, destroying 9,000 of them. The attempt was a complete failure, and James, bitterly disappointed, fell ill, and died of ague. He wrote many works, among others a treatise against tobacco, another on witches, and another on the "divine right of kings." But as a king he prepared great trouble for his people.

Fourth Parliament, 1624.

Disastrous expedition to Holland, 1625.

Death of James I., March 27, 1625.

CHAPTER XVII.

KING AND PEOPLE.

1. Charles I.—All people, except a very few, were full of hope when Charles came to the throne. He was a very different man from his father. Though only five and twenty he was stately and dignified, with dark hair, high forehead, and a grave, melancholy countenance. He was reserved, but gracious in his manner, never giving way to those outbursts of passion and scolding by which James offended his counsellors. Moreover, since Charles had wished for a war with Spain, he had been popular among the people. But those few men, who looked deeper, saw very serious difficulties in the character of the new king. He had the same fixed idea as his father of his prerogative, while he had none of James's frankness and good nature. On the contrary, in spite of his gracious manner, he was both obstinate and insincere. He was a religious man and a good father, but he did not think it wrong to deceive and break his promises to gain his end. "*Pray God,*" said a thoughtful courtier, "*that the king may be in the right way when he is set; for if he were in the wrong he would prove the most wilful of any king that ever reigned.*" Sad and true words; and when we remember how the Commons had already begun to set their will against the king's will, we shall not wonder that Charles's reign was one long quarrel, in which each side grew more and more angry and unjust till the terrible end came.

Character of Charles I.

2. Early Troubles.—The struggle began very soon, for when the first Parliament met, the people were distressed by the disasters in Holland, and mistrusted Buckingham, who had unbounded influence over the king. Moreover, they were irritated that the queen had her priests and Roman Catholic chapel in England. Therefore, though Charles asked for £300,000 to carry on the war, the Commons only granted him

Charles's first Parliament, June 18, 1625.

KING AND PEOPLE.

£140,000; and although it was usual to give the king for life a steady tax called "*Tonnage and Poundage*" on every tun of beer and wine, and every pound of certain articles, they now only gave it for one year. Charles was very angry. He prorogued Parliament (for the plague was raging in London), and bade them meet again in Oxford. Unfortunately before they met, seven ships which Charles had lent to the King of France, were used against the Huguenots at the siege of La Rochelle on the French coast. The Commons reproached the king with giving help to the Roman Catholics, and declared they had no confidence in Buckingham; but Charles would not allow them to discuss his favourite minister, and dissolved Parliament.

<small>Tonnage and Poundage.</small>

<small>Parliament dissolved 1625.</small>

Charles and Buckingham now hoped to gain popularity by carrying on the war with Spain, not considering that they had neither men nor money. A fleet was raised by pressing merchant-vessels into the service, and as there was no regular army in those days, men were called from their homes for soldiers. Sir Edward Cecil, who commanded the forces, had orders to attack some Spanish town, and to seize Spanish treasure-ships coming from America. He sailed into Cadiz Bay and took a fort, and then marched up the country without food. The men got hold of some wine, and became helplessly drunk, and Cecil had to take them back to the ships. He then sailed homewards, and missed the treasure-ships by two days. This expedition gave rise to the well-known nursery rhyme—

<small>Disastrous expedition to Cadiz, Oct., 1625.</small>

> "There was a fleet that went to Spain,
> When it got there, it came back again."

The hoped-for victory had proved a miserable failure, leaving a serious debt, which obliged the king to summon another Parliament.

But before the elections he tried a clever stratagem. He made sheriffs of some of the men who had been most troublesome in the last Parliament, so that they should not be eligible for members. It was all in vain! If he silenced some voices, others would be heard. No sooner had the Houses assembled than Sir John Eliot rose and called for an inquiry into the mismanagement which led to so

<small>Buckingham impeached in the second Parliament, 1626.</small>

many disasters, and the Commons impeached Buckingham. "He has broken those nerves and sinews of our land, the stores and treasures of the king," said Eliot, "his profuse expenses, his superfluous feasts, his magnificent buildings, his riots, his excesses waste the revenues of the Crown. No right, no interest, can withstand him by him came all our evils on him must be the remedies." Charles's only answer was to send Eliot and his supporter, Digges, to the Tower, and when the Commons refused to sit without them, and asked for Buckingham's dismissal, he released Eliot and Digges, but instantly dissolved Parliament before any money had been voted.

King dissolves Parliament.

3. Forced Loans.—Charles was now in difficulties. He had just quarrelled with Louis XIII. of France, partly because he had been obliged to dismiss Queen Henrietta's Roman Catholic attendants, and partly because he felt bound to take the part of the Huguenots of La Rochelle against their king. But to make war he must have money, and though he was levying tonnage and poundage illegally, and fining the Roman Catholic recusants, he was very short of funds. He appealed to the country for a "free" gift of money, but scarcely any one gave. Then some one suggested that though he could not compel people to *give*, he might compel them to *lend*, though it made very little difference, as he was never likely to repay it; so he sent commissioners to every county to require each person to advance money according to his means.

The king levies forced loans, 1627.

It may be imagined what discontent this caused! Under the Tudors the country had been kept at peace and the taxes lightened; even James had only levied money from the customs and from rich men. But now, in order to pay for Buckingham's extravagance and for wars which only ended in disgrace, every man had his private affairs examined and a sum of money forced from him. Eighty gentlemen in different parts of the country would not pay and were imprisoned, and poor men who refused were pressed as soldiers, or had soldiers billeted in their houses.

Great discontent.

At last the preparations for war were complete, and Buckingham sailed to La Rochelle with a fleet of a hundred ships. He besieged the fortress of St. Martins, in the island of Rhé, opposite the town, and if he had succeeded, the war might have been popular, as it was to help the Protestants. But, as usual, all went badly. The French broke through, and carried food to the fortress. Buckingham's troops died of disease, and he was forced to come home for reinforcements. *Buckingham fails to relieve La Rochelle, 1628.*

4. Petition of Right.—A great sadness fell on the English people. They who had been so powerful were now constantly dishonoured before other nations. They who had boasted of law and freedom now saw men imprisoned who had committed no crime. Five country gentlemen who had been sent to prison had appealed to the judges for a writ of *habeas corpus*,[1] which obliged the gaoler to produce his prisoner in court, and show the warrant, stating the charge against him. Now, against these men there was no charge, for it was no crime to refuse to lend money, and the Magna Charta had said that *Five gentlemen appeal against imprisonment.* "*no man shall be taken or imprisoned unless by lawful judgment of his peers or the law of the land.*" Nevertheless, the judges had sent these men back to prison, fearing to displease the king.

Parliament now demanded their release, and Sir John Eliot and Sir Thomas Wentworth spoke bold words. "We must vindicate our ancient liberties," said Wentworth; "we must reinforce the laws made by our ancestors." The Commons then drew up a "Petition of Right" against illegal taxation, benevolences, and imprisonment, asking the king to promise, *first*, that no free man should be asked for a loan without consent of Parliament; *secondly*, that no free man should be sent to prison without a cause being shown; *thirdly*, that soldiers should not be billeted in private houses, and *fourthly*, that martial law should cease. The House of Lords agreed to the petition, and though the king struggled hard against it, he was so pressed for money that he was obliged to give way, and on June 7, 1628, it became law. Throughout the country bonfires and ringing of bells told how the people rejoiced at the vindication of their liberty, and the Commons granted the supplies

---

[1] So called from the first words of the writ *produce the body.*

for which Charles had asked. But when they went on to ask for Buckingham's dismissal, the king refused to listen, and prorogued Parliament for a time.

They had no occasion to impeach the favourite again. Just as Buckingham was starting from Portsmouth on a second expedition to La Rochelle, a fanatic named John Felton, who had been refused promotion in the army, and looked upon Buckingham as a public enemy, stabbed him to the heart with a knife at the door of the public hall, crying, "God have mercy on thy soul." When the confusion was over the assassin was found walking up and down without his hat. He had not attempted to escape, and was afterwards hanged.

<small>Assassination of Buckingham, Aug. 23, 1628.</small>

5. Sir John Eliot.—The hated duke was dead and the people rejoiced. But Charles made Weston, Buckingham's secretary, High Treasurer, and all went on as before. The fleet went to La Rochelle, but had no success, and in 1629 Charles made peace with France. Richelieu had conquered La Rochelle, and immeasurably lowered England's position in the world. In fact, everywhere on the continent the Catholics were gaining ground; and for this reason, the people in England were very uneasy when the king raised Laud, Bishop of Bath and Wells, to be Bishop of London. Laud loved rich decorations, and services with great ceremonial like the Roman Catholics, and always upheld "divine right" and the absolute power of the king. This absolute power Charles was now using to levy tonnage and poundage whenever he chose, seizing the goods of any merchants who refused to pay.

<small>Laud made Bishop of London, 1628.</small>

It happened that some of these goods belonged to a member of Parliament, and, when the House met again in January, 1629, Sir John Eliot advised that the custom-house officers who had taken them should be sent for and punished. The officers pleaded that they had acted by the king's order, and Charles bade the speaker adjourn the House. This was done, but when the members met again, and again an order came to adjourn, they would not listen. The speaker tried to rise, but two members held him down in his chair, and the doors were locked, while Eliot put the vote that "*they were traitors who should bring in changes in religion, or who should take or pay custom duties*

<small>Parliament becomes defiant, 1629.</small>

not granted by Parliament." Just as the members were shouting "Aye, aye," the guards came by the king's order to break open the doors. There was no need; the house adjourned immediately, and a few days later the king dissolved Parliament. He sent Eliot and several other members to prison, but soon released those who made submission. Three only—Eliot, Valentine, and Strode—refused to say anything against the rights of Parliament, and Eliot, after remaining three years and a half in the Tower, died, the first martyr to the cause of liberty. *Tumult and dissolution. Death of Sir John Eliot, 1632.*

6. Wentworth and Laud.—For the next eleven years Charles ruled without a Parliament, and his chief ministers were Weston, Laud and Wentworth. We have seen how such men as Eliot and Pym had risen up to defend the liberty of Parliament; two equally determined men, Wentworth (afterwards Lord Strafford) and Laud, now upheld the despotic power of the king. The question was which would conquer. Wentworth, who was very ambitious, had broken with his old friends directly after Buckingham's death, and sided with the king. He became President of the Council of the North, and ruled with a rod of iron. Laud, who was far more conscientious and single-minded, was unfortunately narrow and bigoted, and these two men first helped to ruin their master, and then died as martyrs to his cause.

For the first five years all was outwardly quiet. Moderate men felt that the Commons had gone too far, and insulted the king; and as Weston was a careful treasurer, and did not oppress the people with taxes, they were content. It was at this time that the inland post-office was first established, and letters were sent by weekly post. Hackney coaches too, which first began to run in 1625, became common, but they were not allowed in the crowded streets; and sedan-chairs were introduced in 1634 for carrying people within the town. A great scientific discovery took place about this time. Harvey, the king's physician, published in 1628 his work on the circulation of the blood. In the country we have a glimpse of peaceful life in the simple-hearted poet-clergyman, George Herbert, who wrote his quaint religious poems in the Rectory of Bemerton in Wiltshire, and went to his rest in 1633, before the troubled times began; while in 1634 the *Inland Post. 1625. Harvey, George Herbert and Milton.*

poet Milton wrote his "Comus" at Horton, in Buckinghamshire, having given up the Church because he would not be allowed to speak his mind freely.

At this time the Puritans were emigrating in large numbers to New England. A thousand were taken by John Winthrop in 1630, and during the next eleven years no less than twenty thousand crossed over the sea. Lord Baltimore, who was a Roman Catholic, also founded a new colony, called Maryland, in 1634, to the north of Virginia. In this colony, although it was founded for Roman Catholic "recusants," the first law was that every one should freely follow his own religion.

Emigrations to America.

Such asylums of freedom were now greatly needed, for at home matters grew worse and worse. Wentworth was sent in 1633 to govern Ireland, where the new "plantations" of English and Scotch made the natives very uneasy. In one sense he ruled well. He called an Irish Parliament, and obtained enough money to pay a well-disciplined army, with which he kept good order. He encouraged trade, and the linen manufactures of the north were started in his time. But he had no respect for promises nor for law. He was anxious to be "*thorough*," as he wrote to Laud, and he paid no heed to the wishes of the people, but put down the Roman Catholic religion with great severity, and tried to colonise Connaught, though the king had given his word it should not be done. Thus his reign was one of terror. So long as his firm hand was over them, the Irish were quiet, but a terrible reaction came, as we shall see, when he left them.

Wentworth's rule in Ireland, 1633-1639.

7. Laud and the Puritans.—The same year that Wentworth went to Ireland, Abbot, Archbishop of Canterbury, who had always been a peacemaker, died. Then Laud became archbishop, and two years later, in 1635, when Weston died, he became really the chief minister in England. He began at once to make many changes towards the old religion, such as putting back the altar to the east end of the church, whereas for a long time it had stood in the middle, restoring painted windows, and replacing the crucifix in Lambeth Chapel. These things alarmed the Puritans,

In our time any one who does not like a church service can go elsewhere, but then no one thought it possible to have different kinds of worship; there was one church, and everyone was forced to attend. So when any one in authority like Laud made changes which most people disliked, trouble was sure to follow. The Puritans had now increased very largely, and Sunday was, by order of Parliament, kept as a much more serious day than formerly. In olden times sports and pastimes went on in most villages, but now the justices of the peace put these down because they led to drunkenness. Laud and the king, paying no attention to the law, determined to restore the games, and ordered the clergy to give this out from the pulpit. They refused, and hundreds of Puritan ministers were in consequence deprived of their livings. Nor was this all, for just at this time three men—Prynne, a barrister, Bastwick, a physician, and Burton, a clergyman—were punished by the Star Chamber for writing pamphlets against Laud's government. They had their ears cut off in the pillory, and were imprisoned for life. These things made many moderate men side with the Puritans. Thus we see that step by step the king and his ministers were losing the love of the people. *Sentences on Prynne, Bastwick, Burton, 1637.*

8. Ship-Money.—Charles had long ago broken his promises given in the "Petition of Right," and had been raising money in the old ways, punishing severely all who resisted. Now, as a fleet was wanted, he commanded all the coast towns to provide him with ships, as they had done for Elizabeth when the Armada threatened England, or to give him "ship-money" instead. This was directly against his promise in the Petition of Right, and when he went farther, and levied the tax in the inland towns as well, a Buckinghamshire squire named John Hampden refused to pay, and appealed to the law. Although all the judges were at that time appointed by the king, five out of the twelve boldly declared that Hampden was right; but as the majority were against him, the tax was continued, and all England was indignant. *King levies ship-money, 1634-1638.* *Hampden appeals.*

9. Laud and Scotland.—Even this storm, however, might

have passed over, if the king and Laud had not just at this time quarrelled with the Scots by ordering them to use the English Prayer-book. Ever since the Reformation the Scots had used the extempore prayer, and now they refused to have a prayer-book thrust upon them.

Charles attempts to force a prayer-book on the Scots.

When the clergy began to read from it in the principal church of Edinburgh, an old woman threw a stool at his head, and there was the same feeling of rebellion all over Scotland. The king sent a message requiring the congregation to submit, but the only result was that they solemnly renewed the National Covenant which had been made in 1557, and gentlemen, nobles and ministers, rode round the country with a declaration, which the people signed wherever they went.

The Covenanters, 1638.

The king was very angry, and marched to the Border. But the Scotch Covenanters were prepared, while the English soldiers sympathized with the Scots, and Charles was warned that they would not fight. So he was obliged to give way, and returned to London, secretly determined to come back and conquer. He sent for Wentworth, now Earl Strafford, to come home. Strafford came, and advised him to call a Parliament, while he himself hurried back to Ireland to bring over his well-disciplined troops.

Lord Strafford recalled to England.

10. The Short Parliament.—Neither Strafford nor the king, however, knew how dissatisfied the people had been growing. Parliament met on April 13, 1640, but only sat for three weeks. They refused to vote any money till their grievances were redressed, and they would not hear of a war with Scotland. So Charles, obstinate as usual, dissolved Parliament, and marched north with such an army as he could muster. The Scots had been beforehand with him; they had invaded Northumberland, and now drove back the English at Newburn, near Newcastle, and out of Durham. Charles found himself obliged to make peace by promising a large sum of money, and this he could not get without another Parliament.

11. The Long Parliament, 1640-1653; 1659-1660.—But now in his difficulties any Parliament was sure to be his master, and the "Long Parliament," which met on Nov. 3, 1640, lasted longer than the king's life. The first thing the Commons did was

KING AND PEOPLE. 169

to set at liberty the men whose ears had been cut off, and the next was to impeach Laud and Strafford. They hated Strafford most, for he had deserted his party, had planned to bring an Irish army into England, and had encouraged the king to act in defiance of Parliament. He was in Yorkshire, and wanted to return to Ireland, but Charles promised that if he would come to London not "a hair of his head should be touched." So he returned, and as he entered the House of Lords he saw Pym, followed by three hundred members, standing at the bar of the House, and bringing the message of his impeachment from the Commons. He was sent to the Tower, and on Jan. 30, 1641, he was tried in Westminster Hall. During the trial young Sir Henry Vane, whose father was a courtier, while he himself was a great friend of Pym, was able, from some of his father's papers, to show that Strafford had proposed to govern the kingdom with the help of an Irish army. Still it was so difficult to convict the minister legally, that the *impeachment* or prosecution according to usual law, was changed to a *bill of attainder*, or special condemnation by Parliament.

Trial and execution of Strafford, 1641.

The bill was sent to the king to sign. Charles refused at first, but an angry crowd gathered round Whitehall, and the queen grew alarmed, so at last, bursting into tears, he appointed a commission to sign the bill which sent his faithful servant to the scaffold. Strafford, far nobler, had written to his master, relieving him from his promise to protect him, yet he felt the desertion bitterly. "Put not your trust in princes," said he, as he prepared for death. He was beheaded on May 12, 1641. Laud was not beheaded till 1645.

2. Important Reforms.—After Strafford's death Parliament made great reforms. A "Triennial Act" was passed ordaining that there must be a Parliament at least every three years, and that no future Parliament could be dissolved without its own consent. The Council of the North, the Star Chamber, and the Court of High Commission, were abolished, and statutes were passed against illegal taxation. There were now two parties in Parliament. One was the court party, formed of those who wished not to be too hard upon the king; the leaders of this party were Lord Falkland—a brave, gentle, and

Triennial Act and other reforms, 1641.

noble spirit—and Hyde, afterwards Lord Clarendon. The other was the Puritan party, with Pym as leader, and he proposed that councillors, judges, and ministers should in future be appointed by Parliament. While this was being discussed, and Charles was away in Scotland, terrible news came from Ireland.

13. Grand Remonstrance.—The Irish, no longer kept under control, had risen and massacred the Scotch and English, killing men women and children, and driving them out to die in the snow or drown in the river. All England shuddered with horror, and a panic set in when the Irish showed a commission bearing the king's seal authorising them to take up arms. Charles had, of course, not dreamed of a massacre, but there is no doubt he had hoped to rouse the Irish against the English Parliament. He succeeded, but not as he wished, for Pym and Hampden pointed out boldly to the House that they could no longer trust the king nor his ministers, and a "Grand Remonstrance" was drawn up, showing all the evils they had suffered for years past, and demanded ministers appointed by Parliament. A violent debate followed from early morning to midnight, and at last the "Grand Remonstrance" was passed amidst an uproar which would have ended in bloodshed but for Hampden's resolute firmness.

Massacre in Ireland.

14. Attempt to Seize the Five Members.—Five days later the king returned from Scotland, and trusting that many members would still support him, he sent to impeach Lord Kimbolton, and five members in the Commons— Pym, Hampden, Holles, Haselrig, and Strode. He promised "on the word of a king," to do no violence, but the Houses would not trust him, and refused to give up the members. The next day he broke his word, and came down to the House with guards and a long train of armed cavaliers to seize the members. As he entered he saw that their seats were empty; they had been sent for safety to the city. "Since I see my birds are flown," said he, " I do expect from you that you will send them unto me as soon as they return hither, otherwise I must take my own course to find them;" and he walked angrily away, the members shouting, "Privilege, privilege," as he went.

He never found the five culprits. London, always powerful, was now entirely on the side of liberty. The city was not in those days a mere mass of warehouses and offices as now. Three hundred thousand people then had their homes between Temple Bar and the Exchange, the merchants in richly furnished houses, the shopkeepers above their stores, together with the 'prentice lads, who cried, "What d'ye lack" at the booths which served as shop-fronts. Each trade had its "Company," such as the Merchant Tailors, the Fishmongers, or the Goldsmiths; and these companies had their trained bands, in which aldermen, shopkeepers, and apprentices were the officers and soldiers. It was under this powerful protection that the five members now met a committee of the House of Commons every day, and after a week were brought back in triumph along the river to Westminster.

London defies the king.

15. Outbreak of Civil War.—By that time it was clear the king was no longer master in London, and he had left with his family for Hampton Court. The queen crossed over to the Netherlands with the elder children, taking the crown jewels to raise money; and on Aug. 22, 1642 the king raised his standard at Nottingham. Civil war had begun.

For the next four years there was fighting all over England. Roughly speaking, the west and north sided with the king, while the east and south held by the Parliament. Sixty-five of the peers and nearly half the Commons rallied round their sovereign. The king's nephew, Prince Rupert, son of the Elector Palatine, commanded the Royal Cavalry, which was composed of gentlemen and their sons, bold, dashing riders known as "Prince Rupert's Horse"; while the whole of the kings party went by the name of the "Cavaliers." The rest of the Commons, together with twenty peers, and many country squires, farmers, merchants, and tradesmen, took the side of the Parliament; and because all servants and apprentices wore their hair cropped short, the cavaliers nicknamed them "Roundheads."

King's party or "Cavaliers."

Parliamentary party or "Roundheads."

At first the king had the advantage. The Earl of Essex, who led the Parliamentary army, wanted to make terms with Charles rather than to overthrow him, and Prince Rupert's dashing horsemen struck

172   HISTORY OF ENGLAND.

terror into the farmers and shopkeepers who had turned soldiers.
At Powick Bridge, and at Edgehill, in Warwickshire,
<small>Powick Bridge and Edgehill, 1642.</small> though neither party conquered, the royal troops had on the whole the best of it, and Essex retreated. Charles followed, till he reached Brentford and threatened London. If he had taken it and all its wealth, the war might have ended; but the trained bands marched boldly out to Turnham Green, and the king's army retreated.

16. Royalist Successes and Reverses.—Charles now made his headquarters at Oxford, and little by little the south-west counties were gained by the royalists. The whole country was at war. In the north the Parliamentary leader, Fairfax, was sorely pressed. In the west the Cornishmen, who were fervent royalists, were defeating General Waller, while Prince Rupert was fighting Essex in Oxfordshire. The Parliamentary council was always hoping to make peace. Pym and Hampden alone saw that the struggle must be fought out, and these two brave men were soon to pass away. On June 18, 1643, Prince Rupert, marching westward against Waller, <small>Death of Hampden, June 24, 1634.</small> defeated Hampden with a small party of horse at Chalgrove in Buckinghamshire, and Hampden rode off the field, his head hanging and his hands on his horse's neck, mortally wounded. After lying six days at Thame, striving to write down his plans for the Council, he died, crying, "Oh Lord, save my country." During the next two months town after town fell to the royalists; Bath, Exeter, Bristol, Dorchester, and many other towns were taken, and Gloucester was closely besieged. The Parliament was in great danger, for the people of London were growing dissatisfied. But a change was at hand. By <small>Parliamentary successes, Falkland killed, Sept. 20, 1643.</small> great efforts a fresh army was collected under Essex, with which he raised the siege of Gloucester. Then turning back, he met the royalists at Newbury in Berkshire, Sept. 20, 1643, and there Lord Falkland fell, crying, "Peace, peace," and found rest in death.

Meanwhile Pym had sent Sir Henry Vane to Scotland for help, <small>League with the Scots, Sept. 25, 1643.</small> and a "Solemn League and Covenant" was signed, in which the Scots promised to fight for the Parliament on condition that the Presbyterian religion was protected. This league was scarcely signed when Pym died, on Dec. 8, worn out with anxiety.

Map V. CHIEF BATTLES AND SIEGES OF THE CIVIL WAR

— Royalist Successes
— Parliamentary D°
— Indecisive

17. Oliver Cromwell.—But another leader was already prepared to take his place. Oliver Cromwell, a stern, zealous, resolute man, the son of a gentleman in Huntingdonshire, had long been watching the troubles of his country. He had sat in the Parliament of 1628, when the Petition of Right was passed; he had spoken in 1641 against the cruelties of the Star Chamber; and when war broke out he began at once to levy a troop to fight in the Parliamentary army. Very early in the war he saw that the rabble collected on their side could never stand against the high-spirited cavaliers; and he formed his troop of gentlemen and freeholders, who fought not for plunder, but for liberty and religion. Among such men each had his own religious opinions, and Cromwell did not care whether a soldier was a Presbyterian, Baptist, or Independent, so long as he loved God and would fight for the Parliament. The result was, that long before Pym died, "Cromwell's Ironsides," as they were called, were as famous as "Rupert's Horse," and wherever they went victory followed. It was entirely owing to them that the first great Parliamentary victory was gained, when seven months after Pym's death, the Scots and Roundheads together, led by General Fairfax, met and defeated the royalists at Marston Moor.

Cromwell's Ironsides.

Battle of Marston Moor, July 4, 1644.

18. Battle of Naseby, June 14, 1645.—Cromwell had now great influence, and saw clearly that the war would not end till the Parliamentary army had more resolute leaders. He told the Council that they must remodel their army, which was led by members of Parliament, and put military officers in their place. This was done; and by what was called the "Self-denying Ordinance," members gave up their commands. The army was reconstructed, and Sir Thomas Fairfax put at its head, and at his special request Cromwell was allowed to remain a short time longer as lieutenant-general. In that short time the work was done. The "New Model," as the army was called, met the royalists at Naseby, in Northamptonshire, and defeated them utterly. Charles fled to Wales, and afterwards to the Scotch army at Newark; and little by little the garrisons all fell into the hands of the Parliament. The Council offered to take back their king if he would give them complete power over the

Self-denying Ordinance.

army for twenty years, and grant freedom of worship to the Puritans. But Charles was still bent on setting one party against another, that he might come back as master. At last the Scots, tired of his intrigues, accepted £400,000 for their expenses in the war, and handed the king over to Parliament, Jan. 30, 1647.

19. The King a Prisoner.—He was lodged at Holmby House, Northamptonshire, and treated with great respect, and he hoped soon to be king again, for the Parliament and the army had begun to quarrel. Now the war was over, Parliament wanted to disband the army, paying them only one-sixth of their due. But the army was composed of men who had made great sacrifices for their religion and liberty, and they refused to disband till they were promised freedom to worship as they chose, till their arrears were paid, and the widows and orphans provided for. In fact they knew that they were the strongest, and one day, while the quarrel was going on, a body of horse, commanded by Cornet Joyce, went to Holmby House, and carried the king off to Hampton Court, so as to have the power in their own hands.

He is seized by the army.

Meanwhile Parliament was invaded by a city mob, and serious riots seemed likely to take place. In this dilemma part of the army marched to London under Cromwell and Fairfax, and determined to make their own terms with the king.

The old story began again. Charles pretended to treat with them, while all the time he was secretly plotting with the Scots and Irish, promising each whatever they wanted if they would rise and support him. He escaped to the Isle of Wight on Nov. 12, where, however, he was again confined in Carisbrooke Castle. But he had succeeded in persuading the Scotch to invade England, and in exciting a royalist insurrection in Wales, Kent, and Essex.

Plots with Scots and Irish.

This second civil war brought the king's ruin. Fairfax put down the insurrection in Kent and Essex. Cromwell put it down in Wales, and then defeated the Scots at Preston. The soldiers came back, determined to put an end to the king who tricked them with promises while he raised war in secret.

Second civil war, 1648.

There was no chance of peace, they said, so long as he lived. It did not matter now that the judges refused to try the king, or that Parliament would not form a court to impeach him. The army was master, and one morning Colonel Pride, with a regiment of soldiers, stood at the door of the House and turned away all who, like Sir Henry Vane, refused to sit in judgment on their king. This was called "Pride's Purge." After it was over only fifty-three members remained, and these appointed one hundred and thirty-five persons to form a court of Justice. Bradshaw, an eminent lawyer, was made president, and Cromwell and his son-in-law, Ireton, were there; but when the name of the great General Fairfax was called, his wife cried aloud, "He is not here, and never will be; you do wrong to name him." *Pride's Purge. Dec. 6, 1649.*

20. Execution of Charles I.—Before this court, to which only sixty-three men came, the king was summoned on Jan. 20, 1649, and impeached as a tyrant, traitor, and murderer. He refused to defend himself—for indeed the trial was a mockery—and sentence was passed that he should be executed. Nine days later he took a tender farewell of his two youngest children, Henry and Elizabeth, the only ones who were in England, and bade Henry never to be made king while his elder brothers Charles and James were alive. "I will be torn in pieces first," answered the brave child, and the father stept out, calm and dignified, on to the scaffold outside a window of Whitehall Palace, and was beheaded, Jan. 30, 1649.

CHAPTER XVIII.

ENGLAND ATTEMPTS GOVERNMENT BY A REPUBLIC.

1. The Commonwealth.—The king was dead, and the few men, not more than eighty, who still formed a Parliament, were all the Government left in the country. They abolished the House of Lords, and declared that a king was unnecessary. Then they elected a Council of State of forty members to carry on the Government, and on May 19, 1649, proclaimed a "Commonwealth" or

"Free State." We must try and put ourselves in the place of this young Commonwealth, which sprang out of the execution of a king, and yet wished to do well for the country. Fairfax and Vane joined it again, now that it was no longer of any use to protest against the terrible deed. Cromwell was there, stern, earnest, and guided in all his actions by the severe commands of the Old Testament. So was Bradshaw, who had condemned his king because he feared he would ruin the country, and Ireton, Cromwell's son-in-law, a brave, upright soldier. These were the leading men, and with them were many honest republicans, such as Marten, Scot, Ludlow, and Hutchinson.

They had a hard task before them. All Europe looked coldly upon them. One of their foreign ambassadors was murdered at the Hague, where Charles Stuart, the king's eldest son, was openly recognised as Charles II. Another was murdered at Madrid almost before they began their sittings. The people at home, too, were

Dangers to the Commonwealth. discontented, because of the heavy war-taxes, and the country was overrun with highwaymen and disbanded royalist soldiers. The general uneasiness was increased by a book called *Eikôn Basiliké*, or the *Royal Image*, really written by a certain Dr. Gauden, but supposed to be the work of King Charles while in captivity. It gave a touching picture of

Eikôn Basiliké. his piety and suffering, and caused many to look upon him as a martyr, and to wish openly that the good old times before the civil war could come back again. Then the Scots had at once proclaimed Charles II. as their king; while the Duke of Ormond, in Ireland, succeeded in uniting the Roman

Scotland and Ireland are royalist. Catholics, the royalists, and even the Protestants of Ulster, in favour of the young prince, inviting him to come over and fight for his kingdom. Lastly, Prince Rupert was in the Channel with eleven royalist ships, which he had been keeping safely in the Dutch harbours, and now brought to

Prince Rupert in the Channel. attack English traders. All these difficulties made the small band of governors afraid to dissolve Parliament, and let the people decide by new elections how they wished to be governed. On the contrary, this fragment of a Parliament determined to go on as they were; and as the most pressing trouble was the Irish rising, they began by sending

Cromwell to Ireland with 12,000 men. Even in this they had a difficulty, for the soldiers mutinied, and only consented to go when they learnt who was to lead them.

2. Cromwell in Ireland.—Cromwell landed in Ireland on Aug. 15, 1649, when only Dublin remained in the hands of the Parliament. In three months he was master of the country. But he conquered by terrible severity. He knew he must do his work quickly, and he believed he was carrying out the judgment of God for the massacres in 1641. So at the siege of Drogheda, with which the war began, he gave his soldiers orders to spare no one bearing arms. On the night of Sept. 11, when they made a breach in the town wall and entered the city, no less than 2000 men were put to the sword. St. Peter's Church, where many had taken refuge, was set on fire, and of those who surrendered every tenth soldier was shot, and the rest sent as slaves to Barbadoes. At Wexford, on Oct. 11, a similar slaughter took place, though not by Cromwell's orders. After this there was less loss of life, for the other towns were terrified and surrendered, yet these two massacres will always remain a stain on Cromwell's memory. *Siege of Drogheda, and Wexford, 1649.*

He stayed nine months in Ireland subduing the country, and meanwhile the Council at home was governing England. Sir Harry Vane was placed at the head of the navy, and under him was the famous Admiral Blake, who was soon to win such splendid victories. Milton, the poet, was made Latin Secretary to the Council, because he could correspond in that language, and Bradshaw was President. *Home Government.*

3. Cromwell in Scotland.—They had soon to deal with a new difficulty, for news arrived that Charles had landed in Scotland. The Covenanters, though they had hanged the royalist Earl of Montrose, were willing to fight for Charles II. when he swore to uphold the Covenant and the Presbyterian religion. The Commonwealth saw at once how dangerous it would be if Charles marched into England with a Scotch army, and they determined to attack him in Scotland. But when they asked Fairfax to command the army he refused, *Charles II. arrives in Scotland, June 24, 1650.*

saying that they had no right to break the covenant with Scotland unless the Scots attacked England.

Cromwell was therefore recalled from Ireland to take the command, and after being received with great honour in London, was sent north with 16,000 men. When he crossed the Border all the people in the south of Scotland fled northwards, having heard of his severity in Ireland, and the country was left desolate. Many returned when they found how well his troops behaved, yet food was very scarce, and when the army drew near to Edinburgh, Cromwell was obliged to retreat to Dunbar, a town on the sea-coast, so as to get his provisions by sea. Here David Leslie, the Scotch general, managed to place his troops on the Lammermuir Hills to the south of the English army, so cutting them off from Berwick and England. Cromwell was in a very dangerous position, his soldiers were sick and starving, and so long as the Scots remained on the hill, he could not attack them. Fortunately for him the Covenanters became impatient, and one afternoon he saw that Leslie was moving his men down towards a little brook, across which there was an easy passage to Dunbar. He knew at once that Leslie meant to attack him, and resolved to begin first. "*Now*," said he to Lambert, one of his generals, "*the Lord hath delivered them into my hand.*" Before daylight the next morning, Sept. 3, 1650, he set his troops in motion, and with the cry, "The Lord of Hosts, the Lord of Hosts," they charged before the Scots were well awake. A hot fight followed for a few minutes on the brook, but a panic seized the Scots, and as the sun rose the army was seen flying in disorder hither and thither. In one short hour they were scattered. Cromwell first ordered a halt and sang the 117th Psalm, and then pursued the fugitives; 3000 were killed, 10,000 taken prisoners, and nearly all the baggage and artillery seized. Edinburgh opened its gates, and Cromwell took possession of the town.

Battle of Dunbar, Sept. 3, 1650.

Nevertheless he was fighting in Scotland for nearly another year. A new army was formed by the royalists and the covenanters, and Charles II. was crowned at Scone on Jan. 1, 1651. At last Cromwell gained possession of Fife, and cut Charles off from the north of Scotland, while, perhaps purposely, he left the way open to England. Charles, weary of the strict Presbyterians, determined to try his fortune among the English. Breaking up his camp he marched southwards through Lancashire towards the west of England, which had always been loyal. On he went with Cromwell following behind; but so few English ventured to join him that when Cromwell overtook him at Worcester Charles had only 16,000 men against 30,000. Then followed the famous Battle of Worcester on Sept. 3, the anniversary of the Battle of Dunbar. The royalists were totally defeated, General Leslie was taken prisoner, and Charles fled in disguise. He was so sorely pressed that he lay one whole day hidden in an oak tree in Boscobel Wood, Shropshire, while the Parliamentary soldiers were passing to and fro underneath. The miller Humphrey Penderell and his four brothers will always be remembered as having concealed him and saved his life; and after a number of adventures he reached Brighton, then a small fishing village, and crossed in a collier vessel to Normandy. *Battle of Worcester, Sept. 3, 1651.* *Flight of Charles II. 1651.*

4. Navigation Act and Dutch War.—From this time the Commonwealth was respected by foreign nations, and treated as the recognised Government of the country. Admiral Blake had already defeated Prince Rupert at sea, and now Vane determined to strike a blow at the Dutch who had supported Charles, and at the same time increase the English navy. In Oct., 1651, a "Navigation Act" was passed, forbidding foreign goods to be brought into England except by English vessels, or vessels belonging to the country from which the goods came. Now the Dutch were the chief carriers from foreign countries, so this Act took the trade from them and gave it to the English ships. While the question was still being discussed with Holland, the Dutch fleet, under Admiral Tromp, met the English fleet, under Blake, in the English Channel. A fight took place, in which the Dutch were defeated, and a naval war began, which lasted two years. After one battle, Nov. 1652, when Tromp gained a victory, he bound a broom to his masthead and sailed down the Channel to show that he had "swept the English from the seas." But he had boasted too soon, for after many battles, in which the Dutch suffered severely, they were completely defeated, and Tromp was killed. From that time to this, England has re- *Dutch completely defeated, Feb. 1653.*

mained mistress of the seas, and to Vane and Blake we owe the rise of our modern English fleet which had begun under Elizabeth.

5. Expulsion of Long Parliament.—But while respected abroad the Commonwealth was beginning to have troubles at home. We must remember that the eighty men who formed the Parliament had never appealed to the people after the king's death, and therefore could not be said really to represent the nation. Many of them were not so honest and upright as Fairfax, Vane, and Bradshaw; and as there was no check upon them, many unjust things were done. The members gave offices to their friends, while they oppressed those who did not agree with them in religion, and the royalists who did not bribe them, and sometimes perverted the laws for their own interests. When Cromwell came back from Worcester he saw much bad government, and wished to put an end to it. He had now an army which was devoted to him, and he and the officers told the members that they ought to dissolve Parliament, and have a proper one elected. But even Vane was afraid to do this, fearing that the army would get the upper hand and the Republic be destroyed; and the members prepared a bill proposing merely to elect others to sit with them. Cromwell objected that this was not an appeal to the nation, and conferences were held by the officers and some of the members to try and come to an understanding.

Abuses in the Government.

Members refuse to allow a new Parliament.

One day, April 20, 1653, when one of the conferences was going on at Whitehall, Cromwell heard that the rest of the members were passing their bill at Westminster. Quick to act, he hurried down to the House with a regiment of musketeers, and leaving them outside, went in and listened to the debate. When the question was put "that this bill do now pass," he rose and paced the floor, praising them at first for what they had done well, and then blaming them for injustice and self-interest. "Come, come," said he, "I will put an end to this. It is not fit you should sit here any longer. You are no Parliament;" and calling in his soldiers, he bade them clear the House. "What shall we do with this bauble," he cried, taking up the speaker's mace which lies on

Cromwell turns out the members, April 20, 1653.

the table as a sign of authority. "Take it away." The members were so taken aback at this sudden dismissal that only Sir Harry Vane found words to remonstrate. "This is not honest," he cried; "yea, it is against morality and common honesty." Nevertheless Cromwell turned them all out, locked the door, and put the key in his pocket, and the next morning some royalist wag stuck a placard on the door, "This house to let, now unfurnished."

6. Instrument of Government.—In this way the Long Parliament was driven out, after lasting ever since 1640, but as it could not legally be *dissolved* without its own consent, we shall hear of it again. Cromwell and the other officers now summoned an assembly, elected by the people under the guidance of their ministers. It was to be a "Godly Parliament," and went by the name of the "Little or Barebone's Parliament," from a member, Praise-God-Barebone who sat in it. Scotland, Ireland, and Wales each sent six members. Some good Acts were passed—one for the relief of debtors, another that births, deaths and marriages should be registered. But the members wished to make so many reforms that they threw the whole Government into confusion; and after sitting five months, they gave back their power to Cromwell. The Council then drew up an "Instrument of Government," making a new constitution, and put Cromwell at the head of the state as Lord Protector.

The rule of the army.

Little or Barebone's Parliament. July 4 to Dec. 16.

Thus within five years of the king's death one man once more ruled the nation, though his power at first was very limited, for his council was elected for life, and he had no veto on the laws. Moreover, he had many enemies. The Royalists and Presbyterians, the Republicans (such as Vane and Bradshaw), and even the Levellers or extreme Radicals, were all against him for different reasons, and plots of assassination and rebellion were constantly springing up. Yet he ruled well and justly during the ten months before a new Parliament assembled. He made a fair peace with Holland, and concluded treaties with Denmark, Sweden, and Portugal, favourable to English trade. He inquired into education, and gave manuscripts and books to the Bodleian Library at Oxford. He made ordinances which were just to all religious sects, except that

Cromwell Protector, Dec. 16, 1653.

he forbade the use of the Book of Common Prayer, and would not allow the royalist clergy to preach in public ; but even these had their private congregations. He cut down the costs of the law-courts so that all men might have justice, and removed heavy burdens from the land, giving advantages to small farmers and yeoman. He united Scotland by an ordinance to England, and the Scots reckoned the eight years of his government as "years of peace and prosperity." Poor Ireland was less happy. Those who were taken in the war suffered death or exile, while those who had borne arms were banished to the dreary province of Connaught to form new homes.

<small>His ordinances.</small>

The new Parliament met Sept. 3, 1654. It was fairly elected, except that Roman Catholics and royalists were shut out ; but it only lasted five months, the republicans were uneasy. Cromwell expected them merely to carry on his work, but they went back and questioned his ordinances, and Vane raised a debate against any one " single person ", being the head of the State.

<small>His first Parliament.</small>

7. Cromwell's Rule.—Cromwell had by this time grown into the belief that he was called by God to rule the nation, and he was afraid the royalists would rise if he did not rule firmly. So he dissolved Parliament Jan. 22, 1655, and a few months later divided England into ten districts, over which he placed military officers, called Major-generals. In fact, he now governed despotically by military rule, and even imprisoned for a short time his old friends, Vane and Bradshaw, because he feared their influence. On the other hand, he left the judges free ; he allowed the Jews to settle again in England, and he protected the Quakers, a sect founded at this time by George Fox, a weaver. He was always unwilling to punish attacks on his own life, and he made no attempt to enrich himself, though he now lived in state at Whitehall.

<small>Major-generals, 1655.</small>

8. Petition and Advice.—In fact, he did not wish to be a despot, and when in 1656 he rebuked the Duke of Savoy for persecuting his Protestant subjects in the Vaudois, and so was drawn into a war with Spain, he again called Parliament together.

But he excluded many members, and required all who were elected to receive a certificate from the Council. This Parliament began amicably. They drew up a "Petition and advice" requiring that the major-generals should be withdrawn, and formed an "Other House," or House of Lords, in which the peers were to be created by Cromwell. *Cromwell's second Parliament, Sept. 17, 1656.* Then they asked Cromwell to take the title of king, by which he would indeed have gained in dignity, but his power would have been more restricted, for the limits of a king's prerogative were defined by the laws. When he refused this honour, fearing to offend the army, they gave him a mantle of state, a sceptre and a sword of justice, and power to name his successor. *Cromwell refuses title of king.* All worked well the first session, but the next time Parliament met some of the old republicans had gained seats in the place of those who were made peers, and they would not work with the new House of Lords, and began to attack Cromwell himself; so he dissolved them on Feb. 4, 1658, and for the rest of his life governed alone.

It was not for many months. He had now reached the height of his power. His fleet, though it failed in an attack on San Domingo, had taken Jamaica from Spain, and Cromwell made it a flourishing settlement, the foundation of our possessions in the West Indies. His army, allied with the French, *Capture of Jamaica, 1655.* defeated the Spaniards in the Battle of the Dunes (1658), when the English gained Dunkirk. All nations sent ambassadors to him as to a king, and the alliance was eagerly sought.

9. State of The Country.—He had brought order and peace into the country, and trade and agriculture flourished. Even the royalists despaired of upsetting this steady government. Yet the people were not happy at heart. The stern Puritan rule galled them; they missed the dances round the Maypole, the races, the cockfightings, the theatres, and the Christmas mummers and good cheer; and many longed for the old days with a king, free Parliament, open-handed country squires, and a gay court. The republicans were discontented because the republic was crushed, the royalists because a usurper was in the place of a king. Cromwell had tried an impossibility. He wanted the people to work with him in building up an earnest, self-governing country, but his standard was too high for his time, and he knew that he had failed, and that after his death his work would be undone. By failing to establish a settled government he had missed his aim. His enlightened despotism gave the English many benefits, but it did not bestow on them the one blessing they longed for—*the undisturbed supremacy of the law of the land.*

10. Death of Cromwell.—Although he was only fifty-nine his health was breaking, and a pamphlet called "Killing no murder," advocating his assassination, made him uneasy, so that he often went about in armour. The death of his favourite daughter, Lady Claypole, gave the final death-blow. A dangerous ague settled upon him, and though prayers were everywhere offered for his recovery, he knew that he must die. On Aug. 30 he offered a touching prayer for the people, asking that God would "give them consistency of judgment, one heart, and mutual love"; and four days after, on Sept. 3, the day of Dunbar and Worcester, the great Protector passed away. His was a strange and complex character, and we shall never know how far ambition and how far religion and patriotism guided him. Yet we must honour him in that he never spared himself in the service of his country. When England was at her lowest he raised her to honour both at home and abroad, and he died without having enriched himself at her expense. He was buried with royal honour in Westminster Abbey.

<small>Cromwell's death, Sept. 3, 1658.</small>

11. Richard Protector.—So great was the Protector's influence that his eldest son Richard was at once named to succeed him. A fresh parliament met on Jan. 27, 1659, and the lawyers gathered round the new Protector. But Richard was a different man from his father, peaceable and sluggish; the army was not satisfied to be governed by a civilian, and Vane protested openly in the Commons against such a weak ruler. Distracted by quarrels, in which he took no interest, Richard listened to the army and dissolved Parliament, April 22. Then the officers recalled that fragment of the Long Parliament which Cromwell had dismissed—the "Rump" or hinder end of a Parliament, as it was coarsely called. The Rump did not want Richard, so he calmly resigned, and retired into private life in

<small>"The Rump." May 7, 1659.</small>

July, after a brief dignity of ten months. But the Rump and the army now disagreed as to who was to have the upper hand. A royalist rising took place, and the soldiers, after subduing it, came back under General Lambert, and guarding the doors of Westminster on Oct. 13, refused to let the members sit. They took the power into their own hands, electing a Committee of Safety from among the officers. <small>Anarchy.</small>

12. Restoration of Charles II.—This again only lasted two months. There was in Scotland another army, led by General Monk, who had once served under Charles I., but had joined the Parliament in the civil war. Monk was a cool, business-like man. He would have been faithful to Richard for Cromwell's sake. But now when he saw anarchy everywhere, he quietly resolved to bring back Charles II. On New Year's Day, 1660, he marched into England, proclaiming that he was coming to bring about a free Parliament. At York he met Fairfax, who had been living in retirement, and though General Lambert brought troops to prevent them from marching south, the soldiers no sooner saw their old commander-in-chief than they deserted to Fairfax, and all resistance was over. Monk entered London, and a month later the Rump was dissolved, and the Long Parliament expired at last. A new and freely elected Parliament met, which was called a "Convention," because it was not called by a royal writ. There were in it so many royalists and Presbyterians that they at once passed a resolution to restore the old government of King, Lords, and Commons, and to invite Charles II. to come and govern them. <small>Monk enters London.</small> <small>Long Parliament expires, March 16, 1660.</small>

Charles had already been in secret correspondence with Monk, and had issued a proclamation at Breda, in Holland, promising a general pardon, religious liberty, and satisfaction to the army; and now, on May 25, he landed at Dover amidst loud rejoicing. On his birthday, May 29, he entered London. The roads were strewn with flowers, the streets hung with flags and garlands, and the fountains ran with wine. The army alone stood sullenly aloof. But the soldiers could not withstand a whole nation mad with joy, and they were men of too earnest and serious natures to excite wanton and useless bloodshed. A few months later the army was disbanded, and these men returned <small>Charles II. returns, May 1660.</small>

quietly to their desks, or shops, or farms. "It seems it is my own fault," said the king slyly, "that I have not come back sooner, for I find nobody who does not tell me he has always longed for my return." Nevertheless, it is very doubtful whether he would have come back, if the Puritan army had not tired out the patience of the nation.

CHAPTER XIX.

THE RESTORATION.

1. Charles II.—No king was ever more heartily welcomed than Charles II. when he came back to "enjoy his own again." The nation was worn out and weary with so many changes, and longed for a settled government. If Charles had only had the good of his people at heart, he might have been a great king. But though he was clever and sagacious, amiable and easy-tempered, with plenty of good sense and judgment, he was not a good man. He was selfish and indolent, and having spent most of his life as an adventurer abroad, he had no true sense of his duty to the country. All through his reign he was aiming at two things. *First*, to have his own way and get plenty of money for his dissolute pleasures without accounting to Parliament for it; *Secondly*, to further the Roman Catholic religion; not because he was deeply religious, but because he wanted to be an absolute king like his friend young Louis XIV of France, and he thought that the Protestant religion made people too independent. He and his brother James, Duke of York, had both been educated as Roman Catholics, though they passed outwardly as belonging to the Church of England. As the English people had striven for centuries to make the king's ministers accountable to Parliament, it is clear that they and the king had directly opposite views.

Character and aims of Charles.

But Charles was far too shrewd to quarrel openly, as his father had done. He was resolved, as he told James, "never to go on his travels again;" so his reign was a confused shifting of power. At one time the king tried to have his will, at another he gave in to Parliament; and through it all, by his careless good-temper, and by sacrificing his ministers whenever it suited him, he managed to keep his throne, and to enjoy life as the "merry monarch" who

"Never said a foolish thing,
And never did a wise one."

2. Clarendon's Administration.—His first chief adviser was Sir Edward Hyde, a royalist who had sat in the Long Parliament, and had been Charles's tutor in exile. He was now made chancellor under the title of Lord Clarendon, and the seven years of his administration were the best of Charles's reign. The "Convention Parliament," which was sitting at the restoration, put to death thirteen of the men who had condemned Charles I. and imprisoned others; and taking the dead bodies of Cromwell, Ireton, and Bradshaw from Westminster Abbey, hanged them on the gallows at Tyburn. After this they passed an "Act of Indemnity," pardoning all others who had fought in the civil war except Vane and Lambert. They next passed to the question of the king's revenue, out of which at that time were paid the expenses of the court, the fleet, the ambassadors, and the judges. They granted him a fixed income for life of £1,200,000, on condition that he should give up certain rights called *military tenures, feudal dues,* and *purveyance*, which had long oppressed the people. This done, they disbanded the army, and then dissolved to make way for a new parliament. Charles, however, who did not feel quite secure with only the trainbands to protect him, quietly kept 5,000 horse and foot soldiers, among whom were the famous body of "Coldstream Guards," which General Monk had formed years before at Coldstream on the Tweed. Charles paid these soldiers himself, and thus formed the first beginning of a *standing army*, though it was not recognised by law.

Act of Indemnity, 1660.

Abolition of feudal tenures, 1660.

First standing army, 1660.

For a time all was rejoicing. The people were so pleased at the king's return that they chiefly elected cavaliers to sit in the new Parliament. The court blazed forth in great splendour; the staid, sober rule of the Commonwealth was forgotten, theatres were opened, revelries of all kinds abounded, and orgies at Vauxhall—a place of amusement first

Cavalier Parliament, 1661-1678.

opened at this time—took the place of sermons and prayer-meetings. With this pleasure-loving life came many evils. Gambling and drinking, duelling and debauchery, were seen everywhere at court. All sorts of follies were allowed, and it was not safe to go out unguarded after dark, because of the mad freaks indulged in even by men of quality in the pitch-dark streets, which were not lighted till towards the end of Charles's reign.

A riotous court.

3. State of the People.—In the country things were better. By degrees many of the royalists settled down in their old homes, and those who had long been divided as Cavaliers and Roundheads, shook hands and forgot their disputes. The people rejoiced to get back their village dances and feasts, and the disbanded soldiers returned to their farms and industries, bringing with them the earnest, serious spirit of the Puritan army. In spite of the numerous coaches now running from the chief towns—while the post ran every other day, or once a week, according to distance,—yet there was really very little intercourse between the country and London, and the political quarrels of this reign did not prevent England from improving steadily. The least prosperous part was the north, where moss-troopers still ravaged the country; where judges could not travel without a strong guard, and bloodhounds were kept to track the freebooters. In fact, it is difficult for us in these days to realize how very unsafe both life and property were in those times.

4. Religious Persecution.—The Scotch border was especially disturbed, because Charles's Parliament did not recognize Cromwell's "Act of Union." The old form of government was restored. Scotland had once more a separate Parliament, bishops were forced upon the people, and those who held to the "covenant" were persecuted without mercy. In Ireland the people suffered from another cause. Those who had served the king in the wars complained that Cromwell's followers had seized most of the land; and though at last, by an "Act of Settlement," the Cromwellians gave up one-third of their gains, these were given away as the Government pleased, and the native Irish received but little.

Grievances of Scotland and Ireland.

THE RESTORATION.

In England the Cavalier Parliament at once restored the Church as it was in Laud's time. The bishops went back to the House of Lords. The Church Service was again used, with some alterations, and from that time to this it has remained the same. But although Charles had promised liberty of conscience to all his subjects, he could not prevent Parliament from passing a "Corporation Act," obliging all officials to renounce the "covenant" and take the sacrament according to the English Church. Moreover, in 1662, an "Act of Uniformity" was passed, allowing no man to hold a living unless he had been ordained by a bishop, and would accept the Prayer-book. All others were turned out of their livings on St. Bartholomew's Day, Aug. 24, 1662, and more than two thousand able men formed congregations in chapels of their own, taking for the first time the name of "Dissenters," as dissenting or separating from the Church.

Corporation Act, 1661.

Even this, however, was not allowed. In 1664 a "Conventicle Act" was passed, forbidding persons to worship in conventicles or chapels; and in 1665 the "Five Mile Act" prevented dissenting ministers from teaching in schools, or coming within five miles of a town. The famous divine, Richard Baxter, who wrote the *Saint's Everlasting Rest*, was one of those driven out; and he tells us that hundreds of clergy with their families were without house or bread, while numbers were imprisoned. It was for preaching in conventicles that John Bunyan, the tinker, lay for twelve years in Bedford gaol, where he supported his wife and family by making metal tags for laces, and in his spare time wrote the *Pilgrim's Progress*. This book and the poems of *Paradise Lost* and *Paradise Regained* which Milton, blind and poor, wrote at this time, give a true picture of the severe Puritan religion of the people.

Acts against Dissenters, 1662, 1664, 1665.

Bunyan and Milton.

During this and the next reign large numbers of Non-conformists emigrated to America, and Charles gave large grants of land to different people, either in payment of old debts or to get more money. It was in this way that Penn, the famous Quaker, received a large territory in payment of a heavy debt, and in 1682 took a body of Quaker emigrants to the New World. Pennsylvania was the first American state in which the Red Indians were treated as equals.

Pennsylvania founded 1682.

5. Royal Society.—But Charles was not entirely mercenary; another charter which he granted does him great honour. As early as 1645, during the civil war, a small group of men, weary of quarrels about *opinions*, determined to study *facts*. They held meetings first in London, and afterwards at Oxford, to discuss questions of science, and there Boyle who improved the air-pump, Hooke, who introduced the use of the microscope, Halley the astronomer, and others explained their experiments and discoveries. After the Restoration Charles II. (who took great interest in science, and a few years later founded Greenwich Observatory) attended some of these meetings, and granted a charter to the members, by which they became "The Royal Society of London." Sir Isaac Newton explained his discovery of gravitation before this society in 1682, and it is now one of the greatest scientific societies in the world.

<small>Foundation of Royal Society, 1662.</small>

It would have been well if all that Charles had done in 1662 had been as wise as his patronage of science. Unfortunately he did three things that year which he had better had left undone. In May he married Katharine of Portugal, who brought the island of Bombay and the fortress of Tangier as her dowry, but she was a Roman Catholic, and the marriage was very unpopular, especially as she had no children, and therefore the Duke of York, also a Roman Catholic, remained heir to the throne. In June he caused the brave Sir Harry Vane, the most moderate and disinterested of all the republican leaders, to be executed on Tower Hill; and this not because anything could be really brought against him, but because, as Charles wrote to Clarendon, "he was too dangerous a man to live." In November, the city of Dunkirk, which Cromwell had taken from Spain, was sold to France, and this made the English people very angry, with Clarendon, especially as they suspected that the king spent the money on his own pleasures.

<small>Marriage of Charles, May, 1662.</small>

<small>Execution of Vane, June 14, 1662.</small>

<small>Sale of Dunkirk, Nov. 1662.</small>

6. Dutch War.—Soon after this the war with Holland broke out afresh. The Dutch and English were always disputing the command of the sea, and New Amsterdam in America had lately been taken by the English and called "New York" after the Duke of York. The leading Dutch statesman, Jean De Witt, was also very sore that Bombay had passed into the hands of England, while Charles hated Holland ever since it had been unfriendly to him in exile. A dispute between English and Dutch vessels on the shores of Africa at last brought matters to a head, and war was declared between England and Holland, and the next year Louis XIV. took the side of the Dutch. The fighting was entirely at sea, and the Duke of York, who was admiral of the fleet, gained a victory off Lowestoft in Suffolk, but unfortunately he did not follow up his advantage. The king had to ask Parliament for a large sum to carry on the war, and they granted £1,250,000 *for the war only*, because they feared it would be squandered by the court. Dutch War, March 1665.

Meanwhile a terrible scourge visited London. In the filthy cities of those days plagues were not uncommon, and in the narrow streets of London, where the upper stories of the houses almost touched, and the clay floors covered with rotten straw, food, and dirt, a hot summer always brought more or less pestilence. The summer of 1665 was hot beyond all experience. In May the plague which had been raging on the continent broke out in London, and went on increasing all the summer, till in September 1500 persons died in one day, and 24,000 in three weeks. On door after door the red cross appeared, to mark the plague within, while the dead-cart, with its muffled bell, passed along at night, and the cry, "Bring out your dead" sounded through the stillness of the almost deserted streets. King, courtiers, members of Parliament, even doctors and clergy fled from the plague-stricken city. Only devoted and earnest men, chiefly the persecuted Puritan preachers, remained to close the eyes of the dead, and comfort the living. Brave General Monk, who had become Duke of Albemarle, Laurence the Lord Mayor, and some others also faced the danger, and remained to keep order and prevent robbery and anarchy from adding to the horrors of the suffering people. Plague of London, 1665.

With the winter the plague died away, after more than 100,000 persons had perished. But trade and prosperity could not return at once, and the weary Dutch war went on. One famous battle in the Downs, between Dunkirk and the north Foreland, with the Duke of Albemarle and Prince Battle of the Downs, 1666.

Rupert on one side, and the Dutch commander de Ruyter on the other, lasted four days without either party gaining the victory.

To add to the troubles, a great fire broke out in Pudding Lane, near London Bridge, by a baker's oven being overheated. An east wind was blowing, and the wooden houses of the crowded streets caught like tinder, and burnt for three days. It was chiefly owing to the energy of the king and the Duke of York that the flames were stopped at last, by blowing up several batches of houses at Temple Bar, Pye Corner, Smithfield, and elsewhere, making gaps which the fire could not cross. The loss was fearful ; 13,200 dwellings and 89 churches were destroyed, as well as the halls of the City Companies, the Exchange, the Custom House, and St. Paul's Cathedral. But in the end the fire was a blessing, for it destroyed the wretched wooden houses, and choked up the foul wells and pipes with rubbish. New brick houses were now built, and the greater part of the water was brought in future from Chadwell springs in Hertfordshire, along a canal called the "New River," which had been completed by Sir Hugh Myddleton in 1619.

Fire of London, Sept. 2, 1666.

New River supply, 1620.

In the midst of all these disasters Clarendon had to apply to the Commons for fresh supplies to refit the fleet ; but they had begun seriously to suspect that the money they gave was wasted on court revels. They insisted on appointing a committee to examine the accounts, and as Charles knew these would not bear examination, he determined to go without the money and make peace. He got Louis to arrange a Peace Congress at Breda, May 1667 ; but before anything was decided, De Ruyter, the Dutch admiral, suddenly sailed up the Medway with sixty vessels, burnt three men-of-war at Chatham, and blockaded the Thames. The people were mad with rage when they found that, after all the money granted, the English fleet could not even defend their own river. They vented their anger on Clarendon, who had long been unpopular both with the king and the country. As soon as the Dutch peace was concluded he was impeached, and fled to France, where he died in exile after writing his *History of the Great Rebellion.* His daughter, Anne Hyde, had been married

Peace of Breda, 1667.

Dutch fleet burns ships in the Medway.

Banishment of Clarendon, 1667.

to the Duke of York in 1661, and was the mother of our two queens Mary and Anne.

7. Cabal Ministry.—When Clarendon fell, the strong cavalier party in Parliament was broken up. Charles in future followed much more his own will, and for the rest of his reign did his best to outwit his Parliament. For some time past those members of the Privy Council who were the more intimate advisers of the king had formed a sort of special committee called the "Cabal" (from the French *cabale*, club). Cabal Ministry, 1667-1673. This committee was the beginning of our present "Cabinet." It happened, curiously enough, that the five cabinet ministers at this time were named Clifford, Arlington, Buckingham, Ashley, and Lauderdale, so that the initials spelt the word cabal. These men were the king's chief advisers during the next six years, and became so hated by the nation that cabal has been a word of reproach ever since.

They were, in fact, the victims of the secret intrigues of Charles. For some time past Louis XIV had been encroaching on the Netherlands, which belonged to Spain. In 1668 he advanced so far that Holland grew alarmed, and De Witt, with the help of Sir William Temple, English ambassador at the Hague, concluded a "Triple Alliance" between the three Protestant countries—Holland, Sweden, and England Triple Alliance, Jan. 1668. —and forced Louis to make peace with Spain at Aix-la-Chapelle. Meanwhile Louis, on his side, hoped to undermine this alliance by a secret understanding with Charles, who was irritated because he could not persuade Parliament to favour the Roman Catholics, or side with France. A secret treaty was signed at Dover between the two kings, in which Charles promised to declare himself a Roman Catholic, and help the French Secret Treaty of Dover, 1670. against the Dutch, if Louis in return would give him £300,000 a year and send French troops to England if the people grew troublesome. Only Clifford and Arlington, who were Roman Catholics, knew of this treaty, and even they did not know the whole. The next year, 1671, Charles got a large grant from the Commons for the fleet, and then prorogued Parliament for a year and nine months.

From treachery he now went on to dishonesty, and by Clifford's advice closed the Exchequer. It had long been the custom for the

13

goldsmiths and bankers of London to lend to the English Government the money which people put into their banks, receiving back both interest and principal out of the revenue. In 1672 the Royal Exchequer owed in this way about £1,300,000, when all England was startled by a Royal Order, declaring that these payments would be stopped. Of course this brought great distress on all the people whose money the goldsmiths had lent, nor was it ever repaid till William and Mary came to the throne.

National bankruptcy, 1672.

While the people were still sore at such injustice the Duke of York openly declared himself a Roman Catholic, and Charles published a "Declaration of Indulgence," suspending all the laws against Roman Catholics and Nonconformists. To crown all, he openly joined Louis, and declared war against the Dutch. At first it seemed as if Holland must be conquered, but De Witt, having been murdered in a riot, young William of Orange, great-grandson of the famous William who had defended the Netherlands in Elizabeth's reign, now came into power. He followed his brave ancestor's example, and persuaded the Dutch to pierce their dykes and let in the sea, and so the allied armies were obliged to retire.

Declaration of Indulgence, 1672.

Second war with Holland, 1672.

8. Test Act.—At last Charles, having no more money, was obliged to let Parliament meet, and face the anger of the Commons. They made him at once give up the "Declaration of Indulgence"; and passed an Act called the "Test Act," requiring all civil and military officials to declare that they did not believe the doctrines of the Church of Rome, and to take the sacrament in the English Church. This obliged the Duke of York to resign his post as admiral, and Clifford and Arlington to retire from office. Ashley, too, who had been made Earl of Shaftesbury, quarrelled with the king, probably because he found out about the secret treaty of Dover. So the "Cabal ministry" broke up, having gained the hatred of the people by the evil done in their time. After this Shaftesbury did all he could to oppose the king. He became the leader of a "country" party or "opposition" in Parliament, and this was the beginning of the division between "ministry" and "opposition" which has continued to our day.

Close of Cabal ministry.

Ministry and opposition.

9. Danby Administration.—Charles, as usual, gave way when he saw Parliament was determined. He chose for his chief minister Sir Thomas Osborne, Earl of Danby, whom the Commons liked, and he made peace with Holland in 1674. The Commons in return granted him liberal supplies. He even allowed Danby in 1677 to arrange a marriage between William of Orange and the Duke of York's eldest daughter Mary. This marriage pleased the people very much, for William and Mary were both Protestants, and as James had no son, Mary was heir to the crown after her father.

Danby administration, 1673-1679.

Marriage of William and Mary, 1677.

But all this time Charles was still secretly treating with Louis. In 1675 he received a yearly pension from him of £122,000, and promised in return not to make any wars or treaties without his consent ; and in 1678, when the Commons urged him to go to war with France, he made another private treaty, receiving £24,000 as a bribe to dissolve Parliament.

Charles receives a pension from Louis.

10. "Popish Plot."—Though all this was secret, yet there was an uneasy feeling in the nation that it was being betrayed, and just then a strange story caused a panic throughout all England. A preacher of low character, named Titus Oates, who had gone over to the Jesuits, declared that he knew of a plot among the Roman Catholics to kill the king and set up a Catholic Government. He brought his tale to a magistrate, named Sir Edmund Bury Godfrey, and shortly afterwards Godfrey was found murdered in a ditch near St. Pancras Church. The people thought that the Roman Catholics had murdered him to hush up the "Popish Plot," and when Parliament met a committee was appointed to examine into the matter. Some papers belonging to a Jesuit named Coleman alarmed them, and so great was the panic that an Act was passed shutting out all Roman Catholics, except the Duke of York, from Parliament. After this no Roman Catholic sat in either House for a hundred and fifty years. But worse followed. Oates became popular, and finding tale-bearing successful, he and other informers went on to swear away the lives of a great number of innocent Roman Catholics. The most noted of these was Lord Stafford, an upright and honest peer, who was executed in 1681, declaring his innocence.

"Popish plot," 1678.

Charles laughed among his friends at the whole matter, but let it go on, and Shaftesbury, who wished to turn out Lord Danby, did all he could to fan the flame.

Meanwhile King Louis had made peace with Holland and Spain at the "Treaty of Nimeguen," and now that he no longer needed Charles's help, he refused to give the pension; and Montague, the English ambassador at Paris, who had reason to be afraid of Danby, showed the House of Commons the despatch in which the pension had been arranged. This despatch had Danby's signature, and a note in the king's handwriting, stating that the despatch was written by Danby at the king's command. The House was thunderstruck. That England's king should be a pensioner of France was too humiliating. Danby was at once impeached, and Charles, to save further discoveries, dissolved Parliament, which had existed for seventeen years and a half.

Treaty of Nimeguen, 1678.

Fall of Danby, 1679.

11. Exclusion Bill.—But the nation was now thoroughly alarmed, and as soon as the next Parliament was elected, in 1679, Danby was sent to the Tower, where he remained five years, and the Commons brought in a bill to exclude the Duke of York from ever coming to the throne because he was a Roman Catholic. Charles, alarmed, sent James out of the country and dissolved Parliament, after it had only sat for two months. In that short time, however, Shaftesbury had passed a most useful Act. It will be remembered that ever since the Magna Charta it had been the right of every Englishman who was arrested to apply for a writ of "Habeas Corpus." But judges and kings had for a long time managed to put aside these writs when it pleased them. Now Shaftesbury brought in a "Habeas Corpus Act" in spite of Charles's opposition, which reformed these abuses, and made the law too clear to be evaded. It effectually provided against illegal arrest, and undue detention in prison before being brought to trial. The gaoler in answer to a writ had to show his warrant for detaining the prisoner; and to allow him his freedom if the offence was bailable.

Habeas Corpus Act, 1679.

Meanwhile the struggle for the Exclusion Bill went on. The next Parliament met in October, and the bill was passed in the

THE RESTORATION. 197

Commons. But in the House of Lords it did not pass, for a very able statesman, Lord Halifax, opposed it. Halifax called himself a "Trimmer" because he was like a man who moves from side to side to balance or trim a boat—he would not let either party go to extremes. Now though Parliament wanted Mary, wife of the Prince of Orange, to be the next sovereign, Shaftesbury was really planning for the Duke of Monmouth, an illegitimate and favourite son of Charles II., to succeed. *Duke of Monmouth.*

This Halifax saw would be a great evil. Monmouth was very popular, and went by the name of the "Protestant Duke," and Shaftesbury pretended that Charles had been married to the young man's mother before he married his queen. Dryden, the great poet of this period, wrote a satirical poem describing Monmouth and Shaftesbury as Absalom and Achithophel plotting for the kingdom. But the king remained *Parliament dissolved, Jan. 1681.* true to the Duke of York, and matters began to look so serious that he again dissolved Parliament.

Then two violent parties arose—the Shaftesbury party, called "Petitioners," who petitioned the king to agree to the bill, and the "Abhorrers," who abhorred the bill. These two parties soon gave each other the nicknames of "Whig" and "Tory." *Whig* meant sour milk or whey, and was a name which had been given to Scotch rebels. The Duke of York's *Whig and Tory.* friends called Shaftesbury's party "Whigs," meaning that they were rebels against the king. *Tory* was a name given to Roman Catholic outlaws in Ireland; and Shaftesbury called the Duke of York's friends "Tories," as being enemies to the Protestants, like the Irish outlaws. Soon these two names lost their real meaning, and have since been used only to mean the party which sides more with the people (*Whig*) and the party which sides with the power of the Crown (*Tory*).

In March 1681 Charles's fifth and last Parliament had met at Oxford, and the Whigs, believing that there was really a conspiracy to bring back Roman Catholic rule, brought armed followers with them. This ruined their cause. People began to be afraid there would be another civil war, and when *Oxford Parliament, 1681.* Charles came with a strong guard to Oxford, and offered that the Princess of Orange should be named regent, and really govern after his death, though James might be called king, he found a strong party to support him. Then all at once, at the end of a week, without warning, he dissolved Parliament, and never had another.

12. Rye House Plot.—His victory was complete. An accusation of high treason was brought against Lord Shaftesbury for plotting with Monmouth, and when the city sheriffs, who were Whigs, chose a grand jury in his favour, Charles found a flaw in the charter of London, and managed to get two fresh sheriffs appointed. By this time, however, Shaftesbury had fled to Holland, where he died the next year, 1683. In his fall he dragged down better men with him. Though their leader was gone, the Whigs still hoped to prevail upon the king. Monmouth had many friends, especially Earls Russell and Essex, Algernon Sidney, Lord Grey, and Lord Howard, and these men formed a confederacy. Whether they meant to urge the people to rise is uncertain, for unfortunately some bold and desperate men, unknown to the party, made a plot to murder Charles and James at the Rye House, a lonely spot in Hértfordshire, on their way from Newmarket to London. The plot was discovered, and though the Whig leaders knew nothing of it, the Crown lawyers took advantage of it to bring them to trial. Essex committed suicide in the Tower, Russell and Sidney were both executed. Lord Russell was a man of noble character, deeply beloved by his friends, who tried to help him to escape. Monmouth even offered to stand his trial by his side, and Lady Russell took the notes in court to help him in his defence. But in those days, when kings made and unmade judges as they pleased, there was little chance of justice in state trials. Russell and Sidney were both condemned, and died bravely for their cause.

Fall of Shaftesbury, 1682.

Execution of Russell and Sidney.

13. Doctrine of "passive obedience."—The Tories now had all their own way. The Duke of York had been employed for some time past in hunting down the unfortunate Covenanters in Scotland. He now returned, and was again made Lord High Admiral, and allowed to sit in the Council without passing the test. The charters of many towns which had supported the Whigs were taken away, and some of the leading Whigs prosecuted and fined. Charles again received a pension from Louis as a bribe not to support William of Orange ; and as he had now a standing army of 9,000 soldiers, besides six regiments abroad, he felt safe. The clergy, too, taught everywhere that "*passive obedience*" to the sovereign was a duty, and Charles seemed almost to have succeeded in becoming an absolute king when death stepped in. On Feb. 2, 1685, he was seized with a fit, and died a few days after. On his deathbed he received the last rites of the Church of Rome from a monk, who was brought secretly to him by the Duke of York. Then, calling in his courtiers and the bishops, he apologised in his old witty way for "being so unconscionably long in dying," and spoke a kind word for his favourite, Nell Gwynne the actress. On Feb. 6, 1685, the "merry monarch" was no more.

CHAPTER XX.

THE REVOLUTION.

1. James II.—The reign of James II. shows how in four years a really well-meaning man could turn a whole nation against himself by sheer obstinacy and faithlessness to his promises. Though Parliament in the last reign had tried to shut him out from the throne, yet, when he declared on Charles's death that he would "uphold Church and State as by law established," everybody seemed satisfied, and he was proclaimed king. The fact was, most people thought that though the new king was a Catholic, yet when he promised to rule according to English law, he would keep his word. Probably he meant to do so at first, but he was a stubborn, narrow-minded man, bigoted and arbitrary ; he could only see his own side of any question, and therefore was quite unfit to govern a free nation.

Every one knew that he was a Roman Catholic, and if he had only quietly followed his own religion, or had even tried to get Parliament to allow other Roman Catholics in England to follow theirs, he might have done much to make all his subjects happy. But he wanted much more than this. *Character and aims of James II.*

He wanted to abolish the Test Act in order to put Roman Catholics into the chief posts in the kingdom, to abolish the **Habeas Corpus Act**, which prevented him from imprisoning those who opposed him, and then, surrounded by his own friends, to bring England back to Roman Catholicism. "I will lose all or win all," he once said to the Spanish ambassador, and he had not sense enough to see that in the way he acted he was sure to lose.

Even before he was crowned he ordered his chapel doors to be thrown open, and mass to be performed in public. He told the bishops that the clergy must not preach against the Roman Catholic religion, and ordered all persons imprisoned for not taking the oaths to be set at liberty.

<small>Arbitrary acts of James II.</small>

This last act was good in itself. The Quaker Penn, who was then in England, and had great influence with James, urged it upon him, and 1200 Quakers, besides twice as many Roman Catholics, came out of prison. But it showed that James meant to act without consulting Parliament, or even the judges, and very soon after he did so in another case. As the revenue was only granted to the king for life, it ceased when Charles died in February, and Parliament did not meet till May. Now it would have upset trade if the custom duties had been stopped for three months, so the minister Lord Guildford proposed to collect them, and to put them aside till Parliament met. But James, determined to establish his power, ordered them to be paid to him direct as they had been to Charles.

2. Monmouth's Rebellion.—Nevertheless the elections were so carefully managed that the new members in the House of Commons were nearly all on the king's side, and a revenue of two millions was voted to him for life without difficulty. The members were specially anxious to show their loyalty because a rebellion had just broken out. Many of those Whigs who had fled to Holland after the Rye House Plot, had urged Monmouth, when Charles died, to cross over to England, and rouse the people against a Roman Catholic king. Monmouth, who was living quietly in Brussels, did not wish to move, but he was over-persuaded. It was finally agreed that the Earl of Argyll, who was also a refugee, should cross to Scotland and call out the Covenanters, while Monmouth went to the west of England.

<small>Revenue voted for life.</small>

Argyll arrived first, on May 2, and his clan of the Campbells

rallied round him. But the leaders who came with him from
Holland interfered too much with his plans, and the king's troops
had heard of his coming, and were prepared to oppose
him, while the Covenanters were many of them afraid   *Failure and death of Argyll, 1685.*
to rise. Argyll's force was scattered, and he was
taken prisoner, sent to Edinburgh, and there executed, refusing
bravely to give any evidence against others. There is a picture in
the lobby of the House of Commons called "The last sleep of
Argyll," showing how one of the covenant lords, who had deserted
his cause, found the earl, who had been true to the last, sleeping
peacefully in his irons an hour before his execution.

All those concerned in the rebellion were severely punished, and
many sold into slavery. In Dunottar Castle the vault is still shown
where the "wild Whigs" were confined before being shipped off to
America.

Monmouth was more successful at first. He was very popular in
the western counties, and no sooner did he land at Lyme in Dorset,
than the people flocked to his standard, shouting, "A Monmouth!
a Monmouth!" By the time he reached Exeter he had 1500 men
with him, and he entered Taunton in triumph, under flags and
wreaths hung along the streets, while a train of young girls
presented him with a Bible and a sword. But only the lower
classes joined him; the gentry and clergy were all for the king, or
thought that if any Protestant interfered, it ought to be the Princess
Mary of Orange and her husband. Many were also
offended that Monmouth allowed himself to be pro-   *Monmouth proclaimed king. June 20.*
claimed King in the market-place of Taunton, though
he had said in his proclamation that he only came to
establish a free Parliament. Meanwhile the king's troops were
hastening against him, commanded by a Frenchman, Louis Duras,
Lord Feversham. He was obliged to retreat, and met them at
Sedgemoor, near Bridgewater. The royal troops were
drawn up in a field protected by a deep trench known   *Battle of Sedgemoor, July 5 and 6, 1685.*
as the Bussex Rhine. Monmouth did not know of this
trench. He started with his army an hour after
midnight to surprise the enemy, and picking his way across the
swamps, threw the outposts into confusion. But the trench stopped
his advance and gave them time to rally, and in the early dawn his

army of peasants and colliers, though they fought desperately, were completely routed. Two days after Monmouth was found half-starved in a ditch. He was taken to London and executed, dying bravely at the last, though he had begged piteously for his life. It gives us a curious picture of the superstition of those days that in his pocket were found spells and charms to open prison doors and preserve him in the battle-field. Two well-known men were in the Battle of Sedgemoor, which was the last important battle fought in England—Churchill, afterwards Duke of Marlborough, was a captain in the king's army; and Daniel Defoe, who wrote *Robinson Crusoe*, fought in Monmouth's ranks.

3. The Bloody Assizes.—The rebellion was at an end, but a cruel revenge followed. Colonel Kirke, a brutal, heartless man, was left in command at Bridgewater.

<small>Kirke's lambs.</small>

His soldiers were ironically called "Kirke's lambs," because, while they had a lamb for their banner, they were ferocious and blood-thirsty. Under Kirke's orders these men hanged whole batches of prisoners with terrible cruelty, and burnt their bodies in pitch. But worse was to come. In September Judge Jeffreys, a man, if possible, more coarse and brutal than Kirke, came with four other judges to try those who had joined in the rebellion. In these "Bloody Assizes," as they were ever after called, no less than 320 people were hanged, and 841 sold into slavery to the West Indies. In Somerset corpses were seen by every roadside and in every village; and children going to school or church might see their father's or brother's head over the doorway. In vain good Bishop Ken begged James to have mercy; the king approved all that was done, while Jeffreys mocked and insulted the unhappy victims with coarse language and brutal jokes. One noble lady, Alice Lisle, was beheaded for merely hiding two fugitives; and only those were spared who secretly bribed the judge with large sums of money. Batches of prisoners were given to favourite courtiers to sell into slavery, and the queen's "maids of honour" received a large sum for obtaining the pardon of the school-girls who presented Monmouth with the Bible and sword.

4. Violation of Test Act.—When all was over James made Jeffreys lord chancellor as a reward, and took advantage of the

THE REVOLUTION. 203

rebellion to add 10,000 men to his army, putting over them several Roman Catholic officers who had not taken the test. Lord Guildford, and Lord Halifax, who was President of the Privy Council, told James that he was breaking faith with Parliament; but he had already arranged with France for a pension, and having a strong army, thought himself safe. He dismissed Halifax, and put Sunderland, an obliging courtier, in his place; and when Lord Guilford died soon after, the infamous Jeffreys, who was a violent upholder of the royal prerogative, had the chief power in the Council.

James appoints Catholic officers.

Just at this time Louis XIV. revoked the Edict of Nantes, and set to work to exterminate the Protestant religion in France. All Huguenot ministers were banished, but the people were forbidden to leave, and regiments of dragoons were sent among them to kill and ill-treat in the most horrible manner any who would not go to mass. The *dragonnades*, as these persecutions were called, were so shameful and cruel that, in spite of all precautions, more than 200,000 Huguenots managed to escape from France into Holland, Switzerland, Germany, and England. Some went into the Church, some into the army, while the whole district of Spitalfields in London was colonized with Huguenot silk-weavers. In fact, by these dragonnades Louis drove the most industrious, skilled, and wealthy of his subjects into foreign lands.

Revocation of the Edict of Nantes Oct. 1685.

This persecution of Protestants by a Roman Catholic king startled the English nation; but James, blind as usual to the feelings of his people, was delighted with what Louis had done. When Parliament met, the Commons reproached him with having appointed Roman Catholic officers contrary to law. But he only scolded them sharply for not trusting him. The Lords were bolder; they told him plainly that he could not put aside or "dispense with" the Test Act of his own will. So, rather than allow further discussion, the king prorogued Parliament Dec. 1685. It never sat again, but was *prorogued* from time to time, and *dissolved* two years later. James always meant to allow the members to sit when they would support him, but that time never came.

Parliament objects to violation of Test Act, 1685.

In this way he prevented public opposition, but still he could not altogether shut people's mouths. The coffee-houses of London were now the chief places where men met daily. A Turkish merchant had first opened a coffee house in Cromwell's time, and they spread rapidly all over the town, each man having his favourite haunt where he met his special friends, who discussed scandal, literature, politics, or religion over their coffee and tobacco-smoke. Popular coffee-houses, such as Wills's in Covent Garden, became almost little parliaments in themselves, and had so much influence that Charles II. had tried to close them in 1675; but there was such an outcry that they had to be opened again, and now people discussed in them daily the strange conduct of the king.

Coffee houses of London.

James, however, cared very little for public opinion. As soon as Parliament was prorogued he privately consulted all the judges as to his "Power of Dispensation." Four of them ventured to tell him that he had no power apart from Parliament. These he dismissed, and put more obedient judges in their place. Then he managed that Sir Edward Hales, a Roman Catholic whom he had made Governor of Dover, should be tried for not taking the test. Hales pleaded that the king had "*dispensed*" with it, and of course the judges, having promised the king, gave a verdict in his favour.

Power of Dispensation.

After this farce James went on steadily, turning out churchmen and putting in Roman Catholics. He began a system called "closeting," that is, taking men into his private room, and asking them whether they would vote against the Test Act. If they would not they were sure soon after to lose their post. James's own brothers-in-law, staunch loyalists, suffered in this way. The elder, Lord Clarendon, was recalled from Ireland, and a Roman Catholic, Lord Tyrconnel, appointed in his place. The younger, Lord Rochester, was dismissed from being high treasurer. Lord Herbert, Rear-Admiral of the Fleet, lost his command, and James even went so far as to summon four Roman Catholic lords and his own Jesuit confessor, Father Petre, to sit in the Privy Council.

Roman Catholics put into office.

He next established an Ecclesiastical Court, something like the old Star Chamber, and put Jeffreys at the head of it. When Compton, Bishop of London, refused to suspend a rector, Dr. Sharp, for preaching a controversial sermon, this court suspended the bishop himself.

Court of Ecclesiastical Commission, 1686.

A new Roman Catholic chapel was now built for the king at Whitehall, and another in the city for one of the foreign ambassadors. Orders of monks began to settle in London, and a large school was opened by the Jesuits in the Savoy. Even James, however, now saw that the people were growing angry. Riots took place in the city, and in order to check any chance of revolt, a camp of 13,000 troops was planted at Hounslow to overawe London. Then, hoping to get the Nonconformists to support him, James published another "Declaration of Indulgence," announcing that Roman Catholics and Dissenters were free to worship as they pleased, and to hold offices without taking any kind of test. A small body of the Dissenters, led by friends of the king, loudly welcomed the Indulgence. But the more thoughtful leaders saw that the kings object was merely to make way for his own party, and they refused to accept a boon which he had no legal right to give. *[Camp at Hounslow. Declaration of Indulgence, April 4, 1687.]*

In vain Pope Innocent XI., a good and wise man wrote advising patience and moderation; in vain King Louis counselled caution; in vain even his own Roman Catholic subjects begged him to govern according to law. James, under the influence of Father Petre, thought that if he only went steadily on, people would see he was working for their good and give way. *[James deaf to warning.]*

5. Attack on the Universities.—He now began to interfere with the universities. He appointed a Roman Catholic, Dr. Massey, to be Dean of Christ Church College, Oxford, suspended Dr. Peachell of Cambridge for refusing a degree to a monk, and expelled the Fellows of Magdalen College, Oxford, because they would not elect a Roman Catholic, Dr. Parker, as their president. A month later he dissolved Parliament, which had not met for two years, and began to prepare for new elections. He asked the lord-lieutenants, deputy-lieutenants, and justices of the peace in each county whether they would encourage the election of members who would vote against the Test Act and penal laws, and those who would not were replaced by others. To crown all, James received the Pope's nuncio or ambassador with great pomp at court. *[Expulsion of Fellows of Magdalen, 1687. New lord lieutenants and officials.]*

The statesmen of England now saw that, unless something was

done, the country would soon be in the hands of a despot, and messengers were secretly sent to Holland to ask William of Orange if he would come and defend the rights and liberties of England. William was quite willing, for he and all the Protestant princes of Europe were seriously afraid of the growing power of Louis XIV., who was James's ally; and it was very important to them that England should remain a strong Protestant country. But two things held William back. First, he wanted to be sure that all parties in England would support him. Secondly, he could not move so long as the French army was threatening the Netherlands. A few months later the way was made clear for him. In Sept. 1688 Louis went to war with Germany, and had work enough on his hands, so William was free.

First suggestions to William of Orange, 1688.

6. Birth of James the Pretender.—Meanwhile great things had happened in England. On June 10, 1688, a son and heir was born to King James. His second queen, Mary of Modena, had been so long without children that no one ever expected this, and the people had been patient under the king's bad government, because they thought that at his death, Mary of Orange would make everything right again. Now this hope was gone, and while James was delighted, the whole nation was in despair. They would not even believe that the child was the queen's son. They said it had been brought into the palace secretly to impose a Roman Catholic prince upon them, and this remained the common belief for many years.

7. Declaration of Indulgence.—A month before this unhappy child was born James had again issued the "Declaration of Indulgence," and ordered all the clergy to read it out two Sundays following in their churches. Now the declaration was certainly illegal, and churchmen thought it wrong besides. So seven bishops, including Sancroft, Archbishop of Canterbury, signed and presented a petition, begging the king not to force their clergy to read it against their conscience. James was very angry, and still more so, when on the Sundays named hardly any clergymen read the declaration, and where they did the congregation walked out of Church. He now ordered the bishops to be tried for seditious libel in presenting a petition against the

Petition of the Seven Bishops.

Government, and, as they would only give their own recognisances, refusing to give bail, they were sent to the Tower.

Then at last the temper of the nation showed itself. The thronging crowds cried, "God bless them," as the bishops' barge passed along the Thames to the Tower, and all England was aroused. One of the bishops was Trelawney of Bristol, and even in the far west the peasants chanted the refrain—

> "And shall Trelawney die, and shall Trelawney die,
> Then thirty thousand Cornish boys shall know the reason why."

8. Trial of the Bishops.—When the day of the trial came the most eminent lawyers pressed forward to defend the bishops, the crowds reached for miles around the courts, and the jury would not have dared to convict them even if they had wished. When the verdict of NOT GUILTY was known the bells rang, the people thronged to the churches, bonfires were lighted, and the crowd not only shouted, but sobbed for joy. James was at Hounslow when a great shout arose in the camp. On his asking what it meant. "Nothing," replied Lord Feversham, "the soldiers are only glad the bishops are acquitted." "Do you call that nothing?" answered the king; "so much the worse for them." Four months later he found out at last that it was so much the worse for him.

9. The Revolution.—The bishops were acquitted on June 30, and that very day Admiral Herbert, disguised as a common sailor, carried a special invitation to William, signed by several noblemen—Earl Danby, who answered for the Tories, the Duke of Devonshire for the Whigs, Bishop Compton for the Church, Lord Russell for the navy, Lord Shrewsbury, Lord Lumley, and Henry Sidney for the people. *Invitation to the Prince of Orange, June 30, 1688.* William now felt sure of support, and on Sep. 30 (when Louis was busy with Germany) he issued a proclamation, which was soon spread all over England, in which he declared he was coming with an army, as Mary's husband, to secure a free and legal Parliament.

At last James was frightened; he put the lord-lieutenants back in their posts and the fellows in their colleges; gave back the charters to the towns and removed Father Petre from the Council. But it was too late! On Nov. 5, 1688, William landed at Torbay with 13,000 men; and though at first *Landing of William, Nov. 5. 1688.*

the people held back, remembering the dreadful consequences of Monmouth's rebellion, in a few days nobles and gentry flocked to his standard. King James was not thrown into any great consternation by the news. He had expected that the invasion would take place in the northern provinces; he now hastened to recall the regiments which had marched in that direction, and to order them to the west. He hoped to cut off the prince from all communication with the rest of the country, and to bring such a large army into the field as would destroy his forces at one blow. On Nov. 19 he joined his army at Salisbury, but, like Richard III., two hundred years before, he found himself all at once deserted by nearly all his supposed friends. Lord Churchill and many other officers with their men joined William's army, and the governors of towns declared themselves on the Protestant side.

James's own daughter Anne, with her husband George of Denmark, fled to Danby at Nottingham, and the unhappy king, forsaken by all, returned to London, sent his wife and child to France, and was starting to join them when some fishermen brought him back. But William was too wise to keep him; he left him very carelessly guarded at Rochester, and James escaped unhindered to France. Before he left he destroyed the writs prepared for the election, and threw the Great Seal into the Thames. He wished to leave confusion behind him, hoping soon to come back with a French army and reconquer his kingdom. Louis XIV received him with honour, and prepared one of the royal palaces for him and his queen.

<small>Flight of James, Dec. 23, 1688.</small>

Thus the Revolution was accomplished without one drop of blood being shed. Even the mob of London, though they pillaged the Roman Catholic chapels offered harm to no one except to the hated Chancellor Jeffreys. He had hidden himself in a public-house at Wapping, and was thankful when the Lord Mayor allowed him to be shut up safely in the Tower, where he died the year after.

<small>End of Judge Jeffreys.</small>

10. Interregnum.—William arrived at St. James's Palace only a few hours after James left it for ever. English, Scotch, and Dutch troops were quartered in different parts of London, and all was fairly quiet again. The House of Peers met, and as there was no

House of Commons, an assembly was formed of any members who had sat in Charles II.'s reign, together with the Lord Mayor, the aldermen, and a committee from the Common Council of London. These two Houses then begged William to govern them for the time, and to send out circulars inviting electors all over England to return members for a Convention; a Parliament could only be summoned by a king. When this Convention met on Jan. 22, 1689, it was settled, after a great deal of discussion, that James had abdicated the throne, and that William and Mary should be proclaimed king and queen, and William alone should govern. William refused to be merely regent, and Mary wished to give up all power to her husband.

11. Bill of Rights.—Before this, however, the Lords and Commons determined to state the limits of the king's power, so that there might be no more disputes. They drew up a "Declaration of Rights," which a few months afterwards became a statute. In this Declaration, after blaming James for trying to destroy the laws, they declared that *the Ecclesiastical Commission Court was illegal, that the king cannot suspend or dispense with the laws, nor raise money, nor keep a standing army without the consent of Parliament; that subjects may petition a king; that all elections of members must be free, and that there must be perfect freedom of speech in Parliament, which should be held frequently to redress grievances and strengthen the laws. That jurymen must be honestly chosen, and in trials for high treason must be freeholders; while excessive fines, and cruel, unusual punishments must not be inflicted.* Lastly the Bill of Rights added *that no papist should ever again hold the crown of England.* These, they said, were the undoubted rights and liberties of the English people, and under these conditions William and Mary were declared King and Queen of England, Feb. 13, 1689. If Mary died William was to go on reigning alone, while Anne and her children were to be the next heirs.

12. William III—The coronation took place on April 11, 1689, and William of Orange, by the free act of Parliament, was the reigning King of England. But he knew he would have to fight for his crown. Louis XIV. was not only James's ally, he was also very anxious to give William trouble in England, that he might not fight against France abroad. So he lent James money and officers to go to Ireland, where Tyrconnel, the Roman Catholic lord-lieutenant, with an army of 20,000 men, was ready to help him to reconquer England. James crossed over to Kinsale, he was being received with shouts of welcome in Dublin, even before William's coronation had taken place in London.

James received in Ireland.

Nor did every one acknowledge William in England. Ever since the Restoration the clergy had been teaching the people that a king reigned by "divine right," and they owed him "passive obedience." Now the people had revolted against their king, and Parliament had elected another. Therefore when all members and officials were called upon to take the oath of allegiance to William, the Archbishop of Canterbury, together with five of the Seven Bishops and a large number of clergy and others, refused. These men were called "Nonjurors"; they were treated patiently, but they could not remain in office, for they would not even read the prayer for King William in the service. They formed themselves into a party and elected their own bishops for nearly a hundred years, till in 1805 the last "nonjuror" bishop died. These men, together with the Roman Catholics and the friends of James, who were now called "Jacobites" (from *Jacobus*, Latin for James), formed constant plots against the Government. They looked upon William as a usurper, and when obliged to drink the king's health, put a bowl of water before them to imply that they drank to the "king over the water."

Non-jurors, 1689-1805.

Jacobites.

In Scotland riots took place for another reason. The Covenanters, who had been so long persecuted, not only declared at once for William, but "rabbled" or drove out the clergy of the English Church, in many cases with great cruelty. When order was restored the Covenanters had the chief power in the Scotch Parliament, and William and Mary were proclaimed king and queen at the Cross of Edinburgh, April 11, 1689. But an old follower of James, Graham of Claverhouse, Viscount Dundee, went off with a few troopers to the

Covenanters "rabble" the English clergy.

Highlands, and calling the Highland chiefs together at Lochaber in Inverness, prepared to fight. As Sir Walter Scott wrote a century later—

> "To the Lords of Convention 'twas Claver'se who spoke,
> Ere the King's crown shall fall there are crowns to be broke;
> So let each Cavalier who loves honour and me,
> Come follow the bonnets of Bonny Dundee."

13. Massacre of Glencoe.—The struggle was not long. General Hugh Mackay was sent against him with an army, and though the Highlanders gained a complete victory in the Pass of Killiecrankie, Dundee was killed in the battle; and after this the Highlanders retired, and forts were built to keep them out of the Lowlands. Two years later a very shameful thing happened. William summoned all the Highland chiefs to take an oath of loyalty before Jan. 1, 1692. By Dec. 31 all had come except the Macdonalds of Glencoe, whose chief Ian Macdonald put it off to the last day, and then went to the wrong place. Unfortunately John Dalrymple, Master of Stair, who was Secretary of State for Scotland, wishing to make an example, took advantage of this to get a warrant from William to root out the men of Glencoe, and sent to the Highlands a regiment composed of the Campbells of Argyll, hereditary foemen of the Macdonalds. The soldiers, after living some days quietly among the people, rose one morning early and shot down nearly the whole clan. It was a treacherous and wicked massacre, and William has been much blamed for not punishing more severely the people who planned it.

Battle of Killiecrankie, July 27, 1689.

14. Civil War in Ireland.—Meanwhile, in Ireland, a civil war was raging between two parties—the native Irish and Roman Catholics on one side, and the Protestant settlers on the other. James came to Ireland because he wished to reconquer England, but the Irish hoped he had come to uphold their religion, and give them back their lands. Tyrconnel had begun by disarming all the Protestants in the south, and they, afraid of being massacred, crossed over in large numbers to England. In the north, where the settlers were more numerous, they gathered to defend themselves at Enniskillen on Lough Erne, and in the town of Londonderry at the head of Lough Foyle. When James arrived before Londonderry in April 1689 the "'prentice boys of Derry" had already shut their gates, and 30,000 Protestants had taken refuge there.

Governor Lundy did, it is true, offer to surrender to James, but the citizens and soldiers were so furious that he had to escape for his life; and the people, led by a clergyman named Walker, and a Major Baker, held the town for William of Orange. This was the beginning of the term Orangemen, which is still so commonly used for the Protestants in the north of Ireland. A long and painful siege of one hundred and five days followed. The Irish army blockaded the town, and a boom or barrier of firewood was formed across the mouth of the River Foyle, so that no provisions could enter. William sent the English fleet to relieve the town, but Colonel Kirke, the commander, would not risk running the blockade. Hunger, disease, and death were destroying the unfortunate people by hundreds, yet, though even horse-flesh was no longer to be had, and the provisions doled out were very near their end, the brave inhabitants still cried, "No surrender."

<small>Siege of Londonderry, April 20, 1689.</small>

At last a sharp order came from England to Kirke that he must attempt a rescue, and, among other volunteers, two brave seamen—Browning, a native of Derry, and Douglas, a Scotchman—offered to run in their ships of provisions. On the evening of July 30, side by side, the ships steered straight at the boom. A strain, a crash, and it gave way. At that moment Browning was shot dead by the enemy. But he did not die in vain; an hour later, the two ships laden with food had reached the starving people, and three days later, the Irish army retreated. The siege of Londonderry was over. That same day Colonel Wolseley scattered another portion of the Irish army at Newton Butler, near Enniskillen, and the north of Ireland was free from James's soldiers.

<small>Relief of Londonderry, Aug. 1, 1689.</small>

In Dublin, however, James still reigned as king, and, having no money, coined shillings and sovereigns of brass, promising to give good coin for them when he had regained his English throne. In his name the Irish Parliament passed severe laws against those Irish who held to William, and declared the property of nearly all the English settlers in Ireland to be forfeited; but these laws had little effect, for

<small>James reigns in Dublin.</small>

William's German general, Marshal Schomberg, had come to Ireland with an army, and though he could do nothing during the winter, he was a great protection to the Protestants.

15. Important Measures.—During the remainder of the year 1689 England was settling down under William. He chose able ministers, among whom were his old friend Lord Danby, who had arranged his marriage with Princess Mary, and Lord Halifax, who kept the balance between the Whigs and Tories. Parliament passed many useful measures. The "Toleration Act" gave the Dissenters permission to have service in chapels of their own provided these chapels were registered; but not the Roman Catholics, for the nation was still too much afraid of them. A revenue of £1,200,000 was voted for the crown; but now for the first time the Commons kept part of this money in their own hands, while they settled £300,000 on William and Mary for life, and only gave them the custom duties of £600,000 for four years. From that time to this Parliament votes annually the supplies for the public expenses of the country, and this secures that they shall meet at least once a year. <small>Toleration Act, 1689.</small> <small>Annual voting of supplies.</small>

A third bill gave Parliament power over the army. It happened that a regiment of Scotch soldiers mutinied, and, as a standing army was illegal, they could only be tried as ordinary citizens. Men saw at once that, in these times of danger, there must be severer discipline than this in the army. So Parliament passed a "Mutiny Bill," giving the officers powers for six months to try soldiers by "Court-martial." <small>Mutiny Bill 1689.</small> When the six months was over the bill was renewed, and continued to be renewed every year, allowing the sovereign to keep and control a certain number of soldiers for twelve months. In 1879 it was superseded by the "Army Discipline and Regulation Bill," but this too has to be renewed every year. So if Parliament did not meet, the sovereign could not legally have either money or army, and thus the nation is protected from such tyranny as James exercised.

16. Close of the War in Ireland.—It was indeed necessary to keep up the army, for Louis was actively helping James. Early in 1690 he sent over a large number of French troops to Ireland, and William saw that he must go himself with more men and fight out his battle with James on Irish ground. He arrived in Belfast on June 14, and on July 1 the famous Battle of the Boyne took place between the two kings. The English soldiers forded the river under a heavy fire and forced the ranks of the enemy, though their general, Schomberg, fell dead at the outset; and William, though wounded early in the battle, led the left wing of the army and gained the day. James, on the contrary, looked on from a distance, and when he saw that the Irish were beaten he fled to Dublin, and sailed from Kinsale to France. "Change kings with us and we will fight you again," said an Irish officer, so ashamed were they of their cowardly king.

Battle of the Boyne, July 1, 1690.

And they did fight for more than a year; till the Irish army, led by French generals, was defeated at Aughrim by the Dutch general, Ginkell. On Oct. 3 Limerick, the last stronghold of the rebels, which was held by a brave Irishman, Patrick Sarsfield, surrendered to Ginkell. In the treaty of Limerick the Roman Catholics were promised freedom of worship, and those who wished were allowed to go with Sarsfield to France. About 14,000 Irish soldiers went, and for a hundred years there was no more fighting in Ireland. But the Protestants, who now had the power, abused it. The promise of the treaty of Limerick was not kept, and the cruel penal laws, which were passed in Anne's reign, kept alive bitter hatred in the hearts of the Roman Catholics.

Treaty of Limerick, 1691.

17. Grand Alliance.—More than a year before Limerick surrendered, William had returned to England, where he was much wanted to carry on the war with France. In 1690 Germany, Spain, Holland, Brandenburg, and Savoy, had all joined in a "Grand Alliance" against Louis; but the allies were so slow, and the French army so strong, that for a long time Louis had the best of the struggle. The very day before the Battle of the Boyne, the French fleet attacked the Dutch and English fleets off Beachy Head, in the English Channel; and because Admiral Herbert, now Lord Torrington, was jealous of the Dutch and would not help them, the French gained a complete victory, sailed down the Channel, and burnt the little village of Teignmouth. The French Admiral de Tourville

Battle of Beachy Head, June 30, 1690.

THE REVOLUTION. 215

hoped that the Jacobites would rise, but the mere sight of a Frenchman on their coasts made the English rally round William, and when he came back from Ireland they were willing and anxious to give him men and money to fight Louis in Flanders. Early in 1692 he crossed over to the Netherlands, leaving Queen Mary to govern in his place.

He was no sooner gone than the Jacobites in England began to plot against him. Though the English had found William useful in putting an end to the tyranny of James, they never really liked him, for he was reserved, harsh-tempered, and unsociable, and he was a Dutchman, though his mother was the daughter of Charles I. Moreover, though he ruled England well, his mind was occupied with foreign wars, and the English disliked to have to pay soldiers to defend Holland. Even Queen Mary was unpopular at first, for people blamed her for taking her father's throne. But she was so gentle and unselfish that in the end she was much beloved. *William unpopular.*

The Jacobites now took advantage of a victory which Louis gained over William at Mons in Flanders, to persuade some of the Tories to treat with King James. Lord Churchill, now Earl of Marlborough, was one of these, and Lord Russell, who was High Admiral in place of Lord Torrington, was inclined to join him. But when the French fleet came into the channel, hoping that Russell would not oppose them, the blood of the English sailor rose. "Do not think," said he, "that I will let the French triumph over us in our own seas;" and he won a brilliant victory off Cape la Hogue, and burnt fifteen French ships. It was when the poor wounded sailors came home after this battle that Queen Mary determined to turn Greenwich Palace into a home for disabled seamen. After her death King William carried out her plan, and sailors lived in Greenwich Hospital till 1865, when it was thought better to give them pensions. The building is now a Royal Naval College. *Jacobite plots. Battle of La Hogue, May, 1692. Greenwich Hospital.*

18. National Debt.—Thus the attacks of France only bound England more closely to William. Year after year, from 1692 to 1697, he went abroad to carry on the war, and as Parliament saw that in fighting abroad he was preventing Louis from putting James back on the throne, they made great efforts to provide him with money. This was not easy, for now that people taxed themselves in Parliament, forced loans could not be raised as they had been by earlier kings. In 1692 the treasury was empty, while money was wanted for the war, and Charles II.'s debt to the goldsmith's was still unpaid. In this dilemma a clever young Whig, Charles Montague, persuaded Parliament to invite rich people to lend them a million pounds, for which they would receive a yearly interest from Government. This debt has gone on till now, and has increased to more than 600 million pounds. The actual money lent will never be repaid till the National Debt is done away with, but the *interest* is so steadily paid that people are glad to leave their money lying invested in this way. If, however, any man wants to have back his *capital* (that is, his whole sum of money invested), he gets a stockbroker to sell his right to the interest to some other man, who gives him say the £100 or £200 which he had invested, and then takes his interest for the future.

19. Bank of England.—In William's reign the National Debt, was still too new for Government to increase it very much, and in 1694 Montague carried out another plan suggested by a Scotchman named Paterson. This was to borrow another million and a half, and to give the subscribers a charter creating them into a National Bank, called the "Governor and Company of the Bank of England," which was to do all the money business of the Government, and get an interest on their money. This bank has been a great success. All Government money passes through it; it keeps the *bullion* or masses of gold and silver till they are made into coins; it pays the interest on the National Debt, and lends money to Parliament when it is wanted. The Bank of England now employs 1100 clerks, and pays £300,000 a year in salaries and pensions. Its banknotes are received like gold all over the world, and "safe as the Bank of England" has become a proverb.

20. Rise of Party Government.—We see by these important bills which were passed for borrowing money, that the House of Commons, in turning out the Stuarts and putting in a king by Act of Parliament, had begun to get back the old power which they had before the time of the Tudors, and William was wise enough to let them use it. But as the two parties of Whig and Tory were now

THE REVOLUTION. 217

very sharply divided, whichever happened to be the strongest grew very troublesome when it did not approve of what was done by the king's ministers. In this difficulty the Earl of Sunderland pointed out to the king that the only way to have a strong Government was to choose the ministers from the party which had the greatest number of members in Parliament. This is how our Government is still carried on. If the ministers cannot persuade a *majority* of the members to vote with them they resign, and the queen calls upon some of the other party to take their place. If they, in their turn, do not feel strong enough, then Parliament is dissolved, and a new one elected. In this way the ministers become the leaders in Parliament, and the choice of the people, as well as the servants of the sovereign.

21. Useful Legislation.—Though William had much trouble with his Parliaments, they passed many useful measures. A new "Triennial Act" decreed that a fresh Parliament must be elected every three years. The law obliging all printed books and pamphlets to be approved by the king's licenser was allowed to drop, and any man might for the future print what he pleased, unless it slandered the Government or other people. One great result of this was that instead of only one newspaper, the *London Gazette*, which had been published for some time, a number of newspapers soon sprang up, and people in all parts of England could learn what was being done and discussed in the great towns.
_{Triennial Act, 1694.}
_{Freedom of the press, 1695.}

Another very important Act did away with the infamous law of treason introduced by Thomas Cromwell in Henry VIII.'s reign, and for the future men accused of treason were allowed to have a lawyer to defend them, and to have a copy of the accusations against them. After this no man could be condemned as Vane, Strafford, Russell, and Sidney had been, without means of defending themselves. Also in 1701 an Act was passed giving fixed salaries to the judges, and declaring that they could not be removed unless they were convicted of doing wrong, or both Houses of Parliament wished it. No sovereign could henceforth dismiss a judge, as James did, because he would not strain the law in the king's
_{Law of Treason, 1696.}
_{Independence of judges.}

favour; but so long as they give just judgment the judges are now free from fear of either king or people.

Still one more great measure we owe chiefly to Montague, who was by this time Chancellor of the Exchequer. This was a new silver coinage. Up to the time of Charles II. silver money was made by simply cutting the metal with shears, and shaping and stamping it with a hammer. Therefore it was quite easy for rogues to shear the coins again, and take off a little silver before passing them. In this way the coins became smaller and smaller, and often a man who received fifty shillings found, on taking them to the bank, that they were only worth fifty sixpences. In Charles II.'s reign a mill worked by horses began to be used for making coins, which had either a ribbed edge or words round the edge, so that they showed if they were clipped; these were called "milled coins." But as the old ones were still used, rogues melted down the good coin or sent it to France, because it was worth more than the clipped money, and so they made a profit. At last the matter became so serious that Montague, and the Lord Chancellor, Somers, consulted with Locke the philosopher, and Sir Isaac Newton, and agreed to coin a large quantity of new-milled money, and *call in the old*. Newton, who was made Master of the Mint, took great care that the new money should be true and good, and in 1696 the change was made. At first it caused great trouble and hardship, but in the end every one received full value for their money, and the loss was made up by putting a tax on window-panes. This tax was continued for various reasons till 1851, and we shall find that many houses built during these hundred and fifty years had few windows and small panes in order to escape the window tax.

New coinage, 1696.

Milled co'ns.

Window Tax, 1696-1851.

22. Peace of Ryswick.—While these useful reforms were being made under William's wise and just Government, he himself had many troubles. In 1694 Queen Mary died of smallpox, and for a time he was stunned with grief. Moreover, the Jacobites took advantage of her death to try and get rid of the "Dutch" king, as they called William. Louis XIV. promised to send over a large French army if the people

Death of Queen Mary, 1694.

THE REVOLUTION. 219

would rise; and early in 1696 a plot was formed to murder William in a narrow lane leading to Hampton Court, on his return from hunting. Fortunately a Roman Catholic gentleman named Prendergast, too honourable to countenance murder, warned the king. *Plot to murder William, 1696.* The plotters were seized and punished, and, as usual, the knowledge that the French wished to invade England made the people only more loyal. William was very popular at this time, for he had gained a great victory (1695) at the siege of Namur, and the English people began to be confident that he would bring the war against France to a successful ending. The attempt to assassinate him made him still more popular. The Lords and Commons bound themselves in an association to avenge his death if he was murdered, and to put Anne on the throne. Thousands throughout the country signed the paper.

The next year, the war with France ended, and King Louis XIV. signed a peace at Ryswick in Holland, in which he gave up all he had conquered since the treaty of Nimeguen in 1678, except the fortress of Strasburg, and acknow- *Peace of Ryswick, Sept. 11, 1697.* ledged William as King of England, promising never again to disturb his Government. After eight years of war the country was at last at peace! Processions, banners, bonfires, and illuminations showed how glad the people were, and King William went in state to St. Paul's, which Sir Christopher Wren had been rebuilding ever since the fire of London, and which was used for the first time on that day, Dec. 2, 1697.

But the peace brought bitter disappointment to the king, for the first thing Parliament did was to reduce the army at once to 10,000 and the navy to 8000 men. The next year they insisted on sending away William's Dutch Guards, and taking *Reduction of the army.* back land in Ireland which he had given to Dutchmen. They were still afraid of any king becoming powerful, and having a strong army. William was sorely hurt at what he considered their ingratitude to himself, and even threatened to go back to Holland and be king no longer. But in the end he gave way, though he warned them that they were leaving England too unprotected.

23. Spanish Succession.—In truth, he knew what they did not, that Louis had made peace, because he hoped to get what he wanted another way. Charles II., King of Spain, though only thirty-five, was weak and sickly, and it was known he could not live long. He had no children, and had an immense inheritance to leave—Spain, Naples, Sicily Milan, the Spanish Netherlands, and the rich Spanish lands in South America. There was no one who had any strict right to succeed him, but there were three princes who were related to Charles, and who for different reasons might equally well be chosen. These were Joseph, eldest son of the Elector of Bavaria; Archduke Charles, son of the Emperor Leopold; and Philip, Duke of Anjou, grandson of Louis XIV Now Louis XIV. knew that the other states of Europe would not like his grandson to have such immense power, and he wanted to make a compact with William to help him in getting at least part of it. This William was willing to do if he could only keep Louis out of the Netherlands. But to make good terms he wanted a strong army at his back, and this was why he was so vexed that Parliament reduced it. Still he did his best. Two treaties were made—by the first the young Prince of Bavaria was to receive the bulk of the Spanish Empire; viz.: Spain, the Netherlands, Sardinia and the Colonies; the Dauphin was to have Naples, Sicily, Finale, and Guipuzcoa; while Archduke Charles was to get Lombardy. This treaty, made without the consent of Charles II., so enraged him, that he made a will and left all his dominions to the Electoral Prince. Unfortunately he died, and a second treaty gave Spain, the Netherlands, Sardinia and the Colonies to the Archduke Charles, and the rest to the Duke of Anjou, except the Milanese, which was given to the Duke of Lorraine, in exchange for the Duchy of that name Louis did not like this, but was willing to make the best of it. Meanwhile the treaty was secret, and the Spanish ministers were not consulted. When they discovered that their lands were being divided without their permission they were very angry, especially with William, and persuaded Charles II. who died six months after the second treaty, to make a will leaving the whole to the Duke of Anjou. Would Louis now stand by his treaty or by the will? The temptation was too great. He knew that William's army was disbanded, so he broke all the treaties into which he had entered with the European powers, and accepted the inheritance for his grandson, who became Philip V. of Spain.

24. Act of Settlement.—At first sight this seems to have very little to do with England, and so the English Parliament thought. They were annoyed with William for having interfered at all and made the treaties. They did not want to go to war about foreign countries; they were far more anxious to settle who should reign after Anne, for she had just lost her last living child the Duke of Gloucester. By an "Act of Settlement" they decided that the English crown should pass on Anne's death to the Electress Sophia of Hanover and her children, she being granddaughter of James I., the only Protestant descendant of the English royal family. It is under this Act that our present Queen holds her crown. *(Act of Settlement, 1701.)*

25. Louis Recognises the Pretender.—But they soon found out that, while providing for a danger far off, they had overlooked one close at hand. All the object of the last war had been to keep the French out of the Spanish Netherlands, and now Louis put French garrisons into the fortresses in the name of his grandson Philip V., and kept the Dutch garrisons prisoner till William acknowledged Philip as King of Spain. Even then Parliament, however, did not wish to fight, though they allowed William to make a "triple alliance" between England, Holland, and the Emperor Leopold to turn Louis out of the Netherlands. At last, one morning they learnt that their exiled king James II. had died in France, and Louis XIV. had *recognised his son as James III. of England.* Then all at once the nation saw how dangerous it was that Louis should be so powerful. That he should try to dictate to them who should be King of England was not to be borne, and the people clamoured for war. William dissolved the Tory Parliament, and another was elected, which at once voted men and money to fight against this French king, who insisted on settling England's affairs. *(Louis secures fortresses in the Netherlands. Triple alliance.)*

But William, who had long been failing in health, was too ill to command this new army; and knowing that Lord Churchill, now Earl of Marlborough, was a military genius, he named him commander-in-chief. Even before war was declared his reign was over. On Feb. 20, 1702, he fell from his horse and broke his collar-bone; and on March 8 this grave, silent man, who had done so much for England, and received so little gratitude in return, passed to his rest.

<small>Death of William, Feb. 20, 1702.</small>

CHAPTER XXI.

THE LAST OF THE STUARTS.

1. Queen Anne.—When William died Anne was proclaimed queen. Her young Roman Catholic half-brother, James Stuart, knew it was hopeless to make any effort to secure the throne. He remained at the French court, and was called King James III. or the "Chevalier de St. George," while in England he was known as "the Pretender." In Scotland he had many supporters, but they could not move.

<small>Anne proclaimed queen.</small>

"Good Queen Anne," as she was called, was a favourite with the English people, who were glad to have once more an English sovereign. She was a slow-minded and obstinate woman, but affectionate and good. Like Queen Elizabeth, she loved her people, and wished to do well for them, while they respected her for the resignation which she had shown when losing her children one after the other. She was much guided by Marlborough, for his wife had been her friend from childhood, and they wrote to each other almost daily, Anne calling Lady Marlborough "Mrs. Freeman," while she called the queen "Mrs. Morley." Anne's husband, Prince George of Denmark, was a dull good-natured man, who did not interfere in politics. The disputes in this reign were not between the sovereign and the people, but between the Whigs and Tories.

<small>Character of Queen Anne.</small>

The Whigs wanted war with France, the Tories wanted only to defend the English shores, and not to fight on the continent. Marlborough was a moderate Tory, but as a general he was eager for war, and so was Lord Godolphin, who was Lord High Treasurer. These two men had the chief influence in the ministry for the next eight years.

<small>Ministry of Marlborough and Godolphin.</small>

THE LAST OF THE STUARTS. 223

2. War of The Spanish Succession.—Very soon after her coronation the queen declared war with France, and Marlborough crossed over to the Netherlands and took Liége. Louis had only the King of Bavaria on his side, while against him he had the DUTCH, who wanted to drive him out of the Spanish Netherlands; the ENGLISH, who required him to send away the "Pretender;" the GERMAN Emperor Leopold, *Grand Alliance at war with France.* who wanted the Spanish possessions for Archduke Charles; the King of PRUSSIA, the King of PORTUGAL, the Duke of SAVOY, and several minor princes. The war was going on at the same time in the Netherlands, Spain, Italy, and Germany. The three men by whose counsels the great Alliance was chiefly guided were Heinsius the Grand Pensionary or leading statesman of Holland, Prince Eugene of Savoy the imperial general, and Marlborough, who was the leading spirit everywhere.

The work Marlborough did was almost beyond belief. He directed the movements both in Flanders' and Spain; he was constantly treating with the ministers at the courts of the different allies, and he crossed from time to time over to England to join in politics and keep up the enthusiasm for the war. He had great faults; he was avaricious, and he had no true sense of honour. He deserted his first friend, James II., at the Revolution, and when William III. was his sovereign, *Character of Marlborough.* he turned back and plotted with James. Yet he was an able statesman, and the greatest general England had before Wellington. He was calm and diplomatic, humane on the battlefield, and quite heedless of danger, while at the same time he knew at once what ought to be done by each of the armies fighting over nearly the whole of Europe. Yet for the first two years he could do but little more than hold Louis in check, for the allies were timid and did not work together.

During these two years very little happened at home. The Tories made a great attack upon the Dissenters, who were all Whigs, hoping to keep them out of Parliament. An "Occasional Conformity Bill" was brought in to prevent *Occasional Conformity Bill, 1702-1711.* Dissenters from taking the sacrament in church (according to the Test Act) merely to get into office, and then going as usual to their chapels. The bill was passed by the Commons, but always thrown out by the Lords till 1711, when at last the Lords gave way, and for more than a hundred years a special favour had to be granted each year in Parliament to allow Dissenters to hold office. In 1704 Marlborough, who wished to keep the Tories in good humour, persuaded Anne to give up to the Church the first-fruits and tenths, which had been paid to the king ever since the Pope had lost them. This money, which is called "Queen Anne's Bounty," is still used to increase the incomes of the poorer clergy.

Queen Anne's Bounty, 1704.

Meanwhile Marlborough was growing tired of the slowness of the allies. King Louis had gathered a large army and sent it to join the Bavarians on the Danube, meaning to risk a great battle near Vienna against the Austrians under Prince Eugene. Marlborough saw the danger at once; he told no one his plans, but marched straight to the Danube, joined Prince Eugene near a little village called Blenheim, and there, fought that famous battle in which two-thirds of the French army, so long thought to be invincible, were killed, wounded, or taken prisoner.

Battle of Blenheim, Aug. 13, 1704.

A few days before the strong fortress of Gibraltar had been taken by Admiral Rooke, and it was clear that the tide of war had turned. Marlborough, who had been created a duke, became the idol of the English people and the terror of France. Parliament gave him a large estate near Woodstock, where he built the splendid mansion called "Blenheim House," and when the next elections took place in 1705, Godolphin and Marlborough had a strong Whig party in Parliament, because the people were in favour of the war.

Taking of Gibraltar, Aug. 3, 1704.

Marlborough went back to Flanders, and gained another great victory at Ramillies in May 1706, taking possession of nine strong fortresses between Flanders and France. The Emperor of Austria even offered to make him governor of the Spanish Netherlands, but the English and the Dutch were both so much against it that Marlborough refused. About the same time the Earl of Peterborough, who was commanding the English army in Spain, took Barcelona, and driving Philip V. back into France, proclaimed Archduke Charles king at Madrid. Defeated on all sides, Louis now began to wish for peace. He offered to give up Spain and the

Battle of Ramillies, May 1706.

Louis proposes peace, 1706.

Netherlands to Archduke Charles, if Philip might keep Naples, Sicily, and Milan. There is no doubt peace ought to have been made. But the war had become popular in England, and the Whigs, who were now the strong party, were afraid they would lose power if it was ended. So they made difficulties, and, for their own selfish ends, drove France to desperation, and wasted men and money for the next seven years in a useless war.

3. State of the Nation.—Happily England was now prosperous enough to bear the burden. In spite of war and the peril of the enemy's ships at sea, commerce was so flourishing that the ministers had no difficulty in borrowing more and more money, and the National Debt increased to fifty-four millions of pounds. This debt was now useful to the Government, because so many people drew interest from it that they were very anxious not to have civil war, for fear they should lose by it. <small>Use of the National Debt.</small> This was shown very clearly when in 1708 the Pretender attempted to cross to Scotland with 4000 French troops. He caught the measles just before starting, and the French ships, going without him, were driven back by Admiral Byng. But this alarm made the "stock" of the National Debt fall 14 or 15 per cent; that is, any man who had lent £100 could only sell his right to another man for £85, because, if there had been a civil war, it was not certain that the interest would be paid. This is even now one of the great safeguards against riots and rebellions in England. So many are interested in having a steady Government which will pay its debts, that the greater number are always on the side of law and order.

The Bank of England, too, was another help both to Government and to trade. It was so much sounder and safer than the goldsmiths' banks had been, that merchants who dealt with it, were more easily able to get credit, and the bank did <small>Stability of credit.</small> an enormous business, and was able to help Government when necessary. This, together with the new coinage, made the country prosperous and the towns increase rapidly. Bristol grew large again by the trade with the West Indies; <small>State of towns and country.</small> Manchester and Norwich, Leeds and Sheffield, became important; and Liverpool, to which many merchants moved after the plague and fire of London, began to take a great place among towns. One unfortunate thing grew out of all this prosperity—the

Decrease of yeoman class. fine race of yeomen, the men who lived and worked on their own land, which had been their fathers' and forefathers' before them, began to die out. So much waste land was enclosed, that farming became less profitable, and the rich merchants were so anxious to buy estates of their own, that the yeomen found it paid better to sell their property and put their money into trade. In this way England lost those simple, stalwart, independent men who had been the backbone of the country ever since Saxon times.

4. Union of England and Scotland.—On the other hand, in the year 1707 England and Scotland were at last made one. Up

Act of Union passed in Scotland, Jan. 1707; in England, March 1707. to that time there had been still heavy duties raised upon any goods passing between the two countries, and as Scotland was a poor land, and had to import many things, this pressed heavily on the people. So they began to grow restless, and being specially angry with the English about a Scotch colony which had failed on the Gulf of Darien because of the English trading laws, they passed a law in the Scotch Parliament in 1703, that when Queen Anne should die they would have one of the Protestant princes for a king, but *not the same one as England.* This would have been very bad, for with two kings once more in the island, war would be sure to follow. So the English gave way about the duties, agreeing to let goods pass free across the border if the Scots would give up their separate Parliament, and send members to the English Parliament, as in the days of Cromwell. At first the Scots were very unwilling, but in 1707 a commission from both countries met, and agreed that the Scots should keep their own Presbyterian Church and their own Scotch laws, but give up their Parliament, and send instead forty-five members to the English House of Commons and sixteen elective peers to the Lords. By this "Act of Union" both countries were

Kingdom of Great Britain. united under the name of "Great Britain." And now once more the Saxon-speaking people were one, as in days of old when North-Humber-land reached to the Firth of Forth. The crosses of St. George and St. Andrew were blended to form the "Union Jack," and in our day Scotchmen and Englishmen are brothers in interest, in nationality, and in good-feeling, while both countries have flourished ever since they joined hands across the border.

5. State of Ireland.—It is painful to turn from this picture to that of the sister-country Ireland. There, as we have seen the Treaty of Limerick was not kept, but the Roman Catholics, cowed and disheartened by their defeat, were treated by England and by the Irish Protestants as cruelly during the next fifty years as ever the Huguenots had been by the Roman Catholics abroad. Penal laws were passed persecuting the priests, for- <small>Penal laws in Ireland.</small> bidding Roman Catholics to hold land, bribing their children to become Protestants, or taking away their means of education. All these, as well as the laws against manufactures and trade in Ireland, drove the people to desperation, and taught them habits of lawlessness from which we are even now suffering.

6. Party Struggles.—All this time the war was dragging wearily on. Marlborough gained three more important victories at Oudenarde, Lille, and Malplaquet; but in Spain the <small>Oudenarde, 1708; Lille, 1708; Malplaquet, 1709.</small> French were again successful, and Philip V. went back to Madrid. Still France was so exhausted that in 1709 Louis again proposed peace, and again the Emperor of Austria and the English ministers refused. But they made a mistake, and Marlborough made a still greater one in asking to be appointed Captain-General of the forces for life. There was nothing the English had dreaded so much ever since the days of Cromwell, as a great man with an army at his back, and they were getting tired of the war and the Whigs.

Just at this time a noisy Tory preacher, Dr. Sacheverell, preached a sermon on "divine right" and the wickedness of resisting a rightful sovereign. The Whigs thought this was an attack on the rights of William III. and Anne, and the ministers impeached Dr. Sacheverell before the House of Lords. He was found guilty, but the nation was so much on his side that the <small>Trial of Dr. Sacheverell.</small> Lords only condemned him not to preach for three years, and to have his sermon burnt. It was a foolish affair, but the people were just then in the humour to quarrel with the Whig ministers. They took Dr. Sacheverell's part, and when he was set free they followed him with shouts of "The Church and Dr. Sacheverell," lighted bon-fires, rang the church-bells and illuminated the streets.

Queen Anne sympathised with the people. She had always been a Tory at heart, and she had just quarrelled with the Duchess of Marlborough, and taken as her friend Mrs. Masham, a cousin of a very able statesman, Robert Harley, who was opposed to the ministers and to Marlborough. Harley, and a brilliant speaker named St. John, began now to attack Marlborough in Parliament, and to cry out that the war should be stopped; and the great political writer Dean Swift helped them with fierce articles in the papers. "Six millions of supplies and almost fifty millions of debt," he wrote, "the High Allies have been the ruin of us." Even the people turned against their idol, and accused him of carrying on the war for his own benefit. At last, in 1710, Anne dismissed the ministry, and appointed Harley as "Earl of Oxford" and St. John as "Viscount Bolingbroke" to be her chief ministers. Parliament was dissolved, and after the elections the House of Commons was full of Tories. A few months later Marlborough was dismissed from his command, which was given to the Duke of Ormond, a strong Tory. Marlborough was even accused of having misused public money; his wife was sent away from court, and he himself left England, an example of a man treated with ingratitude because he relied too much on his great success.

Attack on Marlborough and the Whigs, 1710.

Ministry of Oxford and Bolingbroke, 1710-1714.

7. Peace of Utrecht.—The Tories now began at once to make terms with France, and the peace of Utrecht was signed in 1713. England did not gain as much as she would have done seven years before. Though the French were expelled from the Netherlands and from Germany, yet Philip still kept Spain and Spanish America under a promise that the crowns of Spain and France were never to be united. Austria gained Milan, Naples, and the Spanish Netherlands; the Dutch received a strong line of fortresses to defend their country; England kept Gibraltar and Minorca, and was given Hudson's Bay and Straits, Newfoundland and Acadia, now called Nova Scotia, about which English and French fishermen had been quarrelling for a century. Louis promised solemnly to acknowledge Anne and her successors of the house of Hanover as lawful sovereigns of England, and never again to support the Pretender, who went to live in Lorraine ; and England was given the sole right, for thirty years, of trading in negro slaves with the Spanish colonies, and of sending one merchant ship each year to the South Seas. But the English ministers were so anxious to avoid troublesome questions that they left a stain on English honour. The Catalans, a people in the north-west of Spain, had stood by the allies in the war, and had been assured that their liberty should be protected. But the Austrian emperor did not care to uphold them, and England, though reluctantly, left them to the mercy of Spain, to which, after a long struggle, they were obliged to submit, July 1715.

8. Death of Anne.—Anne's reign was now drawing to a close. She was known to be ill, and every one began to think who would succeed her. Old Princess Sophia of Hanover had died, and her son George, Elector of Hanover, was the Protestant heir named by Parliament in the Act of Succession. As he was a German who could not speak a word of English, the Jacobites secretly hoped they might succeed in proclaiming the Pretender, and even the Tory ministers Bolingbroke and Oxford began to intrigue with him, because they knew that George would favour the Whigs. But the end came before they were prepared. The queen was one day much upset by a violent quarrel between Bolingbroke and Oxford in the Council Chamber, in consequence of which Oxford received his dismissal. Almost immediately afterwards she was seized with apoplexy and died two days later, Aug. 1, 1714. The Whig Dukes of Argyle and Somerset at once consulted with the Duke of Shrewsbury, who was President of the Council, and, though a Tory no friend of the Pretender. Troops were stationed both in London and Portsmouth, and before the Jacobites could make any opposition, George Lewis, Elector of Hanover, and great-grandson of James I., was proclaimed king. George I. proclaimed king.

9. Summary.—We have now left behind us the troubled period during which the Stuarts tried to be absolute kings, and Parliament and the nation withstood them. This struggle, which lasted for nearly a hundred years, from 1603 till the reign of William and Mary, ended in Parliament being more powerful than before, and we shall see that in the reign of George I. it gained new strength. As the new king could not understand discussions in English, he no longer sat in the Cabinet Council, as other kings and queens had done. The leading man among the ministers took his place, with the title of "Prime Minister," and from that time the prime ministers have, under the sovereign, been the real rulers of the country.

Meanwhile during this century the nation had been silently growing in prosperity and in culture. As the country grew richer more people had leisure to cultivate their minds. The English ministers of this period gave pensions and appointments to men of letters, and we find Milton, Newton, Locke, Addison, Swift, Steele, and many others holding posts under Government. This was an age rich in literature. "News-Letters," which afterwards grew into newspapers or journals, had begun during the Civil War, and increased, as we have seen, after 1695, when the press was freed from control. Dean Swift wrote political articles in the *Examiner*, and published his satirical *Tale of a Tub* (1704); Steele published two penny papers, the *Tatler* (1709) and the *Spectator* (1711), in which Addison and others wrote brilliant essays upon things of daily life, and charming sketches such as that of Sir Roger de Coverley. In more serious literature we have Locke's famous essays on the *Human Understanding* (1690) and on *Toleration*. In History Bishop Burnet wrote his *History of his own Time* (1715), and Pepys his delightful *Diary*. At this time, too, stories or works of fiction became popular, such as Bunyan's *Pilgrim's Progress*, De Foe's *Robinson Crusoe* (1719), Swift's *Gulliver's Travels* (1726), and Arbuthnot's *History of John Bull*, in which Englishmen first received that name. Among poets we have Cowley, Milton, Dryden, and Pope, and the satirist Samuel Butler, the author of *Hudibras*. During this and the next century a change gradually took place in literature. At the beginning men wrote in cumbrous or florid style; towards the end they wrote in plain terse sentences, being more anxious to be well understood than to write

[sidenote: Literature of the 17th century.]

fine periods. This was because people were more educated, and writers no longer appealed only to learned men; they had to write for the public. One great and good result of this spread of books, newspapers, and knowledge of all kinds, was that a feeling of toleration began to grow up, leading people to understand that others might differ from them in opinion, and making it impossible that England should ever go back to the old times of persecution and tyranny.

PART VII.

THE EXPANSION OF ENGLAND.

SOVEREIGNS OF THE HOUSE OF HANOVER.

(Or Brunswick Lüneburg. Family name—Guelph.)

CHAPTER XXII.

ENGLAND STRENGTHENED BY PEACE AT HOME AND CONQUEST ABROAD.

1. George I.—Seven weeks after Queen Anne's death, George I. landed with his only son at Greenwich. Though he was a foreigner he was well received, for the nation wanted rest and settled government. If we look back, we shall see that during the twenty-five years which had passed since James II. fled to France there had been two serious wars—one from 1689 to 1697, which kept William III. constantly abroad, and ended in the peace of Ryswick, the other from 1702 to 1713, in which Marlborough gained his victories, and which ended in the peace of Utrecht, only a year before Anne died. England had joined in these wars partly to defend Holland, but chiefly to prevent France from putting James and his son back on the throne, and the cost of these wars in money alone had been so great that the National Debt, begun in 1692, had increased in twenty-two years to nearly *thirty-eight millions* of pounds. What the people now wanted was a king who would let Parliament and the ministers govern the country, and not stir up strife, so as to give the Pretender a chance to return. *[The House of Hanover.]*

George I. was just the man they required. He was fifty-four years of age, awkward and slow, and he cared more for his home in Hanover than for being King of England. But he was honest and well-intentioned; he did his best to reign according to the laws, and interfered as little as possible. He naturally leaned towards the Whigs, who had put him on the throne, and even before he reached England he dismissed the Tory ministers. The new Parliament was nearly all Whig; and Oxford, Bolingbroke and Ormond were impeached for having intrigued with the Jacobites. Ormond and Bolingbroke fled to France; Oxford remained, and was imprisoned for two years in the Tower. *[Character of George I.]* *[Impeachment of Oxford, Bolingbroke, and Ormond.]*

For a long time the people were very restless, for many still held by the Stuarts. (Such serious riots broke out in the Midland Counties that a Riot Act was passed in 1715, decreeing that if any crowd did not disperse quietly after the Act was publicly read, then the authorities might use force, and could not be blamed if any one was hurt.

Riot Act, 1715.

2. Jacobite Rebellion of 1715.—In Scotland and the north of England the rebellion was more serious. The Highlanders rose under the Earl of Mar, and the English Jacobites under the Earl of Derwentwater and Mr. Forster, member for Northumberland. The Duke of Argyle, however, who was sent against them, defeated the Scots at Sheriffmuir, near Stirling, on the same day that the English Jacobites surrendered at Preston in Lancashire. In two months the rebellion was over. The Pretender, who landed in Scotland a month later, was forced to go back to France with Mar. Forster escaped, and young Lord Derwentwater was executed. These riots and the rebellion made the nation anxious to have a strong government ; and in 1716 a Bill was passed allowing the king to keep the same Parliament for seven years, and so the law remains to this day.

Septennial Parliament, 1716.

Meanwhile in France Louis XIV., who had reigned seventy-one years, and had been such an enemy to England, died in 1715, and his great-grandson, a young boy of ten, became Louis XV. So France ceased to trouble our country during the next twenty years ; especially as the Duke of Orleans, who was regent, made an alliance with England and Holland, promising to support the house of Hanover, if these countries would help him to secure the French crown to the line of Orleans, if Philip V. of Spain should break his promise and claim both crowns, in the case of the death of Louis XV. England and France did indeed declare war against Spain in 1718, when Philip threatened Sicily. Sir George Byng defeated the Spanish fleet at Cape Passaro, and the Spaniards tried to invade Scotland in 1719, but the struggle only lasted a short time, and Philip gave way.

Triple Alliance of 1717.

Battle of Cape Passaro, 1718.

3. South Sea Bubble.—Having now peace at home and abroad the English people turned their attention to commerce.

ENGLAND STRENGTHENED. 235

Trade had been spreading even during the wars, and English merchants did business with Turkey, Italy, Spain, Portugal, Holland, Germany, Russia, Norway, the Baltic, America, Africa, and the East Indies. The peace of Utrecht, by putting an end to fighting on the sea, made traffic safer, and those who had hoarded their money in troubled times now wished to use it in trade. Many companies were started which made large profits in manufactures, mining, shipping, and commerce. Among these the most popular was the South Sea Company, which had been formed in 1711 to trade with South America, and which hoped to do such great things, that in 1719 the directors offered to pay off the National Debt, by giving shares in the undertaking to those to whom the Government owed money, if the ministers in return would give them special trading privileges. But the Bank of England also offered to work off the National Debt, and the two companies bid against each other higher and higher, till at last, in April 1720, the Government passed a Bill accepting the offer of the South Sea Company to advance *seven and a half millions of pounds!*

Spread of English trade.

Good men of business knew that it was impossible they could make large enough profits to meet this enormous sum, and Robert Walpole, a sound-headed Norfolk squire, protested in Parliament against the Bill. But in vain! All England went wild to have South Sea shares. Country gentlemen sold their estates to speculate with the money; clergymen, widows, bankers, doctors, lawyers, all pressed forward to buy, till a share of £100 sold for £1000. Besides this, other bubble companies soon sprang up to take advantage of the mania for speculation, and the Stock Exchange became like a great gambling-house. At last the South Sea directors, finding that the smaller companies were spoiling their market, exposed some of them, and in doing this ruined themselves.' When once people's confidence was shaken and they began to examine more closely, it was clear that the enormous profits which had been promised could never be paid.' The shares fell rapidly from £1000 to £135, and at last almost to nothing. The South Sea Bubble had burst, the company failed, and hundreds were ruined. Lord Stanhope, one of the ministers, died

Robert Walpole protests, 1720.

South Sea Bubble bursts, March 1721.

of the shock; another, Lord Sunderland, resigned, and the nation called loudly for Walpole, who alone had opposed the Bill, to put matters straight.

4. Walpole.—The king wisely did as the people wished. A new ministry was formed in March 1721, with Walpole at the head, and with the help of the Bank of England he succeeded in calming the panic, even paying back some of the money. For the next twenty years Walpole was the foremost man in England. He was the first man who was called "Prime Minister," and took the place in the Cabinet which the sovereign had held till then. Walpole was a rough, coarse, country gentleman, with very little learning or originality; he made no great reforms, while he has been much blamed for getting his own way in Parliament by bribing the members. But, on the other hand, he was a clear-headed, practical man, with plenty of sound common sense. He knew that the country was in a very restless state, because the Roman Catholics and Dissenters were irritated by the laws made against them, and because many of the Tory country gentlemen wanted the Stuarts back.

Walpole Prime Minister, 1721-1742.

Now, being a country gentleman himself, Walpole could gather round him the great Whig families, such as the Russells, Cavendishes, and others who favoured the house of Hanover. These families had great power in nominating members to Parliament, and moreover many places where towns had fallen into decay, such as Old Sarum, near Salisbury, still sent members, though there were hardly any people to vote, and the few there were sold the seat to the highest bidder. Thus more than half the members of Parliament were not really chosen by the people, but nominated by the Government, and Walpole had a House of Commons which would do much as he liked.

Whig families and nomination boroughs.

He made use of it to give the country rest. By remaining friendly with the French he kept the Pretender quiet, without repealing the laws against Dissenters and Roman Catholics, he managed that they should not be put in force. There was, indeed, a slight Jacobite conspiracy in 1722, and Atterbury, Bishop of Rochester, was banished for encouraging it; and there was trouble in Ireland because Walpole had given a patent to an

Walpole gives the country rest.

ENGLAND STRENGTHENED.

English ironmaster named Wood to coin farthings and halfpence to the value of £108,000 for circulation in Ireland. The Irish Parliament objected that they should lose by this coinage, and Swift, who disliked Walpole, published seven letters, called the Drapier letters, on the subject, which inflamed the people still more. Walpole, however, wisely withdrew the halfpence, and no evil followed. In this way he kept peace, and taught the people to value a steady Government, under which they could live and work quietly. *Wood's halfpence, 1723.*

When George I. died of a fit of apoplexy in his carriage, on his way to Osnabruck, in Hanover, his son succeeded him without any disturbance; and though the new king did not like Walpole, he found him too useful to be sent away, and the change of kings made no difference to England. *Death of George I., June 10, 1727.*

5. George II.—George II. was a thorough German like his father, though he could speak English. He was stubborn and passionate, and would often have sacrificed England to Hanover; but fortunately his wife, Caroline of Anspach, had great influence over him, and being a clever woman, she saw how valuable Walpole was, and upheld him till her death in 1737. Then towards the end of the reign the great Pitt, afterwards Lord Chatham, took the reins of government, and we shall see that George II.'s reign was an important one in history, because he was, in spite of himself, in the hands of two able ministers, both of whom he disliked. *Character of George II.*

6. Walpole's Trade Policy.—For the next ten years there is very little to relate. Walpole was chiefly employed in economising, and paying off part of the National Debt, while at the same time he also abolished the duties on many articles sent in and out of England. He was the first to see the folly of forbidding the colonies to trade with other countries, and he allowed Georgia and Carolina to export rice to different parts of Europe. By this means the Carolina rice took the place of the inferior rice of Italy and Egypt, and all countries profited by it. He also tried to lighten the *custom* duties paid at our own *Walpole's Finance.*

seaports, and to collect the duties on certain goods as *excise* or inland taxes. If he could have done this, it would have stopped a great deal of smuggling, made London a free port, and doubled English trade. But the people did not understand this, and thought it would be unbearable to have excise officers coming to their shops, and the agitation was so great against the bill that Walpole withdrew it. Still his influence remained very strong, till he made the mistake which so often ruins popular ministers. He liked to have power in his own hands, and being jealous of others, he parted by degrees with nearly all the best men in his Cabinet. The result was that a strong "opposition" party was formed against him, led by such men as Pulteney, afterwards Earl of Bath, Carteret, and Chesterfield, while among the younger men the most eloquent and earnest was William Pitt, a young cornet, who was grandson of a former governor of Madras. This party took the name of the "Patriots," and complained loudly against Walpole's peace policy, and the bribery by which he secured votes. Walpole treated them with good-humoured contempt, although they had the support of Frederick, Prince of Wales, who had quarrelled with his parents. When they talked of patriotism and honour, he laughed at them, saying, "They would grow wiser and come out of that," and he held his ground, till a quarrel with Spain which broke out in 1739 began his fall.

7. The Family Compact.—In fact a secret danger was threatening England, for France was extremely jealous of her trade and her colonies, and in 1733 Louis XV., who had now children of his own, and was no longer afraid of his uncle Philip V., made a "Family Compact" with him that Spain should gradually take away her South American trade from England and give it to France. France in return promised to help Spain to get back Gibraltar. No one knew of the compact at the time, but it was really the beginning of a long struggle between England and France which should have the chief trade and colonies of the world.

It was not difficult for Spain to find an excuse for quarrelling with England. By the Treaty of Utrecht one English ship of 600 tons was to be allowed to trade each year with the South Seas. This

ENGLAND STRENGTHENED. 239

ship had not kept strictly to the bargain. Other small ships hovered near, and brought in goods by night to the large one, so that much more than one shipload was landed. Besides this a number of English goods were smuggled into the Spanish ports of America, and the Spaniards in return used their right of searching ships at sea. This often led to acts of violence, which became worse after the compact with France, and the English grew very indignant. In 1738 a sea-captain named Jenkins came before Parliament and said that his ears had been cut off by the Spaniards in 1731, and that they had abused England and the king. It is very doubtful whether this was true, and Walpole tried hard to keep peace. But the Patriots used the story to stir up the country, and they forced Walpole to declare war against his own judgment. "They may ring their bells now," said he, when the people rejoiced at the war, "but they will soon be wringing their hands." <small>War of Jenkins's ear, 1739.</small>

8. Fall of Walpole.—He was right, but he had better have resigned and let those manage the war who approved of it. The beginning of the struggle did not go well, and people said it was because Walpole was against it. Moreover it soon became mixed up with a much larger war which broke out in 1740 all over Europe, while at the same time a terrible frost in the winter of 1740, and a bad harvest the next summer, brought great suffering both to England and Ireland. Bread rose to famine prices, and the people, always ready to blame the Government, cried out loudly against Walpole. At last, in Jan. 1742, he was obliged to resign. As usual his enemies wished to impeach him, but he had still too many friends. He was raised to the peerage with the title of Earl of Orford, and a pension of £4000 a year. He was the first chief minister who received a title on retiring from office, instead of running the risk of losing his head. This shows how the House of Commons was now beginning to govern the country. In former times there was no means of getting rid of an unpopular minister except by impeaching him. But now that the real power was in the hands of the Commons, a minister could be set aside and at the same time honoured for his past services by removing him to the House of Lords.

9. War of the Austrian Succession.—With the fall of Walpole fell also the policy of peace with France, which had lasted for more than a quarter of a century. The new ministry which was now formed was quite willing to do what George II. had long wanted, and join the war on the Continent to protect Hanover. This war had sprung up because the Emperor Charles VI., having no son, had persuaded the great powers to sign a treaty called the "Pragmatic Sanction," promising that his daughter Maria Theresa should have all his hereditary possessions. But when he died in 1740 none of those who had signed, except England and Holland, were willing to keep their word. Frederick II. of Prussia seized Silesia, the Elector of Bavaria claimed Austria, and France and Spain took his part. Maria Theresa, Archduchess of Austria and Queen of Hungary, fought bravely for her rights, and the "War of the Austrian Succession" lasted nearly nine years. It was in fact part of the struggle for the "Balance of Power" which makes each of the nations on the Continent afraid that some other will grow too strong.

England had an excuse for joining in the war because she had signed the Pragmatic Sanction, and George II. now went himself to fight, and defeated the French in the battle of Dettingen on the Maine. But this brought upon England just what Walpole had tried to avoid. The French at once retaliated by sending 15,000 men to land in England under Charles Edward, son of the Pretender. They never arrived, for a storm scattered the fleet; but the next year when the French, under the famous Marshal Saxe, defeated the English at Fontenoy, Prince Charles Edward made a second attempt, and landed in the Highlands, July 1745, to regain the English crown for his father.

Battles of Dettingen, 1743; Fontenoy, 1745.

10. The '45.—It seemed at first as if all Walpole's work was to be undone. Charles Edward was a handsome, daring young fellow, and the Highlanders rallied round him at once. By Aug. 29 he was at the head of a large army, a fortnight later he had entered the city of Edinburgh and proclaimed his father king, and on Sept. 21 his wild Highlanders cut Sir John Cope's English troops to pieces at Prestonpans, about nine miles from the city. "Bonnie Prince

ENGLAND STRENGTHENED.

Charlie" was now almost master of Scotland, and six weeks later he started with 6000 men to try his fortune in England.

Here, however, he was soon undeceived. The English had enjoyed peace and quiet under the Georges, and they did not want to begin the struggle again. They flocked to look at the young prince and his Highlanders, but they did not join him, and by the time he reached Derby his advisers saw that the English armies would be too strong for him, and persuaded him to retire to Glasgow. He gained one victory at Falkirk, Jan. 1746, but a few months later, in April, his Highlanders were utterly defeated by the Duke of Cumberland at Culloden, on the borders of Inverness. During the next five months Prince Charlie wandered about the Highlands, faithfully concealed by his friends, especially by a lady named Flora Macdonald, who was devoted to his cause. At last in September he escaped back to France. *English do not rise. Battles of Falkirk and Culloden, 1746.*

This was the last Jacobite rising. The Stuarts never again tried to regain their throne. The old Pretender died in 1766, and Prince Charlie died in 1788 at Rome, where his only brother was a cardinal. The Highlanders were very cruelly treated by the Duke of Cumberland after the battle, and three Scotch lords were beheaded. Moreover, laws were made taking away the power of the chiefs over their clans, so as to break the feudal traditions, and bring the people more directly under the sovereign. The Highlanders, forbidden to carry weapons or wear their own peculiar dress, remained very restless and unhappy, till twelve years later, when Pitt carried out the happy idea suggested by a Scotchman, John Duncan, of raising Highland regiments to fight in the wars. Since then there have been no braver or more faithful subjects than the Highlanders. *Disarming of the Highlanders, 1746.*

11. Religious Revival.—During all these years, while wars and rebellions were troubling the country, we hear scarcely anything of the Church or the clergy. Walpole had been chiefly anxious to keep things quiet; the upper classes had grown to care very little for religion or morality; and the country vicars, who were many of them Jacobites, were more interested in politics than in teaching the people, who sank into wickedness and vice as they increased in numbers. It was this sad state of things which led two clergymen, George Whitefield and John Wesley, to preach not only in the churches but in the open air to all who would come and listen. The rough colliers of Bristol, the wretched poor of the cities, the country people in remote villages, gathered in the fields and open spaces to listen to men who were earnest and eager to lead them to a better life. Like the friars in the reign of Henry III., Whitefield and Wesley did the work which the Church was neglecting. From their preaching sprang the "Methodists," now a large and earnest body both in England and America. Their founders were Churchmen, and they aroused the Church of England, so that our English clergy have become devoted earnest teachers and workers among the people both in the quiet villages and in the crowded towns.

Preaching of Whitefield and Wesley. 1739.

For the next eight years politics remained quiet. Henry Pelham, was Prime Minister, and he ruled firmly and well. In 1748 the war on the Continent ended in a peace signed at Aix-la-Chapelle. It had been an enormous expense to England, without any return except the million dollars' worth of treasure which Commodore Anson, who had been sent to plunder the Spaniards, brought back after sailing round the world. It had, however, put an end to the intrigues of the Stuarts, and increased the power of Great Britain on the seas.

Peace of Aix-la-Chapelle, 1748.

12. Minor Reforms.—In 1751 Prince Frederick of Wales died, and his young son George became the heir to the throne. That same year, an Act was passed adopting the *new style* of dating the days of the year. This style had been introduced into Roman Catholic countries by Pope Gregory XIII. in 1582 to correct the old style, by which the year became about three days too long at the end of four centuries. According to the new style, one of these days is cut out at the end of each century (by passing over one leap-year), except at the end of each fourth century, when it is not needed. England did not adopt this style in 1582, and so was now eleven days behind France and Germany; her Sept. 3 was their Sept. 14. It was enacted that in 1752 these eleven days should be skipped over and the new style

Reform of the Calendar. 1751.

adopted. The people found this difficult to understand, and when told that Sept. 3, 1752, was to be called Sept. 14 for the future, there were actually some riots, because they fancied they would really lose eleven days. In this same year, 1752, the year was fixed to begin on Jan. 1 instead of on March 25.' The next year, 1753, deserves to be remembered as the year in which Lord Hardwicke passed an Act putting a stop to the shameful marriages which took place near the Fleet Prison, where disreputable parsons, imprisoned for debt, married any two people who came to them and paid well, without asking any questions. *Hardwicke's Marriage Act, 1753.

13. English East India Company.—But though during these eight years, from 1748 to 1756, England was at peace at home, yet she was struggling with France in two widely distant parts of the world. It will be remembered that Queen Elizabeth granted a charter in 1599 to a company of English merchants to trade in the East Indies, and now for nearly 150 years the East India Company had been founding factories and stations on different parts of the shores of Hindustan. In 1613 they built a factory at Surat on the west coast; and in 1640 another on the east coast called Fort St. George, around which grew up the town of MADRAS (*see* Map VI.) In 1662 BOMBAY near Surat was given to England as the dowry of Charles II.'s queen; while in 1698, in the reign of William III., another English company founded Fort William on the river Hooghley, round which the town of CALCUTTA was built. Lastly, the two companies became one in 1702. Each of these three stations had a governor and a small army, chiefly of native soldiers or *sepoys* (*sepahai*, soldier), to protect the factories, and the traders paid a yearly rent for their land to the *Nawab* or native prince of their district. Over these Nawabs were *Nizams* or governors of provinces, and over all was the Great Moghul of India.

Now the French also had an East India Company, which had built a fort at Pondicherry, about a hundred miles south of Madras, and south of this again the English had a settlement called Fort St. David. The English and French settlers were very jealous of each other, and between 1746 and 1748, when the nations were at war at home, sharp fightingFrench East India Company.

went on here, and the French took Madras, but gave it back at the peace of Aix-la-Chapelle.

In 1748 the Great Moghul of India and the Nizam of the Dekkan or Southern India both died, and the Nawabs began to quarrel among themselves. Dupleix, Governor of Pondicherry, who was an ambitious man, hoped by encouraging these disputes to become master of South India. By putting in a Nizam of the Dekkan and a Nawab of Arcot near Madras, of his own choosing, he did really for a short time hold the country.

<small>Dupleix tries to rule South India, 1749.</small>

It seemed as if the English traders would be driven out from Madras, for their ally, Nawab Muhammad Ali, was shut up in Trichinopoly and besieged by the French. In this peril they were saved, and the foundation of our Indian Empire was laid, by a young clerk of the Company, Robert Clive, who had been sent out in 1744 by his family because he was too wild to be controlled at home. Clive had already fought the French in 1746, and now he formed the daring scheme of relieving Muhammad Ali. With a small band of only 200 English and 300 Sepoys, he marched to Arcot, surprised the garrison, and held the town for fifty days, till the Mahrattas, who were friends of Muhammad Ali, joined him and routed the enemy. Trichinopoly was relieved. Soon after this his superior officer, Major Lawrence, returned from England, and victory after victory forced the French to give up the struggle. In spite of all his efforts Dupleix could not regain his power; he was recalled to France, a peace was signed in 1754, and for a time all was quiet.

<small>Clive saves the English settlement, 1751.</small>

<small>Peace in India, 1754.</small>

14

9. French and English in America.—But the struggle between the French and English only died out in one country to spring up in another. The very year that the peace was signed in India, fighting began in America. The English had now thirteen flourishing colonies in North America, each with its own laws and its own industries. These colonies were all on the east coast. To the north of them were the French, who had colonised Canada, now called the province of Quebec (*see* Map VII.); to the north-west were the North American Indians; and on the south-west was the

French possession of Louisiana. For a long time the country of the Red Indians to the north-west had been a source of dispute. The French governors claimed all the country west of the Alleghanies, and drove out the English settlers. The English penetrated up the valley of the Ohio, and were building a fort in the fork of the river, when Duquesne, Governor of Canada, sent a large force in 1754, which drove them out, and estab-·lished there a French stronghold called Fort Duquesne. George Washington, then a young man of twenty-two, who was sent to retake the fort, had so few men compared to the enemy that after one successful skirmish, he was forced to retire. The Marquis of Montcalm, who now succeeded Duquesne as Governor of Canada, determined to link the three forts Duquesne, Niagara, and Ticonderoga (Map VII.) together by lesser forts, so as to cut off the English entirely from the west. This led the Government at home to take the matter up seriously, and Major-General Braddock was sent from England with 2000 men. Braddock was unfortunate. / As he marched through the woods to capture Fort Duquesne, 700 of his army were destroyed by French and Indians in ambush, and he himself was killed. It was now clear that England and France must fight the matter out.

Fort Duquesne, 1754.

Defeat of Braddock, 1755.

15. Seven Years' War.—Nor was this all, for the war on the Continent had been breaking out afresh. Ever since the peace of Aix-la-Chapelle Maria Theresa had longed to get back Silesia, and Frederick II., King of Prussia, had just learnt that France, Sweden, Russia, and Saxony were willing to help her to crush his growing power. Shrewd and far-seeing, he began the attack by declaring war against Saxony and making an alliance with England; and so it came to pass that England and Prussia on one side, and France, Russia, Austria, and Saxony on the other, began that terrible struggle known as the "Seven Years' War."

Outbreak of the Seven Years' War, 1756.

England was completely unprepared. The army had been greatly neglected, and there were only three regiments fit for service. The nation was seized with a panic lest France should invade England, and the Duke of Newcastle, who had become Prime Minister when his bro-

England overwhelmed with disaster, 1756.

ther, Henry Pelham, died, was a weak, fussy man, quite unfit to face such a time of danger. A great disaster had already taken place. Before declaring war the French had taken possession of Minorca, and Admiral Byng, who was sent with ten ships badly manned, to turn them out, found he was not strong enough to overcome them, and after a slight skirmish was forced to retire. Newcastle, terrified at the anger of the people, promised that Byng should be tried by court-martial on his return to England. Indeed the next year, after Newcastle had gone out of office, Byng was tried, and although the court recommended him strongly to mercy, declaring that though by law guilty he was morally guiltless, yet the gallant admiral was shot on March 14, 1757.

<small>French seize Minorca, April 17, 1756.</small>

<small>Execution of Admiral Byng, 1757.</small>

Scarcely had the nation begun to recover from the loss of Minorca than still more terrible news reached England from India. One of the native Indian princes, Suraj-ud-Daula, Viceroy of Bengal, had quarrelled with the English traders, marched upon Calcutta, seized the city, and thrust 146 English prisoners, on a sultry June night, into the strong-room of the garrison, called the "Black Hole," which was not twenty feet square, and had only two small gratings to admit air. Stifled and shrieking for release, the unhappy prisoners were left to die of suffocation. In the morning only twenty-three came out alive. Then Suraj-ud-Daula put an Indian garrison in Fort William, and forbade any English to live in Calcutta, which he named Alinagore, the "Port of God."

<small>Black Hole of Calcutta, June, 1756.</small>

Never had England been so low as in these years of 1756–1757. Frederick II. was scarcely holding his ground on the Continent— the Duke of Cumberland had retreated before the French army, and agreed at Closterzeven to allow them to occupy Hanover—the French were victorious everywhere in Canada. Englishmen had been murdered in India, and even the great statesman, Chesterfield, exclaimed, "We are no longer a nation!"

<small>Defeat on the Continent, 1757.</small>

16. William Pitt.—The turn of fortune, however, had already begun. It was now that William Pitt, once the leader of the younger "Patriots," and afterwards known as Lord Chatham, came

ENGLAND STRENGTHENED.

to the front. For many years Pitt, by his love for his country, his outspoken earnestness, and his opposition to injustice, as when he spoke vehemently to save Byng, had won the hearts of the people. But George II. disliked him for his speeches against Hanover. In 1756 the Duke of Devonshire, then Prime Minister, chose him as Secretary of State, but the king dismissed him a few months later. The consequence was the Government broke up, and Newcastle, who now had to form a ministry, told His Majesty roundly that he could not govern without Pitt. So George was obliged to yield, and the "Great Commoner," as the nation called him, was Secretary of State for the next four years. During that time, though Newcastle remained Prime Minister, and did all the bribing which was usual at that time to make the members vote with the Government, Pitt had the real power in the State. "I am sure," said he, "I can save the country, and that no one else can;" and it was this confidence which enabled him in four years to raise England from the depths of despair to the height of power. *Administration of Pitt, 1757-1761.* Pitt had many faults; he was violent, vindictive, and often ungrateful, but he was also disinterested, patriotic, and courageous; he steadily refused to enrich himself, and he served his country well.

He came into power in June 1757, and in a very short time the militia was organized all over the country, the navy was strengthened, and the Highlanders were formed into regiments. Pitt utterly refused to recognise the disgraceful convention of Closterzeven; the Duke of Cumberland was recalled, and Duke Ferdinand of Brunswick, an able general, was sent out to command the English and Hanoverians. A yearly subsidy of £700,000 was voted for King Frederick, who now, sure of support, took fresh courage, and routed the French and Germans at Rossbach, in Saxony, Nov. 15, 1757. A month later he defeated a large Austrian army at Leuthen, in Silesia. *Battles of Rossbach and Leuthen, 1757.* It was these victories, and the desperate courage by which he held his position against so many enemies, which gained for the King of Prussia the name of Frederick the Great, and prevented his country from being crushed in those early days, when she was scarcely yet a power in Europe.

248　HISTORY OF ENGLAND.

17. Conquest of Canada.—But while Pitt gave fresh life to the war on the Continent of Europe, he turned his chief attention to America, where England had much more to gain or to lose. He appealed to the colonists to raise armies to attack Quebec and Montreal, and to conquer the west country, winning their sympathy by giving their officers equal rank with the royal officers in the field. From England he sent ammunition, arms, and provisions, as well as his newly-raised Highland regiments. General Abercromby went as commander-in-chief, but Pitt chose out comparatively young though able men, Amherst, Wolfe, and Howe, to act under him. He sent Admiral Boscawen with a fleet to attack Louisburg in the north, and to cut off the Canadians from help by sea.

War in Canada, 1757-1760.

The next three years were eventful for Canada. On July 27, 1758, Louisburg and the whole of Cape Breton fell into the hands of the English. On Nov. 25 Fort Duquesne was retaken by a body of Highlanders and Americans, under General Forbes and Washington. It was at once renamed Pittsburg (Map VII.), after the great minister. The English met, indeed, with reverses at Ticonderoga, where Lord Howe was killed and General Abercromby defeated, but the next year, 1759, Ticonderoga, Crown Point, and Niagara were all taken.

Fort Duquesne taken, 1758.

Meanwhile the brave French commander Montcalm, who received very scanty support from France, was holding Quebec, the chief city of Canada, against Wolfe. Quebec stands on high rocks overhanging the left bank of the river St. Lawrence, and has another river, St. Charles, beside it. To the west of the city is a high rocky plain, the Plains of Abraham, and on the lower ground to the east Montcalm had planted his army. In June 1759 a large fleet, with General Wolfe's soldiers on board, sailed up the St. Lawrence; but neither by bombarding, nor by an attack in which he lost several men, could Wolfe take the city. Disheartened and ill with fever, which also destroyed a large part of his army, he thought he would have to give up the attempt till after the winter. But one day while reconnoitering the north shore above Quebec, he noticed a narrow path winding up the steep to the Heights of Abraham, and resolved to lead his army up by night and surprise the city. At midnight of Sept. 12 his preparations

Taking of Quebec, Sept. 1759.

were made. Two hours later his troops were silently gliding down the St. Lawrence in boats, borne by the current to their destined landing-place, Wolfe's Cove. As the procession moved on, Wolfe softly repeated Gray's "Elegy," written a few years before. He paused on the words,

"The paths of glory lead but to the grave."

"I would rather be the author of that poem," he exclaimed, "than take Quebec." At daybreak the little army stood on the plains, and Montcalm, though taken by surprise, hastened to repulse them. As the French rushed forward the English met them with a deadly volley. Montcalm cheered his troops on, but they were too untrained, and they gave way before the charge of bayonets that followed. "They run, they run!" said an officer to Wolfe, who lay in his arms mortally wounded. "Who run?" asked Wolfe; and when he heard, "Now God be praised," said he, "I die happy." The brave Montcalm, too, died of his wounds; and when he heard his fate he murmured sadly, "So much the better; I shall not live to see the surrender of Quebec." A monument now stands on the Heights of Abraham, on which are inscribed side by side the names of these two brave generals, who died each doing his duty. Though the war went on for another year, till Montreal surrendered, on Sept. 8, 1760, yet the real conquest of Canada, which crushed the power of the French in America, took place under the walls of Quebec.

Death of Wolfe and Montcalm.

18. European Successes.—It was a proud time for Pitt, to whose energy and support so much of the success of his young commanders was due. And this same year brought other victories in Europe. At Minden, in Westphalia, the English and Hanoverians, under Duke Ferdinand, defeated the French, while Admiral Boscawen sunk five French ships off Lagos, in Portugal, that same month. In November Admiral Hawke defeated the rest of the fleet, in the midst of a gale of wind, off Quiberon Bay, on the west coast of France. "We are forced to ask every morning what victory there is." wrote Horace Walpole, son of the late minister, "for fear of missing one."

19. Clive and India.—At the same time tidings came from the other side of the world that another possession was being won for England. Clive had come home in ill-health in 1753, and had only just returned to Madras as Governor of Fort St. David, when the horrible news of the Black Hole tragedy arrived there. It was at once decided to send Admiral Watson and Clive to retake Calcutta; and before six months were over the English flag again waved over Fort William, and Suraj-ud-Daula was forced to sign a peace. But he did not keep his word, and when Clive found that he was plotting with the French to drive out the English from Bengal, and had posted a large army at Plassy, he determined to depose him, and put one of his officers, Mir-Jafir, in his place. Though Clive had only a small army of 3000 men against the Nawab's army of 60,000, he risked a battle at Plassy. It was the first great battle fought by the English in India, and it was little more than a rout. The native army fell quickly into disorder before the English cannon. Suraj-ud-Daula was seized with a panic and fled, and Mir-Jafir was placed on the throne, under the protection of the English. This battle decided the fate of India. Clive remained for three years reducing the country to order, and then returned to England and was made an Irish peer, with the title of Lord Clive. Meanwhile at Madras fighting was still going on. Colonel Eyre Coote defeated the French at Wandiwash, and Pondicherry was taken by the English. Though it was afterwards given back to the French, with its fortifications destroyed, yet the native princes henceforward looked to the English for support and protection. When Lord Clive returned to India in 1765 the Great Moghul invested the East India Company with the office of "Dewan" or collector of the revenue of Bengal, Behar, and Orissa, in return for a yearly tribute of a quarter of a million sterling, and this gave the English great power.[1]

20. Close of the War.—Meanwhile great changes were taking place in England. George II. died Oct. 26, 1760, and his grandson George III. succeeded him. The new king wished for peace, while Pitt wanted to go on further and declare war against Spain, which had secretly promised to help France. The House of Commons, however, was tired of the expense of the war and dreaded more fighting. Pitt, wiser than

Walpole had been, retired sooner than act against his judgment, and the king put the Earl of Bute in his place. Pitt proved right, for only three weeks after he resigned, England was obliged to declare war against Spain. For another year fighting went on, and the army and navy, which Pitt had made so efficient, won brilliant victories over France and Spain. But Bute refused to give Frederick the Great any more money; and he being now supported by Russia, made a separate peace with Maria Theresa at Hubertsburg, by which he kept Silesia. Finally, a treaty was signed at Paris in 1763 between England, France, Spain, and Portugal, which brought the "Seven Years' War" to an end. By it England gained Canada, Florida, and all the French possessions east of the Mississippi except New Orleans, while in India she now became the ruling power. The French restored Minorca to England, but it passed with Florida to Spain not many years after.

War with Spain, 1762.

Peace of Hubertsburg, Feb. 1763.

Treaty of Paris, Feb. 1763.

CHAPTER XXIII.

INDEPENDENCE OF THE AMERICAN COLONIES.

1. Political Condition of England.—When the peace of Paris was signed in 1763, George III. had already been king for three years. The kingdom over which he reigned had now become a great power. "You would not know your own country," wrote Horace Walpole to a friend; "you left it a private little island living upon its means, you would find it the capital of the world." On the other hand, if George III. succeeded to a powerful kingdom, he also succeeded kings who had very little power. George II. had once said, "In England the ministers are king;" and these ministers belonged to the great Whig families who returned half the members to Parliament, and bought up the votes of the rest whenever they wished to pass a Bill. They even held almost regal

England a great power.

252 HISTORY OF ENGLAND.

levées, to which all men came who wished to obtain Government posts and other favours; for as the kings were foreigners they were chiefly guided by the ministers. Thus it had come to pass that Parliament was no longer freely elected by the people, nor had the king much power over it.

<small>Parliament no longer representative.</small>

England was drifting back into the old order of things before the Wars of the Roses, when the great nobles governed the land. The political history of the first twenty years of George III.'s reign is chiefly occupied with the efforts of the king to get back his power over the ministers, and the resistance of the nation, both in England and America, to attacks upon their liberty.

2. Industrial Condition of England.—Meanwhile a great change was coming over the nation itself, for the age of discoveries and inventions which was just setting in brought machinery to take the place of hand work, and increased all industries and manufactures so rapidly that large towns sprang up during the next fifty years where none had been before. In 1761 the flyshuttle enabled the weavers to do twice as much work as before. In 1767-1768 Hargreaves invented the spinning Jenny, and Arkwright the spinning-frame; and these were followed a few years later by Dr. Cartwright's invention of the power-loom, which took the place of hand-labour. Though the ignorant mob again and again broke these machines and burnt the mills, yet the industries of spinning and weaving gained enormously in a few years. Then the discovery that pit-coal could be used for smelting iron, and the invention of Watt's steam-engine in 1769, led to large iron-works and factories being founded near to the coal-mines of the North. England was fast becoming a manufacturing country. There only remained the difficulty of carrying the goods from place to place or to the ports, and this was greatly overcome by the energy of the Duke of Bridgewater. In 1758 the Duke obtained an Act of Parliament allowing him to make a canal six miles long, from his coal-mines at Worsley to Manchester. His scheme was thought mad at first, for his canal had to cross the valleys of the Mersey and Irwell by an aqueduct 290 yards long. But when Brindley, the celebrated engineer, overcame this difficulty, the canal was so

<small>Machinery and Steam power.</small>

<small>First canals, 1758-1760.</small>

INDEPENDENCE OF AMERICAN COLONIES. 253

successful that others were soon made, and goods carried in barges all over England.

The consequence of this great outbreak of industry was that the population increased very quickly, and food became much dearer. There was not then, as now, a large supply of corn and other food coming from abroad, for these were shut out by heavy duties. So corn which during the five years from 1760 to 1764 averaged 30 shillings a quarter, averaged 45 shillings during the following five years, and went on rising rapidly in price for fifty years longer. Those farmers who understood the best ways of raising crops prospered, and more and more waste land was enclosed every year to grow corn, clover, turnip, and other root-crops. *Enclosures of land, 1760-1774.* No less than 700 enclosure Acts were passed between 1760 and 1774. This did good in some ways, for it led to the land being better cultivated, and to good roads being made by which the haunts of highwaymen were destroyed. But, on the other hand, the labourers lost the waste land on which they used to send a horse or cow to graze; and as they had to pay more heavily for food and clothing, they were not so well off as they had been a hundred years before. The great difficulty now began which has increased up to our own day, of the rich growing richer while the poor grew poorer. *Increase of poverty and paupers.* From this time the Poor law, which had been useful in Elizabeth's reign, began to be a burden on the industrious people who had to provide for the paupers.

The time had now come when farming was no longer the chief industry of the country. The manufacturing, mining, and trading classes had increased enormously, and the questions of custom-duties and commercial treaties abroad, and of rates and taxes at home were important, not only to the rich manufacturers, merchants, and farmers but also to the artisans and mechanics in the workshops. Now these were regulated by Parliament, which, as we see, was composed chiefly of the great land-owners and those whom they favoured, who were not elected by the people for whom they made laws. *Growing importance of the middle classes.* This is why we find constantly in this reign that loud complainings and riots often followed some measure passed by the Commons.

254   HISTORY OF ENGLAND.

3. Character of George III.—At first, however, the chief struggle was between the king and his ministers. George III. came to the throne determined to be master. His mother, an ambitious German princess, was very anxious that her son should take back the power into his own hands, and be a father to his people. "George, be a king," was her constant maxim; and during the sixty years of his long reign he tried to follow her advice. He was a simple, conscientious, religious man, and an affectionate husband and father. His quiet home life with Queen Charlotte and their fifteen children, and his patience under sad attacks of insanity, made his people love and respect him, and he was often spoken of as "dear old king George." But with all this he was unfortunately narrow-minded, ignorant, obstinate, and arbitrary, so that his determination to rule by his own will led him into serious blunders. If he did good to England by making the manners more pure, religion more reverenced, and the people as a whole more loyal, on the other hand he gained power over Parliament by wholesale bribery, opposed all justice to Ireland, supported the slave trade, and lost the American colonies.

4. Wilkes.—We have seen that the first thing he did on coming to the throne was to part with Pitt, and to make his own tutor, Lord Bute, Prime Minister, that he might conclude a peace with France. This he did, not so much because he disliked the war, as because he wanted to be free to put down the Whigs at home. The Tories had now quite given up all hopes of a return of the Stuarts, and they were willing to support a king who was a true-born Briton. So George III. made use of his prerogative of giving away honours and offices to form a party known as the "King's friends." Henry Fox, a clever but unscrupulous politician, had joined Bute, and he promised to get a majority in the Commons to vote for the peace. He succeeded. In the year 1762 no less than £82,000 of secret service money was spent in bribery, and the peace was carried by a majority of 319 against 65, in spite of Pitt's remonstrances.

Tory party revived under Bute.

Lord Bute, however, did not keep his power long; he was a Scotchman, and since the rebellion of 1745 the English had mistrusted

INDEPENDENCE OF AMERICAN COLONIES. 255

the Scotch as Jacobites. Moreover, he was a favourite with the king's mother, and this the people did not like, and he turned out all the servants of the Government who had been appointed by the Whigs, even the clerks and excisemen, and put a most unpopular tax on cider. For a long time he had gone about the streets protected by a bodyguard of prize-fighters, and at last he became so alarmed at this unpopularity that he resigned. *Bribery and injustice; Bute resigns.*

The next minister was George Grenville, a Whig, but he did not succeed much better, and the king did not find him easy to control. Though an honest, conscientious man, he made mischief both at home and in America. His first difficulty was scarcely his own fault. The king's speech, made when Parliament was prorogued, had been violently attacked in "No. 45" of the *North Briton*, a paper edited by a worthless but popular man named Wilkes, who was member for Aylesbury. Grenville issued a "general warrant" to arrest the "authors, printers, and publishers of the paper," and Wilkes, with forty-eight others, was put into prison. He soon gained his freedom under the *Habeas Corpus* Act, and proceeded against the Government for arresting a member of Parliament, and for issuing a *general warrant* which did not give names of the people to be arrested. He gained his cause, but Parliament prosecuted him for libel, and serious riots took place. The people shouted for "Wilkes and liberty," and so many libels were published against the king and his mother that 200 printers were prosecuted. Wilkes was wounded in a duel, and crossed over to France, being outlawed by Parliament. From that time, however, no general warrants have ever been issued. *Grenville's Administration, 1763. Arrest of Wilkes. General warrants.*

5. Stamp Act.—This contest was no sooner over than Grenville made another mistake, which was the beginning of the quarrel with the American colonies. For a long time the colonists had really governed themselves, for English ministers paid very little attention to them. But Grenville, as was wittily said, "lost America because he read the American despatches." The foolish law that the colonies might only trade with England had been evaded for a long time, and the colonists made large sums by trading with Spanish

America. Grenville determined to put this down, and at the same time, as the late war in America had been very expensive, he proposed to levy money by a "Stamp Act," obliging legal papers in America to bear a stamp as in England. The colonists were very indignant. It was quite just that they should help to pay for a war which had been incurred on their account, but they had been accustomed to vote their own taxes, and would have given the money willingly if they had levied it themselves. They petitioned against the Act, but it was passed nevertheless in 1765. The consequence was that the Americans, the State of Virginia setting the example, pledged themselves not to buy any goods from England, and several manufacturers were ruined.

Just at this time the king had his first short attack of insanity, and when he recovered he desired that a Regency Bill should be passed to provide a regent in case he was ill again. *Regency Bill, 1765.* The name of the king's mother was left out of this Bill, and the king was so displeased that Grenville was obliged to resign. The new minister, Lord Rockingham, determined to repeal the hated stamp tax, and Pitt, though he was ill, came down to the House and insisted that *as the colonists had no representatives in Parliament to see that just taxes were imposed, England had no right to tax them,* and that the Act ought to be "repealed absolutely, totally, and immediately." *Taxation and representation. Repeal of Stamp Act, 1766.* This was done, and the king invited Pitt to join the ministry, with the Duke of Grafton as Prime Minister.

But Pitt had no longer his old influence. By accepting a peerage, and going to the House of Lords as "Earl of Chatham," he ceased to be the "Great Commoner," and he was in such ill-health that he could not attend to business. In his absence Townshend, the Chancellor of the Exchequer, who thought Parliament had been weak in repealing the Stamp Act, *Townshend's Revenue Act, 1767.* now actually passed a new Revenue Act imposing duties on tea, glass, red and white lead, painters' colours, and paper, imported into America; so the old irritation was set up again.

6. The Middlesex Elections.—Still the colonists loved the old country, and no outbreak occurred as yet. It was in England

INDEPENDENCE OF AMERICAN COLONIES. 257

that the House of Commons next fell into difficulties with the people. In 1769 Wilkes returned from abroad, and was elected member for Middlesex, where the electors were more independent than in many places. The king was so annoyed at this that he pressed the Government to interfere, and Wilkes was imprisoned for the libel which had obliged him to flee to France some years before. Meanwhile serious riots broke out in London. For two nights the mob obliged every one to light up their windows to celebrate Wilkes' election. The Austrian Ambassador was dragged from his coach, and had "No. 45" chalked on the soles of his shoes; and the King's Bench prison, where Wilkes lay, was so furiously attacked that the Riot Act was read, and several persons shot. Nevertheless the House declared that Wilkes was incapable of sitting in Parliament, and when, in spite of this warning, he was elected four times running, they made a great mistake by doing what they had really no power to do. They declared the rival candidate, Colonel Luttrell, to be duly elected, although he had only 296 votes against 1143. This was a direct infringement of the rights of the electors, for if Parliament could choose its members, the nation would cease to have any voice in its own laws. The people were so irritated that the king was insulted when he went to close the session; and when Wilkes came out of prison (April 1770) the word "Liberty," in letters three feet high, blazed on the front of the Mansion House, and he was elected an alderman of the city.

Wilkes elected for Middlesex, 1769.

Parliament infringes the rights of the electors.

7. Liberty of the Press.—The next year, Feb. 1771, the house and the people had another contest, in which Wilkes and the public gained the day. Ever since 1695, when the press was set free, newspapers had become more and more numerous. No less than seventeen were published in London alone, and though it was against a "standing order" of the House that reports of their proceedings should be published, yet most of the important speeches in Parliament appeared regularly in many papers. As no reporters were allowed in the House, these accounts were, of course, very inaccurate and one-sided, and often even insulting to the members. Therefore the

Parliamentary reporting, 1771.

17

Commons determined to put a stop to them, and the Speaker ordered eight printers to be taken into custody for publishing them. Two of these appealed to the law, and were brought before Wilkes and another alderman named Oliver, who discharged them as not having been guilty of a legal offence. Another named Martin, who was a liveryman of the city, gave the Speaker's messenger into custody, because the warrant was not signed by a city magistrate.

This caused a violent quarrel between the city and the House of Commons, during which the Lord Mayor and Oliver were sent to the Tower. The people flocked to cheer them as they went, and when they were released after six weeks, all London was illuminated. Meanwhile the printers remained at liberty. They had gained the battle, for *from that time the proceedings of Parliament have been regularly reported and no one has interfered.* The consequence was that better newspapers soon appeared. In 1770 the *Morning Chronicle* was first published, the *Morning Post* in 1772, and the *Times*, at first as a small square sheet, in 1785. In 1774 Wilkes was again elected for Middlesex, and allowed to take his seat, and in 1782 the Commons acknowledged they had been wrong in interfering for Colonel Luttrell, and struck the proceedings out of their journals.

City and Parliament.

Modern newspapers.

8. Revolt of the American Colonies.—All this time the restless feeling in America was growing stronger. In 1770 Lord North became Prime Minister, and he was willing to do exactly what the king wished. It was now the royal levées which were crowded with people seeking favours, and George felt he was "at last a king."

Restless feeling in American colonies, 1770.

He was all the more determined to be master of the American colonists, and in this Parliament and the people quite agreed with him. The English had always looked upon the colonies as existing for their use, and forgot that men who had faced hardship and privation to make new homes ought to be the first to benefit by their labour. America was now like a grown up son who has a right to govern his own life, but it was only such great men as Lord Chatham and Burke the Irish orator who understood this. In 1770 Lord North took off all the taxes except the one on *tea*, and this the king

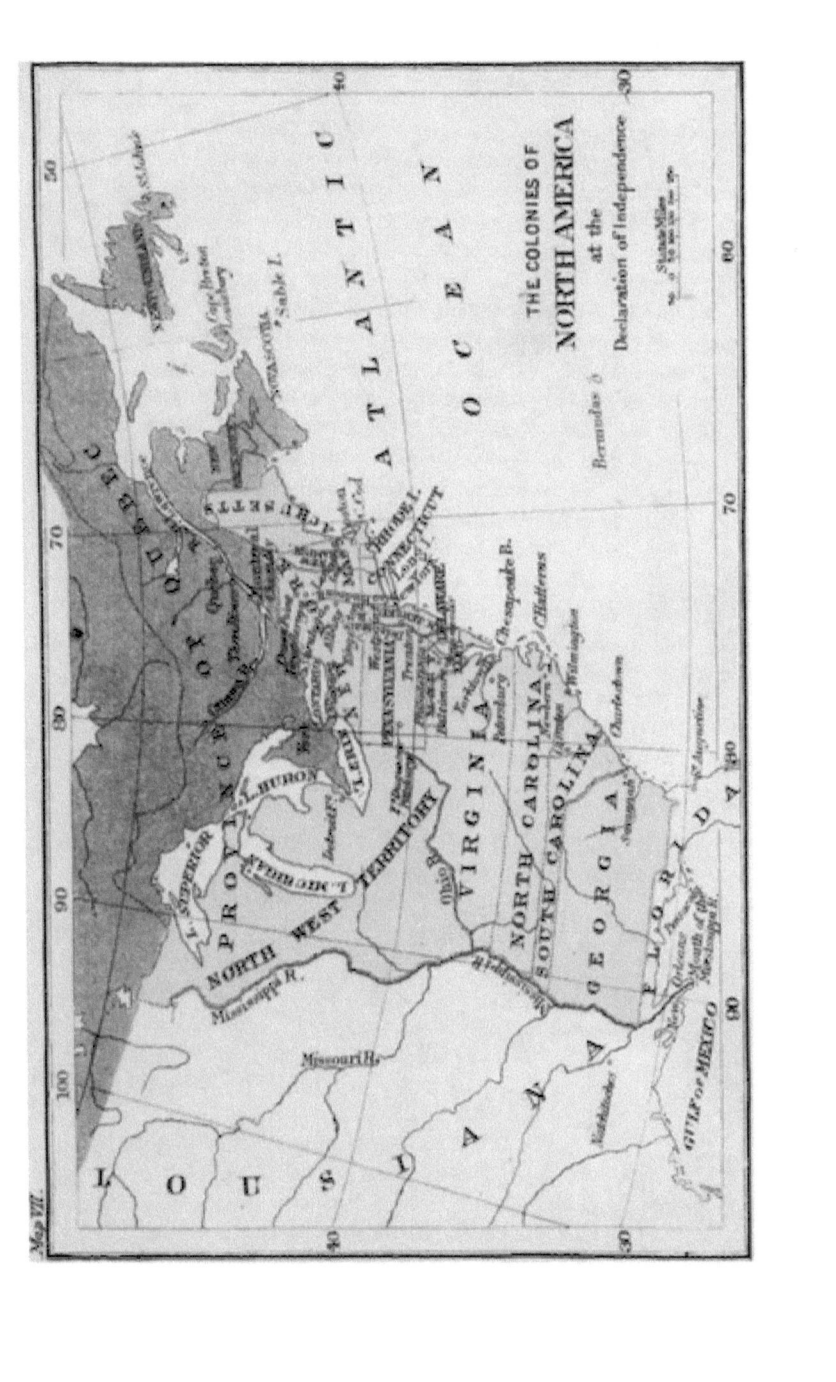

INDEPENDENCE OF AMERICAN COLONIES.

resolved to keep, though it brought in little more than £300 a year. Yet on the very day this was decided in London, a riot had taken place in Boston between the citizens and the soldiers, in which some people were killed. A wise man would have seen, when this news reached England, that it was the wrong time to irritate the colonists unnecessarily.

Still, however, another three years passed by without an outbreak. The Americans steadily refused to buy tea, and at last the East India Company suffered by the loss of trade. So Lord North took off the *English duty* on all tea which passed through to America, but he left the American duty as before. The consequence was the India Company tried to force their tea into America, and on Dec. 16, 1773, a large cargo arrived at Boston, Massachusetts. The colonists determined not to let it in, and as the ships entered the harbour a body of men disguised as Red Indians leaped on board, opened the chests with their hatchets, and emptied all the tea into the water. To punish this offence Lord North passed a Bill in 1774 to close the port of Boston, and to shut out all trade from the city; and another to annul the charter of Massachusetts, and appoint a Council named by the Crown. *[Throwing of tea into Boston Harbour, 1773.]*

From this time war was certain, though it did not break out for another year. Even Franklin, the American philosopher and statesman, who had come to England to try and mend matters, went back disheartened. In Sept. 1774 a council of fifty-five men, elected from all the thirteen colonies except Georgia, met at Philadelphia and resolved to cease trading with Great Britain till the rights of Massachusetts were restored. At the same time they organised a militia in case they should have to fight. Still the king would not yield. Parliament in 1775 declared that a rebellion existed in Massachusetts, and on April 19 the first blood was shed, when the Governor, General Gage, who had been sent to enforce the new measures, despatched some soldiers to destroy a store of arms belonging to the colonists at Lexington, near Boston (*see* Map VII.) The farmers and mechanics, who had long forseen that the struggle must come, were ready. A small band of determined men, gathered on a hillock by *[First Congress in America, 1774.]* *[War begins April 19, 1775.]*

Concord River, encountered and drove back the troops. On a monument, erected in 1836 on the scene of this skirmish, stands engraved the first verse of Emerson's Concord Hymn—

> "By the rude bridge that arched the flood,
> Their flag to April's breeze unfurled;
> Here once the embattled farmers stood,
> And fired the shot heard round the world."

For the next eight years the English army and the colonists were fighting against each other in America. A month after the battle of Concord, Congress appointed as commander-in-chief the same George Washington of Virginia who had seized Pittsburg in 1754, and who from this time forward faced suffering and privation, remained calm and self-reliant in defeat as in success, and sacrificed everything for the good of his troops and the freedom of his country. "First in war, first in peace, and first in the hearts of his countrymen," he clung to the union with England till this was no longer possible, and then became the President of a free United States in 1789.

George Washington.

This time was, as yet, far distant, though war had begun. Before Washington reached the army, the battle of Bunker's Hill near Boston had taken place, in which, though the colonists were beaten, yet they proved triumphantly that the "Yankees were no cowards." During the next year the war went on with varying success. The English defeated an American invasion of Canada in 1775; but Lord Howe was, on the other hand, forced by Washington to abandon the blockade of Boston in 1776. Gradually the colonists became sternly resolved to break off from the mother country, and this resolve gained strength when it was known that England had engaged German troops to carry on the war.

Battle of Bunker's Hill, May 1775.

On July 2, 1776, Congress, led by great and earnest men, such as John Adams, Franklin, and Sherman, voted that the united colonies should be free and independent states, and Thomas Jefferson of Virginia drew up a Declaration of Independence ending in these solemn words, "*We, the representatives of the United States of America, in Congress assembled, appealing to the Supreme Judge of the world for the rectitude of our intentions, solemnly publish and declare that these*

Declaration of Independence, July 4, 1776.

INDEPENDENCE OF AMERICAN COLONIES. 261

United Colonies are, and of right ought to be, Free and Independent States." The next year, the English army, under General Burgoyne, was surrounded at Saratoga and forced to surrender, and France, eager to avenge the humiliation of the Seven Years' War, entered into an alliance with the colonists. <small>Burgoyne's army surrenders at Saratoga, Oct. 17, 1777</small>

Lord Chatham had long foreseen that this would happen, and though broken with age and disease, he came down to the House, to urge that full redress should be given to the colonists. But in vain! Then on April 7 occurred that memorable scene in the House, when the aged statesman rose for the last time to plead for reconciliation with America, and to bid defiance to his old enemy France. The Duke of Richmond made a weak speech in reply. Chatham strove again to rise, but speech failed him, and he fell back in a swoon. A month later, he died, and his death put an end to all hope of peace. <small>Death of Chatham, 1778.</small>

The next four years were very troubled ones for England. In 1779 Spain joined France against her, and besieged Gibraltar, which General Eliott defended successfully for three years, till he destroyed the enemy's fleet with red-hot shot, and was relieved by Lord Howe. In 1780 Russia, Sweden, and Denmark, entered into an armed neutrality to prevent the English from searching their vessels for "*contraband of war*," that is for goods belonging to an enemy, and Prussia and Holland joined them soon after. <small>Siege of Gibraltar, 1779-1782.</small>

10. Domestic Troubles.—Nor was the danger only from abroad, for the troops had been taken from Ireland for the American war, and as the French threatened an invasion, the Irish raised a volunteer corps, chiefly of Protestants, to protect the country. This corps increased very rapidly up to 100,000 men, and with such an army the Irish, who had been so long oppressed by restrictions on their trade, could venture to follow the example of America. Henry Grattan, a noble and eloquent speaker moved in the Irish Parliament that they ought to have the free right of exporting their goods to other countries; and Lord North, harassed on all sides, passed a Bill in 1780 giving them this right for wool and glass. <small>Grattan obtains free export for Ireland, 1780.</small>

In England the uneasy feeling showed itself in another way. In 1778 Parliament had repealed some of the more oppressive laws against the Roman Catholics. This offended the extreme Protestants, and Lord George Gordon, a weak-headed fanatic, led 60,000 people to the House of Parliament to petition against the Bill. It was the first monster petition ever presented to Parliament, and it was not a success. The badly-governed mob insulted the Lords, and broke into the lobby of the Commons, till they were turned out by main force. On their way back riots broke out, and London was for four days in the hands of the mob. Roman Catholic chapels were burnt, and a fearful scene took place in Holborn, where a distillery was broken open and set on fire, the rioters rolling drunk in the flames. Order was restored at last only by the help of 10,000 troops.

<small>Gordon riots, 1780.</small>

Lord North's government was becoming very unpopular, for the war expenses were very heavy, trade was stopped, and Burke complained loudly in Parliament of the money lavished by Government in pensions and bribery. Then in 1781 came news of another terrible disaster to the English army in America. Lord Cornwallis with 4000 men had been cut off from supplies by Washington on land, and the French fleet by sea, and was driven by famine to surrender at Yorktown, Oct. 18, 1781.

<small>Surrender of English army at Yorktown, Oct. 18, 1781.</small>

11. Home Rule in Ireland.—It seemed as if England would be crushed under her many enemies. Lord North in despair exclaimed, "It is all over," and resigned in March 1782. The new ministers hastened to quiet the Irish by repealing Poyning's law which gave the English Parliament power over any Bills passed in Ireland, and began at once to arrange a peace with America, France, and Spain. This was not easy, for Spain claimed Gibraltar, and France demanded Bengal, and both these were of great value to England. Fortunately, before anything was arranged, Admiral Rodney, one of England's greatest seamen, met Count la Grasse going with the French fleet to seize Jamaica, and utterly defeated him, and the raising of the siege of Gibraltar happened a few months later.

<small>Repeal of Poyning's law, 1782.</small>

<small>Rodney's naval victory, 1782.</small>

12. Treaty of Versailles.—These victories gave England the chance of an honourable peace, and in the Treaty of Versailles, Jan. 1783, France gained nothing, and Spain only Minorca and Florida. England kept her strong fortress of Gibraltar, the key to the Mediterranean. Already in Nov. 1782 articles of peace had been signed between England and the United States, by which England kept only Canada, Nova Scotia, and Newfoundland, and freely acknowledged the independence of the United States. This treaty was ratified on Sept. 3, 1783, after the peace with France was concluded. *(Treaty of Versailles, Jan. 1783.)*

Thus ended the attempt of George III. and his minister to force taxation upon a powerful colony. Had they only been wise enough to give reasonable freedom to the colonists, America might perhaps still have been part of the British Empire. From this time forward her history is separate from that of Great Britain; yet the love of the old country remains strong in American hearts, and England, on her side, is proud of the powerful nation which sprang up from her shores.

13. Convict Settlement in Australia.—It is remarkable that, even while America was breaking away, the first step was being taken towards new colonies on the other side of the world. In 1768, not long after Townshend passed his unlucky "Revenue Act," Captain Cook, a native of Yorkshire, was sent by the Royal Society to Tahiti, an island in the Pacific Ocean, to observe a transit of Venus across the sun. As Cook returned he visited New Zealand, which had been discovered and named by Tasman in 1642. After sowing some seeds *(Cook's voyages, 1768-1778.)* and casting some pigs loose on the island, Cook went on to Australia (then called New Holland), and exploring the south-east part, planted the British flag there and called the country New South Wales. In 1787, eight years after Cook had been murdered at Hawaii, it was decided to make New South Wales a convict settlement, and in 1788 Captain Arthur Philip was sent there with 850 convicts, men and women. He went first to Botany Bay and then on to Port Jackson, where he remained and called the settlement *Sydney*, after Viscount Sydney, the colonial secretary. The convicts suffered terrible hardships at first, being often even without food, and though they were criminals, we should remember they acted as pioneers in a country which has now become one of the finest British colonies.

14. Warren Hastings.—Meanwhile changes which were taking place in India brought the trading settlements in that country under the English Government. After Lord Clive came home in 1767 the English traders used their power to oppress, and extort money from the natives, and so many complaints were made of their injustice and tyranny that the ministers interfered and appointed Warren Hastings, who was Governor of Bengal, to be Governor-General over the three Presidencies, Bengal, Bombay and Madras. Hastings had a difficult task. His power was not clearly defined, and Sir Philip Francis, one of the East India Council, sent out to rule with him, thwarted him in every possible way. On the whole, he ruled justly and well. He protected the natives by appointing English collectors in the place of the extortionate native Zemindars, and did much to stop bibery in the law-courts. He waged a difficult war against the Mahrattas, the men of the great Hindoo empire of the Dekkan, and made peace with them in 1782; and that same year he sent a sepoy force by land, and Sir Eyre Coote by sea, to defend Madras, which had been almost conquered by a military adventurer Hyder Ali, backed by the French. Coote succeeded against great odds in defending the place till Hyder Ali died at the end of the year, and the peace of Versailles in 1783 put an end to the war between France and England.

Warren Hastings Governor-General of India, 1773.

First Mahratta war, 1779-1782.

Defence of Madras, 1782.

Thus in 1784 when Warren Hastings returned to England, he left the British possessions in India strong and at peace, and the people of Bengal reverenced him as a conqueror, protector, and friend. But in gaining his ends he had not always used just means. The East India Company at home pressed constantly for money, and in order to supply this, Hastings lent his English troops to the Vizier of Allahabad for a sum of £400,000, to attack a free Afghan tribe, the Rohillas, whose country was destroyed, and they themselves enslaved; and he was said to have used cruelty and oppression towards the native princes to extort money. For these and other acts he was impeached at the Bar of the House of Lords in 1787, and Burke, who felt very strongly that English rule in India ought to be just and merciful, was one of his chief accusers. The trial began in 1788, and lasted at intervals for more than seven years. At last in 1795 Hastings was acquitted. Those who blamed him, probably understood very little the difficulties he had to overcome, and he should be remembered as the chief Englishman after Clive who established British rule in India.

Trial of Warren Hastings, 1787-1795.

15. Pitt and Fox.—The inquiry, however, into the abuses of English rule in India led to the better government of the country. There were now two great statesmen on the opposite side of the House of Commons. One was the younger Pitt, who was son of the Earl of Chatham, and who became Prime Minister in 1783. The other was Charles James Fox, son of the Henry Fox who had supported Bute and afterwards became Lord Holland. Fox was a gambling, dissolute man, but a clever, eloquent statesman, with an ardent love for his fellowmen, and a hatred of oppression and wrong. He brought in an India Bill in 1783, which was thrown out by the Lords. Now Pitt brought in a second India Bill, which appointed a Board of Control, composed of six members of the Privy Council, to overrule the East India Company in political matters, and protect the natives. This Bill was passed, and from that time India was far more justly governed, and became really a part of the British Empire.

India Bill passed, 1784.

CHAPTER XXIV.

THE FRENCH REVOLUTION—NAPOLEON AND ENGLAND.

1. Government of the Younger Pitt.—The year 1784, in which the India Bill was passed, was an important year for England, for in March a strong ministry was formed, with one of England's greatest statesmen at its head. When young William Pitt, then only twenty-four years of age, accepted office in Dec. 1783, the Whigs, with Fox as their leader, laughed at him as a "mere boy," and little thought that he would remain Prime Minister for seventeen years. He had not even a majority in the House, and five times he was outvoted. Still he fought on, for he knew that the people outside the House were on his side, and he hoped to break down the bribery and corruption of the great Whig houses, by showing that he meant to reform abuses and govern well. He was right ; for when Parliament was dissolved in March 1784 the new elections gave him a large majority, and for the next eight years, while England was at peace, he did great things for the nation.

<small>The younger Pitt Prime Minister. 1783-1800.</small>

A very remarkable book, called *The Wealth of Nations*, had been published by Adam Smith in 1776, which taught that every man ought to be allowed to gain as much as he can by his labour, and that laws which check trade between one country and another are hurtful. Pitt had studied this work, and one of the first things he did was to lower the duty on tea and spirits, and to make the collection of all taxes much more simple, as Walpole had wished to do. This lessened the temptation to smuggle, so that merchants brought in their goods openly through the custom-house, paying the proper duties, and the revenue was so increased that Pitt was able to take off many oppressive taxes. He would have gone further, and made the trade between England and Ireland free ; but the Irish Parliament now passed its own laws, uncontrolled by England, and while the English merchants were jealous of the Irish, the Irish on their side would not yield on any point. The Irish patriots, Grattan, Flood, and Curran, refused to accept the Bill as it was passed in England, and so lost what they might have

<small>Pitt's finance.</small>

<small>Ireland rejects Pitt's Bill for free trade, 1785.</small>

gained because they could not have all they wanted. Pitt was more successful in making a commercial treaty between England and France, abolishing many of the duties on goods passing between the two countries.

England had not been so prosperous for a long time as in this early part of Pitt's ministry. The struggle with America was over, and trade went on briskly; India opened a new market for English goods, machinery enabled the manufacturer to produce everything much more rapidly, and the factories gave work to large numbers of people. Moreover, Pitt began by economy and honesty to reduce the National Debt. He published an account of all money received and paid by Government, Reduction of National Debt. and when he borrowed he did so openly, by public contract, so that he got the loan at the lowest price, and prevented the jobbery by which officials had formerly often pocketed a good deal of public money. He even tried to reform the House of Commons itself by bringing in a Bill to take away the members from those boroughs where there were scarcely any electors, and give them to the largest counties, and to the cities of London and Westminster. But his Bill did not pass, for those who gained money by the boroughs opposed the scheme, and the nation Pitt's Reform Bill rejected. 1785. was so prosperous that people cared very little about the elections. It seemed indeed as if a period of peace and prosperity had set in for a long time to come. Though the king had a second attack of insanity at the end of 1788, it passed away while Pitt and Fox were disputing how much power the Prince of Wales, who bore a very bad character, should have as Second Regency Bill, 1788. Regent, and whether Parliament had the right to control him. Fortunately the king's recovery settled the matter, and the people rejoiced as he went to return thanks at St. Paul's. They felt safe under Pitt's government, and wanted no change. They little suspected that trouble was at hand from quite a new quarter. In July 1789 the French Revolution broke out, and upset all Europe, causing war and confusion for the next quarter of a century.

2. French Revolution.—For a long time the nations all over Europe had been beginning to feel that Government ought to be as much for the good of the middle and working classes as for kings and nobles. In England wise reforms had been made from time to time to satisfy this feeling; but in France for the last hundred and fifty years the oppression of the people had become worse and worse.

<small>Oppression of lower classes in France.</small> The laws were so unjust that taxes were heaped on the farmers and labourers, while the nobles paid none, but lived at Court, caring nothing for their estates except to wring money out of them. Labourers had to work for many days every year on the roads and estates of their landlord without receiving any pay, cottages and farms fell into ruin, and constant famines added to the misery of peasantry. Vice and extravagance reigned in the towns side by side with the most cruel want, while France itself was growing poorer and poorer.

At last Louis XVI., called together the Great Assembly of France called the "States General," to try and raise <small>States General assembled, May 5, 1789.</small> money to carry on the Government. But this only brought the discontent to a head. The Commons, or "Third Estate," as they were called, forced the other Estates—that is the Parliaments of the Nobles and Clergy—to meet with them as a "National Assembly." An insurrection broke out in Paris, July 14, 1789, in which the great French prison called the "Bastille" was stormed, and a revolutionary commune set up to govern the city. A few months later the mob fetched Louis from <small>Imprisonment and death of Louis XVI., 1789-1793.</small> Versailles, and he remained practically a prisoner in Paris for three years. At last in 1792 Austria and Prussia invaded France, hoping to put him back on his throne, but the French army was too strong for them, and the excited mob of Paris massacred whole masses of royalists on Sept. 21, 1792, and ended by bringing their king to the guillotine, Jan. 21, 1793. So died Louis XVI., and the "Reign of Terror" began, in which one party after the other murdered all who differed from them, among others the poor queen Marie Antoinette.

All this time England had looked on quietly. Many English people were at first glad that the French had rebelled against the selfish nobles. Fox gloried in the Revolution, and even Pitt thought in the beginning that it would pass over, and was anxious not to interfere. But Burke by his speeches and <small>Effect on England.</small> writings excited the people of England against the revolutionists, imagining that the overthrow of kingship in France would lead to the same result in England and other

THE FRENCH REVOLUTION. 269

European countries. The revolutionists grew bolder and bolder, they defeated the Austrians in the Netherlands, took possession of Savoy and Nice, and threatened to invade Holland, which was protected by a treaty with England. Then Pitt was obliged to remonstrate, and on Feb. 1, 1793, within a month of the death of Louis XVI., France declared war against England, Holland, and Spain.

3. War with France.—For the next nine years England was continually at war with the French republic, while other nations joined first one side and then the other in a most bewildering manner. At first England, Spain, Holland, Austria, and Prussia were united in one coalition, for which England had to provide a large part of the money. The allies were very unsuccessful. Though Lord Howe gained a great victory over the French fleet off Brest, yet on land the French were everywhere victorious. In 1795 they conquered Amsterdam and captured the Dutch fleet. The stadtholder of Holland fled, and the Dutch republicans joined the French and proclaimed a republic. The King of Prussia, too, who had carried on his part of the war by means of large supplies from England, retired from the contest, and Spain, jealous of the English fleet, joined the French. It was at this time that the English took possession of the Dutch settlements at the Cape of Good Hope, and of Ceylon and Malacca, the Dutch settlers being glad to be saved in this way from falling into the hands of France.

Lord Howe defeats the French fleet, June 1, 1794.

French take Amsterdam and the Dutch fleet, 1795.

England takes the Cape of Good Hope, Ceylon, and Malacca, 1795

Austria was now England's only ally, and she required four millions and a half for her expenses. Pitt would willingly have made peace if he could, for the cost and losses of the war were bringing great suffering on England. In less than three years the heavy drain on the country had checked all prosperity, and the country banks would, many of them, have been obliged to stop payment if Pitt had not passed a Bill in 1797 to authorize the Bank of England to pay any sum above twenty shillings in bank-notes instead of gold and silver. This Act lasted for twenty-two years. Taxes were heavy, trade was almost at a standstill, and two bad harvests brought serious famine. The

Effects of the war on England.

London mob ran after the king's carriage crying, "Bread, bread;" and riots, angry meetings, and seditious writings increased every day.

Pitt, on the other hand, was alarmed at the sympathy which some of the workmen's clubs and societies showed for the French revolutionists, and began to rule harshly. The *Habeas Corpus* Act was suspended, so that men could be imprisoned without a trial. One bookseller was punished for publishing Tom Paine's *Rights of Man*, a book attacking royalty; another was imprisoned for a pamphlet on reform, and three leading men, Horne Tooke, Hardy, Thelwall, and others were accused of exciting the people against Parliament and tried for high treason, but were acquitted.

Pitt becomes despotic.

4. Trouble in Ireland.—Nor was this all, for a French invasion was attempted in Ireland. In 1782 Grattan had succeeded, as we saw, in forcing Lord North to repeal the laws which gave the English Parliament power over the Parliament of Ireland, so that the Irish had "Home Rule," and could pass what laws they pleased. Now as Roman Catholics and Protestant Dissenters could not be elected to this Irish Parliament, nearly all the members belonged to the Protestant aristocracy. There were very few patriots who, like Grattan, dealt fairly with the Roman Catholics or the Irish peasants. The consequence was that the Roman Catholic gentry and the Irish tenants, who were ground down by the stewards of absent landlords, broke out into riots and outrages, and a kind of civil war sprang up between the "Orangemen," (so called from William, Prince of Orange,) who founded lodges in the north of Ireland in 1790, and the "United Irishmen," a society composed of Roman Catholics and Protestants, who joined together in 1791 to secure their civil and religious rights. The chief leaders of the United Irishmen, Hamilton Rowan, Wolf Tone, and Lord Edward Fitzgerald applied to the French for help, and it was agreed that a French army under General Hoche should invade Ireland. On the night of December 16, 1796, thirty-eight ships sailed from Brest, carrying 15,000 troops, with the intention of entering the mouth of the Shannon in Ireland, and the port of Bristol in England. Had they arrived it would have been a very serious matter; but

Orange Lodges, 1790.

United Irishmen, 1791.

THE FRENCH REVOLUTION. 271

in the darkness one large ship went down, a gale drove part of the fleet into Bantry Bay, where a fog shut them in for four days, and they waited in vain for General Hoche, who never arrived. He had been driven back by the storm into the harbour of La Rochelle, and the fleet returned without ever invading Ireland. *French invasion of Ireland, 1796.*

All these troubles made Pitt very anxious for peace, and he tried to come to terms with the French "Directory," as the Government was now called. But fresh revolutions had been taking place in Paris, and the French, elated by their victories abroad, refused to give up Belgium, Holland, or those parts of Italy which their young Corsican general, Napoleon Bonaporte, had taken from the Austrians. Moreover they were planning a joint attack of the Dutch, French, and Spanish fleets to sweep the English ships from the Channel, leaving the country defenceless. It was clear that England must go on with the war or lose her commerce and power, and the merchants and wealthy men answered readily Pitt's appeal for money to defeat the French. *Pitt tries in vain for peace, 1796.*

5. Naval Victories.—And now came a time when England's fleet, great ever since the days of Elizabeth, saved England in her peril, and showed that her sailors had lost none of the old spirit of their ancestors, the Anglian sea-rovers, the hardy Norsemen, and the Danish vikings. Before the Dutch fleet could put to sea, Admiral Sir John Jervis, with Nelson as his commodore, met the Spanish fleet off Cape St. Vincent, defeated it, and drove it back to Cadiz. Still the French and Dutch fleets remained unconquered, and it was well that bad weather prevented the Dutch from joining the French, for just at this time the English sailors broke out into mutiny at Spithead and the Nore. The men, who were badly fed, badly paid, and harshly treated, had some real grievances, and the Admiralty wisely set these right while they sternly put down the rebellion. After a few of the worst ringleaders had been punished, the remainder of the fleet returned to their duty, and a few months later fought bravely in an obstinate battle under Admiral Duncan, utterly defeating the Dutch fleet off Camperdown, in Holland. *Battle of St. Vincent, Feb. 14, 1797. Mutiny at the Nore, May 1797. Battle of Camperdown, Oct. 11, 1797.*

These naval victories put an end to the attempt to destroy the English fleet. But the French, who had just made peace with Austria at Campo Formio, were still eager to crush their one great rival, England. Napoleon Bonaparte was now Commander-in-Chief of the larger part of the French army, and while he pretended that he was preparing to attack the English shores, he was really persuading the Directory to let him take the army to Egypt, and push on to harass the English in India. He had in fact determined to become the ruler of France, and seeing that he could not yet seize power at home, he wished to gain great victories abroad and return as a conqueror.

The man who spoiled his campaign was England's greatest admiral, Horatio Nelson. From his early boyhood, when at thirteen he left his father's rectory in Norfolk to enter the navy, Nelson had put his whole heart into his profession. Now, after a long experience, he found himself at forty years of age sent to chase and defeat the man who was already England's most formidable enemy.

Battle of the Nile, Aug. 1, 1798. For more than two months he tried in vain to find the fleet in which Napoleon's army had sailed; but at last, he came upon it at anchor in the Bay of Aboukir, in the delta of the Nile. The French thought their position was secure; but Nelson, by sending some of his ships right between them and the shore, put them between two fires, and won the famous "Battle of the Nile." The ships being destroyed, the French army was left stranded in Egypt, and Napoleon determined to attempt the conquest of Syria. Crossing the desert, he stormed Jaffa, and marched on and laid siege to Acre, but here he was stoutly repulsed by the Turks, assisted by Sir Sidney Smith. Retreating to Egypt, he next defeated the Turks at Aboukir, near Alexandria, and then hearing that the French were being defeated

Napoleon made First Consul, 1799. in Europe, he left the command of the army to his generals and returned to France, where he was made First Consul. After a few months he went off again to fight the Austrians in Italy, and, defeating them at Marengo, June 1800, forced them to make peace at Luneville, Feb. 1, 1801.

6. Union of Great Britain and Ireland.—England now stood once more alone, for Russia, who had joined her for a little while, quarrelled about the right of search in ships, and war broke out in the Baltic. Pitt, moreover, was no longer Prime Minister, and the reason for this we must now relate.

Ever since the French invasion of Ireland had failed the country had been very unquiet, till at last an organised rebellion broke out, which ended in the rebels being routed and their camp taken at Vinegar Hill in Wexford, June 21, 1798. Even after this a French squadron landed a body of troops in Mayo, which were defeated by Lord Cornwallis, who was Lord Lieutenant of Ireland. Fitzgerald was killed and Wolfe Tone was hanged. <small>Irish Rebellion of 1798.</small> Pitt now determined to abolish the Irish Parliament altogether, and by an Act of Union to bring Irish members to sit in the English House, as the Scotch members had been brought in Queen Anne's reign. By wholesale bribery and a liberal distribution of titles and honours, he succeeded in passing the Act through the Irish Parliament, and won over the Roman Catholics by promising to give them equal rights with the Protestants. On Aug. 2, 1800, the "Act of Union" received the royal assent, and on the last day of the eighteenth century, Dec. 31, 1800, the king closed the British Parliament, to reopen it in Jan. 1801 as the "Imperial Parliament," in which a hundred Irish members took their seats in the House of Commons, and four Irish bishops and twenty-four Irish lords in the House of Peers. The Cross of St. Patrick was added to those of St. George and St. Andrew on the Union Jack, and from that time till now the laws for England, Scotland, and Ireland have all been passed in the Imperial Parliament. <small>The Union Jack.</small> Unfortunately the king let himself be persuaded that it was against his coronation oath to allow Pitt to bring forward a Bill giving the Roman Catholics the rights which he had promised. Thus one great sore remained <small>Resignation of Pitt, Jan. 1801.</small> unhealed, and Pitt, who felt bound in honour to keep his word, could only resign his post.

7. **Peace of Amiens.**—The shock of his resignation drove the king again out of his mind for a short time, and Pitt, sorely grieved, hastened to give his help to Mr. Addington (afterwards Lord Sidmouth), who had been Speaker of the House, and now became

Prime Minister. England was still fighting against great odds, but a short peace was at hand. Sir Ralph Abercromby defeated the French in the battle of Alexandria, and the English being strengthened by fresh troops from India, the whole French army was forced to capitulate. Meanwhile, on April 2, Nelson had overcome the Danish fleet at Copenhagen. The fight was so obstinate that Sir Hyde Parker, who was in command, gave the signal for retreat, but Nelson, putting his telescope to his blind eye, declared that he could not see the signal, and fought on to victory. At this time Napoleon was actually collecting boats and rafts at Boulogne to attack England, but the disasters in Egypt led the French to seek a temporary peace. At the treaty of Amiens, signed March 1802, France gave up the south of Italy, and England relinquished all her conquests except Ceylon and Trinidad, while the English kings dropped the title of "King of France," which they had held since Edward III.

Battles of Alexandria and Copenhagen, 1801.

Peace of Amiens, March 1802.

8. Trafalgar—But no treaty could check the restless ambition of Napoleon. In a few months he had annexed Piedmont and Parma, and sent a French army into Switzerland; and when the English Government remonstrated, he called upon them to expel all the French refugees living in England, and to give up Malta to the Knights of St. John. It was clear that he meant mischief, and the ministers had no choice but to declare war. From this time till 1815 England was engaged in a continual struggle with Napoleon. In 1804 he became Emperor of France, which he had, ever since he became First Consul, ruled with a firm hand, giving her good laws, and putting an end to riot and disorder, so that she once more became a great power. But this did not content him. He wished to be master of Europe, and as England was the one free country which baffled him, his chief ambition was to crush her. "Let us be master of the Channel for six hours," said Napoleon, "and we are masters of the world."

Napoleon as Emperor at war with England, 1803-1815.

England rose bravely as her difficulties increased. Pitt became Prime Minister again in 1804; more than 300,000 volunteers

THE FRENCH REVOLUTION. 275

organised themselves to protect their country, and Nelson started off to the West Indies in pursuit of the French and Spanish fleets. Meanwhile these fleets had turned back, by Napoleon's orders, to attack England, and to protect the host of flat-bottomed boats in which he hoped to send a force of 100,000 men across the Channel. *Napoleon attempts to invade England, 1805.* But Sir Robert Calder met the Spanish fleet off Cape Finisterre and drove it back into Cadiz, and Nelson, who had returned in hot haste, met the French fleet off Cape Trafalgar on Oct. 21, 1805. Then occurred the memorable battle in which the great commander laid down his life. "*This day England expects every man to do his duty.*" *Battle of Trafalgar, Oct. 1805.* So ran Nelson's famous signal, hoisted before the action began, and the words will ring for ever in the ears of Englishmen. Wounded by a musket ball on the deck of his own ship, the *Victory*, the brave admiral died even as he learnt that the French were defeated. He had done his work nobly, and his last simple words of command, coming from a man who had obeyed them all his life, were the best legacy he could leave to his country.

England had now lost her greatest admiral, and her most trusted statesman was soon to follow. Pitt lived to hear of the victory of Trafalgar, but bad news reached him not long after. Napoleon had crushed the armies of Austria and Russia at Austerlitz, near Vienna, Dec, 2, 1805. "Austerlitz," wrote Wilberforce, "killed Pitt." He died Jan. 23, 1806, at the early age of forty-seven, after a life of faithful devotion to his country. *Battle of Austerlitz and death of Pitt.*

9. Abolition of the Slave Trade.—On Pitt's death Fox joined Lord Grenville in a ministry known as "The Ministry of all the Talents," which will always be remembered because it carried one great measure for which Pitt and his friends had long been struggling. This was the *abolition of the slave trade.* *Ministry of all the Talents, 1806.* Ever since the preaching of Whitefield and Wesley, which roused many to lead a religious life, a more tender feeling had been growing up for the suffering of human beings. In 1773 John Howard, an earnest philanthropist, began to devote his life to visiting the wretched *Prison reform.*

and filthy gaols of England, and trying to better the condition of the prisoners; and a noble woman, Mrs. Fry, followed his example forty years later. Meanwhile in 1788 three men, Wilberforce, Thomas Clarkson, and Zachary Macaulay, formed an association to put down the trade in negro slaves from Africa to America. This trade had fallen chiefly into English hands, and the horrors of it were almost too dreadful to relate. The poor negroes, snatched from their homes, were packed on narrow shelves between the decks of a ship, often suffering from hunger, thirst, suffocation, and all kinds of cruelty, and were only brought into the air on the upper deck from time to time, and lashed to make them leap and take exercise. The brutal men who dealt in them only cared to keep them alive in order to sell them, and the sick were murdered or thrown overboard without mercy. Yet so much money was made by this trade that it was only after twenty years of constant struggle in Parliament, that at last in 1807 an Act was passed forbidding any Englishman or English vessel from carrying slaves for sale. Fox, who had laboured all his life to abolish the slave trade, did not live to see the Act passed. He died Sept. 3, 1806. This Act, though it put a stop to the trade, did not abolish slavery in the English colonies; that went on till 1833, twenty-seven years after.

Abolition of the slave trade, 1773-1807.

Death of Fox, 1806.

10. The Berlin Decree.—While England was thus reforming her laws, Napoleon was working to destroy her commerce. After another victorious struggle with Russia and Prussia in 1806, in which he won the famous battle of Jena, he remained master of nearly the whole of Europe. He now passed a decree at Berlin, declaring a blockade of all the English ports, and forbidding the nations on the Continent to trade with England. This was a severe blow to British merchants, and the ministers retaliated by declaring all the ports of France and her allies under blockade, and by seizing the Danish fleet at Copenhagen, Sept. 1807, because they had heard that Napoleon was about to use it against England. This blockade brought great trouble with the United States, for their vessels trading with France were liable to be seized. In 1812 Congress, irritated by this restriction, and by search made in their ships for English deserters, declared war against Great Britain, and hostilities continued till 1815.

11. Peninsular War.—Meanwhile on land Napoleon was everywhere successful, and he gave crowns and countries to his brothers and relations over the greater part of Europe. But the time was coming when he was to receive a check. In May 1808 disputes in the royal family of Spain gave him the opportunity of getting the crown for Joseph Bonaparte, while he also attacked Portugal, and the Regent of that country fled to Brazil. But he had now made the greatest mistake of his life. The proud Spanish people, indignant at having a mere adventurer forced upon them, rose everywhere in rebellion, and appealed to England for help. Napoleon seizes the crown of Spain, and invades Portugal, 1808.

A short time before this happened Sir Arthur Wellesley (afterwards Duke of Wellington) had returned from waging a successful war against the Mahrattas in India from 1803 to 1805, and had been made Secretary for Ireland. George Canning, a rising statesman, who was now minister for foreign affairs, determined to listen to the cry of Spain, and to oppose Napoleon in the Spanish Peninsula. Two small armies were at once sent to Portugal under Wellesley and General Sir John Moore, and the war known as the "Peninsular War" began. Unfortunately the troops sent were too few, and Wellesley and Moore were put under the control of the Governor of Gibraltar and another senior officer. So although Wellesley gained a victory over the French General Junot at Vimiero, Aug. 21, 1808, he was not allowed to follow it up, but a Convention was made with the French at Cintra, Aug. 30, and Wellesley was recalled to England. Peninsular War begins, 1808.

Sir John Moore, who remained, was ordered to advance into Spain and join the Spanish troops, but on his road he learnt that Napoleon had come himself, and having swept away the Spanish army was advancing on Madrid. Moore, who was a brave and experienced officer, and had only 25,000 men with him while Napoleon had 70,000, saw that he must go back to the coast and re-embark his men. His retreat was one of the most masterly ever recorded in war. He took his way to Vigo, with Napoleon in hot pursuit, and on his road, learning that the harbour was not fit for his troops to embark, he turned off to Corunna, a seaport in Galicia. When he arrived there, on Jan. Retreat and Battle of Corunna, 1809.

10, he found that the fleet had been detained by contrary winds, and before it came up on the 14th, the French army, under Marshal Soult, had arrived, and was drawn up for attack. At midday on the 16th the French gave battle. Steadily and firmly the English met them; the French were repulsed on all sides, and the English army were all embarked by midnight, leaving 3000 Frenchmen dead on the field. But the brave English general who had saved his troops was killed himself, and there on the lonely battlefield his comrades buried him in sorrow and silence—

Burial of Sir John Moore.

> " Not a drum was heard, not a funeral note,
> As his corse to the ramparts we hurried;
> Not a soldier discharged his farewell shot
> O'er the grave where our hero we buried.
>
> " Slowly and sadly we laid him down,
> From the field of his fame fresh and gory,
> We carved not a line, and we raised not a stone,
> But we left him alone with his glory."[1]

When news of the destruction of the Spanish army and of Moore's retreat reached England the nation almost lost courage, but Canning, gathering together a stronger army, sent Wellesley at once back with it to Portugal. From this time, during the next four years, Wellesley was steadily employed driving Napoleon's best generals out of Spain. He was as yet not nearly so famous as Napoleon; he was badly supplied with troops and provisions, and he had no ambition except to do his duty. But he believed that he had right on his side, that in the end he should conquer this tyrant who was overrunning all Europe; he was thoughtful and careful of his men, while Napoleon shed blood recklessly; and he never allowed his troops to plunder the people, but paid for all he took. Patiently, step by step, he showed that the French armies could be conquered, and so broke the spell by which Napoleon held all nations in his power.

Wellington and Napoleon.

He defeated Marshal Soult at Oporto on May 12, and Marshal Victor at Talavera, July 28, 1809, for which victory he was created Viscount Wellington. Then retreating into Portugal, he constructed

---

[1] From Wolfe's *Burial of Sir John Moore*.

that winter three famous lines of fortresses, known as the lines of Torres Vedras; so that when Marshal Massena was sent in 1810 to drive the English army into the sea, he was first repulsed at Busaco, Sept. 29, 1810, and then found himself before the first line of defence, which he could not pass. Unable to find a way of attack, and short of food, for Wellington had purposely cleared the country of cattle and crops, Massena lost 45,000 men from skirmishes, disease, and hunger, and was forced to retreat into Spain. Here the Spaniards gathered in small armed bands called "guerilla bands," and harassed the French among the hills and forests, while Wellington and his generals, advancing steadily, won a long succession of battles. The most famous of these were the storming of the two fortresses of Ciudad Rodrigo and Badajos in 1812, the battles of Salamanca and Vittoria in 1812 and 1813, and the long siege of St. Sebastian in the winter of 1813, which put an end to the power of the French in Spain.

Wellington's victories in Spain, 1809-1813.

12. Russian Campaign.—Wellington's victories, however, did more than merely free the Spaniards; they gave Europe courage to rise against their common foe. Napoleon, still bent on conquest, had marched into Russia in 1812, and after a fearful battle at Borodino, Sept. 7, 1812, had pushed on to Moscow. But the Russians burnt the city; and Napoleon's soldiers, having neither food nor shelter, were forced to march back in the bitter winter through endless miles of snow, dying by thousands as they went. Out of 400,000 men 20,000 only returned. Napoleon's army was destroyed while Russia was pursuing him in the rear, and Austria and Prussia rose on his flank. Hastening back to France, he gathered an army and returned, actually winning three more battles at Lutzen, Bautzen, and Dresden. But his enemies were closing around him, and at Leipzig, after three days fighting he was utterly defeated, Oct. 19, 1813. He was forced to fall back on the Rhine, and during the early part of 1814 struggled vigorously against the overwhelming numbers of his enemies. But when at last the victorious allies entered Paris, he gave way, and abdicating, was banished to the island of St. Elba, April 28, 1814.

Burning of Moscow and retreat of the French, 1812.

Abdication of Napoleon.

13. **Waterloo.**—Then the brother of Louis XVI. was placed on the French throne under the title of Louis XVIII., because the young dauphin who died during the Revolution had been called Louis XVII. The war, however, was to see yet another famous battle. After eleven months of an unsettled peace, all Europe was startled by the news that Napoleon had escaped, landed at Cannes, and, welcomed on all sides by his old comrades, was marching to Paris. In three weeks he was emperor again and the king had fled. The allies lost no time. In April, Wellington, who had been at a Congress in Vienna, was already in Brussels, and armies from England, Prussia, Austria, and Russia were gathering for an attack. England and Prussia alone were ready, and Napoleon hoped to defeat them separately before they could meet. He did repulse the Prussians at Ligny on June 16, but on that same day Wellington successfully opposed Marshal Ney at Quatrebras, and took up a strong position on the heights of St. Jean, above the little village of Waterloo, nine miles from Brussels.

<small>Napoleon returns, March 1815.</small>

On the 18th, Napoleon and Wellington met for the first time face to face in battle. Wellington had a very difficult army to command, his veteran soldiers had nearly all been sent to the American War, so his English troops were young and inexperienced, while more than half his forces consisted of Netherlanders, Hanoverians, Nassauers, and Brunswickers. His allies the Prussians were still a long way off, though their general Blucher, had sent word to Wellington on the 17th that he would join him early the next afternoon. When Napoleon began the battle at midday on the 18th, Wellington could only hope to hold his ground till help arrived. Time after time now in one part, now in another, the French cavalry charged against the immovable squares of British infantry, and fell before their deadly fire. But the day wore on, and at four o'clock the wearied troops watched in vain for their allies. At last, about five, it was evident that the French were fighting with the Prussians somewhere out of sight. On they came, and at seven o'clock the French made one last desperate charge on the English lines, and then fled in confusion. The Prussians had come up just in time to secure a great victory. More than 25,000 French soldiers lay on the field of battle, and even the English lost 13,000. But the war was over at last. Napoleon fled

<small>Battle of Waterloo, June 18, 1815.</small>

to Paris and abdicated in favour of his son. He then tried to escape from France, but finding all the ports guarded, he gave himself up at Rochport to Captain Maitland, of the English ship *Bellerophon*. He was placed in the island of St. Helena, this time safely guarded, and there he died, May 5, 1821. Louis XVIII. returned to Paris, and the allies occupied France for the next three years, till all fear of revolution was over. From that day to this though Frenchmen and Englishmen have been a long time learning to understand each other, whenever they have fought it has been as allies and never as enemies.

<small>Death of Napoleon, 1821.</small>

14. Condition of the Nation.—The English nation went almost mad with joy when peace was proclaimed. For the last twelve years they had strained every nerve in the war of freedom, and for the last three of these years they had been at war with the United States, in which they run a great risk of losing Canada, and had only just made a peace early in 1815. Though trade had to a certain extent prospered because England was almost the only country in which war was not actually going on, and because she had most of the carrying trade on the sea, yet the enormous taxes, the high price of corn, and the long wearing anxiety of the war, had tried every one sorely. In 1810 the king had gone hopelessly out of his mind, and never afterwards recovered, and the Prince of Wales became Regent. Parliament had been so much occupied with the war that the Prime Ministers, the Duke of Portland (1807-1809), Mr. Perceval (1809-1812), and Lord Liverpool (1812-1821) had no chance of making useful reforms, while the alarm and uncertainty caused by the French revolution had made all classes suspicious of each other. Now as soon as the first excitement of peace was over the nation began to feel the effects of the long war.

<small>Peace of Paris, 1815.</small>

<small>Prince of Wales Regent, 1810-1820.</small>

The national debt had increased to 840 millions, and pressed heavily upon the country. Though a Bill had been passed in 1819 by which the Bank of England began again to pay in gold, there was still a great deal of paper money in the country. Disbanded soldiers and sailors returned home to swell the numbers of the unemployed, the manufacturers who had provided stores for the war had no work for their men, and the more peaceful trades were at a low ebb. The farmers and landowners, alarmed at the fall in the price of corn, persuaded Parliament to pass a Corn-Law in 1815 forbidding foreign corn to be imported under 80s. a quarter, and the consequence was that when a bad harvest came in 1816 it caused a famine. Riots broke out everywhere,—among the agriculturists in Kent, and the colliers and miners in the Midlands and the west of England, while at Nottingham the Luddites or machine-breakers rose with fresh violence. The next four years were full of trouble. A paper called the *Weekly Political Register*, published by William Cobbett, taught the workmen to think that a reform of Parliament would cure all their evils. Political meetings became so many and so threatening that Government again suspended the Habeas Corpus Act, and a riot at Manchester, in which more than fifty people were badly wounded by the Hussars, caused Parliament to pass six severe laws against the freedom of the people, which were known as the "Six Acts."

<small>Oppressive Corn-Law, 1815.</small>

<small>Manchester Massacre, Aug. 1819.</small>

The Regent too was very unpopular. He had married in 1785 a beautiful widow, Mrs. Fitzherbert, but this marriage was not legal because she was a Roman Catholic, and because a "Royal Marriage Act" passed in 1771 allowed none of the royal family to marry under twenty-five without the king's consent. So the Prince deserted Mrs. Fitzherbert in 1795 and married a coarse, vulgar woman, Princess Caroline of Brunswick, with whom he soon quarrelled. Their only child, Princess Charlotte, who was very much beloved, married Prince Leopold of Saxe-Coburg, but died Nov. 6, 1817, and her only child died with her. Thus there was no direct heir to the throne, and when the next year three of the king's sons married, the only one who pleased the people was the Duke of Kent, who married the sister of Prince Leopold, the widower of Princess Charlotte. The only child of this marriage was our present queen, Alexandrina Victoria, who was born May 24, 1819. Her father died eight months after.

<small>Death of Princess Charlotte, 1817.</small>

<small>Royal marriages.</small>

15. Summary of George III.'s Reign.

—And now the long life of George III. was drawing to a close. Blind and insane, the poor old king was still beloved in spite of all the mistakes he had made, and when he sank to rest on Jan. 29, 1820, in the eighty-second year of his age and sixtieth of his reign, the nation grieved sincerely. Since he came to the throne as a young man determined to "be a king," great things had happened. A large part of America had been lost; India had been gained by the English Government; Pitt had reformed abuses and raised the country; Napoleon had done his best to ruin it; and Nelson and Wellington had saved it. Ireland had become one with England in government, as we trust she will be one day in heart. Englishmen had washed their hands of the infamous trade in negro slaves, and in 1816 the English and Dutch bombarded Algiers and forced the "Dey" or native prince to release all the Christians whom he had captured and made slaves during the troubled times.

Death of George III., 1820.

Side by side with these political events, inventions and discoveries had advanced rapidly. In 1807 two Americans, Fulton and Livingston, moved a vessel up the Hudson from New York to Albany by means of a steam-engine, and in 1813 a steam-tug towed two vessels along the Clyde Canal. Steam-carriages had also been attempted, but as yet without success. Trade and manufacture had increased enormously with the invention of new machinery, and the command of the English over the sea. In science, great men such as Lamarck, Cuvier, and Lavoisier in France, and Herschel, Davy, and Priestley in England, were making grand discoveries in their quiet studies, while all Europe was raging with war.

Discoveries and inventions.

In literature this was the greatest age since Elizabeth's reign. Adam Smith's *Wealth of Nations* appeared in 1776. Robertson's *Histories* of Scotland, of the Emperor Charles V., and of America, were written between 1759 and 1777, and Gibbon's famous work on the *Decline and Fall of the Roman Empire* appeared from 1776 to 1787. The great Samuel Johnson (1709-1784), sharp of tongue but kindly of heart, published his great *Dictionary* in the reign of George II., yet he lived to grieve for the death of Goldsmith (1728-1774), whose *Vicar of Wakefield, Deserted Village*, and other works, were all written in the reign of George

Literature.

III. Among plays we shall never find more charming comedies than Goldsmith's *She Stoops to Conquer*, or Sheridan's *Rivals* and *School for Scandal;* nor were actors wanting to render these and more serious plays, for Garrick and Foote, Kemble and Mrs. Siddons, belong to this time. Most remarkable of all, however, was the sudden outburst of poets. Cowper, Burns, Shelley, Keats, and Byron then lived and wrote, while Campbell, Coleridge, Wordsworth, Southey, Walter Scott, and Tom Moore were famous as poets long before George III. died. The British Museum, which began from a collection of valuable books left by Sir Hans Sloane in 1753, and was increased by the Royal Libraries of George II. and George III., was now already becoming a large library of reference for the nation, and the Elgin marbles which were bought by the nation and placed there in 1817 first brought ancient art before the British public. Lastly, Sir Joshua Reynolds and Gainsborough stand pre-eminent among painters, and Chantrey and Flaxman among sculptors; while in humbler though graceful art Josiah Wedgewood produced the beautiful pottery known as Wedgewoodware, for which Flaxman drew the designs. When George III. died everything promised well for the future social and intellectual development of England. The two things still greatly needed were reforms in Parliament and in the laws of trade.

Art.

CHAPTER XXV.

THE HISTORY OF OUR OWN TIMES.

1. Trial of Queen Caroline, 1820.—We have now arrived at a period which our grandfathers and our fathers can remember. There are indeed few men alive who were at the battle of Waterloo, for the youngest old enough to have been there, would now (1890) be over ninety years of age. But there are many who as children remember the coronation of George IV. and the trial of Queen

Caroline. This unhappy woman, neglected by her worthless husband, had been living abroad for the last six years. Now when she wished to take her place as queen the king bade the ministers bring in a Bill to dissolve the marriage. After a long trial, in which the celebrated lawyer Brougham defended the queen, the Bill was dropped. But the king refused to let Queen Caroline's name be read in the Church service, and when she tried to enter Westminster Abbey at the coronation she was driven back. She died a few days afterwards, and the English people, who pitied her, disliked King George more than ever.

2. Holy Alliance.—This did not, however, much matter, for George IV. and his brother William IV., who reigned after him, did not interfere much in the government of the country. For nearly forty years after the battle of Waterloo England was at peace, with the exception of one naval battle fought in defence of the Greeks against Turkey and Egypt in Navarino in 1827, and some local wars in India, Africa and China. Of these forty years the first seven were full of anxiety and distrust. Ever since the French revolution the sovereigns of Europe were so afraid that their subjects would force them to establish free governments that in 1815 the Emperors of Russia and Austria and the Kings of Prussia, France, and Spain, entered into a "Holy Alliance," binding themselves to help each other in crushing any attempts at rebellion in any country. Insurrections had already been put down in this way by a French army in Spain and by an Austrian army in Italy, and though England did not join this Holy Alliance, yet every one knew that Lord Castlereagh (afterwards Lord Londonderry), who was Foreign Secretary, would have wished to join it, while the "Six Acts" passed in 1819 made the people afraid that the English Government too would become tyrannical. *England at peace.*

George IV. had been king for a month only, when a conspiracy was formed by twenty-five men, led by one Thistlewood, to murder all the ministers at a dinner at Lord Harrowby's house. The conspirators were arrested in a stable in Cato Street, Edgeware Road; four of them were executed, and five transported for life, and there the matter ended. But it *Cato Street conspiracy, Feb. 23, 1820.*

showed that the nation was uneasy, and indeed the feeling of alarm was so great, that when Castlereagh went out of his mind in 1822 and committed suicide, just as he was starting to join a congress at Vienna, the people could not help being relieved at his death. They were not far wrong, for, he had been the chief leader among those who wished to keep the people down, instead of finding out the reason of their discontent. With his death a new policy began, which was a happy one for England.

<small>Suicide of Castlereagh, Aug 12, 1822.</small>

3. Canning, Peel, and Huskisson.—Lord Liverpool had been Prime Minister ever since 1812, but several changes had taken place in the men who served with him, and now, in 1822, Robert Peel, the son of a cotton-spinner, became Home Secretary; Canning, whose policy had defeated Napoleon in Spain, took Lord Londonderry's place as Foreign Secretary; and the next year William Huskisson, who had already held minor posts in the Government became President of the Board of Trade. These three men belonged rather to the great middle class of England than to the landowners, and they understood better what reforms were needed.

Canning, who was a disciple of Pitt, wished before all things to keep England at peace and to leave each nation free to settle its own government. He refused at once to have anything to do with the Holy Alliance, and, on the other hand, though he sympathised strongly with the Greeks who were struggling to throw off the Turkish yoke, and with the South American colonies, Mexico, Peru, and Chili, which were trying to get free from Spain, he would not interfere between a country and its rulers. But when the South Americans had gained their freedom by their own efforts, he acknowledged them as independent states, and sending British Consuls there, declared that England would not allow any foreign nation to assist Spain in reconquering them. A few years later, in 1826, when a French army threatened to join Spain in an attack on Portugal, the Portuguese applied to Canning for help, and he at once sent troops, by which means war was prevented. The same feeling of justice which made him uphold the weak abroad, led him at home to try, though unsuccessfully, to give the Roman Catholics their rights, and to better the condition of the slaves of the West Indian planters.

<small>Canning's foreign policy.</small>

Meanwhile Peel, as Home Secretary, set to work to improve the criminal law of England. This was terribly severe, for no less than 200 different crimes, many of them very slight, were punished by death. A man or woman could be hanged for stealing a piece of cloth from a shop, or stealing a fish from a pond, as well as for forgery or murder. The consequence was that the number of executions was very great, batches of twenty or more being hanged in a row at one time; while, on the other hand, many went unpunished, because juries often would not convict a man who would be put to death for a trifling crime. Already in 1808 Sir Samuel Romilly had tried to alter these unjust laws, and had abolished hanging as a punishment for pocket-picking, and after his death Sir James Mackintosh took up the work. At last in 1824 Peel succeeded in doing away with the punishment of death for more than a hundred smaller crimes, and little by little the laws were made more just.

Reform of criminal laws, 1808-1824.

Perhaps, however, for the good of the whole nation, the most useful reforms were those made by Huskisson in the laws which were crippling the trade of the country. The Navigation Laws of Cromwell were still in force, which gave all the carrying trade to English ships, and put heavy duties on all goods brought in by foreign vessels. This might answer for a time, but in the end other countries retaliated and laid heavy duties on goods brought to them in English ships, and in this way trade was much hindered. Huskisson succeeded in passing a "Reciprocity of Duties" Bill, by which English and foreign ships had equal advantages in England whenever foreign nations would do the same by English vessels coming to their ports. He also reduced the duties on silk and wool, so as to make them more just both for the growers and the manufacturers; and at the same time he caused those Acts to be repealed which allowed magistrates to fix the wages of workmen, and which prevented men who were seeking work from travelling to different parts of the country. He had great difficulties in carrying these measures, for the merchants, manufacturers, wool-growers, and even the workmen, each cried out because the advantage was not all on their side. But in the end the traders found their trade doubled, and the workmen that they could make

Reciprocity of Duties Bill, 1823.

Trade Reforms, 1824.

better bargains, while the public bought their goods at a fairer price.

4. Commercial Crisis.—At first, however, these good effects were counteracted by the sudden increase of trade with all countries as soon as they had settled down after the war, and especially with the new-freed South American colonies of Brazil and Mexico. As usual, every one flocked in to make a profit, joint-stock companies were started, money was invested in all kinds of foolish schemes, such as a company of milk-maids to milk the wild cattle of Buenos Ayres and make butter, which the inhabitants did not care for when it was made. The speculation was almost as wild as at the time of the South Sea bubble. Then after about a year the reaction came. Between sixty and seventy banks stopped payment in six weeks, and the panic was only checked by the Government coining sovereigns at the rate of 150,000 a day, and persuading the Bank of England to advance money to the merchants on the security of their goods. The depression which followed brought great distress to the middle and lower classes. The poor were once more at the point of starvation, and it was not surprising that they broke out into riots, smashed machinery, and clamoured so lustily for food that at last the Government ordered foreign corn to be let in below the legal price. There was not enough in the docks to do much good, but the little relief it gave, made men begin to see how cruel it was to shut out foreign corn from the people merely to raise the price for the benefit of the farmers and landlords. In 1828, when Huskisson was Secretary for the Colonies, a law was passed by which the duty on corn *fell* as the price rose, and *rose* as the price fell, so as to press less heavily on those who bought in scarce seasons. This was called a "sliding scale" of duties, and was the first step towards free trade in corn, which was not yet to come for another weary eighteen years.

Speculation caused by sudden increase of trade, 1824.

Scarcity of food, 1825, 1826.

Sliding scale duties on corn, 1828.

5. Emigration.—Meanwhile the distress had another very important effect; the want of work and of food led the Government to think of helping people to go to the colonies. Since the beginning

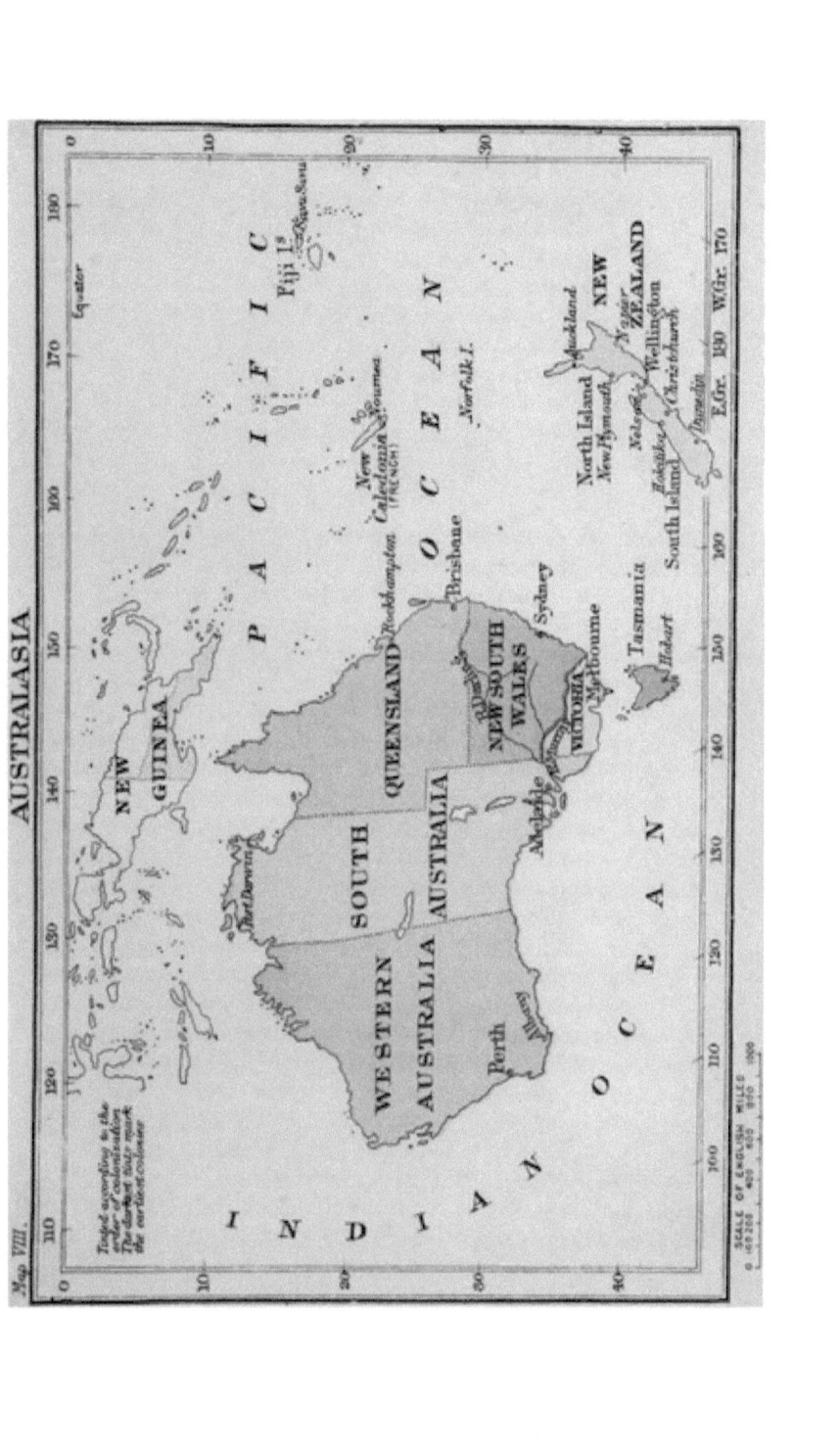

of the century sums had been given from time to time to assist paupers to emigrate to Canada, and 5000 people had been sent to the Cape in 1814; and now, when working men and labourers cried out for more work than could be found at home, the Colonial Office began as part of its business to attend to emigration. Very little was done at first, but a committee was formed to inquire into the matter, and the report which was made to Parliament encouraged many to emigrate at their own expense. In 1826 as many as 13,000 people went to Canada, the Cape, and Australia, and the numbers from that time always increased in years of scarcity at home. Thus a "greater Britain" began to grow up beyond the seas.

Emigration, 1826.

5. Foundation of Australian Colonies.—In Australia, NEW SOUTH WALES had already become a flourishing colony. In 1803 Lieutenant M'Arthur had bought Merino sheep at the Cape, and had settled as the first "squatter" on the large open tracts of New South Wales. In 1810 Colonel Macquarie, who was sent out as governor of the convict settlement, saw that the best way to govern, was to give freedom to those convicts who earned a good character, and he employed them in making roads and opening up the country around *Sydney*. In 1822, when he returned to England, and Sir Thomas Brisbane took his place, many free emigrants had already made their home in the colony. Then came the bad times of 1826, and numbers more flocked out. The rich pastures to the north of New South Wales were then first peopled around the convict settlement of *Brisbane*, and thus the colony arose which, when it was divided off from New South Wales in 1859 was called QUEENSLAND. After some time Eastern Australia became so prosperous that the people refused any longer to receive convicts, who were for the future sent to WESTERN AUSTRALIA which had been colonised since 1829, but did not flourish because of bad management. These were the only Australian colonies in George IV's reign, except that free settlers began to arrive in the convict island of Van Diemen's Land, now called Tasmania. But looking on a little farther, we find towards the end of William IV.'s reign a settlement called SOUTH AUSTRALIA being formed, its capital being named *Adelaide*, after William IV.'s queen; while in 1835 a body of men settled on the shores of Port Philip, and called their first town *Melbourne*, after the Prime Minister of that day. In 1851 this last settlement was divided off from New South Wales and called VICTORIA, after the Queen. The earliest of these settlements were only in their infancy in the troubled year of 1826, but it was partly the distress and suffering of that time which led so many to venture into new lands where labour met with a better return.

7. Repeal of Test and Corporation Acts, 1828.—The next year, 1827, Lord Liverpool, a prudent and able, though not a brilliant statesman, who had been Prime Minister for fifteen years, had a stroke of palsy and resigned; and people hoped that Canning, who took his place, would do much for England. But unfortunately Canning too fell ill, and died, and after a short interval, during which Lord Goderich was Prime Minister, the Duke of Wellington became head of the Government.

<small>Death of Canning, 1827.</small>

If this had happened a few years earlier, it would have been very bad for the country, for Wellington was a better general than statesman, and would have liked to rule Parliament as he ruled an army. But Canning, though dead, had left behind him a spirit of freedom and justice which could not be checked, and during Wellington's administration two great measures were passed in spite of his wishes. The first was the repeal of the "Test and Corporation Acts," which for nearly 150 years had prevented dissenters from holding offices in towns or under Government, except by a special Act passed each year. In 1828 Lord John Russell proposed and carried the repeal of these oppressive laws. The second was the "Roman Catholic Emancipation Bill." Since 1817 Roman Catholics had been allowed to enter the army and navy. It was clear that they could not long be shut out of Parliament, but though two Bills were passed in the House of Commons to admit them as members, the Lords always threw them out. A large number of the Roman Catholics were Irish, and in 1823 a "Catholic Association" had been formed in Ireland, whose leader, Daniel O'Connell, was a clever, eloquent barrister. But the disputes between the Association and the Orangemen were so bitter that in 1825 the Association was suppressed for three years, and though Sir Francis

<small>Wellington's administration, 1828-1830.</small>

<small>Catholic Association, 1823.</small>

Burdett passed another Bill to relieve the Roman Catholics, the Lords threw it out, and nothing was done. At last, when Canning died, the Irish, who knew that Wellington and Peel were both against Roman Catholic emancipation, grew very restless. O'Connell was elected member for Clare in June 1828 by an enormous number of votes. He could not take his seat because he was a Roman Catholic, yet Government knew he could be elected again and again, and, moreover, that he would persuade the Irish to elect Roman Catholic members in other parts of Ireland. *Election of O'Connell, 1828.*

8. Catholic Emancipation Bill, 1829.—The question could no longer be put aside. For several months Parliament discussed it, and in the end, March 5, 1829, the Roman Catholic Emancipation Bill being again passed in the House of Commons, the Lords gave way. A few years later, in 1833, another Act enabled Quakers and others who thought it wrong to take an oath to *affirm* instead; but it was not till 1858 that all injustice was removed, by the oath being so altered as to allow Jews also to sit in Parliament.

As soon as the Roman Catholic Emancipation Bill was passed, O'Connell was again elected for Clare, and took his seat.

8. William IV.—In June 1830 George IV died. His death made very little change except that his brother William IV., a simple, genial sailor, who "walked in London streets with his umbrella under his arm and frankly shook hands with old acquaintances," was a favourite with the people. This was fortunate, for a fresh revolution had broken out in France against the king, Charles X., who had tried to govern despotically. Charles abdicated and came to Great Britain, where he lived in Holyrood Palace which William lent him; and his cousin Louis Philippe, Duke of Orleans, was made Captain-General of France and afterwards king. About the same time Belgium broke away from Holland, and two years later took Leopold of Saxe-Coburg, the widower of Princess Charlotte, to reign over them. *Character of William IV.* *Second French Revolution, 1830.*

10. Reform Bill.—All this stir among other nations roused the English people to cry out again for the reform of Parliament. It was evidently unjust that large towns, such as Birmingham,

Manchester and Leeds, should have no member to speak for them, and show what laws were necessary for the growing masses of people living in them, while owners of parks and forests, with only a few scattered villages here and there, had control over nine or ten small boroughs, and nominated for them what members they pleased. Yet Wellington could not be persuaded to listen to a Reform Bill, and spoke so strongly against it that he became extremely unpopular, so that the king's visit to the city had to be postponed because it was not safe for the duke to go with him without a powerful escort. The new Parliament, elected as usual on the change of kings, had a large number of reformers in it, and William IV. was so clearly on their side, that Wellington had to resign. From that time he became popular again, for the people loved their "Iron Duke," who had fought for them so bravely, though they did not like his politics, and many of his political friends were vexed at him for passing the Roman Catholic Emancipation Bill. He lived for another twenty-two years, till 1852, and his bent form riding in the park was familiar to many who had not been born when he fought the battle of Waterloo. When he died the whole nation went into mourning, and the touching respect shown at his funeral showed how England loves her great men.

<small>Wellington resigns, Nov. 16, 1830.</small>

Lord Grey, the man upon whom the king now called in 1830 to form a Government, had never ceased for the last forty years to urge that Parliament should be reformed, and the men he chose as his colleagues were as eager as himself. How familiar the names are to us! Lord Brougham, Lord Melbourne, Lord Palmerston, Lord John Russell, the Hon. Mr. Stanley, afterwards Lord Derby, and Lord Lansdowne. All these men have been leaders in public life within living memory. But there was still a battle of more than a year to be fought before a reformed Parliament could be obtained. The First Reform Bill was introduced by Lord John Russell on March 1, 1831. It was only carried by one vote, (302 to 301), and was defeated in "Committee," that is when each separate part of the Bill is discussed. Then the ministers persuaded the king to dissolve Parliament, that the people might be able to express their wishes in the new elections.

<small>Lord Grey's Administration. 1830-1834.</small>

<small>First Reform Bill, March 1831.</small>

What they wanted was plain enough. The lords, the clergy, and the army and navy were chiefly against the Bill, but the manufacturers, the educated middle class, the townspeople, and the workmen, who wanted members to speak for them in Parliament, were all for reform. Excitement ran very high; "the Bill, the whole Bill, and nothing but the Bill, was the election cry; and in the end so many reformers were elected that the Second Reform Bill was carried through the Commons on Sept. 2, 1831, by a majority of 109 (345 to 236). But when Lord Grey brought it into the House of Lords they rejected it. Second Reform Bill, Sept. 2, 1831.

Outbursts of indignation came from all parts of the country, and meetings were held everywhere in support of the Government. At one large meeting in Birmingham the speakers declared that they would pay no more taxes till the Lords gave way, and serious riots took place at Derby, Nottingham, and Bristol. People began to talk gravely of the fear of a revolution. When Parliament met in December it was with serious faces, and the Third Reform Bill was brought in, slightly altered, and was passed on Dec. 18, by the large majority of 162. When the Lords still rejected it in committee by a majority of 35, Lord Grey asked the king to say that unless it were passed he would create enough new peers to outvote the opposition. He refused at first, but as Wellington could not form a government, Lord Grey had his way, and several Lords who were against reform, seeing that opposition was useless, stayed away on the next occasion, so that the Bill was carried by a majority of 84 (106 to 22).

By this Bill fifty-six small boroughs, which had 111 members between them, had to give them up altogether, and thirty others had only one member instead of two. Weymouth and Melcombe Regis lost two. The 143 seats which were thus set free were given chiefly to the counties and large towns of England, and the rest to Scotland and Ireland. Householders in boroughs paying a £10 rental, and tenants-at-will in counties paying £50 a year rent, were given votes—besides copyholders and leaseholders for a term of years. The only thing to be regretted was, that the reform, instead of being freely granted, when it was clear that justice required it, was so long delayed. It was during this struggle for reform that the names of *Conservative* for those who wished to keep to the old laws, and *Liberal* for those who wished to give freely what the people asked, took the place of the old names Tory and Whig; the name of *Radical* had sprung up long before, in 1819, when, during the riots and distress after the war, a body of men in Parliament wished to go to the *root* of things and make thorough reforms.

Terms Conservative, Liberal, and Radical.

11. Important Acts and Reforms.—For the next five years the Liberals had the chief power in Parliament except for a few months, from Nov. 1834 to April 1835, when there was a Conservative Government under Sir Robert Peel. During these five years many useful reforms which had been begun before were completed and others introduced. The victory was at last gained for which Wilberforce had struggled so long. An Act was passed abolishing slavery in all the English dominions, and a year after, Aug. 31, 1834, all slaves belonging to British subjects in all parts of the world were free, though they remained till 1838 apprenticed to their old masters. Wilberforce, who was in his seventy-fifth year, lived long enough to hear that the Bill had passed the second reading, and then died, thankful that his work had succeeded. The English nation had to pay twenty million pounds to compensate the owners who lost their slaves, but the money was well spent.

Abolition of slavery, Aug. 30, 1833.

That same year, 1833, Lord Ashley, afterwards Lord Shaftesbury, succeeded in passing Acts which protected the children who worked in factories from overstrain and ill-treatment, and an annual grant of public money was first established to be given to those schools which were teaching the children of the poor. Thirty thousand pounds had been given in 1831 for education in Ireland. In this year too the trade with the East Indies was thrown open to all merchants.

Factory and Education Acts, 1833.

In 1834, the poor-law was altered, not before it was necessary. The old poor-law had become a very heavy burden. The idle and reckless were living upon those industrious and saving workers who paid the poor-rate. The new

New Poor-Law, 1834.

poor-law ordered workhouses to be built all over England, and obliged those who could not keep themselves and their families to go into the workhouse, unless there was some very good reason for giving them money in their own homes. By this change the rates were less heavy, wages rose, and the labouring classes were better off. The number of paupers has from that time steadily diminished, so that there are not now half as many compared to the population as there were fifty years ago.

In 1835, when Lord Melbourne was Prime Minister, the government of towns was reformed. The mayor and aldermen were for the future (except in the city of London) elected by the ratepayers of the town, and the town councils were obliged to publish accounts of the public money they spent. In 1836 a bill was passed causing all births, deaths, and marriages to be registered at the office of a Registrar-General, and allowing dissenters to be married in their own chapels or before the registrar of the district. *Municipal Reform, 1835.*

While all these reforms were being made in Parliament, the nation outside had not been standing still. In 1816, only a year after the battle of Waterloo, London was first lighted by gas. This did more to prevent robbery and violence in the streets than all the hanging had done; and when, in 1829, Sir Robert Peel had abolished the old watchmen, and introduced policemen, (long called "Peelers" and "Bobbies" after his name), the streets became comparatively safe both by day and night. The roads, too, all over England and Scotland were greatly improved by the new system, introduced by a blind Scotchman named MacAdam, of making them of broken stone after a sound foundation had been obtained. Upon these *macadamized* roads coaches could run ten or twelve miles an hour, instead of crawling along as formerly, and carriages and waggons no longer sank wheel-deep in the mud. *Gas and Police.* *Macadamized Roads.*

Lastly, the first great English railway was opened between Liverpool and Manchester, George Stephenson, the son of a poor collier, who had risen to be a leading engineer, had triumphed over all difficulties, and made a locomotive engine, which moved a train at the rate of thirty-five miles an hour along a line of rails which he had *Opening of Liverpool and Manchester Railway, 1830.*

carried even across a famous bog called the Chat Moss. One sad event, however, cast a gloom over the grand day of opening. Huskisson, who had done so much for English trade, got out of his compartment to speak to the Duke of Wellington, from whom he had long been estranged. As he stood at the door of the Duke's carriage, a train came up on the other track, and he was struck down and killed. Probably, however, Huskisson himself would have reckoned his own death a small thing in comparison with the great benefit that day first gave to the country. Machinery and steam, which had for some time past been the servants of man in the workshop, the mine and the manufactory, were now brought into play to carry his goods far and wide by land and sea.

These advances caused the upper and middle classes to grow more and more wealthy, and with greater wealth came improvements of all kinds in the streets, buildings, and other arrangements of all the great towns. The markets of London were rebuilt, the streets better paved and made more cleanly, Regent's Park was laid out, Hyde Park and St. James' Park were replanted and made healthy breathing places among the crowded thoroughfares. The Zoological Gardens were opened in 1828. University College and King's College were founded. Last, but not least, the care of the helpless received attention, and a large asylum was built at Hanwell, where poor lunatics lived comfortably and were kindly treated, instead of being chained down and neglected as formerly.

Lunatic Asylum

Now, too, men who had wealth to spare began to thirst after more knowledge and to wish to give it to others. In 1823 the first "Mechanics' Institute" was founded in London by a body of gentlemen, of whom Dr. Birkbeck was the chief. Other towns followed the example, and while Government was giving grants for educating children, these institutes were giving instruction to grown-up workmen in the evening hours. Soon it was found that books were needed which these men could read, and in 1825 Lord Brougham and others founded the "Society for the Diffusion of Useful Knowledge," which published simple and cheap works on history, science and other subjects. In

First Mechanics' Institute, 1823.

Useful Literature.

1836, the revenue stamp on newspapers was reduced to one penny, so that newspaper reading was much more widely spread.

12. Suffering of the Working Classes.—And yet, with all these increased advantages for the upper class of the working people, the poorer classes both in town and country remained unhealthy, miserable, ignorant, and often in great distress; and in 1837, when William IV died, there was great suffering and discontent in England. The truth is that when great changes are made there is always suffering for a time, and it falls chiefly on those who are poorest and least able to change quickly with the altered conditions. In the twenty years of peace over which we have now passed things had advanced very rapidly. The sudden outburst of trade, the use of machinery, the invention of railways were all in the end great blessings to the very poorest. But for the moment they threw many out of work, by altering the places where labour was wanted, and the kind of labour to be done, so that wages were often actually lower and less easy to earn than before. Food was still very dear, and the rates very high, for the changes in the poor-law had not yet done much to take the burden off the industrious workmen, while those who had depended on the outdoor relief given under the old law, were of course badly off. The labourers on the farms could scarcely buy barley or rye bread, while meat, except a little salt pork, never came within their homes, and in many districts the people only just kept their families from starvation.

CHAPTER XXVI.

ENGLAND AND HER COLONIES.

1. Victoria.—At five o'clock on the early morning of June 20, 1837, the young Princess Victoria was awakened from sleep to receive the Lord Chamberlain and the Archbishop of Canterbury, who came to tell her that she was Queen of England. She had only celebrated her eighteenth birthday a month before, but she had been carefully trained to be self-reliant and conscientious, thoughtful for others, and strict in the performance of duty. As she was the only child of the Duke of Kent, fourth son of George III., whose elder sons had no heirs, it had long been known that she would succeed to the throne; and England owes a deep debt to the widowed Duchess of Kent, who in quiet seclusion so brought up her young daughter that she became a just ruler, a sympathising queen, a loving wife, a pure and noble example, a sovereign who, after fifty-three years of rule, reigns not only in name, but in the hearts of her subjects.

As the laws of Hanover required a male heir to succeed to the throne, that country now became separated from the English Crown, and the Duke of Cumberland, the Queen's uncle, became King of Hanover. This was a great advantage, for now at last England was free from any possessions in Europe which were likely to involve her in foreign quarrels, and we shall see that the only serious wars during the next fifty years arose, directly or indirectly, out of our possessions in India and Africa. Our history during this time deals chiefly with attempts to make our laws just and wise at home, and to give good government to our colonies.

Hanover becomes separate from England, 1837.

2. Rebellion in Canada, 1837.—The first question which sprang up was that of Canada. This country was divided by Pitt in 1791 into two provinces, Upper and Lower Canada, each with a governor and Council appointed by the Crown, and an assembly elected by the people. The system did not work well either in

ENGLAND AND HER COLONIES. 299

Upper or Lower Canada, because the Council and Government were not responsible to the people, and the Assembly had not full control of the revenues and the expenditure. Great difficulties arose, which ended in a rebellion in Lower Canada, which spread into Upper Canada in 1837, just as the queen came to the throne. The country was put under martial law, and the Earl of Durham, a very able and upright man, was sent out as Governor-General to report on the best way of remedying the evils existing. Unfortunately he not only reported, but acted very much on his own authority, in settling difficulties and restoring order. The Government at home sent out a sharp rebuke, which so irritated him that he resigned and came back, without waiting for permission. He died in July 1840 a disappointed man. *(Lord Durham Governor-General. 1838.)*

Nevertheless his scheme was adopted, and, moreover, laid the foundation for all the free constitutions which England has given to her new colonies. The two Canadas were united in 1840 and allowed to govern themselves, all their officials being responsible to an Upper and Lower House, answering to our Houses of Lords and Commons. The only hold which England still kept was by appointing a Governor-General to represent the Queen. Twenty-seven years later, in 1867, all the British possessions in North America were allowed to join Canada in one great federation, called the "Dominion of Canada." *(Constitution of Canada, 1840. Dominion of Canada, 1867.)* Nova Scotia and New Brunswick joined in 1867; Hudson's Bay Territory was acquired and Manitoba was formed in 1870; British Columbia and Prince Edward's Island joined, the one in 1871, and the other in 1873; so that now a country of 3,500,000 square miles forms one grand Dominion under the British Crown, and one long line of rail, the Canadian Pacific Railway, opened in 1886, carries the traveller from Nova Scotia on the shores of the Atlantic, to British Columbia on the Pacific, without ever leaving British soil. Newfoundland is now the only North American British colony which has not joined the Dominion.

3. Inventions and Reforms.—This history of this new country has carried us all through Victoria's reign, for this great railway was only finished in 1886. We must now go back to the beginning, and see what rapid advances were made during the first few years in the old country. In 1837 the first electric telegraph was patented by Wheatstone and Cooke, and used on the Blackwall railway. In 1838 ships worked entirely by steam crossed from England to New York, carrying coal enough for the whole voyage; and in 1839 Mr. Hill, afterwards Sir Rowland Hill, persuaded the Government to carry out his scheme for a penny postage all over the United Kingdom. This was a grand step, for hitherto the people, who could best afford to pay, namely, members of Parliament, had the right of franking their own and their friends' letters,—that is, of putting their name on the envelope and sending the letter free of cost; while the poor man had to pay from sixpence to one shilling and fourpence to send a letter to the country, according to the distance. In 1839 a postage of fourpence for half an ounce was introduced, and on Jan. 10, 1840, a letter could go to any part of England, Scotland, and Ireland for one penny

Electric telegraph, 1837.

Penny postage, 1839-1840.

4. Rise of the Chartists.—Still the early part of this reign was not without its troubles. The poorer class, as we have seen, were scarcely able to live, and reforms were much needed. But the ministers had such a small majority in the new Parliament, elected on the Queen's accession, that they were not strong enough to pass fresh measures, and as Lord Melbourne was an easy-going man, who always wanted to "let things alone," the people thought he was teaching their young sovereign to be careless about their distress. Moreover, the workmen were discontented because the shop-keepers had been given votes for members of Parliament, and they had not. Only a few weeks after the Queen's coronation, which took place June 28, 1838, a large meeting was held at Birmingham, and a declaration was drawn up, called by O'Connell the "People's Charter." It asked for six reforms. 1. For all men to have votes; 2. For a fresh Parliament to be elected every year; 3. For voting by ballot; 4. That a man might sit in Parliament without having land of his own; 5. That members of Parliament should be paid; 6. That the country should be divided into equal electoral districts. Numbers 3 and 4 of these demands have since become law, and so many men are now allowed to have votes that the first clause is almost satisfied; so also is the sixth clause by the Reform Bill of 1885. The "Chartists," as those were called who signed the Charter, did great mischief by exciting riots in Birmingham, Sheffield, Newport, and other places.

5. Anti-Corn-Law League.—Meanwhile a small knot of thoughtful men were discussing how to attack the real evil which oppressed the country. On Sept. 18, 1838, a meeting was held in Manchester, and an Association formed to press on the Government to take the duties off foreign corn. This was the beginning of the Anti-Corn-Law League, of which the chief leaders were Richard Cobden, a clear-headed, upright cotton-printer of Manchester, and his friend John Bright, who was a carpet manufacturer at Rochdale. For the next five years these two men, and those who worked with them, taught the public by pamphlets, lectures, and speeches how unjust these corn-laws were towards the poor. For if, by opening the ports and letting in foreign corn, the poor man could buy his bread for half the price, then the other half, which he had to pay because the ports were closed, was actually a tax levied on him for the farmers' benefit. Thus those who were almost starving were indirectly paying money to those who were well-to-do. Yet the anti-corn-law lecturers had great difficulty at first in persuading their hearers, for the landowners and farmers thought the scheme would ruin the country, by making it not worth the farmer's while to cultivate his land, and even the workingmen were far more eager for the Charter than for the repeal of the corn-laws. But the facts were so clear and so well put that at last the nation began to be convinced. Lord Melbourne had already proposed a lower fixed duty on corn, and when he could no longer secure a majority in the House, and resigned in 1841, Sir Robert Peel, who succeeded him with a Conservative ministry, saw that something must be done.

6. Marriage of the Queen.—The young Queen was very sorry to part with Lord Melbourne, who had been a faithful adviser to her. But she had now the best of friends and advisers in a good husband. In Feb. 1840 she had married her cousin, Prince Albert of Saxe-Coburg, whom she loved sincerely. It was a happy marriage for England. The Prince, like herself, had been educated to be good and true. Devoted to his wife and to her people, he made her life happy by his affection and support, and did much for the prosperity of England by encouraging science and art, and gathering around him the intellectual men of the time. At the same time he was careful never to interfere between the Queen and her people, but put his own ambition entirely aside, and was content to do good without seeking applause.

7. Difficulties at Home and Abroad.—The new ministry had hard work before them. O'Connell as Lord Mayor of Dublin began in Ireland an agitation for Repeal of the Union, which was only ended by his arrest and trial in 1843-1844. Scotland was agitated by the great dispute in the Presbyterian Church, which led to the "Free Kirk" being established in 1843. The Chartists were holding meetings all over the country, and there had been a war going on in China since 1839, because British traders sold opium to the Chinese against the wish of their Government. This war came to an end in 1842, but before it was over, terrible news came from India of a massacre of a whole British force in Afghanistan.

<small>Opium war with China, 1839-1842</small>

For a long time past the English had been gradually annexing more and more of India, till only the Punjab and Afghanistan (see Map VI.) lay between them and those parts of Asia where the Russians had great influence. The English Government had always been afraid that the Russians would make an alliance with the Afghans and attack India; and to prevent this Sir Alexander Burnes was sent, in 1837, to Kabul to make a commercial treaty with the Afghans. While he was there it was suspected that the Afghan chief, Dost Muhammad Khan was intriguing with the Russians, and Lord Auckland, then Governor-General of India, very unwisely sent an army, deposed Muhammad, and put another chief in his place. The result was that the Afghans—a fierce, warlike and treacherous people—murdered Sir Alexander Burnes, and six weeks later Sir W. Macnaughten also, who was treating with them. After this General Elphinstone could no longer hold his position at Kabul, and determined to return to India, having received a promise from Akbar Khan, the

<small>Disasters in Afghanistan, 1841.</small>

Afghan chief, that the army should be allowed to retreat safely. In spite, however, of this promise, the Afghans hid themselves on the rocks on each side of the Koord Kabul Pass, and picked off the soldiers below as they marched by It was a terrible story, and only one man, Dr. Brydon, escaped to tell it, and arrived half dead at the fortress of Jellalabad, which was held by Sir Robert Sale, between Koord Kabul and the Khyber Pass. England, it is true, avenged the insult, and an army, under General Pollock and Sir R. Sale, retook Kabul, and rescued the women and children who had been left behind. But 4500 regular troops and 12,000 camp followers lay murdered in the awful pass, and English power in the East had received a severe blow.

Added to these disasters abroad there were financial difficulties at home. Lord Melbourne's ministry had left the Treasury with a debt of two millions and a half, which had to be made good, and to meet this difficulty Peel determined to levy an "income-tax," by which everyone who had more than £150 a year should give so much in the pound of their income to the Government. This tax was only to last for three years, *Income-tax established, 1842.* and not to be more than 7d. in the pound, but in 1845 it was renewed for another three years, and has never since been taken off. The highest it has ever been was 1s. 4d. in the pound in 1855-1857, and the lowest 2d. in the pound in 1874-1876.

8. Repeal of the Corn Laws.—On the other hand, Peel did all he could to reduce the duties on foreign imports, and especially on corn. Still, however, the distress continued, and worse was to follow. In 1845 the harvest failed in England, and the potato disease broke out and destroyed the chief food of Ireland. Famine was close at hand, and the nation called loudly for the ports to be opened and foreign corn to be let in. *Bad harvest and potato disease, 1845.* 'Peel, who had become gradually convinced that Cobden was right, now proposed to bring in a Bill to repeal the duties on corn, and as he could not persuade the other ministers to agree with him, he resigned and advised the Queen to call upon Lord John Russell, who had written a strong letter against the corn-laws to take his place. *Peel supports free trade, 1845.* What now followed helps to show the difficulties of a Prime Minister, for

Lord John Russell could not form a ministry, because his chief supporters, Lord Grey and Lord Palmerston, who both wanted free trade in corn, could not agree about foreign affairs. So the Queen asked Peel to come back to office, and this is why the corn-laws were repealed by a Conservative, and not by a Liberal minister.

<small>Lord John Russell cannot form a ministry.</small>

It was soon known that Peel meant to bring in his Bill, and the excitement all over the country was intense. Cobden now at last saw the result of his labour ; at a meeting held at Manchester no less than £60,000 was subscribed in an hour and a half to help the cause. On Jan. 22, 1846, Peel explained in an eloquent speech why he gave up "Protection," and proposed to bring in "Free Trade," and on June 25 the Bill passed the House of Lords, and the corn-laws were repealed. The duty was to decrease gradually till Feb., 1849, when only a fixed duty of one shilling a quarter remained. This last shilling was taken off in 1869. This was Peel's last great reform, for his old friends were very angry with him, and Disraeli (afterwards Lord Beaconsfield) attacked him severely. A "Protection" party was formed in Parliament, and when Peel wanted to bring in a "Coercion Bill" to stop crime in Ireland, this party joined the Liberals against him. The very night on which the Lords passed the repeal of the Corn-laws, Peel was obliged to resign, and Lord John Russell became Prime Minister.

10. End of Chartist Agitation.—The next eight years, from 1846 to 1854, were chiefly remarkable for four things—the downfall of the Chartists, the annexation of the Punjab, the discovery of gold in the colonies, and the great International Exhibition of 1851. In 1848 another revolution broke out in Paris, King Louis Philippe fled to England, and a republic was established. All Europe was very unsettled. In Italy, Austria, and Prussia, insurrections took place, and the sovereigns were forced to grant Parliaments to their people. In Ireland, where there had been a terrible famine in 1847, an extreme party called the "Young Irelanders," broke out into rebellion under Smith O'Brien, but was quickly suppressed. In England the Chartists thought they could now agitate for their Charter A petition was drawn up, said to be signed by more than

<small>Disturbed state of Europe, 1848.</small>

five million people, and Feargus O'Connor, member for Nottingham, called a monster meeting on Kennington Common on April 10, 1848, proposing to march to the House of Commons to present the petition. All London was in a panic ; the Government forbade the procession ; the Duke of Wellington stationed soldiers out of sight in all parts of London, and 200,000 gentlemen were sworn in at the different vestry halls as special constables to prevent disturbance. But the whole thing came to nothing. Only twenty-five thousand people assembled, and the procession was not formed. The petition was carried in a cab to Westminster, when it was found that there were less than two million signatures, and that many of these were mere shams. In truth, ever since 1842, the country had been growing more prosperous, and the people cared very little for the Charter now that they had food to eat. From this time no more was heard of the Chartists.

The next year, 1849, the Navigation laws were repealed altogether, and in 1850 England lost one of her best and wisest statesmen. Sir Robert Peel was killed by a fall from his horse, much to the grief and dismay of the nation. *Death of Sir R. Peel, 1850.*

10. Extension of Territory.—Meanwhile on the other side of the world British territories were growing. In 1843 Sir Charles Napier conquered the native princes of Scinde, and annexed that province. In 1845 and 1849 the Sikhs, a warlike race living in the Punjab, a country nearly as big as England, which lies to the north-west of Hindustan, quarelled among themselves and made war upon the English frontier, causing serious trouble. At last, after Lord Gough had won the battle of Goojerat on Feb. 21, 1849, the Governor-General of India, Lord Dalhousie, annexed the whole province and put it under a board of three men—Col. Henry Lawrence, his brother John Lawrence, and Charles Grenville Mansel. The firm and just rule of the two brothers soon won the respect of the brave Sikhs, who eight years later did good service to the English. *Annexation of the Punjab, 1849.*

The discovery of gold in 1849 in California, which had just become a possession of the United States, and in 1851 in Victoria, Australia, was an advance of quite a different kind. The question of the effect of a rise and fall in the price of gold is a very difficult one, about which those who know most do not entirely agree. But two things are certain—the discovery of gold in the colonies in 1851 made things cheaper at home, and by causing a great excitement led many to emigrate, not only to the gold-fields, but to other settlements besides. The history of the colonies begins from this time to be very important. The Cape of Good Hope colony, though it lay on the road to India, advanced the least, because the Dutch Boers, who had settled there before the English came, were always quarrelling with the natives, and involving the English in petty wars. Still, in spite of skirmishes with Kaffirs and Zulus, the English territory was increasing. Natal had become a British colony in 1843, and Cape Colony was given a constitution in 1850, though it did not entirely manage its own affairs till 1874.

Discovery of gold, 1849-1851.

Cape Colony Constitution, 1850.

In Australasia things advanced more quickly. The natives of Australia were so low and degraded that they gave way rapidly before the white men, while in New Zealand the intelligent Maoris soon became good and peaceable citizens. In 1837 Edward Gibbon Wakefield, who was afterwards secretary to Lord Durham in Canada, had formed a company in London to colonise New Zealand; and his brother, Colonel Wakefield, went to the north island and settled a colony at Port Nicholson, on Cook's Straits, round which grew up the province of WELLINGTON. In 1839 the English Government declared New Zealand to be a crown colony, and in 1840 the Maori chiefs made a treaty at Waitangi, giving Great Britain the sovereignty of the islands, while they kept their own lands and forests, except where they were paid for them. The next settlement was that of AUCKLAND in the north, close to the Maori country. Then followed the settlements in the south island,—NELSON in 1841, OTAGO in 1848, and CANTERBURY, with its capital Christchurch, in 1850. As Wakefield's system was not to *give* but to *sell* land to settlers, using the money in making roads and bridges, the early New Zealand colonists were chiefly men with some savings to start them in life. The only great checks to the prosperity of the country were the wars with the Maoris

Colonisation of New Zealand, 1839-1850.

Treaty of Waitangi, 1840.

from 1861 to 1868. Since then the natives have been thoroughly friendly with the English, and have their own Maori, members in the New Zealand Parliament.   *Maori wars, 1861-1868.*

Thus there were now seven Australasian colonies—New Zealand, Tasmania, and the five settlements in Australia. In 1850 Lord John Russell had passed a Bill allowing New South Wales, Victoria, South Australia, and Tasmania to choose their own constitution under an English governor, and in a few years the others followed, New Zealand receiving hers in 1852. Meanwhile the gold-fever of 1851 carried a long stream of emigrants to these colonies, and set up the constant movement to and fro between them and the old country, which, while their government was free, bound them in heart and interest to England.   *Australian Colonies Bill, 1850.*

11. The First Great Exhibition.—That same year, 1851, was the year of the "Great Exhibition of the Industries of all Nations," which Prince Albert, then Prince Consort, chiefly planned and carried out in order to give a living, picture of the point which industry had reached all over the world, and to encourage English workmen in knowing what other nations could produce. The Crystal Palace, which now stands in the grounds at Sydenham, is the same building which Sir Joseph Paxton erected for this brilliant display. It was a great success, and was very useful both then and afterwards by leading to other exhibitions. But instead of marking, as many people hoped, the beginning of a new era when wars would cease, and nations would only struggle with each other in peaceful work, it proved to be rather the close of thirty-five years of peace, after which came troubles. Since then many greater exhibitions have been held—the last, in 1889, in Paris, being the most successful of all. It was held to commemorate the revolution of 1789.

The Exhibition had scarcely closed when all England was alarmed by the news that Prince Louis Napoleon, who had been for three years President of the French republic, had filled the streets of Paris with troops, shot down all who resisted, imprisoned his political opponents, and persuaded the French people to make him Prince President for ten years. A year later he became Emperor as Napoleon III. All those who remem-   *Coup d'état in Paris, Dec. 2, 1851.*

bered the trouble and misery worked by the first Napoleon feared that the same story would begin again, and young Englishmen began to form themselves into volunteer regiments to protect their country. But Lord Palmerston, who was Foreign Secretary, knew Louis Napoleon well, and had no fear of his attacking England, where he had lived for many years. He was right, for all his life Napoleon III. remained a firm ally to England. Yet Palmerston was wrong in upholding the *coup d'état* (as the massacre of Dec. 2 was called), and the Queen was very much displeased with him.

<small>First English volunteers, 1852.</small>

12. The Eastern Question.—But though England did not have trouble with France, war in Europe was near at hand. In 1852 Russia and Turkey quarrelled about the Holy Places at Jerusalem, and about the protection of Christians in those countries on the Danube over which Turkey ruled. The Russian Emperor, Nicholas, thought the matter might be settled if the English would help him to seize these countries, and he in return would help them to take Egypt and Candia. England, however, refused to appropriate her neighbour's lands, and the European powers tried hard to persuade the Russian Emperor to keep the peace. But Nicholas was violent and headstrong, and thought that England would not fight. So when the Turks refused to give him power to protect the Christians of Turkey he sent Russian troops into the Danubian principalities. The Turks then crossed the Danube and defeated the Russians on land, while the Russians in return burned the Turkish fleet at Sinope, Nov. 30, 1853. Most people now agree that it would have been better if England had not interfered in the quarrel; and the Prime Minister, Lord Aberdeen, did all he could to keep peace. Lord Palmerston, however, though he was now Home Secretary, and had not the control of foreign affairs, had great influence among the ministers, and he was very anxious to put an end to the Russian power in the Black Sea, while the English people remembered how Russian intrigue had helped to bring about the disaster in Afghanistan. So the English and French fleets, which had passed through the Dardanelles, now entered the Black Sea to defend the Turks, and on March 28, 1854, war was declared by England and France against Russia.

13. Crimean War.—If the war itself was not a mistake, the way it was carried out was full of blunders. It took place chiefly in the Crimea, which is a small peninsula jutting out from the south of Russia into the Black Sea; though hostilities also went on in the White Sea, where Archangel was blockaded, in the Baltic, and in Russian Armenia, where Kars was gallantly defended by the Turks under General Williams, and only surrendered at the close of the war. The allies, reaching the Crimea on Sept. 13, 1854, gained their first victory on the river Alma on Sept. 20, and, if they had only pushed on, they might have entered Sebastopol, the great fortress of the Crimea. But the French general, St. Arnaud, refused to follow up the victory, and the English general, Lord Raglan, gave way. This gave Todleben, the great Russian engineer, time to strengthen the fortress and so the war was prolonged for more than a year. Both the English and French soldiers behaved splendidly. It was here, at the fight of Balaclava, that the famous "Charge of the Light Brigade" was made, in which six hundred men, whose officer mistook the order given, charged boldly into certain death against the whole Russian army rather than hesitate to obey a command. Again at the battle of Inkermann, on Nov. 5, the Guards and a few British regiments kept the whole Russian army in check till the French came and the battle was won. But the loss of life was terrible for want of good generalship. Then came the long tedious siege of Sebastopol, lasting through a bitter winter, in which the soldiers were badly clothed and left without necessaries through bad management at home. Stores of food were sent where they could not be landed; a cargo of boots arrived which were all for the left foot; sickness broke out, and there were no blankets for the men to lie on; and the contractors who supplied provender for the horses filled the trusses of hay with manure. Amidst all this confusion and disorder one name will be ever gratefully remembered. Sidney Herbert, the Minister of War, asked Miss Florence Nightingale, who had studied nursing, to take out a band of ladies to nurse the sick and wounded. As soon as she reached the hospital at Scutari all fell into order; wounds were properly bandaged, the

Crimean War, 1854-1856.

Charge of the Light Brigade, Oct. 25, 1854.

Confusion and mismanagement.

Miss Florence Nightingale.

sick were nursed, the dying comforted; and tender, cultivated ladies, taught by her example, have from this time given their help on all the battlefields of Europe.

Meanwhile the nation at home grew very impatient at the accounts of misery and neglect, and began to call loudly for Lord Palmerston to take the lead of the Government. As soon as Parliament met, Lord Aberdeen resigned, and Lord Palmerston became Prime Minister Jan. 1855. Things had already begun to go better as the authorities gained experience; the siege was carried on successfully all the next summer, till on Sept. 8, 1855, the Russians left the town and blew up the forts—Sebastopol was taken. The next spring peace was made, and in the Treaty of Paris, Russia promised not to keep a fleet in the Black Sea.

<small>Treaty of Paris, March 30, 1856.</small>

14. Discontent in India.—For a few months England was at peace, with the exception of a war in China; and then all at once an awful blow fell. There had been, for a long time, a smouldering discontent among the natives of India, partly because the English had annexed so many states, especially Oude in 1856, and partly on account of the insolent treatment received from their conquerors. A curious accident brought this discontent to a head in 1857. A new rifle had been invented a short time before, in which greased cartridges were used, and the Sepoys thought that this grease was the fat of cows, to use which is sacrilege to the Hindus, or the fat of pigs, which is unclean to the Muhammadans. In vain the Indian government changed the grease to smooth paper, in vain the officers reasoned with the men; they thought the English wanted to make them lose their caste. In February and March 1857 two slight outbreaks occurred at Barrackpore. After this all was quiet for a time, but the local magistrates noticed that *chupaties,* or little baked cakes, were being mysteriously passed from village to village. At last, on May 3, 1857, some Sepoys mutinied and were imprisoned by Sir Henry Lawrence, and on May 12 three regiments rose at Meerut near Delhi, fired on their officers, and tramping off to Delhi, took the aged native king, who was the heir of the old Moghuls, out of his palace, where he was living on an English pension, and proclaiming him emperor, roused the native regiments to murder their officers and join the insurrection.

<small>Grievances of Indian Sepoys.</small>

15. Indian Mutiny.—In a few days half Upper India was in a blaze, and a few thousand Englishmen had to stand against millions of maddened natives. Fortunately Lord Canning, son of the great statesman, was Governor-General, and he was brave, calm, and able. Two things will always be uppermost in the minds of those who remember this awful time; one is the never-to-be-forgotten horror of the wretched massacres of English men, women, and children; the other, the noble and devoted conduct of the governors, generals, and all concerned. Sir John Lawrence, who was then governor of the Punjab, at once disarmed his Sepoys, and, heedless of his own danger, sent his British troops to besiege Delhi, with the help of his faithful Sikhs. Sir Henry Lawrence, who was governor of Oude, finding that the rebels were too strong for his small force to overcome them, fortified the governor's residence at Lucknow, and brought all English people in to stand a siege. He was killed by a shell a month later, but his dying words were "Never Surrender."

At Cawnpore the brave old commander, Sir Hugh Wheeler, was deceived. He thought he could trust a native prince, Nana Sahib, and asked for his help. But the Nana, when he came, put himself at the head of the mutineers, and attacked Wheeler, who took refuge in some old barracks with only 500 men and 500 women and children. They could not even get a drop of water without crossing the fire of the Sepoys to reach the well, and at last Wheeler was forced to accept Nana Sahib's offer to let them retreat in boats on the Ganges. But the Nana had never meant them to escape. No sooner were they in the boats than they were shot down, and 250 women and children, who remained alive, were carried back to the town. There, sick and terrified, they remained for eighteen days, and then, on July 15, when brave General Havelock, was close at hand to help them, the Nana, fearing a rescue, sent in men who cut them all to pieces, and their bodies were thrown into the well of Cawnpore. *Massacre of Cawnpore, July 15, 1857.*

Englishmen were nearly mad when they heard the news, and Canning had great difficulty in preventing them from taking cruel revenge. But he was firm; he punished severely all who could be proved guilty, but he would not let Englishmen stain their honour with innocent blood, and indeed many of the natives were loyal and true, and saved *Justice of Canning.*

English women and children at the risk of their own lives. Soon the tide turned. Delhi was taken in September, even before fresh troops arrived, and the war remained chiefly at Lucknow, which had been closely besieged for four months. The people there were starving, and expected every day to be massacred, but they held out, and help was coming. Sir James Outram, with Havelock, who had been gaining victory after victory with his Highland regiments, relieved the Residency, and bearded soldiers cried like children as they took the little ones in their arms, and thanked God that they were saved from the horrors of Cawnpore. Sir Henry Havelock died soon after, but Outram defended the place till Sir Colin Campbell came in November with a larger force, and removed the English garrison to a place of safety. In April 1858 the city itself was at last taken.

Relief of Lucknow, Sept. 23, 1857.

16. India under the Crown.—Little by little the rebellion was crushed, after a splendid campaign by Sir Hugh Rose in Central India during the hot season of 1858 ; and meanwhile the mutiny had hastened a change which had been long intended. In June 1858 the East India Company ceased to exist, the territories of India were transferred to the Crown of England, and the Queen was proclaimed sovereign of India. The Company's army became part of the Queen's army, and Lord Canning, who had been Governor-General, became the first "Viceroy" or representative of the Queen. After this the country was greatly improved under Canning, and afterwards under Sir John, who had become Lord Lawrence. New canals were made, telegraphs sprang up over the country, and no less than 1360 miles of railway were laid down before 1862. The cultivation of cotton was encouraged, and large quantities were sent to supply the mills at Manchester. In spite of terrible famines in 1866, 1873, and 1877, much was done to relieve the sufferings of the poorer natives, while public schools and colleges were opened in every province. Little by little the natives were admitted into the public service of the country, and, under Lord Northbrook and Lord Mayo, the laws were made more just and the taxes lighter. In 1875 the Prince of Wales made a royal progress through the country, and in 1877 the Queen took the title of "Empress of India." In 1878, when there was a danger of war

End of the East India Company, 1858.

Victoria Empress of India.

with Russia in Europe, Indian troops first crossed the sea to Malta ; and in 1882 they actually fought side by side with English soldiers in Egypt, and took part in the triumphal procession in London. Thus little by little this great country of the East, which was full of ancient learning when Britain was inhabited by savages, is becoming more and more closely linked to the little island of the West, which is the centre of the British Empire. What our power in India may become in the distant future no one can tell, but our greatest statesmen and our royal princes have done their best to establish a peaceful and beneficent rule.

17. Recent Wars.—Since the Indian Mutiny the chief wars in which England has been engaged have been—1st, a war with China in 1855, which broke out again in 1860, when the English and French entered Pekin ; 2d, the Abyssinian expedition, under Sir Robert Napier in 1867, to rescue some Englishmen from King Theodore; who was killed in his stronghold ; 3d, the successful expedition of 1873, under Sir Garnet Wolseley, against the Ashantees on the Gold Coast, who had attacked tribes protected by England ; 4th, another disturbance in Afghanistan, when Sir Frederick Roberts, 1879-1880, made a brilliant march across the country to avenge the murder of the English envoy, Sir Louis Cavagnari, which happened much in the same way as the murder of Sir Alexander Burnes thirty-seven years before ; 5th, two unsatisfactory wars against the Zulus and the Boers in 1879-1881 ; 6th, the war in the Soudan, 1884-1885, to support the Khedive against the Arabs, when, for the first time in history, a European army ascended the Nile in boats, manned in part by Canadian boatmen. It was in this war that the hero, Charles George Gordon, lost his life in Khartoum. Besides these there were in 1888 some "small wars" on the north-west frontier of India, in Tibet, and at Suakim, when British troops were sent to assist the Egyptian garrison against the Dervishes under Osman Digna. None of these wars, however, have had any great effect on the English people, and in the few pages we have left, we must try and learn what the last quarter of a century has done for England.

Wars in Afghanistan and Africa, 1867-1886.

18. Reform Bills.—During this time the Conservatives and Liberals have changed places several times, the leaders being first

Lord Derby and Lord Palmerston, with a few months' government under Lord John Russell, when Palmerston died in Oct. 1865 ; and afterwards Disraeli and Gladstone. Though the two parties have of course differed in many things, they have both done their best to improve the condition of the working classes in England, and give all English subjects their fair share of power. In 1858 the Conservatives, under Lord Derby, carried a Bill admitting Jews to Parliament; and in 1867 a Reform Bill was passed giving votes to householders in boroughs who had paid their rates, and to lodgers who paid £10 rent; though in the counties, tenants had to pay £12 a year rates, to entitle them to a vote. In 1872 the Liberals, under Gladstone, passed the "Ballot Act," so that no one can know which way a man votes; and in 1884, Mr. Gladstone passed the "Representation of the People" Bill, which gives votes to all householders and lodgers who have lived for a year in the same house and paid their rates, whether they live in town or country. Thus workmen and labourers, even in small villages, have now a voice in the government of the country, and about two million and a half of voters have been added to the roll of electors. The next year, 1885, a Redistribution Bill was passed, which regulated the number of representatives, and divided the country into more equal electoral districts.

Reform Bills, 1858-1-85.

Meanwhile troubles in other lands brought anxiety in England. In 1858 an Italian named Orsini tried to assassinate the French emperor by throwing bombs into his carriage, and the French were so angry because some of the conspirators found a refuge in England, that people were afraid there would be a war between England and France. This led Lord Palmerston to encourage the Rifle Volunteers, who now increased rapidly and were put under the War Office, thus becoming part of the British Army. No war came, however, and in 1860 Cobden arranged a useful commercial treaty between England and France. Even the terrible war between France and Prussia in 1870 left England at peace, and during the siege of Paris and the outbreak of the Commune, Napoleon III. found refuge in England, where he died Jan. 1873.

Orsini bombs, 1858.

Volunteers organized, 1858.

War between France and Prussia, 1870.

19. American Civil War.—In 1861 came another trouble. While all hoped that England and America were being drawn nearer together by the Atlantic cable, along which a message had passed in 1858 from our Queen to the President of the United States, the States themselves were drifting into a civil war. The Northern States did not allow slavery, but the Southern States still had slaves, and they were very sore when in 1850 the new State of California adopted laws forbidding slavery. Still up to 1860 the Presidents of the United States had been chiefly on the side of the South. In that year the Abolitionists succeeded in electing Abraham Lincoln, a just and moderate man, who would not have favoured the slave owners, though he would have respected their laws. Upon this the Southern States wished to secede and form a confederacy of their own, and a war broke out which lasted four years. Now as the raw cotton used by English manufacturers came chiefly from the Southern States, whose ports were soon blockaded by the North, thousands of men and women in the cotton factories of Lancashire were thrown out of work and almost starved, before cotton could be got from Egypt and India. In spite of all the funds which were raised for them, they suffered terribly, but they bore it most patiently, and even sympathised with the war, because they thought that no men ought to be slaves. The higher classes of England were not so wise. They sympathised chiefly with the South, and many vessels, among which was the famous *Alabama*, were built in English ship-yards and allowed to go to the Southerners to be used in the war. At last in 1865 the North conquered, and slavery was abolished, though noble Abraham Lincoln was shot by an assassin. The Americans had now time to complain to the English Government for having allowed ships to be built for the rebels, and in the end England had to pay three million pounds in compensation for the mischief which the *Alabama* had done. *[Cotton famine in Lancashire, 1861. The Alabama claims.]*

20. Minor Events.—While all this was going on, two events of some importance happened in England. On Dec. 14, 1861, the Prince Consort, "Albert the Good," died of typhoid fever. It was not till he was gone that the nation really knew how he had loved and laboured for them, *[Death of the Prince Consort, 1861.]*

counselled their Queen, encouraged science and art, and trained
<small>Marriage of the Prince of Wales.</small> his children to the higher duties of life. The other event was the marriage of the Prince of Wales, on March 10, 1863, with Alexandra, daughter of the King of Denmark.

During this time events followed quickly. There had been trouble in Ireland, where the "Fenians" broke out into rebellion and tried to seize Chester Castle in England. Many were taken <small>Outrages in England and Ireland.</small> prisoners, and soon after a conspiracy was formed to blow up the wall of Clerkenwell prison, where they were confined. A great explosion did take place among the crowded houses of the poor, but the prisoners did not escape. There were also outrages quite as bad in Sheffield among English workmen, who, having formed "trades unions" to make better terms with their masters, injured or even killed those workmen who would not obey them. The Government, after punishing the outrages, wisely made laws which allowed the best trades unions to exist legally, and so prevented secret conspiracies.

During the next few years many Acts of Parliament were passed for the good of the nation. Ever since the fearful outbreaks of Asiatic cholera in England in 1832, 1848, and 1853, great efforts had been made to purify the houses and streets of the poor, and <small>Public Health Act, 1866.</small> more attention paid by all classes to laws of health. In 1866 the Sanitary or Public Health Act gave the public officers power to insist on drains being properly made to each house, and all unhealthy matter cleared away; and to see that not more than a fair number of people lived in each room or house. It is probably partly owing to these reforms that there has been no serious epidemic of Asiatic cholera in England for the last thirty years, although in 1884, 1885, and 1886 hundreds of thousands have died of it on the Continent, while in England, on the contrary, the death-rate has been growing less since 1880, at the rate of about 41,000 a year.

21. Important Acts.—In 1869-1870 great things were done for Ireland. The State Church was disestablished, and Catholics and Protestants placed on an equality; while in 1870 Mr. Gladstone passed an Irish Land Act, giving the tenants a much fairer hold on their land. In 1870 Mr. Forster passed an English Education Act, which appointed that wherever there were not enough schools for all children to be educated, a School Board should be formed, and Board Schools built and kept up by a rate. The principle of *cumulative* voting was for the first time recognized by this Act ; for it was enacted that at every election (for a School Board) every voter should be entitled to a number of votes equal to the number of members to be elected, and might give all such votes to one candidate, or might distribute them among the candidates as he should think fit. Previous to this, schools for the masses were principally under the control of the churches, and though doing much good, did not at all meet the wants of the people. A few years later another Act obliged every child to be sent to school and there are now twice as many children in the elementary schools of England, Scotland, and Ireland as there were in 1875. By this means the mass of ignorance and vice is being slowly reduced, and no one can now grow up without being taught to read, write, and obey. Besides this, Schools of Science and Art have been founded all over the country, where higher teaching can be had for very little expense. In the upper classes, too, education is now much more considered, especially for women. In schools of the present day girls are trained to know more of the facts of history, art, science, and other subjects, which are of importance in training the mind to understand the realities of life and its duties ; while there are colleges for women both at Oxford and Cambridge, and wives and mothers are no longer content to be ignorant on subjects which are of interest to their husbands and sons. In 1871 religious tests were abolished in the Universities of Oxford, Cambridge, and Dublin, so that now a Churchman, a Dissenter, a Catholic, a Hindu, or a Muhammadan can all enter and study there. That same year the Queen, on the advice of Mr. Gladstone, did away with "purchase" in the army, so that now a man cannot *buy* promotion, but rises in his turn because he has served his country long and well. In 1888 a Local Government Bill was passed which created a system of County

Side notes: Irish Church disestablished, 1869. Land Act, 1870. Education Act, 1870. Education of women. Religious Tests and Army Purchase, 1871. Local Government Bill, 1888.

Councils, having under their control the administration of many local affairs, such as drainage, maintenance of roads and advancing of money for emigration purposes.

In 1874 Disraeli, who was created Lord Beaconsfield in 1876, became Prime Minister for the second time, and under his rule an Act in 1877 allowed the colonies of Natal, the Cape, the Orange Free Republic, and the Transvaal to become one federation. This Act has, as yet, produced no results. England has done her best to make up for the wrongs Ireland suffered in the past, and Mr. Gladstone, who had again become Prime Minister in 1880, passed another Irish Land Bill in 1881. On May 6, 1882, Lord Frederick Cavendish, who had gone to Ireland longing to do good to the country, was basely murdered in Phœnix Park, Dublin, together with Mr. Burke.

Murder of Cavendish and Burke, 1882.

At last, in 1886, Mr. Gladstone, joined Mr. Parnell, the leader of the Irish members, and tried to pass a "Home Rule" Bill. He was defeated, and Parliament was dissolved. In the new elections a large number of his party lost their seats. These elections brought the Conservatives back into power, with Lord Salisbury as Prime Minister. What will be the end, and how England can best help those among the Irish who suffer patiently from the great poverty of the country, time alone can show.

Home Rule defeated, 1886.

22. English Problems.—Nor are we without our troubles in England, for as the population increases there are a larger and larger number of people who can only just make a living by producing luxuries for the rich, and when bad times come, like those from 1879 to 1886, and the upper classes have less to spend, there is much suffering. In 1889, the men working in the dock yards of London, goaded to desperation by ill-treatment and low wages, "struck," and after a long struggle, during which the men acted with great moderation, their demands were conceded, and their wages increased. Men of all ranks, and all over the world, felt a strong sympathy in this movement, which was, on the whole very successful. The farmers, too, find it difficult to make their farms pay, now that corn and other food come in so cheaply from abroad, and there is little doubt that in time Parliament must in some way alter the land-laws,

ENGLAND AND HER COLONIES.   319

so as to be more just to all. Meanwhile every one must have patience ; not only statesmen, but many noble men and women of all classes, are devoting their lives to helping those who will help themselves, and trying, by better dwellings, better schools, better arrangements for the employment of labour, and wise emigration to the colonies, to lessen the number of struggling poor.

23. Advances in the last fifty years.—Lastly, the past fifty years have been so rich in inventions, in science, in art, and in literature, that it is impossible even to give a sketch of them here. The most important of these to the country as a whole have certainly been machinery, steam transit by railways and steamships, and the electric telegraph. The first of these has enabled goods to be manufactured a hundredfold more rapidly than formerly, and fifty workmen to be employed where there was one before. The second, the railroads and steamships, have brought distant countries close to us, so that passengers and goods which formerly were more than six weeks in going to America, and six months in reaching India and Australia, now cross the Atlantic in eight days, and are in India in little more than three weeks after leaving the British shores. The last, the electric telegraph, has been in many ways the most marvellous of all. In olden days a merchant had often to wait for nine months before he could learn anything about the sale of his goods in India or Australia, and the statesman was equally in the dark as to what might be going on in lands which it was his duty to govern. Now either of these can learn everything he needs to know in a few hours, and can get quicker and more certain information about matters going on in New York, Melbourne, or Calcutta, than he could in the days of Elizabeth as to what was taking place in Dublin or Edinburgh. In this way England, once confined within the limits of one small island, now stretches out her arms all over the world.

Rapid communication.

Electric telegraph.

And as in matters of daily business, so in the realms of thought and knowledge, we have advanced very rapidly in the last fifty years. Photography, the electric light, the spectroscope, revealing the nature of distant worlds, the telephone, carrying from a distance the actual tones of a friend's voice to our ear, the phonograph, recording sounds, have all been invented within living memory. Researches into ancient history and the deciphering of Egyptian and Assyrian inscriptions have thrown light on the past; while the

<small>Science and literature.</small> discoveries of geology and biology, in which Lyell, Darwin, and Herbert Spencer have led the way, have opened new paths of thought, which can be followed by every man if he will, now that books are sold so cheaply, and free libraries, which were first opened in 1850, enable all men in large towns to read without expense. And truly for those who care really to cultivate their minds and strive by study to grow wiser and better, there is no lack of good and wholesome reading. In history, writers such as Grote and Lord Macaulay have been followed by Green, Freeman, Gardiner, and Lecky. In Political Economy, John Stuart Mill, Fawcett, Cairnes and others, have led men to think clearly. In Philosophy and Art, Carlyle teaches us to hate what is false, and Ruskin to love what is beautiful. In Fiction, Thackeray and Dickens, Charlotte Brontë and George Eliot, have made us sigh and laugh, while Tennyson and Browning have filled our hearts with the dream-thoughts of poetry. Nor can men take up books of travel, or even the daily newspaper, without learning that courage, the love of adventure, and the spirit of self-sacrifice, still, as of old, inspire Englishmen to noble deeds. True to the old wandering spirits of the Teutons, Englishmen have in our day faced dangers at the North Pole and in the heart of Africa. Sir John Franklin and Livingstone have died in pursuit of discovery, and Charles George Gordon took his life in his hand and went alone to Khartoum to perish with the people whom he had so much loved, if he could not save them. Quite recently (1890) Henry M. Stanley returned from his heroic and successful expedition to Equatorial Africa, to rescue Emin Pasha. His discoveries in the Congo region are likely to lead to great results, in extending trade, commerce, and civilization.

24. Conclusion.—We have now followed the English nation from the time when the Angles, Jutes, and Saxons first landed from flat-bottomed boats on the British shores, to the present day when English ships visit English ports all over the world. No doubt these possessions bring difficulties with them. Russia still threatens us in Afghanistan, while the Suez Canal, which opened to us in 1868 a nearer road to India, makes us deeply interested in the vexed "Eastern Question." But at a Congress at Berlin in 1878, Lord Beaconsfield, three years before his death, made a treaty with all European nations, which has only lately saved us from war, and efforts to settle the Afghan boundary peaceably have been recently successful. As a result of this Congress, Cyprus was placed under the protection of England, and thus practically has become a British possession. A dispute with the United States about the fisheries of Canada has been under arbitration, but a settlement has not yet been reached. Moreover, if anxiety comes with large possessions, strength comes with them as well, even though we are often obliged to make new acquisitions in order to protect those we already possess. For this reason North Borneo, the eastern half of New Guinea, the island of Socotra and Burmah, have only very lately been added to our empire.

In 1886 another Exhibition was held in London, this time not of "all nations," but of the productions of "India and the Colonies," and for the first time people at home have realised how far the power of England extends. True, from Europe there was little except from Malta and Cyprus. But *Colonial and Indian Exhibition.* from ASIA came all the riches of India, and the products of Ceylon, the Straits Settlements, North Borneo, and Hong-Kong. From AUSTRALASIA came gold and silver, copper, iron, tin, wool, wine, and grain. AFRICA sent diamonds and ostrich-feathers from the Cape, ivory and gold ornaments from Sierra Leone and the Gold Coast, and magnificent wood from the Mauritius. From NORTH AMERICA Canada sent all her many products, from the fur-seals of Hudson's Bay to the splendid timber of the Canadian forests. From CENTRAL AMERICA British Honduras sent mahogany and sugar. From SOUTH AMERICA British Guiana contributed gums, oils, and bark; while the WEST INDIES, with their spices, rum, sugar, and lovely basket-work, presented at every turn the name of one of their numerous islands. And besides all these products native to the countries themselves, the number of manufactured articles of all kinds, many of them better than our own, showed that the Englishman, in settling in other lands, has not lost his skill or cunning in workmanship or in inventive power. We saw that the high hopes raised by the Great Exhibition of 1851 were soon destroyed, for where different races and nations with widely different interests are concerned, it will probably be some time before war will entirely give place to reason and friendly arbitration. Let us hope that the Exhibition of 1886 may be of better omen; for the inhabitants of India and the colonies are all subjects of the same Empress-queen, and in the Australasian and Canadian colonies at least, nearly all are English in speech, in race, and in heart.

<small>Unity of English-speaking people.</small>

Surely there is every encouragement to lead the English-speaking race to look forward hopefully to the future; and if a watchword is needed to bind together England's sons in all parts of the world, it is found in Nelson's noble words—

"ENGLAND EXPECTS EVERY MAN TO DO HIS DUTY."[1]

THE LEADING FACTS

OF

CANADIAN HISTORY.

BY

W. J. ROBERTSON, B.A., LL.B.

CHAPTER I.

EARLY SETTLEMENT OF CANADA.

1. Dominion of Canada.—If we take a map of North America we shall find that by far the greater part of its northern half is named the Dominion of Canada. On the east there is the Atlantic Ocean, on the west the Pacific, on the south the Great Lakes, and on the north the Arctic Sea. The only parts of this vast territory not in Canada are Alaska, a portion of Labrador, and the island of Newfoundland. Its area is about 3,500,000 square miles, and is somewhat larger than the United States lying south of it. But the name Canada, has only very recently been applied to this territory, for less than twenty-five years ago that name was used to point out the Provinces marked Quebec and Ontario on the map. Then the Provinces of Nova Scotia, New Brunswick, Prince Edward Island, Manitoba, and British Columbia were from time to time added, and these with the great North-West Territories make up the present Dominion of Canada.

<small>Provinces of the Dominion of Canada.</small>

2. Early Inhabitants.—Who the first inhabitants of America were, we do not know, but we do know that they were not English, French, or the ancestors of any of the white or black people now living in Canada and the United States. Nor were the people now known as North American Indians the first to inhabit this

324 LEADING FACTS OF CANADIAN HISTORY.

Continent, as many remains exist of an earlier and more civilized race.

<small>Mound Builders.</small> Heaps of earth of curious shapes are found all over North America, (many of them in the neighborhood of Lake Superior) and these "mounds," as they are called, contain the bones of men and other animals, stone axes, copper tools, well shaped pottery and a variety of other articles, made with a great deal of skill and taste. Then on the shores of Lake Superior we find old mines where copper had been taken out in large quantities a great many years ago. Large trees have grown over the rubbish that fill these mines, and this shows that a long time has passed since the miners were at work. Whence these clever and industrious people came we do not know, but it is thought they were originally from the south of Asia.

3. North American Indians.—The "Mound Builders" were followed by a fiercer and ruder people that cared for little except hunting and fishing, making war and roaming the forests. Very little interest was taken by them in tilling the soil, a few tribes growing small quantities of maize or Indian corn in clearings in the dense forests which covered most of the country. The principal tribes were the Algonquins, inhabiting the region from the Atlantic to Lake Superior; the Hurons, principally found in the Georgian Bay District, and the Five Nation Indians or Iroquois, occupying the middle and western part of the State of New York. These tribes were much alike in their appearance, manners, and customs. Tall, sinewy, copper-colored, with straight black hair, black eyes, high cheek bones—they were keen of sight and hearing, swift of foot, fond of war, cruel to their enemies and generally true to their friends. The Algonquins lived almost entirely by fishing and hunting, dwelt in wretched tents called wigwams, and were often on the verge of starvation. The Hurons and

<small>Red, or North American Indians.</small> Iroquois tilled the soil to some extent, and laid up stores of corn for the seasons when game was scarce. They often lived in villages, in large bark houses occupied by several families, and were much more comfortable and prosperous than the Algonquins. Indian women did all the work and drudgery; the men when not hunting, fishing, or fighting, lived a lazy life, and spent their spare hours sleeping, gambling, and

EARLY SETTLEMENT OF CANADA.

story-telling. Such were the people the first European settlers found in the greater part of North America.

4. Discovery of America.—Little was known of America, until Christopher Columbus, a native of Genoa in Italy, persuaded Isabella, the Queen of Castile in Spain, to give him ships to find his way to India, by sailing westward instead of round the Cape of Good Hope. This was in 1492, A.D. *(Christopher Columbus.)* Long before this, in the tenth century, the people of Iceland had made their way to the north-eastern coast of America, and seemed to have sailed south as far as Massachussetts. These visits did not lead to any settlements being made, and were very soon forgotten, so that Columbus is the *real* discoverer of America. After a long voyage he came to an island and thought he had reached India. This mistake led to the group, of which this island is one, being called the West Indies. But Columbus did not reach the mainland as soon as John and Sebastian Cabot, two navigators sent out by Henry VII. of England, who explored the coast of Labrador and Newfoundland in 1497-98. A little later a Florentine named Amerigo Vespucci visited the New World and wrote an account of his travels. This led to the new continent being called America. *(Origin of Name.)*

5. Jacques Cartier.—France, unlike Spain and England, did not take much interest in the work of exploring America until 1534, when Francis I. sent out from the sea-port of St. Malo, the famous sea captain, Jacques Cartier. Cartier sailed to Newfoundland, entered the straits of Belle Isle and passed into the Gulf of St. Lawrence. *(Jacques Cartier, first voyage, 1534.)* He landed at Gaspé, and erected a cross bearing the arms of France, to indicate that he had taken possession of the country for the French King. The next year he made another visit and entered the Gulf on St. Lawrence's Day, and for this reason he named the Gulf and the great river which empties into it, the St. Lawrence. Sailing up the river he came to an Indian village, Stadacona, situated near where now the city of Quebec stands. Continuing his voyage he reached another Indian village, called Hochelaga. This village was situated at the foot of a beautiful mountain covered with trees, and he named it Mont Royal—hence the name of our great commercial city, Montreal. After a short stay Cartier returned to Stadacona, and spent the winter there. His men suffered terribly from cold and scurvy, but were treated with the utmost kindness by the Indians. In the spring he returned to France, taking with him by force a number of Indian chiefs who were never permitted to go back to their own people—a base reward for their hospitality. Six years after, Cartier and Sieur de Roberval made an attempt to colonize Canada, but their efforts were fruitless; and France, occupied with other matters of greater interest at home, sent out no other expedition for nearly fifty years.

6. Champlain.—At last in 1603, Samuel De Champlain, a distinguished naval officer, and Pontgravé, a merchant of St. Malo, were sent out to open up a trade in furs with the Indians and at the same time to attempt to civilize them and convert them to Christianity. They found no traces of the Indian villages Stadacona and Hochelaga and after a short stay, having reached the rapids of St. Louis, returned to France with a cargo of furs. For the next few years the efforts of the French were directed to establishing a colony in Acadia (now Nova Scotia), at Port Royal. Failing in this attempt, Champlain and Pontgravé were despatched to the St. Lawrence to build a fort at a suitable point for trade with the Indians. This led to the founding of the city of Quebec at the foot of the cliff Cape Diamond, in 1608. Champlain then proceeded westward, and meeting a war party of Algonquins and Hurons, was induced by promises of a profitable trade to join an expedition against the Iroquois. He ascended the Richelieu river and discovered Lake Champlain, and near Lake George had his first encounter with the Iroquois. Again in 1615, he joined a war party of Hurons against the Iroquois; but was unsuccessful in the attack, notwithstanding the advantage of fire-arms. These unprovoked assaults taught the Iroquois to hate and distrust the French. Later on, when the Iroquois obtained possession of guns and were skilled in thier use, a terrible revenge was taken on the weak Canadian colony. In nearly all the wars that followed between the English and French settlers in America, the brave and adroit Iroquois were found fighting on the side of the English. Champlain spent much time in exploring the country to the north and west, making

Founding of Quebec 1608.

his way up the Ottawa across to the Georgian Bay, and thence down to Lake Ontario.

7. Company of One Hundred Associates.

—So many companies were anxious to engage in the profitable fur trade of Canada, and so much rivalry and ill-feeling existed among them, that Cardinal Richelieu, the principal minister of Louis XIII, decided to give the sole right to engage in the trade to a Company known as that of the "One Hundred Associates." Besides the fur trade, this Company was given the control of the coast and inland fishing. In return for these grants, the Company bound itself to bring out six thousand colonists and settle them in Canada, at the same time making provision for the support of a Roman Catholic clergy who were to look after the religious welfare of the colonists, and to labor to convert the Indians. Tradesmen and mechanics were to be taken out to Canada to build houses and make all necessary articles for the use of the settlers. Champlain was made governor of the young colony, but did not keep his position long; for war broke out between England and France, and England sent Sir David Kirke with a fleet to take Quebec. Twice Kirke appeared before the fort, and on the second occasion, in 1629, captured it. For three years England held Canada, and then, peace being restored, gave it back to France, not considering the country of much value. Champlain again took charge of the colony, and labored unceasingly to make it prosperous, and to bring the Indians to a knowledge of Christianity. In this he was partially successful, but his work was cut short by death, A.D. 1635. Champlain is rightly considered the Founder of the colony of New France or Canada*.

1627.

---

* Canada, is a word of Indian origin, and is supposed to mean "a collection of huts."

CHAPTER II.

CANADA UNDER FRENCH RULE.

1. Indian Missions.—To understand the history of Canada during the greater part of the seventeenth century, we must bear in mind that a two-fold object was constantly kept in view by the French Kings: *first*, the establishment and extension of the colony at the expense of the English settlers in America; and *secondly*, the conversion of the Indians to the Roman Catholic faith. The French Kings and their ministers wished to profit not only by the fur-trade of America, but to build up on this continent a colony where the religion of the Roman Catholic Church should be held and practised by the whole population, Indian as well as French.

By far the most interesting portion of the history of French Canada is the story of the Jesuit missions among the Indians. Full of holy zeal for the salvation of the Red men, missionary after missionary of the religious society called Jesuits, made his way to the Hurons in the Georgian Bay district, to the Algonquins to the north and up the Ottawa, and to the fierce Iroquois in the Mohawk Valley.

Among the Algonquins they suffered want and hardship, dwelling in wretched tents full of smoke and filth and often ill-treated and despised by the people they were trying to benefit. At first their efforts were of little avail; even the Hurons, the most intelligent, kindly, and well-to-do of the Indian tribes thought the missionaries brought them trouble in the shape of drought, sickness, and ill-success in hunting and war. But no amount of failure could discourage these patient and unselfish men. After a while the Indians began to respect them, and then came a general willingness to be baptized and to accept the religion taught by the missionaries. It was not long before nearly all the Hurons became converts to Christianity, and left off their heathen practices and habits. Two names will always be remembered in connection with these Huron Missions, those of Father de Brébœuf and Father Lalement; the first strong in frame, brave of heart, and capable of enduring any amount of hardship; the second, delicate, refined, loving, and unselfish. Other missionaries took their lives in their hands and went among the cruel and treacherous Iroquois, hoping to do some good to the fiercest enemies of the colony. But little, however, came of these missions. The Iroquois did not trust the French, and the missionaries after a brief stay were either murdered or compelled to escape for their lives. The name of Father Jogues, who suffered, first mutilation, and later on, death, at the hands of the Iroquois, is one that shines bright on the roll of Martyr missionaries.

De Brébœuf.

2. Indian Wars.—The story of Indian Missions is also a part of the story of Indian Wars. The Algonquins and the Hurons were the friends of the French, while the Iroquois were bent on the destruction of the feeble colony and its allies. The Hurons lived in populous villages between the Georgian Bay and Lake Simcoe, and were said to number thirty thousand people, most of whom accepted Christianity through the labours of Jesuit missionaries. St. Ignace, St. Louis, St. Joseph and St. Marie, were among the most important of these missions. In 1648, St. Joseph was surprised by the Iroquois, while most of the Huron hunters and warriors were absent. Seven persons were captured and killed, the missionary, Father Daniel, meeting his fate while ministering to the dying. The next place to fall was St. Ignace; then St. Louis was attacked. Here Fathers Jean de Brébœuf and Gabriel Lalement, refusing to leave their helpless flocks, were made prisoners and put to the most cruel tortures. Brébœuf's nails were torn from his fingers, his body hacked with knives, red hot hatchets hung round his neck, his gums seared, and finally, his heart cut out, no word or token of pain escaping from his lips. His tortures lasted four hours. Lalement, so delicate, sensitive, and frail, was tortured for seventeen hours before his sufferings were ended in death. St. Marie was the next object of attack. It was manfully defended by a few Frenchmen and Hurons, and after a fierce conflict the Iroquois retreated.

Destruction of Huron Missions.

Martyrdom of Brébœuf and Lalement.

The Huron missions were destroyed, and the people were scattered. An effort to transfer the missions to Isle St. Joseph or Christian Island, near Collingwood, and gather the terror-stricken Hurons together again, ended the following spring in another dreadful massacre on the mainland, by the Iroquois, where the Hurons had come in search of food for their starving families. Ten thousand Hurons had perished, a few came to Quebec with the missionaries, the rest were scattered far and wide among other tribes in the north, east and west. The once powerful, brave and intelligent Hurons, as a nation, ceased to exist; and with them perished the principal fruits of the Jesuit Missions.

3. Growth of New France.—Let us now return to what was going on in the colony, during this period of Indian strife and bloodshed. The Company of One Hundred Associates did not carry out what it had promised to do; very few settlers were brought out by it, and its attention was almost entirely taken up with the trade in furs. It sent out scarcely one thousand colonists, much less the six thousand it had promised. The population grew very slowly, so slowly that in 1662, it had less than two thousand souls. But a great interest was taken in the spiritual welfare of the colony, and out of this interest came the founding of Montreal as a mission, in 1642, by a number of devoted men and women, who came from France for that purpose. Here, the little band prayed and fought, for the Iroquois lay in wait, night and day, right under the guns of the rude fort to kill and scalp the unwary. Many a sad and heroic tale comes down to us of this troublous time. The story of Dulac des Ormeaux and his sixteen companions recalls the bravest deeds of the best days of the ancient Greeks and Romans. Hearing that a large number of Iroquois were coming down the lakes and rivers to attack the feeble garrisons on the St. Lawrence, these young men determined to sacrifice their lives and save the colony. They made their wills, confessed their sins, received the sacrament and took a sad farewell of their friends in Montreal. Then, with a few Christian Hurons and Algonquins they took possession of an old fort near the Long Sault rapids, on the Ottawa. Here they awaited the descent of the Iroquois, prepared to sell their lives dearly.

Founding of Montreal, 1642.

Pass of the Long Sault, 1660.

Soon two hundred came down in their boats, and landing, attacked the little band in their hastily constructed breastwork of logs. For days the unequal struggle lasted. The Hurons deserted to the Iroquois in dismay. Dulac and his companions fought on until worn out with want of sleep and nourishment, the four that were left alive fell into the hands of the enraged savages. Three were mortally wounded and were burnt alive, the fourth was saved for Indian tortures. The Hurons who so basely deserted to the enemy found no mercy at the hands of the Iroquois, and were put to death. Thus perished Dulac and his companions, but not without saving the colony. The Iroquois were checked and disheartened and for a time the settlement had peace.

The colony, as already stated, made slow progress. Governor after Governor was appointed to no purpose; the Company of One Hundred Associates was doing nothing to further its interests, and Indian raids threatened the very existence of the settlements. In 1659, the Abbé Laval came to Canada. His arrival marks a new era in the life of the colony. Zealous, devoted, able and enthusiastic, for many years he laboured in the interests of the Church, and his influence did much to mould the future of Canada. His first stay was a brief one; he was anxious to prevent the sale of brandy or "fire water" to the Indians, but the traders found it too profitable to be given up, although its effects on the Indians were frightful. Finally, Laval sailed to France to get the French King to stop the wretched traffic, and to have the Governor who refused to put the law in force against the offenders recalled.

Laval in Canada.

4. Royal Government.—Up to this time *fur companies* aided by the leading clergy, had governed the colony. Now a change was decided upon. The ONE HUNDRED ASSOCIATES lost their charter, and Canada was placed under the government of the French King. This change was due largely to the influence of Laval at the French Court, and took place in 1663. A Governor, Intendant and Bishop were appointed, and these aided by a Supreme Council, acted under the instructions of the King. The Governor was at the head of military affairs; the Bishop, of Church affairs; and the Intendant, of legal and money affairs. The

Governor and the Bishop appointed the members of the Council, at first four, but afterwards increased to twelve in number. The Intendant made laws for the people, and published them at the church doors or from the pulpit. Even such small matters as pew rents, stray hogs, fast driving, family quarrels, were dealt with by him. The Bishop, too, took an active part in the affairs of the colony, and because the duties of the Governor, Bishop and Intendant, were not very clearly stated, frequent quarrels took place between these, the chief officers of the King. The law in force was very different from the law of England, and is known as the CUSTOM OF PARIS, the same law that prevailed at that time in France. It is still in force in Quebec Province and suits the French people better than our English laws. The colonists had nothing to say in making their own laws, they had no Parliaments or Municipal Councils, everything was managed for them by the King, through the Governor, Bishop, Intendant, and Supreme Council. To hear complaints and settle disputes, courts were established at Quebec, Three Rivers and Montreal, these courts being under the control of the Supreme Council, and presided over by the "seigneurs" or holders of large tracts of land from the

<small>Military Tenure.</small> King by *Feudal* or *Military tenure*. These seigneurs were gentlemen who came out to Canada from France, enticed by the offer of large grants of land for which they paid by bringing out settlers and giving their services in times of war, in defence of the colony. They generally settled near Quebec, Three Rivers, and Montreal, along the banks of the St. Lawrence, so as to have the river always near at hand to bring in and take out what they bought and sold. Besides, when attacked by the Iroquois, they could more easily escape to one of the forts by water than by land.

5. Talon.- M. de Mezy, was the first Governor, Laval the first Bishop, and Talon the first Intendant. Talon was a very able man and used his power and talents in the interests of the colony. But, unfortunately Laval and the Governor could not agree, and

<small>Carignan regiment settles in Canada.</small> De Mezy was recalled. A new Governor, De Courcelles took his place, and about the same time the Marquis de Tracy was sent out with the famous Carignan regiment to help the colony in their struggles against the Iroquois. A

number of settlers also came, bringing sheep, cattle, farm implements, and a few horses, so that the population was increased by two thousand persons. This new strength enabled the settlers to attack their enemies, the Iroquois, and two expeditions, the one in the winter, and the other the following summer, invaded the Mohawk territory, fired the villages of the Indians, and destroyed the stores of grain, kept by them for a winter supply of food.

These attacks annoyed the Governor of New York, who thought it an invasion of English territory—but they had the effect of giving the colony peace for eighteen years. The Iroquois allowed missionaries to go to them, and some of them accepted their teachings, and became less barbarous. Canada now made better progress. Talon did his utmost to utilize the natural resources of the country and to promote trade with the West Indies. He also sent out exploring expeditions to Hudson's Bay, the Great Lakes, and the Mississippi of which he had heard from the Indians. He induced many of the soldiers to settle in the colony, *Talon's administration.* and gave grants of land to the officers and men. As women were few in number, the French Government sent out a large number of young women to become wives for the soldiers and settlers. As soon as these ship-loads of women arrived, the men who wanted wives came down to the vessels, and chose their partners. These curious marriages generally turned out well—the couples thus brought together living fairly happy and contented lives. Some serious drawbacks to the success of the colony must be noted. One was the sale of "fire-water" to the Indians and settlers, although Laval did his best to have it stopped. Another was the tendency of young men to take to the woods, to live and trade with the Indians. These "*Coureurs du Bois,*" as they were called, often became more savage than the Indians themselves, dressed in Indian fashion, and took Indian wives. Once used to this mode of life, it was found impossible to bring them to settle down and till the soil. The trade in furs was too profitable to be abandoned for civilized life. Then again, the colony suffered by its trade being placed in the hands of a few men, *Paternal government.* who enriched themselves at the expense of the people.

So, it happened that Canada did not grow as fast as the English colonies to the south of them, simply because the government did not allow the settlers sufficient freedom in managing their own affairs.

6. Discoveries in the Great West.—The Jesuit missionaries were the first explorers of the far West. They united the work of discovery with their mission labors, just as Livingstone and Moffat in recent years, have done in Africa. Talon was anxious to prevent the English from extending their trade westward, and with this in view, he established trading-posts and missions at Sault Ste. Marie and other points. Before, however, his great plans could be carried out, he returned to France, and left to his successors the task of discovering and exploring the Mississippi.

Talon returned to France in 1672 and about the same time Courcelles the Governor also asked to be recalled. The new Governor, Louis de Buade Count de Frontenac, is the most striking figure in the history of New France. No Governor was so successful in his dealings with the Iroquois; they feared and respected him, at the same time giving him their regard and confidence. He treated them as children, threatening them with punishment if unruly, and rewarding and encouraging them if they behaved well. He made a great display of force when treating with them, and managed to impress them with the greatness and power of the French King, the "Great Father," across the Big Waters. He was not so successful with his COUNCIL, for his hasty temper and haughty bearing, together with his attempts to control everything and everybody, led to many a scene in the Council Chamber, and caused bitter quarrels in the colony. His rule however, will be always remembered with gratitude for, as long as he was Governor, Canada was safe from Indian attacks. More important still were the discoveries in the west in his time by Joliet, a merchant, Marquette, a missionary, and Robert Cavelier, Sieur de la Salle. Father Marquette, who lived and labored among the Indians on the shores of Lake Superior and Michigan, was joined by Joliet, and these two brave men, in bark canoes, with five men, went down the mighty Mississippi, until they reached the Arkansas river. Fearing to fall into the hands of the Spaniards, they returned and Joliet brought the news of his discoveries to Quebec. The story of his

Character of Frontenac.

Joliet and Marquette. 1673.

exploit filled La Salle who had obtained a grant of land at Lachine (so-called it is said because La Salle thought the St. Lawrence led to China) with the desire to explore the West. Before Joliet made his great discovery, La Salle had found his way to the Ohio, although his doings at this time are not very well known. Courcelles had planned building a fort at the foot of Lake Ontario, where Kingston now stands, and his successor in office carried out his plan, and founded Fort Frontenac. This fort served as a trading-post, and also as a check on the Iroquois in time of war. At first the fort was of wood—afterwards La Salle, in 1674, built it of stone and promised to keep it up, if he were granted the privilege of engaging in the fur trade. It was from this point that he set out to find his way to the Mississippi. After years spent in braving the dangers of the wilderness, and overcoming obstacles which would have daunted most men, he succeeded in 1682 in launching his canoes on the Father of Waters—the broad Mississippi. In the month of April he reached the Gulf of Mexico, and took possession of the Great South and West in the name of Louis XIV. under the title of Louisiana. _{La Salle explores the Mississippi.}

Five years after, La Salle was basely murdered by some treacherous followers, while engaged in a venture to found a colony at the mouth of the Mississippi.

7. Frontenac.—Let us now turn to what was going on in Canada under Frontenac's rule. The colony was at peace with the Indians—but Frontenac quarrelled with his Intendant, with the Governor of Montreal, with Laval and the Jesuits, in fact with everybody that would not do as he wished. His conduct was so violent and unjust, that many complaints were made to the King. Laval and the missionaries were anxious to stop the sale of liquor to the Indians, but Frontenac was too greedy of gain to forbid it. At last, after ten years of disputing and wrangling, the King grew wearied and Frontenac was recalled (1682). _{Frontenac's first Administration. 1672-82.}

But not for long. The Iroquois were soon on the war-path again, incited by the Governor of New York, Colonel Dongan. The English colonists were anxious to take away from the French the trade with the Indians, and they generally succeeded in keeping on good terms with the Iroquois, who saw that the English colonies were growing much more rapidly than the French settlement. It needed but the treachery of Denonville, one of Frontenac's successors, to bring on the colony a terrible calamity. To gratify a whim of the King, he seized at Fort Frontenac fifty Iroquois chiefs, who had come to a friendly meeting, and sent them in chains to France to work at the galleys. He followed up this outrage by leading two thousand men into the country of the Senecas, one of the five nations of the Iroquois. For several days he pillaged and burned their villages, destroying their food supplies, and putting many to death.

The Five Nations soon united to punish the French. Fort Niagara, at the mouth of the Niagara River, and but recently built, was levelled to the ground. Fort Frontenac had to be abandoned and burnt, with all its stores and trading vessels. The Island of Montreal was surprised, and more than a thousand of its inhabitants were killed or carried off prisoners for further torture. This is the *Massacre of Lachine*, 1689. The colony was in despair, and its people had to take shelter in the forts of Quebec, Three Rivers and Montreal.

Massacre of Lachine. 1689.

To save the colony from perishing Frontenac was again despatched to Canada as Governor. He brought with him the chiefs seized by Denonville, and sent them back to their tribes to act as peacemakers. At this time a war arising out of the English Revolution of 1688 was going on in Europe between England and France. Frontenac determined to punish the English colonists for the part they had taken in stirring up the Iroquois to attack the French settlements. Bands of French and their Indian allies made frequent raids into New York, New Hampshire and other border colonies, scalping and murdering the defenceless people. Schenectady in New York and Salmon Falls in New Hampshire were burned to the ground, and their inhabitants butchered. For years this cruel border warfare lasted, leaving a dark stain on the early history of the American settlements.

In 1690 an effort was made by the British colonists to drive the French out of Canada. Sir Wm. Phips was sent by Massachusetts to capture Port Royal in Acadia (Nova Scotia). This he accomplished, and then sailed up the St. Lawrence to take Quebec. Before this, however, an expedition under the command of Colonel Winthrop had been sent to take Montreal. Sickness and a lack of supplies led to its failure and it returned to Albany. But Phips reached Quebec and demanded its surrender. The demand met with a haughty and indignant refusal from Frontenac, who had prepared for a spirited defence. In vain Phips opened a furious fire on the town and landed his raw soldiers on the Beauport shore. He was driven back with heavy loss by the French and their Indian allies, and compelled to beat a retreat to Boston. Thus ended the second attempt by the English to capture Quebec. Meanwhile the savage border warfare *Sir William Phips attempts to take Quebec, 1690.* went on unchecked. The Abenaquis Indians aided the French in the work of murder—the Iroquois, the English. A single incident will give us a glimpse of the savage nature of this warfare. Hannah Dustin of Haverhill, taken prisoner in one of these border raids, avenged the murder of her week-old child by slaying ten out of twelve of her sleeping Indian captors, and then succeeded in escaping to the British settlements. These were the days when both French and English offered prizes to the Indians for human scalps. Little wonder that the border settlements did not prosper. The Treaty of Ryswick (1697) put an end for a short time to the war between England and France, and each country restored to the other its conquests. The next year saw the death of Frontenac in his 78th year. His memory was cherished as the one man whose energy saved Canada when on the verge of ruin.

8. State of the Colony.—The War of the Spanish Succession in Europe, which broke out in 1702, was the signal for a renewal of the horrors of border warfare between Canada and the English colonies in America. Not until the Treaty of Utrecht in 1713, did the settlers along the frontier again breathe freely. This treaty gave Acadia, Newfoundland and Hudson's Bay Territory to England, while France kept Canada, Cape Breton and Louisiana. For over thirty years the colony had rest, and a chance to grow and prosper. The principal Governor of this time was Vaudreuil, whose term of office began in 1703. He foresaw that a fierce struggle must take place between the French and the English for control of the North American continent, and he laid his plans accordingly. The fortress of Louisburg in Cape Breton was begun; Quebec, Montreal and Fort Frontenac were strengthened, and a new stone fort was

built at Niagara. Trade, ship-building and manufactures were
encouraged, and we find even woollen and linen goods among the home productions. Canada, at this time, exported largely to France and the West Indies such products as staves, tar, tobacco, flour, pease, and pork. She brought in rum, sugar, molasses, and most of the manufactured goods she needed. Roads were opened up between the parishes, and a letter-post established. Law was better administered than in the earlier days of the colony. With all these improvements it made but slow progress. The feudal system of land tenure, while good for military purposes, did not encourage the peasants who held the land from their seigneurs, to make many improvements. The people had no say in making the laws, and the general want of education kept the colony in a dull and lifeless state. Young men tired of the quiet, home-life of the farm took to the woods, and lived and traded with the Indians. In 1702-22, Quebec had a population of seven thousand, and an agreeable society, whose principal element was the military class. Montreal had about two thousand inhabitants, and the whole of Canada about twenty-five thousand. The whole country to the west was a forest with a few trading posts and forts at Kingston, Niagara, and Detroit.

Condition of the people.

9. Braddock's Expedition.—Vaudreuil died in 1725, and was succeeded by the Marquis de Beauharnois. In his time Fort Frederic, at Crown Point, on Lake Champlain was built, and soon became an important post in the wars between the rival colonies. No new stirring events took place until the outbreak of the War of the Austrian Succession, which brought England and France once more into conflict. It was not long before their colonies were engaged in a deadly struggle, a struggle that lasted, with a brief intermission, until the flag of England floated over the walls of Quebec. In 1745, Louisburg was taken after a brave defence, by an army of New England farmers and fishermen under Sir William Pepperell. The French tried to retake this, the second strongest fortress of the New World, but without success. Peace was for a short time restored in 1748, and Louisburg, to the great annoyance of the people of New England, was given back to France. In these days, it often happened that while the mother

Louisburg taken, 1745. Restored, 1748.

countries, France and England, were at peace, their children in India and America carried on a bitter strife. Not until 1756 was war once more declared in Europe; yet, in 1754, hostilities broke out in the valley of the Ohio. The French claimed the Great West, and sought to shut in the English to the strip of territory between the Atlantic and the Alleghany Mountains. To carry out this plan, a fort was constructed at a point where two branches of the Ohio River meet, the Monongahela and the Alleghany. This fort got the name Du Quesne, from the French Governor of Canada at that time. The English colonists of Virginia sent George Washington, a young officer and surveyor, to build another

LAKE COUNTRY AND WESTERN FORTS.

fort near at hand. Unfortunately Washington fired upon a party of French and Indians who came to warn him that he was encroaching on French territory. This act was the beginning of the final struggle for the mastery of the New World. General Braddock was sent out from England with two regiments of regular

troops and was placed in command of the militia of the colonies. He thought he knew more about bush warfare
than such men as Washington, and would take no
advice. He was so stubborn and arrogant that many
of the best militia officers would not serve under him. The French
too, made preparations for the conflict. Baron Dieskau brought to
Canada a strong military force, and was accompanied by the last
French Governor of Canada, De Vaudreuil, a son of the former
Governor of that name.

Braddock sent to America, 1754.

In the spring of 1755, Braddock began his march from Virginia
to Fort Du Quesne. He had a force of two thousand men, regulars
and colonial militia, but his movements were hampered by taking
a long train of baggage-waggons and artillery. One hundred
men with axes went before to cut down trees and make a road for
these to pass over. The journey was a slow and weary one,
and the French garrison at Fort Du Quesne was well aware of
Braddock's movements. As he neared the fort, an ambuscade of
French and Indians was formed, with the hope of checking his
march. In spite of repeated warnings from Washington and others,
Braddock neglected to take the most ordinary precautions against
surprise. Passing through a thickly wooded defile, a sudden hail of
bullets was poured into the astonished and dismayed ranks of the
British regulars. On all sides was heard the terrible war-whoop of
the Indians, and the work of destruction began. The British
soldiers huddled together and fired their muskets into the air or
into their own ranks. They were mown down by the bullets of the
concealed French and Indians—without being able to
offer any defence. Braddock had five horses shot
under him, and was mortally wounded. Fortunately
for the regulars, the colonial forces, used to Indian modes of
fighting, took shelter behind the trees and fought the enemy in
their own fashion, and kept them at bay. This enabled the terror-
stricken soldiers who survived, to escape from the defile. More
than one-half had fallen—the remainder, panic-stricken, fled, and
paused not till they had put forty miles between them and the
dreaded enemy. Braddock was carried in a dying condition on a
litter from the field, and that night with his life paid the penalty of
his folly.

Braddock defeated, 1755.

CANADA UNDER FRENCH RULE.   341

Fort Niagara, the forts on Lake Champlain, and Beauséjour in Acadia, were also marked out for attack by the English. The expedition against Niagara never reached its destination—Beauséjour was not able to make any defence and was easily taken; and Baron Dieskau was defeated and made prisoner near Lake George by Colonel William Johnson, at the head of a body of colonial militia and Mohawk Indians. This Colonel Johnson was a remarkable man in many respects. He had acquired a wonderful influence over the Mohawks, and was made one of their great chiefs. He built two great strongly fortified houses in the Mohawk valley, and made them headquarters for the surrounding Indians—one of whose daughters, the famous Molly Brant, sister of Joseph Brant, he married in Indian fashion. Johnson was made a knight for his victory over Dieskau, and received a large grant of money from the Crown.

Sir William Johnson defeats Baron Dieskau, 1755.

10. Capture of Quebec.—The next year (1756) war was formally declared between England and France, and the struggle went on with increasing bitterness in America. This war is known as the *Seven Years' War*, and was carried on in Asia, America, and Europe simultaneously. The French sent out as Commander-in-Chief, the famous Marquis de Montcalm, an officer of great skill, courage, and energy. The English had by far the greater number of men, and the greater wealth and resources, but for a time they were badly officered and led. Their first Commander-in-Chief was the Earl of Loudon, who proved a wretched failure. Another general, almost equally unfit, was Abercrombie, who allowed Oswego to fall into the hands of Montcalm. A still greater disaster befell the English at Fort William Henry, on Lake George. After a spirited defence the garrison was allowed to go out with the honors of war, engaging not to serve against the French for eighteen months. Montcalm promised them protection against attacks by his Indian allies, who sought victims to scalp and torture. The Indians crazed by liquor, fell upon the retreating garrison with their women and children, and in spite of the efforts of Montcalm and his officers, murdered or carried off prisoners the most of them. Almost equally disastrous was the attempt made by Loudon, aided by a large fleet and force, to take Louisburg.

Seven Years' War begins.

Massacre of Fort William Henry, Aug. 9, 1757.

These repeated failures, added to a general want of success in other parts of the world where the war was carried on, led to a change in the British government, and William Pitt, was placed in charge of England's foreign affairs. Very soon a change was noted. Pitt had determined he would drive the French out of Canada, and he made his preparations accordingly. He chose good men to command, and gave them an energetic support. Amherst was made the Commander-in-Chief, and Boscawen was put at the head of the fleet in America. Under Amherst were placed Wolfe, Lawrence, and Whitmore, officers young in years, but full of energy and courage. One mistake Pitt did make : he left Abercrombie in charge of the army intended to operate along Lake George and Lake Champlain.

William Pitt becomes War Minister of Britain.

The first fruits of Pitt's policy was the capture of Louisburg. Against this strong fortress was sent a fleet of over one hundred and fifty vessels, and an army of twelve thousand men, under the command of Amherst and Wolfe. After a siege of seven weeks, in which Wolfe greatly distinguished himself, the garrison of five thousand men surrendered, and were sent prisoners to England.

Capture of Louisburg, 1758.

But victories were not all on the side of the English. A large force under General Abercrombie was repulsed with heavy loss while trying to take Ticonderoga, or Carillon, on Lake Champlain. The defeat was due to the death in the early part of the fight of young Lord Howe, and to the utter folly and rashness of Abercrombie, in ordering his brave troops to attack the French protected as they were by felled trees and a breastwork of timber, with sharpened stakes pointing outward. In this battle Montcalm proved his skill as a general, and the English lost two thousand men, many of them Highlanders, who for the first time in their history, served in the foreign wars of Britain. The campaign of 1758, closed with the easy capture of Fort Du Quesne, by a force sent against it under General Forbes. Forbes, falling sick, was borne on a litter across the Alleghanies with his army. Finding winter approaching, he sent Washington ahead with a smaller force, to take the fort before it could get help. On the 25th of November, without a blow being struck, Du Quesne was taken

Ticonderoga, 1758.

CANADA UNDER FRENCH RULE. 343

possession of by Washington, and named Fort Pitt, in honor of England's greatest War Minister.

The year 1759 opened with great efforts put forth by Montcalm to save Canada to the French. The prospects of the colony were gloomy enough. The mother country gave but little assistance; in fact, she was not able to give much. So many men in Canada were drawn into the army, that the farms were only half-tilled, and the crops were scanty and poor. To add to the miseries of the people, the internal affairs of Canada were under the control of the worst official of French Rule. This was the Intendant Bigot, whose whole career was one of extortion, fraud, and lewdness. Monopolies plundered the poverty-stricken people; grain, cattle, and horses were seized and sold abroad, and the money put into the pockets of Bigot and his tools. Every man between the ages of sixteen and sixty was drafted into the army to defend the colony. Montcalm labored ceaselessly to put Quebec and the other fortresses in the best possible condition for defence, but he was hampered by the Governor and the Intendant. Meanwhile a plan of campaign had been arranged by the British, which was to bring the war to a close by one great and united effort. Amherst was to proceed along the line of Lakes George and Champlain, and take Ticonderoga and Crown Point. General Prideaux, aided by Sir William Johnson and his Indians, was to attack Niagara, while to Wolfe was given the heavy task of assaulting Quebec. Amherst and Prideaux having performed their allotted tasks were to join Wolfe at Quebec. Prideaux was killed while besieging Niagara, and the honor of taking the fort fell to Sir William Johnson. Amherst found little opposition at Ticonderoga and Crown Point, the French falling back on Quebec for the final defence. Amherst, however, lingered at these points, building and strengthening forts to secure the line of Lakes George and Champlain.

State of Canada.

Plan of Campaign to take Canada.

Early in 1759, Wolfe sailed from Louisburg to Quebec with his army of less than nine thousand men. Saunders and Holmes commanded the fleet, while Wolfe was assisted by an able staff of officers, Townshend, Monckton and Murray. Landing at the Island of Orleans, Wolfe anxiously viewed

Wolfe reaches Quebec, 1759.

for the first time the rock fortress, Quebec, the greatest stronghold of France in the New World. For miles on both the east and west of Quebec, Montcalm had fortified the banks of the St. Lawrence. Between the St. Charles and the Montmorency were more than thirteen thousand men of all ages, and the walls of Quebec itself bristled with guns. Who could hope to capture this Gibraltar of America, with such a small force as Wolfe had at his command? Yet, Wolfe, weakened as he was by a fatal disease, did not shrink from the effort. Soon he seized a strong position opposite Quebec, Point Levi, and there Monckton fixed his batteries. The French made fruitless efforts to dislodge the British fleet, by sending fire-ships down the river, but these were taken in tow by the sailors and did little harm. The batteries from Point Levi began to play upon the doomed fortress, and soon a great part of Quebec was in ruins. Nevertheless, Montcalm strong in his position on the north shore, with entrenchments from Quebec to the river Montmorency, defied every effort of Wolfe to land his troops. On

<small>Wolfe attempts to land at the Montmorency, 31st July.</small> the 31st of July, a desperate attempt was made to gain a footing and storm the heights near the Montmorency; but to no purpose, Wolfe was compelled to retire with heavy loss, and his chagrin and grief brought on a fever.

It looked as if Quebec could not be taken, and winter was approaching which would bring relief to the garrison. Then it was one of Wolfe's staff, Townshend, proposed to climb the steep banks of the St. Lawrence, at a point some three miles above Quebec. The plan was adopted, and steps were at once taken to carry it into effect. Early in September, Wolfe managed, under cover of a pretended attack on the opposite (Beauport) shore, to have the main part of his army and fleet moved above Quebec. Taking advantage of a dark night, and knowing that a small body of French soldiers were coming down to Quebec from Montreal with a supply of provisions, Wolfe's fleet dropped silently down the river, escorting thirty barges laden with sixteen hundred men. With muffled oars they glided down the stream, hugging the north shore. The sentries along the bank were deceived, their challenges being correctly answered (a French deserter having given the English the proper countersign), and they thought it was the convoy expected from Montreal. As the boats glided on, Wolfe, weak with his recent illness, and filled with mingled hope and anxiety,

SIEGE OF QUEBEC.

softly repeated several stanzas of Gray's "Elegy" written but a year before. Pausing on the words

"The paths of glory lead but to the grave,"

he exclaimed! "I would rather be the author of that poem than take Quebec." In the early morning, of the 13th September, he landed at what is now known as Wolfe's Cove. His active Highlanders were soon at the top of the path leading up the cliff. The French guard was quickly overpowered, and at daybreak Wolfe and his little army stood ready for battle on the Plains of Abraham. Montcalm, who had been expecting an attack below the city on his lines at Beauport, as soon as the news was brought him broke up his camp, and without waiting for reinforcements hurried to meet Wolfe. Had he remained in the city it is doubtful if Wolfe could have taken it before the coming winter. But his impetuous temper led him astray, and marching through Quebec he flung himself on Wolfe's veterans, who

The British land at Wolfe's Cove.

Battle of Plains of Abraham, 13th Sept., 1759.

stood calmly awaiting their gallant leader's orders. Not until the French were within forty paces did Wolfe give the command to fire, then, at the given signal, a well-directed volley of musketry, followed by a fierce charge of bayonets, caused the French to give way, and the victory of the Plains of Abraham was won. It was a dear victory to both English and French, for their brave leaders both fell in the conflict. Wolfe, wounded first in the wrist, then in the chest, lived long enough to know that the victory was won, and his heroic task done. "They run, they run," said an officer holding <small>Death of Wolfe and Montcalm.</small> in his arms the dying general. "Who run?" asked Wolfe; and when he heard, "Now God be praised" said he, "I die happy." Montcalm was carried fatally wounded into Quebec, and when told his fate murmured sadly, "So much the better, I shall not live to see the surrender of Quebec." He died before midnight, and was buried in a grave <small>Quebec surrenders Sept. 18, 1759.</small> made by the bursting of a shell, a fitting close to the career of a brave soldier and a true patriot. Five days after, on the 18th September, Quebec surrendered, and Canada practically ceased to be a French possession.

CHAPTER III.

LAYING THE FOUNDATIONS OF THE CANADIAN CONSTITUTION.

1. Peace of Paris, 1763.—General Murray took the command of the British army after the death of Wolfe, and De Lévis succeeded Montcalm. Though Quebec had fallen, the Governor, Vaudreuil, and De Lévis, were not willing to surrender Canada to the British without a struggle. The walls of Quebec had been partly beaten down, and a great portion of the city had become a mass of ruins by the cannonading of the British, and Murray, fully expecting an assault from the French, at once began to put the fortress into as good a condition as possible. His army, especially the Highlanders, suffered much from the cold, which was very severe that winter. The French in Quebec and the British army were on very friendly terms, and much kindness was shown to the suffering soldiers by the inhabitants, the nuns knitting long hose to protect the unfortunate Highlanders from the effects of the frost and cold. Towards spring De Lévis advanced with an army of seven thousand men to re-take Quebec, and Murray was foolhardy enough to march out of the city against him. The British numbered but three thousand men, (so much had they suffered during the winter) and in the second battle of Plains of Abraham, they were defeated and compelled to retreat, in haste, within the walls of Quebec. The siege lasted some time longer, until the St. Lawrence becoming free of ice, a British fleet sailed up the river, and De Lévis, in despair, returned to Montreal. *Second Battle of Plains of Abraham, 1760.* In September, Murray and Amherst united their forces before Montreal, and Vaudreuil and Lévis feeling the impossibility of defending the city with the few weary and disheartened men at their disposal, surrendered all Canada to England, on the 8th of September, 1760.

Three years later the Seven Years' War was brought to a close, and Canada was formally given to England ; France ceding all her possessions in America east of the Mississippi except New Orleans, and the islands of St. Pierre and Miquelon near Newfoundland. Besides these great territories England gained largely in India and other parts of the world. The treaty that closed this war is known as the Peace of Paris. *Peace of Paris, 1763.*

2. Conspiracy of Pontiac.—About the time this treaty was made, a very strange and remarkable plot took place. Its object was the seizure of all the British forts along the Upper Lakes and in the Great West, and the holding them for the French. A famous Indian chief, Pontiac, who did not want the British to rule in Canada, and who did not know that the French had given up all hope of recovering it, stirred up the Indian warriors in the valley of the Ohio, and along the line of the Great Lakes, to seize the rude forts in the West recently handed over by the French to the British. A short time after the Peace of Paris was signed, a sudden and almost simultaneous attack was made on these forts, and in nearly every instance they fell into the hands of the Indians, their garrisons being murdered or made prisoners.

Detroit was besieged for over a year by thousands of Indians, who managed to prevent supplies and assistance coming to the garrison. At last a strong force came to the relief of the brave defenders of the fort, and the Indians sullenly withdrew. Fort Pitt and Niagara also, were able to hold their own against the dusky warriors, and the Indians finding that French power was at an end in America, ceased hostilities. Pontiac, a few years later, while drunk, fell by the hands of a treacherous Illinois Indian.

Seige of Detroit by Pontiac, 1763-64.

Two things make this conspiracy remarkable in Indian history. One is the vastness of the scheme planned and carried out by Pontiac with so much skill and success; the other is the determination shown by the Indians in the siege of Detroit, their usual mode of warfare being to capture forts, if at all, by surprise, and not by a long siege.

3. Military Rule.—There was an interval of more than two years between the surrender of Canada by the last French Governor and the Peace of Paris, and during that period the colony was governed by *Military Rule*. General Murray ruled over the district of Quebec; General Gage, that of Montreal; and Colonel Burton, that of Three Rivers. A Council of Officers met twice a week, and settled all disputes. The people were allowed the free use of their religion, and were treated justly and kindly. The French militia, who had been called from their homes to defend the colony against the British were allowed to go back to their farms and occupations, and the regular soldiers were sent to France.

State of the colony.

Canada was in a sad condition at this time. The people had been taken from their usual occupations to defend the country, and their farms had gone untilled, except by the women and the feeble men and boys who were unfit to carry a musket. Bigot, the last Intendant, and a host of greedy followers had plundered the people of the little they had, and the colony was flooded with a worthless paper money. Not many more than sixty thousand inhabitants were scattered along the line of the St. Lawrence between Montreal and Quebec. Peace brought Canada a measure of prosperity. Farms could now be tilled without fear of interruption from enemies, English or Indian.

FOUNDATIONS OF THE CANADIAN CONSTITUTION. 349

Many of the principal inhabitants returned to France, some of them like Bigot, to answer for their misdeeds to the French King, and to receive merited punishment. Gradually the colony settled down to steady industry, and the mild rule of Murray and his brother officers lessened any feeling of soreness arising from passing under the government of their old-time enemies.

4. The Quebec Act.—After the Peace of Paris, King George III., proclaimed Canada a British province, and promised the French inhabitants the right of free worship, and the "free exercise" of their religion. They were also left in undisturbed possession of their property, and were given in every way the same rights and privileges as the King's subjects of British birth, except that they were excluded from holding public office, because the laws of Great Britain at that time did not allow a Roman Catholic to hold offices in the gift of the State. An effort was made to induce British people to settle in Canada by offering them land grants, and the protection of British laws. A promise, also, was made of British parliamentary institutions as soon as the circumstances of the country would permit; that is, the people of Canada would be allowed to have their own Parliaments, and make most of their own laws. In the meantime the country was governed by a Governor and Council, the latter composed entirely of men of British birth, many of them military officers. The British settlers for many years were few in number, yet they had all the power, and the French had no voice in managing the affairs of the colony. Again, English law was introduced into the courts, and the English language used. Trial by jury was unknown to the French, and they did not like the system. They preferred to be tried directly by a Judge, in a language they understood. On the other hand the English settlers wanted British law in both criminal and civil cases. They did not like the French way of buying and selling land, and settling disputes about property. General Murray the first Governor after 1763, and his successor Sir Guy Carleton, both, tried to befriend the French, and in so doing displeased the English settlers. To please the former they allowed French civil law—that is the law relating to property and inheritance—to prevail; while the demands of British settlers were met by giving them English criminal law,

Government of Canada 1763-74.

which includes trial by jury. The consequence was both English and French were dissatisfied, and after considerable delay and many complaints, the British parliament tried to remedy the evil by passing in 1774 what is known as the Quebec Act.

Quebec Act 1774 — This Act extended the boundaries of Canada from Labrador to the Mississippi, and from the Ohio river to the watershed of Hudson's Bay. It gave the French the same political rights as the British, regardless of their religion. It gave the Roman Catholic clergy the right to collect tithes (the tenth part of the produce) and their "accustomed dues" from their own people. The French law or Custom of Paris was made the law in civil cases—and English law, the law in criminal cases. The Government was to consist of a Governor and Council, appointed by the Crown. The Council was to consist of not less than seventeen and not more than twenty-three members, the majority being of British birth.

5. Canada invaded by the Americans.—Another reason for passing this law must now be mentioned. The English colonies in America had for many years felt it a grievance that Britain should endeavor to force them to trade exclusively with her. Nearly everything they sold had to go first to England, and they had also to buy the most of their manufactures from the people of the mother country. At that time all European nations thought that their colonies existed for the good of the mother countries, and so they tried to keep the colonial markets for their own trade. So long as the French held Canada the English colonies had to depend upon Britain for aid against the French and their Indian allies; but when Canada became a British possession their fear of attack from the north and west was removed, and the colonies felt more independent of England, and more inclined to resent any interference with their freedom. Not long after the conquest of Canada, England tried to tax the American colonies, claiming that as the war in America was for their special benefit they should bear a portion of the expense. The colonies thought the tax unjust, because they were not represented in the British Parliament. After several efforts had been made to settle the difficulty the colonies revolted, and declared

Declaration of Independence, 1776.

themselves independent of Great Britain. Sir Guy Carleton saw what was coming, and he also knew the American colonies would try to get Canada to join in the revolt against England. There was a fear lest the new French subjects of the King should take sides with the discontented English colonies. To prevent this, the Quebec Act was passed, giving the French so many rights and privileges. A few months after this Act was passed the people of Canada were invited by the American colonists to send representatives to a Congress at Philadelphia, to protest against the invasion of their liberties. The Canadians of British birth were known to be discontented with the Quebec Act, because it gave them the French civil law, and did not secure them the protection of the Habeas Corpus Act, which all British subjects highly valued. Nevertheless, very few of the English in Canada were willing to aid in a revolt against Britain, so the invitation to the Congress was refused, and Canada remained loyal to the British Crown.

War began between the colonies and the mother country in 1775, and the Americans sent troops into Canada, with the hope that the Canadians would rise in arms and aid them in throwing off the yoke of England. But they were disappointed, for while the French would do nothing to defend Canada, they would do but little to help the Americans. *Invasion of Montgomery and Arnold* Two expeditions were sent against Canada—one, by way of Lake Champlain, to take Montreal; the other, under General Benedict Arnold, by way of Maine, to capture Quebec. Governor Carleton could not defend Montreal, and escaped to Quebec, there to make a final stand. The Americans united their forces under Generals Montgomery and Arnold, and advanced against the famous old fortress; but Carleton had taken wise precautions to defend the city. On the last day of the year, at four o'clock in the morning, in a blinding snowstorm, an attack was made on the Lower Town. But it was of no avail; Montgomery was killed, and four hundred of the Americans were hemmed in and taken prisoners. Arnold remained near Quebec throughout the winter, and then, with his forces terribly reduced by sickness and disease, retreated. Thus ended the fifth and last siege of Quebec. Soon after, the arrival of a strong body of

British troops, under General Burgoyne, forced the Americans to leave Canada, which was troubled no more by invaders during the Revolutionary War. This war came to an end in 1783, by England acknowledging the Independence of the United States (as they were now called) in the Treaty of Versailles. By this treaty the boundaries of Canada as far west as the Lake of the Woods were fixed. Canada lost the fertile territory lying between the Ohio and the Mississippi, and received as her southern boundary the middle of the Great Lakes, the St. Lawrence, the forty-fifth parallel of north latitude, and the St. Croix River in New Brunswick. The boundary between the present State of Maine and New Brunswick was left very vague, and this gave rise to serious trouble at a later date.

Boundaries of Canada fixed 1783.

6. United Empire Loyalists.—The close of the Revolutionary War brought a large increase of population to Canada. Many of the American colonists remained loyal to England during the struggle for independence, and when the war was over, these people found themselves looked upon with dislike and suspicion by their republican neighbors. So harsh was the treatment they received that the British Parliament took pity upon them, and voted them a large sum of money (over £3,000,000) in consideration of the losses they had borne by remaining loyal to the British Crown. Besides this grant of money they were given large and valuable tracts of land in Nova Scotia, New Brunswick, and in Western Canada, (now Ontario). It is said that over twenty-five thousand left the United States and settled in the British colonies, and of these ten thousand came to Upper Canada, settling chiefly around the Bay of Quinté, along the Niagara River, and the St. Clair.

Settlement of U.E. Loyalists. 1784.

Each U. E. Loyalist received two hundred acres of land free; so did each of his sons on coming of age, and each daughter when she married. They were given provisions for three years, in addition to clothing, tools, and farming implements. Disbanded soldiers and half-pay officers also came to Canada, and received grants of land and aid for a time from the Government.

7. The Constitutional Act of 1791.—All these years the

FOUNDATIONS OF THE CANADIAN CONSTITUTION. 353

people of Canada had been without a Parliament, although George III., in 1763, had promised them that as soon as possible they would be given the same rights of self-government, as enjoyed by other British subjects. The French portion of the population had never known any other form of government than that of a Governor and Council, and therefore did not feel the need of a change. But the British population were discontented with the Quebec Act, and its French law of buying, selling and holding property, especially land. This discontent rapidly grew greater when British settlers began to take up land in Western Canada. These wanted the British law of "freehold," that is, the right of every man holding land to have it as his own. According to the French system, the farmers held the land as tenants from their "seigneurs" and had to give for its use, money and work, besides being subject to a great many petty exactions and services. They could not freely sell or will the land without paying the "seigneur" or getting his consent. On the other hand, they could not be turned out of their holdings by being unable or unwilling to pay their debts. Again, the British settlers wanted the protection of the Habeas Corpus Act, Trial by Jury, and other British laws; and the need of these was felt during the harsh and tyrannical rule of Governor Haldimand, who succeeded Carleton in 1778. The complaints from Canada became so pressing and frequent, that William Pitt, (a son of the great war minister of that name) who was the Prime Minister of England at that time, brought in a Bill to give Canada representative institutions. The Bill also aimed at settling the difficulties that had arisen out of the difference of the language, laws, religion and customs of the two races in Canada. It proposed to divide Canada into two Provinces, Lower Canada and Upper Canada. The former was French Canada, while the latter was settled mainly by a British population. The boundary line between the two Provinces began at Point-au-Baudet, on Lake St. Francis, extended north to Point Fortune on the Ottawa, and then continued along that river to its head waters and Hudson's Bay Territory. Roughly speaking, it made the Ottawa River the dividing line. Each Province was to have a Governor, an Executive Council, a Legis-

Boundary between Upper and Lower Canada.

lative Council and a Legislative Assembly. The Governor and the two Councils were appointed by the Crown, but the Legislative Assembly was elected for four years by the people.

In Lower Canada the Legislative Assembly was to have not less than fifty members, and the Legislative Council fifteen. In Upper Canada the former was to have not less than sixteen members, and the latter seven. The Executive Council was chosen to advise the Governor, and the Legislative Council corresponded in a measure to our Dominion Senate, or the British House of Lords. Both Councils were independent of the people, and could not be removed, if they did wrong, by the people's representatives, the members of the Legislative Assembly. The British parliament kept the right to impose taxes or duties for the regulation of commerce; but the Canadian parliaments had the power to collect them. They could also impose taxes for public purposes, such as building roads, bridges, public buildings, and providing education for the people. Unfortunately, the money arising from the sale of wild lands, from timber and mining dues, and from taxes on goods coming in the country was under the control of the Governor and his Executive Council, and this left the people of Canada with very little power to get rid of a bad Government. The Quebec Act was to remain the law until repealed by the Provinces; but in Upper Canada all land was to be held by "freehold tenure," and English criminal law was to be the law for both Upper and Lower Canada. Provision was made for founding a Canadian nobility and an Established Church. One-seventh of the Crown lands was set aside for the support of a "Protestant clergy" in both Provinces; but the Roman Catholic clergy in Lower Canada were left with the power given them by the Quebec Act, to collect tithes "and their accustomed dues" from their own people in support of the Roman Catholic Church.

Terms of the Constitutional Act.

The Bill did not become law without strong objections being made by leading men of British birth in Lower Canada. It was also strongly opposed by Charles James Fox, Pitt's great political rival, who foresaw very clearly the result of attempting to govern Canada by Councils not responsible to the people. He also objected

Constitutional Act passed. 1791.

to the clauses relating to titles of nobility and granting Crown lands for the support of a Protestant clergy; and he pointed out what would be the effect of dividing Canada into separate Provinces, one French and the other British. Nevertheless, in spite of these and other objections, the Bill was passed by large majorities in the British Parliament, and became law in 1791. The new Constitution went into force in Canada the following year.

CHAPTER IV.

THE WAR OF 1812.

1. The Beginning of Parliamentary Government.—When the Constitutional Act was passed Canada had a population of one hundred and fifty thousand, of which about twenty thousand belonged to the Western Province. There were few villages or towns then in Upper Canada, the more important being Kingston and Newark (now Niagara). Newark was chosen as the place of meeting for the first Parliament of Upper Canada; but a few years after, in 1797, Parliament was moved to the village of York, or Toronto, because Newark being situated at the mouth of the Niagara river, and just opposite an American fort, it was not considered safe for the seat of Government to be so near the guns of a possible enemy. On the 17th September 1792, twenty-three men came, mostly from farm and store, to Newark to form a Legislative Council and Assembly; seven belonging to the Council and sixteen to the Assembly. They were busy men, and time was precious, so they set to work in earnest. The Governor Sir John Graves Simcoe was equally sturdy and energetic, and equally anxious to build up the Western Province. The first session saw English Civil Law and Trial by Jury introduced, and bills passed to collect small debts, to regulate tolls for millers, and to erect jails and court-houses in the four districts in which the Province was divided. These districts were the Eastern or Johnstown; the Midland or Kingston; the Home or

Parliament of Upper Canada meets Sept. 17, 1792.

Legislation of the First Parliament of Upper Canada.

Niagara; and the Western or Detroit. The session lasted less than two months. Parliament met the next year in May, and passed bills offering rewards for wolves' and bears' heads; and what was more important, provided for the doing away with slavery in Upper Canada. There were not many slaves in the province, but the Act passed in 1793, forbade the bringing of any more slaves into the country, and made all children, who were slaves, free at the age of twenty-five. During the time Parliament met at Newark, a government newspaper, the *Gazette*, was started—the first newspaper in Upper Canada.

The Parliament in Lower Canada met in December, 1792, at Quebec, and was composed of fifteen members of the Legislative Council and fifty of the Legislative Assembly. Of the latter, fifteen were of British origin, the rest were French.

<small>Parliament of Lower Canada meets December, 1792.</small>

It was soon found that there were two languages used by the members, so it was decided that a member could speak in either language; but all notices, bills, laws and other papers must be printed in both English and French, and thus the law has remained ever since. Too soon, jealousies and ill-feeling arose between the two races, and the newspapers on both sides helped to increase the mutual dislike. The Lower Canadian Parliament did not pass any law against slavery, but in 1803, Chief Justice Osgoode gave a decision to the effect that slavery was against the laws of England, and this led to the few slaves (about three hundred) in the Province being set free.

2. Founding of Upper Canada.—As already stated, there were only twenty thousand people in Upper Canada in 1791, and this small population was scattered along the St. Lawrence, around the Bay of Quinté and along the Niagara and St. Clair rivers. Settlers preferred to take up farms near the rivers and lakes, because it was very difficult to get in or out of the settlements except by water. The land was covered with forests, and every farm was a bush farm. The settler had to chop down the trees before he could plant or sow a crop of any kind. The fallen trees had to be burnt, and among the blackened stumps, with a rude "drag," drawn generally by oxen, he covered up the "seed." Sometimes his crop was planted and tended with the spade and hoe. His dwelling place was a log-hut or "shanty," often built in a small "clearing" in the heart of the forest, and covered with bark or "troughs." There, sheltered by the trees from the rude winter, his family lived, every member able to work doing something to lighten the settler's toil, and improve the common lot. Fortunately, the soil was fertile, and for the amount of seed sown the crop was plentiful. Mills for grinding grain of any kind were very scarce, and often the settler had to make his own flour or meal by pounding the grain in the hollow of a hard-wood stump, or by using a steel hand-mill, provided in these days by the Government. Instances were not rare of a man trudging forty miles to get a bushel of wheat ground by a grist-mill, and then trudging home again with his load lightened by the miller's toll. Roads were few and rough, made, as they were, through the woods. Frequently there was nothing more than a "blazed" path for the foot-traveller or the solitary horseman. In other places swampy and low ground was bridged over by logs laid side by side, forming the famous "corduroy roads" our fathers and grandfathers tell about, and the remains of which are to be found in many localities to-day. The daily life of these hardy people (for they usually had good health and strong frames) was very simple and free from luxury of any kind, unless the abundance of game and fish may be called such. They wore home-made clothing, had very rude furniture, often, also, home-made, and rode in carts and sleds drawn by oxen. Yet, notwithstanding these hardships, they lived happy, contented lives. They were very sociable with their few neighbours, helped each other in their "logging bees," and their house and barn "raisings," which gatherings were sometimes marred by the rather free use of distilled liquors. Once in a long time, they were visited by a travelling preacher, who, by almost incredible toil, made his way to the "sheep" scattered in the "wilderness." Then, in some rude log-cabin, the few settlers gathered together to listen to a sermon, have their children baptized, and perchance, other solemn religious rites performed. Of education, there was little or none. Not that the settlers despised it, but the inhabitants were too few, too busy, and too poor to employ competent teachers and send their children to school after they could help on the farm. Later on, as we shall find, the Government tried to help the people in this respect, but the aid they got for many years was of little value. Old and worn-out pensioners took to teaching to get a scanty livelihood, and paid for their "board" and small salary by giving the youths of the school district a very imperfect knowledge of reading, writing and arithmetic. The salary of the teacher was too small to enable him to pay for his board, so it was arranged that he should "board around" among the different families sending their children to the school. The prudent teacher usually managed to spend the most of his time in the homes where the most comfort prevailed.

3. Political Discontent.—The early settlers cared little for politics, aside from the aid the Government could give in the way of building roads, bridges, and opening up the country for settlement. Nevertheless the defects of the Constitutional Act were soon so apparent and hurtful, that the people of both Upper and Lower Canada began to complain. In both provinces, the Executive Council and the Legislative Council did not consider they were responsible to the people, and used their power to further the interests of themselves and their friends. Judges and other salaried officials were often members of these councils, and the union of law-making and law-interpreting did not work well. The governors, as a rule, took the advice of their Executive Councils and paid no attention to the remonstrances of the Legislative Assembly. There was no way of getting rid of these men, who abused their trust by putting their needy friends into government offices, and by granting wild lands to speculators, who hoped by holding the lands until the neighbouring settlers made improvements, to be able to sell at a good profit. They were also accused of spending corruptly the money intended for the U. E. Loyalists and other settlers, and for the Indian tribes. In our days, the people's representatives would refuse to vote any money for the public expenditure, until their wrongs were righted ; but, at that time, such a course was impossible, for nearly all the revenue was under the control of the Governor and his Executive Council. In Lower Canada, besides these abuses, they had to contend against race jealousies and religious animosities. The British in that province usually were on the side of the Governor and the Councils—while the French supported the Legislative Assembly, the majority of which was French. The Assembly demanded that judges should not sit in Parliament, and after a struggle the Governor and Legislative Council yielded. Another demand was that the revenue of the Province should be expended by the Assembly. This, however, was not granted for many years. But the quarrels between the Assemblies and the Governors were, in 1812, dropped to meet a pressing common danger. *Judges in Lower Canada disqualified from being members of Parliament, 1811.*

4. Cause of the War of 1812.—To explain this danger we must refer to what had been going on in Europe for nearly twenty years. In 1793 England was drawn into a war with France, and, except for a brief period in 1802-3, there had been a continuous struggle against the power of the French General and Emperor, Napoleon Bonaparte. In 1806, when Napoleon had conquered the most of Europe, he issued a "decree" from Berlin in Prussia to the effect that English goods were *Berlin decree 1806.* not to be bought or sold on the Continent of Europe, and that other nations should not trade with England. England, who had been for many years the mistress of the sea, retaliated by forbidding all neutral nations to trade with France, and threatening their vessels with seizure if they did not call at English ports. These "Orders-in-Council," as they were called, were very hard on American vessel owners who could not trade with either England or France without their vessels being liable to seizure. Besides, England, anxious to secure men for her navy, stopped American vessels on the seas, and searched them for runaway sailors and British subjects. It was said that this was often a mere pretext to take American sailors to man British war-ships. The American Congress complained loudly against England's abuse of power, but got no redress. At last the United States, which just then was governed by the Democratic party—a party, from the time of the Revolution, always hostile to England and friendly to France—declared war, although the hateful "Orders-in-Council" were repealed within a few days of the declaration.

5. The Campaign of 1812.—The declaration of war was made on the 18th of June, and was very much against the wishes of a considerable portion of the American people. The New England

States were anxious for peace, for war to them meant loss of trade and injury to their commerce. Consequently they refused to give any active aid, and thus, although the population of the United States was eight millions, and that of Canada only about one quarter of a million, the difference in numbers did not really show the difference in military strength of the two countries. The United States hoped to take Canada with very little effort; for it was known that only 4,500 regular soldiers were in the colony, and a few militia scattered all along a frontier of fifteen hundred miles. It was also known that England was too busy fighting Napoleon in Spain to be able to give the Canadians any immediate help. When the war broke out, Sir George Prevost was the Governor-General of Canada, and General Sir Isaac Brock the acting Lieutenant-Governor of Upper Canada, in the absence of Mr. Francis Gore then in England.

The American plan of campaign was to invade Canada with three armies. One was to cross at Detroit, a second at the Niagara frontier, and the third, by the way of Lake Champlain. These were the armies of the West, the Centre, and the North respectively, General Dearborn being the Commander-in-chief.

Plan of Campaign of the Americans.

The first blow was struck at Fort Michillimackinac at the entrance of Lake Michigan. This post was held by the Americans, and was important on account of its trade with the western Indians. Acting under orders from General Brock, Captain Roberts with a small body of men from St. Joseph, took the fort by surprise, and by so doing secured the support and confidence of the Indian tribes of the West and North-west. On the 12th of July, the American general, Hull, crossed over from Detroit, and by a proclamation, invited the Canadians to throw off the yoke of England; but the invitation met with no response. General Brock immediately sent Colonel Proctor with a few regulars to Fort Malden, near Amherstburg. Here Proctor was joined by the famous Indian chief, Tecumseh, who brought a number of warriors to help the English in the struggle against the Americans. Tecumseh was a Shawnee, and for years had sought to unite the various Indian tribes against the Americans, for he saw very clearly that the Indians were being

Tecumseh.

pushed back, further and further, by the steady encroachments of the white people. At this time, Tecumseh was in the prime of his noble manhood, and wielded a great influence over the Indian tribes, who believed him to be of supernatural birth.

For a short time, Hull remained in Canada, and then getting afraid of Indian attacks, returned to Detroit and shut himself up, in that strong fort. On the 5th of August, Brock set out for Detroit, with a small force of regulars and York militia. A week later he reached Amherstburg, and there met Tecumseh with seven hundred warriors. Tecumseh sketched for Brock, on a piece of birch bark, the plan of Detroit, and it was resolved to attempt its capture, although Brock had only fourteen hundred men, half of them Indians, while Detroit was defended by over two thousand. Brock demanded the surrender of the fort, and the demand being refused, crossed the river and made preparations for an attack. Greatly to the surprise of the English and the Indians, and the garrison itself, Hull surrendered the fort and the territory of Michigan without a shot being fired, he and all his men being made prisoners. Brock sent the regulars of Hull's army to Montreal as prisoners of war; the militia were allowed to return home. A large quantity of military supplies, ammunition and cannon, fell into the hands of the English, which proved a very timely aid to Brock in carrying on the war. Brock then returned to Toronto, and found that General Prevost had agreed to an armistice, by which the war was stopped for a time on Lake Champlain and the Niagara frontier. This gave the Americans an opportunity to collect their armies and carry supplies along Lake Ontario to Niagara. Before the month of August ended, war was renewed, and the Americans gathered six thousand men under General Van Rensselaer at Lewiston, opposite Queenston, on the Niagara river, with the intention of invading Canada. To oppose this force, Brock had only fifteen hundred men, mostly militia and Indians. Brock's troops were scattered all along the Niagara river from Fort George, at its mouth, to Queenston seven miles up the stream. His men were kept on a constant watch against attempts of the Americans to cross.

Surrender of Detroit by Gen. Hull.

On the 13th of October, in the early morning, the American army began crossing the river at a point below Queenston Heights. The few regulars and militia stationed there poured a destructive fire into the boats of the Americans as they approached the shore, many of which were sunk, and their occupants killed or taken prisoners.

<small>Battle of Queenston Heights, 13th Oct., 1812.</small> The Canadians thought they had driven back the invaders, when it was discovered that a large force of Americans had under cover of the night made their way to the top of Queenston Heights. Hearing the sound of firing, Brock, who was at Fort George, galloped in hot haste for the scene of conflict, leaving his *aides* to follow him, and hurrying forward the troops as he sped past them. When he reached Queenston and saw that the Americans had succeeded in getting a footing on the Heights, he put himself at the head of a small body of men and rushed up the mountain side eager to dislodge the enemy. While cheering his followers on he was struck in the breast by a musket ball, and fell mortally wounded. His tall figure and bright uniform had made him a mark, all too good, for the American riflemen. His brave soldiers, though few in number, were anxious to avenge his death, and again made an attempt to dislodge the foe—but only to be driven back with heavy loss. Among those who fell in this second attempt was Brock's *aide-de-camp*, Colonel MacDonnell of Glengarry, a noble young man only twenty-five years of age, whose life was full of promise. Soon after General Sheaffe arrived from Fort George with three hundred men and some artillery. All the men that could be mustered were now marched through the fields back of Queenston, and unperceived they ascended the Heights, and concealed themselves among the trees. The Americans in the meantime were landing fresh troops, and carrying off their dead and wounded. About three o'clock in the afternoon the British moved rapidly through the woods against the unsuspecting Americans. A number of Indians who were in the Canadian army, as soon as they saw the enemy raised the terrible war-whoop, and rushed on their prey. The rest of the troops joined in the shout and the onslaught. The Americans gave one volley and then fled. But there was no escape, save by the brow of the mountain overhanging the river. In their terror many of the enemy threw themselves over the precipice, only to be dashed on the rocks, or drowned in the river. The American shore was lined with their fellow-countrymen, but no

help was given. Soon two American officers ascended the mountain side bearing a white flag, and with difficulty the slaughter was brought to an end. One thousand Americans were made prisoners and a hundred slain. Thus dearly was the death of Brock avenged. In one of the batteries of Fort George, amid the booming of minute guns from friend and foe, Brock and MacDonnell side by side found a resting place. A month's armistice was unwisely agreed to by General Sheaffe, which enabled the Americans to gather troops for another attack on the Niagara frontier. Towards the end of November, General Smythe, who succeeded Van Rensselaer, attempted a landing near Fort Erie, but his men were driven back by a small force of Canadians. This ended the attempts, in 1813, of the army of the Centre to gain a footing on Canadian soil.

Nor was the army of the North under General Dearborn more successful. In November, Dearborn advanced with an army of ten thousand men by way of Lake Champlain to take Montreal. The French Canadian militia under Major de Salaberry, felled trees, guarded the passes, and used every possible means to check his advance. At Lacolle, near Rouse's Point, a British outpost was attacked by Dearborn's troops, but in the darkness of the early morning, his men became confused and fired into each other's ranks. When they discovered their mistake, disheartened and cowed, they returned to Lake Champlain, and Dearborn finding the Canadian militia on the alert, gave up his attempt on Montreal and retired to Plattsburg. *Dearborn defeated at Lacolle, Nov., 1812.*

To sum up:—The results of the land campaign of 1812 were the capture of Detroit, the surrender of Michigan, the great victory at Queenston Heights, and the repulse of Dearborn at Lacolle by a small body of Canadian militia. On the sea, however, the Americans were more successful, gaining several victories over British men-of-war, and controlling the great lakes.

6. Campaign of 1813.—General Sheaffe succeeded General, Brock as Lieut.-Governor of Upper Canada, and the Parliaments of both Provinces met to vote money for the defence of the country. They issued Army Bills, or promises to pay, instead of gold and silver and this paper money was not to be exchanged for coin until the war was over. The Americans made great preparations this year to conquer Canada, and, as in 1812, placed three large armies on the frontier. That in the west was led by General Harrison; that on the Niagara frontier by General Dearborn; and that in the east by General Hampton. A regiment of British soldiers arrived in the depth of winter from New Brunswick to help the Canadians. The war was continued throughout the winter; Major Macdonald capturing Ogdensburg, with a large quantity of arms and supplies, and Colonel Proctor in the west, defeating General Winchester in a battle at Frenchtown a place about twenty miles south of Detroit. Vessels were built on the lakes by both sides, but the Americans were the sooner equipped, and sailing out of Sackett's Harbor General Dearborn, and Commodore Chauncey with two thousand men attacked and captured York, which was defended by only six hundred men, regulars, militia, and Indians. General Sheaffe retired from the old French fort at York, to Kingston, taking the regulars with him, and was replaced in Upper Canada by General de Rottenburg, Sheaffe's conduct at York being blamed. Having taken York the American fleet and army sailed across Lake Ontario to the mouth of the Niagara river to take Fort George. General Vincent with fourteen hundred men held the fort for some time against Dearborn, and then, his ammunition failing, retreated to a strong position on Burlington Heights, having first spiked his guns, and blown up his magazine. Fort George was now taken possession of by the Americans. While Chauncey was at Fort George, Sir George Prevost and Sir James Yeo, a naval officer just arrived from England, crossed the lake from Kingston with a large force and attacked Sackett's Harbor, hoping to destroy the naval stores there. When on the point of success, Prevost withdrew his men, imagining the Americans were trying to entrap him. These disasters were more than balanced by two brilliant exploits, one at Stoney Creek, near Hamilton, the other at Beaver Dams. At the former place, on the fourth of June, Colonel Harvey, of General Vincent's army, with seven hundred men, made a night attack on four thousand Americans who had advanced from Fort George to drive Vincent from his post on Burlington Heights. The attack was completely successful, the Americans taken by surprise, after a brief resistance, retreating hastily with the loss of four cannon, and one hundred and twenty prisoners, including two generals. At Beaver Dams (near the present town of Thorold), Lieutenant Fitzgibbon with a small force was stationed. General Dearborn hoped to surprise this post, and for that purpose sent six hundred men from Fort George, under Major Boerstler. A Canadian heroine, Mrs. Laura Secord, became aware of the plan, and set out on foot to warn the British of the intended attack. To avoid the American sentries she had to walk twenty miles, a journey that took all day, from early morning till sunset. Fitzgibbon, warned, made such a skilful arrangement of his few men in the woods, that the Americans thought they were surrounded by a large force, and, after a brief resistance, surrendered to only one half of their own number of men. The Americans were now, in turn, besieged in Fort George by Vincent and his small army. *Beaver Dams.*

Two serious disasters now befell the Canadians. Captain Barclay, with six British vessels, was defeated on Lake Erie by Commodore Perry, with nine American vessels; and this loss compelled Colonel Proctor and Tecumseh to abandon Detroit and retreat into Canada, as their supplies could no longer come to them by the lakes. Proctor was closely followed by General Harrison with a large force drawn from the west, many of them Kentucky riflemen accustomed to border warfare. Tecumseh urged Proctor to make a stand against the Americans, but Proctor continued his retreat until he reached Moraviantown, on the Thames river. There, at last, Tecumseh persuaded him to prepare for battle on a favourable ground. Soon Harrison and his men appeared, and a fierce battle began. Almost at the beginning of the fight, Proctor fled and left Tecumseh and his Indians to uphold the honour of British arms. Tecumseh and his warriors fought with desperate courage and great skill, but they were soon overpowered and Tecumseh was killed. *Battle of Moraviantown, and Tecumseh killed, Oct. 5th, 1813.* Had Proctor stood his ground, the battle of Moraviantown might have ranked in our history with that of Queenston Heights, and other brave deeds. The few of Proctor's men, that escaped, fled and joined General Vincent. The Americans had now possession of the western part of Canada, and hoped soon by two large expeditions to take Montreal. The first of these, nine thousand strong, under General Wilkinson set out from Sackett's Harbour, in boats, expecting to take Kingston and Prescott, and then float down the St. Lawrence and make a junction with General Hampton, who was to approach Montreal by Lake Champlain. Kingston was not molested, and Wilkinson was so annoyed by the Canadians along the bank of the St. Lawrence, that he landed below Prescott with four thousand men, to beat back his enemies. Here, in an open field, called Chrysler's Farm, with only eight hundred men Colonel Morrison and Colonel Harvey, the hero of Stoney Creek, inflicted so heavy a defeat on the forces of Wilkinson, that they were glad to return to their own side of the river. The other expedition under General Hampton, with three thousand men, had been defeated by Colonel de Salaberry, with four hundred Canadian militia, at the battle of Chateauguay. These two victories put an end for a time to the attempts to take Montreal.

<small>Battle of Chrysler's Farm 11th Nov., 1813.</small>

<small>Chateauguay 26th Sept., 1813.</small>

CHATEAUGUAY AND CHRYSLER'S FARM.

In Upper Canada, General Vincent had been compelled by the defeat of Proctor, to retreat again to Burlington Heights, and the

Americans had the control of the Niagara peninsula. But the bad news from the east led the American general, McClure, to abandon Fort George; not, however, before he had committed the inhuman act of burning the village of Niagara, turning the people out of their homes in the depth of a very severe winter. After the retreat of the Americans to their own side of the river, the British under General Drummond, arrived on the frontier, and determined to avenge the burning of Niagara. Fort Niagara on the American side was surprised, and three hundred prisoners taken. Lewiston, Black Rock, Buffalo, and other American villages were burned, the destruction of Buffalo closing the campaign of 1813. *Buffalo burned, Dec. 30th, 1813.*

7. 1814 and the Close of the War.—The winter of 1814 was used by the Canadians to carry, on sleds, supplies from Montreal to Kingston and Toronto for the troops in the west.

The Americans had gained a footing in the western peninsula by their success at Moraviantown, but General Harrison returned to Detroit and took no further part in the war. Lower Canada was the first to be attacked this year. In March, General Wilkinson with five thousand men tried in vain to take a strong stone mill at Lacolle defended by five hundred Canadians. He was repulsed with heavy loss, and retreated to Plattsburg. In May, General Drummond and Sir James Yeo made a successful raid on Oswego, and carried off a large quantity of supplies. The Niagara frontier was the scene of two bloody battles. The Americans, four thousand strong, crossed at Buffalo, took Fort Erie and then pushed on to Chippewa. General Riall, with two thousand men, tried to check their progress, but was defeated at the battle of Chippewa. He then retreated to Lundy's Lane, now a street in the village of Niagara Falls South. The American soldiers began plundering and burning the buildings of the farmers, and destroyed the pretty village of St. David's. They then advanced against Riall at Lundy's Lane. General Drummond heard of the invasion, and the battle at Chippewa, and hurried from Kingston to aid General Riall. He reached Fort Niagara on the morning of July 25th, and with eight hundred men pushed forward to Lundy's Lane. At five

Lacolle Mill, 30th March, 1814.

Chippewa, 5th July, 1814.

Lundy's Lane, July 25th, 1814.

o'clock in the afternoon he met General Riall retreating before a strong body of American troops under Generals Brown, Ripley, and Scott. Drummond at once stopped the retreat, and faced the foe.

THE NIAGARA FRONTIER.

The Americans were four thousand strong, the Canadians had three thousand. From five o'clock till midnight the battle raged. The utmost stubbornness and courage were shown by both armies in the fierce stuggle for the British guns. General Riall was taken prisoner and three American generals, Scott, Brown, and Porter, were wounded. At last, worn out in the vain effort to force the British position, the Americans retreated, leaving their dead to be burned by the victors, for the number of slain was so great that burial was impossible. The loss to the enemy was nearly nine hundred; to the British about the same. The scene of this battle, the best contested and bloodiest of the whole war, is marked to-day by a little church and graveyard in which many a Canadian hero sleeps.

The war was drawing to a close. The Americans after the battle retired to Fort Erie which they held for some time in spite of the attacks of General Drummond, and then withdrew across the river. In the mean time the war in Europe had been brought to an end by Napoleon's defeat and his retirement to the island of Elba. England could now assist Canada, and in August sixteen thousand men arrived. A great expedition was planned against Plattsburg, in which eleven thousand men, and the fleet on Lake Champlain were to take part. Sir George Prevost led the land army, and Captain Downie commanded the British flag-ship. Prevost waited for the British vessels to attack the American fleet

Failure of attack on Plattsburg, 11th Sept., 1814.

before proceeding against Plattsburg which was defended by a small force. Unfortunately the British ships were defeated and many of them destroyed in the engagement that followed, and Prevost, without any good reason, retreated without striking a blow. His officers were so chagrined that they broke their swords, vowing they would serve no longer. Meanwhile, in August, the British had entered Chesapeake Bay, captured Washington, the capital of the United States, and burned the public buildings, including a valuable library. This was in revenge for the burning of Niagara by General McClure. At last, on the 24th of December, 1814, the Treaty of Ghent was signed, which restored to the United States and to Canada their losses, but did not settle the points in dispute which led to the war. Two weeks after the peace was made in Europe, a bloody battle was fought at New Orleans, where the British general, Pakenham, endeavored to carry by assault a strong line of entrenchments defended by General Jackson. The English general did not know that the war was over, and many of Wellington's veterans fell in the worse than useless contest.

<small>Treaty of Ghent, Dec. 24th, 1814.</small>

CHAPTER V.

THE STRUGGLE FOR RESPONSIBLE GOVERNMENT AND THE REBELLION OF 1837-38.

1. Growth of the Colony.—The war of 1812 brought no territory or glory to the Americans, save the victories they won on the lakes and the high seas. They had been defeated in most of the battles on land; their trade and commerce had been greatly injured by British vessels, the New England States had threatened to leave the Union, and a very heavy public debt had been contracted. Canada, too, suffered by her farmers being taken away from their farms to serve in the militia, many of them never returning to their homes, and many others returning wounded and crippled. To the latter the Government gave small pensions for life; and the widows and orphans of the killed received small grants of money.

The country was too poor to pay heavy pensions, or to recompense families for the loss of their bread-winners. During the war the British Government had spent large sums in the colony, and this for a time seemed to make it prosperous. But when the struggle was over, and the expenditure ceased, the effects of the cruel conflict began to be felt. For a few years there were hard times, and these were made worse by the failure of the wheat crop in Lower Canada. So great was this failure that the Governor, on his own authority, took the public money to help the farmers to buy seed, and the Lower Canadian Parliment, the next year, voted a still larger sum. But the colony soon recovered its prosperity, for the soil was fertile and the people were hardy and industrious. Efforts were made to bring in settlers by offering free passages across the ocean and one hundred acres of land to each man, besides giving him help the first year of his settlement on a farm. Very unwisely Americans were not allowed to become citizens of Canada, the Government fearing and disliking them. This was one of the bad effects of the recent war. The years from 1815 to 1820 saw a great many people settle in Canada from Great Britain and Ireland. The county of Lanark was settled about this time by immigrants from Scotland, and the failure of the crops in Ireland brought in 1820 many Irish to Canada.

Immigration.

There was a growth not only in population but also in trade, commerce, and manufactures. In the absence of good roads, grain and other products of Upper Canada had to be taken down to Montreal and Quebec by water. The rapids of the St. Lawrence prevented vessels from coming up, so large flat-bottomed or "Durham" boats floated down the river from Kingston to Montreal, laden with goods. These boats were then sold as it did not pay to bring them up the rapids. After a while, as the trade grew larger, canals were built between Kingston and Ottawa, and along the St. Lawrence below Prescott. These we know as the Rideau and Lachine Canals. Further west a more important work was begun in 1819. This was the building of a canal between Lakes Erie and Ontario to overcome the obstacle to navigation caused by the Falls of Niagara. Hon. W. H. Merritt, of St. Catharines, had the honor of proposing and carrying out the project, which was finished in 1829. Very

Inland Navigation and Canals.

STRUGGLE FOR RESPONSIBLE GOVERNMENT. 371

early in the century steamboats came into use on the lakes and rivers, the credit of which must be given largely to the Hon. John Molson of Montreal. Quebec became noted for shipbuilding, and a brisk trade in timber with the Old World sprang up at this port. The manufacture of potash and pearlash was a profitable industry; but grain crops, in the absence of good roads, could not find a ready market. Then, as now, there was considerable smuggling along the frontier between Canada and the United States, and in consequence the revenue suffered considerably.

To meet the demand for money to carry on the growing trade of the country, Banks were founded, among the earliest being the Banks of Montreal, Kingston, and Quebec; and a little later the Bank of Upper Canada. The population, and therefore the trade, of Upper Canada grew more rapidly than that of Lower Canada, and this led to disputes between the Provinces. After the Constitutional Act of 1791, it was arranged that Upper Canada was to have as her share one-eighth of the customs duties collected at the chief ports of Lower Canada. Thirteen years later the proportion was changed to one-fifth, and then, in 1822, there still being dissatisfaction, the British Parliament passed the Canada Trade Act, which gave Upper Canada £30,000 of arrears due by Lower Canada, and arranged for a more just division of the revenue in the future. *Founding of Banks.*

Education was improving very slowly. Governor Simcoe had planned the founding of a college in his time, and for that purpose brought from Scotland, John Strachan, a young but clever school teacher to be its head. When Strachan arrived he found Simcoe had left the colony, and he started a grammar school at Cornwall, where many of the most noted men of Upper Canada were educated. In 1807, the Parliament of Upper Canada voted £500 for the support of eight *grammar* schools; and in 1816, *common* schools were granted £6,000 to help in paying teachers and in buying books. In 1823, McGill University in Montreal was organized for teaching, and four years later we have the beginning of King's College at York. In 1829 Upper Canada College was founded to prepare pupils for the coming University. Few people, at that time, could afford to give their sons a college education, so these young universities for many years had but little to do. *Educational growth.*

2. Political Abuses and Troubles.—Canada had no more wars with foreign nations, and her history, save for political troubles, since 1814 has been the history of growth in wealth, in population, and in enterprises for opening up the country to settlement, and for utilizing her natural resources. But, of political struggles, from the day she became a British colony until the present, she has had her full share. The war of 1812 had hardly ceased when a political struggle began which ended in rebellion and bloodshed ; also, fortunately, in better and freer government. We have now to tell very briefly the causes of this strife, and how it resulted.

In Lower Canada, as already stated, great discontent was aroused by the action of the Governors and the Councils in refusing to allow the Legislative Assembly to control the expenditure of the revenue arising from timber and mining dues, the sale of crown lands, and the taxes collected at the Customs-house. The Assembly offered, if it were given the control of all the revenue, to provide for the necessary expenses of the Province, including the payment of the salaries of judges and other civil officers. This offer, however, the Governors and their advisers would not accept, and the Assembly then tried to stop the supplies. But the Governor took the money from the treasury, without asking permission, to pay the necessary salaries and expenses. The British parliament was petitioned to redress these grievances, and to pass an Act giving the Legislative Assemblies the control of the expenditure of all public money. Little heed was given in England for some time to these complaints, as the Governors and their Councils generally succeeded in keeping their side of the case well before the British government. Besides this trouble about the control of public money, there was the more serious difficulty due to the difference of race, religion, and language in the population. The British element disliked the French, and sided with the Governors and their Councils ; while the French elected the most of the members of the Assembly. The Councils were mainly British, and the Legislative Assembly, French. In 1828, an effort was made by the Home Government, by a half-measure, to settle the difficulty arising from the control of the revenue. This measure proposed

Causes of Discontent in Lower Canada.

to give the Assembly the control of the duties on goods, in return for a permanent support of the judges and other officials. It did not grant the control of the other revenues, nor did it make the Legislative Council elective, and therefore subject to the control of the people. So this effort to conciliate the people failed, and the discontent was increased by a harsh measure passed by Lord John Russell in 1837, which refused the just demands of the people.

Turning to Upper Canada, we find much the same troubles and abuses as in Lower Canada. There was, however, for some time, an important difference in the political situation. In Lower Canada the Assembly was bitterly opposed to the Government; but, in Upper Canada the Assembly contained so many Government officials, such as postmasters, sheriffs and registrars, that the majority of the members supported the Governors and their advisers. A small but increasing number of the members complained of the abuses of the time, and were treated by the ruling body as malcontents and traitors. It was not safe to say anything in the press or on the floor of Parliament against the Government and their management of affairs. The men who for many years really controlled the province were known as the Family Compact, on account of the closeness of the alliance they had formed to get and retain the offices of the Government. Many of them were U. E. Loyalists, who prided themselves on their loyalty to British institutions. Others were emigrants from the mother country, who, unwilling to make a living by hard work on bush farms, managed through the influence of friends in the Old Land to get office in or under the Government. Very soon this Compact of office-holders came to believe that it had a right to manage the affairs of the Province, fill all the offices and make profit out of the wild lands for themselves and their friends. The management of these lands was one of the great grievances of the settlers. Not only were large grants given to the friends of the Compact for purposes of speculation, but a company of British capitalists, called the Canada Land Company, bought up large tracts which it held without making any improvements. The County of Huron suffered more than most places from this bad policy, as for many years this fine, fertile district was left

<small>Discontent in Upper Canada.</small>

<small>Canada Land Company</small>

uncleared and unsettled. Then, land had been set aside in each township as Clergy Reserves and for the support of common schools. So much uncleared land coming between the farms of settlers made it difficult to construct roads and fences, and separated the farmers so much that they could not form school districts without a great deal of trouble and inconvenience.

Then again, there was great discontent because the English Church clergy claimed that they alone were entitled to share in the Clergy Reserves grant. The Church of Scotland also claimed a share, as it was the established church of Scotland, and after some dispute its claim was recognized. This left out the Methodists, Baptists, Roman Catholics and other denominations, and, therefore, did not mend matters much. In 1836, Sir John Colborne, the Governor, and his Executive Council, endowed fifty-seven rectories of the Church of England with a part of these church lands. This was done because the Reform party (the party opposed to the Family Compact) was in the majority in the House of Assembly, and it was feared something might be done to prevent the Church of England from getting the benefit of the endowment.

The Clergy Reserves question.

As already stated, for a time the Family Compact controlled the Legislative Assembly. This did not last long, for the abuses of power were so great that the people began to elect as members men who tried to remove the evils from which they were suffering. In 1824 this Reform party elected a majority of the members, and chose one of their own number as Speaker, or Chairman of the Assembly. The most prominent members of this party at this time were Dr. Rolph, Peter Perry, and Marshall Bidwell. At this time also the noted William Lyon Mackenzie began to make his influence felt. Mackenzie was a Scotchman who had emigrated to Canada a few years before— had been a storekeeper in different places—and then had come to Toronto to start a newspaper. His paper, "The Colonial Advocate," attacked the abuses of the Family Compact so fiercely that a gang of ruffians seized his press and threw it into Lake Ontario. This made Mackenzie and his paper more popular than ever, and he was elected member of the Assembly for the County of York, the most populous county in the Province. On

William Lyon Mackenzie

the floor of the Assembly he made himself very troublesome to the Executive Council, and was continually unearthing frauds and scandals in connection with the public accounts, and the management of such works as the Welland Canal. Another man of a higher character and better judgment was elected, a little later, in the town of York. This was the fair-minded and moderate patriot, Robert Baldwin. In 1830 the elections resulted in favor of the Family Compact, and it used its majority in the Assembly to have Mackenzie expelled from the House for a breach of parliamentary privilege. Mackenzie was re-elected, and again expelled, and once more elected. He was then sent to England with petitions to the King for a redress of grievances. In 1835 the election gave a majority to the Reform party, and the next year the Governor, Sir John Colborne, resigned his position and left the province.

3. The Rebellion in Lower Canada, 1837-38.—Meanwhile matters were hastening to a crisis in Lower Canada. The French were much under the influence of M. Papineau, an eloquent speaker and writer, who had the power to stir the feelings and passions of the *habitants*. There had been a deadlock in Parliament, as the Assembly had refused to vote money for the payment of judges and other officials, and the Governor had taken what was needed out of the treasury without the consent of the Assembly. As soon as it was known that Lord John Russell had carried through the British Parliament resolutions opposed to granting the Canadian people their rights, the excitement in Lower Canada was very great, and broke out in a revolt, under the leadership of Papineau and Dr. Wolfred Nelson. The rebels were poorly prepared for a rising, and the revolt was soon suppressed by Sir John Colborne and his regulars. *St. Denis.* Engagements took place at St. Denis on the Richelieu, where Lieutenant Weir was shot by the rebels while attempting to escape from his captors; at St. Charles, where the rebels were defeated; and at St. Eustache, on the Ottawa, where many of the rebels were burned in a church.

The constitution of Lower Canada was now suspended, and a Special Council, half of the members of which were English and half French, was created to govern for the time being. Lord Durham, a nobleman *Lord Durham sent to Canada.*

of great intelligence and fair-mindedness, was sent out from England to examine into the cause of the rebellion, and to report to the Home Government. On his arrival, he at once began to inquire into the true state of affairs in both Provinces, and corrected several abuses in the management of the crown lands. He found a great many political prisoners in the jails, and not thinking it wise to try them before the ordinary courts, or by courts-martial, he released the most of them, and banished Nelson and eight others to Bermuda. He forbade Papineau, who had fled to the United States, to return to Canada, under pain of death. In doing these things, Durham acted without authority, and he was blamed by the British Parliament, which annulled his sentences. Durham was so chagrined at this seeming insult that he resigned his position and returned to England in broken health. His important work was, however, the drafting of a Report on the state of Canada, containing a great many valuable suggestions about the best way of governing colonies. He advised that Canada should be given *Responsible Government*, that is, the Governor should choose for his advisers the men having the confidence of the people's representatives. Besides, he recommended that Canada should have only one Parliament instead of two, and suggested the Union of all the British provinces in North America under one Parliament. Later on, it will be seen that this Report had a very great influence. After Durham had left Canada, Sir John Colborne became Administrator. The people of Lower Canada despairing of justice once more broke out in revolt, and a few slight engagements took place. Once more the rebellion was crushed—this time with considerable loss of life and property. Twelve of the leaders were tried by court-martial, and executed at Montreal. This ended the rebellion in Lower Canada.

Lord Durham's Report.

4. Rebellion in Upper Canada, 1837.—After Sir John Colborne's retirement in 1836, from the governorship of Upper Canada, the British Government by a curious mistake sent out as his successor, Sir Francis Bond Head, a man who had never taken any interest in politics, and who was quite ignorant of the state of affairs in the Province. At first the Reformers thought Sir Francis would be friendly to their

Sir Francis Bond Head.

STRUGGLE FOR RESPONSIBLE GOVERNMENT. 377

cause, but, like all preceding governors, he soon came under the influence of the Family Compact. He invited leading Reformers to join the Executive Council and the invitation was accepted. But he would not listen to the proposal that the Council should be responsible to the Assembly, and, in consequence, the Reform members of the Council resigned. Soon after this there was a general election, and Sir Francis threw himself into the contest with great zeal and effect. He made the people believe that their loyalty was at stake, and succeeded in having Mackenzie and other Reform leaders defeated at the polls. Mackenzie and some of his associates now despaired of having the grievances of the people removed by peaceable means, and unwisely listened to the suggestions of Papineau to join in a revolt. As if to encourage them, Sir Francis Head sent all the regular troops from Upper to Lower Canada to aid in suppressing the rebellion there, leaving York and its armory wholly unprotected. Mackenzie began to stir the passions of the people by articles in his paper, and by violent speeches. Soon the disaffected began arming and drilling throughout the western part of the province, and, although warned of what was going on, Sir Francis refused to take any steps to stop these dangerous proceedings. In fact the Governor acted as if he wished to hasten a revolt. Finally it was arranged that a rising should take place on the 7th December, that York should be surprised, the government buildings and armory seized, the Governor and Council taken prisoners, and then a republican form of Government established. It so happened that the leaders of the revolt in York, Dr. Rolph being the chief, changed the time for attack from the 7th to the 4th, without informing all the leaders outside of the change.

On the day appointed, about four hundred men gathered at Montgomery's Tavern, four miles from Toronto. They were badly armed, worn with travel, and disappointed at the mistake in their plans. Still, had they marched at once on York, it could easily have been surprised and captured; but Rolph, either through fear or treachery, counselled delay until more men arrived. Before this could happen the rebels were discovered, and steps taken to defend the town, the armory, and the government buildings. It was now too late to attempt a surprise. The next day Mackenzie wished to attack at once; but

Montgomery's Tavern.

Rolph still counselled delay, promising support from friends in the town if the attack were delayed until after dark. The night attack was a failure, and the following day Colonel McNab having arrived from Hamilton with a number of loyalists, a force of nine hundred men was sent against Mackenzie, who with four hundred men stood his ground near Montgomery's Tavern. The conflict was brief and decisive—the few rebels, without proper arms or support, being easily defeated and scattered. Mackenzie, with a reward of £1,000 on his head, escaped with great difficulty ; and after many exciting adventures in travelling from York round the head of Lake Ontario to the Niagara frontier, crossed the Niagara river, and found refuge on American soil.

5. The "Patriot" War, 1837-38.—Besides Mackenzie, Rolph and some other leaders thought it prudent to leave Canada. Still others were taken prisoners, and during the administration of Sir George Arthur, who succeeded Sir Francis Bond Head, Lount and Matthews were hanged at Toronto, an act of severity for which there was but slight excuse.

Mackenzie, unfortunately, did not rest content with the failure of his schemes. He now gathered together, at Buffalo, a number of ruffians and sympathizers from the slums of Americans cities, promising them land and bounties after they had liberated Canada. These men took possession of Navy Island, about two miles above Niagara Falls, fortified it, and made preparations to invade Canada.

Burning of the "Caroline" Dec. 28th, 1838. Colonel McNab defended the Canadian shore with a number of militia and Indians. A little steamer, the "Caroline," was used by the "Patriots" to carry supplies from Buffalo to Navy Island, and McNab determined to capture and destroy it. This he did by sending a party of men under Lieutenant Drew across the river at night, who cut the vessel from her moorings, set her on fire, and allowed her to drift over the Falls. This act of violence greatly incensed the United States Government, but an apology by the British Government smoothed over the difficulty. A little later, Navy Island was abandoned, and the frontier at Detroit and on the St. Lawrence, became the points of attack. A number of Americans crossed at the former place, took possession of Windsor, and marched on Sandwich. Colonel Prince met them with a body of militia,

GROWTH OF RESPONSIBLE GOVERNMENT. 379

defeated them, and shot four prisoners without a trial. On the St. Lawrence the most important event was the landing of a number of Americans at Windmill Point, a little below the town of Prescott. They took possession of a strong stone windmill, from which they were driven with some difficulty. The garrison, about one hundred and thirty in number, surrendered; about fifty were killed—the Canadians losing thirteen killed and a number wounded. *Battle of Windmill Point Nov. 16th, 1838.* The leaders of this raid, Von Schultz and nine of his companions, were tried and executed. The "Patriot War" was over, and Mackenzie was an exile. After many years of hardship and suffering, he was pardoned and allowed to return to Canada, and once more entered political life.

CHAPTER VI.

THE GROWTH OF RESPONSIBLE GOVERNMENT.

1. The Act of Union—1840.—The rebellion had failed because the Canadian people were loyal; nevertheless, it called the attention of the Home Government to the need of a change in the Government of the Colony. The influence of Lord Durham's report now began to be felt, and it was decided by the British Government to unite the two Provinces of Upper and Lower Canada under one Parliament. To bring this about, Charles Poulett Thompson was sent out as the Governor of Canada. No great difficulty was met with in Lower Canada, because the Lower Canadian Parliament had been suspended on account of the rebellion, and the Special Council that was acting in its place was quite willing to aid in bringing about the desired union. But the French were not quite so willing, for they feared the loss of their influence as a race. Their petitions against the union were not heeded, and the Council passed a strong resolution in favor of uniting the Provinces.

In Upper Canada the Assembly was prepared to support the project, but the Family Compact which controlled the Legislative and Executive Councils did not like the idea of losing its power, and bitterly opposed the proposed measure. Mr. Thompson, with great tact and skill, made the Compact feel that the British Government was anxious for the change, and by appeals to their loyalty induced the members of the Legislative Council to pass a resolution in favor of Union. A Bill stating the terms of the Union was now drawn up, approved of by the Parliament of Upper Canada and the Council of Lower Canada, and sent to the Imperial Parliament to be made into a law. The Bill passed the British Parliament in 1840 ; but the Union did not take place till February, 1841.

By the terms of the Union, Upper and Lower Canada were to have but one Parliament, composed of a Legislative Council with not less than twenty members appointed by the Crown for life, and a Legislative Assembly of eighty-four members—forty-two from each Province. The Executive Council was to consist of eight members, who were to be *responsible* to Parliament ; that is, the Governor was instructed by the Home Government to choose his advisers from the political party having a majority in the Assembly. The Assembly was given the control of all the revenue ; but had to make a permanent provision for the payment of judges and for other necessary expenses of government. The judges now became independent, like the judges in England, and could not be dismissed without good cause. Thus most of the demands of the people were conceded, although some years had to pass before Canada got a full measure of responsible government.

<small>Terms of the Union.</small>

2. The Municipal Act of 1841.—For his services in bringing about the Union Mr. Thompson was made a peer, with the title of Lord Sydenham. The first united Parliament met at Kingston in 1841, and it was found that the election, which followed the Union, had resulted in the two political parties being of nearly equal strength. Lord Sydenham tried to govern by means of an Executive Council composed of members of both parties ; but the Reform element, finding it difficult to work harmoniously with their political opponents, resigned office, and the Government became a Conservative Government. Nevertheless, in spite of the difficulty experienced in working the new machinery, many important measures were passed the first session.

Of these, the most important was the Municipal Act, which gave local self-government to the villages, towns, townships and counties of Upper Canada. The people of each municipality could now manage such matters as building roads, bridges, jails and court-houses, through men elected for that purpose, and who were called councillors in villages, towns and townships, and aldermen in cities. Other measures were the taking over of the Welland Canal as a government work, the placing of public works under the control of one of the members of the Executive Council or Ministry, and the encouragement of numerous enterprises for the development of the country. Unfortunately for Canada, Sydenham died from the effects of a fall from his horse, and one of the best and safest guides in political affairs Canada has ever had was removed, Sept. 19, 1841.

Municipal Act passed, 1841.

3. Sir Charles Metcalfe.—The British Government that appointed Sydenham was a Liberal Government, but it had lost power, and a Conservative Government appointed his successor. This was Sir Charles Bagot. He was a Conservative, but he pursued the same policy as Sydenham, and during his short term of office, tried to carry out the principle of responsible Government. He formed a new ministry, the principal members of which were Mr. Baldwin, Mr. Lafontaine and Mr. Francis Hincks. This was the first Reform Ministry of Canada. Bagot died in 1843, and was succeeded by Sir Charles Metcalfe, whose political experience had been gained in India and Jamaica. He was an able and upright man but utterly unfitted by his previous training for governing a colony where the people wished to manage their own affairs. He soon got into trouble with his Ministry and the Assembly. He claimed the right to make appointments to government offices, such as registrarships and shrievalties; but his advisers objected on the ground that they were responsible for all such appointments, and therefore, should recommend the persons to be appointed. As the Governor would not yield, Messrs. Baldwin and Lafontaine and all the members of the Executive Council, except one, resigned. For some time Metcalfe tried to govern without a ministry, as the Conservatives were not strong enough in the Assembly to form a Government. At length he succeeded in getting Mr. Draper to take office and form a Ministry, and then dissolved the Assembly and had a new election. In this election Sir Charles Metcalfe took an active part, and managed to get a small majority in favor of his Ministers and his policy. Soon after this, he asked to be recalled, on account of ill-health, and Earl Cathcart acted as Governor until Lord Elgin arrived in 1847.

<small>Gov. Metcalfe opposed to Responsible Government.</small>

4. Ashburton Treaty.—While Canada was thus slowly working out a free system of government some important events of another character had taken place. In 1842, England and the United States settled the boundary line between Maine and New Brunswick and between Canada and the United States as far west as the Lake of the Woods. The map that showed the boundary decided upon in 1783 had been lost, and disputes had arisen about the line between the State of Maine and New Brunswick. After various fruitless efforts to get a satisfactory decision Lord Ashburton and Daniel Webster were appointed by the British and United States governments respectively to decide what was the right boundary line. The result of the negotiation was that Webster succeeded in getting for the United States the lion's share of the disputed territory. The treaty gave seven thousand square miles to the United States and five thousand to New Brunswick. It fixed the forty-fifth parallel of latitude as the dividing line as far as the St. Lawrence, and then traced the line up that river, and through the great Lakes as far west as the Lake of the Woods. From that point west the forty-ninth parallel of latitude was to be the boundary to the Rocky Mountains. The treaty also had a clause providing for the sending back to their own country of escaped criminals accused of arson, forgery, piracy, robbery and murder. This is known as the first "Extradition Treaty."

<small>Ashburton Treaty, 1842.</small>

5. Educational Progress in Upper Canada.—More important than the Ashburton Treaty was the great change made in our Public School system by Dr. Egerton Ryerson. In 1839 the Parliament of Upper Canada had set aside two hundred and fifty thousand acres of land for the endowment of *grammar* schools; but little provision had been made for the *common* or, as we now

GROWTH OF RESPONSIBLE GOVERNMENT. 383

call them, the public schools. In 1841 Parliament granted two hundred thousand dollars a year for educational purposes; but three years later it repealed the Act. In 1844 Rev. Egerton Ryerson, a Methodist clergyman, who had taken an active part in journalism and politics, was appointed Chief Superintendent of Education for Upper Canada. He at once began to lay broad and deep the foundations of our Public School system. He crossed the Atlantic many times to examine the schools of Scotland, England, Prussia, and other European nations, and wisely selected from each system what was best adapted to a new country. His scheme was submitted to Parliament in 1846, and its main features adopted. Later on, in 1850, it was improved: and from that time to the present our Public School system has undergone many changes, all of which were intended to make it as perfect as possible. This system now provides for the free education of every child at the expense of the public; and gives each locality or district a large measure of control over its own schools, subject to the inspection and oversight of the Government. *Common School System Introduced, 1846.*

In the meantime some progress had been made in higher education. In 1841 Victoria University, at Cobourg, got its charter, and the same year Queen's College, Kingston, was founded. Both these colleges were denominational—Victoria being connected with the Methodist body, and Queen's with the Church of Scotland. King's College, Toronto, had been founded as a Church of England institution, and was put under the charge of Dr. Strachan. But the growing strength of other religious denominations soon compelled the adoption of a more liberal policy, and, in 1849, the University of Toronto (as it was now called) became a non-denominational institution and was opened to all classes of the people on the same easy terms. Dr. Strachan was not satisfied with the change, and at once took steps to establish a college under the control of the Anglican Church. The result of his efforts was the founding of Trinity University, Toronto, in 1853.

6. Lord Elgin's Administration.—When Lord Elgin reached Canada he found a bitter party conflict going on. The Draper Administration was weak and tottering to its fall. Its opponents were led by Messrs. Baldwin and Lafontaine, and the country was disquieted by an agitation over the "Rebellion Losses Bill," and by a demand from the more extreme Reformers for a different policy with regard to the Clergy Reserves. In 1840 a partial settlement had been made of the latter question by giving one half of the proceeds of the Reserves to the Church of England and the Church of Scotland, and the remaining half to the other religious denominations. This did not satisfy a large portion of the people, who thought the land should be sold, and the money received used for educational and other purposes. The other cause of disquiet, the Rebellion Losses Bill, was a measure intended to make good to the loyalists in Upper Canada the losses they had sustained by the rebellion of 1837-38. The Draper Government proposed to take the money received from certain taxes and pay the losses with it; but the members from Lower Canada demanded that the losses in Lower Canada should also be paid. An attempt was made in 1847 to satisfy the people of Lower Canada by voting a sum of money to the loyalists; but the amount was so small that it had no effect in quieting the agitation. In 1849 the Draper Government was defeated at the polls, and the famous Baldwin-Lafontaine Administration came into office.

Rebellion Losses Bill, 1849.
The Rebellion Losses Bill was once more brought into Parliament—this time by a Reform Government. It was a more sweeping measure than that of the previous administration, and proposed to pay a large sum to the injured loyalists of Lower Canada. At once a great outcry was raised that rebels were to be paid as well as loyalists, and the country was wild with excitement. Nevertheless, the Bill passed both Houses, and was assented to by Lord Elgin, who felt it his duty to act on the advice of the government, supported as it was by a large majority of the members of Parliament. This course did not please the opponents of the bill, a number of whom were foolish enough, in their excitement, to cause riots in Montreal and Toronto. In the former

Parliament Buildings burned at Montreal, 1849.
city Parliament was in session, when an infuriated mob broke in, drove out the members and ended by setting the Parliament buildings on fire. The mob prevented all attempts at saving the contents, and a very valuable library containing documents of great importance was burned. Lord Elgin was pelted with rotten eggs and stones when driving

through the city, and some of the leaders of the agitation in their excitement went so far as to talk openly of annexation to the United States. Lord Elgin asked to be recalled; but the Imperial Government commended his actions, and refused his request. As a consequence of this riot, Parliament met no more in Montreal, its sessions being held alternately every four years in Quebec and Toronto.

Soon after his arrival, in 1847, Lord Elgin announced at the opening of Parliament that the duties in favour of British goods had been removed by the British Parliament and that henceforth Canada would be free to *Commercial Freedom.* place on goods coming into the country such duties as she wished. At the same time the Governor advised the building of a railroad from Halifax to Quebec. We shall find that it took many years to carry this proposal into effect. The same year saw a great immigration of people from Ireland due to the terrible failure of the potato crop in that unhappy land. Thousands of ill-fed and ill-clad people were crowded into the vessels crossing the Atlantic, and, in consequence, fever and pestilence broke out in the ships. When they reached Canada this pestilence spread along the frontier and many people besides the poor immigrants died.

7. Commercial Progress.—Let us now see what the people of Canada had been doing since the Union in opening up the country and in acquiring wealth. We have already pointed out that for a long time Canada had few means of taking her products to distant markets, and was dependent on the boats that navigated her lakes and rivers. This state of things now began to change rapidly. The need of better means of carrying goods and the products of farm and shop to market led to the building of railroads through the more thickly settled parts of the country. The first line built was one between La Prairie and St. *Railway era.* John's in Lower Canada, which was opened for traffic in 1836. The first road begun in Upper Canada was the Northern Railway, the first sod of which was turned in 1851. Then came in rapid succession the Great Western and the Grand Trunk, the latter receiving from the Government important aid. These roads helped very much in opening up for settlement the north, west, and east of Canada, and made the farms of the settlers much more valuable. In 1852 the Municipal Loan Fund Act was passed, which gave the Government power to lend money to towns, villages, and other municipalities for local improvements, such as roads, bridges, and public buildings. The terms were very easy, and many municipalities got so heavily in debt that they were unable to pay back to the Government either principal or interest. There are many municipalities in Canada that yet feel the burden of a foolish extravagance at this time. Besides, there was in Canada, as elsewhere, a kind of railway craze, and a great deal of money was spent on roads that did not pay for their construction. Parliament was too free in making grants to railroads and other public works, and the result was that Canada began to have a heavy public debt, which has ever since been steadily growing. In 1851 another event of importance took place : the Canadian Government was given the control of the Post-office, and immediately established a uniform rate of postage—threepence on every half-ounce—and, besides, introduced the use of postage stamps. Before this, when a letter was sent or received, postage had to be paid in money. In 1846 England adopted Free Trade as her policy, and a few years after threw open her markets to all countries on the same terms. For a time this injured Canadian farmers and producers, who had not as good means of carrying their products to English markets as the Americans. But with the building of railroads and the establishment of better lines of steamships the evil was lessened, and Canada prospered greatly, increasing rapidly in both wealth and population. This prosperity was partly due to a very important treaty made in 1854, through the tact and wisdom of Lord Elgin. In that year Canada and the United States agreed upon a Reciprocity Treaty, by which the products of the sea, the farm, the mine, and the forest could be freely exchanged. The United States obtained the right to fish in many of Canada's waters and the use of the St. Lawrence and Canadian canals ; while Canada, in return, was given the right to navigate Lake Michigan. The treaty was to continue ten years from March, 1855, and after that could be ended by twelve months' notice from either party.

8. The Clergy Reserves and Seignorial Tenure.—

Meanwhile, political agitation was going on over two burning questions. One was the old grievance of the Clergy Reserves, which the Baldwin-Lafontaine Administration hoped had been settled in 1840. But a strong and growing body of the more radical Reformers, led by George Brown, the editor and manager of the *Globe*, a powerful political newspaper, wished to take the Reserves away from the denominations and use them for the general good of the Province. The other question, that of Seignorial Tenure, was one of great interest to the people of Lower Canada. It was seen that holding land under the old French system of feudal tenure was a great hindrance to the prosperity of the farmers of that Province; the services and payments by the peasants to the "seigneurs" having become a grievous burden as the Province became better settled and the land more valuable. It was found impossible to dispose of one question without dealing with the other; so in 1854, the Reform Government of Mr. Hincks having been defeated by a temporary union of the extreme wing of the Reformers with the Conservatives, the new Conservative Ministry of Sir Allan McNab, brought in two bills : the one to divide the Clergy Reserves among the different municipalities of Upper Canada according to population, the proceeds to be used by them for local improvements or for educational purposes ; the other, to abolish Seignorial Tenure, and to allow the land in Lower Canada to be held by the people as *freeholds*. In both cases compensation was made by Parliament for the losses the clergy and the seigneurs suffered by the change. In this way two grievances of long standing were happily removed, and the last link uniting Church and State in Upper Canada was broken. Two other political changes must be noted. In 1853, the population having increased greatly since the Union, the number of members of the Legislative Assembly was increased from eighty-four to one hundred and thirty, each Province still having an equal number of members. Three years later, the Legislative Council became an elective body, the existing members retaining their positions for life. The population of Upper Canada was now fully one million and a quarter, and that of Lower Canada about three hundred thousand less.

Clergy Reserves and Seignorial Tenure Acts, 1854.

9. A Political Dead-Lock.—A curious state of affairs now arose in Canada. The old political parties became shattered, and new alliances were formed. In Upper Canada the more advanced Reformers gained great influence, and began agitating for a change in the basis of representation in Parliament. They claimed that as Upper Canada was more populous and wealthy than Lower Canada, and paid more taxes, it should send more members to Parliament. Against this it was urged that at the time of the Union Lower Canada had a larger population, greater wealth, and a smaller public debt than Upper Canada—yet, it was given the same number of representatives. It was, therefore, contended that Lower Canada should continue to have as many members of parliament as Upper Canada. The agitation was continued for many years, and parties became nearly equally divided on the question of "Representation by Population" as it was called. On the one side was a majority of the members from Upper Canada, and a minority from Lower Canada; while opposed to the new policy was a minority from Upper Canada, and a majority from Lower Canada. John A. Macdonald and George Etienne Cartier were prominent leaders of the Conservative party; George Brown, William McDougall and A. A. Dorion the principal advocates of "Representation by Population" and the Reform policy. Several administrations were defeated in the years between 1858 and 1864, and finally it became evident some change in the constitution must take place if good government was to continue.

Representation by Population agitation.

10. Steps towards Confederation.—In 1864 a dead-lock of political parties was reached, and the leaders of both sides recognizing the danger, dropped their feuds, and united to form a Coalition Government, which had for its object the Confederation of the Provinces of Upper and Lower Canada, and, if possible, also those of the Maritime Provinces. The principle of this Confederation was suggested by the form of Government in the adjoining Republic; the object aimed at being to give the several Provinces the control of their own local affairs, matters of general interest to be managed by a common parliament in which all the provinces would be represented. Several things helped along the movement. In 1860 George Brown had proposed in Parliament the principle of such a scheme, but his resolution was lost by a large majority. The country was not then ready for its adoption. But when, in 1864, circumstances forced the policy on both parties, it was found that not only Canada but the Maritime Provinces were discussing Confederation A Conference or gathering of delegates from these provinces was called to meet in September at Charlottetown, in Prince Edward Island, to arrange for a union, and the Canadian Government asked and received permission to send delegates. At this gathering the Confederation of all the Provinces was seriously discussed. It was decided to call another Conference at Quebec in November, and to invite all the provinces to be present through their delegates. The Conference met, and after much deliberation, the outlines of a scheme of Confederation were approved of by Upper Canada, Lower Canada, Nova Scotia, and New Brunswick. Prince Edward Island and Newfoundland had withdrawn from the Conference, the terms proposed not being agreeable to them. The delegates separated to report to their respective Parliaments, which soon after, in 1865, agreed to the scheme and made the necessary arrangements to get the consent of the British Parliament. In 1866, delegates from the different provinces met in London to draft a Bill for submission to the Imperial Parliament. This Bill was finally passed on the 28th February 1867, and, under the name of the British North America Act, is the law which defines our present constitution. It came into force on the 1st of July, 1867. But its passage was not satisfactory to all the provinces. Nova Scotia was brought into Confederation against its will—its Government having accepted the terms without asking the consent of the people. Remonstrances and petitions were sent to the British Parliament; but they were of no avail. The British Government thought that the discontent would soon die away, and that the British possessions in America would be safer and stronger under Confederation, against possible attacks from the United States, than existing as colonies independent of each other.

Charlottetown Conference 1864.

Quebec Conference, 1864.

British N. A. Act passed, Feb'y. 28th, 1867.

11. Minor Events of Importance.—Before giving the

terms of this Confederation Act, we must notice some things of less importance, which had taken place while Canada was working out her future form of government. In 1854 our Volunteer system was introduced. Before this the Militia had very little drill, and when danger threatened the country, its defence, for a time, depended upon the few regular troops stationed in Canada. Now the young men were encouraged to volunteer and form companies and regiments under their own officers, so that, should an invasion be attempted, there would always be thousands of active men, with some knowledge of drill, ready to resist. In 1858 Bytown or Ottawa, on the Ottawa river, became the fixed place for Parliament to meet. This site was chosen by the Queen, and its choice gave rise to much dissatisfaction on the part of the larger cities. More important to the welfare of the country was the introduction in 1858 of *decimal* currency, whereby we began to reckon in dollars and cents instead of in pounds, shillings and pence; and the completion of a long bridge across the St. Lawrence at Montreal, which was opened by the Prince of Wales in the summer of 1860, under the name of the Victoria Bridge.

Volunteer System begun, 1854.

Decimal Currency introduced, 1858.

In 1861, a civil war began in the United States between the Northern and Southern States, and lasted for four years. It affected Canada in many ways. For a time it made good prices for nearly all the Canadian farmer had to sell, raised the wages of mechanics, and gave good profits to the merchants. On the other hand, there was a serious danger of a war between England and the North, arising out of the sympathy and secret help the people of England gave the South. Many Canadians crossed the frontier to fight in the armies of the North, and many Southerners took refuge in Canada, some of whom made raids across the border into the villages and towns of the North. These raids created a bad feeling towards Canada, so that when the war was over and the Reciprocity Treaty expired in 1866, the United States Government refused to renew it. Canada also suffered from the ill-will of the American Government in another way. On the 1st of June, a body of ruffians called Fenians, and belonging to a secret society having for its object the separation of Ireland from Great Britain, crossed the frontier at

Reciprocity Treaty expires, 1866.

Black Rock, took possession of the ruins of old Fort Erie, and threatened the Niagara peninsula. A number of Volunteers from Toronto and Hamilton were at once sent to join some regular troops under Colonel Peacock, at Chippewa, but before they could accomplish this they met the raiders at Ridgeway, and, in a badly managed skirmish, were driven back with several killed and wounded. *Ridgeway, June 1st., 1866.*

Soon after, Colonel Peacock with the regulars arrived, and the Fenians recrossed to the American side, leaving a few stragglers behind, some of whom were captured, tried, and condemned to death. Their sentences, through the clemency of the Crown, were changed to imprisonment in the Penitentiary. Attacks were also threatened at Prescott, St. Albans and other points on the border, but the watchfulness of the Canadian volunteers prevented any serious attempt being made to invade the country. After a long delay the American authorities put a stop to these raids, which, had the feeling of the United States towards Canada been more friendly, might never have taken place. In one way these attacks did good. They made the British Provinces feel the need of a closer union, and this, doubtless, hastened the formation of the Confederation. *Effect of Fenian raids.*

CHAPTER VII.

NOVA SCOTIA AND NEW BRUNSWICK.

1. Nova Scotia.—We have now to trace the history of a new and larger Canada. Henceforth it is the Dominion of Canada about which we must speak. We must, also, drop the old names Upper Canada and Lower Canada, and use instead for these provinces—the new names Ontario and Quebec. For when Nova Scotia and New Brunswick joined in the Confederation, it was decided, to prevent confusion, to change the names of the provinces of Old Canada. *Change in names of Upper and Lower Canada.*

In many respects the history of Nova Scotia and New Brunswick is very similar to that of Upper and Lower Canada. As in Lower Canada, the first settlers of Nova Scotia were French, the first settlement being made by De Monts, in 1605, at Port Royal (now Annapolis), a little earlier than that at Quebec by Champlain. The Cabots, it is said, first discovered the country, and on that ground Nova Scotia was claimed as an English possession.

<small>Port Royal founded, 1605.</small> The little colony at Port Royal did not prosper, and in 1614 an English expedition from Virginia took the fort, destroyed it, and then sailed away. At that time the province was called Acadia, and included the present provinces of Nova Scotia and New Brunswick, but in 1624 it was given by England to Sir William Alexander, and he named it Nova Scotia. Between 1624 and 1713 Port Royal changed ownership many times, belonging alternately to the English and the French until the Treaty of Utrecht, when it passed finally into the possession of the English.

At this time its name was changed to Annapolis, in honor of the English Queen Anne. Not only Port Royal, but all Acadia, was by this treaty given to the English. English settlers <small>Halifax founded, 1749.</small> slowly found their way to the Province, and the city of Halifax was founded in 1749. But the French inhabitants and the Micmac Indians were not satisfied with the change of ownership, and plots against British rule were entered into between the French inside and the French outside the Province. All efforts to get the Acadians to take the oath of allegiance to the British king failed, and as the English settlements in the Province were in constant danger of attacks from the neighboring French and their Indian allies, it was decided to re- <small>Expulsion of Acadians, 1755.</small> move the Acadians from their homes and carry them to a French colony at the mouth of the Mississippi. This severe sentence was carried out in 1755. The sad story of the Expulsion of the Acadians is told in the beautiful and pathetic poem "Evangeline," by Longfellow. The constant fear of attacks from the French was removed when, in 1758, the strong fortress of Louisburg, in Cape Breton, was captured by Wolfe. The conquest of Canada and the Peace of Paris followed, and Nova Scotia, Cape Breton, and Prince Edward Island were surrendered to the British. Until 1784 Nova Scotia, New Brunswick, Prince Edward Island, and Cape Breton formed one Province. Then New Brunswick, Prince Edward Island, and Cape Breton became separate Provinces, but the last named was again joined to Nova Scotia in 1819. A Constitution was given to Nova Scotia in 1758, so that it had representative institutions many years before Lower Canada. It was to be governed by a joint Executive and Legislative Council, appointed by the Crown, and by an Assembly elected by the people. This form of Government did not succeed much better than the similar form in the two Canadas, and for the same reason. *[New Brunswick, Cape Breton, and P. E. Island secede.]*

The Revolutionary war of the United States caused some discontent and excitement in the province, and efforts were made to turn the people over to the side of the revolting colonies; but without success. After the war many U. E. Loyalists settled in Nova Scotia; and soon the new settlers began to agitate for a more just and liberal form of government. The agitation was carried on in much the same fashion as in Upper Canada, but it did not lead to rebellion. The same abuses existed as in Upper and Lower Canada, and after a severe political struggle, in which Joseph Howe played an important part, Responsible Government was granted in 1848. *[Responsible Government secured, 1848.]* Nova Scotia had made considerable progress by this time; her fisheries, forests, mines, and fertile lands being sources of wealth. Her inhabitants were remarkably strong, vigorous, and intelligent people, many of them being of U. E. Loyalist and Scotch descent. Her schools and colleges were generously supported by the Government, and education, before Confederation, had become pratically free to all her people. Of her colleges, King's, Windsor, was founded in 1788, and Dalhousie, Halifax, in 1820.

Railways were gradually introduced, but not to the same extent as in Upper Canada; and an Intercolonial Railway between the different British Provinces of North America had often been suggested. This, in brief, was the state of affairs when Nova Scotia through her delegates at the Quebec Conference consented to become part of the Dominion of Canada. These delegates, however, did not represent the opinions of the people of Nova Scotia, and a bitter agitation against Confederation began under the old Reform leader, Joseph Howe. In vain the Province, through its Assembly, petitioned against the Union, and sent Howe to England to oppose the passage of the British North America Act. The British Government would not listen to the appeal, and Nova Scotia entered Confederation much in the same fashion as old Scotia entered the Union with England over one hundred and fifty years before. Let us hope that our Confederation may have the same happy results as the Union of 1707.

<small>Nova Scotia opposed to Confederation.</small>

2. New Brunswick.—Until 1784 New Brunswick was a part of Nova Scotia, and its history to that time is therefore the history of Nova Scotia. Its earliest settlements were at the mouth of the St. John River, and like the settlements at Port Royal were made by the French. After the American Revolutionary War, thousands of United Empire Loyalists settled in the province; many of them in the neighbourhood of the present city of St. John. These new settlers were dissatisfied because they were not given fair representation in the Legislative Assembly, and petitioned to have a new province formed independent of Nova Scotia. In 1784 the Home Government granted their petition, and the result was the formation of the present province of New Brunswick, with a government similar to that of Nova Scotia. Fredericton became its capital, although its chief town was St. John. The people of this province did not pay the same attention to farming as the settlers of the other provinces, because the very valuable timber and fisheries of the country made it more profitable to engage in lumbering and fishing than in tilling the soil. In 1809, Britain laid a tax on timber brought from the Baltic, and in this way encouraged the timber trade of New Brunswick.

<small>United Empire Loyalists settle in New Brunswick, 1784.</small>

Its ports became noted not only for their timber trade, but also for ship-building. After the war of 1812-14, many disbanded soldiers settled in the province, and, as in Upper Canada, received liberal grants of land. But a serious disaster in 1825, checked the prosperity of the province. The summer of this year was very hot and dry, and bush fires raged fiercely. On the 7th of October, a terrible wave of fire

<small>Great Fire, 1825.</small>

swept over the country, from Miramichi to the Bay of Chaleurs. Five thousand square miles of forest and farm, village and town, were made desolate, and hundreds of lives were lost. The political atmosphere, too, was troubled for many years. The struggle for responsible government took place in this province as elsewhere in British America, and New Brunswick had its Family Compact as well as Upper Canada. But, unlike Upper Canada, its rights were won without rebellion and bloodshed. In 1837, the control of the revenue was given to the Assembly, and in 1848, responsible government was fully conceded. In these struggles for freedom to manage its own affairs, Lemuel Allan Wilmot took a prominent part as a champion of the people. The dispute about the boundary line between Maine and New Brunswick kept the province in a state of alarm and uncertainty for years; and at one time it was feared that the quarrels along the border for possession of the disputed territory would lead to war. The Ashburton Treaty, in 1842, resulted, as we have seen, in taking away from New Brunswick a large territory which rightfully belonged to it. In the twenty years before Confederation, by means of railways and steamboats, great progress was made in opening up the country; in extending the trade of the province, although the timber trade was threatened with injury by the removal of the duties from timber exported from the Baltic to England; and in improving the educational system of the province. Good public schools were established; and among other colleges, the University of Fredericton and Mt. Allison College at Sackville, were founded. The former is a state college, the latter is connected with the Methodist denomination.

Responsible Government 1848.

Ashburton Treaty 1842.

The story of the Union with the other provinces has already been told. As in Nova Scotia there was strong opposition to Confederation, and in the first election held after the Quebec Conference, the Confederation party was badly beaten at the polls. For a time it seemed as if New Brunswick would refuse to proceed any further with the scheme, but the Home Government was anxious for Confederation, as also were the Governor and the Legislative Council. These influences, aided by the alarm caused by the Fenian invasion, helped

Confederation accepted, 1866.

to bring about a change in the popular feeling, and another election being held the Confederation party was successful. Union resolutions were now passed, and delegates sent to London to aid in framing the British North America Act.

CHAPTER VIII.

CANADA SINCE CONFEDERATION.

1. The British North America Act.—We must now give the terms on which the four Provinces, Ontario, Quebec, Nova Scotia, and New Brunswick, agreed to share a common lot. The principle of their union was that each Province should manage its own local affairs, and leave to the Dominion the control of matters which were of common benefit and interest. To carry out this principle it was necessary to have local Legislatures or Parliaments, as well as a general or Dominion Parliament. This part of the scheme was suggested by, if not borrowed from, the system of government existing in the United States. But in several very important respects the United States model was not copied. Perhaps the most important difference was the retention of Cabinet or Responsible Government in the management of all our affairs, whether belonging to the Dominion or to the Provinces. Again, in the United States each State is free to make its own laws, so long as it does not go beyond the bounds of the Constitution; but in Canada it was agreed that the Governor-General, on the advice of his Ministers, should have the power to *veto*, or forbid from becoming law, any measure passed by the local Parliaments, if these measures were thought to be hurtful to the general welfare of the Dominion. The Provinces were given the control of many matters such as education; the appointment of courts of justice (but not of the judges); the management of Crown lands within the Province; asylums and jails; the regulation of the sale of intoxicating liquors; and the general power of enforcing the laws. They were permitted to raise a revenue by *direct* but not by *indirect* taxation ; that is, they could impose such taxes as were paid only by the people on whom they were placed, but not such taxes as duties on goods coming in or going out of the country, which are called *Customs*, or taxes on articles made in the country, which we call *Excise*. Custom and *Excise* duties are supposed to be paid eventually by the people who buy the goods and use them, and not by the seller or manufacturer. One of the important benefits expected to come from Confederation was the removal of the barriers preventing the different Provinces from trading with each other. To make it impossible for one Province to tax the goods coming into it from another Province, the Dominion Parliament was given the sole right of raising a revenue by Custom or Excise duties. This, however, would make it very difficult for the Provinces to collect money enough to defray their expenses; therefore it was arranged that the Dominion should pay the Provinces annually a large sum out of its revenue, in return for the right to collect these duties. Besides this right of *indirect* taxation the Dominion kept the control of the Militia, the Post-office, the currency, the penitentiaries, the appointment of judges, the construction and management of the more important public works, and the control of all Crown lands not belonging to any of the Provinces. To carry out this scheme it was necessary to have a good deal of political machinery ; so each Province was given a Lieutenant-Governor, appointed by the Governor-General of the Dominion for a term of years, a Legislature elected by the people for four years, and, if the Province wished it, a Legislative Council or Senate. Of the four Provinces Ontario was the only one that felt content to do without a Legislative Council. In each Province there was to be an Executive Council, or Ministry, responsible to the people through their representatives in the Legislature. The Dominion Parliament was to have, as its head, a Governor-General, appointed by the Crown; a Senate, composed of members from the different Provinces, and appointed by the Governor-General for life, and a House of Commons elected by the people. Each Province was given a certain number of senators, Ontario being given twenty-four, Quebec twenty-four, and Nova Scotia and New Brunswick twenty-four ; in all, seventy-two. The number of members of the House of Commons, at the outset, was to be one hundred and eighty-one, of which Quebec sent sixty-five, Ontario eighty-two, Nova Scotia nineteen, and New Brunswick fifteen. A census was to be taken every ten years, and the number of members given to each Province was to be regulated by the population; Quebec to send sixty-five, and the other Provinces in proportion to their population. In this way the problem of "Representation by Population" was solved. The real government of the Dominion was to be in the hands of an Executive Council, chosen by the Governor-General from the political party having a majority in the House of Commons, and was to consist, at first, of thirteen members. The Governor-General could reserve any law passed by the Dominion Parliament for the sanction of the Home Government; and, on the advice of his Council, could, within a year from the time of its passing, veto any bill passed by a local Parliament. This power of veto was given because it was feared that the Provinces might pass laws injurious to the Dominion as a whole, or hurtful to the rights of some of the people in them. Having settled the terms of the political partnership, it was thought that there would be a closer union if a railroad were built between the Maritime Provinces and Quebec. It was, therefore, agreed that the long-talked-of Inter-Colonial Railway should be constructed from Halifax to Quebec, the British Government to give its aid in carrying out the costly scheme.

2. New Provinces.—The principal events of our history since confederation must now be told very briefly, for this part of our history is so recent, that we cannot say yet, which of its events are the most important, or whether some things that have taken place since confederation are for the good of Canada, or not.

The first Governor-General of the Dominion was Lord Monck, and his Prime Minister was Sir John A. Macdonald, who had taken a leading part along with the Hon. George Brown in carrying through the Confederation scheme. His principal colleagues were Sir George E. Cartier from Quebec, the Hon. Chas. Tupper from Nova Scotia, and the Hon. S. L. Tilley from New Brunswick. The first Prime Minister of Ontario was the Hon. John Sandfield Macdonald, the Lieutenant-Governor being the Hon. William P. Howland. The majority of the people of the Dominion were content to give the new constitution a fair trial, except the people of Nova Scotia. In the first parliament elected after the union, the members from that province were nearly all opposed to confederation, and had to be quieted by the grant of "better terms."

In 1868, steps were taken to get possession of the vast territory held by the Hudson Bay Company in the North-West. This territory, known as "Prince Rupert's Land," had been given to the Hudson Bay Company in 1670 by King Charles II. of England, and had been used by it, for two hundred years, to carry on a profitable trade in furs. The value of this territory was but little known, and the Company fearful of losing its charter always strove to make the English people believe that it was fit for nothing except grazing buffaloes, and providing trapping grounds for Indians. A very few settlers had made their way into this unknown and lone land—the only settlement of importance being at Red River where Lord Selkirk had founded a colony in 1811. The whole population numbered but ten thousand souls, and was gathered mainly at the different trading-posts.

The charter of the Company was expiring, and the Canadian Government induced the British Parliament to pass an Act by which the North-West or Hudson Bay Territory could be surrendered to Canada, on payment of the just claims of the Company. Canada offered to give the Company three hundred thousand pounds sterling, one twentieth of the land, and the right to retain their trading privileges. The offer was accepted. Unfortunately, little thought was given to the small settlement of French and half-breeds on the Red River when taking possession of the country, and making provision for its future government. Surveyors were set to work near Fort Garry at the junction of the Red and Assiniboine rivers, and the inhabitants became alarmed lest their lots and homes should be taken from them. The necessary steps were not taken to quiet their fears, and when Hon. Wm. McDougall endeavored to enter the new Province of Manitoba, as its Governor, he found his way barred by an armed force. The chief leaders of the revolt were Louis Riel, a Frenchman, with some Indian blood in his veins, and M. Lepine. A Provisional Government was formed by these men, and they made prisoners of all who were supposed to be

Acquisition of the North-West, 1870.

Red River Rebellion, 1869-70.

in sympathy with the Canadian government. Among others thus seized was Thomas Scott, a brave, outspoken, loyal subject. For some reason or other Riel had taken a strong personal dislike to Scott, and, after giving him the form of a trial, had him sentenced to be shot. The sentence was carried out under circumstances of great brutality, in March 1870. When the news reached Ontario there was great excitement, and when, a few months after, volunteers were called for, to go with General Wolseley to crush the rebellion, thousands of young men offered their services. Only the best fitted to endure hardship were chosen, and when, after a long and trying march over what was known as the Dawson Road, they reached Fort Garry, they found the rebels scattered and everything quiet.

Thomas Scott murdered, 1870.

Many of these volunteers received grants of land in the new province and became permanent settlers. Soon there began to rise at Fort Garry a prairie city which, to-day, is the fine flourishing capital of the province of Manitoba—the city of Winnipeg. In 1870 the "Manitoba Act" was passed. It defined the limits of the Province of Manitoba, and stated how it was to be governed. Its form of government is very much the same as that of Ontario; and, like Ontario, it decided to do without a "Second Chamber" or Legislative Council. It was given the right to send four members to the House of Commons, and was allotted two senators. The next year saw the admission of another province to the Confederation. This was British Columbia on the Pacific Coast, which, separated from the rest of the Dominion by the Rocky mountains, made it a condition of becoming a part of the Dominion that a railway should be constructed across the prairies and through the Rocky Mountains, so as to connect British Columbia with the Eastern provinces. Although the population of this new province was very small, it was given six members in the House of Commons and three in the Senate.

Manitoba Act passed, 1870.

British Columbia joins the Confederation, 1871.

Two years after, still another province was added to the growing Dominion. Prince Edward Island, which in 1866 refused to become a part of the Confederation, was now willing to cast in its lot with the other provinces. This little island with its hardy and intelligent population formerly belonged to Nova Scotia; but in

1784 it received a separate government. Its history before 1873 was much the same as that of Nova Scotia and New Brunswick, except that it had trouble in connection with the way its land had been parcelled out to a number of men called "proprietors," who did not live on the island, and yet refused to give up their claims to those who were the actual tillers of the soil. The Legislative Council of Prince Edward Island was elective; in this respect it differed from the other provinces. On entering Confederation it was given six members in the House of Commons and four in the Senate. No new territory has since been added to the Dominion; but the North-West has been divided into districts, and given a form of government, consisting of a Lieutenant-Governor and Council, in which the people have a slight control over their own local affairs. They have also been given representation in the House of Commons—four members at present being returned from the four districts, Assiniboia, Alberta, Saskatchewan and Athabasca.

Prince Edward Island admitted, 1873.

3. Political Changes.—The party struggles that embittered the politics of Canada before Confederation were dropped for a short time after the Union of the provinces, only to be renewed with almost equal intensity at the general election of 1872. The Government of Sir John A. Macdonald had aroused strong opposition by its share in the Washington Treaty, and its mode of dealing with the proposed Pacific railway. Several points were in dispute between England and the United States, and between the United States and Canada. During the Civil War between the North and South the English authorities had carelessly allowed some vessels, fitted out in British ports, to escape to sea, where they were used by the South to attack and plunder the merchant vessels of the North. The most notorious of these vessels was the "Alabama," which did a great deal of harm to the shipping of the North. After the war was over, the United States claimed damages for injuries caused by this vessel, and the matter was left for peaceable settlement to a "Joint High Commission" of which Sir John A. Macdonald was a member. Canada was greatly interested in this Commission, for she had claims against the United States for injuries inflicted by the Fenians. Besides, the ownership of San Juan, an island on the Pacific coast, and the boundary line between Canada and Alaska were in dispute. The Americans, too, were anxious, now that the Reciprocity Treaty was no longer in force, to get fishing privileges in Canadian waters. The Commision met, in 1871, at Washington, and agreed to submit the Alabama Claims to arbitration, the result being that the United States received $15,500,000 for the supposed injuries inflicted by the Alabama on her commerce. The claims of Canada for damages on account of the Fenian raids were not even considered; but England, as a slight compensation, agreed to guarantee for Canada a loan of £2,500,000.

The dispute about the island of San Juan was left to the Emperor of Germany for his decision, which was given the next year in favor of the United States. The Treaty also gave the United States the use of Canadian fisheries for twelve years, in return for the use of their fisheries, and the right to sell fish and fish-oil in United States markets. As this was not considered enough for the use of the valuable Canadian fisheries, a commission was to meet at Halifax later on and decide what sum of money should be paid the Dominion by the United States as an equivalent. This Halifax Commission met in 1878, during the Mackenzie Administration, and awarded $5,500,000 to Canada; the success of this negotiation being due largely to the fact that it was conducted on behalf of Canada by Canadians; Sir Alexander Galt being the principal Canadian representative.

Washington Treaty, 1871.

Halifax Commission, 1878.

The other cause of political feeling, the building of the Pacific Railway, arose out of the agreement with British Columbia, when that province entered Confederation, that an all-rail route should be built in ten years from Ontario to the Pacific. Many thought such a bargain could not be carried out, that the time was too short, and the cost too great. The elections of 1872 were fought mainly on this issue, and resulted in a majority for the government. The next year Mr. Huntington, the member of Parliament for Shefford, made a formal charge in Parliament that the government had agreed to give a charter to Sir Hugh Allan to build the Pacific Railway, in return for large sums of money to carry the elections. The charge, and the publication of certain letters bearing upon this alleged corrupt bargain, caused great excitement in the Dominion, and after a fierce struggle in Parliament, the government resigned.

Pacific Scandal, 1873.

The Governor-General, Lord Dufferin, called upon the Hon. Alexander Mackenzie, the leader of the Liberal Party, to form a government. Mr. Mackenzie accepted the trust, and after forming a ministry, of which the principal members were the Hon. Edward Blake from Ontario and the Hon. A. A. Dorion from Quebec, asked for a new election. This took place in January, 1874, and resulted in giving a very large majority to the new government. Mr. Mackenzie continued in office till 1878, when his government was defeated on the question of a trade policy for the country. There was a general commercial depression at this time and Canada, with other countries, felt the pinch of hard times. A great many thought that the industries of the country would be benefited if the tariff was raised and foreign goods competing with Canadian products kept out. This policy of "protection" was opposed by the Mackenzie government, but, when the elections took place in September 1878, it was found that the doctrines of the "National Policy" were very popular, and, in consequence, Sir John A. Macdonald, who had advocated them, was once more called to be Prime Minister of Canada. That position he held till his death, which took place June 6th, 1891. He was succeeded in the Premiership by Hon. J. J. C. Abbott, who at the time of writing holds the office. ^{"National Policy" adopted, 1878.}

4. Important Laws.—Amid all this strife many measures became law, some, at least, of which will likely remain for years on the Statute-book. In 1874, during the Mackenzie Administration, a Ballot Act was passed, which provided for secret voting by ballot, instead of "open voting." This reform was introduced to prevent bribery and intimidation, which were very common under the old system of "open voting." It is very doubtful whether the Act has had all the effect on bribery it was expected to have. Another and a later law bearing on elections was the Dominion Franchise Act, which made the right to vote for member of the Dominion Parliament the same throughout the Dominion. Previous to this Act the franchises for Dominion elections were the same as the franchises in the several Provinces. This Act was passed in 1885, and, besides making the franchise uniform, it greatly increased the number of voters, so much so, ^{Ballot Act, 1874.} ^{Uniform Franchise Act, 1885.}

that now nearly every man twenty-one years of age, and over, has a vote. Before this was passed another measure, which created a great deal of ill-feeling, became law. This was the Redistribution Bill of 1882, which seriously changed the boundaries of the constituencies of Ontario, for the purpose, it was said by the Government, of equalizing the number of electors in the different constituencies. The Liberals complained that the changes were made so as to give their Conservative opponents an unfair advantage in the coming elections.

Among other political measures since Confederation we must notice the increase in the number of representatives in Parliament—there being now ninety-two from Ontario, sixty-five from Quebec, sixteen from New Brunswick, twenty-one from Nova Scotia, six from Prince Edward Island, five from Manitoba, six from British Columbia, and four from the North-West Territories. A Supreme Court of Appeal was established in 1875, to avoid the expense of taking appeals from Canada to the British Privy Council; although appeals are yet allowed to the Privy Council, and are frequently taken there. Then again, in 1879, a new tariff was framed, which greatly increased the duties on foreign goods; and although every session changes are made, yet they are generally arranged for the purpose of "protecting native industries."

5. Provincial Legislation.—Though many important laws have been passed by the Dominion Parliament, equally important measures have been enacted by the Provincial Legislatures. These laws deal with a great many subjects, such as education; the regulation of the liquor traffic; aid to railways; the establishment of asylums for the deaf, dumb, blind, and insane; the better management of prisons; the sale of timber limits; mining regulations; and improvements in our municipal laws. In Ontario, under the long administration of Hon. Oliver Mowat which began in 1872, two very important laws have been passed—one dealing satisfactorily with the indebtedness of municipalties to the Municipal Loan Fund, and the other, with the regulation of the liquor traffic. The latter, popularly known as the Crooks' Act (so called from the Hon. Adam Crooks, its framer), has done a great deal to lessen drunkenness, vice, and crime. Then again, the franchise has been greatly extended in the different

Municipal Loan Fund Debt Bill and Crooks' Act.

provinces, and voting by ballot, except for school trustees, has been made compulsory. Unmarried women and widows in Ontario, with the necessary property qualification, have been given the right to vote in municipal elections, but not in elections for members of either the Provincial or Dominion Parliament. In Prince Edward Island the difficulty with the "proprietors" has been settled in the interests of the people. Quebec has, by the payment of four hundred thousand dollars, disposed of the "Jesuit Estates" question, while Manitoba has secured the right to build railways within her borders. Ontario has had several legal conflicts with the Dominion as to her proper boundaries, her right to regulate the liquor traffic, and for right to control the crown lands in her territory, all of which questions have been decided by the British Privy Council in favor of the Province. The exercise of the right to *veto* provincial laws has caused some friction between the Provinces and the Dominion ; but the wise decisions of the British Privy Council have led to a strong feeling in the Dominion against interfering with provincial legislation. To avoid any undue influence being exercised by the Dominion over the Provinces, members of the Dominion Parliament are not allowed to be members of Provincial Legislatures.

6. The North-West Rebellion.—One painful incident in our history must now be told. In 1885 a number of French Half-breeds, who had settled on the Saskatchewan River, in the Northwest, rose in revolt against the Dominion, and induced several Indian tribes to join them. The cause of this rebellion was the fear these people had that their lands were to be taken from them and given to the incoming settlers. Surveyors had been sent among them, and this excited fears, which were not regarded until it was too late to prevent mischief. There were also complaints of ill-treatment and neglect of duty by Dominion officers in the North-West, and the petitions of the half-breeds and Indians did not receive prompt attention from the proper authorities. The result was that the excited half-breeds sent for Louis Riel, who was living in the United States, to advise and lead them. One false step led to another, until the discontent broke out in an attack, led by Gabriel Dumont, North-West Rebellion 1885.

on some armed Police and volunteers at Duck Lake, in March, 1885. Several of the volunteers were killed, and open rebellion spread over a wide district, a number of Indian chiefs with their followers joining in the revolt. A large force of volunteers, under General Middleton, was sent in the depth of winter 'from Quebec and Ontario to crush the rebellion. Aided by the Mounted Police, and the volunteers of Manitoba and the North-West, the rising was speedily brought to an end, the last important and decisive engagement taking place at Batoche, where Riel was captured. Many lives were lost in the campaign, and great hardships were endured by the volunteers, half-breeds, and settlers, before this needless outbreak was suppressed. Riel and several Indians were tried for treason and murder; some, among whom was Riel, were executed, the remainder being either imprisoned or pardoned. The execution of Riel caused great excitement in Quebec, where considerable sympathy was felt for the people he so sadly led astray. The rebellion had its uses—for an inquiry was made into the grievances of the Indians and half-breeds, and many of the causes of complaint removed.

Execution of Riel 1885.

7. Material Progress.—Since Confederation there has been a marked change in the material condition of the country. Railways now reach nearly every part of the older Provinces, whilst the territories in the North-West and British Columbia have been connected with the great world of trade by the Canadian Pacific Railway. This great enterprise was completed in 1886, the first sod being turned in May, 1881. A portion of the road had been partly built by the Mackenzie Government; but after that Government was defeated the contract was given to a strong company of capitalists, the chief members of which were Canadians, the company agreeing to build the road for a subsidy of $25,000,000, and 25,000,000 acres of land in the fertile districts of the North-West. The company has shown great energy and ability, so that the Canadian Pacific Railway, with its numerous branches, its large traffic and its connecting steamships on the lakes and on the Pacific, is now one of the most important lines in the world. Then again, the Grand Trunk has gradually obtained the control of many lines

Canadian Pacific Railway completed, 1886.

formerly independent, the most important being the Great Western and its connections. These two companies—the Canadian Pacific and the Grand Trunk—now control nearly all the roads in Canada, except the Intercolonial, which was built by the Government, at a great cost, to connect the Western provinces with those down by the sea.

Canals, too, have been deepened, widened, and straightened; the new Welland Canal, constructed by the Mackenzie Government, being a very important public work. Great harbour works have been undertaken and built, and lake and ocean vessels have been wonderfully improved, although Canada has as yet no line of fast steamships crossing the Atlantic. In all our cities and larger towns Street Railways are to be found; while electric lighting, and machinery worked by electricity are among recent industrial changes.

Turning to the farms of Canada, we find that the most fertile portions of Ontario and Quebec have been cleared and tilled, and that thousands of the farmers of the older Provinces are finding their way to the rich prairies of Manitoba and the North-West, where the forests are few and the soil easily brought into cultivation. Large towns and villages now dot the face of Ontario, while the two cities of Montreal and Toronto are rapidly increasing their population, wealth, and trade. The population of Canada has increased until it is now estimated at five millions, and of this Ontario is thought to have two millions. This is a part of the bright side of our material condition. Against it we have to place the tendency of so many of our young men to leave Canada for a home in the United States; the increasing difficulty our farmers experience to make farming pay; and the want of a large foreign market for our manufactures.

8. Literary and Social Progress.—Perhaps it is because the energies of the Canadian people have been directed so largely towards overcoming the difficulties met with in settling a new country, that we have so few great writers of prose or verse. Our Public and High Schools are efficient, and our Universities with their too small endowments, are doing a good work; yet, of native Canadian authors, there are none who rank with the great writers of the Mother Country. Nevertheless, there are many good writers of verse, some clever journalists and essayists, and not a few historians who have done good and faithful work. Every year the number of those who seek literary and scientific fame is increasing, and with greater wealth and leisure, the growth of higher and nobler ideals, and the development of a stronger national sentiment, Canada may hope yet to have among her sons and daughters, worthy rivals of Shakespeare, Milton, Macaulay, Scott and George Eliot. The love and practice of art in its various forms is also becoming more and more apparent; Canadian artists already having won fame and distinction in song and painting. With the increase of education, wealth, leisure, and foreign travel, there has been a marked change in the customs and habits of the people. 'Social refinement and luxury have in recent years greatly increased, and a type of character is being gradually developed which is distinctly national. With her magnificent resources of soil, forest and mine; her strong, hardy, intelligent, and vigorous people; her relatively pure, simple, and healthy domestic life; her free systems of education; and her excellent form of government, Canada certainly possesses the promise and potency of a great nation.

APPENDIX.

HOW WE ARE GOVERNED.

1. Parliamentary System.—As already explained the Dominion of Canada was given its form of Government in 1867. Its constitution is to be found in the British North America Act, which cannot be changed without the consent of the British Parliament. In its main features our constitution is much like that of the Mother country, although some of its principles are evidently borrowed from the constitution of the United States.

To understand this Act, we must bear in mind what was sought in procuring its passage. The central idea was that there should be a common Parliament for the whole Dominion taking the charge and control of all matters of common or general interest, at the same time leaving each Province the control of all matters of a merely provincial or local nature. This was secured by giving the Dominion a Federal Parliament composed of a Governor-General appointed by the Crown, a House of Commons elected by the people, and a Senate appointed by the Governor-General in Council for life. The Dominion Parliament was to have the right to make laws on all matters relating to the public debt and property, trade and commerce, raising money on the credit of the Dominion by loan or taxation, the postal service, militia, fisheries, navigation, banks, currency, coinage, bankruptcy, marriage and divorce, criminal law, public works for the Dominion, and, in common with the Local Legislature, agriculture and immigration. The right to impose indirect taxes such as customs and excise was left in the hands of the Dominion Parliament. The Governor-General is the link which connects us with the Crown, and he is supposed to represent the sovereign. He is appointed, generally, for five years, and is paid by the Canadian people. Like the Queen, he can commute or do away with the sentences of a Court of Justice, and must refuse or give his assent to every Bill which goes through both Houses of Parliament. He is the proper person to open, prorogue, or dissolve a Parliament, and he is the official head of the army and navy. In his name, too, all the appointments to the Bench, the Senate, and the Lieutenant-Governorships of Provinces are made. But in all these acts, the Governor-General is simply following out the counsel of his advisers, the Dominion Cabinet or Ministry.

The Ministry, which is really responsible for all the things done in the Governor-General's name, is composed, generally, of thirteen men, each of whom must be a member of one of the Houses of Parliament. The Ministry must have the confidence of Parliament, and should it lose that confidence it must resign and give way to those who possess it. Each minister is supposed, unless it be the President of the Council, to have the charge of some Department of the public service, and to be responsible for its management. The Ministry, as a whole, is responsible to Parliament for the acts of its individual members.

The members of the House of Commons must be elected at least every five years, although, as often happens, a general election may take place before that time expires. The number of members in the Commons depends upon the population of each Province, compared with the population of Quebec. Quebec has always 65, and the other Provinces in proportion. At the present time, Ontario has 92; Quebec, 65; Nova Scotia, 21; New Brunswick, 16; Manitoba, 5; British Columbia, 6; Prince Edward Island, 6; and the North West Territories, 4; a total of 215 members.

The members of the Commons do not require any property qualification, but they must be British subjects. The right to vote for them is regulated by a Dominion Franchise Act, and is limited to men of twenty-one years of age, who must either have a small income, or be the owner or tenant of some property. Nearly every man who is a British subject has now a vote for members of Parliament. Voting, since 1874, takes place by ballot. The House of Commons, like the British House of Commons, has the sole right of bringing in money-bills.

The Senate consists of 79 members, appointed for life or good conduct. A Senator may, however, lose his right to a seat by absence from the sessions of Parliament, or by insolvency, for he must possess a property qualification. The Senate must assent to all bills before they become law, and it can introduce any bill except money-bills. The British North America Act fixes the highest number of Senators that may be appointed; if more should be needed the British Parliament would have to give its consent. There are now 24 Senators from Ontario, 24 from Quebec, 10 from Nova Scotia, 10 from New Brunswick, 4 from Prince Edward Island, 3 from British Columbia, 2 from Manitoba, and 2 from the North-West Territories.

The Dominion Parliament is subject to the British Parliament, inasmuch as all laws made by it can be annulled by the British Government. Nor can the Canadian Parliament make any treaty of commerce without the consent of the Mother country.

Turning now to the Provincial Parliaments or Legislatures we find very much the same form of government. At the head of each Province is a Lieutenant-Governor, appointed by the Governor-General in Council for five years. His duties are, in his sphere, the same as those of the Governor-General.

The Local Legislature may consist of one or two Houses, as the people of each Province may choose. Ontario, Manitoba, and British Columbia have but one House each, the other Provinces thinking it necessary to have Legislative Councils as well as Legislative Assemblies. The members of the Councils are appointed for life by the Lieutenant-Governor in Council, or really by his advisers, the members of the Provincial ministry or cabinet, except in Prince Edward Island, where they are elective. The Ministry of each Province occupies the same position in Provincial affairs, as the Dominion ministry occupies in Dominion affairs. The number of the members of the Ministry depends upon the work to be done, and generally ranges from five to seven. A general election must take place at least every four years for the Legislative Assembly, except in Quebec, where the term has been extended to five years.

The duties of these Provincial Parliaments are very important, as the B.N.A. Act gives them the control of education, direct taxation, the administration of justice, asylums, jails, and a host of other matters, not the least important being the making of laws for the improvement of our municipal institutions. They cannot, however, levy duties such as excise and customs, and the laws they make can be *vetoed*, or forbidden, by the Governor-General in Council, within a given time from their passage. In brief, the relations between the Provinces and the Dominion are supposed to be much the same as those between the Dominion and the Mother country. Like the Dominion Parliament, the Local Legislature must meet annually. Elections to the Legislative Assemblies take place by ballot, and each Province makes its own franchise laws. In all the Provinces, however, the qualification is so low that few men are without a vote. Women, as yet, have not been given the right to vote.

In the Provinces as well as in the Dominion, the members of Parliament are elected from districts called *constituencies*, and generally *only* one member is returned from a constituency.

Canada is said to possess Responsible Government, which means that when the Ministry of any Province or of the Dominion ceases to retain the confidence of its Parliament it must resign; and then the Lieutenant-Governor or Governor-General, as the case may be, must choose a new body of advisers, which possesses the confidence of Parliament. Parliament in turn must represent the people, otherwise the members would not be elected by them.

2. Judicial System.—To interpret the laws and put them in force, Judges, Magistrates, Sheriffs, and other officers are appointed. The duty of appointing the Judges rests with the Governor-General in Council, but the appointment of Magistrates, Sheriffs, Bailiffs, and the creation and organization of Courts of Justice are in the hands of the Lieutenant-Governor in Council. So we say, briefly, that the Judges who interpret the law and pass sentences are appointed by the Dominion Government, while the carrying out or administration of the law is under the control of the Provincial Governments. There are a great many kinds of courts, and also many kinds of judges, in Canada, beginning with the court of the humblest magistrate and ending with the Supreme Court of Canada, where cases from all parts of Canada are heard and settled. There is an appeal, however, from this highest Canadian Court to the British Privy Council. Our judges hold office for life or good conduct, and cannot be dismissed except by petition of both Houses of Parliament. The courts of the different Provinces differ somewhat in their organization and, so far as Quebec is concerned, in the law they interpret and enforce. The Criminal Law is the same for all the Provinces, but the Civil Law, as it is called, is very different in Quebec from that in any other Province. The Quebec Civil Law is based on French law or the CUSTOM OF PARIS, while the Civil Law in the other Provinces is based upon English Law. Nevertheless each Province makes laws suitable to its own needs, and this leads to a considerable variety in the laws relating to property and trade.

3. Municipal System.—Besides the Federal Parliament and the Local Legislatures, there are several other law-making bodies which come into even closer contact with the people. It would obviously be very inconvenient to have every little matter of a local nature brought before the Dominion Parliament or the Local Legislature for discussion and settlement, and therefore power has been given to the people in the different Provinces to elect men whose duty it shall be to make laws and regulations for small districts. For instance, in Ontario, where this local government is very fully carried out, the Province is divided into villages, towns, townships, counties, and cities. Each village, town, township, and city elects annually by ballot, a certain number of men, whose duty it is to look after the interests of the district or locality they represent. These men form what is called the "Council," and they are known as "Councillors" in the villages, towns, and townships, and as "Aldermen" in the cities. The presiding officer of the "Council" in villages and townships is the "Reeve," and in towns and cities the "Mayor."

In villages and townships, the Council is composed of five men, the Reeve, Deputy-Reeve, and three others. In towns and cities, of the Mayor and generally three Aldermen for each ward or section of the town or city. The Council is limited as to its powers of taxation by the laws of the Province, and its power to make by-laws or binding rules is also strictly defined by statute. Nevertheless, its power and usefulness are very great, as all questions relating to repairs on roads and highways, to the maintaining of order by constables and a police, the levying of taxes for school purposes and local improvement, and a host of other matters come before the Council. In Quebec taxes for school purposes are levied by the School Boards, not by the Municipal Councils. Besides the village, town, township, and city, there is the county, which includes a number of township and all villages within its area. Sometimes, unless a separation has taken place, the towns within the county form a part of it for municipal purposes. The county has also a Council made up of the Reeves and Deputy-Reeves of the villages and townships. The County Council looks after matters of common interest to the villages and townships, and has to draw from them the money it expends. The chairman of the County Council is elected by its members, and is known as the "Warden."

The right to vote for aldermen and councillors is confined to ratepayers; and widows and unmarried women with the requisite property qualifications have the right of voting in municipal elections.

Municipal systems much the same as that of Ontario are in operation in Quebec, the Maritime Provinces, Manitoba, and British Columbia. In Quebec, we have villages, towns, "parishes," townships, and cities, the councils of which are elected by the people, while the Mayors are appointed by the Councils, except in cities and towns, where they are elected by the ratepayers. There are also County Councils in Quebec, composed of the Mayors or presiding officers of the villages, parishes and townships. The local councils are composed of seven members, holding office for three years and elected by open vote. There is an important difference between the working of the Municipal system in Ontario and Quebec, for whereas the most of the money spent on local improvements in Ontario is raised by the municipalities themselves, in Quebec a great deal is left to the Local Legislature, which gives large grants for roads, bridges, and other local needs. Nevertheless, large powers are given to the councils in the matter of taxation, and in making local improvements.

In Prince Edward Island, and also in Nova Scotia, the Local Legislature transacts a great deal of the business which in Ontario and the other Provinces is left with municipal councils.

4. **Educational System.**—If the Municipal systems of the Dominion are much alike, so also are the Educational systems. Each Province, by the Confederation Act, is given entire control of its own educational work, but no change can be made which would affect the rights enjoyed by any class before the British North

America Act came into force. In Ontario the educational system is a very complete one, beginning at the Kindergarten and running up through Public and High Schools to the Provincial University, all of which are under Government control and inspection, and are, in whole or in part, supported by grants of public money, either from the Local Legislature, or from the Councils of the various municipalities. The Public Schools are intended to give a good English education, the High Schools and Collegiate Institutes to continue this education, the Normal, Model, and Training Schools to fit teachers for their profession, and the University to complete the educational edifice. But besides these Schools and Colleges which are under Government control, there are a great many other schools and colleges which are under private control, many of which are doing excellent work, especially in the field of higher education. The Public and High Schools are only partly supported by Government grants, the most of the money needed for their maintenance being raised by taxation from the people who get the benefit of them. The expenditure of this money and the management of the schools, subject to Government restrictions, is in the hands of School Boards, whose members, the Trustees, are usually elected by the ratepayers, although High School Trustees are appointed either by Town, City, or County Councils.

In Ontario, and in some other Provinces, a Separate School system is established. In Ontario and Quebec, Roman Catholics and Protestants have their own schools, which are supported by their own taxes, and which, like the Public Schools, receive Government aid and are subject to Government inspection and control. One difference may be noted between the provinces : in Ontario most of the schools are Public Schools, and nearly all the Separate Schools are Roman Catholic, while in Quebec there are few Public Schools where the children of both Roman Catholics and Protestants are educated together. In Manitoba an effort is, at present, being made to withdraw Government aid from all but Public Schools.

In Ontario educational matters are under the management of a Minister of Education, who is a member of the Local Government ; but in Quebec and the other Provinces, this work is done by a Council of Public Instruction, acting generally through a Superintendent, or other executive officer or officers. In Quebec the

Council of Public Instruction is made up of a Roman Catholic and of a Protestant Committee, each committee looking after its own schools. Model, Normal, and High Schools, together with numerous Academies, furnish a training for teachers and an excellent secondary education.

In Quebec, as in Ontario, the schools are largely dependent on local support, but the Universities in Quebec are not so dependent upon the State as the Provincial University of Ontario, and are supported mainly by endowments.

In Manitoba, British Columbia, and the North-West Territories, the Ontario system has been copied in its main features, and in the Maritime Provinces, very liberal provision is made by the Local Legislatures for educational purposes.

INDEX TO ENGLISH HISTORY.

ABERCROMBY, General defeated, 248
Abercromby, Sir R., victorious, 274
Abolition of slavery, 294
Aboukir, Battle in Bay of, 272.
Abyssinian expedition, 313
Acre, siege of, 272.
Act of Indemnity, 187; of Settlement of English Crown, 221; of Succession of Henry VIII, 127; of Supremacy, 122; of Uniformity, 128, 129, 136, 189
Actors of Geo. III.'s reign, 284
Adam Marsh, the friar, 63
Addington, Prime Minister, 274
Addison's writings, 230
Addled Parliament, 155
Afghanistan, Wars in, 302, 313
Agincourt, Battle of, 97
Agriculture in time of Elizabeth, 138
Aix-la-Chapelle, Peace of, 242
Akbar Khan, Afghan chief, 302
Alabama claims, 315
Albans, Battle of St., 102
Albert, Prince, 301; death, of 315
Albion, old name of England, 4
Aldermen, origin of, 11
Alexandria, Battle of, 274
Alfred the Great, 16-18; his laws, 17
Alice Perrers influences Edward III., 83
Allegiance, Oath of, 139
Alma, Battle of the, 309
Alva, Duke of, threatens England, 143
America, emigrations to, 155, 166; struggles with French in, 245; civil war in *1861*, 315; voyages of discovery to, 116, 138, 147
American colonies, quarrel with, 256; first Congress and war begins, 259; Declaration of Independence, 260
Amiens, Treaty of 1802, 274
Anderida taken by Cissa, 8
Angles were heathen, 12; settlement of the, 9
Anglesey, Druids slain in, 5; origin of name, 16
Angevin kings, 48
Anjou, Duke of, King of Spain, 220
Anjou lost to England, 56
Anne Boleyn, 120; married, 122; beheaded, 124
Anne of Cleves, divorce of, 125
Anne, Queen, crown settled on, 209; proclaimed queen, 223; and Duchess of Marlborough, 222; her "Bounty," 224; death of, 229
Anselm, Archbishop, 40; Rome, 40

Anson's voyages, 242
Anti-Corn-Law League, 301
Arabella Stuart, conspiracy for, 156
Archangel, blockade of, 309
Arcot, Clive takes, 244
Argyll, revolt and death of, 201
Arkwright invents spinning frame, 252
Armada, Spanish, 145, 146
Army, takes the power from Parliament, 175; first standing, 187; Discipline Act, 213; reduced by Parliament, 1697, 221; purchase abolished, 317
Artevelde, James von, 78
Arthur, King, defeats the Saxons, 8
Arthur, murder of Prince, 56
Arundel, Archbishop, persecutes Lollards, 94
Arundel, Duke of, beheaded, 87
Aryan, origin of Celts, 4
Ashantee, expedition to, 313
Asia, products of colonies in, 321
Assizes of Clarendon and Northampton, 50
Athelney, Alfred the Great hid in, 17
Athelstan called Emperor of Britain, 19
Atlantic cable, first message along, 315
Attainder, Bills of, 102; of Lord Strafford, 169
Atterbury, Bishop, banished, 236
Auckland settlement, N.Z., 306
Augustine converts Ethelbert, 13
Austerlitz, Napoleon's victory at, 275
Australasia, products from, 321
Australia, convicts in, 263; foundation of colonies of, 289; South founded, 289; Western colonised, 289
Australian Colonies Bill, 307
Austrian Succession War, 240

BABINGTON, Anthony, plot of, 144
Bacon, Roger, 62
Bacon, Sir Francis, 147; impeached, 158; his *Novum Organum*, 158
Badajos stormed, 279
Balaclava, Battle of, 309
Baliol, John, King of Scotland, 71
Ballot Act passed, 314
Baltic, English fleet in the, 309
Baltimore founded, 166
Bank of England, 216, 225
Bannockburn, Battle of, 75
Barebone's Parliament, 181
Barnet, Battle of, 105
Baronets first created, 157
Barons rebel against William II., 39; Henry I., 42; Stephen, 46; Henry II., 52

410 INDEX.

Barons' War, 65, 66
Barrows of early races, 3
Basques, early men allied to, 3
Bastile stormed, 268
Battle, trial by, 44
Battles, see under special names
Bautzen, Battle of, 279
Baxter, Richard, divine, 189
Beachy Head, Battle of, 214
Beaconsfield, Lord, 314, 318, 321
Beauforts, rule of the, 94, 95
Becket, Thomas, chancellor, 49; quarrels with Henry, 51; murdered, 52
Bede, first English historian, 14; his history translated by Alfred, 18
Bedford, Duke of, Protector of England, 98; death of, 99.
Belgium made a separate kingdom, 291
Bellerophon, Napoleon gives himself up on the ship, 281
Benevolences first raised, 105; renewed, 115
Berlin decree, 276
Bernicia, kingdom of, 9
Bill of Rights. 209
Birkbeck, Dr., founds institutes, 296
Bishops resist unlawful taxes, 55; trial of the, 207
Black Death of 1348, 81
Black Hole of Calcutta, 246
Black Prince, his battles, 78, 79, 80; death, 84
Blake, Admiral, 177; his victories over the Dutch, 179
Blanchard, Alan, of Rouen, 97
Blenheim, Battle of, 224
Bloody Assizes, 202
Blue-Coat School founded, 129
Boadicea, 5
Board Schools established, 317
Bodleian Library, 181
Boers, difficulties with the, 306; wars against, 313
Bolingbroke, Henry of, 87; banished, 88; becomes Henry IV., 109
Bolingbroke (St. John), 228, 229
Bombay, 243; given to England, 190
Bonaparte, Joseph, King of Spain, 277
Bonaparte, see Napoleon
Bonner, Bishop, 129, 131
Borneo, North, annexed, 321
Borodino, Battle of, 279
Boston, riot in, 259; tea thrown into harbour, 259
Bosworth Field, Battle of, 110
Bounty, Queen Anne's, 224
Boyne, Battle of the, 214
Braddock, Defeat of General, 245
Bradshaw, president at Charles I.'s trial, 175
Breda, peace of, 192
Bretigny, Treaty of, 79
Bretwalda, or overlord, 13, 14
Brigade, Charge of the Light, 309
Bright, John, 301
Brindley, makes canals, 252

Brisbane founded, 289
Britain, races of, 2, 5; Roman conquest of, 5
British Museum founded, 284
Britons, homes of, 5; religion of, 5
Brontë, Charlotte, 320
Brougham, Lord, defends Queen Caroline, 285; on useful literature, 296
Browning, poet, 320
Bruce, Robert, 71, 73, 75; murders Comyn and is crowned king, 73; wins Battle of Bannockburn, 75
Brydon, Dr., reaches Jellalabad, 303
Buckingham, Duke of, 156; impeached, 162; fails to relieve La Rochelle, 163; assassinated, 164
Bunker's Hill, Battle of, 260
Bunyan, John, 189
Burdett, Sir F., upholds Catholic emancipation, 290
Burgesses in Montfort's Parliament, 65
Burghers, increased power of, 22
Burgoyne's army surrenders, 261
Burgundy, Duke of, murdered, 97
Burke accuses Warren Hastings, 265; defends American Colonies, 258; on French Revolution, 268
Burleigh, Lord, Secretary of State, 135, 142; death of, 147
Burnes, Sir A., murdered, 302
Burnet, Bishop, his writings, 230
Burns, the poet, 284
Bute, Earl of Prime Minister, 251; resigns 255.
Butler, Samuel satirist, 230
Byng, execution of Admiral, 246
Byron, the poet, 284

CABAL Ministry 193; fall of, 194
Cabinet, formation of the, 193
Cabot, voyages of, 116
Cade, Jack, rebellion of, 101
Cadiz, failure of expedition to, 161
Cædmon, poet, 13
Cæsar, Julius, came to Britain, 4
Calais, English after one hundred years' war, 99; siege of. 79; loss of, 132
Calcutta, built, 243; Black Hole of, 246; Clive retakes, 250
Calder, Sir R., defeats Spanish fleet, 275
Calendar, reform of the, 242
California, gold found in, 305
Calvin, Scotch followers of, 136
Campbell, the poet, 284
Camperdown, naval victory off, 271
Canada, conquest of, 248; constitution given to, 299; Dominion of, 299; Pacific Railway, 299; products from, 321; rebellion in 1837, 298; struggle with French in, 245
Canals first made, 252
Canning, G., enters on Peninsular War, 277; Foreign Secretary, 286; his foreign policy, 286; death of, 290
Canning, Lord, first Indian Viceroy, 312; conduct in Indian Mutiny, 311

INDEX. 411

Canterbury, origin of name, 8
Canterbury Settlement, N.Z., 306
Canute, see Cnut
Cape Breton taken, 248
Cape of Good Hope Colony, 306 ; passes to England, 269 ; federation of, 318
Capital and labour, 81
Caractacus, 5
Carlyle, 320
Caroline, Queen, marriage of, 282 ; trial of 284
Carr, Robert, Earl of Somerset, 155
Castlereagh (Lord Londonderry), suicide of, 286
Castles, building of Norman, 35 ; destroyed by Henry II., 49
Cassiterides or Tin Islands, 4
Cassivelaunus, 4
Catalans, England deserts the, 229
Catesby starts Gunpowder Plot, 154
Catholic Association formed, 290 ; Emancipation Bill passed, 291
Catholics excluded from Parliament, 195 ; plot against Elizabeth, 143, 144 ; Test Act against, 194 ; put into office by James II., 204
Cato Street conspiracy, 285
Cavagnari, Sir L., murdered, 313
Cavalier Party, 171 ; Parliament, 187
Cavendish, Lord F., murdered, 318
Cawnpore, massacre of, 311
Caxton, William, the printer, 106
Cecil, Lord Burleigh, 135, 142, 147
Celts in Britain, 3
Central America, products of, 321
Ceorls or freemen, 11
Ceylon taken by English, 269
Chancellor, origin of name, 37 ; first Great, 67
Chantrey, sculptor, 284
Charing Cross, one of Eleanor's crosses, 67
Charles I. fails to marry Infanta, 156 ; marries Henrietta Maria of France, 159 ; his character, 160 ; his struggles with Parliament, 160-165, 168-175 ; signs Strafford's warrant, 169 ; flees to Scots, 173 ; prisoner of Parliament, 174 ; intrigues with the Irish and Scotch, 174 ; confined in Carisbroke, 174 ; executed, 175
Charles II. proclaimed in Scotland, 176 ; crowned in Scotland, 178 ; his flight to France, 179 ; his restoration, 185 ; his character, 186 ; his marriage, 190 ; closes Exchequer, 193 ; war with the Dutch, 191, 194 ; receives pension from France, 193, 195 ; death, 199
Charles V. of Spain, genealogy of, 119
Charles VII. and Jeanne Darc, 99
Charlie, Bonnie Prince, 240
Charlotte, death of Princess, 282
Charter of Henry I., 42 ; the Great, 58, 89 ; the People's, 300
Chartists, rise of the, 300 ; of 1848, 304
Chatham, Lord. see Pitt
Chaucer, works of, 82
Chesterfield despairs of England, 246

Chevalier St. George, the Pretender, 222
China, wars with, 302, 310, 313
Chippenham, Peace of, 17
Chivalry, age of, 78
Cholera, outbreaks of, 316
Christ Church, Oxford, founded, 119
Christianity brought to England, 12
Christians, Dey of Algiers releases, 283
Chronicle, Saxon, 18, 40, 41, 44, 47
Chupaties passed in India, 310
Church-lands pass to nobles, 124, 133
Cintra, Convention of, 277
Circuits established,
Cissa and Ella, 8
Cistercians settle in England, 44
City and Commons quarrel, 254
City Companies, 171
Ciudad Rodrigo stormed, 279
Civil war, outbreak of, 171 ; in United States, 315
Clare, O'Connell elected for, 291
Clarence, death of Duke of, 106.
Clarence, Earl of, see Hyde.
Clarendon, assize of, 50 ; Constitutions of, 51.
Clarkson, T., denounces slavery, 276
Claverhouse, rebellion of, 210
Clergy, trial of the, 50 ; would not sit in Parliament, 70
Clerkenwell prison blown up, 316
Clive, Robert, saves India, 244 ; retakes Calcutta, 250 ; made a peer, 250
Closterzeven, convention of, 246
Cloth, English taught to weave, 80
Clyde, first steam-tug on the, 283
Cnut, King of England, 24
Cobbett, William, 282
Cobden, 301, 304 ; arranges French Treaty, 356
Coffee-houses of London, 204
Coinage, debasement of the, 128 ; calling in of base, 137 ; new, 218
Coins, gold, first used, 80 ; of Alfred's grandson's dug up in Rome, 18
Coke sent to prison, 158
Colet, lectures of, 117
Coleridge, the poet, 284
Colonial Office takes up emigration, 289
Columbus, discoveries of, 116
Commercial treaty with France, 314
Common Pleas, Court of, 68
Commons gain a share in making laws, 76 ; gain power over money grants, 93 ; in Montfort's Parliament, 65 ; summoned to Parliament, 70 ; sit separate from Lords, 81, 89
Commonwealth, abuses of the, 180 ; Acts passed by the, 179 ; proclaimed, 175
Compurgation, 11
Concord, Battle of, 260
Conservative, term first used, 294
Constantinople, Greeks flee from, 117
Constitutional Government, rise of, 230
Conventicle Act, 189
Convention Parliament, 187
Convict settlements, 263

Convocation of Clergy, 70
Cook's voyages, 263
Cooke, inventor of telegraph, 300
Coote, Sir Eyre, in India, 254
Copenhagen, English seize Danish fleet at, 276; naval battle of, 274
Copernicus, 146
Corn-laws, oppressive, 282; League against the, 301; repealed, 304
Corn, sliding scale of duty on, 288
Cornwallis, Lord, surrenders at Yorktown, 262
Coronation of the Queen, 300
Corporation Act, 189; repealed, 290
Cotton famine, 315
Council of Eleven, 86
Council of the North abolished, 169
Court of High Commission, 152; abolished, 169
Court-martial established, 213
Covenant, First, signed, 136
Covenanters of Scotland, 168; rabble English clergy, 210
Cowper, the poet, 284
Cranmer, rise of, 122; Protestant reforms of, 127; imprisonment, 130; burnt, 133
Crecy, Battle of, 78
Crimean War, 309
Cromlechs, 3
Cromwell, Oliver, 173; his "Ironsides," 173; subdues Ireland, 177; fights Charles II. in Scotland, 178; defeats him at Worcester, 179; closes the Long Parliament, 180; made Protector, 181; his ordinances, 181, 182; appoints major-generals, 182; refuses the Crown, 183; his death, 184; character, 184
Cromwell, Richard, 184
Cromwell, Thomas, his administration, 121-125; destroys the monasteries, 124; executed, 125
Crown jewels lost in Wash, 59
Crown Point taken, 248
Crown settled on Anne, 209; on the House of Hanover, 211
Crusades, 41; Richard goes to, 54
Culloden, Battle of, 241
Cumberland, Duke of, at Closterseven, 246
Curia Regis, King's Court, 43
Cuthbert, Monk of Montrose, 13
Cyprus, 321

DALHOUSIE, Lord, annexes Punjab, 305
Danby's administration, 195; his fall, 196
Danegeld, first paid, 23; London exempt from, 44
Danes invasions of, 15; murder King Edmund, 15, Treaty of Wedmore with, 17; massacre of 1002, 23
Darnley, murder of, 140
Darwin, Charles, 320
David II. of Scotland taken prisoner, 81
David of Scotland fights for Matilda, 46
Death-rate decreasing in England, 316
Declaration of Indulgence, 205; of Independence, 260; of Rights, 209

Defoe, Daniel, 202
Deira, Kingdom of, 9
Dekkan, war in the, 254
Delhi, Siege of, 311
Deptford Dockyard built, 118
Derby, Lord, Prime Minister, 314
Derwentwater, Lord, executed, 234
Despenser, Lady, carries off Earl of March, 93
Despensers, favourites of Edward II., 76
Dettingen, Battle of, 240
Devonshire, riot in, 128
Dey of Algiers forced to release Christian slaves, 283
Dickens, Charles, 320
"*Dieu et mon Droit*" first used, 78
Directory, French, at war with England, 271
Dispensation, James II. claims power of, 204
Disraeli, 314; opposes free trade, 304
Dissenters, Nonconformists first called, 189
Divine right, question of, 151
Domesday Book, 37
Dominicans in England, 62
Douai priests incite rebellion, 144
Dover, secret treaty of, 193
Downs, Battle of the, 191
Dragonnades in France, 203
Drake, Sir Francis, 138, 144, 146
Dresden, Battle of, 276
Dress of people in the fifteenth century, 96
Drogheda, siege of, 177
Druids, 5
Dryden, the poet, 197
Dudley, Earl of Warwick, Protector, 129
Dudley, Lord Guildford, 130, 132
Dunbar, Battle of, 178
Duncan, Admiral, at Camperdown, 271
Dundee, revolt of Viscount, 210-211
Dunes, Battle of the, 183
Dunkirk, sale of, 190
Dunstan, government of, 21
Dupleix tries to subdue India, 244
Duquesne Fort attacked, 245; taken, 248
Durham, Lord, Governor of Canada, 299
Dutch towns redeemed, 157
Dutch wars, 179, 190, 194

EARL, origin of term, 23
East Anglia founded, 9
East India Company, 146, 243; ceases, 312
East India Company of France, 243
Eastern Question, 308, 321
Ecclesiastical Commission, Court of, 204
Edgar the Peaceable, 21; his laws, 23
Edgecote, Battle of, 104
Edgehill, Battle of, 172
Edict of Nantes, 146; revoked, 203
Edinburgh, origin of name, 9; treaty of, 137
Edith the Saxon ancestor of our Queen, 42
Edmund, Edred, and Edwig, 15, 21
Edmund martyred by Danes, 16

INDEX. 413

Edmund Ironsides fights Cnut, 23
Education Acts, 294, 317
Edward the Elder conquers Danelagh, 18
Edward the Martyr, 22
Edward the Confessor brought up in Normandy, 26; his reign, 26-27
Edward I., as prince, fights the barons, 65; escapes from prison, 66; goes to crusades, 66; *crowned king*, 66; summons first complete Parliament, 69; yields right of taxation to Parliament, 72; death of, 74
Edward II., favourites of, 74, 76; dethroned and murdered, 76
Edward III.'s minority, 77; claims and fights for French crown, 78; gives up his claim, 79; institutes Order of Garter, 79; imports Flemish weavers, 80; death of, 84; sons of, 86
Edward IV. made king, 103; escapes to Flanders, 104; returns, 105; puts Duke of Clarence to death, 106; dies, 106
Edward V., 106; reigns three months, 107; murder of, 108
Edward VI., 125; made king, 127; prayerbook of, 127, 136; his grammar schools, 129; founds Blue-Coat School, 129; death of, 130
Edwin, the Christian overlord, 13
Egbert, King of all the English, 14
Egyptian monuments deciphered, 320
Eikon Basiliké, 176
Eleanor, Queen of Henry II., 49, 52
Elector Palatine, son-in-law of James I., 157
Electric telegraph invented, 300; changes worked by the, 319
Eliot, George, novelist, 320
Eliot, Sir John, 158; sent to Tower, 162; death of 165
Elle and Cissa, 8
Elliot, Gen., defends Gibraltar, 261
Elizabeth, Queen, born, 122; sent to the Tower, 132; character, 134; finds England weak 135; leaves it strong, 172; architecture in her reign, 138; refuses to marry, 139, 141; excommunicated, 142; association to protect, 144
Elphinstone retreats from Kabul, 303
Ely, Isle of, refuge of the patriots, 36
Emigration in *1826*, 288
Emma of Normandy, 26
Empress of India, Victoria, 312
Empson and Dudley, 115
Enclosures in George III.'s time, 253
England, area of, 1; first called Englaland, 21
English arrive in Britain, 7; early villages and laws, 10-11; first use of term, 10
English Church organized, 13
English patriots' revolt, 35, 36
English-speaking people, spread of, 322
Eorls or Ethelings, 11
Erasmus, the reformer, 117
Essex, origin of name, 9
Essex, first Earl of, in Ireland, 148; insurrection and execution of, 148; Earl of, leader of Parliamentary army, 171
Ethelfled conquers Danish boroughs, 18
Etheling Edgar, chosen by patriots, 30
Ethelings or Eorls, 11
Ethelred the Unready buys off the Danes, 23
Ethelwulf, 15
Eton School founded, 101
Evesham, Battle of, 66
Exchequer Court, 44, 68
Exchequer closed by Charles II., 193
Excise Bill, failure of, 238
Exclusion Bill, struggle for the, 196-198
Exhibition of *1851*, 307; Indian and Colonial of *1886*, 321
Excommunication of John, 57

FACTORY Acts, 294
Fairfax, leader of Parliamentary army, 173-175
Fairs, annual country, 62
Falkirk, Battle of, *1298*, 72; *1746*, 241
Falkland, Lord, 165; death of, 172
Family compact between Spain and France, 238
Famine in England, 75; in Ireland, 303
Farm, rise of the, 80
Farthings first coined, 67
Fawcett on Political Economy, 320
Fawkes, Guy, 154
Felton, assassin of Buckingham, 164
Feudal System, 34; tenures abolished, 187
Field of the Cloth of Gold, 120
Finisterre Cape, Spanish fleet driven from, 275
Fire of London, 192
Fisher, Bishop, beheaded, 123
Fitz-Alwin first mayor of London, 54
Fitzgerald, Lord E., leads Irish rebellion, 270; is killed, 273
Fitz-Herbert, Mrs., wife of the Prince Regent, 282
Fitz-Peter, Geoffrey, justiciar, 55, 58
Five-Mile Act, 189
Flambard, Ralph, a cruel justiciar, 39; arrested, 42
Flanders, wool trade with, 80, 89, 120
Flaxman, sculptor, 284
Flemings come to England, 38; colonise Pembroke, 44; one cause of "Hundred Years' War," 78; settle in Eastern counties, 80
Flodden Field, Battle of, 118
Folk-land becomes Kings-land, 34
Folkmoot, 11
Fontenoy, Battle of, 240
Forster passes Education Act, 317
Fotheringay, Queen of Scots in, 144
Fox, C. J., rival to Pitt, 265; his India Bill, 265; joins the ministry, 275; his death, 276
Fox, Henry, upholds Bute, 254
France, Hundred years' war with, 78; Henry V. Regent of, 97; title of king of, given up by England, 274; joins Ameri-

can colonists, 261; war between Germany and, 314
Franchise, limited in fifteenth century,100; of 1885, 314
Francis I. of France, 118
Francis, Sir Philip, thwarts Warren Hastings, 264
Franciscans in England, 62
Franklin, Sir John, 320
Frederick, Prince of Wales, dies, 242
Frederick the Great, 247
Free Companies of France, 79
Free trade in corn, 304
Freeman, historian, 320
French crown, Edward III. claims, 78
French Revolution, 1789, 267; the second, 1830, 291; the third, 1848, 304
Friars, Black and White, 62
Frith-guilds established, 19
Frobisher discovers straits, 138
Fulton invents a steamboat, 283
Fyrd, Saxon military service, 53

Gainsborough, painter, 284
Galileo, 146
Gardiner, Bishop, 129, 131
Gardiner, historian, 362
Garter, Order of the, 79
Gascoigne, Judge, and Prince Henry, 95
Gas, introduction of, 296
Gaunt, John of, 83, 84, 86
Gaveston, Piers, rules, 74; beheaded, 74
George I. proclaimed king, 229; character of, 233; death of, 237
George II., character of, 237; wins Battle Dettingen, 240; death of, 250
George III. succeeds, 250; character of, 254; quarrels with America, 258; hopelessly insane, 281; death of, 283
George IV., his quarrel with Queen Caroline, 285; death of, 291
General warrants abolished, 255
Gibbon's Works, 284
Gibraltar, siege of, 261; raised, 262
Gilbert, Sir H., voyage of, 138
Ginkel, Dutch general in Ireland, 214
Gladstone, W. E., passes Ballot Act and Reform Bill, 314; fails to carry Home Rule, 318
Glencoe, Massacre of, 211
Glendower's rebellion, 92-93
Gloucester, Thomas, Duke of, 87
Gloucester, rule of Humphrey, Duke of, 98-100; murder of, 101
Godolphin, administration of, 222
Godwin, Earl of Wessex, outlawed, 26
Gold, discovery of, 305
Goldsmith's Works, 284
Goojerat, Battle of, 305
Gordon, C. G., death of, 313, 340
Gordon riots, 262
Gough, Lord, in India, 305
Grammar schools founded, 129
Grand Alliance against Louis, 223
Grand Remonstrance, 170

Grattan, Henry, the Irish patriot, 262; refuses Free Trade Bill, 266
Great Britain, union of, 226
Great Contract, 155
Greek Testament, spread of the, 117
Green, historian, 320
Greenwich Hospital built, 215
Gregory, Pope, and the Angles, 12
Grenville, George, minister, 255
Gresham, Sir Thomas, 138
Grey, Lady Jane, 130, 132
Grey, Lord, arrest and execution of, 107, 108
Grey, Lord, administration of, 293, 30
Grosseteste, Bishop of Lincoln, 63
Guerilla bands of Spain, 279
Guiana, products of British, 321
Guilds, formation of, 22
Guthrum, leader of the Danes, 17
Gunpowder Plot, 154
Gunpowder, changes from use of, 111
Guy Fawkes, 154

"Habeas Corpus" Act, 196; suspended, 282
Hackney coaches first run, 165
Hadrian, wall of, 6
Halfpennies first coined, 67
Halifax, Lord, the Trimmer, 197, 213
Hampden, 158, 170; appeals against ship-money, 167; his death, 172
Hampton Court, built by Wolsey, 119; conference at, 1604, 153
Hanover, George, Elector of, succeeds to English throne, 229; Princess Sophia of, dies, 229; becomes separate from England, 298
Hanseatic League, 110
Hanwell, asylum at, 296
Harfleur, siege of, 97
Harley, Earl of Oxford, 223
Harold I., Danish King, 24
Harold II., the Saxon, governs England, 23; becomes king, 29; his death, 30
Harrowby, Lord, conspiracy to murder ministers at his house, 285
Harthacnut, Danish king, 24
Harvest fails in 1845, 304
Harvey, physician of Charles I, 165
Hastings, Battle of, 30
Hastings, execution of Lord, 108
Hastings, Warren, 264, 265
Havelock, General, 312
Hawarden Castle, Welsh attack on, 68
Hawke defeats the French, 249
Hawkins carries slaves to America, 138
Health Act, 316
Heathen names given to week-days, 12
Hedgeley Moor, Battle of, 108
Hengest and Horsa, 8
Henry I., character, 41; marries English Princess, 42; his charter, 42; his son drowned, 45; death, 45
Henry II., 48-53; great possessions of, 49; establishes juries, 50; quarrel with

INDEX. 415

Beckett, 50, 51; Lord of Ireland, 52; his rebellious sons, 52; death, 53
Henry III., character and marriage, 63; accepts crown of Sicily for his son, 64; quarrels with barons, 64-66; a prisoner, 65; death, 66
Henry IV., (Bolingbroke), 86; banishment and return, 88; descent of, 89; rebellions against, 92-93; death of, 94
Henry V., a beloved king, 95; alien priories granted to, 95; wins Battle of Agincourt, 97; made Regent of France, 97; dies young, 98
Henry VI., succeeds while a baby, 98; character, 100; insanity of, 101-102; prisoner in the Tower, 103; reigns again, 104; dies in Tower, 105
Henry VII., character, 113; marries Elizabeth of York, 113; extorts money, 115; rules without Parliament, 115; death of, 117; his chapel, 117
Henry VIII., his marriages, 118, 122, 124, 125, 125; his character, 117; builds a navy, 118; intrigues with France and Spain, 120; writes against Luther, 120; declared Supreme Head of the Church, 122; destroys the monasteries, 124; his death, 126; coinage debased in his reign, 128
Henry, son of James I., dies, 156
Heptarchy, use of term, 10
Herbert, Admiral, 207; as Lord Torrington loses Battle of Beachy Head, 214
Herbert, George, poet, 165
Hereford, Henry Bolingbroke, Earl of, 88
Heresy, first man burnt for, 94
Hereward-the-Wake, 36
Hexham, Battle of, 103
Highlanders, disarming of, 241
Hill, Sir Rowland, 300
History of the World, by Raleigh, 156
Hoche, General, threatens Ireland, 271
Holland, failure of expedition to, 159; wars with, 179, 190-191, 192; naval war with, 191
Holy Alliance of *1815*, 285
Holy League, Henry VIII. joins the, 118
Home Rule Bill defeated, 318
Homildon Hill, Battle of, 93
Honduras, products of, 321
Hooper, Bishop, burnt, 133
Horne Tooke tried for treason, 270
Hotspur, Harry, killed, 93
Hounslow, James II plants troops at, 205
Howard, John, visits gaols, 275
Howard, Lord, defeats Armada, 145
Howe, Lord, killed, 248
Hubert De Burgh defeats the French, 61; dismissed by Henry III., 63
Hubert, Walter, justiciar, 55
Hubertsburg, Peace of, 251
Hudibras written, 230
Hudson's Bay Territory, 299
Huguenots introduce silk weaving, 203
Hundred Years' War begins, 78; ends, 99

Hundreds were groups of townships, 11
Hus-carls of Cnut, 24
Huskisson, W., 286; passes Reciprocity of Duties Bill and trade reforms, 285; killed, 296
Hyde, Anne, mother of Queen Mary and Queen Anne, 193
Hyde, Earl of Clarendon, 170; his administration, 187; his *History of the Rebellion*, 192; his fall, 192
Hyde Park replanted, 296
Hyder Ali attacks Madras, 264

IBERIANS, early men allied to, 3
"*Ich Dien*," use of motto, 79
Ida founds Bernicia, 9
Idwal, King of Wales, gives wolves' heads, 22
Ierne, old name of Ireland, 4
Impositions, illegal, of James I., 155
Income-tax established, 303
Independence, Declaration of, 260
India, English settlements in, 146, 243; war with French in, 244, 250; under Warren Hastings, 264; Mahratta wars in, 264, 277; Bill passed, 265; Mutiny in, 311; brought under the Crown, 312; canals and railways in, 312; Prince of Wales visits, 312; products from, 321
Indian troops in Malta and Egypt, 313
Indulgence, Declaration of, 194
Inkermann, Battle of, 309
Interdict, England under an, 57
Interregnum in *1688*, 208
Ireland, people and language of, 1; Henry II. Lord of, 52; invaded by Edward Bruce, 76; mistaken laws for, 83; Richard II. visits, 87, 88; brought under England, 148; massacre in, 170; supports Charles II., 176; suffered at Restoration, 188; civil war in, 212; James II. reigns in, 211, 212; penal laws in Anne's reign, 227; French attempt to invade, *1796*, 270; rebellion in, 273; union with England, 273; potato disease in, 303; Young, 305; Land Act, 317; Church disestablished, in, 316; murders in, 318
Irish, missions of, in England, 13; reject Free Trade Bill, 266
Iron-works grow up, 252
Isabella, Queen of Edward II., 74, 76, 77
Italy, learning brought from, 117

JACK Cade's rebellion, 101
Jack Straw's mob, 85
Jacobite rebellions, *1715*, 234; *1745*, 240
Jacobites, 210; plots of, 215
Jamaica taken from Spain, 183
James I., crowned on stone of Scone, 151; character of, 151; quarrels with Puritans, 153; discovers Gunpowder Plot, 154; rules without Parliament, 155; executes Sir W. Raleigh, 156; his struggles with Parliament, 157, 159; death of, 159

416   INDEX.

James II., early life 186, 194, 195; character of, 199; reinstates mass, 199; appoints Catholic officers, 203; claims power of dispensation, 204; expels fellows of Magdalen, 205; birth of his son, 206; escapes to France, 208; reigns in Ireland, 211, 212
James, Prince of Scotland, brought up in England, 93
James IV. of Scotland, 113
Jane Seymour, marriage of, 124
Jarrow monastery, 14
Jeanne Darc, her mission and death, 98-99
Jeffreys, Judge, 202, 208
Jenkins' ear, War of, 239
Jervis, Admiral, defeats Spanish fleet, 271
Jews, settle in England, 38; expulsion of, 63; admitted to Parliament, 291, 314
John Ball preaches equality, 85
John Bull, History of, 230
John, King, plots against Richard I., 55; loses Normandy, 56; quarrels with the Pope, 57; struggle with his barons, 58; signs Magna Charta, 59; death, 59
John, of Gaunt, Duke of Lancaster, 83, 84, 86
Johnson Samuel, 233
Joint-stock companies of 1824, 238
Journal Book of Parliament, 158
Judges made independent, 217
Juries established, 50
Justiciars, Flambard, 39; Roger of Salisbury, 43, 46; De Lucy, 49; Longchamp, 54; Hubert Walter, 55; Fitz-Peter, 55, 56; Peter des Roches and Hubert de Burgh, 61; office of, ceases, 67
Jutes land in Britain, 8

Kaffir wars, 306
Kars defended by General Williams, 309
Katharine of Aragon marries Prince Arthur, 116; and afterwards Henry VIII., 118; divorced, 122
Katharine Howard, marriage and execution of, 125-126
Keats, the poet, 234
Kenilworth, dictum of, 66
Kenneth, King of the Scots, receives Lothian, 21
Kent, Duke of, father of Queen Victoria, 282
Kent, kingdom of, founded, 8
Ket, rebellion of Robert, 123
Khyber Pass, disaster near, 303
Kilkenny, statute of, 83
Killiecrankie, Battle of, 211
King's Bench instituted, 68; College, Camb., founded, 101; College, London, founded, 296; Court, 37, 44
Kings, elected, 12
Kirke, Colonel, sent to relieve Derry, 212
Kirke's lambs, cruelty of, 202
Knights in Montfort's Parliament, 65
Knox, John, 137
Koord Kabul massacre, 303

Labourers, statute of, 81
Laets, landless men, 11
La Hogue, Battle of, 215
Lambert Simnel, imposture of, 113
Lancastrians, wars of the, 102
Land Act for Ireland, 317
Lanfranc, Archbishop, 37; crowns William II., 38
Langland, author of Piers Plowman, 82
Langton, Stephen, Archbishop, 57; upholds the charter, 58; his death, 62
Language, Norman words in our, 43
La Rochelle, siege of, 163, 164
Latimer, Bishop, 129; burnt, 133
Laud, Bishop of London, 164, 166; quarrels with Puritans, 167; executed, 169
Law against heresy, 94; of treason amended, 217
Law-courts, organization of, 68
Lawrence, the brothers, 305; Sir Henry dies in Lucknow, 311; Sir John, during mutiny, 311; improves India, 312
Laws collected under William I., 36
Laws of Alfred the Great, 17; of Edgar, 21, 24
League of Parliament with the Scots, 172
Learning of Henry VII.'s reign, 117
Leases first granted, 80
Lecky, historian, 320
Legate, Pope's, first received in England, 57; Henry III. did homage to, 61; received by Mary, 132; by James II., 205
Leicester, Earl of, 139, 144
Leinster, conquest of, 52; plantations, 148
Leofric of Mercia, 24; his grandsons patriots, 35
Leopold, King of the Belgians, 291
Leuthen, Battle of, 247
Lewes, Battle of, 65
Lexington, battle near, 259
Liberal, term first used, 294
Libraries of George II. and III., 234
Ligny, repulse of Prussians at, 220
Limerick, Treaty of, 214
Lincoln, Abraham, 315; shot, 315
Lincoln, Battle of, 61
Lille, Battle of, 227
Lisle, Alice, executed, 202
Literature, Society for Diffusion of, 296; of seventeenth century, 230; in George III.'s reign, 253; of our time, 320
Liturgy, English, introduced, 126
Liverpool, Lord, Prime Minister, 281, 286; resigns, 290
Livingston, Chancellor, invents steamboat, 233
Livingstone, 320
Llewellyn refuses homage, 67
Loans, Forced, of Charles I., 162
Locke's Works, 230
Lollards, 84, 83, 94; rising of the, 96; laws against, repealed, 127
London, "Lynn-din," 5; alarming growth of 1604, 152; charter of, 44; plague and fire of, 191-192; rebuilt by Alfred, 18; train-bands oppose Charles I., 171, 172

INDEX.   417

Londonderry, Lord, suicide of, 286
Londonderry, siege of, 211; relief of, 212
Longchamp, Justiciar, deposed, 54
Lord Mayor's Show, first, 101
Lords Appellant and Richard II., 87
Lords, Cromwell's House of, 183; of the Congregation, 136; sit separate from Commons, 81, 89
Lothian given to Kenneth, King of Scots, 21
Louis of France invades England, 59; returns to France, 61
Louis XIV. revokes Edict of Nantes, 203; intrigues for Spanish crown, 220; secures fortresses in Netherlands, 221; recognizes the Pretender, 221; at war against Marlborough, 223-225; makes peace, 228; dies, 234
Louis XVI. executed 268
Louis XVIII. placed on throne by the allies, 280
Louis Philippe comes to England, 304
Louisburg taken, 248
Lucknow, relief of, 312
Luddites, 282
Luneville, treaty of, 272
Luther, preaching of, 117, 123; Henry VIII. refutes, 120
Luttrell, Col., chosen by Parliament: 257
Lutzen, Battle of, 279
Lyell, Sir Charles, 320

M'Arthur, Lieut., brings sheep to Australia, 289
Macadamized roads, 295
Macaulay, Z., denounces slavery, 276
Macaulay's History, 320
Macdonald, Flora, 241
Machinery, effects of, 253, 297
Mackay, General, defeats Dundee. 211
Mackintosh, Sir J., reforms criminal law, 287
Macnaughten, Sir W., murdered, 302
Macquarie, Colonel, employs convict labour on roads in Australia, 289
Madras, origin of, 243; defence of, 264
Magdalen, James II. expels Fellows of, 205
Magistrates, origin of county, 69
Magna Charta, 58, 89
Mahratta wars, 264, 277
Maintenance, custom of, 111
Major-generals, 182
Malacca captured by English, 269
Malcolm III. upholds the patriots, 35
Maldon, Battle of, 22
Malplaquet, Battle of, 227
Manchester massacre, 282
Manitoba founded, 299
Mansel, C. G., in India, 305
Maori, chiefs, treaty with, 306; wars, 306; members in N. Z. Parliament, 306
Mar, rebellion under Earl of, 234
March, Earl of, 92, 93; his estates restored, 95
Marches, Lords of the Welsh, 67

Margaret, heir to Scotch throne dies, 70
Margaret, wife of Henry VI., 101; wore a red rose, 104; fought for her husband, 102, 103, 104
Maria Theresa in Seven Years' War, 245
Marie Antoinette executed, 268
Marlborough, Duke of, 202; ministry of, 222; character, 223; wars of, 223-225, 227; dismissed from command, 228
Marlborough, Duchess of, 222
Marriage Act, Hardwicke's, 243
Marshall, William, Earl of Pembroke, 61
Marston Moor, Battle of, 173
Mary, Queen of England, childhood of, 120; proclaimed queen, 130; character, 131; marriage, 132; persecutes Protestants, 133; death, 134
Mary, Queen of Scots, 119; set aside in Henry VIII.'s will, 127; sent to France, 127; claims English throne, 135; goes to Scotland, 137; marries Darnley, 140; escapes to England, 141; a prisoner, 141; beheaded, 145; compared with Elizabeth, 142; plots in favour of, 143, 144
Mary of Guise, Regent of Scotland, 136
Mary, Queen, wife of William III., 209; builds Greenwich Hospital, 215; dies, 218
Maryland, colony of, 166
Mass, riot in favour of the, 128; restored by James II., 200
Massacre of St. Bartholomew, 143
Massena, Marshal, in Peninsular war, 279
Massey, Dr., made Dean of Christ Church, 205
Matilda of Anjou, daughter of Henry I., 45; fights for English Crown, 46
Matilda of Boulogne, wife of Stephen, 46
Mayflower, voyage of the, 153
Mayo, Lord, 312
Mayor, first, of London, 54
Mechanics' Institutes, 296
Melbourne, Lord, 295; resignation of, 301; treasury debts left by, 303
Melbourne founded, 290
Members of Parliament paid, 70
Mercia or March-land, 10
Methodists, rise of, 242
Middle Ages of England, 110
Middle class, progress of, 105
Middlesex, origin of name, 9
Mill, John Stuart, 320
Milled coins, 218
Militia established, 53
Milton, 166; Latin Secretary, 177; his *Paradise Lost*, 189
Ministers powerful under the Georges, 252
Ministry and opposition, origin of, 194
Minorca passes to England, 228; loss of, 246
Moghul, Great, of India, 243
Mona or Anglesey, Druids slain in, 5
Monasteries and towns, 14; destruction of the, 124
Monk, General, enters London, 185; faces the plague, 191

27

418 INDEX.

Monmouth, Duke of, aims at the throne, 197; his rebellion, 200; proclaimed king in Taunton, 201; executed, 202
Monopolies, abolition of, 148; revived, 157
Montague, Charles, starts National Debt and Bank of England, 216; makes new coinage, 218
Montague, exposes the secret pension, 196
Montcalm defends Quebec, 248; his death, 249
Moore, Sir John, sent to Spain, 277; dies at Battle of Corunna, 278
Moore, Tom, the poet, 284
Moots of Early English, 11
More, Sir Thomas, 117; as chancellor, 121; execution of, 124
Morkere, Earl of Northumbria, 35
Morte d'Arthur, printed by Caxton, 106
Mortmain, statute of, 68
Mortimer, Lord, 76; hanged, 77
Mortimer's Cross, Battle of, 103
Moscow, retreat of French from, 279
Mountjoy, Lord, in Ireland, 148
Mowbray, Earl, beheaded, 93
Muhammad Khan deposed, 302
Municipal reform, 295
Murray, Regent of Scotland, 141
Mutiny at the Nore, 271
Mutiny Bill, 213
Mutiny, Indian, 311
Myddleton, Sir H., completed New River, 192

NANA Sahib, 311
Napier, Sir C., conquers Scinde, 305; Sir R., in Abyssinia, 313
Napoleon I., goes to Egypt, 272; made First Consul, 272; Emperor, 274; threatens England, 272, 274; issues Berlin decree, 276; invades Portugal, 277; his retreat from Moscow, 279; defeated at Leipzig, 279; banished to Elba, 279; his return, 280; Battle of Waterloo, 280; death at St. Helena, 281
Napoleon III., his coup d'état, 307; his death, 314
Naseby, Battle of, 173
Natal, a British colony, 306
National Assembly in France, 268
National Debt begins, 216; a safeguard against rebellion, 225; offer to pay off, 235; increase of, 281
Navarino, Battle of, 285
Navigation Act passed, 179: laws repealed, 305
Navy created by Henry VIII., 113
Nelson at Cape St. Vincent, 271; wins Battle of the Nile, 272; in Battle of Copenhagen, 274; Battle of Trafalgar, 275; his death, 275
Nelson Settlement, N.Z., 306
Neolithic men, 3
Netherlands, revolt of the 142; Louis XIV. attacks the, 221
Neville Cross, Battle of, 81
New Brunswick joins the Dominion, 299

New Forest laid out, 37
New Guinea, part of annexed, 321
"New Model" army, 173
New South Wales founded, 289
New River supply, 192
New Zealand colonised 306
Newcastle, Duke of, sacrifices Byng, 246; Prime Minister, 247
Newfoundland not in the Dominion, 229
Newspaper, first weekly, 159
Newspapers, modern, 253
Newton, Sir Isaac, 190, 230
Niagara taken, 248
Nightingale, Miss Florence, 309
Nimeguen, Treaty of, 196
Nithing, Saxon term, 39
Nobles, blending of English and Norman, 43; destruction of old, 110; life of Early English, 20
Nomination boroughs, 236
Nonconformists, persecutions of, 153; laws against; 189; Indulgence granted to, 205; marriages allowed in their chapels, 295
Non-jurors, 210
Nore, mutiny at the, 271
Norfolk, origin of name, 9; rebellion in, 128
Norfolk, Duke of, plots against Elizabeth, 142
Normandy, duchy of, 25; fish and timber trade with, 80; lost to England, 56
Norman Conquest, 30
Normans, flock to England, 26; origin of, 25; revolt of English against the, 35
North, Lord, ministry of, 258-262
Northampton, Battle of, 102
Northbrook, Lord, 312
Northmen, 15; same as Normans, 25
Northumberland, Warwick, Duke of, 129; proclaims Lady Jane Gray, 130; executed, 130
Northumbria founded, 9
Northumbrian rebellion, 1065, 28;
Nova Scotia passes to England, 229; joins the Dominion, 299

OATES, Titus, plot of, 195
O'Brien, Smith, 304
Occasional Conformity Bill, 224
O'Connell, Daniel, 290; takes his seat for Clare, 291; and the Chartists, 300; on repeal, 302
O'Connor, Feargus, 305
Odo, Bishop, conspires, 33
Offa, King of Mercia, 14
Oldcastle, Sir John, and the Lollards, 96
Opposition and ministry, origin of, 194
Oporto, victory of, 278
Opium war, 302
Ordainers, the Lords, 74
Ordeal, 11
Orange Lodges founded, 270
Orangemen, 290
Ordinances of Cromwell, 182

INDEX. 419

Orleans, Siege of, 98 ; the maid of, 99
Ormond, Duke of, put in command, 228 ; impeached, 233
Orsini bombs, 314
Otago Settlement, N. Z., 306
Oude annexed, 310
Oudenarde, Battle of, 227
Outram, Sir J., defends Cawnpore, 312
Overbury, Sir Thomas, poisoned, 156
Oxford, Earl of, *1710*, 228-229 ; impeached, 233
Oxford, first students at, 50 ; Parliament, *1688*, 197 ; Provisions of, 64

PAINE, Tom, his *Rights of Man*, 270
"Painted Chamber" of Commons, 81
Palæolithic men, 2
"Pale" in Ireland, 114
Palmerston, Lord, 304, 310, 314 ; upholds *coup d'état*, 308 ; presses on Crimean War, 308
Pandulph, Pope's legate, 57
Panic of *1824*, 288
Paris, Treaty of, *1763*, 251 ; *1815*, 280 ; *1856*, 310
Paris, Archbishop, 136 ; collects Saxon chronicle, 147
Parliament, first so called, 63 ; the Mad, 64 ; Simon de Montfort's, 65 ; first complete, 69 ; gains right of taxation, 72 ; first *prorogued*, 74 ; takes control of Government, 81 ; the Good, 83 ; ruled by great lords, 86 ; the Merciless, 87 ; Bills not to be altered by the king, 95 ; gives crown to Henry IV., 89 ; decline of, 100 ; of the "Bats," 100 ; the seven years', 121 ; quarrels of James I. with, 154, 155, 157, 158 ; quarrels of Charles I. with, 160-165, 168-178 ; Addled, 155 ; the Short, 168 ; the Long, 168 ; signs league with Scots, 172 ; and army quarrel, 174 ; driven out by Cromwell, 180 ; Barebone's, 181 ; Cromwell's, 182, 183 ; Long expires, 185 ; Cavalier, 187 ; exclusion of Catholics from, 195 ; opposes violation of Test Act, 203 ; rise of party government in, 216 ; infringes rights of electors, 257 ; Irish, 212, 270, 273
Parma, Duke of, threatens England, 145
Partition treaties, *1697*, 220
Party government, rise of, 194
Passive obedience taught, 199
Passaro, Battle of Cape, 234
Paston letters, 105
Paterson suggests Bank of England, 216
Patriot Party in Walpole's time, 238
Paupers, increase of, 253
Pavia, Battle of, 120
Paxton, Sir J., built Crystal Palace, 307
Peace, Keepers and Justices of, 69
Peasant Revolt, 84
Peel, Robert, Home Secretary, 287 ; reforms criminal law, 287 ; introduces police, 295 ; on corn-laws, 301, 303 ; levies income-tax, 303 ; carries free trade, 304 ; death of, 305

Pelham, Prime Minister, 242
Pembroke, Marshall, Earl of, 61
Penal laws in Ireland, 229
Peninsular War, 277-279
Penn, the Quaker, 189, 200
Pennsylvania founded, 189
People, growing power of the, 58 ; their lives in thirteenth century, 61, 62 ; demand freedom, 85 ; prosperity of in fifteenth century, 95, 96 ; suffer from increase of grazing land, 123 ; tired of strict Puritanism, 183 ; rejoiced at Restoration, 185 ; suffering of, in *1837*, 297
Perceval, Prime Minister, 281
Percies, rebellion of the, 93
Perkin Warbeck, imposture of, 114, 115
Perrers, Alice, 83
Peter des Roches, guardian of Henry III., 61
Peter's Pence sent from England, 18
Petition of Right, *1628*, 163
Pevensey, English fight for William II. at, 39
Philip VI. of France, 77
Philip of Spain, Mary's husband, 132 ; sends Armada, 145
Phœnicians visited Britain, 4
Photography, 319
Picts and Scots, 6 ; defeated by Saxons, 8
Piers Plowman, Vision of, 82
Pilgrim Fathers, 153
Pilgrimage of Grace, 125
Pinkiecleugh, Battle of, 127
Pitt (the elder), 237 ; minister under Newcastle, 247 ; successes of, 249 ; retires, 251 ; becomes Earl of Chatham, 256 ; his death, 261
Pitt (the younger), Prime Minister, 265 ; tries to give free trade to Ireland, 266 ; reduces the National Debt, 267 ; fails to pass Reform Bill, 267 ; becomes despotic, 270 ; resigns, 273 ; death of, 275
Pittsburg, Fort Duquesne called, 248
Plague of London, 191
Plantagenet line of kings, 48
Plantations of Ulster and Leinster, 148, 155
Plassey, Battle of, 250
Plot to murder William III., 219
Poets of George III.'s reign, 284
Poitiers, Battle of, 79
Pole, Cardinal, Archbishop of Canterbury, 132 ; death of, 134
Police, introduction of, 295
Political Economy, works on, 321
Poll-tax, first, 84 ; people resist the, 85
Pondicherry taken by English, 250
Poor-law established, 137 ; new, 294
Pope, Paul IV., 133 ; Gregory XIII. reformed the calendar, 242 ; power of the, in England ends, 122
Popish Plot, 195
Portland, Duke of, Prime Minister, 281
Portsmouth dockyard built, 118
Post, first Inland, 165 ; Penny, 300
Potato disease, 303

Poundage and tonnage, 161
Power-loom invented, 252
Powick Bridge, Battle, 172
Poynings' Act in Ireland, 114; repealed, 262
Præmunire, first statute of, 83; second, 87
Prayer-book brought into use, 127, 128, 136
Presbyterians, 153
Press, freedom of the, 217
Preston, Scots defeated at, 174
Pretender, birth of the, 206; recognized in France, 221; threatens Scotland, 225; lands in Scotland, 1715, 234; the Young, 1745, 240
Pride's Purge, 175
Prince Edward's Isle joins Dominion, 299
Prince Consort, death of the, 315
Prince of Wales in India, 312; his marriage, 316
Printing introduced into England, 106
Privateers, English, 143
Proclamation, illegal, of James I., 155
Prorogation of Parliament, 74
Protection party formed, 304
Protector, Oliver Cromwell as, 181; Richard Cromwell as, 184
Protestant party formed, 125
Protestants, Queen Mary persecutes, 133
Prynne and Bastwick pilloried, 167
Pulteney leads opposition, 238
Punjab annexed, 305
Puritans, angered by Laud, 166, 167; emigration of, 153; rise of the, 146, 152
Pym, 158; leads Grand Remonstrance, 170; makes league with Scots, 172; death, 172

QUAKERS, allowed to affirm, 289; rise of the, 182
Quatrebras, Battle of, 280
Quebec, taking of, 249
Queensland made a separate colony, 389
Quiberon Bay, Battle of, 249

RADICAL, use of term, 294
Railways, first opened, 295
Raleigh, Sir Walter, 138, 146; disaster and execution of, 156, 157
Ramillies, Battle of, 224
Rebellion, of Jack Cade, 101; of Ket, 128; Wyatt's, 132; in Norfolk, 1549, 128; against Henry IV., 92-93; against suppression of monasteries, 124
"Recusants," fines levied on, 154
Reform, agitation for, 292; Bill, the first, 292; second and third, 293
Reforms of 1867, 1868, 1885, 314
Regency Bill, 256; the second, 267
Regent, Prince of Wales made, 281
Regent's Park laid out, 296
Religious, Revivals, 47; tests abolished, 317
Renard Simon influences Mary, 131
Repeal, O'Connell urges, 302

Revenue Act, 256
Revenue, life, voted to James II., 200
Revolt in Netherlands, 142; in north of England, 142
Revolt of peasants, 84
Revolution, French, 1848, 304; the English, 207
Reynard the Fox printed by Caxton, 106
Reynolds, Sir J., painter, 284
Richard, Earl of Cambridge, beheaded, 95
Richard, Duke of York, protector, 104; his claim to the throne, 102
Richard I., 53; ransomed, 55; death, 55
Richard II., 84; quells the rioters, 85; struggle with his uncles, 86-88; absolute king, 88; banishes Bolingbroke, 88; disgrace and death, 88-89; his body removed to Westminster, 95
Richard III. (Duke of Gloucester), becomes protector, 107; crowned king, 108; good laws of, 109; death on Bosworth Field, 110
Ridley, Bishop, burnt, 133
Ridolfi Plot, 142
Right, Petition of, 163
Rights, Declaration or Bill of, 209
Riot Act passed, 234; read, 257
Riots of 1791, 270; of 1816-1819, 282; of 1825-1826, 288;
Rivers, Lord, arrest of, 107; execution of, 108
Robert of Normandy, barons rebel in favour of, 39; goes to crusades, 41; imprisonment, 42
Roberts, Sir F., in Afghanistan, 313
Robertson's Histories, 283
Robin Hood, days of, 61-62
Robinson Crusoe, 230
Rodney's naval victory, 262
Roger of Salisbury, 43; imprisoned by Stephen, 46
Rohillas, cruel treatment of, 264
Rolf or Rollo the Viking, 21
Roman rule in Britain, 5, 6; names of towns, 6
Romilly, Sir S., reforms criminal law, 287
Rose Sir Hugh, in Central India, 312
Roses, Wars of the, 89, 101-110
Rossbach, Battle of, 247
Rouen, Siege of, 97
Roundheads, 171
Rowan, Hamilton, Irish leader, 270
Royal Exchange built, 138
Royal Marriage Act, 282
Royal Society founded, 190
Rump Parliament, 184
Rupert, Prince, his horse, 171; attacks the Commonwealth, 176; fights the Dutch, 191-192
Ruskin, 320
Russell, execution of Lord, 198
Russell, Sir J., 314; carries repeal of Test Act, 290; Prime Minister, 304; his Colonies Bill, 307
Russia and Turkey, 308
Rutland, Earl of, murdered, 102

INDEX. 421

Ruyter, De, burns English ships, 192
Rye House Plot, 198
Ryswick, Peace of, 219

SACHEVERELL, Dr., trial of, 227
St. Albans, Battle of, 102
St. Bartholomew, Massacre of, 143
St. Helena, Napoleon at, 281
St. James's Park replanted, 296
St. John, Viscount Bolingbroke, 228; impeached, 233
St. Paul's, meeting of barons in, 58; rebuilt by Wren, 219
St. Sebastian, siege of, 279
St. Vincent, naval victory at, 271
Salamanca, Battle of, 279
Salisbury, Countess of, beheaded, 125
Sanitary reforms, 316
Saratoga, English army surrenders at, 261
Sarsfield, Patrick, holds Limerick, 214
Savoy Palace, burnt by the mob, 85
Savoy, Duke of, persecutes Protestants, 182
Sawtre, W., burnt at the stake, 94
Saxons settlements, 8, 9
Saye, Lord, murdered, 101
Schomberg, Marshal, commands in Ireland, 213
Science in George III.'s reign, 283
Science and Art Schools, 317
Scotland, contest with Edward I., 70-74; governed by English Council, 71; free, 75; proposed union with, 155; proclaims Charles II. king, 176; united with England under Cromwell, 182; separated by Charles II., 188; Pretender threatens, 225; final union under Anne, 226
Scots, language of, 1; origin of, 6; refuse the prayer-book, 168; invade Northumberland, 168
Scrope, Archbishop, beheaded, 93
Scutage or shield-money, 49
Sebastopol, siege of, 309
Sedgemoor, Battle of, 201
Selden sent to prison, 158
Self-denying Ordinance, 173
Senlac Hill, Battle of Hastings on, 29
Sepoy, origin of name, 243; mutiny, 310
Septennial Parliaments, 234
Serfs gradually gain freedom, 80
Settlement, Act of, 221
Seven Years' War breaks out, 245
Shaftesbury, opposes Charles II., 194; brings in "Habeas Corpus" Act, 196; supports Monmouth, 197; his fall, 198
Shakespeare, 56, 147
Shelley, the poet, 284
Sheppey, Danes winter in, 15
Sheriffmuir, Battle of, 234
Ship-money levied by Charles I., 167
Shire, Knights of the, 65, 70, 100
Shire-reeve or sheriff, 19
Shires, grouping of hundreds, 19
Shrewsbury, Battle of, 93
Sidmouth, Lord, 273

Sidney, execution of Algernon, 198
Sidney, Sir Philip, 147
Sikhs, conquest of the, 305; faithful in the mutiny, 311
Silk-weaving brought to England, 203
Simnel, Lambert, impostor, 115
Simon de Montfort, 63; his Parliament, 65; his death, 66
Sir Roger de Coverley, 230
Six Acts passed, 282; oppressive, 285
Slave trade, Lanfranc tries to abolish, 37; abolition of, 276
Slavery, abolition, 294
Slaves in England, 11
Sloane, Sir Hans, 284
Sluys, Battle of, 78
Smith, Adam, his *Wealth of Nations*, 301
Socotra annexed, 321
Solway Moss, Battle of, 119
Somerset, Duke of, protector, 1547, 127; executed, 129
Somerset House built, 123
Sophia, Princess, of Hanover, dies, 229
Soult, Marshal, defeated at Oporto, 278
Southey, the poet, 284
South Sea Bubble, 235
Spain, James I. intrigues with, 156; war with, 1762, 251
Spanish Armada threatened, 144; arrives and is defeated, 145
Spanish Succession, 219-220
Spectator published, 230
Spectroscope invented, 319
Spencer, Herbert, 320
Spenser, poet, 147
Spinning-jenny invented, 252
Spithead, mutiny at, 271
Spurs, Battle of the, 118
Stafford, Lord, executed, 195
Stamford Bridge, Battle of, 29
Stamp Act, 256; repeal of, 256
Standard, Battle of the, 46
Stanhope, Lord, dies, 235
Stanley, 320
Star Chamber instituted, 114; abolished, 169
States General of France, 268
Statute of Kilkenny, 83; of labourers, 81; of Mortmain, 68; first, of Præmunire, 83; second of Præmunire, 87
Steam-boats, first invented, 283
Steam-power, changes worked by, 319
Steele publishes *Spectator*, 230
Stephen, misery of England under, 47, 48
Stephenson, George, engineer, 295
Stone periods, men of the, 2, 3
Stonehenge, 3
Strafford, Lord, *see* Wentworth
Strongbow conquers Leinster, 52
Stuart Arabella, 156; Henry, Lord Darnley, 140; James (old Pretender), 206, 222, 234; Charles Edward (young Pretender), 241
Succession, Act of, 127
Suez Canal, 321
Suffolk, origin of name, 9

Suffolk, murder of Duke of, 101
Sunderland, Earl of, advises party government, 217; ruined by South Sea Bubble, 236
Supplies, annual voting of, established, 213
Supremacy, Act of, 122; bishops refuse oath of, 136
Suraj-ud-Daula, 246, 250
Sussex, origin of name, 19
Sweating Sickness, *1479*, 105
Sweyn overcomes England, 23
Swift, his writings, 230, 237
Sydney settlement founded, 263; roads made round, 289

TALAVERA, Battle of, 278
Talents, Ministry of all the, 275
Tallies, in Exchequer Court, 43
Tasmania settled, 289, 307
Tatler published, 230
Taunton, Monmouth proclaimed in, 201
Taxes, heavy under William II., 39; bishops resist unlawful, 55; right of levying, conceded to Parliament, 72
Telephone invented, 319
Temple, Sir W., at the Hague, 193
Tenchebrai, Battle of, 42
Tennyson, poet, 320
Test Act passed, 194; James II. violates the, 202; deposes those who will not vote against the, 204; repealed, 290
Teutons, origin of, 7
Tewkesbury, Battle of, 105
Thackeray, 320
Thegns of Early English, 12; a new nobility, 19
Theobold, Archbishop, reconciles Stephen and Henry, 48; rules England, 48
Theodore of Tarsus in England, 13
Thirty Years' War, 157
"*Thorough*" rule of Laud and Wentworth, 166
Throgmorton plots against Elizabeth, 144
Ticonderoga taken, 248
Titus Oates, 195
Todleben fortifies Sebastopol, 309
Toleration Act, 213
Tonnage and Poundage, 161
Torres Vedras lines of fortress, 279
Torrington, Lord, *see* Herbert
Tory and Whig, 197
Tostig outlawed, 28
Tower, 107, 108
Towns, origin of, 14; Roman names of, 6; Danish names of, 24; English, 24
Townshend's Revenue Act, 256
Towton, Battle of, 103
Trade, growth of, 80; in Elizabeth's time, 138; spread of, 235
Trades unions, outrages of, 316
Trafalgar, victory of, 275
Train-bands of London, 171, 172
Treason, unjust law of, 122; amended, 217
Treaty of Wedmore, 17; of Wallingford, 48; of Paris, ; of Troyes, 97; of Utrecht, 228; of Versailles, 26

Trial, by battle, 44; of the bishops, 207
Triennial Act, 169, 217
Trichinopoly, relief of, 244
Trimmers, the, 197
Trinidad, English keep, 274
Trinity House founded, 118
Triple Alliance of, *1668*, 193; of *1701*, 221; of *1717*, 234
Tromp, Admiral of Dutch fleet, 179
Troyes, treaty of, 97
Tudors, summary of reigns of, 149
Turks at war with Russia, 308
Turnham Green, train-bands defend, 172
Tyler, John, of Dartford, 84; Wat, 85
Tyrconnel, Lord Lieutenant of Ireland, 204, 210
Tyrone, Hugh O'Neill, Earl of, 147

ULSTER plantations, 148, 155
Uniformity, Acts of, 128, 129, 136, 189
Union Jack, 227, 273
United Irishmen, 270
United States, at war with England, 276; peace made with the, 281; submarine cable to, 315; civil war in, 315
University College founded, 296
Utrecht, Peace of, 228

VAGRANCY, law against, 123
Van Dieman's Land, 289
Vane, Sir Harry, 169; his mission to Scotland, 172; head of the navy, 177; opposes Cromwell, 181, 182; executed by Charles II., 190
Vasco de Gama's voyage, 116
Vauxhall opened, 187
Verdict, or truly said, 50
Versailles, Treaty of *1783*, 263
Victoria, Australia, founded, 290; gold found in,
Victoria, Queen, born, 282, 298; her marriage, 301; Empress of India, 312
Victory, Nelson's ship, the, 275
Vienna, congress at, 280
Vikings or creek dwellers, 15
Villas, Elizabethan, 138
Villeinage dies out, 86
Villeins, ceorls sink into, 20
Villiers, George, Duke of Buckingham, 158, 161, 162, 163, 164
Vimiero, victory of 277
Vinegar Hill, Battle of, 273
Vittoria, Battle of, 279
Volunteers of *1804*, 274; of *1859*, 308; officially organized, *1859*, 314
Voyages of discovery, 138

WAITANGI, N. Z., treaty of, 306
Wakefield, Battle of, 102
Wakefield, E. G., his colonial system, 306
Wales, language of, 1; subdued by Harold the Saxon, 29; conquests in, 40; conquered by Edward I., 67-68; first English Prince of, 68; brought under English law, 122

INDEX. 423

Wales, Prince of, his marriage, 316 ; visit to India, 312
Wallace, Scotland's hero, 71 ; hanged, 73
Wallingford, Treaty of, 48
Walls of Hadrian, 6
Walpole, Horace, on England, 251
Walpole, Robert, opposes South Sea scheme, 235 ; Prime Minister, 236 ; finance of, 237 ; fall of, 239
Walter Scott, Sir, 284
Waltheof the Patriot executed, 36
Wandiwash, Battle of, 250
War, Hundred Years', 78, 96
Warbeck, Perkin, 114
Wards, parishes united into, 22
Warren Hastings, 264 ; trial of, 265
Warwick, the king-maker, 103, 104 ; killed, 105
Washington, George, 245 ; American commander-in-chief, 260
Waterloo, Battle of, 280
Wat Tyler's rebellion, 85-86
Watt invents steam-engine, 252
Wedgewood's pottery, 284
Wedmore, Treaty of, with Danes, 17
Wellesley, Sir A., in second Mahratta war, 277 ; sent to Portugal, 277 ; as Wellington, Duke of, compared with Napoleon, 278 ; his victories in the Peninsula, 279 ; meets Napoleon at Waterloo, 280 ; Prime Minister, 290 ; opposes reform, 290 ; death of, 292
Wellington, N. Z., founded, 306
Welsh or *strangers*, 10
Wentworth, Lord Strafford, 158, 163 ; his rule in Ireland, 166 ; proposes Irish troops, 168 ; trial and death, 169
Wesley, preaching of, 242
Wesleyans, rise of, 242
Wessex, origin of name, 9 ; rise of kings of, 14
West Indies, products from, 321
Westminster Abbey built, 27 ; rebuilt, 63
Weston, Treasurer of Charles I., 164
West Wales, Britons driven to, 10
Wexford, siege of, 177
Wheeler, Sir Hugh, in Cawnpore, 311
Wheatstone, inventor of telegraph, 300
Whig families support Walpole, 236
Whig and Tory, 197
Whitehall Palace built by Wolsey, 119
" White Chamber " of Lords, 81
Whitefield, preaching of, 242
White Sea, hostilities in the, 309
Whittington, Dick, 96
Wiclif, teaching of John, 82 ; his death, 90
Wilberforce, W., denounces slavery, 276
Wilkes arrested, 255 ; elected for Middlesex, 257

William, son of Robert of Normandy, 45 ; killed, 45
William the Conqueror, 26, 28-31 ; birth and character of, 83 ; confiscates English land, 34 ; lays waste North Country, 36 ; collects English laws, 36 ; makes landowners swear allegiance, 37 ; makes New Forest, 37 ; orders Domesday Book, 37 ; his death, 38
William II. (*Rufus*), character, 31 ; quarrel with Anselm, 40 ; wars with Robert, 41 ; his death, 41
William, son of Henry I., drowned, 45
William of Orange, 1569, 142, 143
William of Orange (afterwards William III.) invited to invade England, 206, 207 ; landing of, 207 ; marriage of, with Mary, 195, proclaimed in England, 209 ; in Scotland, 210 ; fights James in Ireland, 214 ; fights in Netherlands, 215 ; unpopular, 215 ; plot to murder, 219 ; makes triple alliance, 221 ; his death, 222
William IV., 291
William the Lion taken prisoner, 53
Williams, General, defends Kars, 309
Window tax, 218
Winthrop, John, emigrates Puritans, 166
Witangemot, 11
Wolfe, General, killed at taking of Quebec, 249
Wolfe Tone leads rebellion in Ireland, ; is hanged, 273
Wolseley, Sir G. in Ashantee, 313
Wolsey, administration of, 119 ; suppressed some monasteries, 124 ; death of, 121
Women, higher education of, 317
Wood's halfpence, 237
Woolwich dockyard built, 118
Worcester, defeat of Charles II. at, 179
Wodsworth, the poet, 284
Wyat's rebellion, 132

YEOMAN class, decrease of, 226
Yeomen of North England, 20
York, James, Duke of, 186 ; declares himself a Roman Catholic, 194 ; attempts to exclude him from the throne, 196
York, murder of young Duke of, 108
Yorkists, rebellions of, 113 ; wore white rose, 102
Yorktown, English army surrenders at, 262

ZEMINDARS, native collectors, 264
Zoological Gardens opened, 296
Zulus, wars against, 305, 313
Zutphen, Battle of, 147
Zwingli, teaching of, 123

INDEX TO CANADIAN HISTORY.

ABENAQUIS, 327
Abercrombie, Lord, 341; defeat of, 342
Abraham, Plains of, 345-346-347
Acadians, expulsion of, 392
Acadia colonized, 392
Alabama Claims, 401-2
Allan, Sir Hugh, 402
Alaska, 323, 401
Alexander, Sir Wm., 392
Algonquins, 324-326
America, discovery of, 325; origin of name, 325; whence peopled, 325
American Revolution, 350-352
American War of 1812-14, causes of, 359; events of, 359-369.
American Civil War, effects on Canada, 390-391
Amherst, General, 342-343, 347
Annapolis, 392. See Port Royal
Arbitration, 402
Arctic Sea, 323
Arnold, Benedict, besieges Quebec, 351-352
Arthur, Sir George, 378
Ashburton Treaty, 382
Asia, 324
Atlantic, 323, 324

BAGOT, Sir Charles, 381
Baldwin, Robert, 375, 381, 384, 387
Barclay, Captain, 363
Batoche, 406
Beauharnois, Marquis de, 338
Beaver Dams, exploit at, 365
Belle Isle, 325
Berlin Decree, 359
Bidwell, Marshall, 374
Bigot, M., 343, 348
Blake, Edward, 403
Boundary disputes, 382
Braddock, General, defeat of, 340
Brébœuf, 329; his martyrdom, 329
British Columbia, 323, 400, 492, 406
British North America Act, 389, 397-99
Brock, General, Governor of Upper Canada, 360; captures Detroit, 361; death of, 362
Brown, George, 387-388
Burgoyne, 352

CABOTS, The, 325
Canada, discovery of, 325; origin of name, 327; under Hundred Associates, 327-331; Royal government, 331, et seq.; surrender of, 347; Canada Trade Act, 371; American invasion of, 350-51, 359, 369; rebellion in, 375-378; Dominion of, 323, 397
Canada Land Company, 373
Canadian Pacific Railway, 406
Carignan Regiment, 332
Carillon, fall of, 342
Carleton, Sir Guy, 349, 351
Caroline, destruction of the, 378
Cartier, Jacques, 325; explores St. Lawrence, 325; at Hochelaga, 325; winters at Quebec, 326
Cartier, Sir George E., 388, 397
Cathcart, Earl, 382
Census, 398
Champlain, Samuel de, 326; founds Quebec, 326; discovers Lake Champlain, 326; explores the Ottawa, 327; discovers Lakes Huron and Ontario, 327; surrenders to Kirke, 327; death, 327
Charlottetown Conference, 389
Chateauguay, Battle of, 366
Chauncey, Commodore, 364
Chippewa, Battle of, 367
Chrysler's Farm, Battle of, 366
Clergy Reserves, 354, 374, 384, 386-387
Colleges, 371, 383, 393, 396
Colborne, 374, 375; suppresses rebellion, 375, 376
Columbus, Christopher, 325
Commission, Joint High, 401
Company of the Hundred Associates, 327, 330, 331
Confederation proposed, 388, 389; adopted, 389
Constitutional Act, 352-353
Courcelles, M. de, 332, 335
Coureurs du bois, 333
Crooks' Act, 404
Crown Point, 343

DALHOUSIE COLLEGE, 393
Dawson Road, 400
Deadlock, Political, 387-88
Dearborn, General, routed at Lacolle, 363; at York, 364; beleaguered in Fort George, 365
De Mezy, 332
De Monts, 392
Denonville, M. de, 336
De Tracy, 332
Detroit, Pontiac at, 348; captured by Brock, 361
Diamond Cape, 326
Dieskau, defeat of, 341

INDEX. 425

Dominion Franchise Act, 403
Dorion, A. A 388
Draper, 379, 383
Drummond, General, 367, 368
Duck Lake, 405
Dufferin, Lord, 403
Dumont, Gabriel, 405
Du Quesne, Fort, 339-340 ; fall of, 342
Durham, Lord, 375-376 ; his report, 376, 379
Dustin, Hannah, 337

EDUCATION IN CANADA, 358, 371, 382-3
Elgin, Lord, 382, 383 ; mobbed, 384 ; makes Reciprocity Treaty, 386
Erie, Fort, Battle of, 367 ; Fenians at, 391
Erie, Lake, Battle on, 365

"FAMILY COMPACT," The, 373, 374, 375, 377, 379
Fenians, The, 390 ; invasion of, 391 ; repulse of, 391 ; trials, 391
Fishery Award, 402
Fitzgibbon, Lieutenant, gallant exploit of, 365
Five Nations, The. See Iroquois
Fort Garry, 399, 400
French Town surprised, 364
Frontenac, 334, 335 ; second administration, 336-337 ; death of, 337
Frontenac, Fort, founded, 335
Fur Companies, rival, 327
Fur Trade, 326, 328, 333

GALT, Sir A. T., 402
Geneva Arbitration, 402
George, Battles of Lake. See Ticonderoga
George, Fort, 361, 362, 363, 364, 365
Ghent, Treaty of, 369
Gore, Francis, Governor of Upper Canada, 360

HALDIMAND, General, 353
Halifax founded, 392
Hampton, General, 366
Harrison, General, invades Upper Canada, 365
Head, Sir Francis, 376, 377 ; awaits rebellion, 377 ; recalled, 378
Hincks, Francis, 381, 387
Hochelaga, 325
Howe, Joseph, 393-394
Howe, Lord, 342
Hudson's Bay, 350
Hudson's Bay Company, 399
Hudson's Bay Territory, 353, 399 ; ceded to Canada, 399
Hull, General, surrenders, 361
Huntington, Mr., charges of, 402
Hurons, 324, 326, 328, 329, 330
Huron Missions, 329 ; destroyed, 329, 330

IMMIGRATION, large, 352, 370, 385
Indians, the mound-builders, 324 ; characteristics, 324 ; wars, 329 ; tribes, 324 ; locations, 324. See Hurons, Iroquois, etc.
Intendant, the, duties of, 331-332
Intercolonial Railway, 398, 407
Iroquois, 324 ; wars with, 326, 329, 330, 331, 332, 335, 336, 337

JESUITS in Canada, 328 ; missions of, 328-330 ; explorers, 334
Jogues, Father, 329
Johnson, Sir William, 341, 343
Joliet, 334
Judges, appointment of, 380

KING'S COLLEGE, Toronto, 371, 383 ; Windsor, 393
Kingston, seat of Government, 380
Kirke, Sir David, captures Quebec, 327

LACHINE, massacre of, 336
Lafontaine, Sir L. H., 381, 383
Lalemant, Father, 328-329
La Salle, 334 ; his explorations, 334-335 ; death of, 335
Laval, Abbé, 331, 332, 333
Legislatures, local, 396, 397, 398
Lepine, 399
Lévis, De, 347
Loudon, Lord, 341
Louisburg, siege of, 338 ; second siege, 342
Lower Canada, rebellion in, 375-376
Loyalists, United Empire, 352, 373, 393 394
Lundy's Lane, Battle of, 367-368

MACDONNELL, Colonel, 362-363
Macdonald, J. Sandfield, 388, 398
Macdonald, Sir John A., 388, 398, 401 ; resigns Government, 402 ; again Premier, 403 ; dies, 403.
Macdougall, Hon. William, at Red River, 399
Mackenzie, Hon. Alexander, 403, 406, 407
Mackenzie, William Lyon, 374, 375 ; rebels, 377 ; attacks Toronto, 378 ; at Navy Island, 378
Manitoba Act, 400
Marquette, 334
McClure burns Niagara, 367
McGill College, 371
McNab, Colonel, and Sir Allan, 378, 387
Metcalfe, Sir Charles, 381
Michilimackinac, 360
Miramichi, great fire of, 394
Missions, Huron, 329 ; destruction of, 329
Monck, Lord, 398
Montcalm, Marquis de, 341, 342, 343, 344, 345, 346
Montgomery, General, 351
Montmorency, fight at, 344
Montreal named, 325 ; founded, 330 ; surrender of, 347 ; Parliament buildings burned, 384

426   INDEX.

Moraviantown, Battle of, 365-366
Mound-builders, The, 324
Mounted Police, The, 405-406
Municipal Act, 381
Municipal Loan Fund, 385, 404
Murray, General, at Quebec, 346, 347; military governor, 348, 349

NAVY ISLAND, 378
Nelson, Wolfred, 375
New Brunswick, 394: organization of Government, 394; great fire in, 394; boundary disputes, 395; anti-Confederate, 395; education in, 395
Newfoundland, 323
New Orleans, Battle of, 369
Niagara, Fort, captured from the French, 343; seat of Government (Newark), 355; captured by Americans, 364; burned, 367
North-West Rebellion, 405-406
North-West Territory, 399
Nova Scotia colonized, 392; Acadians expelled from, 392; anti-Confederate, 394; Constitution granted, 393; "Better terms" granted, 399; education in, 393

OGDENSBURG, 364
Ontario, Province of, 391
Ormeaux, Dulac des, heroism of, 330
Oswego taken, 341
Ottawa selected as seat of Government, 390

"PACIFIC SCANDAL," The, 402; Pacific Railway, 401, 402, 406
Packenham, General, at New Orleans, 369
Papineau, Louis, 375
Paris, Peace of, 347
Parliament Building at Montreal burned, 384
Parliament, First, of United Canadas, 380
"Patriot" War, 378
Pepperell, William, captures Louisburg, 338
Perry's victory on Lake Erie, 365
Phips, Sir William, attacks Quebec, 337
Pitt, William, 342, 353
Plains of Abraham, 345, 346, 347
Plattsburg, attack on, 369
Pontiac, Conspiracy of, 347-348
Port Royal founded, 326, 392; pillaged, 392
Pontgravé, 326
Prevost, Sir George, 360; at Sackett's Harbour, 364; retreat from Plattsburg, 369
Prince Edward Island enters the Dominion, 400
Prince of Wales in Canada, 400
Proctor, Colonel, at French Town, 364; at Moraviantown, 365, 366

QUEBEC founded, 326; captured by Kirke, 327; besieged by Phips, 337; Wolfe before, 344, 345; fall of, 346; Quebec Act, 349; besieged by Arnold, 351-352; Quebec Conference, 389
Queenston Heights, Battle of, 362

RAILWAYS—Northern, 385; Grand Trunk, 385; Intercolonial, 398; Canadian Pacific, 401, 402, 406; Great Western, 385; Lake Champlain and St. Lawrence, 385
Rebellion Losses Bill, 384, 385
Reciprocity Treaty, 386
Redistribution Bill, 403
Red River Settlement founded, 399; rebellion, 399-400; Red River expedition, 400
Representation by population, 388
Resolutions, the Ten, 373
Responsible Government, growth of, 379-384
Revolutionary War, causes of, 370
Riall, General, at Chippewa, 367; at Lundy's Lane, 368
Richelieu, Cardinal, 327
Ridgeway, fight at, 391
Riel, revolt of, 399-400
Roberval, 326
Rolph, Dr., 377-378
Russell, Lord John, 378
Ryerson, Rev. Dr., 382-383
Ryswick, Peace of, 337

SACKETT'S HARBOUR, attack on, 364
Sackville College, 395
Salaberry, De, 366
Salle, La. See La Salle
San Juan difficulty, 401
Schenectady (Corlaer) sacked, 336
Schultz, Von, 379
Scott, Thomas, shot, 400
Secord, Mrs., bravery of, 365
Seignorial Tenure, 332; abolished, 387
Selkirk, Lord, 399
Seven Years' War, 341
Sheaffe, General, 362, 363, 364
Simcoe, Governor, 355
Six Nations, The. See Iroquois, etc.
Smythe, General, 363
Stadacona, 325-326
St. John founded, 394
St. Lawrence discovered, 325
St. Marie, Mission of, 329
Stoney Creek, Battle of, 364
Strachan, Rev. Dr., 371, 383
Southern Raiders, 390
Supreme Council, the French, 331
Sydenham, Lord, 379, 380, 381

TALON, M., 332; able administration of, 333
Tecumseh, 360, 361; death of, 365
Ten Resolutions, The, 373

INDEX. 427

Thompson, Hon. Charles. See Lord Sydenham
Ticonderoga, attacks on, 342 ; fall of, 343
Tilley, S. L., 398
Timber trade, 371, 395
Toronto captured, 364 ; attacked by rebels, 376 ; seat of Government, 355, 385
Tracy, Marquis de, 332
Trinity College, 383

UNION SCHEME, 379; Union Act, 380 ; Union accomplished, 380
Upper Canada, settlement of, 352 ; early legislation, 355 ; founding of, 356-357 ; "Family Compact" in. 373, 374, 375, 377, 379; rebellion in, 376, 377 ; union with Lower Canada, 380
Utrecht, Treaty of, 337
Universities, Canadian. See Colleges

VAUDREUIL, Marquis de, 337, 340
Versailles, Treaty of, 352

Vespucci, 325
Victoria Bridge, 390
Victoria College, 383
Vincent, General, 364, 365

WAR of 1812-14; causes of, 359 ; events of, 359-369
Washington burned, 369 ; Treaty of, 402
Washington, George, 339
Weir, Lieut., 375
Wilkinson, General, 366 ; defeated at Chrysler's Farm, 366 ; at Lacolle Mill, 367
William Henry, Fort, massacre of, 341
Wilmot, L. A., 395
Windmill Point, Battle of, 379
Wolfe, General, 342; before Quebec, 344-345 ; slain, 346
Wolseley, Colonel, 400

YEO, Sir James, 364
York captured, 364 ; Parliament at, 355

www.ingramcontent.com/pod-product-compliance
Lightning Source LLC
Chambersburg PA
CBHW021421300426
44114CB00010B/589